HOME EDUCATORS ASSOCIATION

The Virginia Homeschool Manual

Edited by Janice P. Campbell
Executive Editor, Anne Miller

2248-G Dabney Road • P.O. Box 6745 • Richmond, Virginia 23230-0745
804-278-9200 • FAX: 804-278-9202 • office@heav.org • www.heav.org

Virginia Homeschool Manual:
A Comprehensive Guide to Home Education in Virginia

Janice P. Campbell, Editor
Anne Miller, Executive Editor
Book Design and Layout by Anne Miller
Cover Design by Anne Miller and Susannah Miller

Publishers Cataloging-in-Publication
Virginia homeschool manual: A comprehensive guide to home education in Virginia / edited by Janice P. Campbell and Anne Miller

Home schooling—United States—Handbooks, manuals, etc. 2. Education, Parent participation—United States—Handbooks, manuals, etc. I. Campbell, Janice P. II. Miller, Anne P. III. Title.

ISBN: 978-0-9723765-1-8

Home Educators Association of Virginia
2248-G Dabney Road
P.O. Box 6745
Richmond, Virginia 23230-0745
www.heav.org

Printed in the U.S.A.

ISBN: 978-0-9723765-1-8

Table of Contents

The book you are holding represents the Virginia Homeschool Manual. In it, you will find essential information on each of the topics we have covered. But there's more! The CD that accompanies the manual contains many more articles we just couldn't fit into the book. These articles are listed on the back of each section title page for easy reference. Each article was carefully chosen by a section coordinator to enhance your understanding of a particular topic, and we encourage you to fully explore the CD. You'll find a complete, searchable Table of Contents when you open the CD, and we know you'll appreciate the wealth of information gathered there. Simply insert the CD into your computer, and start exploring!

SECTION G - TESTING AND EVALUATIONS

SECTION H - HIGH SCHOOL AT HOME

SECTION I - COLLEGE AND COLLEGE ALTERNATIVES

SECTION J - SPECIAL-NEEDS EDUCATION

SECTION K - GIFTED EDUCATION

SECTION "H" - EXTRACURRICULAR ACTIVITIES

SECTION I - SUPPORT GROUPS

SECTION N - THE VIRGINIA LAW

SECTION K - GIFTED EDUCATION

SECTION L - EXTRACURRICULAR ACTIVITIES

SECTION M - SUPPORT GROUPS

SECTION N - THE VIRGINIA LAW

SECTION O - GREAT RESOURCES

Introduction

The manual you are holding is the result of nearly two years of hard work and dedication on the part of many people. When HEAV asked me to undertake the revision of the manual, I never imagined the 300+ page manual would evolve into more than 1000 pages of information and inspiration! I am grateful to the HEAV board members for their patience during this lengthy process, and I am thankful for the contributions and input of each member of our volunteer staff, without whom this manual would be much less comprehensive and useful than it is.

My vision for the manual was that it should be a "curriculum fair in a binder." It should contain not only the basic information it has always offered, but it should also provide the type of encouragement, inspiration, and counsel that homeschoolers receive at the annual HEAV Convention in Richmond. In order to accomplish this, I, along with Anne Miller and Yvonne Bunn, made a list of the subject areas we needed to cover, and assembled a volunteer team of experienced homeschool mothers who were willing to share their expertise in a particular subject. Each volunteer became a section coordinator, writing and pulling together articles that provided a broad overview of her section topic.

When the coordinators turned in their sections, I was thrilled to see that each section reflected the personality and knowledge of its coordinator. Reading the manual was like receiving personal counsel from a group of experienced homeschool moms. Of course, with such a large project, there were challenges to meet, but each volunteer persevered, in sickness and in health. We obtained permission for articles we hoped to use, and found other articles when permission was denied, and we spent many, many hours editing, polishing, and proofreading each article.

The greatest challenge came, however, when we realized we had far more information than would fit into one binder. There was nothing we were willing to leave out, so we chose a solution that wouldn't have been feasible just a few years ago—we decided to put as many pages as possible from each section into the manual, then place the remaining articles on a CD, so that readers could read and print the remaining articles from their computers. I realize it's not a perfect solution, but it is the solution that allowed us to keep manual costs within bounds, and still provide all the valuable information the coordinators had gathered. I encourage you to explore the CD—at a friend's home or the library if you have no computer at home—in order to appreciate the scope of the wisdom each coordinator has offered.

The attractive, readable design of this edition of the manual is due to countless hours of work by Anne Miller, who graciously added this enormous task to her heaping plate of responsibilities. She took the hundreds of pages I sent her, transformed them into the attractive format you see here, and oversaw the printing and production of the book. I am so grateful for her tireless attention to detail, her pleasantness in the face of onrushing deadlines, and her ever-delightful sense of humor. I can think of no one else with whom I'd rather undertake a task of this magnitude.

It's been an enormous undertaking, but I am delighted to have had a part in creating the new manual. I'm grateful for each of the volunteers who shared in the task; for the HEAV board, which instigated the project; and for my family, who became quite accustomed to sharing the dining room table with chunks of the manual-in-progress. Most of all, I'm grateful to the Lord for His presence in my life, and for the opportunity to pass on the knowledge and encouragement I've received as a homeschooler. I hope you will find the help, knowledge, and inspiration you seek within these pages.

Janice Campbell
Editor, *The Virginia Homeschool Manual*

Manual Staff

TAMMY BEAR: *SUPPORT GROUPS* SECTION COORDINATOR

Tammy Bear and her husband, H.T., have homeschooled their five blessings (Heather, India, Taylor, Zachary, and Jacob) for ten years. Tammy has served homeschoolers in her area by being president, vice-president and membership coordinator for the Tri-Cities Home Educators for the last six years. She has also served as newsletter editor, along with her husband. Tammy has co-coordinated a Cooperative Learning And Specialized Studies (CLASS) program for homeschoolers in her area. She and her husband are the Exhibit Hall coordinators for the HEAV convention. She has been a speaker at numerous mother/daughter retreats. Tammy enjoys reading and knitting in her quiet time, and spending time with her husband and little bear cubs up on the Blue Ridge Parkway viewing God's beauty.

VICKI BENTLEY: *BEGINNING THE HOMESCHOOL JOURNEY* SECTION COORDINATOR

Vicki Bentley, the mother of eight daughters, foster mom of over fifty since 1985, and grandma to fourteen wonderful grandbabies (so far) has homeschooled 17 children over the last 15 years, with the strong undergirding of her husband Jim. She led a local support group of over 250 families for 14 years. She has served on the executive board of the Home Educators Association of Virginia and helps to coordinate their annual convention. Vicki has addressed state and national conventions, university teacher organizations, and many mothers' groups. She is the author of *My Homeschool Planner*, the Family Chore System, *Home Education 101: A Mentoring Program for New Homeschoolers*, and various articles. Vicki has a heart for moms, and offers strong practical wisdom and encouraging words. You can contact her through www.HomeEducation101.com, or at vicki@everydayhomemaking.com.

BETH WRIGHT BESS: *GIFTED EDUCATION* SECTION COORDINATOR

Beth lives in Virginia with her husband and their three exceptionally/ profoundly gifted children. Their oldest son began taking classes at the College of William and Mary when he was twelve. Beth's publishing credits include articles about early college classes and gifted education appearing in *Gifted Education Press Quarterly* and on the Davidson Institute's website, *PG Cybersource*. Beth has spoken about early college and homeschool gifted education at homeschooling conventions, both local and statewide. She has lectured on the same at William and Mary and the University of Virginia. Beth is currently writing a book about early college classes.

YVONNE BUNN: *THE VIRGINIA LAW* SECTION COORDINATOR

Yvonne Bunn is executive director of Home Educators Association of Virginia (HEAV). She has a degree in elementary education, and, prior to homeschooling for the past 16 years, taught in private Christian schools. She and her husband George have five children.

Yvonne has been on the HEAV board since 1990, and has worked as HEAV's Director of Government Affairs. She initiated Governor George Allen's proclamation of Virginia Home Education Week and has coordinated HEAV's "Day at the Capitol." She most recently spearheaded HEAV's effort in the General Assembly to pass the first homeschool license plate in the nation with the logo "Education Begins at Home."

Yvonne has spoken at numerous "How to Begin Homeschooling" conferences throughout Virginia as well as National Christian Home-School Leadership conferences in Phoenix, Arizona, and Williamsburg, Virginia. She also participated in a week-long series on HSLDA's nationally syndicated "Home-School Heartbeat." In 1992 Yvonne received Home School Legal Defense's "Outstanding Service" award.

JANICE CAMPBELL: EDITOR; *COLLEGE AND COLLEGE ALTERNATIVES* AND *TEACHING TIPS* SECTION COORDINATOR

Janice, along with her husband, Donald, has homeschooled their four sons since the late 1980's. She graduated *cum laude* from Mary Baldwin College with a Bachelor of Arts in English, and is the author of *Transcripts Made Easy*, a transcript workbook that includes free e-mail support.

Before taking on the task of editing the manual, Janice was a columnist for *Home Education Learning Magazine* (HELM), and editor of *The Virginia Home Educator*. She continues to write and edit, and offers *Beat-the-Clock Essay Workshops* to prepare homeschoolers for high school essay writing and standardized tests. Her website, www.everyday-education.com, is designed to provide homeschooling information and inspiration.

JANICE GOLDSTEIN: ASSISTANT TO THE EDITOR

Janice and her husband, Bruce, have three children and have been homeschooling for over 11 years. Their oldest, Joelle, graduated from college last year, is married, and living in Connecticut. Josh, 19, graduated from homeschool last June and is taking classes at community college. This leaves Adam, the only one still schooling at home. In addition to homeschooling and housework, Janice teaches Hebrew at her Messianic congregation, and Spanish to middle school and high school age homeschoolers. She is a registered nurse and is studying to be a Health and Wellness Consultant in Complementary and Alternative Medicine. Last, but not least, she is a Master Gardener, and writes a column for a local newsletter on growing and using herbs.

DARLENE LEVY: *EXTRACURRICULAR ACTIVITIES* SECTION COORDINATOR

Darlene and her husband, Bob, have always homeschooled their three children, with a casual "everyday learning" approach. Morgan, 16, now attends a Community College; Austin, 14, and C. Reid, 11, share lessons at home...and on the road!

Darlene works part-time with a short-term international exchange program, as well as being a part-time mystery shopper; both being jobs that include her children. Under the pseudonym "The Imperfect Homeschooler," she is a freelance writer for *Homeschooling Parent Magazine* and *The Bayith Educator*. The editor and founder of Tidewater Homeschool Information Support, she is also involved with two local groups, Homeschoolers In Support and Peninsula Family Schools.

Darlene is known to always have a coupon, a camera, a crochet hook, or a computer at her fingertips. In lieu of cleaning house, she enjoys scrapbooking, gardening, listening to books on tape, traveling, and raising bantam chickens.

ANNE MILLER: MANUAL LAYOUT AND DESIGN, EXECUTIVE EDITOR, AND *HIGH SCHOOL AT HOME* SECTION COORDINATOR

Anne Miller and her husband, Jeff—a designer and builder of homes—have always homeschooled their eight children (six boys and two girls, ages nine to 24). Two of the Miller children have received master's degrees, one in business administration, the other in electrical engineering, and two are seniors in mechanical engineering.

Anne has served homeschool families through HEAV for almost 17 years and is in her fifth term as president. She is also the director of publications, and the former editor of *The Virginia Home-School Manual, Fifth and Sixth Editions*. Anne is a speaker, writer, editor, and graphic designer who loves gardening and working with her husband in their construction business.

JUDITH MUNDAY: *SPECIAL-NEEDS EDUCATION* SECTION COORDINATOR

Judith Munday has taught special-needs students in Virginia for over twenty years in private, public, and Christian school settings. She is married to Dr. John C. Munday Jr., and their three children and their families, which include five grandchildren and one on the way, love the Lord. In 1968, Judith received a Master of Education from the University of Illinois and, in 1985, a Master of Arts in Education degree from CBN (now called Regent) University. Since her retirement in 1999 from the Chesapeake Public Schools, Judi has been serving special-needs students and their parents through her business, H.I.S. Place for Help in School. Her website, www.hishelpinschool.com, is a source of useful teaching strategies and helpful information.

SARAH OLBRIS: *TESTING AND EVALUATION* SECTION COORDINATOR

The writer of the testing section, Sarah Olbris, is the wife of a native Virginian. Together, Dwayne and Sarah have four children and have been married 18 years. They have been homeschooling for ten years. Sarah has experience in public schools as well as in homeschool. She has been testing homeschoolers (groups and individuals) since the late 1980's and doing evaluations and portfolio evaluations since the mid to late '90's. She has worked with gifted, average, and learning disabled children. She brings many years of experience to this section and hopes it will be beneficial to you.

KARYLENE OLLENBERGER: *PLANNING AND RECORD KEEPING* SECTION COORDINATOR

Karylene and her husband, Randy, have homeschooled their children for the last ten years, including two through high school. She has a Bachelor of Science degree from Radford University. She returned to school after the birth of her fourth child to become a registered nurse, obtaining a diploma from Riverside School of Professional Nursing. She worked part-time for seven years while homeschooling, but currently is a stay-at-home mom. She has been a tutor at the Three Rivers Homeschool Cooperative for the last five years. She is the designer and partner for "Add Ons—Historical Timeline Characters," which produces large-size paper doll historical character figures for small hands.

JANELL RARDON: *FAMILY FOUNDATIONS* SECTION COORDINATOR

Mrs. Janell Rardon resides in Suffolk with her husband, Rob, their three children, Candace, Brooke, and Grant, and Abraham, their faithful golden retriever. As a homeschooling parent, Janell has worn many hats in the homeschooling community, serving as enrichment program coordinator, support group leader, community liaison, curriculum specialist, workshop leader, writing coach, and teacher.

Her passion as a Christian communicator and author is to equip the family to thrive; enabling each member to discover its creative potential, purpose, and passion. When a spare moment arises, you will find Janell hidden away in her rubber-stamping workshop, creating beautiful cards and gifts!

Janell is available to speak to homeschooling groups and ministries, and has many study guides and bible studies available.

HEAV: Your State Organization

Compiled by Yvonne Bunn

HEAV: Who We Are and What We Do

ome Educators Association of Virginia is a statewide, non-profit association of homeschooling parents and grandparents who have worked together since 1983 to promote and protect home education in Virginia. Although the members of the Executive and Advisory Boards have changed over the years, the mission of HEAV has remained the same—to provide information, legislation, and resources on a statewide level, to all Virginia parents desiring to teach their children at home. HEAV serves ALL homeschoolers—regardless of their religious or philosophical beliefs. Membership is—and always has been—open to all.

As homeschooling has matured in Virginia, so has our organization. It was not until a year after our founding that the homeschool statute as we know it today took effect. At that time, most people had never heard of anyone teaching at home. And for those who did begin to take responsibility for the education of their children, opposition was common. Over the years, homeschooling has changed drastically! Today it is not uncommon for the clerk at the grocery store or the mechanic fixing the car to know a friend or have a close relative teaching at home.

Through the years, HEAV has continued to work for better homeschool laws in Virginia. As explained in the law section of this manual, numerous changes have been made to the homeschool statute. Please take special care to read through the law section and become familiar with your rights as parents. It is also important that you understand the requirements of the homeschool laws.

As you read this manual, we ask that you remember to pray for the HEAV board, volunteers, and staff. If you are interested in serving on the Board, Advisory Board, or any one of our numerous committees, please contact our office and we will gladly send you a copy of our constitution and an application.

Board meetings, which are open to all HEAV members, are held quarterly. Give us a call at 804-278-9200, or e-mail us at office@heav.org, for the date and time of our next meeting. Also, contact us if you have any comments or suggestions for future editions. May God bless you as you seek to train and educate your children. We hope you find this manual helpful.

—Yvonne Bunn

HEAV PHILOSOPHY
We believe:
- God gives parents the primary right and responsibility to educate their own children;
- Parents have the right to educate their children in conformity with their own moral and religious convictions;
- Parents have the right to freely choose schools, tutors, co-ops, or other means necessary to educate their own children in keeping with their convictions;
- Parents as home educators can provide a high-quality education through individualized instruction;
- Parental love and understanding, patience to teach until a child learns, and parental awareness of the needs of the whole child are more important than teacher-certification requirements;
- Home education provides the family with excellent opportunities to strengthen spiritual values, grow in personal responsibility, and develop leadership qualities in their children.

HEAV STATEMENT OF PURPOSE
The purposes of HEAV, which shall operate within the context of a biblical worldview, shall include but are not limited to the following:
- Help and encourage parents to fulfill their God-given rights and responsibilities to educate their own children;
- Provide information and advice to homeschooling parents regarding home education and family life;
- Support and protect the rights of parents to teach their children at home through legislative initiatives and contact with representatives in the Virginia General Assembly and United States Congress;
- Educate the general public, educators, and elected officials through personal contacts, the media, lectures, seminars, workshops, conventions, and newsletters concerning the benefits of home education and the Constitutional right of parents to educate their own children;
- Provide information to home-educating parents, the general public, the media, and elected officials regarding the Virginia Code, pending legislation, and court cases as they relate to homeschooling;
- Direct interested parents to local homeschool support groups for support and encouragement;
- Assist homeschool support groups by providing information, resources, leadership workshops, and training seminars.

AREAS OF SERVICE
Lobbying and Legislative Activities
- **Public policy**—These issues are the main focus of HEAV's Director of Government Affairs. HEAV stays abreast of issues affecting homeschool families, and disseminates information to the homeschool community via mail, phone, e-mail, speakers, and our printed materials.
- **Day at the Capitol**—Sponsored by HEAV, it brings approximately 500

students and parents to Richmond to tour the Capitol, Executive Mansion, and Supreme Court. During visits when the General Assembly is in session, homeschoolers can talk with their own representatives, observe committee meetings, and see the live session. At other times, parents and students can participate in an interactive chamber presentation where students learn how a bill becomes a law by sitting in the chamber and debating then voting on a mock bill.

- **Virginia Home Education Week**—the fourth week of every January—was proclaimed by former Governor George Allen at HEAV's request.
- **HEAV legislative volunteers and paid lobbying staff** work with legislators during the year, and have a constant presence at the General Assembly when the legislature is in session.
- **On-line bill monitoring**—We look for any surprise legislation that may affect our right to home educate, and we track new bills introduced during the session.
- **Networking**—HEAV works closely with the Virginia Department of Education, local school boards, and local school superintendents, as well as numerous state and national homeschool and pro-family organizations throughout the year.
- **E-mail legislative updates and alerts**—When necessary, we send parents the information they need to help wisely shape the public policy that will affect them as homeschooling families.
- **The first homeschool license plate in the nation**—HEAV initiated legislation and worked for passage of a license plate bill. After receiving 350 orders, the Virginia DMV imprinted our HEAV-designed homeschool license plate with the legend, "Education Begins at Home." These plates can be purchased at www.dmv.state.va.us.

Convention/Seminars
- **Annual State Convention and Educational Fair**—A yearly convention is provided by HEAV with a participation in excess of 10,000 people. The purpose of the convention is to support, encourage, and equip homeschool moms and dads. It is planned for the new homeschooler as well as the veteran. This event presents nationally known speakers; workshops; a curriculum exhibit hall; a used-curriculum sale; a children's program; a support-group leaders' luncheon; a single-parents' luncheon; special tracks for teens, for veteran homeschoolers, and for parents with special-needs children. It includes one day of free workshops for interested parents and beginning homeschoolers.
- **High school graduation ceremony**—The graduation is complete with caps and gowns, "Pomp and Circumstance," diplomas presented by parents to their graduate, and a commencement speaker.
- **Support group leader seminars**—In order to equip leaders and provide timely information, HEAV sponsors leadership seminars.
- **Homeschool Success Seminars**—HEAV's popular Homeschool Success Seminars cover a wide variety of subject matter—everything from how

to begin, to how to choose curriculum, to the Virginia law and testing requirements, to high school at home, to getting organized. Find the latest Homeschool Success Seminars at **www.heav.org/events/seminar/ index.html.**

Communications
- **Resource contact**—HEAV is a resource for a variety of groups and organizations such as colleges; radio, television, and print media; the Virginia Department of Education; school boards; and legislators. We provide information packets, articles, speakers, and other materials.
- *The Virginia Home Educator*—This informative, free news magazine is published quarterly and includes state, local, and national news; informative articles; resources; and reviews. For a free subscription, sign up at **www.heav.org**, or e-mail us at **office@heav.org**.
- *The HEAV Virginia Homeschool Update*—Our free weekly e-mail newsletter includes concise information on current topics and upcoming events of interest to homeschoolers. (You may sign up for this free service on our website at **www.heav.org**.)
- **The Legislative Update**—The *Legislative Update* provides timely information by e-mail on legislative matters and is sent as needed during the General Assembly session.
- **Website at www.heav.org**—We have a comprehensive site designed to assist homeschoolers with information on the Virginia homeschool law, how to begin homeschooling, testing, resources, required forms, and information to help parents homeschool from kindergarten to college.
- **The Virginia Homeschool Manual**—The manual is the only resource of its kind for home educators in Virginia! This comprehensive manual is a must for every homeschool household.
- **Statewide list of local support groups**—HEAV maintains a list of support groups to help connect new homeschoolers, and those new to the area, with groups in their vicinity.
- **"Homeschool's Cool" tote bags**—Designed and sold by HEAV, these bags promote home education in a fun and graphic way.

Support Groups
- We actively promote regional and local support groups through referrals, our website support-group directory, and our magazine.
- We offer regional and local support groups the opportunity to publicize their events and news in the *Virginia Home Educator,* as well as in our weekly e-mail newsletter, the *Virginia Homeschool Update.*
- We provide regional and local support groups with training, resources, information, intercommunication, and encouragement.
- To help keep regional and support-group leaders informed, we send free copies of the *Virginia Homeschool Update,* the *HEAV Legislative Update,* the *HEAV Leader Letter,* and *The Virginia Home Educator* magazine to support groups.
- HEAV sponsors leadership-training seminars to serve leaders so they can better serve homeschoolers.

- HEAV sends representatives, speaking on a wide variety of topics, to visit local support groups. (Give us a call if you'd like someone to speak to your group!)

Education

- We distribute thousands of pieces of free information to parents around the state every year.
- We sponsor numerous **Homeschool Success Seminars** throughout the state during the year. We present them to interested parents and groups at colleges, churches, museums, libraries, the state convention, and at the HEAV Office and Resource Center in Richmond.
- HEAV also continues to make new resources available for the equipping of home educators. These resources are for sale through our office and resource center and our website e-store.
- We offer an extensive selection of CDs and MP3s on a variety of home-schooling subjects. Titles are listed on our website at **www.heav.org.**
- We also publish the manual you are holding in your hands, *The Virginia Homeschool Manual.* HEAV's manual is on the shelves of libraries throughout the state.
- HEAV works to educate the general public, the media, pastors, state and private educators, school boards, judges, attorneys, and state legislators about the benefits of home education and the constitutional right to home educate.
- We take steps to present home education in the best possible light through personal contacts, newspaper interviews, lectures, seminars, conventions, radio and television interviews, printed materials, and by sponsoring **Virginia Home Education Week** and **Day at the Capitol.**

Special Events

- **Museums and Historical Sites**—HEAV partners with museums across the state by arranging many FREE and reduced-cost Homeschool Open House events for parents and students. We encourage museums to offer discounted membership prices for homeschool families and reduced pricing for special educational programs. These outstanding "field trips" are held around the state and announced in HEAV's free weekly *Update.* A slideshow of special "Homeschool Days" can be found on HEAV's website under "Events."
- **Box Tops for Education**—HEAV is the state coordinator for homeschoolers in Virginia. Through this fund-raising program, support groups raise money for local projects as well as the state organization.
- **Conferences and Homeschool Days**—HEAV has participated in many special events and presentations: the first Army Education Summit, Smithsonian Museum docent presentation, Busch Gardens Homeschool Day, the Virginia Association of Museums statewide conference, Homeschool Legal Defense National Summit, the Virginia Conservative Leadership Conference, Six Flags Homeschool Day, the Virginia Association of College Registrars and Admissions Officers statewide conference,

International Children's Festival, and many HEAV-sponsored home-school days at museums and historical sites around the state.

Operations

A major milestone was reached in 1996 when HEAV was able—through the generous help of local support groups and donors—to move our operations into a real office in Richmond. Previously, our "office" operated out of the homes of dedicated homeschooling parents in Front Royal.

Because of the thousands upon thousands of phone calls and e-mail messages, the enormous volume of mail, and those ever-critical administrative details, we then hired an office manager who orchestrated the day-to-day details of running our office.

A second major milestone was reached in 1998—again through the incredibly generous support of homeschooling families and support groups—allowing us to hire an executive director. Our director oversees all the operations and events that are sponsored or conducted by HEAV.

Even though HEAV has paid staff in several key positions, much of HEAV's work is still done by volunteer moms, dads, teens, and grandparents who are willing to serve. (So if you'd like to volunteer, we can always use your help—please e-mail us at **volunteer@heav.org**.)

Each year, our board members and office staff answer questions, provide counseling, offer referrals, and fill thousands of requests for free homeschool information. Our office is open from 10:00 a.m. to 4:00 p.m, Monday through Friday. You may contact us at 804-278-9200.

Board and Advisory Board

Our Board of Directors provides leadership, accountability, and direction for the Home Educators Association of Virginia (HEAV). The Board is made up of homeschooling parents, grandparents, and other dedicated individuals who volunteer their time, energy, talents, and resources to help promote and protect home education in Virginia. All board members endorse the HEAV Statement of Philosophy.

Volunteers

Hundreds of volunteers work with us each year and are the backbone of HEAV. All our board members began as volunteers and they—with a multitude of others—continue to volunteer untold hours of service to Virginia home-schoolers. Volunteers make up a majority of the Convention staff. They also help organize HEAV events and participate in presentations. They work at our office and work from their homes; they make phone calls, make contacts for us, help with mailings, do computer work, do data entry, write articles...the list of their activities seems endless. Their selfless work is an encouragement and an example to all of us.

If you're interested in working with us as a volunteer, please visit **www.heav.org/support-homeschoolers/volunteer**, or e-mail us at **volunteer@heav.org.** We'll make sure your strengths and interests fit the job. We would love to have your valuable help!

Key Virginia Information

COMMONWEALTH OF VIRGINIA
- To obtain any government telephone number: 804-786-0000
- To write or FAX your representatives fill in their names now and use this page as a reference when needed.

Governor

The Honorable_____

Governor's Office

P.O. Box 1475

Richmond, Virginia 23212

804-786-2211

Fax: 804-371-2655

Salutation:

Dear Governor_____

Lieutenant Governor

The Honorable _____

900 East Main Street

Fourteenth Floor

Richmond, Virginia 23219

804-786-2078

Fax: 804-786-7514

Salutation:

Dear Lieutenant Governor_____

State Senator*   District #_____

_____

_____

_____

_____

State Delegate*   District #_____

_____

_____

_____

_____

Senate Address

The Honorable _____

General Assembly Building

Richmond, Virginia 23219

Fax for all: 804-786-4640

Salutation: Dear Senator _____

House Address

The Honorable_____

P.O. Box 406

Richmond, Virginia 23218

Fax for all: 804-786-6310

Salutation: Dear Mr., Ms., Mrs. ____

OTHER KEY STATE OFFICES:

Attorney General	804-786-2071	Fax: 804-786-1991
Secretary of Education	804-786-1151	Fax: 804-371-0154
Department of Education	804-225-2020	Fax: 804-786-5389

If you do not know who your delegate or state senator is, you can call your local library, or voter registrar's office, or the State Board of Elections (800-552-9745).

Virginia General Assembly Information

Information 804-786-7281

Bill Status 804-786-5435

Bill Room.. 804-786-6984

Legislative Information—Senate 804-698-7410

.... Toll-free: 1-888 892-6948

Legislative Information—House.. 804-786-6530

....Toll-free: 1-877 391-FACT

House Clerk.. 804-698-1619

Senate Clerk 804-786-3838

Legislative Services for Senate 804-698-7410

Legislative Services for House.. 804-698-1500

Recorded Schedule of Meetings (during session)............................. 804-371-8664

Toll-Free Opinion Hot Line 1-800-889-0229

Fax to the Governor.. 804-371-2655

Fax to the Lieutenant Governor 804-786-7514

Governor's Office 804-786-2211

Lieutenant Governor's Office 804-786-2078

Fax to Senators 804-698-7671

Fax to Delegates.. 804-786-6310

WEB-SITE ADDRESSES
General Assembly
http://legis.state.va.us
Legislative Information System
http://leg1.state.va.us
Bill Search: House and Senate Bills and Resolutions
http://leg1.state.va.us/991/bil.htm
Code Of Virginia Searchable Data Base
http://leg1.state.va.us/000/src.htm
Homeschool Statute
http://leg1.state.va.us/cgi-bin/legp504.exe?081+ful+CHAP0364

Key Federal Information

U.S. Capitol Switchboard

      202-224-3121 (To reach U.S. Senators or Congressman)

The White House

      1600 Pennsylvania Avenue, NW
      Washington, D.C. 20500
      202-456-1414
      Opinion Line: 202-456-1111
      president@whitehouse.gov
      vicepresident@whitehouse.gov

World Wide Web

      The White House www.whitehouse.gov
      U.S. Senate   www.senate.gov
      U.S. House   www.house.gov

Bill Status (Status of legislation awaiting action from the White House.)

U.S. Senate and House: (update on legislation)	202-225-1772
White House Executive Clerk:	202-456-2226
For copies of pending legislation in the Senate:	202-224-7860
For copies of pending legislation in the House:	202-226-5200

U.S. Senator _____

      Phone: _____
      Fax: _____
      E-mail: _____

U.S. Senator _____

      Phone: _____
      Fax: _____
      E-mail: _____

U.S. Congressman*   *District #_____*

      _____
      Phone: _____
      Fax: _____
      E-mail: _____

U.S. Senate Address	House of Representatives Address
The Honorable_____	The Honorable_____
The United States Senate	The United States House of Representatives
Washington, D.C. 20510	Washington, D.C. 20515
Salutation: Dear Senator_____	Salutation: Dear Congressman_____

* Contact your voter registrar, library, or State Board of Elections (1-800-552-9745) to obtain this information.

Order Your Homeschool License Plate Now!

Y ou can now order your official Commonwealth of Virginia homeschool license plates. Encourage others to homeschool and have fun by displaying your specialized license plate!

The HEAV-sponsored license-plate—"Education Begins at Home"—is the first homeschool license plate in the nation!

The cost of the plate is $10 per year in addition to the registration fee for the vehicle. A random numbering system will be used unless you would like to personalize your homeschool plate with an alphanumeric combination of your choice (additional $10 fee).

To order your homeschool license plate, simply go to www.heav.org/ events/lplate, then follow the link to the DMV site. Your homeschool license plate can now be ordered online with a credit card. You can also order a sample plate for displaying in your homeschool!

Day at the Capitol: A Hands-On Government Classroom

Day at the Capitol is both a day to learn about the Virginia legislative process and a day to make a positive impression on our legislators! This annual HEAV sponsored event brings almost 500 parents and students to the Capitol for a fun-filled, educational day.

Our HEAV lobbyist gives an up-to-date review of important legislation from the session, several guest legislators share key information about good citizenship and current issues, then parents and students tour the Capitol, Executive Mansion, and Supreme Court. During visits when the General Assembly is in session, homeschoolers can meet with their legislators, attend committee meetings, and view the legislative session from the gallery. During post-session visits, families can sit in legislators' chairs in the chamber and debate and vote on a mock homeschool bill during the hour-long chamber presentation. During this time, experienced House and Senate staff members explain the history of the oldest continuous legislative body in America. They willingly answer questions from eager homeschoolers.

Another highlight of the day is the Capitol grounds scavenger hunt—a family search for answers to questions about Virginia's history.

During the afternoon, HEAV representatives deliver gifts to the Governor, Lt. Governor, and Attorney General, as well as special gifts of appreciation to key committee members and legislators. In past years, homeschooled students have delivered candy-filled, apple-shaped containers with heart-shaped tags proclaiming "Education Begins at Home."

Often we are able to visit with the Governor. Recently, a parent from Farmville, reported, "We happened to be up in the Rotunda, when who should come out but the Governor, who graciously let us have a photo shoot with him...!" Another family had a chance to shake hands and have their picture taken with the Governor when he walked in while they were touring his office!

Our Day-at-the-Capitol schedule has included a performing arts group singing patriotic songs in the Rotunda as House and Senate members walked through on their way to the General Assembly sessions. The Young Musicians of Virginia—talented homeschoolers from the Tidewater area—have given resounding performances in the Capitol Rotunda as well.

Don't miss this yearly opportunity to give your students a hands-on opportunity to learn about state government. This is home education at its best!

HEAV Conventions Grow with Homeschooling!

For the past twenty-seven years, HEAV has been serving homeschooling parents by offering an annual homeschool convention. During this time, we've seen tremendous growth in home education—as well as our convention attendance, which has grown from several hundred parents in the early years to more than 10,000 attendees!

For each convention, HEAV brings in nationally known keynote speakers who are experts in their fields. We also include a wide variety of workshop speakers, both from Virginia and other states, to cover numerous practical topics. Topics include everything from how to teach reading, to how to manage college at home, to how to live on one income!

Convention begins with special FREE sessions on Thursday to give much needed information to parents who are interested in home education but may not have yet made a decision to homeschool. Others who are ready to begin homeschooling can glean foundational information from these FREE practical sessions: *Introduction to Homeschooling; How to Begin: What You Really Need to Know; How to Choose Curriculum;* and *Know the Law: Notifying and Testing Demystified.*

During the past several years, we have added a new dimension to the Convention—a children's program. Not only does it meet a need for childcare, but this Scripture-based program builds great character while the children are having loads of fun. One mom commented, "This is great! The Convention has become a family event."

Our workshops include information about a variety of homeschooling interests. We have special workshops for teens that meet their interests and help prepare them for the future. We schedule a beginner's track to help new homeschooling parents with the basics. We have inspiring workshops for dads, as well as workshops that offer special tips for teaching children with learning disabilities. We include a Single Parents' Luncheon, underwritten by HEAV, and hosted by a dedicated single parent who homeschooled her daughter alone. We often showcase the musical talents of homeschoolers, and have even had workshops for grandparents!

At a recent convention, attendees included more than 10,000 parents, grandparents, teens, children, speakers, and vendors. Interestingly, at one convention, registration included 509 people from 25 other states, plus one person from Europe and three people from Haiti!

The Exhibit Hall is a beehive of activity during every Convention. Vendors from across the country display thousands of items, giving new and veteran homeschoolers the opportunity to see their materials *before* purchasing them.

The Used Curriculum Sale is always a winner with its fantastic bargains. At a recent convention, more than 47,000 items were available for sale. This number doesn't include the tables of *free* merchandise. Thousands of bargain hunters attended this sale during the two-day event.

Graduation is always an exciting and encouraging conclusion to the Convention. With almost 200 graduates and approximately 2500 guests, graduation brings tears and excitement as parents present diplomas to their graduates. At the conclusion, the graduates joyously throw their hats into the air to the cheers of their families and friends!

We regularly receive heart-warming and encouraging words from many parents:

"You all put on a first-class shindig!"

"Well-orchestrated! The Convention does reinforce that we have made the right decision with regard to educating our children."

"Thank you for providing much-needed encouragement to homeschoolers!"

"You all have thought of everything! The Used Curriculum Sale was amazing; the Exhibit Hall, excellent!"

"I came as a grandparent and got so much out of the Convention myself! This was so inspirational. I am a public school teacher and my daughter homeschools."

"Excellent blend of spiritually motivating and academically driven presentations...as always, we're coming away uplifted and nourished for our continuing journey!"

Of course, HEAV could never provide a convention like this without our volunteers who work so hard to make it possible. We owe a tremendous debt of gratitude to our convention director, convention coordinators and volunteers—from those who worked endless hours during the months prior to Convention, to those who donated money on the spot to help others. What a blessing you are to us! Thank you for working with HEAV to serve your fellow homeschoolers in such practical ways.

Look for convention information in the spring issue of the *Virginia Home Educator* magazine! There are special perks for registering early—like discount admission and early entrance into the Used Curriculum Sale! Don't miss this great opportunity to re-charge your batteries, buy curricula, and prepare for another great year!

Support HEAV!

Yvonne Bunn

WHAT *IS* HEAV? WHAT DO YOU DO? AND WHAT DO I GET FOR MY MEMBERSHIP FEE?

Have you ever wanted to ask us these questions? Don't feel bad. We often hear them. We sometimes get so busy we forget to introduce ourselves!

HEAV has been Virginia's state homeschool organization for the past 27 years. We are a not-for-profit 501(c)(3) organization with an office in Richmond run by staff and volunteers. A full-time executive director oversees all the operations of the organization. A volunteer board of experienced home-educating parents directs the organization with input from an advisory board—all from different areas of the state.

HEAV PROVIDES MANY SERVICES FOR VIRGINIA HOMESCHOOLERS. WE...

- Actively promote home education in the Commonwealth of Virginia;
- Provide homeschool representation to the Department of Education, the Governor's office, the Virginia General Assembly, and state and national pro-family organizations;
- Counsel new and veteran homeschoolers and refer them to knowledgeable sources of information;
- Work with approximately 200 local support groups;
- Provide information on testing and referrals;
- Offer some of the best homeschool resources (books, audio, and video-tapes) to help homeschoolers;
- Provide an HEAV website with updated information and links to other helpful sites;
- E-mail free *Legislative Updates* and alerts;
- Publish a quarterly magazine, *The Virginia Home Educator*, with home-school news, encouragement, recognition, and help. The magazine is sent to 14,000 to 20,000 Virginia homeschool families and support group leaders;
- Give members a free classified ad in the *Virginia Home Educator;*
- Send the free information-packed *Virginia Homeschool Update* by e-mail each week;
- Publish the *Virginia Homeschool Manual: A Comprehensive Guide to*

Home Education in Virginia that includes everything you need to know to educate your children at home in Virginia;

- Produce and sell "How to Begin Homeschooling" and "The Virginia Law" CDs and MP3s for new homeschoolers;
- Sponsor the annual three-day HEAV Virginia Homeschool Convention with more than 100 workshops, many nationally known speakers, and the largest new-and-used curriculum fair in Virginia;
- Offer discounts on conventions, seminars, books, tapes, videos, *et cetera;*
- Offer a $20 Homeschool Legal Defense membership discount;
- Have a year-round Director of Government Affairs and full-time lobbyist in Richmond during General Assembly sessions;
- Monitor the state legislature during legislative sessions; and
- Introduce legislation that will benefit and protect the rights of home-educating parents.

We hope this gives you a better idea of who we are and what we do? HEAV didn't happen over night, and it didn't happen without the help of several thousand supportive HEAV members. Please join us in making homeschooling better for Virginia parents. Your $35 yearly membership fee helps make it all happen. **Please fill out the membership information on page B-18, or on our website (www.heav.org), today!** We need your help to protect the rights of homeschooling parents and to help us keep home education strong in Virginia!

Beginning the Homeschool Journey

Compiled by Vicki Bentley

Additional articles on the CD
BE SURE TO CHECK OUT THESE OTHER GREAT ARTICLES ON THE CD!

Each article in the book and on the CD has been carefully chosen by the section coordinator to increase your knowledge and understanding of this subject, so don't forget to use and enjoy the parts of the manual on your CD, as well as the part you are holding.

Please note that the page numbering on the CD is different from that of the hard-copy manual.

Meet Your Travel Agent
An Introduction

I admit it—I am "geographically challenged." I have been known to make a cell-phone call from the parking garage after the HEAV Convention, frantic because I cannot find the exit after four attempts. Two years ago, driving home from Pittsburgh to Petersburg, I phoned my husband (collect!) at work to ask, "If I'm on Skyline Drive, have I missed a turn?" When we were first stationed at Fort Lee, I called him at work to ask where Emporia was. When he told me it was near North Carolina, I meekly inquired, "Does that mean I'm not near Fort Lee anymore?"

Go ahead and laugh. But I've finally determined why I have this problem. I can follow directions (okay, GOOD directions), but I have trouble figuring out *where I am* in relation to *where I'm trying to go.*

Now, if I asked you for directions, what's the first thing you'd probably want to know? Right—you'd want to know where I was trying to go. To get somewhere, I need to know where I'm starting and where I'm trying to go, so I can determine the best course to get me there.

That's our goal in planning this home-education journey, too. Though you may feel "geographically challenged" because you don't know where you are, where you're going, or how you're going to get there, this chapter is designed to help you choose your destination, plan your journey, and select the best route to get there.

Homeschooling is not just an education choice; it is a lifestyle of learning—the Journey of a Lifetime!

—Vicki Bentley

Pre-Trip Planning Checklist
I feel overwhelmed! Where do I begin?

Vicki Bentley

ood planning is the key to any successful road trip. Most of these items will be covered in greater detail later in this section and/or in other sections of this manual, but this checklist will give you a basic overview as you prepare for this journey!

RESEARCH HOMESCHOOLING
- Read all you can about home education. [See list of suggested resources at the end of this chapter.]
- Consider subscribing to homeschooling publications. Attend a state convention (or obtain tapes from the workshops, if this is a mid-year decision).
- Read, read, read.
- Attend an HEAV How-to-Begin seminar in your area.
- Check out home-education websites on the Internet. [See resource list for a starting point.]
- Attend a local support-group meeting and ask lots of questions—other parents often love to talk about homeschooling! Most importantly, talk to other homeschoolers to find out what they do, how, and why.
- And read, read, read!

RESEARCH THE VIRGINIA LAW
"Yes, Virginia, it *is* legal to homeschool." Basically, you should:
- Familiarize yourself with the statutes of the Virginia Code that regulate home education. [See the Virginia Law section of this manual for more detailed information.]
- Comply with either the Certified Tutor statute, the Religious Exemption statute, or the Homeschooling statute.
- Be aware of any deadlines you must meet. For example, under the Home-schooling statute, you should file your "Notice of Intent to Provide Home Instruction" with your superintendent of schools by August 15—unless the decision is made after the deadline, in which case you may send it in as soon as practicable; also, you must submit proof of progress by August 1 of the following year.

- Keep copies of any paperwork you send, and it's a good idea to mail everything "certified; return-receipt requested." Be sure that any paperwork you submit is free of spelling or grammatical errors (and coffee stains).

JOIN SUPPORT ORGANIZATIONS

You don't have to make this trip alone! Consider membership in the national, state, and local organizations that exist to help you. Some suggestions:
- State organizations such as Home Educators Association of Virginia (HEAV) (www.heav.org; 804-278-9200).
- Home School Legal Defense Association (www.hslda.org; 540-338-5600).
- Local support groups.
- Specialized support groups, such as those for families of special-needs children, or those based on particular interests such as sports, 4-H, *et cetera.*

SET GOALS

Why are you homeschooling? What is your idea of an education?
- Determine where your child is now—academically, spiritually, physically, and emotionally/socially; this is your starting point.
- Set measurable, attainable goals for each child. Discuss with your spouse and your child (if appropriate) how these objectives fit into the "big picture" of his future.
- Set personal and family goals.
- Evaluate activities and curriculum against goals.

CHOOSE CURRICULUM

By definition, your curriculum is your "course of study."
- Look through catalogs, magazines, curriculum guides, and books. [See resource list at the end of this section.]
- Talk to other homeschoolers about what worked for them and why, as well as what didn't work and why.
- Attend state-convention workshops/exhibit halls and local curriculum fairs.
- Go to used-book sales and used-curriculum shops.
- Evaluate your child's learning styles. [See article on learning styles.]
- Decide which method(s) seem to fit your family best at this point in time (you may overlap—methods are not mutually exclusive!).
- Keep evaluating all your choices against those goals you have set for your family and for each child.

PURCHASE SUPPLIES
- Homeschool resource books.
- Basic home reference materials.
- School supplies such as paper, pencils, pencil sharpener, rulers, pens, notebooks of some sort (and the proverbial red pen!).
- Filing or organizational supplies to keep your paperwork in order.
- Bookshelves and/or storage cabinets—designate "a place for everything."
- Other necessary items as specified in your curriculum.

ESTABLISH A SCHEDULE

- Decide on your school year (at least 180 days). For example, we home-school for eight weeks on, one week off, August through June, taking a four-week break in December and again in July. My reasoning is that I can do anything for eight weeks at a time, and then I have a week to re-group for the next session! Taking only one month off in summer keeps the girls on their toes academically.
- Have at least a framework for academic and character progress during the year.
- Have a family chore schedule in place, or a plan to keep the house manageable.
- Write out daily/weekly plans so you know that your expectations are realistic! [See Planning and Record Keeping section for more details.]

The Biblical Basis for Home Education

Gregg Harris

Five principles of educating our children are revealed clearly in the fountainhead of all biblical texts on education, Deuteronomy 6:4-9. In this passage we find the purpose of education, the primary site of instruction, the specific curriculum, the designated faculty, and the most effective methods of instruction. By looking at these principles, we can see the biblical basis for home education.

WHY SHOULD WE TEACH OUR CHILDREN AT HOME?

The purpose of educating children is so they will live a godly life, not so they will make a good living: *"The Lord our God, the Lord is one. Love the Lord your God with all your heart and with all your soul and with all your strength. These commandments that I give you today are to be upon your heart. And you shall teach them diligently to your sons."*

Our primary educational goal is to model and impart an ardent love for God and His commandments. A thorough knowledge of His Word is to saturate our thinking and influence our choices as we meditate on His will for us. Our knowledge of God and our attitudes toward Him are to be passed on to our children through our example and our diligent teaching so that they will adopt them for their own. The result will be children who are prepared to live a godly life. Preparation for making a living, while important, is a secondary goal.

WHERE SHOULD EDUCATION TAKE PLACE?

The site for instruction is the godly home. *"And you shall teach them diligently to your sons and shall talk of them when you sit in your house and when you walk by the way and when you lie down and when you rise up."*

The home is the primary location for instructing children. God does not say, "Do this until society gets around to organizing schools for your children." God could have unveiled a formal classroom school program in this passage, as elaborate as the temple worship, but He chose not to.

Educators readily acknowledge the unique needs of each individual child. That is why they ask for smaller student-to-teacher ratios. A home setting guarantees this. But notice that the Scriptures do not make the home a "container" for education. There is no constraint in God's command, merely focus. Homeschooling does not take place only in the home. Much is learned while traveling "by the way." This can include field trips and outings of all sorts.

WHAT CURRICULUM SHOULD BE USED?

The curriculum of instruction is the whole counsel of God on every aspect of life. *"And these words which I am commanding you today shall be on your hearts... and you shall teach them..."*

What are "these words" which Moses commanded Hebrew parents to teach their children? What topics of study did they include? A perusal of the book of Deuteronomy reveals a very complete and well-rounded curriculum. While offering over ten chapters of history, the book also addresses various aspects of art, warfare, marriage, child bearing, economics, ecology, criminal justice, education, health, agriculture, government, the poor, safety, ownership, dress codes, business, self-defense, dietary rules, singing, the attributes of God, and much more. And then we have the rest of the Bible.

John Milton, a devout Puritan leader of the 17th century, wrote, "The end then of learning is to repair the ruins of our first parents by regaining to know God aright, and out of that knowledge to love Him, to imitate Him, to be like Him. I call therefore, a complete and generous education that which fits a man to perform justly, skillfully, and magnanimously, all the offices, both private and public, of peace and war."

All aspects of a godly life are appropriate subjects of study. The curriculum is life itself, illuminated by the Bible and lived out by those who are older and wiser. With this in mind, respond to whatever is happening in your life with the confidence that it all has something good to contribute to your child's education. When my wife gave birth to twins last year, the lesson plans for my two older sons changed drastically. But now I can see what has happened is better than what we had planned. God put twins in our curriculum.

WHO SHOULD TEACH OUR CHILDREN?

The designated faculty are the parents of the child. *"And you shall teach them diligently to your sons..."*

God holds parents responsible for the character training and education of their own children. Fathers, especially, are designated as the ones obligated to *bring up their children in the discipline and instruction of the Lord* (Ephesians 6:4). As in the case of Eli, if a father fails to restrain his children in their crimes, by referral to civil authorities if need be, he becomes guilty as well (I Samuel 3:13).

WHAT ARE THE MOST EFFECTIVE INSTRUCTIONAL METHODS?

The most effective methods of instruction are tutoring and the personal example of the parents. *"And you shall teach them diligently to your sons and shall talk of them when you sit in your house and when you walk by the way and when you lie down and when you rise up."*

Any experienced teacher knows that tutoring is the teaching method of choice. It is personal, tailored to the needs of the individual child, and responsive to ups and downs in the student's ability. The Hebrew term for "diligently" is impregnated with a sense of sweat and determination. Firm direction of studies is expected. Though instruction need not always be given formally, it should always be given intentionally.

The joy and enjoyment of learning are not evinced by a proper sense of obligation. The context of the home assures that the learning will be accomplished on a flexible schedule. Homes, unlike classrooms, are part of the real world where life comes at you from all directions and without much warning.

How can anyone study in an average household? It does require a certain kind of self-discipline. But if children cannot develop good study habits in the real world of home life, their studies will end as soon as their schooling years are over. Lifelong, self-directed students are developed in the furnace of life's daily routine, not in the artificial setting of the school campus. Experience has shown that once a child becomes a dedicated student at home, he is able to get more out of any course of study he takes later on.

Deuteronomy requires diligent instruction from parents in the home, and it requires children to honor and obey their parents. Together these two commandments set the stage for a lifestyle of home-centered education. This alone would be an improvement over conventional classroom instruction. But Moses goes on, under the inspiration of the Holy Spirit, to add another effective educational method: the power of companionship to make the parental example more accessible to the child.

In addition to sessions of diligent instruction, parents are commanded to talk about various subjects of study in the context of the parents' necessary routine. *"As you sit in your house and as you walk by the way and as you lie down and as you rise up"* speaks of the casual inclusiveness whereby parents take their children with them to do whatever has to be done on any given day.

This passage is talking about including the children in our work as well as in our recreation. When we have chores to do or errands to run, we can take our children with us and talk to them about the things that are in their studies and on our hearts. This principle of companionship, more than any other, gives children full advantage of having parents.

WALKING WITH THE WISE

In addition, Proverbs 13:20 states, *"He who walks with the wise grows wise, but a companion of fools suffers harm."* Youth gangs, drug abuse, the occult, teenage materialism, gluttony, and laziness are the fruits of the companionship of fools in age-segregated schools. We call it youth culture. God calls it harm.

On the other hand, great achievements in theology, the arts, the sciences, various professions, skilled trades, and any other worthy endeavors are the consequence of walking with the wise. The greatest achievers are those who have developed a love for their field through the power of companionship with a mentor, friend, or family member. They have an enduring delight in what they do and they devote themselves to it with or without any other incentives.

God is raising up men and women who, for the sake of love, are willing to keep on doing what is right for the rest of their lives. Where do such men and women come from? Certainly they are gifts of God to the church. But God knits these gifts together in a secret place, and then turns them over to parents to nurture and train.

The goal of education is a life, not a living; its best location is a home where life goes on, not in a classroom; its curriculum is the Word of God as it illuminates every part of life; its faculty consists of fathers and mothers; and its methods of instruction are one-to-one tutoring and including the child in the daily companionship of serving God. There is no better way of following these principles than homeschooling. Christian homeschooling is "on-the-job training" for the Christian life. That, more than anything else, is its biblical basis.

Gregg Harris is a Christian husband and father of seven children. Gregg is an internationally recognized author and conference speaker whose work helped to start the Christian homeschooling movements in the U.S., Canada, Australia, and Mexico. Beginning in 1981, his workshops, together with his bestselling book, The Christian Homeschool, have helped to launch over 180,000 families into teaching their children at home. Gregg lives with his wife Sono and the younger of their seven children i Gresham, Oregon, where he serves as a teaching elder of Household of Faith Community Church, a cluster of three age-integrated congregations (www. hoffcc.org).

Biblical Principles for Home Education

Many parents home educate their children because of sincere religious beliefs. This reference section is a compilation of various Scriptures that may be used to support the teaching and training of children at home.

THE EDUCATION OF CHILDREN

God is the Source of Truth

Exodus 34:6	Psalms 100:5	John 15:26
Isaiah 38:19	Psalms 119:142, 151	John 16:13
Psalms 25:5	John 1:14, 17	John 17:17, 19
Psalms 36:9	John 8:31,32	I John 4:6
Psalms 40:11	John 14:6	I John 5:20
Psalms 86:11		

God is the True Teacher

Job 36:22	Proverbs 2:6	Micah 4:2
II Chronicles. 6:26, 27	Isaiah 2:3	Mark 6:34
Psalms 32:8	Isaiah 28:9	Luke 11:1
Psalms 86:11	Isaiah 48:17	Luke 12:12
Psalms 94:10	Isaiah 50:4	John 14:26
Psalms 119:64	Isaiah 54:13	Acts 1:1
Psalms 119:65-68	Jeremiah 31:33, 34	I John 2:27
Psalms 119:102		

God Gives Children to Their Parents

Genesis 30:1-24	I Samuel 1:20	Psalms 127:3, 4
Genesis 33:5	Psalms 107:38	Isaiah 29:23
Genesis 48:8, 9	Psalms 113:9	Malachi 2:15

Educational Responsibility Belongs to Parents

Genesis 18:18, 19	Psalms 34:11	Proverbs 6:20-23
Exodus 33:5	Psalms 78:1-11	Proverbs 13:1
Deuteronomy 4:5-10	Proverbs 1:8	Isaiah 38:19
Deuteronomy 6:1-9	Proverbs 2:1-5	Joel 1:3

Deuteronomy 11:18-21   Proverbs 3:12   Ephesians 6:1-4
Deuteronomy 31:12   Proverbs 4:1   Colossians 3:20
Deuteronomy 32:45, 46   Proverbs 4:20-27   I Thessalonians 2:11

We Are to Teach the Ways of God

Leviticus 10:8-11	Proverbs 13:10	I Corinthians 4:17
Deuteronomy 31:12, 13	Proverbs 19:27	I Corinthians 11:14
I Samuel 12:23	Proverbs 22:17-21	Galatians 4:2
Job 34:4	Ezekiel 44:21-23	Colossians 1:28
Psalms 1:1, 2	Matthew 21:23	I Timothy 2:7
Psalms 34:11	Matthew 25:14-30	I Timothy 3:15
Psalms 86:11	Matthew 28:18-20	I Timothy 4:11
Psalms 119:32	John 7:16-18	I Timothy 6:12
Psalms 119:35	John 21:15	II Timothy 2:15
Psalms 132:12	Acts 5:42	Titus 2:4
Psalms 143:10	Acts 15:35	Titus 2:12
Proverbs 9:9	Acts 18:11	Titus 3:1

We Are Not to Teach Ungodly Ways

Deuteronomy 20:18	Proverbs 21:16	I Corinthians 14:20
Psalms 1:1	Jeremiah 10:1, 2	II Corinthians 6:14-17
Proverbs 1:15	Ezekiel 23:36, 37	II Corinthians 11:3
Proverbs 4:14	Romans 12:2	Colossians 2:8

Our Faithfulness Yields Fruit in Our Children's Lives

Genesis 17:7	Proverbs 20:7	Psalms 112:1, 2
Proverbs 13:22	Proverbs 22:6	I Corinthians 7:14
Proverbs 14:18, 26		

Our Disobedience to God Brings Consequences in Our Children's Lives

Exodus 20:5	Deuteronomy 28:15-68	Proverbs 29:15
Deuteronomy 21:18-21	Judges 2:10-15	

God has a Plan for Education

Psalms 22:30, 31	Proverbs 4:7	I Corinthians 1:30
Psalms 78:2, 3	Proverbs 22:17-21	Galatians 3:24
Psalms 145:4	Romans 2:18	II Timothy 2:1, 2

ACADEMIC SUBJECTS
Language

Genesis 1:3, 27	Romans 10:13, 17	II Timothy 3:16
Genesis 2:7,19, 23	I Corinthians 10:31	Titus 2:8
Genesis 11:9	Colossians 4:6	Hebrews 1:1, 2
Deuteronomy 17:19	I Thessalonians 5:17	I Peter 1:19-21
Psalms 119:11	I Timothy 4:13	I Peter 3:15
Matthew 12:36, 37	II Timothy 2:15	Revelation 1:3

Mathematics

Genesis 1:5
Genesis 2:10-14
Genesis 6
Exodus 25-28
II Chronicles 1-6

Psalms 90:12
Malachi 3:6
Malachi 3:10
Matthew 18:22
Matthew 25:14-30

Luke 14:28
Romans 14:12
I Corinthians 14:40
I Corinthians 16:1, 2
Revelation 21:12-17

Science

Genesis 1
Genesis 2:7
Genesis 10:1-30
Genesis 14-16
Genesis 15:5
Numbers 22:28
Joshua 10:12
I Kings 4:33

II Chronicles 2:1-18
Job 22-38
Psalms 107:23, 24
Ecclesiastes 1:6, 7
Isaiah 40:5, 61
Jeremiah 8:22
Ezekiel 40:5, 6
Mark 5:41

John 1:3
John 17:17
Colossians 1:16, 17
Colossians 2:8
I Timothy 6:20
Hebrews 1:3
II Peter 3:3-9

History

Genesis 1:1, 27
Genesis 2:7
Genesis 3
Genesis 6-9
Joshua 4:20-24
Psalms 76:6-12

Ezekiel 22:25-29
John 3:16
Acts 16:6-10
Romans 2:1-6
Romans 3:10, 23
Romans 5:8

Romans 10:9,10, 13
I Corinthians 1:19-25
II Peter 2:13
Revelation 10:6
Revelation 21:1

Economics

Genesis 2:8-14
Genesis 3:17-19
Leviticus 27:30-34
Deuteronomy 28
Proverbs 3:9, 10
Proverbs 14:23

Proverbs 22:7
Proverbs 31:10-31
Ecclesiastes 5:18-20
Isaiah 48:17
Matthew 6:19-34
Matthew 18:23-35

Matthew 22:21
Luke 12:33, 34
Luke 16:10,11
II Corinthians 9:6-11
I Thess. 4:10-12

Sociology

Genesis 2:20-25, 29
Genesis 9:6
Exodus 20:3, 4, 7
Exodus 20:14-16
Exodus 21:24

Leviticus 18:22, 23
Leviticus 19:20
Deuteronomy 6:4-8
Psalms 139:14-16
Proverbs 6:16, 17

Matthew 19:6
Ephesians 5:3-33
Ephesians 6:1-4
II Thessalonians 3:16

Law

Exodus 20
Psalms 1:2
Psalms 2:10, 11

Psalms 19:7
Psalms 37:31
Psalms 119:1-8

Romans 3:19
Romans 6:23
James 1:25

The Arts

Genesis 1:1	Psalms 104	Romans 1:22, 23
Exodus 20:4, 5	Ecclesiastes 3:11	I Corinthians 10:31
Psalms 19:1-6	John 1:3	Ephesians 2:10
Psalms 90:17		

Music

Genesis 4:21	Psalms 40:3	Isaiah 44:23
I Kings 4:29-32	Psalms 100:1	I Corinthians 10:31
II Chronicles 5:12, 13	Psalms 104:33	Ephesians 5:18, 19
Job 35:10	Psalms 137:4	Colossians 3:16
Psalms 28:7	Proverbs 29:6	James 5:13

Physical Education

II Samuel 1:23	I Corinthians 6:19, 20	I Timothy 4:8
I Chronicles 12:1-7	I Corinthians 9:25, 27	II Timothy 2:3
Isaiah 40:28-31	I Corinthians 15:51-55	

Health

Exodus 15:6	Proverbs 3:23	Jeremiah 17:14
Leviticus 15	Proverbs 4:20-22	John 4:46-53
Leviticus 25:18	Proverbs 28:7	Acts 27:34
Psalms 41:4	Isaiah 6:10	I Corinthians 6:19, 20
Psalms 119:117	Jeremiah 3:22	James 4:14, 15
Proverbs 2:11	Jeremiah 8:22	

Career Education

Matthew 6:24-34	Ephesians 4:1	I Timothy 6:1-3
I Corinthians 3:11-23	Ephesians 6:5-9	Hebrews 11:13, 14
I Corinthians 10:31	James 4:12	II Thess. 3:4-13
II Corinthians 5:14-20		

Psychology

Genesis 1:27	John 10:10	Galatians 5:22, 23
Genesis 2:7	Romans 5:8, 9, 12	Ephesians 2:8, 9
Ecclesiastes 12:7	Romans 6:23	Ephesians 5:18
Matthew 5:3-12	Romans 7:14-25	I Thessalonians 5:23

God Gives Teachers to His Church

Isaiah 30:20	I Corinthians 12:28	II Timothy 2:2
Jeremiah 32:33	II Corinthians 6:1	II Timothy 2:24
Matthew 4:23	Ephesians 4:7-16	James 3:1, 2
Romans 12:1-8	Colossians 3:16	I Peter 4:10, 11
I Corinthians 3:9		

Principles of Learning

Psalms 119:71, 73

Proverbs 1:5

Isaiah 50:4

Romans 15:4

Philippians 4:9

II Timothy 3:14

Education Should Lead to Knowledge and Wisdom

Proverbs 16:23

Ecclesiastes 12:9

Daniel 2:21

Psalms 37:30

Psalms 119:66

Proverbs 1:7

Proverbs 2:1-10

I Corinthians 14:31

Proverbs 4:7,13

Proverbs 8:9, 10

Proverbs 9:10

Proverbs 21:11

Proverbs 22:17

Proverbs 23:12

Proverbs 29:25

Titus 3:14

Romans 15:14

Colossians 1:9, 10

I Timothy 2:4

II Peter 1:5, 6

The Student: Our Final Product

Proverbs 20:11

Matthew 5:14-16

Matthew 5:48

Matthew 6:19-21

Matthew 10:16

John 14:9

John 15:4, 11

Acts 27:22

Romans 12:10, 13-17

Romans 13:1-9, 14

Romans 14:3

Romans 15:1, 2, 13

Romans 16-19

I Corinthians 1:10

I Corinthians 2:14

I Corinthians 3:17

I Corinthians 4:6

I Corinthians 5:13

I Corinthians 6:1,7

I Corinthians 6:13

I Corinthians 6:18, 20

Galatians 5:22, 23

Ephesians 2:10

Ephesians 3:19

Ephesians 4:13, 25, 26

Ephesians 5:18

Philippians 2:12

Philippians 3:16

Philippians 4:6, 7

Colossians 1:27, 28

Colossians 3:20

I Thessalonians 2:9

I Thess. 4:11-13

I Thess. 5:14-18

I Thessalonians 5:21

II Thess. 3: 6,10

I Timothy 4:8, 16

I John 2:15-17

Myths About Socialization

Rick G. Boyer

Of all the objections raised to home education, the most common is the question of social development. How can children learn to relate to other people if we don't send them to school? The answer: Naturally and successfully! The fact is that the age-peer social grouping of our schools is unnatural and often destructive of home-taught values. Home educators can protect their children from the effects of this social aberration if they recognize it as such and are prepared to refute its surrounding myths.

Myth: *Schools provide children with plenty of healthy social experience.*
Fact: *Schools isolate children from normal social situations and expose them to negative socializing factors.*

My early years in school contained little social experience. I recall sitting in a desk in a roomful of children all the same age and not being permitted to socialize to any significant degree. Except for a few minutes of hyperactivity at recess and a half hour at lunch, we were anything but social. Class discussions were initiated and guided by the teacher. We didn't select the timing or the topic, nor did we feel free to say exactly what was on our minds. Compared to the real world of home and neighborhood, school was social deprivation. We were actually removed from what really goes on in society by being placed in the artificial environment of a classroom.

The school setting not only lacks positive social experience, it contains some very negative socializing factors as well. Peer pressure is the most commonly recognized of these, but it is not alone. A child is deeply influenced by his teacher, too, and the younger the child, the greater the teacher's degree of influence.

This is a sobering thought to a person of my age, because the generation who were students in the sixties are now the teaching and administration cadre of the public schools. The moral relativism of the Vietnam generation now guides many of our teachers. The curriculum has now become anti-social as well. Sex education encourages students to use others for selfish pleasure. The only obligation is to "protect" themselves and their partners from pregnancy and/or disease. (This, of course, can only be guaranteed by chastity, an overlooked detail.) Death education (along with abortion) is mental preparation for euthanasia. "Values clarification" is teaching children that some people are more valuable than others—if there is one too many in the bomb shelter, take a vote and eject one.

Myth: *Home educators should involve their children in social activities with their own age groups to compensate for their "lack of social contact."*
Fact: *Age-segregated groups foster negative social attitudes while age-integrated family groups encourage mutually-beneficial interaction.*

Research, experience, and logic all confirm that an age-peer social environment is destructive of healthy attitudes toward self and others. A situation in which children are constantly compared to each other teaches them that success comes not by doing one's best but by being like someone else. Another argument against age segregation is the need of the different age groups for contact with each other. This applies not only to consecutive generations, but also to those closer in age.

An experiment was conducted in which 6th graders with reading problems were assigned to teach 1st grade children how to read. The result was that the 6th graders greatly improved their own reading, and the 1st graders learned to read better than their peers taught by the teachers. That experiment illustrates our point: Children benefit from interaction with others who are either older or younger than they are.

Family bonding, so desperately needed in our day, is also frustrated by the segregation of age groups. It is common knowledge that to an adolescent among his peers, it is not acceptable to treat a sibling with affection or to respect and appreciate a parent's advice. In most traditional societies, grandparents help their children rear the grandchildren, giving old age a purpose, children the benefit of wisdom, and young parents relief from shouldering the whole burden. Age-peer-oriented mass education, with its ever-increasing demands on a child's time, has made this concept a faded memory in America. We are a poorer and shallower society for it.

Myth: *One of the important things children learn in school is how to get along with all types of people.*
Fact: *Children in school are more likely to develop habits of unkindness and disrespect for anyone who is "different."*

School children spend much time in the presence of other people, but it is an unnatural, contrived environment where students are separated from the rest of society and have little meaningful communication even with each other. And they certainly aren't learning to "get along." Even well-meaning attempts by teachers to encourage tolerance of others' differences cannot withstand the strong peer pressure to conform and the cruel rejection of those who don't.

Myth: *Children learn to stand up for their beliefs by dealing with their peers' antagonism in school.*
Fact: *Almost all children and adolescents are unready to stand against the overwhelming pressures they face in school.*

Do they stand? Does the average fourth grader take issue with his teacher when told that man evolved from monkeys? Does the average high-school athlete tell his buddies to spare him the locker room jokes because he's a Christian? Surely some do, but not most.

Younger children especially revere their teachers, or at least the teacher's authority. Students of high-school age have lost much of their starry-eyed trust of adults, but for them, peer pressure is almost irresistible. Certainly there are notable exceptions, but it is unusual for a high-school student even in a Christian school to take a clear stand apart from his godless or lukewarm fellows. People tend to become average for the group they are in. As the Bible says, "Bad company corrupts good morals" (I Cor. 15:33, NAS).

Another factor to consider is readiness. When I say that children face too much pressure in school, someone often objects, "But they have to learn to deal with it sometime." True. They will have to learn to drive, too. But not at five or six years of age!

As adults we often forget just how much pressure is on children in school. Children and adolescents in peer groups often say and do things to each other that can only be described as vicious. And it is usually the shy ones, the small ones, the insecure and backward children—in short, the ones who are least able to "deal with it"—who get the brunt of the bullying and ridicule. This is a pressure adults do not have to face. When I was in school, I was one of the smallest boys. This and my insecure personality made me the target for bullying, ridicule, and social exclusion. I have never been subjected to such treatment anywhere else. Even with years of experience in construction, I have never known adults to treat each other the way children treat their peers.

School is a pressure cooker to which no child should be subjected. The damage done by the philosophy expressed in these four myths is unfortunately not limited to children in schools. Many home educators still equate social development with segregating children to their own age group. These parents contrive all sorts of "extracurricular activities" for their children to be involved in for the sake of "normal socialization."

What children really need is their natural habitat. They need to spend time with their families in the real world: home, church, neighborhood, market, and work. They need to see others of all ages going about the real business of living. Further, they need guidance from parents, grandparents, and siblings rather than being thrown into an indiscriminate mix of companions. Proverbs 13:20 is the answer to the myths of socialization: "He who walks with wise men will be wise, but the companion of fools will suffer harm."

Pioneers in the home education movement, Rick and Marilyn Boyer have taught their children at home since 1980. They have fourteen children, including seven who have completed high school, and one college graduate, and four grandchildren (so far!). Their ministry to parents includes authoring eleven books on homeschooling and Christian parenting, as well as speaking at conventions. The Boyers' "sure you can" philosophy has met with a warm welcome from thousands of parents who appreciate the message that home education does not have to be complicated. Read more about the Boyers at www.thelearningparent.com.

Charting Your Course

Vicki Bentley

hen I mention the word *curriculum*, what comes to mind? The word *curriculum* simply means course of study (its root translates from the French *courir*, to run, and Latin counterparts). In mapping out your homeschool course, you must determine where you plan to go, where you are now, and ascertain the best way to get from here to there (lest you be "lost in the parking garage, if you recall my example). This can be overwhelming! But don't despair. Take a "rest stop" to determine your philosophy of education, which will guide you in the rest of your travels.

Why are you homeschooling? Is this something you feel called to do, or are you trying it out for a year? This will steer your curriculum choices somewhat. If you are planning to put your child into public school at some point, you will probably want to use a fairly conservative approach, possibly a pre-packaged curriculum (maybe a correspondence course), or you may want to compare your customized curriculum to the grade-level Standards of Learning for our state. For placement (knowing where to begin), determine what your child already knows versus what is covered in the material. Just because he is a first grader doesn't mean he has to be constrained to covering first-grade reading skills again if he is already reading well above grade level.

NOTE: If you are removing a child from a conventional school setting and you have a concern that he is not up to the cognitive levels indicated by his grade level, I highly recommend having him take a standardized test to provide a baseline for you. That way, at the end of the year, you have a starting point against which to evaluate his progress. (See Testing section of this manual.)

If you are committed to homeschooling for at least several years, you will be responsible for setting the long-term standards for your child's education. What is your concept of an education? What skills, knowledge, and/or experience will your child need in order for you to consider him ready to be on his own? If you can't think that far ahead right this moment, at least consider what you want him to have accomplished by the end of this year. Later in this section is a worksheet you can use to set a few goals for your child. These goals should be measurable—how will you know when they have been accomplished? Discuss with your spouse and your child (if appropriate) how these objectives fit into the "big picture" of his future.

This is also a good time to set some goals for yourself and for your family in general. As you choose activities and curriculum for your child(ren), evaluate these against the goals you have set for this year. Will this activity move you closer to your stated objective? Is a good activity or book or class keeping you from having time to do what is best? Maybe it is something that can wait until another time.

Will you use a packaged curriculum to get started? Or will you choose various books and games that fit into your plan? Are there some subjects that you can teach to all the children at one time in a multi-level approach? Do you prefer the security and continuity of a traditional textbook approach, or do you like the idea of an integrated unit study approach? Maybe the patriotism of the Principle Approach excites you, or possibly your maternal instincts go into overdrive when you read about Charlotte Mason's gentler approach to learning. As you read, you may find that the Classical Approach sounds like what you equate with homeschooling, or maybe you are attracted to the relaxed approach of studying what is of interest in your family at the moment. Feel free to borrow and re-arrange from all these different approaches; they are not mutually exclusive. That's one of the wonderful benefits of home-schooling—you can create a custom curriculum!

There is no one "right" way to homeschool, no "perfect" curriculum. What works for one family may not be the best for another, or what works for you one year with one child may not work for the next. Don't compare your children to the support-group leader's children or your friend's children; compare your family only to God's ideal for your family. Let the ideas in the following articles guide you to prayerfully map out a course to help your children learn about God's world from God's perspective, so they can figure out where they fit into His plan.

Have a great time along the way, and be prepared for an incredible journey!

Where Do We Go From Here?

Setting and Attaining Your Goals

Vicki Bentley

Ask yourself, "Why are we homeschooling?" Have an overall purpose in mind, then set your goals to accomplish that purpose over the year. This will be quite valuable in January, when you may be weary and feel like quitting. Put your reasons in writing!

According to Luke 2:52, "Jesus grew in wisdom and stature, and in favor with God and man." (NIV). What progress would you like your child to make in those four areas this year? Remember: while your *purpose* could be defined as your aim (for example, for your child to grow up to be a godly person), your *goals* should be measurable (to read one chapter of the Bible a day, to keep a prayer notebook, to be kinder to siblings, *et cetera*). If you don't create measurable goals, how will you know when a goal has been reached?

WHAT TYPES OF GOALS SHOULD BE SET?

Intellectual: Try to set specific goals for each child so your studies will have direction. Rather than broad or vague goals such as "to learn phonics," you may aim for him to improve reading speed, read ten biographies, keep a journal, start a family newsletter, learn about three foreign countries, improve multiplication speed, *et cetera*.

Physical: Don't limit physical education to learning a sport. An active PE program is healthy, but go a step further by including activities such as learning to prepare nutritious snacks, walking as a family, working on a construction project, improving hygiene, learning how the body systems work, and so forth.

Spiritual: This is a good time to focus on particular character traits and then plan appropriate activities and/or units to reinforce or teach these goals. For example, if you want to see your student improve in patience, you might include activities such as knot-tying and puzzles. Gratefulness or compassion for others could be encouraged by establishing a pen-pal relationship with a missionary's kid or by taking healthy snacks or small gifts to local nursing-home residents. You could set specific goals for Bible memory work or Bible reading, as well.

Social: For a younger child, goals set in this area could be as basic as learning good telephone manners. This is a good time to identify potentially positive traits that are being misdirected. An overly-organized, compulsive, impatient child could become a very efficient person. The child who is always being taken advantage of is probably very patient with others and probably has a servant's heart (assuming he has a healthy, godly self-image). A spendthrift or wasteful child could learn to use his generosity to further God's kingdom. Look for ways to encourage the gifts to be used appropriately without breaking the child's spirit. This is also a good opportunity to evaluate outside activities and decide how the family's time will be most wisely spent. Are those outside activities helping to meet your goals? Could some of those activities be saved for another time, or dropped altogether?

Once you have set your goals, choose your curriculum and schedule accordingly. There are many excellent resources available, but you don't have to use them all! Be selective—you are choosing the tools to help you lay a firm foundation and build wisely. Sketch out the year so you have a rough outline, then flesh out that outline each week (or each grading period, or whatever works best for you) with activities and assignments to accomplish your goals. Then take time throughout the year to evaluate your progress and possibly make adjustments. Ask yourself, "What is working and what is not working, and why? What can I adjust to meet our goals?"

Excerpted and adapted from *My Homeschool Planner* by Family Resources. Used by permission.

10 Rules of Thumb for Choosing Teaching Materials

Chris and Ellyn Davis

R ULE #1: INVEST IN YOURSELF FIRST.
Like it or not, you are the glue that will hold this homeschooling endeavor together, so you need to develop a strategy for staying sane and on top of it all (even if it means scheduling a nap every afternoon). You wouldn't dream of trying to build a house without a plan, the right materials, and the necessary tools. Homeschooling is like building a house—you need to determine your plan, gather your materials, and be sure you have the right tools for the job. Take some time to read, to look around, to compare. Invest in some of the "tools of the trade" like the "must haves" and parent resources. Begin rearranging your house so it will accommodate study without becoming too cluttered or stressful. Think through what you will do with infants and toddlers during school times; how you will handle meals, cleaning, and laundry; and how you will deal with the other changes schooling at home brings. Don't feel guilty about spending money on yourself. After all, if you were a professional teacher, you (or your parents) would have spent tens of thousands of dollars getting you ready to stand before a classroom of children. So think in terms of what will make you more confident and able to create a learning environment for your household. What will smooth your way mentally, emotionally, physically, and spiritually? Remember that teaching your children at home is going to be quite an adjustment for you as well as for your children. Take care of yourself. Don't overcommit. Stay at home. Find ways to make life easier for yourself.

RULE #2: CONSIDER YOUR SITUATION.

Your first priority is to find where your children are physically, emotionally, mentally, and academically. Start with where they are and build on that. Often children taken from a public-school setting have problems with self-esteem, peer dependency, academic "burnout," and/or the adjustment from classroom to home. The most harmful thing you can do with a damaged child is to jump into academics. Take time to become reacquainted with your children, to "wash away" the institutional effects, to determine their learning strengths and weaknesses. You may want to just cover the necessities of academics (language arts and math) for the first few months to a year, or start out with one or two subjects and gradually add more.

A farm family will have many opportunities for "hands on" learning in the areas of math, science, economics, **et cetera**. A city family has access to museums, libraries, cultural events, and more support-group activities. You can make the most of the real-life learning opportunities God gives you, perhaps never needing textbooks and teaching materials in certain subject areas. We once had a missionary call us, bemoaning the fact that she lived in a large foreign city and her children weren't able to do much nature study. She completely overlooked all the wonderful opportunities her children had to learn foreign languages, history, and geography, and to interact with other cultures. So, look around. God may have already arranged a learning environment for you that is better than a classroom.

RULE #3: CHOOSE TEACHING MATERIALS SUITED TO THE LEARNER.

Textbooks developed for classroom use tend to be "teacher directed" and chalkboard oriented, seldom taking into account children's interests or the different ways children perceive and process information. Different children have different learning strengths and weaknesses that the perceptive parent will take into account when choosing teaching materials. For example, visual learners may do well with workbooks, while auditory learners need songs or spoken instruction, and kinesthetic learners need to manipulate objects

RULE #4: CHOOSE MATERIAL YOU LIKE, OR YOU WILL RESIST USING IT, NO MATTER HOW GOOD IT IS.

All teaching materials have a bias, not just in the subject matter, but also in the way the subject matter is presented. Every teaching parent, whether he or she recognizes it or not, has an educational philosophy—some set of values and beliefs about what and how children should be taught. Sometimes we will have an unexplained inner resistance to certain teaching materials. It could be that this inner resistance arises from a conflict between our educational philosophy and that of the teaching material. Trust the Holy Spirit and choose from your spirit as well as from your head. No matter how much your friends rave about a particular product, don't buy it if you don't really like it yourself. A key question to ask is: "Does just looking at this curriculum make me feel tired or pressured?"

RULE #5: AVOID PROGRAMS THAT REQUIRE A GREAT DEAL OF TEACHER PREPARATION.

Unless you are a researcher type or high-energy person, you will be frustrated by programs with detailed teacher's manuals to wade through, supplemental books or seminars that are necessary to fully utilize the program, or lots of activities to prepare beforehand.

RULE #6: EXPECT TO "WASTE" TIME, ENERGY, AND PROBABLY SOME MONEY.

You will soon discover that often it is you, not your children, who are being educated. So loosen up and accept the fact that some of what you buy may be a total waste of time, energy, and money. This is all a part of learning what works for you and for your children. Consider it payment of your tuition in the University for Home-Educating Parents.

RULE #7: BE AWARE THAT THERE ARE VARIOUS SCHOOLS OF THOUGHT CONCERNING THE TEACHING OF ANY SUBJECT.

Some examples: In math, there are programs that are primarily problem solving with manipulatives and programs that are primarily problem solving on paper. In reading, there are programs that focus on learning phonics before learning to read, programs that focus on learning the rules while learning to read, and programs that focus on just learning to read and letting the rules come later. Each school of thought has produced excellent mathematicians, readers, and spellers, but sometimes products will be advertised as better than the rest because they follow a particular school of thought.

RULE #8: REALIZE THAT THERE IS NO PERFECT CURRICULUM.

What works with one child won't necessarily work with another. What worked one year may not work the next. Your family's needs and interests will change. Buy materials that meet present needs. Mold the curriculum to the child, not the child to the curriculum. Also, be aware that not all books in a series are equally good. For example, the fourth-grade level of a particular program may be excellent, but this does not mean the other levels are.

RULE #9: GOD GAVE YOU **YOUR** SPECIFIC CHILDREN BECAUSE THERE IS SOMETHING IN YOU THAT HE WANTS IMPARTED TO THEM.

Teaching materials are only tools to help you impart yourself to (to disciple) your children. You can trust the Lord to lead you to materials that will help you best disciple each child. Beware of adult peer pressure; many of your relatives and friends will criticize your decision to homeschool. Don't feel you need to live up to their expectations. Other homeschooling parents may pressure you to try their favorite curriculum or intimidate you with their children's achievements. Remember, you know your children's needs better than anyone else and you are best qualified to help them reach their full potential.

RULE #10: REMEMBER THAT TEACHING MATERIALS ARE OFTEN THE LEAST IMPORTANT ELEMENTS OF YOUR HOMESCHOOL.

Books are easy to discard if they don't work, but attitudes and destructive family dynamics are not. Five reasons families fail at home education are:
1. They lack the personal conviction to persevere through the difficult times,
2. The father is not involved,
3. The children are undisciplined and resist parental instruction,
4. The parents cannot handle the added responsibilities, or
5. The family has unrealistic expectations.

The best teaching materials in the world are going to take a back seat to the attitudes and family dynamics in your household.

The Five D's of Education:
A Home-Centered Learning Model

Clay and Sally Clarkson

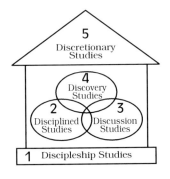

THE HOME-CENTERED LEARNING MODEL

The model is designed so that you provide a range of coordinated learning experiences for your children, moving from more structured learning to more unstructured learning, and from more teacher-directed learning to more child-directed learning. This kind of balanced approach allows you to have input and direction at any level in your children's lives, while at the same time giving them freedom to explore and discover on their own. That balance is important for your child to develop a self-motivated desire to learn, independent of always being told what they must think and study. It gives them the freedom to discover the person that God is making them.

The five focused study areas of the Home-Centered Learning model provide an integrated plan of home education. The house illustration shows how the five areas work together.

1. DISCIPLESHIP STUDIES   *THE SOLID FOUNDATION OF THE HOUSE.*
The study of the Bible.
Doctrine, wisdom, Bible knowledge.
Purpose: To shape your children's hearts to love God and to study and know his Word.

2. DISCIPLINED STUDIES   *THE FIRST CENTRAL STUDY FOCUS.*
The study of the "basics."
Learning skills (reading, writing, math, thinking)
Purpose: To develop your children's foundational learning skills and competencies in language arts, math, and reasoning.

3. DISCUSSION STUDIES   *THE SECOND CENTRAL STUDY FOCUS.*
The study of the humanities.
Literature, history, fine arts
Purpose: To feed your children's minds by giving them the best in living books and fine arts.

4. DISCOVERY STUDIES   *THE THIRD CENTRAL STUDY FOCUS.*
The study of learning.
Nature, science, creative arts, all interests
Purpose: To stimulate in your children a love for learning by creating opportunities for curiosity, creativity, and discovery.

5. DISCRETIONARY STUDIES   *THE UNIQUE FINISHING OF THE HOUSE.*
The study of living.
Home and community life, field trips, life skills
Purpose: To direct your children in developing a range of skills and abilities for adult life according to their gifts and your family's circumstances and resources.

Excerpted or derived from *Educating the WholeHearted Child*, © 1994, 1996 Whole Heart Ministries (P.O. Box 3445, Monument, CO 80132, www.wholeheart.org. Used by permission.

Know Your Students: Identify Their Personal Learning Styles

Inge Cannon

Educators have many ways of defining and describing the way people process information including learning personalities, modalities, and styles. The simplest to understand and apply involves three categories: lookers, listeners, and movers.

Lookers (technically termed visual/spatial learners) process information best when they see it. Listeners (called auditory learners) are most efficient when they can hear information, and movers (kinesthetic or tactile learners) function best when they can physically interact with information in a hands-on way.

It is helpful for a teaching parent to know his own learning style as well as the innate learning style of each child in the family for several reasons:

1. A teacher will tend to choose curriculum that appeals to his own best way to learn because that's what makes the most sense to him. If the children's styles are different, the materials may not make as much sense to them.

2. It is common for curriculum (e.g., a phonics or math program) to work extremely well for one child, and therefore, the parent thinks that subsequent children should do even better since he now knows how to teach the material. Then comes the shock! Child number two or number three is wired completely differently and thus needs a different approach.

3. Effectiveness of communication (even between spouses) is enhanced when we present new or complicated information in the manner the receiver uses best.

The entire population of the world is not divided into three learning groups, however. Thus, some children do very well with two of the three styles. Occasionally a child is equally adept at all three. Sometimes people need to get certain kinds of information one way and other kinds of information in a different way. Furthermore, there is no such thing as one "right" kind of material for a given learning style.

However, there are more and less efficient ways to use what you have. If your child is not learning what you want him to learn one way, try another method. Feel free to adapt the materials you have to the methods that will help you travel past the roadblocks in your child's mind.

The following check list will help you identify the tendencies of learners in each group. Remember that one child will not demonstrate all the characteristics within a category. If you check off most of the characteristics in one category, you will, however, have confidence that your child probably does best in that area *at this time*.

Your goal as a teacher should be to make your children eventually comfortable with all three means of getting information. After you have presented a new idea through the child's preferred style, review the material with some of the other methods to increase your child's flexibility.

VISUAL/SPATIAL LEARNERS (LOOKERS)
- Tend to be quiet and often need to be coaxed into answering questions.
- Are excellent "copycats," functioning best when they "see" what is expected of them.
- Are especially observant of details and can frequently find items lost by others.
- Will take copious notes, even when teacher promises to provide handouts.
- Are visually organized, easily remember where things are, and need to have everything in its place.
- Can assemble most things without help from instructions.
- Will catch your typographical errors and recognize if they have worked on or seen a page of material before.
- Make it a priority to look neat and be color-coordinated.
- Are very aware of spatial relationships and thus able to create well-spaced drawings, diagrams, and graphs.
- Doodle on note paper when talking.
- Tend to have a vivid imagination.
- Will have a large reading vocabulary at an early age.
- Given a choice, would most like to watch television or read a book in their spare time.
- Are easily distracted by visual stimuli (e.g., a new bulletin board or a bird outside the window).
- Respond favorably to visible rewards.

Visual/Spatial Learners Flourish When:
- Taught with books and pictures.
- Allowed to work challenging puzzles.
- The teacher demonstrates the skill to be learned (models it)—"show me."
- Shown the word before hearing what it is.
- Shown a picture of the actual object.
- The position of tongue and lips is demonstrated when new words are presented.
- Doing self-checking materials.

- Taught with the following aids:
    - Flashcards, matching games
    - Puzzles (of every kind)
    - Dictionaries
    - "How to" books with diagrams
    - Charts, maps, pictures, graphs
    - Written directions
    - Wall strips, desk tapes, timelines
    - Well-defined assignments

Note: If you can't have the visual learner observe the concept or skill you are teaching, help him visualize it in his mind.

Visual/Spatial Learners Tend to Struggle With:
- Creative writing.
- Reading beyond the literal meaning.
- Applying arithmetic to word problems.
- Forming a hypothesis and testing it with experiments.

AUDITORY LEARNERS (LISTENERS)
- Love to communicate and can generally "talk your ear off."
- Remember jingles, poems, and television commercials effortlessly.
- Continually keep a rhythmic pattern going by tapping or making sounds.
- Usually sing beautifully and have excellent pitch memory.
- Generally remember names of people they've met or heard about.
- Find it easy to express themselves verbally.
- Tend to read aloud or subvocalize while reading.
- Often sound older than their chronological age (as a result of their ability to process language patterns with "tape recorder accuracy").
- Tend to sort out their problems by talking about them.
- Sound out words and are, therefore, usually phonetic spellers.
- Tend to be poor test takers because they can't sort out visual material fast enough.
- Enjoy listening to a radio, record player, or tapes in their spare time.
- Respond well to phonetic reading programs, usually demonstrating excellent word attack skills.
- Find it easy to follow oral directions.
- Are easily distracted by background noises.
- Respond favorably to verbal praise.

Auditory Learners Flourish When:
- Told every step of the skill to be learned.
- Allowed to move their lips or subvocalize to increase reading comprehension.
- Neurological impressions are combined in reading: read orally to student while he points to the word being read.
- Memorizing rules, plays, poetry, *et cetera*

- Taught with the following aids:
    Audiocassettes
    Music, rhythm instruments
    Rhymes
    Clapping/keeping a beat
    Echo games (singing & rhythm)
    Creating conversation for puppets
    Field trips with interview focus
    Integrated content (interdisciplinary)

Auditory Learners Tend To Struggle With:
- Reading technical or nonfiction writing.
- Rewriting and editing written work.
- Properly researching footnotes.
- Paying attention to detail for accuracy in math, science, and history.

KINESTHETIC/TACTILE LEARNERS (MOVERS)
- Relate to others more comfortably in action and body than in words.
- Tend to live in perpetual motion, rarely sitting still—often called "hyperactive."
- Try to touch everything they see or walk past.
- Use lots of gestures and facial expressions when talking.
- Tend to show anger physically (e.g., by stomping feet and slamming doors).
- Prefer to try things out by touching and feeling, even as they get older.
- Often make paper airplanes and fans out of their papers.
- Prefer to be playing, jumping, running, or wrestling in their spare time.
- Have excellent muscle coordination in sports which require skills in balancing.
- Can successfully maintain balance while blindfolded.
- Are most distracted when they must be still or things get "too quiet."
- Tend to dislike long-range goal setting and complicated projects.
- Are excellent at taking gadgets apart and can put them back together again.
- Find listening a difficult challenge.
- Respond more favorably to a "pat on the back" than to "stars" or a favorable comment.

Kinesthetic/Tactile Learners Flourish When:
- Their learning experiences allow many opportunities to do or feel (touch).
- They can demonstrate or model a task for other students.
- Taught through role playing or pantomime. They love short, dynamic presentations.
- Pointing with fingers to follow or anchor words in early reading.
- They are kept moving with appropriate activities. They love construction.

- Taught with the following aids:
  - Finger plays
  - Tracing motions (in the air, on paper, on the wall or floor)
  - Tactile experiences with sandpaper, sand, clay, water, ***et cetera***
  - Travel/field trips
  - Felt pens (texture)
  - Math manipulatives (blocks, rods, chips, play money)
  - Plays and dramatic interpretation
  - Puppet theater
  - Conducting motions in music
  - Timelines and maps that he makes himself
  - Key: Variety in methods with lots of hand-on activities

KINESTHETIC/TACTILE LEARNERS TEND TO STRUGGLE WITH:

- Concentrating on phonics, grammar, and math rules.
- Reading for information.
- Doing analytical work.
- Proofreading their work.
- Doing research-related writing.
- Completing long-term projects in science and history.
- Understanding the relevance of their work to other academic goals.

Dr. Ronald and Inge Cannon operate Education PLUS, a speaking and publishing ministry for homeschool families. (www.edplus.com). Inge's workshop, "Learning Styles," is available on audiocassette.

The Cannon's primary focus is training parents to implement the many benefits of a discipleship lifestyle in home education. They offer many training tools to inspire and empower parents—particularly in the area of crafting apprenticeship programs, choosing high school curricula, and presenting academic credentials for homeschool graduates (transcripts, resumes, portfolios, *et cetera*). Visit their websites for more information: www.homeschooltranscripts.com and www.edplus.com.

Common Teaching Approaches

Chris and Ellyn Davis

 ll homeschooling materials fall into two main categories: traditional textbook curricula and non-textbook curricula.

THE TRADITIONAL APPROACH

In the Traditional Approach, graded textbooks or workbooks follow a scope and sequence that covers each subject in 180 daily increments over a span of 12 years. Teacher's manuals, tests, and record-keeping materials are usually available that correspond to each of the texts. Textbook curricula assume you will run your homeschool like an institutional school.

Worktext programs present textbooks in consumable workbook format. The student learns his lesson, is given assignments, and is tested all in the workbook. The worktexts include tests or checkpoints to ensure that the material in each section is mastered before the student moves on to the next. Worktexts also allow more independent study and require minimal teacher preparation time and supervision.

Video programs are also available that are actual classrooms on video. The child follows along with the video as if he or she were attending an actual classroom, and uses the accompanying textbooks or workbooks.

Traditional curricula are also available on computer. Many satellite schools as well as universities now offer computer courses on CD or through the Internet.

Most of the textbook and worktext programs used in private Christian schools are available to homeschoolers. They each share a distinct doctrinal perspective, and usually contain strong elements of essentialism.

Some questions to ask yourself before trying the traditional, textbook approach are listed below. "Yes" answers indicate this approach may work for you and your child:

1. Did my child perform well in a school classroom?
2. Does my child like to complete assignments and to have defined goals?
3. Is my child academically oriented?
4. Will my child complete assigned tasks with a minimum of prodding from me?
5. Am I the kind of person who will follow through with the lesson plans and pace of the course of instruction?

Some additional questions to ask before using the workbook approach with your child:

1. Does my child read well and have good reading comprehension skills?
2. Can my child work well independently?
3. Can my child learn without a lot of variety in the teaching materials?

Strengths of the Textbook/Worktext Approach:
- Everything is laid out for ease of use.
- Follows a standardized scope and sequence.
- Has definite milestones of accomplishment.
- Testing and assigning grades is easy to do.

Weaknesses of a the Textbook/Workbook Approach:
- Is geared to the "generic" child. Does not take into account individual learning styles, strengths and weaknesses, or interests.
- Assumes that there is a body of information that comprises an education and that this information can be broken down into daily increments.
- Treats children's minds like containers to be filled with information.
- Focuses on transmitting information through artificial learning experiences.
- Is teacher-directed and chalkboard-oriented.
- Different-aged students study different material.
- Expensive when teaching multiple children.
- Discourages original, independent thinking.
- Has a high "burn out" rate.

NON-TEXTBOOK APPROACHES

Although there are a number of excellent textbook and worktext programs available, many home educators object to the fact that textbooks are teacher-directed, chalkboard-oriented, and seldom take into account different teaching approaches or the different ways children receive and process information.

John Gatto says, "Real books educate. School books school." With textbooks, parents may feel they are "bringing the classroom home," instead of educating their children in a way that is uniquely home-based. These parents have found alternative teaching approaches that allow them to tailor their homeschooling to their family's particular needs. On the following pages we briefly explain the five most-common non-textbook teaching approaches:

- **The Classical Approach** is derived from successful courses of study throughout history, and recently was revived through the writing of Dorothy Sayers.
- **The Principle Approach** is based on the premise that our nation is a unique and vital link in the westward chain of Christianity.
- **The Living Books and Life Experiences Approach** of Charlotte Mason treats children as persons, not as containers to be filled with information.
- **The Unit Study Approach** integrates several subject areas around a common theme.
- **Unschooling** assumes that children are natural learners and gives them resources from which to learn.

THE CLASSICAL APPROACH

The Classical Approach to education has produced great minds throughout history, and has strong elements of perennialism. The modern proponent of the Classical Approach was British writer and medieval scholar Dorothy Sayers. As the Nazis rose to power in the 1930s, Sayers warned that schools were teaching children everything except how to think. Because young adults could no longer think for themselves, Sayers felt they could be easily influenced by tyrants. To remedy this, Sayers proposed reinstating the classical form of education used in the Middle Ages.

In the Classical Approach, children under 18 are taught tools of learning collectively known as the *Trivium*. The Trivium has three parts, each part corresponding to a childhood developmental stage.

The first stage of the Trivium, the *Grammar Stage*, covers early elementary ages and focuses on reading, writing, and spelling, the study of Latin, and developing observation, listening, and memorization skills. The goal of this stage is to develop a general framework of knowledge and to acquire basic language arts and math skills.

At approximately middle-school age, children begin to demonstrate independent or abstract thought (usually by becoming argumentative or opinionated). This signals the beginning of the *Dialectic Stage* in which the child's tendency to argue is molded and shaped by teaching logical discussion, debate, and how to draw correct conclusions and support them with facts. The goal of this stage is to equip the child with language and thinking skills capable of detecting fallacies in an argument. Latin study is continued, with the possible addition of Greek and Hebrew. The student reads essays, arguments, and criticisms instead of literature as in the Grammar Stage. History study leans toward interpreting events. Higher math and theology begin.

The final phase of the Trivium, the *Rhetoric Stage*, seeks to produce a student who can use language, both written and spoken, eloquently and persuasively. Students are usually ready for this stage by age fifteen.

Here are some questions to ask yourself before trying the Classical Approach with your child:
1. Does my family like to read good literature?
2. Are my children intellectually oriented and comfortable with a rigorous academic program?
3. Am I a learner? Am I comfortable learning alongside my children so I can teach them things I never studied?
4. Do I like to study and discuss ideas that have influenced civilization?

Strengths of the Classical Approach:
- Is tailored to stages of mental development.
- Teaches thinking skills and verbal/written expression.
- Creates self-learners.
- Has produced great minds throughout history.

Weaknesses of the Classical Approach
- Very little prepared curriculum available.
- Requires a scholarly teacher and student.
- May overemphasize ancient disciplines and classics.

THE UNIT STUDY APPROACH

A Unit Study takes a theme or topic (a unit of study) and delves into it deeply over a period of time, integrating language arts, science, social studies, math, and fine arts as they apply. Instead of studying eight or ten separate, unrelated subjects, all subjects are blended together and studied around a common theme or project. For example, a unit study on birds could include reading and writing about birds and famous ornithologists (language arts); studying the parts, functions, and life flight (science and math); determining the migration paths, habitats, and ecological/sociological impact of birds (social studies); sketching familiar birds (art); building bird houses or feeders ("hands on" activities); and so forth.

Several fine prepared unit study curricula are available, but it is easy to prepare your own unit studies around areas of interest. History is the logical core curriculum around which to build ongoing unit studies. History provides a framework for all other subjects because it follows a progression and covers every other subject (except possibly math), like art, music, science, literature, and so on.

Here are some questions to ask yourself before trying unit studies with your children:
1. Am I a creative person?
2. Do I like trying to make everything interesting and fun?
3. Do my children have a variety of interests and learning styles?
4. Can I live with the fact that there may be "gaps" in my children's education?
5. Do I have the time and energy to be the driving, creative force behind the development of units?

Strengths of the Unit Study Approach:
- All ages can learn together.
- Children can delve as deeply or as lightly into a subject as they like.
- The family's interests can be pursued.
- Students get the whole picture.
- Curiosity and independent thinking are generated.
- Intense study of one topic is the more natural way to learn.
- Knowledge is interrelated, so is learned easily and remembered longer.
- Unit studies are fairly easy to create.

Weaknesses of the Unit Study Approach:
- It is easy to leave educational "gaps."
- Hard to assess the level of learning occurring.
- Record keeping may be difficult.
- Prepared unit-study curricula are expensive.

- Do-it-yourself unit studies require planning.
- Too many activity-oriented unit studies may cause burn-out of teacher and student.
- Subjects that are hard to integrate into the unit may be neglected.

THE LIVING BOOKS APPROACH

The Living Books Approach is based on the writings of Charlotte Mason, a turn-of-the century British educator. Miss Mason was appalled by several tendencies she noticed in modern education: (1) the tendency to treat children as containers to be filled with predigested information instead of as human beings; (2) the tendency to break down knowledge into thousands of isolated bits of information to be fed into "container" children; and (3) the tendency to engineer artificial learning experiences. She believed in respecting children as persons, in involving them in real-life situations, and in allowing them to read really good books instead of what she called "twaddle"—worthless, inferior teaching material. She considered education a failure when it produced children able to "do harder sums and read harder books" who lacked "moral and intellectual power." Children were to be taught good habits, to be involved in a broad spectrum of real-life situations, and given ample time to play, reflect, and create.

Mason's approach to academics was to teach basic reading, writing, and math skills, then expose children to the best sources of knowledge for all other subjects. This meant giving children experiences like nature walks, observing and collecting samples of wildlife; visiting art museums; and reading real books with "living ideas" because they made the subject "come alive," unlike textbooks that tend to be dry and dull and assume readers cannot think for themselves.

Here are some questions to ask yourself before trying the Charlotte Mason Living Books method:

1. Does our family love to read, both alone and together through reading aloud?
2. Do we love to go to the library?
3. Am I comfortable with a more of "free-form" approach to learning?
4. Will I follow through with teaching my children good habits and character qualities?
5. Do I trust my children to learn on their own?
6. Will I follow through with exposing my children firsthand to nature and to great art?

Strengths of the Living Books Approach:
- Treats children as active participants in the learning process.
- Exposes children to real objects and books instead of interactions with distilled information.
- Encourages curiosity, creative thinking, and a love of learning.
- Eliminates meaningless tasks and busywork.

- Developmentally appropriate.
- Stresses formation of good character and habits.

Weaknesses of the Living Books Approach:
- Tends to be very child centered.
- Very little prepared curriculum.
- May neglect higher-level studies because of its emphasis on art, literature, and nature study.
- May become too eclectic.

THE PRINCIPLE APPROACH

The Principle Approach is an effort to restore to American Christians three vital concepts: the knowledge of our Christian history; an understanding of our role in the spread of Christianity; and the ability to live according to the Biblical principles upon which our country was founded. The Principle Approach is a way of living life, not just a way of educating children.

Developers of the Principle Approach rediscovered seven Biblical principles upon which our country was founded and by which many of the Founding Fathers were educated. The seven principles are as follows: (1) Individuality (God has created distinct differences in people, nations, *et cetera*.); (2) Self Government (Government starts in the heart of man.); (3) Christian Character; (4) "Conscience is the Most Sacred of Property;" (5) The Christian Form of Government; (6) How the Seed of Local Self Government is Planted; (7) The Christian Principle of American Political Union.

Four emphases are unique to this educational approach. First, there is a recognition of God's Hand (Providence) in history. Second, there is the understanding that God has ordained three governmental institutions (the home, the church, and civil government) through which He unfolds His purposes and manifests Christ on this earth. Third, each Christian is responsible for extending God's government. Fourth, the student assumes responsibility for learning and for applying knowledge to his own life.

The Principle Approach may be applied to the study of any subject with the use of notebooks to record "the 4 Rs" (*Researching* God's Word; *Reasoning* from the researched Biblical truths/principles; *Relating* the truths and principles discovered to the subject and the student's character; and *Recording* the individual application of the Biblical principles to the subject and the student).

Here are some questions to ask yourself before trying the Principle Approach:
1. Do I have a real concern for the application of Christian principles to my family and my nation?
2. Will my child assume responsibility for a great deal of learning on his/her own?
3. Does my child like to express him or herself through writing?
4. Am I willing to undertake extensive biblical research and teaching preparation?

Strengths of the Principle Approach:
- Students learn to think "governmentally."
- Students become self-learners.
- Students learn to apply biblical principles to the whole of life.
- Students create their own "textbooks."

Weaknesses of the Principle Approach:
- May present a narrow view of life and of history.
- Focuses mainly on American history.
- Requires a great deal of teacher preparation.
- Prepared curriculum available in a few subjects.
- Extremely literal approach to Scripture.

THE UNSCHOOLING APPROACH

On the one hand, the Unschooling Approach was defined by John Holt, a 20th century American educator who concluded that children have an innate desire to learn and a curiosity that drives them to learn what they need to know when they need to know it. Holt believed that both desire and curiosity are destroyed by the usual methods of teaching. In his book, *Teach Your Own*, Holt wrote: "What children need is not new and better curricula but access to more and more of the real world; plenty of time and space to think over their experiences, and to use fantasy and play to make meaning out of them; and advice, road maps, and guidebooks, to make it easier for them to get where they want to go (not where we think they ought to go), and to find out what they want to find out."

On the other hand, Unschooling refers to any less-structured learning approach that allows children to pursue their own interests with parental support and guidance. The child is surrounded by a rich environment of books, learning resources, and adults who model a lifestyle of learning and are willing to interact with him. Formal academics are pursued when the need arises. Christians who favor less structured schooling, but with definite goals, prefer to be called "Relaxed Home Educators," not "Unschoolers."

Some questions to ask yourself before trying the Unschooling Approach:
1. Am I comfortable with few pre-set goals and little structure?
2. Do my children have strong interests in particular areas?
3. Does my family have a lot of natural curiosity and love learning?

Strengths of the Unschooling Approach:
- Takes little planning.
- Captures the child's "teachable moments."
- Children have access to the real world, plenty of time and space to figure things out on their own.
- Children are less likely to become academically frustrated or "burned out."
- Children can delve into a subject as deeply or as shallowly as they desire.
- Provides a discipleship model of learning.
- Creates self-learners with a love of learning.

Weaknesses of the Unschooling Approach:
- May neglect some subjects.
- Hard to assess level of learning.
- Lacks the security of a clearly laid out program.
- Is extremely child-centered.
- Difficult to explain to others.
- May be overly optimistic about what children will accomplish on their own.

THE MIXED APPROACH

Many homeschoolers use a blend of the different approaches. For example, they may use traditional math and science textbooks, but build unit studies around historical periods that include language arts, music, art, and philosophy, and then choose a computer program to teach typing.

Reprinted from catalog with permission: The Elijah Company, 1053 Eldridge Loop, Crossville TN 38571; www.elijahco.com.

Navigating the Used Curriculum Route

Vicki Bentley

Buying used curriculum is sort of like taking a shortcut when I drive: If I am familiar with the area through which I'm being re-routed, I can save some time; but if I get lost trying to take a shortcut, I may end up woefully behind! By the same token, I can really stretch my homeschool budget by finding great used-curriculum values. Yet I haven't effectively saved money if a particular pre-owned purchase is not the wisest choice for my family. Here are some ways to "know the shortcuts" when navigating the used curriculum options, and save in the long run.

SET GOALS - Have a list of the goals you have set for your children. Know what you are looking for and why, whether new *or* used. Keeping those objectives in front of you as you shop can help you select bargain items that will best meet your needs for the year.

MAKE A LIST - Shopping without a list can be just as disastrous on the swap boards or in the resale shop as it can be in the grocery store! Make a list of the items in which you are most interested, with several alternative selections noted. Having a second or third choice pre-selected helps me to think quickly at a yard sale or curriculum swap. I make a list of all the topics we're covering this year in our units, so I can stay focused on my more immediate needs, and I can better resist the temptation to snatch up a bargain that won't really be useful to me for another year or two.

BE SPECIFIC - Specific titles are very useful, if possible. One year I accidentally purchased three "different" copies of the same well-known science book because the publisher had changed the cover several times and I didn't recognize the title as a book I'd already purchased!

KNOW YOUR AUDIENCE – Consider your own teaching style and your children's learning styles. Just because something was recommended by a friend and is 50% off doesn't mean you will be comfortable using it or your kids will "get it." On the other hand, this may be a good time to try something new, when it isn't a tremendous monetary investment.

KNOW THE PRICES - Do some research to familiarize yourself with the retail prices so you'll be better able to recognize a bargain. I go through my catalogs and mark prices on my wish list so I'll know who sells which items for what prices. That way, I'll know if a used item is enough of a reduction to warrant not getting it new. Also, ask around to determine what sort of discount would be considered fair in the used market for your particular needs. A reference book that might not often be found in the used market can command a price closer to retail than can a book that parents sell off regularly to buy the next grade level. Know what you are willing to pay.

KNOW THE PUBLISHERS – Some publishers make such minor changes in books from time to time that an older edition may work fine for your purposes. Other times, the books may have been revised enough that other materials with which you have to coordinate them (workbook, teacher's manual, quizzes, etc.) may no longer be compatible. When "new models" come out, call the publisher and ask about both the extent of the revisions and how compatible your other components will now be.

LOOK AT THE DATES – Check the copyright dates in the books. Determine if you are willing to go with a little older book in some subjects (say, history or art or language) to be able to splurge for the latest in science or computer technology. Publishing dates can be important if you already have three parts of your A Beka history program and just need another set of tests and quizzes, while you may be more than willing to settle for a five-year-old set of *World Book* encyclopedias for $5 at a library sale instead of shelling out more money for the newest version.

BE CREATIVE – We have picked up books/magazines free or "dirt cheap" and cut out the pictures to illustrate stories, make posters, etc. I've heard of others who have cut out timeline figures from discarded books.

CHEAPER ISN'T ALWAYS A BARGAIN - A friend of mine recently purchased a public school math book because it was a little less expensive than the Saxon she really wanted, then found that she would have to pay $70 for a public school teacher's key for the course. This comes back to knowing what you want and how much it will cost you.

(By the way, the teacher's book may or may not be necessary; some texts have answers in the backs or you may be able to determine the correct answers. Some teacher books have not only answers, but super teaching ideas. If you aren't comfortable without it, consider buying it.)

REMEMBER THAT MOST SALES ARE FINAL – While most dealers of new materials will allow a refund or exchange of items still in resaleable condition if you change your mind, the average re-seller is generally not able to offer that luxury because he is already shaving his margin by selling at a discount. Or the homeschool neighbor you bought the book from has probably already applied your book money to the electric bill. Be pretty sure of what you want, buy with confidence, and if it ends up not working out for you, list it on the swap board or in your homeschool-newsletter classifieds!

TRY TO GET A PREVIEW – If you aren't sure you are able to absorb a loss if it doesn't work out, try to borrow a copy of the book or material from a friend to look over for a few days, or to try for a week or two. Then you'll know if you're comfortable enough with the purchase of a particular used item to risk not being able to return it for a refund.

WHERE TO LOOK – Ask your homeschool friends for recommendations of used book dealers and good swap boards (they are multiplying on-line!). HEAV's e-mail update often announces used-curriculum sales across the state. Check homeschool-magazine ads and yard sales. Our weekly *Trading Post* paper sometimes has curriculum listed, as do some of the on-line auction houses and book sellers. There are several sources listed later in this chapter.

VISIT BOOK ANNEXES – Our local public school system regularly purges textbooks that were replaced with newer ones. The older books go to an annex building which is opened for the public to take what they would like, free of charge. Use this source judiciously, as many public school textbooks may not be suitable for your home use. But I have picked up dictionaries, typing books for keyboard practice, books on local history, **et cetera**, and a few moms have gotten desks, maps, and more. Check with your local school district for more information.

MAKE YOUR NEEDS KNOWN – Let local curriculum dealers and the moms in your support group know that you are on the lookout for certain items. People often have things on their shelves that they don't realize may be of value to others. Swap boards often have "Wanted to Buy" sections as well as "For Sale" listings.

TAKE A FRIEND – Especially (but not *only*) if you are a fairly new homeschooler, it can be a big help to ask a veteran homeschooler (especially one familiar with curriculum) to accompany you on your excursion. She can help you to focus on your list, explain whether or how some items may be able to substitute for others, help you know what questions to ask of a seller, and guide you on prices. There's comfort in a second set of eyes to help navigate—it's like having someone to "ride shotgun" while you're taking that "shortcut to savings"!

Reprinted from *Practical Homeschooling* magazine, Volume #51, P.O Box 1190, Fenton MO 63026-1190. Used by permission.

Travel Budget
What will all this cost me?

Vicki Bentley

If you are considering home education, you are very likely a single-income family, and if you're like most of us, your budget is pretty tight. Although I have read that the average homeschool family spends about $500 per student per year, I have never personally spent nearly that much. My most expensive year was my first year, when I used a pre-packaged curriculum and spent over $600 for three children (okay, with inflation, maybe it would be $800 now!). As we have accumulated non-consumable materials ("living books" or textbooks vs. workbooks), our home library has grown to the point of just adding a few supplemental materials each year.

Homeschooling costs more than public school, but less than private school. That may seem trite, but $500 can sound like a burden or a relief, depending on your previous education experience. What are some of the expenses that you should consider in drawing up an education budget?

CURRICULUM IS THE BROADEST CATEGORY AND WILL MOST LIKELY BE YOUR LARGEST EXPENSE:

- Least expensive—Some parents keep costs to a bare minimum by borrowing or renting curriculum from a friend or a support group, using public school textbooks, using the library, or using all-inclusive basic curricula (such as thick grade-level workbooks available at discount stores, *et cetera*). E. D. Hirsch's *Core Knowledge* series or the State Standards of Learning used with library books would be examples of these options.

- Moderate—A reasonable estimate would be about $250-350 per child, including games, software, and books. You can keep your bill down to a reasonable amount by selecting your materials from a variety of publishers. Some or all of these materials can be purchased used at about a thirty- to fifty-percent savings. Many publishers waive shipping if you purchase from them at curriculum shows (A Beka and Bob Jones University Press both offer this discount, often at shows held at area hotels throughout the spring).

  Another budget saver is multi-level and/or reusable curriculum. Those dollars seem to stretch if you can use the same content-area program for all or most of your students (examples: KONOS curriculum, Diana

Waring's history guides, *Bible Study Guide for All Ages*, Greenleaf Press, *Five in a Row*, *Student Of the Word*, Janice Van Cleave's science books, *Beautiful Feet* guides, *et cetera*). The same applies if you can re-use the material for a later student (such as math textbooks, *Learning Language Arts through Literature*, most unit study guides, or other non-consumable items). Example of a bare-bones generic curriculum for grade seven, at full retail pricing:

Saxon *Algebra 1/2*	$75
Learning Language Arts through Literature	$25
Janice Van Cleave's *Earth Science for Every Kid*	$12
Land of Fair Play (with tests, answer keys)	$13
Total	$125
	(Let's say $100 with tax)

If you didn't re-use this package for another child, you could re-sell all of it for approximately 50-75% of your original cost (in decent shape, of course), bringing back $60-$90 of your original $125 investment (I subtracted approximately $3 for the consumable *Land of Fair Play* tests). If you re-use it and then sell it, your per-child rate goes down tremendously.

- Most expensive—The most expensive route would be school-by-satellite, video courses, correspondence schools, or all-inclusive curriculum packages. These can run anywhere from $500 to almost $1000 per student. However, this is still less than the cost of private school.

TESTING OR EVALUATION FEES

Standardized tests cost about $25-$45 per student; if you would like to hire someone else to actually administer the test, plan to pay an additional $25-50 per student. A private evaluation can cost from $50 into the hundreds, depending on your evaluator. You may also choose to have your child tested in the local public school system if the school is testing at your child's grade level (be aware that the results will be sent to the school).

PROFESSIONAL MEMBERSHIPS
- Local support group—$0 to $30 per year, depending on the group
- Home Educators Association of Virginia—$35 per year
- Homeschool Legal Defense Association—$115 per year ($95 if you are a member of a discount group, such as HEAV or participating support group)

HOME LIBRARY (NOT SPECIFICALLY CURRICULAR)
- Resource books for parents (consider it in-service training): $20-100
- Homeschool magazine subscription for mom and dad: $15-18/year
- Children's resource books/magazines (*God's World*, *Nature Friend*, *et cetera*): $10-20

ANNUAL STATE CONVENTION

- Full three-day registration for parents, two elementary children, and one teen: $155 (parents only would be $55 if HEAV members; price above includes Children's Program and Teen Track)
- On-site accommodations—Marriott Hotel (2 nights): ~$220
- Food/parking: varies

EXTRACURRICULAR LESSONS

In our area, music lessons cost approximately $15 per hour (group rates are considerably less). Our homeschool band is $285 per year, plus instrument, for a total of about $485. Ballet or gymnastics classes are about $25 per month for nine months, for a total of $225. Individual or family membership in a gym or the local YMCA will vary. Local sports association fees also vary, from $8 for our homeschool softball league to several hundred dollars for varsity sports. I have recently paid $25 per two-hour class for my daughter to take oil painting from a local artist, while one of our moms teaches a weekly drawing class for $45 per month. Our support group's learning co-op fee is $10 per family per month (for supplies).

SCHOOL SUPPLIES AND OTHER "SCHOOL AREA" ITEMS

This figure will depend on whether you buy brand-name binders or budget spirals, how many children you are outfitting with supplies, *et cetera*. Needs and desires will vary from family to family: desks, sofa, computer, file cabinet, bookcase or storage unit, paper, hole punch, stapler, tape, pens and pencils, markers, dry erase markers and board, lesson planning book, file folders, pencil boxes, notebooks, erasers, globe, paints, calculator, scissors, glue, science equipment, *et cetera*. Many of these items will be one-time purchases, while others will need restocking each year.

MISCELLANEOUS

Field trips, gas money, admission for activities such as skating or bowling, phone calls, school photos, yearbook, co-ops, outside classes, anything else that is not listed above. Again, these are not necessarily critical items.

Sample for three children in a satellite program (K, 2nd, and 8th):

Curriculum	$700	
Annual testing	75	(often included in program)
Professional memberships	150	
Home library	65	
Annual convention (parents)	75	(commute; includes lunch)
School supplies	150	
Art lessons (1 mo, oldest) & softball	64	
Miscellaneous	50	
Total	$1329	

At $443 per student for the year, this is still less than the average. In subsequent years, the supplies may cost substantially less because you are buying basically just paper and pencils, or you may forego extra lessons, or put together your own curriculum package for considerable savings of up to several hundred dollars.

Be sure to purchase your core curriculum first, then add items from the other categories as your budget allows. Once you have an idea of what you plan to spend, divide it by 52 and set that much aside each week in a "homeschool budget" fund. If you have a lump sum of money at a particular time each year (such as tax time), consider setting your budget amount aside then. Many of these purchases can be made as funds allow, so you might purchase school supplies in August, join the support group in September, pay for band in monthly installments, register for the state convention in April, pay for testing in May, buy curriculum in June, *et cetera*. Because I buy very little curriculum at this point, I have actually begun a homeschool year with no resources or curriculum outlay, paying as we went for memberships, classes, *et cetera*.

Last, but certainly not least, pray about the needs you have for your homeschool and ask God to provide for these things.

(Prices were accurate at the time of printing; some prices may have changed since publication.)

On the Road!
Some practical ideas for homeschooling
Vicki Bentley

You have researched your options, set some goals, charted a course—now you're off! In this portion of our "itinerary," you will find some helpful suggestions for actually "getting in gear" and moving toward that destination!

Here are some "Secrets of Success" that Yvonne Bunn shares with new and prospective homeschoolers in her How-to-Begin seminars:

- Start your day with God, and pray often with your husband about your needs, concerns, frustrations, and breakthroughs. Stay teachable; you'll be tested in new areas.
- Eliminate frustrations by making time for yourself. A quiet time before the family is up will set the tone for your day, while a 15-20 minute reading break or rest time in the afternoon will give you added energy for the remainder of the day. Before academic time, take care of the things that bother you most—dirty dishes in the sink, unmade beds, laundry, so your mind will be clearer to focus on studies.
- Be patient with your children and with yourself. Watch for signs of frustration in your child, such as crying, complaining, or becoming angry. For example, never completing library books may indicate that the reading level is too difficult and the child may be frustrated. Areas of frustration (math or language arts, for example) are obvious when a skill is undeveloped (learning gaps) and a child has difficulty accomplishing a given task. If you are frustrated with your child, take a break and pray! Maybe a different approach or your husband's perspective will help. You might even need to drop the task for a while and come back to it in a few days or weeks, when the child might be readier to absorb the material or concept.
- Know the balance between organization and flexibility. Have a plan and work it—but expect interruptions! Don't compromise time spent teaching basic skill subjects and Bible/character. Establishing a workable routine will give your children security; you can schedule visits, appointments, special activities, *et cetera,* for the afternoons, after

optimal earlier (morning) learning time. And don't answer the phone during school time! Take it off the hook or get an answering machine.

- Use family resources and develop good relationships with neighbors, grandparents, and other relatives. Older children can help younger children, and grandparents can participate in special-interest areas. Neighbors may be more helpful if they perceive you as friendly and open, and if your children respect them and their property.

- When we start out, sometimes we only know to do what we experienced, so we tend to bring the classroom into our homes. It's okay to simply create a learning environment in the sanctuary of our homes, and to enjoy learning along with our children. Education begins with the parent!

Roadblocks to Avoid
Common Mistakes Homeschoolers Make
adapted from Yvonne Bunn's How-to-Begin seminar

ome of the common mistakes that parents make in homeschooling usually stem from misconceptions, fear, and unrealistic expectations.

MYTH #1: "THERE IS ONLY ONE WAY TO HOMESCHOOL."

Children have different learning styles, parents have different teaching styles. What works for one child or one family may not work for another, regardless of how wonderful the material is. Your friend who homeschools next door may seem to have the perfect situation and use the best curriculum, but that doesn't mean it's right for you. Another friend may be very structured, or yet another may seem to be able to just put together the right program of study with just a library card. There is freedom in doing what works for your family! (If you don't believe me, read *A Survivor's Guide to Homeschooling* by Luanne Shackelford and Susan White.)

MISCONCEPTION #2: "THIS IS THE WAY I WAS TAUGHT. IT WORKED FOR ME SO IT WILL WORK FOR THEM."

Don't take things too seriously—remember to encourage and appreciate the joy of discovery. Read those sections about learning/teaching styles again, and find the key that will unlock their minds—it may be different from the key that unlocked that world of learning for you. Make learning fun and be enthusiastic about it yourself—it's contagious!

UNREALISTIC EXPECTATION #3: "I THOUGHT I'D BE ABLE TO USE THIS CURRICULUM WITH ALL MY CHILDREN."

Anticipate change; do what's best for your family. Different children learn in different ways, and your family goes through different stages. The curriculum is a tool; make it work for you. You are free to change methods, curriculum, your schedule, and even your philosophy of education!

FEAR #4: "I'M SO AFRAID I'LL MAKE A MISTAKE AND RUIN MY CHILDREN."

We all make mistakes; hopefully we learn from them. We are blessed to have a God of grace! We can admit that we've made a mistake, re-direct our steps, then move on. If you are afraid that you will leave gaps that ruin your children, remember that it is not your job to teach your child everything there is to learn; it is your job to teach your child how to learn.

DOUBT #5: "MAYBE THIS WASN'T SUCH A GOOD IDEA AFTER ALL...."

Keep your vision by reviewing the goals you first established. Don't be distracted by your children's (especially teens') lack of purpose and direction, especially if you are treading in new waters. Because a young person often doesn't yet have the wisdom and experience to make important life decisions during the teen years, he should not necessarily be the one who determines the kind of education he receives. God made fathers the head of their family, with the responsibility to direct their children, not vice versa. Parents, be careful of peer pressure yourself. Don't seek the approval and acceptance of others. Do what is right for your family—you are accountable to your spouse and to God.

Keep your eyes on the road before you, check your map as necessary, get roadside assistance if needed, and you'll avoid the major roadblocks!

Roadside Assistance
Help and encouragement along the way
Vicki Bentley

New and veteran homeschoolers: You don't have to travel alone! When you hit the occasional rut, or blow a tire, or lose your way (figuratively speaking, of course), there is assistance along the way! Here are a few of the groups available to "roll up their sleeves" and help:

HOME EDUCATORS ASSOCIATION OF VIRGINIA

Home Educators Association of Virginia is committed to providing information, resources, and other support. Their lobbyist and bill reader help to protect your interests during legislative sessions; HEAV works independently and/or with other organizations to introduce legislation to benefit homeschoolers across Virginia. They offer a large annual convention with speaker workshops, a huge exhibit hall with nearly 300 booths of homeschool curriculum/materials, a gigantic used-curriculum sale, a statewide graduation ceremony, and much more. The office staff is available to answer questions, supply resources and information, and encourage you. The quarterly magazine and weekly e-mail newsletters will inspire you and keep you abreast of homeschool happenings in Virginia. HEAV's Homeschool Success Seminars travel around the state to help new and veteran homeschoolers on their journey. Check them out at www.heav.org or 804-278-9200.

HOME SCHOOL LEGAL DEFENSE ASSOCIATION

Home School Legal Defense Association consists of over 55,000 member families, supported by more than 50 dedicated staff members, who have banded together to ensure that our right to educate our families is respected and protected. The lawyers are all homeschooling dads with over 57 years of combined legal experience defending homeschool families. For $115 (or less, if you are a member of a discount group, such as HEAV) per year, this is a sort of "legal insurance policy" with homeschool-law experts. Even if you never use their legal services, their staff is available to answer questions, you will receive their quarterly *Court Report*, and your funds will help defray the legal costs of those who might be in a less homeschool-friendly environment than you are.

LOCAL SUPPORT GROUPS

Local support groups can provide mutual encouragement and information, field trips, co-op or tutoring opportunities, and SOCIALIZATION. Many support groups offer sports activities, academic or extracurricular clubs, field trips, yearbook/newspaper staff opportunities, in-service training for parents, family picnics, science fairs, open houses, end-of-year ceremonies and celebrations, newsletters, e-mail information loops, and more. For information about groups in your area, check with local homeschoolers or check under "Support" at HEAV's website, www.heav.org. [See Support Groups section of this manual for more information.]

NATIONAL CHALLENGED HOMESCHOOLERS ASSOCIATED NETWORK (NATHHAN)

National Challenged Homeschoolers Associated Network (NATHHAN) is a supportive networking organization of over 12,000 families with special-needs children. A quarterly magazine, lending library, and NATHHAN family directory are available for a nominal annual membership fee ($25). Find out more at www.NATHHAN.com or call 208-267-6246.

NATIONAL BLACK HOME EDUCATORS (NBHE)

National Black Home Educators (NBHE) provides information about starting homeschooling, helps families network with other families, and assists families with resources such as books, music, speaking information, and curriculum. For more information, contact Eric or Joyce Burges at 13434 Plank Road, Baker LA 70714; e-mail contact@nbhe.net; or visit www.nbhe.net.

Family Foundations

Compiled by Janell Rardon

Additional Articles on the CD

BE SURE TO CHECK OUT THESE OTHER GREAT ARTICLES ON THE CD!

Each article in the book and on the CD has been carefully chosen by the section coordinator to increase your knowledge and understanding of this subject, so don't forget to use and enjoy the parts of the manual on your CD, as well as the part you are holding.

Introduction:
The Sacred Trust

trust *(n)—That which is committed to one's care.*
"Never violate a sacred trust."
—Webster's 1828 *Dictionary of the English Language*

While attending a seminar over a year ago, I heard the speaker pose a question to all attendees, *"What do you pound the table over?"* A simple question with serious overtones. She wanted us to examine our passions, our hearts, and our mission. Driving home, I considered the issue in great detail and concluded two things:

1) I pound the table over helping others develop a life of spiritual abundance, holiness, and righteousness by developing their relationship with Jesus Christ, and
2) I pound the table over helping families develop strong, stable and spiritually-enabled homes; homes in which their children can be masterfully crafted into Christ's servants and witnesses in a dying world.

Several weeks later, I discovered a powerful story tucked away in Judges 9:50-57. Here, I read of a woman—locked away in a strong tower in the middle of Thebez (a fortified city of Ephraim near Shechem). With the news that Abimelech—a Philistine ruler and enemy of Israel—and his army were en route to destroy the city—all the inhabitants of Thebez (men, women, and children) raced to the strong tower for safety. Locking the door behind them, they all headed for the roof tower to wait. As Abimelech came to the entrance to set the strong tower on fire, the woman of Thebez dropped a millstone from the roof of the tower—crushing Abimelech's head and leaving him for dead. Abimelech, not yet dead, commanded his armor-bearer to slay him so that it wouldn't be said of him that he died at the hand of a woman.

Several significant thoughts emerged in my heart after meditating upon this passage:

- Who was this woman?
- What gave her the strength and fortitude to stand against Abimelech?
- Why did she drop the millstone?
- Did she have children she was protecting?

I concluded by challenging myself, "Shouldn't I be as vehement against the prevailing evil confronting my home, family, and community?" She wasn't alone in that tower—the entire city of Thebez was locked in there with her.

"Every parent who dares to take upon himself the awful responsibility of calling a human life into being, who places himself in God's hands as the instrument of divine creative power, assumes a trust which should exclude every form of selfishness. Beyond the right of being well born, every child has the right to the best training his parent can give. He has the right to the personal care of both father and mother, a care which can never be delegated to others without serious loss to both parent and child. It is a part of holy intimacy...."
—Philip E. Howard, grandfather of Elisabeth Elliot

Just imagine the righteous anger that provoked her act of justice.

Evil confronts my home and family on a consistent basis. Day in and day out. Times have progressed, but the fact remains that evil is real, evil is raging, and evil is in hot pursuit of my children.

What does this mean to us, as parents and homeschool teachers? I believe it conveys the strong message that we must be proactive, ambitious, and tenacious in fortifying our homes, not lacking in zeal towards this mission.

Let's pause for just a moment before we continue to look at Webster's definition of **_fortify_** (v.t.):

1. To surround with a wall, ditch, palisades or other works, with a view to defend against the attacks of an enemy; to strengthen and secure by forts, batteries, or other works of art.
2. To strengthen against any attack.
3. To confirm; to add strength and firmness to.
4. To furnish with strength or means of resisting force, violence or assault.

Key words here are: surround, strengthen, confirm, add, furnish—all verbs that imply action on our part. I believe they imply hard work, as well. Raising a strong family is hard work. Homeschooling your children is hard work. But hard work reaps great rewards in the long term. Charles Spurgeon says it best:

> "Give us the first seven years of a child, with God's grace, and we may defy the world, the flesh and the devil to ruin that immortal soul.
>
> Those first years, while the clay is yet soft and plastic, go far to decide the form of the vessel. Do not say that your office, you who teach the young, is in the least degree inferior to ours, whose main business is with the older folks.
>
> No, you have the first of them, and your impressions, as they come first, will endure last; oh, that they may be good, and only good! Among the thoughts that come to an old man before he enters heaven, the most plentiful are those that aforetime visited him when he sat upon his mother's knee.
>
> The teachings of our childhood leave sharp impressions upon the mind, which remain after seventy years have passed. Let us see that such impressions are made for the highest ends."

The tragedy of September 11, 2001 was a clarion call to all of us. There is no way to avoid the sobering truth that life is short, life is fragile, life is a gift. In her well-written book, _Choices_, Mary Farrar writes:

> "Some of you are in the midst of fighting for your own home even as your read. You are fighting for your marriage, for your children. Perhaps even the battle seems hopeless, the blaze beyond your ability to vanquish. Very simply, we are all in the midst of the fight of our lives. Amazing what a crisis will reveal about the hidden character of a nation—or an

individual. Values surface quickly in the middle of a crisis, don't they? Whether we realize it or not, the critical choices we make in times of crisis can become matters of life and death. I submit to you there is nothing in this world more important than our homes, our marriages, and our children. Nothing. There is not one ministry or job or accomplishment or calling that is more important."

She continues,
   "The family is not just an arm or a finger. It is the very heart. And everyone knows if you have a bad heart, you are in serious trouble."

What better time can there be for self-examination and evaluation than today? In light of all that has happened in the world, take the time. As parents, we must first and foremost prepare *ourselves,* for our children will follow us. Dig deep and ask the hard-hitting questions about the sanctuary of your home and family. Is it all you want it to be? Perhaps you are well on your way or perhaps you've lost your way. David Campbell writes, "If you don't know where you are going, you'll probably end up somewhere else."

It is my hope that the following "Twelve Foundational Stones" will guide you and your family exactly where you want to go. It may be a rough journey at times, but one thing is certain—God is an ever-present help to each of us. He assures victory to all who have a heart towards Him.

—Janell Rardon

Foundation Stone 1: Vision
Casting the Vision

Janell Rardon

"The greatest tragedy in life is not death, but life without reason. It is dangerous to be alive and not know why you were given life. The deepest craving of the human spirit is to find a sense of significance and relevance. The search for relevance in life is the ultimate pursuit of man. Conscious or unconcious, admitted or unadmitted, this internal passion is what motivates and drives every human being, either directly or indirectly. It directs his decisions, controls his behavior and dictates his responses to his environment."

—Myles Munroe, In Pursuit of Purpose

"Where there is no revelation [vision], the people cast off restraint."

—King Solomon, Proverbs 29:18

Prior to embarking on the homeschooling adventure, I encourage you and your spouse to sit down, preferably somewhere quiet, and discuss the following questions:

1. Why are we considering homeschooling?
2. Why is our family taking this alternate route to education?
3. Why are we NOT taking the traditional route, via public or private school?
4. What circumstances led us to this place?
5. Do we realize that we must prune our lives in order to make room for homeschooling? Ask: What must I lay down in order to bring more peace and order into my home PRIOR to "adding" the education of my child/children into the picture? (Remember, it isn't "car-schooling" or "enrichment-program schooling" but HOMEschooling.]
6. What do my children need [I stress "need" here] in the form of social activities, friendships, church involvement, extracurricular sports, musical training, community outreach, *et cetera*.?
7. Will I have enthusiasm for teaching my children and be dedicated to seeking out opportunities and strategies for maximizing this opportunity? (See Debra Bell's *The Ultimate Guide to Homeschooling*, published by Thomas Nelson, for an in-depth look at this.][1]
8. What will this decision require of me (Mother, Father] and of our marriage? How will we safeguard the sanctity of our marriage from the demands of homeschooling? (See *Foundation Stone 5: Where Are You?* for more on this subject.]

George Barna comments in his powerful book, *The Power of Vision*, that "vision is a picture held in your mind's eye of the way things could or should be in the days ahead. It is not somebody else's view of the future, but one that uniquely belongs to you."[2] The key here being that God's plan for your family is tailor made—fitted perfectly—unlike anyone else's. Don't compete. Don't compare (only in respect of raising your own standard or when in need of help]. Don't stray from the path you've chosen.

An anonymous writer penned these significant words about the importance of vision:

"A vision without a task is a dream;
A task without a vision is drudgery;
A vision with a task is the hope of the world."

WRITING YOUR FAMILY MISSION STATEMENT

We've heard that before, haven't we? Vision has a plan. Vision has a future. Vision awaits activity. First and foremost, as parents, it is essential to draft a family mission statement. Habukkah 2:2 writes, "Record the vision, and inscribe it on tablets, That the one who reads it may run." In her national best-seller, *The Path: Creating Your Mission Statement for Work and for Life*, Laurie Beth Jones suggests three simple elements of a good mission statement:

1. A mission statement should be no more that a single sentence long.
2. It should be easily understood by a twelve year old.
3. It should be able to be recited by memory when under pressure.

She continues by adding, "all great leaders in history have had missions that were no more than a single sentence long. Abraham Lincoln's was to preserve the Union. Franklin D. Roosevelt's was to end the Depression... Mother Teresa's was to show mercy and compassion to the dying. Joan of Arc's was to free France. Nehemiah's was to rebuild the wall."[4]

To help you get started, these three guides will make the entire process more pleasing and help you in drafting your mission:

1. **Vision and Values:** Ask yourself: What does our family stand for? What values, principles, causes are important to us? Proverbs 24:3-4 says, "Any enterprise is built by wise planning, becomes strong through common sense, and profits wonderfully by keeping abreast of the facts." You have to know what you stand for. Where do you want your family to be this time next year? in five years? in ten years? We have always said to our children, "You are a Rardon. What does that stand for?"

2. **Purpose and Passion:** Does your family have a particular interest or shared passion? If so, this should definitely be included in your mission statement. Perhaps you are a military family, pursuing advancement in this endeavor. This purpose would definitely harness certain opportunities and requires incredible grace, focus, and determination. Perhaps you operate a family-owned business. This, too, would harness certain decisions and require constant maintenance and care. All of these interests affect the homeschool and, in turn, effect the family; therefore, it is of vital importance to know your purpose.

3. **Discipline and Determination.** This guide will help you stay on track. We will discuss this in more depth in *Foundational Stone 9: Obedience*, but for now, remember that you must know where you are going OR you will end up somewhere else. I am constantly reiterating **my** mission: *To train my children spirit, soul, and body for their future stations in life;* and my **family** mission: *To stand strong, true, and able as a family of faith.* Regardless of the opportunities that unfold before me, I

*"You must realize that your fulfillment in life is dependent on your becoming and doing what you were born to be and do. Anything less makes life your enemy and death your friend. It is essential, vital, crucial and necessary that you understand this fundamental principle of purpose and pursue it with all your heart. For without purpose, life has no heart. Remember, **those who don't know where they are going will probably end up someplace else."***

—Myles Munroe, In Pursuit of Purpose

"A personal mission statement acts as both a harness and a sword, harnessing you to what is true about your life, and cutting away all that is false."
—Laurie Beth Jones, The Path (Introduction, xvii)

must put blinders on and remember my mission. This will be true for your family. Your mission statement will be the banner your family holds high as the waging war of this world buffets your home front.

FACING THE CHALLENGE

Challenges will come. They will come in all shapes, sizes, people, places and even from those who love you most. Expect them. In light of this, remember the following:

> *"When God is going to do something wonderful, He begins with a difficulty. If it is going to be something very wonderful, He begins with an impossibility!"* —*Charles Inwood*

and

> *"When faced with a mountain, I WILL NOT QUIT! I will keep on striving until I climb over, find a pass through, tunnel underneath, or simply stay and turn the mountain into a miracle, with God's help!"* —Rev. Robert Schuller, *The Possibility Thinker's Creed*

Every veteran homeschooler can share their challenges. The days are full of them. Hence, the importance of knowing your mission. When the obstacles stand in your way, you will have the fortitude to press through them because you know where you are going. The year after I graduated from college, I was seriously homesick for my college friends still there. I had made plans to visit them and was so excited about returning. The weather forecast for that day was bleak—"a major snowstorm." After work, I made the decision to try and beat the storm. *"I am going to Harrisonburg."* That was my mission. Leaving Chesapeake late afternoon, all was fine. Then I hit Williamsburg and snow. Contemplating turning back, I kept saying to myself, *"I am going to Harrisonburg."* Knowing this was probably an insane idea, in the naivete of my youth, I pressed on. Nine-and-a-half hours later, I arrived, completely exhausted from the fight. A four-hour trip took nine-and-a-half hours. I still don't know how I did it. As I look back, I see God's hand, sending trucks ahead of me that forged a path in the dark and a single mission statement, *"I am going to Harrisonburg."*

Now, I know I wouldn't want my daughters to be so naive, but there is great power in the fortitude of pressing forward when difficulty arises. Be confident of one thing—God will see you through each and every difficult passage of homeschooling. He will not leave you or forsake you. Lean on, depend on, rely on and hope in His promises for your family.

Write your mission statement and stand strong on it. Face the challenges one by one; knowing that victory will come. In the words of Winston Churchill:

> ***"Never, never, never give up."***

End Notes

[1]Debra Bell. *The Ultimate Guide to Homeschooling, 2001 Edition.*

[2]George Barna. *The Power of Vision.*

[3]Laurie Beth Jones. *The Path: Creating Your Mission Statement for Work and Life.*

[4]Laurie Beth Jones. *The Path: Creating Your Mission Statement for Work and Life.*

Foundation Stone 2: Flexibility
Think Change

Janell Rardon

"Without change there can be no breakthroughs, without breakthroughs, there can be no future...."
—Anonymous

One afternoon, my children and I were shopping, when a framed picture caught my eye. In bold print the words, "THINK CHANGE" blared out at me like a loud siren. I immediately walked over and stood in front of it. "*Think change*," I repeated to myself. "*Think change*." Interesting concept. A paradox of sorts, because who likes change? I certainly don't. Not real change. I don't mind changing purses, changing socks, changing bed linens, changing from winter to spring clothes, but what about changing jobs, changing homes, changing churches, changing families (as is required after a loved one dies and a remarriage occurs, or a family member divorces), perhaps changing habits or behavioral patterns? Yes, what about changing habits? Habits become entrenched and are tenacious when it comes to uprooting them.

Initiating true change, from the inside out, is painstaking work. It involves making a resolution written in stone. As I began meditating on these two little words, "*think change*," I began learning big lessons about myself and about God. I realized that God has required His children to allow Him to change us, to free us to be who He created us to be, and to appreciate Him. As written in Romans 12:2, we are to spend our days being transformed— completely changed—by the renewing of our minds. Why? So we will be prepared to meet God face-to-face in eternity.

Flexibility—that quality of being able to bend or yield to arguments, persuasions, or circumstances—is a rare jewel in the crown of a family, especially one that homeschools. No two days will be alike. No two years will be alike. No two children will be alike.

At first, this was a difficult concept for me to grasp. Having taught in a traditional elementary school setting, I was used to an organized, controlled teaching environment. *Bulletin Boards. Neat rows of desks. Bookshelves lined with all the materials I needed. Copier. Secretary at my disposal. Schedules. Lunch with my peers. Paycheck. Weekends off.*

At the onset of my homeschooling, somewhere in my mind I thought it would be the same. So, imagine my shock when I didn't get a paycheck after the first two weeks of school and my students didn't leave at 3:15p.m.! Flexibility. Adjustment. Think Change.

"Success can only be defined by purpose and measured by obedience. Success has more to do with being than doing. To be successful is to finish the originally intended assignment according to the plan and the specifications of the creator. Purpose is thus the key and the foundation of success. It is the only true source of fulfillment and the only accurate measurement in life. Therefore, success cannot be determined by the opinions of others about your actions, but by the satisfaction of the One who gave you the assignment."
—Myles Munroe, The Pursuit of Purpose

Learning to be flexible is an area that needs constant attention. Webster says that to be flexible is to be "capable of being turned or forced from a straight line or form without breaking." Think of a straight line. Constantly moving forward. Very often, we are like that straight line. We have a plan and nothing is going to interfere with that plan. But life doesn't always work out that way. What do we do:

- When the curriculum we spent our hard-earned money on doesn't seem to be working?
- When a learning disability we feel unable to handle emerges in a child?
- When our husband loses his job and finances become strained?
- When Mom finds out she is pregnant and difficulties force her to bed rest?
- When the plan we had to organize the home goes awry and is stalled?
- When our "ideal" of homeschooling doesn't prove to be unfolding?

What do we do when the rapids of change force their way upon our families? Three things: We slow down our pace, we make room for adjustments by being flexible, and we pray. I have found the following difficult passages to hold very important lessons for our family. Mrs. Charles E. Cowman, author of *Springs in the Valley*, writes:

> *"This is an ingredient in God's plan of dealing with us. We are to enter a secret chamber of isolation in prayer and faith that is very fruitful. At certain times and in certain places, God will build a mysterious wall around us. He will take away all the supports we customarily lean upon, and will remove our ordinary way of doing things. God will close us off to something divine, completely new and unexpected, and that cannot be understood by examining our previous circumstances. We will all be in a place where we do not know what is happening, where God is cutting the cloth of our lives by a new pattern, and thus where He causes us to look at Him."[1]*

Several years ago my family and I attended Dean Shostar's *Glass Armonica Concert*. Prior to attending this special Christmas event, I had never heard of this instrument. All who attended marveled at its ability to pierce through the *noise of the 21st century* with a hushed reverence and serenity. Its perfect pitch provoked a sense of calm. Here, in the midst of the busy preparations of the Christmas season, my little family sat—surrounded by a sea of soft, soothing sounds. I left that concert reflecting on the "perfect Pitch" of the glass, so finely tuned. Mr. Shostar had to be extremely careful not to touch anything that might cause stress to the glass, keeping it from performing to its best. The sound was pleasing, so refreshing, so deeply pure that I felt something inside of me being awakened: perhaps a call to sharpen my ear to hearing the voice of the Lord. Sometimes life just gets *so noisy* that we forget how to truly listen. In studying this issue, I came across a beautiful passage of scripture, found in Isaiah 50: 4-5:

> *The Sovereign Lord has given me an instructed tongue, to know the word that sustains the weary. He wakens me morning by morning,*

wakens my ear to listen like one being taught. The Sovereign Lord has opened my ears, and I have not been rebellious."

Theologian F. B. Meyer instructs us, *"We must be taught before we can teach. We shall never do our best work for God until we accustom ourselves to receive and take His messages."*

Dean Shostar's *Glass Armonica Concert* opened up an opportunity to sit down and think. In order to bring about true and lasting change, one must have ample time to sit down and think—time without noise and distractions.

Homeschooling will force changes upon you and your family. This is a given. I recently counseled a group of young women interested in homeschooling, and was heartened by one woman's brutal honesty. Through tears, she remarked, "I don't want to homeschool. Being a mother is hard, very hard." I felt myself tearing up as well, because I've known her pain. Mothering is one of the most challenging endeavors I have ever endured. I encouraged her to seek God and ask Him to change her. He can and will bring about the true, lasting change that will enable us to be all He intended us to be.

A. W. Tozer wrote, "The widest thing in the universe is not space; it is the potential capacity of the human heart. Being made in the image of God, it is capable of almost unlimited extension in all directions. And one of the world's greatest tragedies is that we allow our hearts to shrink until there is room in them for little beside themselves."[2]

Don't expect all the changes to come at once. Cast your ideals, preconceived notions of homeschooling, expectations of your children and your mate, and personal perfectionism at the feet of the One who will enable you to accomplish all that is required of you. Remember that "success cannot be determined by the opinion of others about your actions, but by the satisfaction of the One who gave you the assignment."[3]

End Notes
[1] Mrs. Charles E. Cowman. *Springs in the Valley.*
[2] A. W. Tozer. *The Pursuit of Holiness.*
[3] Myles Munroe. *The Pursuit of Purpose.*

Foundation Stone 3: Order

The Still Axis

Janell Rardon

"The French have an expression: Reculer pour mieux sauter. This means that you have to step back, retreat a little, if you're going to successfully jump over something. Want to jump across a ditch? You don't just walk to the edge and then leap. You walk to the edge, gauge the distance, and then retreat a bit to give yourself room to get a full running start before you leap. Sometimes we can't take the next leap forward unless we take the time to step back first. Where will you get the strength to sauter [leap forward] if you can't allow yourself to reculer [pull back]?"

—Mira Kishenbaum, The Gift of a Year

"Good order is the foundation of all things."

—Anonymous

Sometimes we can't take the next leap forward unless we take the time to step back first." [1]
　　　　　　　　　—Mira Kishenbaum

We're going to step back now. We're going to rewind and take a good, long look at the condition of our lives and those with whom we live—physically, spiritually, emotionally, and naturally, i.e., our homes, our physical environment.

In order to move forward, we must do this. One of the greatest areas of conflict in many lives is found in this area—order. There isn't a great deal written on this topic, but it is at the very core of all life's processes. We all know God is a God of order. He established the heavens and the earth according to an orderly system. His creativity was displayed through a systematic order of events. Reading through Genesis, the first book in the Bible, we see this order in action; *"on the first day; on the second day; on the third day and so on."*

He had a plan. He followed that plan. He completed His work. He rested. Twenty-four/seven—that is God's design; His ordered amount of time for us to accomplish our day's work. I tell my children all the time that God gives us twenty-four hours in which to accomplish all the day entails. One solar day, twenty-four hours, and no more. I encourage them to listen for adults to comment, "There isn't enough time in the day...." My response, "Oh, yes! God, our infinite source of wisdom, designed the day and that must be good enough for us." If we can't accomplish "our agenda" for the day, then we must step back, look over it and make adjustments.

Listen to the words from Dr. Richard Swenson's best-selling book, *The Overload Syndrome*, and see if they ring true:

"Life in Modern-day America is essentially void of time and space. Not the Star Trek kind. The sanity kind. The time and space that once existed in the lives of people who regularly lingered after dinner, helped the kids with the homework, visited with the neighbors, sat on the lawn swing, went for long walks, dug in the garden, and always had a full night's sleep. People are exhausted. A mother of four from La Grange, Illinois, said: 'I'm so tired, my idea of a vacation is a trip to the dentist. I just can't wait to sit in that chair and relax.' People are stressed. People are breaking the speed limit of life. People are overloaded. We need more time. We need more space. We need more reserves. We need more buffers. We need time to rest and space to heal." [2]

The overloaded, overburdened, discontented lifestyle dictated by the demands of modern cultural expectations and advancements has seeped slowly and subtly into the body of Christ—luring us away from the authenticity and intimacy that God created us to have, both individually and corporately. We were not created to "do" but to "be" one with Him, daily communing and relating to the One who created us. It isn't only a matter of simplification of lifestyle but sanctification of heart, mind, body, and soul.

This truth confirms the reality that I have witnessed in my own life, years ago, and in the lives of countless men and women with whom I come in contact. One common theme seems to weave itself through every plea: Each hungers after something "deeper" in their lives; all desire to push away the hustle and bustle in order to embrace the peace and power that a God-focused, Spirit-led life provides. All hunger for a sense of order, but just can't seem to find "the time" or "the energy" to get it.

This is where we step back. This is where we "think change." This is where we make a plan, stop the madness, and pray. *You see, God desires that we live a well-ordered, peace-filled, abundant life. It is His heart.* How do I know this? It is recorded throughout Scripture. Through my own experiences, I am completely convinced that God doesn't want us frazzled, frustrated, and falling apart. His desire is that we be full and overflowing with His virtues.

By now, you're asking, "How? How is this possible?" *Well, let's take a step back.* Let's grow in our understanding of order and develop a plan for implementing the changes necessary to grow in this area.

WHAT IS ORDER?

Order is "the regular disposition or methodical arrangement of things." All of creation demonstrates this order. I think of the brown pelicans that I watched one summer while vacationing in Hatteras, North Carolina. They flew in such a beautiful pattern of order...one leading.... others following. The lead pelican would flap once and soar...then the next...and the next...in the choreographed pattern danced by this flock of birds. They weren't fighting each other, trying to outdo one another, stressing out about who leads the pack or who wins the race; just working together in a God-ordained fashion of flight.

Order must begin within the soul. God always, I believe, works from the inside to the outside. Anne Morrow Lindbergh, in her brilliant work, *The Gift of the Sea*, suggests we "strive to be the *still axis* within the revolving wheel of relationships, obligations and activities."[3] I fondly call this "the wheel of activity." *Do you feel as though your wheel of activity is spinning madly?* It can happen so quickly. Every "yes" is a spoke on the wheel. Before you know it, your wheel is bulging with activities; all good, but are they all necessary? How can we bring order to the confusion, and quietness to the chaos?

Think for a moment upon the nucleus of Anne Morrow Lindbergh's statement: "the still axis within." A family with children will, at times, feel as though it is spinning out of control. Life gets busy. Very busy. But when we have ordered our world, we can remain calm and centered. May I suggest the following scripture as a guideline that may facilitate a greater sense of order within the realm of your soul:

"Aspire to lead a quiet life, to mind your own business, and to work with your own hands, as we commanded you, that you may walk properly toward those who are outside, and that you may lack nothing."

—1 Thessalonians 4:11:

Three things are noted within this scripture that are highly significant when it comes to leading a well-ordered life:

1. **Aspire to lead a quiet life.** To aspire is "to pant after an object, great, noble, or spiritual." Matthew Henry writes, "We should be ambitious and industrious (about) how to be calm and quiet in our minds, in patience to possess our own souls, and to be quiet towards others; of a meek and mild, a gentle and peaceable disposition, not given to strife, contention or division. Satan is very busy to disquiet us, therefore, let us study to be quiet." Satan hunts down God's people; the righteous are his daily target practice. He loves to entangle us in a web of busyness and preoccupation.

   I am speaking from great experience here, for I have never made it my ambition to lead a quiet life, but—for the last few years—God has been directing my path to this very place, demanding, as a good Father would, that I take full account of my activities, obligations, and responsibilities. He has required my full attention. After several years of tremendous physical challenge, I finally got the message: Slow down or burn out. The one dominating mission for me has been that of educating my children. *The conviction to homeschool is one that requires the pruning of competing activities and obligations.*

2. **Eliminate unsolicited involvement in the affairs of others.** My husband always cautions me to not "poke my nose" where it doesn't belong. "Hold your tongue and walk away," he wisely counsels. I am learning to wait until asked before offering my opinion. Good rule of thumb. You will be amazed at how much emotional clutter is deleted from your life, leaving you ample energy to complete your daily routine with more grace and patience. Does this mean you don't help others? Absolutely not. It means that you don't involve yourself in everybody's business. Do not answer the phone every time it rings. The world will rotate without your help. Stay true to your mission statement. Be flexible when a real need arises. Focus.

3. **Cease from striving.** Striving can be positive, but very often we strive to excel for the wrong reasons. It brings unrest when accompanied by a need to prove ourselves, to compete with others, or to fill something within ourselves that only Jesus can fill. I check myself by asking a simple question: *What is the motivation for what I'm doing? Are my motives love-based or performance-based? If no one in the whole world noticed what I've done today, would God's praise be enough?*

Yes, God sends encouragers and support groups, but our service at home must be grounded in humility and love. Very often, we want to "do what everyone else is doing," or "what is expected of us," so we forego our sense of reason; bringing stress and strain upon our families.

The following words penned by Victoria Moran in *Shelter for the Spirit* give great food for thought:

> *"We live in a place and time when it takes courage and determination to give home priority status, or even realize that it might be a good idea to do so. Most of us are gone a lot, and when we do come home, we're often tired—weary from a variety of activities and torn by conflicting commitments. Sometimes we actually seek these activities out because they don't ask as much of us as the demands at home. Besides, achievement in the outer world is often accompanied by a level of fanfare that domestic accomplishments seldom receive. Even so, there are pioneers among us who are engaged in a sort homesteading of the heart. These are young people who are redefining home for themselves after experiencing a familial environment that was frightening or belittling. These pioneers include all the people who are making day-to-day, domestic choices based on loving convictions. **A home is a signature, distinct and recognizable.** The love put into it may be the greatest accomplishment of a lifetime."*[4]

In conclusion, as you read through these words, may you sift through them; taking whatever pearls you might find that will enable you to strengthen your home and family. We all make mistakes, we all fall short of the glory of God, but with God's sovereign grace flowing freely, we can become exactly who He has designed us to be. I believe with all my heart that the key to a strong family, and to life itself, is discipline...and order precedes discipline.

The resources listed at the end of *Foundational Stone #4: Taking Baby Steps* have blessed me immensely on my road to finding true order in my soul. Each resource has served as both mentor and friend; plowing up the fallow, weed-laden field in my heart and soul and planting seeds of strength, stability, and success in their place.

End Notes
[1]Mira Kirshenbaum. *The Gift of a Year.*
[2]Dr. Richard Swenson. *The Overload Syndrome.*
[3]Anne Morrow Lindbergh. *The Gift of The Sea.*
[4]Victoria Moran. *The Shelter for the Spirit.* *
Not specifically based on "Christian values—proceed with this in mind. I gleaned what I felt was appropriate and applicable.

Foundation Stone 4: Organization
Taking Baby Steps

Janell Rardon

Foundation Stone #4 will address the monumental subject of organization. There are many opinions concerning this subject. I will attempt to bridge the broad spectrum of information with a few simple suggestions that may help you bring organization into your home. Assess your situation and ask yourself the following questions:

1. Is your home a "palace of peace"—"a castle of chaos"—or a "dungeon of drudgery?" Am I the "queen of clean"—the "princess of packrats"—or a "servant to slothfulness?"
2. What is your dream for your house/life/family?
3. What space in your home environment needs your attention most? What would you like to tackle first? *Think baby steps.*
4. Is there a habit you would like to break or begin in your daily routine? For example, *"If I could get started just 30 minutes earlier in the day, I feel I would have better control over my life. I need to hit the snooze button two fewer times!"*

As you read, concentrate on this one space or habit. Christine Field, homeschooling mom of four, writes:

> *"Spending a season on organization may mean the difference between survival and giving up on homeschooling. The frustration caused by disorganization is a major stumbling block for many homeschoolers. Being organized is a tool. It's a blessing, not a prison. If you like the way things are going in your home, if you feel like you are accomplishing what needs to be done, if the children are productive and self-motivated, then you probably don't need an organizational overhaul. On the other hand, it you are stressed out, your children are at loose ends and whiny, if you can't even remember your goals for the year, then a season of organization is in order."[1]*

I really love her idea of "a season of organization" because the organization process requires diligence, patience, and time. Having twins, a four-year old, and a 1900-square-foot house propelled my search for gaining mastery over my living environment. I received another eye opener in the aftermath of my mother-in-law's sudden death. Having to sort through all her belongings, drawer by drawer, was daunting. I remember crying, asking myself, "If I died today, would I want my loved ones to see the condition (the messes) I had shoved into my drawers?" These troubling life experiences fueled my ambition and kicked me into action to simplify and de-clutter.

When we discuss being organized, we are not talking about "cleaning up our messes" but finding a system that is right for us; one that will help transform our "castle of chaos" into a "palace of peace." Julie Morgenstern offers us a great working definition of organization:

"Organizing is the process by which we create environments that enable us to live, work and relax exactly as we want to. When we are organized, our homes, offices, schedules, (and I add our schoolrooms), reflect and encourage who we are, what we want, and where we are going."[2]

The very definition of the word *organize* supports this:
1) to construct so that one part may *cooperate* with another.
2) to distribute into suitable parts and appoint proper officers, so that *the whole may act as one body.*

I don't know about you, but there are days when I feel as though I am at war with my home. Nothing seems to be cooperating. It doesn't take long for things to get disheveled. In my frustration, I took action.

First, I created a motto:

CLEAN IT UP!
Commit to a plan
Lean on God's power
Emerge energized
Act Immediately!
Never quit
Implement intentional living
Train family members
Upkeep, Upkeep, Upkeep!
Pace yourself, Prune activities, Provide time for the task, Pray

Secondly, I carved out time.

Psalm 90:12 says, "Teach us to number our days aright, that we may gain a heart of wisdom." Twenty-four/seven. TIME. It takes time to bring order into our homes and it takes time to keep it there. Find a day, a week, a season of time, where you can shut yourself off from the hurriedness of life to get organized, or at least, to develop a plan of action. Wage an all-out assault on the war zone. Mark off a significant amount of time to get this initial work done. Perhaps you could hire a sitter or recruit family and friends to watch the children for awhile, so you can work!

Where do you start? At the beginning, with the basics. You must repeat to yourself, "*Take baby steps.*" You can't and won't organize the entire house in a day. It will take time. Find one area that needs immediate attention and begin there. If you can't afford to hire an organizational specialist (which may be money well spent), I suggest the following simple steps:

1. **Improve the efficiency of your home**. Key word: SIMPLIFY. Read some of the books suggested in the resource section and outline several different methods of or approaches to simplification. Ask yourself, "What can I live without?" Or, if you are a packrat, "What must I live without?" If you just can't bear to discard, call in an objective person to sit beside you. Every time I shop, I ask myself, "Will this item be in a garage sale this time next year?" "Is there a place for this in my home?" It is amazing what we can live without. Victoria Moran suggests going through every room, with pencil and paper in hand, writing down all of those items that feed your soul and nurture your spirit; eliminating everything else.

2. **Recall your family mission.** What is important to your family? Identify the areas of your home and the items that are most essential to the well-being of each family member. Every family has a unique personality and mission. For example, homeschooling is a major part of my daily life, so I need a homeschool room that is functional, stimulating, well organized, and conducive to learning.

   Perhaps your family has a gift for hospitality and entertains frequently. The kitchen and dining area would play a key role. Therefore, concentrate on having these areas highly functional and efficient.

3. **Work as a team.** Ephesians 4: 16 records, "From him (Jesus) the whole body, joined and held together by every supporting ligament, grows and builds itself up in love, as each part does its work." Teamwork is most essential to the success of an organization program. Every family member must be committed and cooperative, from the youngest to the oldest. Parents, this will be the most challenging aspect of implementation—training your children to work. Make it fun. Make it rewarding. For a stimulating discussion on this subject, I recommend *"Children and Chores"* with Jean Lush. Published by Focus on the Family, this audiocassette, #CT394, can be ordered through them, either by phone or on the Internet at www.family.org.

In conclusion, I sense we've only scratched the surface of this enormous topic, but I hope you have gleaned at least one helpful idea. Purposing to point you in the right direction, I leave you with a simple, yet profound truth found in Proverbs 15:6, *"The house of the righteous contains great treasure."* Crown each room in your home with prayer; inviting joy, laughter, peace, grace, patience, faith, cooperation, vision, *et cetera*, to take permanent residence. This is our inheritance.

SUGGESTED RESOURCES

Organizing From the Inside Out and *Time Management From the Inside Out* by Julie Morgenstern, www.juliemorgenstern.com

The Messie's Manual by Sandra Felton, www.messies.com

Creating a Beautiful Home by Alexandra Stoddard*

The Peaceful Home Video Series by Elisabeth Elliot

Children and Chores audiocassette by Jean Lush. Published by Focus on the Family, www.family.org

Take Time for Your Life and *Stand Up for Your Life* by Cheryl Richardson,* www.cherylrichardson.com

A great help for anyone who hasn't learned the valuable gift of caring for one's self. We discuss the value of not being drained and depleted. These resources give practical tips and tools for healthy care of ourselves.

Sink Reflections by Marla Cilley*

This book and website provide lessons and free reminder e-mails that teach home organization and maintenance in a supportive, friendly way, www.flylady.net

*Not specifically based on "Christian" values—proceed with this in mind. I gleaned what I felt was appropriate and applicable.

End Notes

[1] Christine Field. *Help for the Harried Homeschooler.*

[2] Julie Morganstern. *Organizing From the Inside Out.*

Foundation Stone 5: Marriage
Where are You?

Janell Rardon

"As typical Christian home-schoolers we seem to have all the ingredients for perfect families: Two parents in the home, strong commitment to the family as the key unit in society, convictions that won't quit in the face of persecution, beliefs that if God says it, we'll do it—period. It would certainly appear that we have all it takes for great marriages and great families...I believe that homeschoolers are going to face an unusual degree of satanic temptations and attacks simply because we have unusually high prospects for spiritual success with our children.

And those prospects have multiplied potential for long-range impact on generations to come. The enemy of our soul is going to take every opportunity to break up our marriages because of the dynamic potential our families represent.

— Mike Farris, A Sacred Foundation

xperts all agree that the greatest gift a husband and wife can give their children is a happy marriage. Jay Kessler adds:

"The primary relationship between a husband and a wife is the foundation on which kids build their sense of security, their identity, and learn to relate to others. This prepares them to eventually relate to their own spouse. Couples are virtually helpless in relating to one another in later life if they have not observed a healthy relationship between their own parents. In fact, it is only through a great deal of effort and relearning that people are able to overcome a dysfunctional family life. Therefore I repeat: The relationship between husband and wife is primary. Kids need to understand that mom and dad have something special going on. They need to know that your marriage is solid and that there is nothing anybody can do to divide you from one another."[1]

Jay Kessler's words ring true—it takes a great deal of effort and relearning in order to overcome a dysfunctional family of origin. Both my husband and myself were raised in the home of alcoholic fathers. Having strong mothers, a strong faith, and a gracious God has enabled us to face our difficulties and somehow surmount the residual effects of this type of home environment.

Blindly, we embarked on our adventure of raising a Christian family. Both committed, we began to "relearn" and read all we could about marriage, family, and relationships. Through great effort and, at times, turbulent waters, we fought to remain focused on the task. As mentioned before, raising a strong family is hard work. Maintaining a life-giving marriage is hard work, as well.

God initiated the marriage covenant. It was His idea. Genesis 2:7 records God's creation of man. It continues as God placed man, Adam, in the Garden of Eden to work it and take care of it. *But something happened.* God saw that it wasn't good for man to be alone. Genesis 2:18-25 records the creation of a help meet for man. While Adam slept, God created a woman, Eve, for him. Now he was complete. I have written in the margin of my Bible — "woman completes man; not competes." *This is the essence of marriage.*

So many times, we forget this essential truth. Marriage is a partnership in every sense of the word. Two hearts join together to complete one another.

It seems that the pace of life in the 21st Century has eroded this vital principle. How many days do we just pass our mates in the hallway with a quick glance or smile—so rushed that we can't even pause for a hug? How many days are we so engrossed in our projects, planning, or outside activities that we don't even see one another? This happened to me. Finally, my husband quietly came to me and said, *"Where are you? I miss you. Do you think you could schedule me in?"* Stunned, it was almost as if I heard the Lord saying the same thing. *"Where are you? I miss you. Do you think you could schedule me in?"*

Pained by this confrontation, I remembered the words of God to His beloved creation, Adam, in Genesis 3:9, "Where are you?" God had always communed with Adam in the cool of the evening. This particular evening, He couldn't find Adam. He was hiding. Why? Because Adam was ashamed. We all know the story—Adam and Eve had partaken of the forbidden fruit.

Within these verses, lies a strong message for each one of us. Especially homeschooling parents. We get so entangled in all the responsibilities of nurturing, caring, educating, and transporting our children that we place our marriages on the back burner. The danger lies in the fact that one day our children will grow up and leave our homes. They will be gone. And there we will be, husband and wife. It is imperative that we have a marriage relationship that has been nurtured.

HOW CAN WE SAFEGUARD OUR MARRIAGES?

1. **Ask, "How can I bless my mate?** Focus on how you can be a blessing to your spouse rather than how your spouse should be a blessing to you. If both of you have the same giving attitude, you will both be blessed. But don't wait for your spouse to bless you. When you focus on getting your needs met through your spouse instead of from God, you will always come up short."[2] Love notes, phone calls, flowers, 15-minute "time-outs" from the children, dates, candlelight coffee breaks, *et cetera.* Don't forget that the small things are really the big things.

2. **Keep a storehouse of energy for intimacy and connection.** Intimacy, derived from the Latin root, *intimus*—meaning "within," is defined as "inmost; inward; near; close in friendship." My husband says, "I married you because I enjoy being with you." Isn't that the essence of God's heart in Genesis, "communing in the cool of the day?"

   How can we give to one another if we are emotionally, physically, and spiritually drained? *It is impossible.* We must guard our inner resources. If we fall into bed drained (on a consistent basis) with nothing left to give, we are doing too much. Mike Farris boldly says, "Stop leading a support group." I add, "Prune your activities, obligations, and responsibilities. No matter how worthy, how great, how important, there is nothing more important than your marriage. Nothing."

   Times may come where normalcy is stalled or interrupted due to a death in the family, a busy time with work, a deployment, a new baby, caring for an elderly parent, *et cetera*, but this should be for a "season," and special care and understanding given during this period.

"The first responsibility of parents is to provide a loving and happy home. And the most important relationship in the home is the marriage bond, which takes primacy over the parent-child relationship. The security of a teenager [and, I add, child] and the quality of the parent-child bonding are largely dependant on the quality of the marital bonding. You can see how important it is to assure the best possible relationship between husband and wife, since this is the basis for seriously attempting to relate to a teenager [or child] in a more positive way."
—*Ross Campbell,* Parents' Guide to the Spiritual Mentoring of Teens

3. **Marriage is a give-and-give relationship.**[3] Marriage requires a 100% giving of self at all times. It is hard, I know, but this is truth. Who likes to die to self? Who likes to esteem others higher than self?

4. **Play together.** Laugh. Stay young. Remember the times when you were falling in love. Take the time to be together. Budget it! Do not forsake this essential ingredient. Life is very serious, I know, but don't take it so seriously all the time.

5. **Hug and kiss ten times a day.** My husband and I heard this seemingly silly prescription for marriage boredom at a Zig Ziglar conference many years ago. He assured each attendee that if they implemented this simple practice into their marriage courtship—they would both be happier and more fulfilled. Another study proved that men who were kissed prior to leaving for work were more productive and content. Silly? All I say is "try it!" See what happens.

6. **Learn your partner's love language.** In *"The Five Love Languages: How to Express Heartfelt Commitment to Your Mate,"* Gary Chapman lists five significant love languages: words of affirmation, quality time, gifts, acts of service, and physical touching.[4] When I discovered my husband's love language was quality time, an entire window of understanding opened up for me! I realized how important it was for me to spend time "being" with him.

7. **Deal with underlying "issues."** Don't sweep things under the carpet. In five years you'll have a huge obstacle to surmount. If you need counsel, find it. Don't be ashamed to ask for help. None of us is perfect, therefore, there will be times when we need to deal with some issue of our sin nature. I suggest praying together, and seeking counsel as needed.

8. **Cover your marriage with prayer, both corporately and individually.** Joining together as man and wife in prayer is powerful. Joining together with your children (during family altar) and praying for your marriage allows them to witness your covenant as a "three-fold" cord (Ecclesiastes 4: 12). Hearing your mate assure you that he is praying for you builds great security and rest.

In conclusion, remember the words of Solomon (Ecclesiastes 4: 9-12, NIV):
"Two are better than one, because they have a good return for their work; If one falls down, his friend can help him up.
But pity the man who falls and has no one to help him up!
Also, if two lie down together, they will keep warm.
But how can one keep warm alone?
Though one may be overpowered, two can defend themselves.
A cord of three strands is not quickly broken."

End Notes
[1]Jay Kessler. *Raising Responsible Kids.*
[2]Mike Farris and L. Reed Elam. *A Sacred Foundation.*
[3]Mike Farris and L. Reed Elam. *A Sacred Foundation.*
[4]Gary Chapman. *The Five Love Languages.*

Foundation Stone 6: Devotion

Thirty Minutes of Silence

Janell Rardon

"Quiet time spent grooming the soul affects a home in two powerful ways. First, it gives a sense of peace to the person who engages in it, and one peaceful person can have a profound effect on a household. It means at least one person is passing around more serenity than irritation. It initiates a positive ripple effect that can change the dynamics of relationships.

The second way that quiet, awareness-expanding pursuits benefit a home is that their repeated practice removes tension from the atmosphere. The tranquility and joy that people who meditate realize in their lives can not only be perceived; it can spill over into the place where they meditate, the way a woman's perfume can delicately scent a room through which she's walked."

—*Victoria Moran,* Shelter for the Spirit

Proverbs 24: 3-4 instructs, "By wisdom a house is built, and through understanding it is established; through knowledge its rooms are filled with rare and beautiful treasures." Serenity of soul is a rare and beautiful treasure. I completely agree with Victoria Moran that *"one peaceful person can have a profound effect on a household."* [1] A vital ingredient in the success of the homeschool is found in this truth.

Are you moving through life with more serenity than irritation? *Not just on a good day; every day.* On a typical day, are you an optimist or a pessimist? Is your soul running on empty with nothing to give, or is it full and brimming with care and concern for others?

These are necessary questions. How can we serve our families, churches and communities if we are empty? I faced this question with great care and knew that I needed to withdraw for a season in order to find the answer. Responsibilities compound, obligations mount, and all of a sudden we find ourselves in the midst of a whirlwind, drained of any positive emotion. Why? Because in the midst of the whirlwind, *we forget to take care of ourselves and our relationship to God.*

Having always been a disciplined individual, I'd never dismissed my quiet time with God, but the deeper disciplines of practiced silence, journaling, and meditation had lain dormant. Honestly, I was too tired, too run down, and too burned out to even consider these options. Then, I read a powerful Scripture. *Revelation 8:1.* It reads:

> *"When He opened the seventh seal, there was silence in heaven for about half an hour."*

Silence for half an hour. Thirty minutes. After the September 11 tragedy at the World Trade Center in New York City, "moments of silence" were being held throughout the world. One such memoriam was held at The New York Stock Exchange, but this time it was for two minutes. I remember watching as this usually hectic, hustling world marketplace was silent. It seemed like forever. Absolutely no noise or movement. It was profound. I couldn't help but reflect on Revelation 8:1 and how profound that must have been. Matthew Henry comments:

"Great things were upon the wheel of providence, and the church of God, both in heaven and earth, stood silent, as became them, to see what God was doing."[2]

The entire population of heaven stood silent for thirty minutes to see what God was doing. If this was a principle heaven deemed important, I decided I must integrate this practice into my daily life. Beginning each day with five or ten minutes of complete silence in the confines of my closet, I slowly saw the cares, demands, pressures, and drivenness of my soul dissipate. Over the course of several months, I had trained myself to a full thirty minutes of silence.

Was this easy? No. My mind raced like a champion horse, wanting to avoid the silence, the quiet, the solitude. But, I emerged from this time of communion with God stronger, wiser, and more equipped to handle the whirlwind.

Very often, a homeschooling household can become this whirlwind. Music lessons. Dance classes. Enrichment programs. Field Trips. Boy Scouts. Girl Scouts. Sewing. 4-H Club. Soccer. Swimming. Baseball. Coops. Enrichment Programs. The list goes on and on. While these are all good things, herein lies the challenge: *Are we moving through these activities with more serenity than irritation? Are all these wonderful, exhilarating activities and opportunities robbing us of our quiet time with God? Are they crowding an already busy household?*

Devotion, defined as "a solemn attention to the Supreme Being in worship; a yielding of the heart and the affections to God," should be the first priority of our day. From the youngest to the oldest in our homes, we can, through much training and repetition, inaugurate "thirty minutes of silence" in our daily routine.

1. **Lay the Groundwork**. Your children may ask—I know mine did—over and over again, *"Why do we need a quiet time?"* They need to know why you are enforcing this principle. I began by reading biblical accounts and scriptures concerning this vital spiritual discipline. *Daniel. Moses. Psalm 23. Psalm 46:10. Elijah. Jesus.* All examples of coming away to a secluded place to meet with God.

2. **Start Slowly.** Begin by setting apart 5-15 minutes, a small portion of time, in a place where the house is quiet—no mechanical devices, turn the answering machine volume off, no talking, no interaction—everyone in their room or space and quiet. Wean your family into practicing a period of silence.

3. **Be consistent.** Training requires repetition and consistency. Eventually, and I reiterate *eventually,* it will be something they look forward to. One initial reason we chose to homeschool was to bond as a family. After many years, my oldest and I began to chuckle, "We've got way too much bonding going on!" So, our quiet time became a refuge, a time where everyone retreated to their space and could recharge.

4. **Eliminate Static.** Static is defined as "noise produced in a radio or television receiver by atmospheric or other electrical disturbances." Spend

"Precisely because the Lord is present with us, we can relax and let go of everything, for in His presence nothing really matters, nothing is of importance except attending to Him. We allow inner distractions and frustrations to melt away before Him as snow before the sun. We allow Him to calm the storms that rage within by saying, 'Peace, be still.' We allow His great silence to still our noisy hearts."—Richard Foster, The Celebration of Discipline

"Mary has chosen what is better, and it will not be taken away from her."
—Luke 10:42

a few moments evaluating the present "static cling" in your family life:

5. **What are my greatest distractions?** (See Luke 10:40) Please take a serious moment to reflect on this definition of distraction: Distraction is "confusion from a multiplicity of objects crowding on the mind and calling the attention different ways." Distraction is definitely my greatest enemy. Every day there are always "a multiplicity of objects" trying to call my attention "different ways." They consistently try to get me off the track of homeschooling. Distraction wears many faces: housework, church duties, community service, friendships, solicitors, telephone calls, opportunities, experiences, and many more. Proverbs 4:25 has proven a wonderful antidote for this problem: "Let your eyes look straight ahead, fix your gaze directly before you." This word helps to adjust the focus and defeat the distraction.

6. **What is causing disturbance?** (See Psalm 42: 5,11) Disturbance is an "interruption of a settled state of things; disorder; any disquiet or interruption of peace." Well, any mother of young children will respond to this with a loud, resounding, "Yes!" How many times a day, or even an hour, are there interruptions of peace when young children are present? This is to be expected and often welcomed, but what *other* areas of your home or life are causing "unnecessary" interruptions of peace? Can you pinpoint them?

7. **Where is there chaos and confusion?** (See Galatians 1:7; 5:10) Confusion and chaos can be defined as "disorder." What areas of life seem to be causing chaos? Once again, pinpoint them. C.S. Lewis writes in *The Screwtape Letters*:

    "Music and silence are two things Hell and its' inhabitants detest. No square inch of infernal space and no moment of infernal time has been surrendered to either of those indomitable forces, but all has been occupied by noise—Noise, the grand dynamism, the audible expression of all that is exultant, ruthless and virile. We will make the whole universe a noise in the end."[3]

    Screwtape, the senior devil, was writing this to his young nephew apprentice, Wormwood. Lewis captures the essence of the devil's work in this passage by noting that silence is one "of those indomitable forces" that terrifies the underworld.

5. **Don't quit!** This journey towards training our children in this discipline can be laborious and wearisome. Please, take courage and persevere! I can attest the path was arduous, but the reward has been sweet.

Last, but not least, let us remember that Elohim, Creator God, took the time to rest. After creating the entire universe, which I believe must have taken quite a bit of energy; He decided to implement the principle of rest. I imagine He must have known man's tendency to overwork. Setting the example for all time, He rested, enjoying the fruit of His labor.

Foundation Stone 7: Prayer
He Simply Prayed

Janell Rardon

"And Manoah said, 'Now let thy words [God's] come to pass. How shall we order the child? and how shall we do unto him?'"

—Judges 13:12, KJV

"...Manoah's sense of need at once found expression in prayer.

He believed in God as the living God, as the hearer of prayer. He believed that where God gave a charge or a work, He would give the grace to do it right; that where God gave a child to be trained for His service, He would give the wisdom needed to do so aright. Instead of letting the sense of unfitness and feebleness depress him, or the sense of his obligation set him to work in his own strength, he simply prayed. To him, prayer was the solution to difficulties, the supply of need, the source of wisdom and strength."

—Andrew Murray

Prayer is the cornerstone of the homeschooling family. I have found no better dissertation on the subject of prayer than the words of a 19th Century South African Revivalist, Andrew Murray, penned in *"Raising Your Child for Christ."* Murray's family emigrated from Scotland to South Africa, to where his father was pastor to a church. It was a godly family where prayer was normal and hymns were sung around the house. Most of all, Andrew's father prayed for revival. Every Friday evening he would read accounts of the great movings of the Holy Spirit in history to his family. Then he would go to his study and with tears pour out his heart to God for a similar outpouring on South Africa. Those experiences marked young Andrew deeply. He grew up and became a pastor.

Murray's keen insight into Manoah's petition to God concerning the raising of his son, Samson, leads us to several significant truths and bears repeating:

1. **Manoah's sense of need *at once* found expression in prayer.**
   At once. Manoah turned immediately to God for assistance. He didn't pick up a phone. He didn't read a book. He didn't go to counsel. *All good things, but first he went to the throne of God.*

2. **He believed in God as the hearer of prayer.** Isaiah 50:4-5 says, "The Sovereign Lord has given me an instructed tongue, to know the word that sustains the weary. He wakens me morning by morning, wakens my ear to listen like one being taught. The Sovereign Lord has opened my ears, and I have not been rebellious." God hears our prayers. It may feel as though they are bouncing off the ceiling, and that He is millions of miles away, but He hears.

3. **He believed God would give the grace to accomplish the task he had been called to complete: the training of Samson. He believed in God's power to enable him to do the job right.**
   "What God orders, He pays for." Have you heard that expression? I can't begin to tell you how many times I have felt inadequate, discouraged, downtrodden, negative, and insecure over the daunting task of homeschooling my three children. These feelings always propel me straight to the feet of Jesus, for it is only through His enabling and

empowering that I can complete it. I proclaim His faithfulness. Daily, He has proven to be my Sufficiency. *Note: He even brought a high-school math tutor to live across the street! God is good!*

4. **He believed that where God gave a child to be trained for His service, He would give the wisdom needed to do so.**
We lack. God supplies. That is the economy of the Kingdom of God. James 1:5 (NIV) says, "If any of you lacks wisdom, *he should ask God, who gives generously to all without finding fault, and it will be given to him*." And Philippians 4:19 (NIV), "My God *will meet* all your needs according to His glorious riches in Christ Jesus." Once again, observe the definite nature of these verses…"it *will* be given"…"*will* meet all"…definite promises to those who believe.

5. **He simply prayed.** Manoah refused to let his unfitness and feebleness trap him into a spiral of negative emotions. Neither did he allow a sense of obligation and responsibility to force him to take matters into his own hands, unlike those who tend to rely on their own merits, education, personality, or natural abilities. It sounds so simple, I know, but the greatest training and preparedness comes at the feet of Jesus. Praying. Seeking. Submitting.

6. **He saw prayer as three things:**
   1) The solution to difficulties
   2) The supply of need
   3) The source of wisdom

With a solid confidence in the power of prayer, Manoah proceeded to "order the days of Samson." Many others followed this pattern throughout history:

Casper Ten Boom (father of Corrie and Betsie): Every morning at 8:30 a.m., he read from the "big brass-hinged Bible" after breakfast. This act of faithfulness proved to be the foundation stone that enabled Betsie and Corrie to endure the unimaginable hardships of Nazi concentration camps.

Rev. Clarence Chambers and wife, Hannah (father and mother of Oswald): Challenged by D. L. Moody and Ira Sankey in 1874 (the year of Oswald's birth), their lives changed. Hannah had

> *"four children in school and four younger ones at home. Her budget was meager and money was scarce, but none suspected that anything less than the abundance of the Almighty was theirs. She greeted each day with joy and each crisis with the assurance that the Lord would provide. Oswald learned to pray at a young age. But because of his earnest faith in God, his prayers seemed to go beyond mere form. His brother Franklin described Oswald's prayers at the age of five as 'very original' and recalled times when the older children, along with their mother, would tiptoe up the stairs at night and sit quietly to hear him pray as he knelt by his bed."*[2]

Charles Spurgeon: Sent to live with his grandparents at the age of one, he sat in his grandmother's lap while she read the Bible and prayed, and listened to his grandfather's preaching.

Hudson Taylor: As he listened to missionaries tell their grand stories of life on the mission field around the dinner table in his home, their vision was infectious and marked young Hudson's heart with a passion for mission work.

Katharine Gillingham (mother of Elisabeth Elliot): She

> "*did not think of herself as deeply spiritual. She would have protested if anyone had said she was. But she was certainly hungry for God, deeply conscious of her own weakness and need of Him. Called to be a mother,* entrusted with the holy task of cooperating with God in shaping the destinies of six people, *she knew it was too heavy a burden to carry alone.* She did not try. *She went to Him whose name is Wonderful Counselor, Mighty God, Everlasting Father. She asked His help.*"[3]

We, too, are "*entrusted with the holy task of cooperating with God*" concerning the shaping of our children's destinies. This is a heavy burden to carry alone. Therefore, let us remember not to try. We need to come to the feet of Jesus, who will hear our prayer. In His time, in His way, in His wisdom, He will answer.

End Notes

[1]Information gathered from Revival Fires. Available through: www.jesus.org.uk

[2]David McCasland. *Oswald Chambers: Abandoned to God.*

[3]Elisabeth Elliot. *The Shaping of a Christian Family.*

Foundation Stone 8: Academics
Educating the Human Spirit

Janell Rardon

The training of a child begins early, but when can we begin to teach him? What greater joy for a mother than a low rocking chair and a wee baby in her arms to sing to? Let his little ears hear her sing 'Jesus Loves Me' or 'Away in a Manger' or 'Savior, Like a Shepherd Lead Us.' The rocking rhythm automatically gets songs and verses into a child's mind. Soothed by the motion and his mother's love, he is more open and can learn without effort. An appreciation of good literature can be instilled early. Peter Rabbit and Benjamin Bunny, Squirrel Nutkin, and Jeremy Fisher soon become friends of the children. They also loved the catchy swing of the poems by A. A. Milne. And we wore out two Bible story books. In teaching young children, it is well to remember the words of Isaiah 28:10, 'For precept must be upon precept, precept upon precept, line upon line, line upon line, here a little, there a little.' It is thus our patient God has dealt with us; so we must deal with our little ones, repeating often the Word of God so that it will be hidden in their hearts so they 'will not sin against God.'"[1]

Those interested in learning more about homeschooling often ask me, "Where do I begin?" "At the feet of Jesus," I quietly respond. How can we shape our children's lives without first coming to the Lord for His plan of action? "Vision is of God. A vision comes in advance of any task well done."[2] In *Foundational Stone #1: Vision*, we addressed the importance of writing down our vision for our family. Now, we will do so for each child.

Prior to the school year (sometime before purchasing curriculum), I come aside for a time to pray. True success comes when we kneel before God and ask Him to reveal to us His plan for our children and homeschool. Using a simple acrostic, I begin:

Vision and Values
Individuality of Child
Character Development
Time To Teach
Obtain Wise Counsel
Read, Research, and Refrain from Overindulgence
Yield to God's Leading

To assure victory in selecting your academic program(s) for the year, these seven guidelines will make the entire process more pleasing. Let's break it down:

1. **Vision and Values**. Ask yourself the following questions:
   - What do I want (child) to learn this year?
   - What character qualities need to be strengthened? Refined?
   - What weak areas (academically) need tutorial attention?
   - What strong areas need a place to flourish?
   - Can I give (child) the adequate tools to grow in that area?
   - Do I need to look for outside help in the form of a mentor, tutor, or enrichment group?
   - There deficits (academically) that need special attention? Therapy? Evaluation?
   - What extracurricular activities can be pruned? Added?

   Proverbs 24:3-4 says, "*Any enterprise is built by wise planning, becomes strong through common sense, and profits wonderfully by keeping abreast of the facts.*" Common sense. Keeping abreast of the facts. Good, sound advice for any one embarking on the journey of homeschooling.

   Forecasting a plan of action enables you, the consumer and educator, to stay focused and on track when entering the exhibit hall at conventions or regional seminars. When I *see* all the wonderful, new resources available to me each year, I become visually stimulated and senseless...so I need a strict plan. Schedule in some flexibility, because there might be something that will come along mid-year that you will want to add in, but for the most part, you have a framework. Incorporate your family values, vision, and ministry. Plan field trips to correlate with your curriculum selections. Plan family vacations and get-aways that will enhance your studies.

2. **Individuality of Child/Children.** As stated, every family entity is unique and different. Billy Graham once stated, "To know the will of God is the highest of all wisdom." Study your child and know who they are in Christ, what gift/talents are emerging from their lives, what their bent or disposition is, and what they like/dislike. Choose curriculum that suits their learning style. *What is a learning style?* Consult Cheri Fuller's book, "*Opening Your Child's Nine Learning Windows,*" (see Resources Section) for a complete examination of the different learning styles.

3. **Character Development.** Isn't this one of the greatest reasons we all choose to homeschool? We want to give our children the opportunity to develop strong character. When you write your plan of action, choose character traits that you want to zero in on. I developed a Bible study entitled, "Marks of Greatness," in which we studied the lives of great men and women of God—dissecting their lives, learning from their achievements and mistakes, studying their choices, examining their character, and applying these truths to our own lives. *Child Evangelism Press* offers great resources for this type of Bible study (see Great Resources Section).

"Be strong and of good courage."

—*Joshua 1:9*

4. **Time To Teach.** One of the most important questions I am asked is, "How much time do I have in my day to actually sit down and teach my child/children?" I highly recommend reading "The Challenges of Homeschooling" in Debra Bell's best-selling manual, *The Ultimate Guide to Homeschooling.* There are many factors that determine how much time you have to teach one-on-one: number of children; ages of children; husband's involvement; single-parenting; family dynamics (sick parent, physical challenges); ministry obligations; family business, *et cetera.* All of these will affect your choices.

5. **Obtain wise counsel.** Never underestimate the biblical principle of mentorship. Titus 2 instructs the older to teach the younger. Find a veteran homeschooler who exemplifies what you would like to model your homeschool/family after. Ask them to mentor you and take you under their wing. Perhaps they would even go with you to convention and help you find your way. Sit down at their kitchen table and talk, ask questions, and pray. "Visiting a veteran" will prove your most valuable "conference workshop" session, and will bring you great return on your investment.

6. **The Three R's. Read** daily, **research** the market, and **refrain** from overindulgence. Prior to convention, read as many catalogs, materials, and websites as you can. Resources and opinions can overwhelm, that is why I suggest visiting a veteran. Every retailer and curriculum representative honestly believes their product/system/materials are the best, so you must be secure in your vision and firmly adhere to your plan of action. Ask yourself: Does this product/book/system enhance and fulfill my objectives for the year? Buy only what your plan of action requires. **One thing to remember**: You don't have to teach everything in one year! This is what used to get me into trouble: Everything looks exciting, fun, interesting, challenging. This is the time to review your forecasted plan (now mine is sketched out for years) and stay firm.

7. **Yield to God's leading.** As a Christian homeschooler, I have the great privilege of God's guidance, protection, and leadership. "Guide me in your truth and teach me, for you are my God my Savior, and my hope is in you all the day long" it says in Psalm 25:5. Let God guide your every move. Elisabeth Elliot writes of four ordinary methods by which "God nudges us in the path of righteousness." They are:
   a. circumstances
   b. common sense
   c. godly counsel
   d. biblical principles

These are a good rule of thumb when planning your curriculum. Don't discount good, wholesome "common sense." As I said, I tend to be a visionary and need my husband's wise, common sense to pull me down to earth. His practical bent balances my visionary one.

One thing I always try to remember is that I am training my child in skills that will carry over into their future station in life, be it in business, the professions, the workforce, the home, higher education, the community, ministry, missions, or the armed forces.

Academic training is essential training for any of these areas of service. 2 Timothy 2:15 shouts the battle cry of our mission as parents who are shaping the legacy of learning in each of our children, *"Be diligent to present yourself approved to God, a worker who does not need to be ashamed, rightly dividing the word of truth."*

End Notes
[1] Elisabeth Elliot. *The Shaping of a Christian Family.*
[2] George Barna. *The Power of Vision.*
[3] Lawrence Katz, Ph.D. and Manning Rubin. *Keep Your Brain Alive.*

Foundation Stone 9: Obedience

Obedience is Better than Sacrifice

Janell Rardon

R ecorded in Genesis 22 is the amazing account of a young boy's whole-hearted devotion and obedience to his father. Young Isaac, the child of promise, was told by his father, Abraham, to travel up Mt. Moriah to make a sacrifice to God. Undoubtedly, Isaac had participated in building altars countless times with his father, but this time was to be different. *Isaac was to be the offering.* Climbing the mountain, Isaac asked a simple question, *"Father? The fire and the wood are here, but where is the lamb for the burnt offering?"* Just imagine Abraham's heart. It must have sunk deep within his chest.

Isaac illustrated for generations to come the beautiful picture of submission. It truly baffles my mind how a young boy, probably under the age of twelve, would crawl upon an altar, knowingly, and lie down. Can you imagine? We see no evidence that Isaac resists, runs, or rebels from this commandment. He doesn't complain, he simply asks a practical question concerning the supplies for the sacrifice.

Isaac's obedience is the fruit of Abraham's faith. By lying prostrate upon Mt. Moriah's altar, Isaac's very position demonstrates to us his humility and complete resignation to his father's commandments. F. B. Meyer writes concerning Isaac that "he caught his father's spirit. We do not know how old he was; he was at least old enough to sustain the toil of a long march on foot, and strong enough to carry up the hill the wood, laid upon his shoulders by his father. Inspiration draws a veil over that last tender scene—the father's announcement of the mission; the broken sobs; the kisses, wet with tears; the instant submission of the son, who was old enough and strong enough to rebel if he had a mind. Then the binding of that tender frame; which, indeed, needed no compulsion, because the young heart had learned the secret of obedience and resignation."[1]

The account of Genesis 22 is laden with gold nuggets. Abraham exemplified three significant truths that we, as parents, can model in our parenting:

1. **Isaac testified that we are not to withhold anything from God.** When God asks, we must obey. The first time. This is wholehearted obedience. This principle must be learned early on in a child's life. Continually repeat, *"Please obey the first time. I will not repeat my words more than once, (child's name). If necessary, you will receive the conse-*

quence for not obeying immediately." Counting to five, constantly repeating commands, and tirelessly pleading are not training your child to obey wholeheartedly.

2. **Isaac learned that at every Mt. Moriah, God will provide.** Moriah actually means, "The Lord Provides." Because Abraham didn't withhold anything, God speaks to him, saying:

> *"I swear by myself, declares the Lord, that because you have done this and have not withheld your son, your only son, I will surely bless you and make your descendants as numerous as the stars in the sky and the sand on the seashore."*

God always provides. *Money for curriculum. Help for a struggling student. Food for the table. Gas for the car. Creative ideas for saving money.* Take a minute and write down all the many ways God has provided for you to stay home and teach your children. I would guess they are manifold.

3. **Isaac learned to lie down on altars.** We might call this "submission" in its greatest form. Derived from the Latin root, *submitto*—sub or under, and *mitto*, to send—submission simply means, "resignation." Resignation is "a quiet submission to the will of Providence. Submission without discontent, and with entire acquiescence (submission with apparent content]." Herein lies the truest goal of the education process; Training our children to submit to God.

Once again, I return to Andrew Murray's wise advice on training our children in obedience:

> *"Education has been variously defined as fully developing a child's faculties, fitting him to fulfill his destiny, developing in him all the perfection of which he is capable. Training is a word of deep importance for every teacher and parent to understand. Training is not telling, not teaching, not commanding, but something higher than all of these (without which the teaching and commanding often do more harm than good). It is not only telling a child what to do, but showing him how to do it and seeing that it is done, taking care that the advice or the command given is put into practice and adopted as a habit.*
>
> *Success in education depends more on forming habits than inculcating rules. The child should come to feel it quite natural that in all things he should do the parent's will. And so the habit of obedience is formed; this becomes the root of other habits."*[2]

The habit of obedience was evident in young Isaac. Abraham's training manifested as a sweet, fragrant fruit for years to come. May God enable us to follow in the footsteps of this great patriarch of our faith. May our children, as Isaac, obey wholeheartedly—honoring their parents with a life well-lived.

End Notes
[1] F.B. Meyer. *Abraham.*
[2] Andrew Murray. *Raising Your Children For Christ.*

"Christian contentment is that sweet, inward, quiet, gracious frame of spirit, which freely submits to and delights in God's wise and fatherly disposal in every condition."
—*Jeremiah Burroughs*, The Rare Jewel of Christian Contentment

Foundation Stone 10: Relationships
Training the Tongue

Janell Rardon

It is never too early to start training our little ones to use their words wisely. Proverbs 18:21 says, "Death and life are in the power of the tongue: and they that love it shall eat the fruit thereof." What great power lies in this small member of our bodies, the tongue. As we read in James 3:5, "Even so, the tongue is a little member, and boasteth great things. Behold, how great a matter a little fire kindleth!" One small word accompanied by a wrong attitude or lack of restraint can kindle hurt, pain, brokenness, and hate. Name-calling and harsh words can bring death to character. God has entrusted mankind, the highest form of life, with the blessed ability to communicate. How are we, God's children, maintaining and nurturing this power? Is our conversation growing weeds and thorns or producing fruit that is ripe and plentiful?

Consider for a moment the proverb, "Death is in the power of the tongue." Can you recall a name or comment that was made to you as a child that left a lasting scar and even deep-seated wounds? How many times do we see our children engaging in this type of "conversation warfare," degrading one another with rude, harmful comments? It seems the warfare begins earlier and earlier, often right after a child begins talking.

On the flip side of Proverbs 18:21, we have "Life is in the power of the tongue." Concurring with this is Proverbs 16:24, "Pleasant words are as a honeycomb, sweet to the soul, and health to the bones." Consider in your own life words that have given you life, hope, and a reason to persevere. Perhaps it was one of your teachers who sparked purpose into you, giving you vision for your future. Perhaps your father or mother encouraged you in some gift, talent, attribute, or spiritual gifting. God gives the gifts of edification, encouragement, and wisdom for the purpose of enlarging the heart (Hebrews 3:13; 1 Corinthians 12: 12-28).

Creating an awareness of this by modeling kindness ensures success. Dr. Patricia Morgan writes, "The next generation will not be fathered by persuasive pulpiteers and public orators, but by committed adults who will spend quality time with them, imparting life both by instruction and by example."[1] While studying the writings of Amy Carmichael, I came across two powerful watchwords that I have since implemented as guidelines for

"While in our family there were plenty of times of uproarious laughter, times when we were allowed to play Hide and Seek in the house on a rainy day, times when we could not help shouting, running, jumping, and thundering up and down the stairs, we were taught to think first—was someone asleep, was Daddy studying, did Mother have a head ache?

Quiet was the general rule. Gentle voices, soft footsteps, the quiet closing of doors contribute to the peace of the home.

Learning these simple things is learning to look to the interests of others rather than to one's own. If we thoughtlessly slammed a door (it was hard to remember that big screen door in the summertime) we were asked to come back into the house and do it right."

—Elisabeth Elliot, The Shaping of a Christian Family

the conversations in our home. First, she suggests (concerning our words) asking yourself the following questions:

- Is it true?
- Is it kind?
- Is it necessary?
- Does it (conversation) have the seedbeds of eternity in it? and then,
- In our dealings with others, it is "Never about; always to"?

Meaning, if we find ourselves hurt, offended, angry, upset, or disheartened by someone—we go to them first. This prohibits gossip, unnecessary pain, and broken relationships. Undoubtedly, we will fall in this area. Our tongue needs constant training, supervision, and guarding. That is why we need the grace of God, which we will discuss more in *Foundation Stone #11, Grace: Sowing Seeds of Grace*.

With the above guidelines in mind, I also suggest knowing God's heart concerning the use of our words. In *The Shaping of the Christian Family*, Elisabeth Elliot poses the question, "What does family love look like?" She refers us to Paul's words in Philippians 2: 2-7(NIV):

"Being like-minded, having the same love, being one in spirit and purpose. Do nothing out of selfish ambition or vain conceit, but in humility consider others better than yourselves. Each of you should look not only to your own interests, but also to the interests of others. Your attitude should be the same as that of Christ Jesus: Who, being in very nature God, did not consider equality with God something to be grasped, but made himself nothing, taking the very nature of a servant."

Herein lies the three-fold cord of family relationships: being like-minded, having the same love, and being one in spirit and purpose (unity). All members of a family, each uniquely designed and fashioned with individual personalities, must be committed to family unity; daily exercising the principle of Jude 20: "Build yourselves up in your most holy faith and pray in the Holy Spirit. Keep yourselves in God's love as you wait for the mercy of our Lord Jesus Christ to bring you to eternal life."

THE FAMILY ALTAR

"Soonest taught soonest learned," writes Elisabeth Elliot, "Training six children is not six times as difficult as training one, for the younger ones learn even more quickly from each other than they do from their parents."[2] One of the greatest training tools we implemented began many years ago, when our twins were only three. Gathering together, usually on someone's bed, we began praying together. Restless and wiggly, the twins slowly learned obedience and stillness.

Our "family altar" time has now been occurring nightly, with exceptions here and there, for over eight years. Bringing the cares of the day, relational struggles, neighborhood concerns, world issues, church matters, health issues, *et cetera*, before the throne of God as a family has been a time of tremendous blessing. I offer no formula for success, only admonition to begin. Just start. Gather your family together and pray. It may not be easy or "feel" as though you are accomplishing anything eternal, but in time the fruit will begin to blossom. Sow the seed, water the ground, and trust the Son for the harvest.

Another training tool is Scripture memorization. The "relearning" process we discussed in *Foundation Stone #5: Marriage* can be hastened by learning what God's word says. Full of promises, answers, and hope, it proves to be an incredible tool for holding one another accountable. Consider memorizing:

- Proverbs 18:21, "Death and life are in the power of the tongue."
- Proverbs 10:11, "The tongue of the righteous is a fountain of life."
- Proverbs 16: 24, "Pleasant words are as a honeycomb, sweet to the soul."
- Psalm 37:30, "The mouth of the righteous utters wisdom, and his tongue speaks what is just."
- Proverbs 10:21, "The lips of the righteous nourish many."
- Proverbs 10:31, "The mouth of the righteous brings forth wisdom."
- Proverbs 10:32, "The lips of the righteous know what is fitting."
- Proverbs 12:6, "The speech of the upright rescues them."
- Ephesians 4: 29, "Do not let any unwholesome talk come out of your mouths; but only what is helpful for building others up according to their needs, that it may benefit those who listen."

"A happy family is heaven on earth," reads a page from my daily calendar. As I tell my children over and over again, there's enough evil outside the walls of our home, let's make the inside of our home a safe, loving place. *Let's be "kind and compassionate to one another, forgiving each other just as, in Christ, God forgave you."*

End Notes
[1]Dr. Patricia Morgan. *Raising Children of Destiny.*
[2]Elisabeth Elliot. *The Shaping of a Christian Family.*

Foundation Stone 10: Relationships
It's All About Me

Leslie Vernick

I was feeling miserable. God had recently exposed my lack of love for a particular person in my life and to top it off, I was mad at myself over some mistakes I had made. Wallowing in self-hatred, I wandered over to my colleague's office for support and advice. As I poured out my story she gently stopped me. "Leslie, you're being way too hard on yourself. You know you'll never be able to love others very well until you first love yourself." I nodded in agreement.

Sound familiar? We've all heard that. There's even a verse somewhere in the Bible that says that, isn't there? Not really, though Mt. 19:19 is often used to support this idea: "Love you neighbor as yourself." As a Christian counselor, I have worked with hundreds of men and women over the years who believed, as I did, that the pathway toward good mental health and spiritual growth was through increasing our love for ourselves. However, when we believe we must love ourselves more in order to love God or others enough, we have been deceived.

IT'S ALL ABOUT GOD.

The Bible never instructs or commands us to love ourselves. If anything, Scripture warns us against thinking more highly of ourselves than we ought (Rom.12:3) or thinking only of ourselves (Phil. 2:3-4). Yet this doesn't mean we are to despise ourselves, either. Whether we are absorbed in self-adoration or immersed in self-hatred, we are still focused on self. Life does not center around our wants, needs, or desires. Nor does it revolve around our faults, defects, or weaknesses. A life that is centered on self, whether it is in pursuit of pleasure or avoidance of pain, will never be one immersed in God.

And God wants us to be immersed in Him. He longs for us to know Him and to love Him with all of our heart, mind, strength, and will (Mk. 12:30). He wants us to understand who we are and to look at all of life from His perspective (Prov. 3:5-6). When we do, self-esteem is no longer an issue. Mother Teresa said, "Knowledge of God gives love, and knowledge of self gives humility." As we focus on loving Christ, we gain a humble self-acceptance and are set free from our inordinate self-love. Jesus' love enables us to forsake our self-preoccupation and freely reach out to others (2 Cor. 5:14).

Over the years God has revealed areas where I have been self-absorbed and self-focused. The apostle Paul warns us that in the last days "people will be lovers of themselves, lovers of pleasure rather than lovers of God—having a form of godliness but denying its power" (2 Tim. 3: 1-5). The following questions may help you evaluate your self-focus. Perhaps you will discover the same thing I did. My problems were usually not a result of loving myself too little, but of loving God and others too little and myself too much.

DO MY PRAYERS REVOLVE AROUND ME?

For far too long, my prayers consisted of one-way conversations. I was talking with God, but I wasn't bothering to wait for an answer. Much like a young child with her parents, most of my prayers were self-centered as I asked God to relieve me from a burden or to do something I could not make happen by myself. God was my helper, not my Lord. Oswald Chambers said:

> "Spiritual lust makes me demand an answer from God, instead of seeking God Who gives the answer....Whenever the insistence is on the point that God answers prayer, we are off the track. The meaning of prayer is that we get hold of God, not of the answer."

As I began to get my eyes off my own agenda, desires, and plans and started reflecting upon who God is and loving Him, my prayers began to shift as well. I longed to pray with Paul, "I want to know Christ" (Phil. 3:10). Beyond enjoying His gifts, I hungered to know the Giver.

When was the last time you were awestruck by the presence of God as you prayed? He loves the times we simply want to be with Him and are not just asking for His blessings or help.

ARE MY WANTS THE DRIVING FORCE IN MY LIFE?

"I'm just not happy and fulfilled in my marriage anymore," cried Carl, a 30-something executive, with two young children. "I married too young and for all the wrong reasons. We were never meant to be together and we have nothing in common. I love God but I just can't imagine He would want me to live the rest of my life unhappily married to a woman I don't love. I just want to be happy."

Carl is facing a battle of loves. He loves God, but he also loves himself. Quite naturally, he doesn't want to suffer in an unhappy marriage the rest of his life. These feelings aren't sinful, but they are now beginning to rule his decisions. At the moment, Carl loves himself too much; his concern is only for himself. He is not thinking of God's glory, his wife, or his children.

The desire for happiness or relief from pain can easily lead us to focus inordinately on self. John Calvin says that "the evil in our desires typically does not lie in what we want, but that we want it too much." God isn't opposed to our personal happiness but He describes a way of attaining it that is diametrically opposed to the world's way. God's prescription for a happy heart does not come in a pretty package tied with the bows of self-love; rather, it is often bound with the chords of self-sacrifice and self-denial.

Jesus tells us "Blessed are those who hunger and thirst for righteousness, for they will be filled" (Mt. 5:6).

Sadly, many of us hunger and thirst after happiness, not righteousness. We are content to linger at a table laden with cheap substitutes instead of feasting on the Bread of Life.

AM I ANGRY OR DESPONDENT WHEN I DON'T GET WHAT I EXPECT?

Flinging her Bible to the floor, Janet stormed about my office. "I'm sick and tired of living God's way. What good has it done? I'm 36 years old and I've never been with a man because God has said to wait until marriage. My biological clock is ticking away, and I may never get married and have a child. It's just not fair."

Janet's disappointment and pain were legitimate; God certainly understood. However, her hurt turned to rage because she expected a reward for her commitment to God's moral standards.

Sometimes our understanding of God reminds me of my old S & H Green Stamp books. When I was a child we diligently saved those stamps and pasted them into special redemption books. We could cash them in for prizes after we had filled enough books. With a similar mindset, we try to collect obedience stamps from God. Eventually we think we've filled enough books, and we expect God to cash them in for what we want. When He doesn't "redeem" our obedience as we'd hoped, we become angry, discouraged or cynical.

Paul tells us how he was able to enjoy freedom even when he experienced difficulties and hardships. He wrote,

> *Therefore we do not lose heart. Though outwardly we are wasting away, yet inwardly we are being renewed day by day. For our light and momentary troubles are achieving for us an eternal glory that far outweighs them all. So we fix our eyes not on what is seen but on what is unseen. For what is seen is temporary, but what is unseen is eternal.*
>
> *—2 Corinthians 4:16-18*

Paul understood that life's biggest reality is eternal reality. When I am depressed or angry because life is not going as I expect, my attention is focused on me and on today's reality. I have lost the eternal perspective. I have forgotten that life is not about me but about God. I am loving myself too much.

AM I EXCESSIVELY SELF-CONSCIOUS? DO I FEAR FAILURE OR CRITICISM?

At first glance, people who defer to others, hang in the shadows, don't reach out, and refuse ministry responsibilities may seem to suffer from a lack of self-love. If we look closely, however, we will see that they are just as preoccupied with self as someone who is self-centered. They simply manifest it differently: One in prideful demandingness, the other in a self-protective withdrawal. Our natural tendency is to promote the self, defend the self, protect the self, and hide the self—all because we innately care about ourselves much more than we love God or love others.

A number of years ago I was severely criticized for something I wrote. It was so painful that I hesitated to ever write again. I didn't need to have more self-love or higher self-esteem to start writing again. What I needed was to take my eyes off myself and focus them on Christ. Only then could I be free from my self-conscious fear of failure and criticism. When I know that my adequacy comes from Christ rather than myself, I can reach out and take risks (2 Cor. 3:5). It is in Christ's love, not my own, that I feel secure.

IS SELF-FULFILLMENT MY HIGHEST AIM?

Awhile back I attended a conference on spirituality and psychotherapy for Christian therapists and spiritual directors. Most of the weekend was devoted to the development of the self. Spiritual maturity was defined as having a good sense of who I am, a healthy sense of myself in relationship to others, and an understanding of myself in process. It sounded good. Yet as I reflected further, I wondered: Could a person achieve spiritual maturity without a relationship with God? By this definition, one could.

Certainly a clear sense of who we are is necessary for growth and maturity. Taking honest stock of ourselves leads us to recognize our sinful hearts, as well as our gifts and abilities.

But sooner or later we will come to a fork in the road. One path seeks to glorify the self; the other path seeks to glorify God. The path of self-exaltation and self-fulfillment looks very inviting. Many sincere people smile and draw us forward with encouragement and affirmation. Jesus, however, cautions us that this path will ultimately lead to the loss of our true self (Lk. 9:24).

The other path is much more desolate and lonely. Travelers walking it must be willing to die to their self-orientation, and commit to serving and glorifying Christ alone (Mt. 7:14). As we do this we find that Jesus does not just redeem us, He restores us—thereby revealing our true self. Ponder the words of Thomas á Kempis in *Imitation of Christ:*

For indeed by loving myself amiss, I lost myself, and seeking Thee alone, and purely loving Thee, I have found both myself and Thee.

Leslie Vernick is the Director of Christ-Centered Counseling and the author of *How to Act Right When Your Spouse Acts Wrong* and *The TRUTH Principle* (WaterBrook). You can reach Leslie through her web site at www.leslievernick.com

This article first appeared in *Discipleship Journal* magazine Issue 127, Jan/Feb 2002, published by Navpress, Colorado Springs, Colorado.

Foundation Stone 11: Grace
Sowing the Seeds of Grace
Mrs. Teresa Gregus and Janell Rardon

Grace may be defined as "appropriately, the free, unmerited love and favor of God, the *spring and source* of all the benefits men receive from him." Homeschoolers need the gift of God's grace. *Day in and day out.* Homeschooling is a daily routine that can, and I stress *can*, be daunting in its' daily demands. Quite frankly, the twenty-four hour cycle of "things to be done, things to be undone, things to be redone" can be, at times, overwhelming. I wish it weren't true. But, it is. Therefore, we need the gift of grace to be in full operation in our homes.

Daniel Webster once wrote,

"Any work we undertake is bound to decay or crumble—with the exception of teaching, especially spiritual instruction." He continued:

"If we imbue (people) with high principles, with just fear of God and love of their fellow-men, we engrave on those tablets something which time cannot efface, and which will brighten and brighten to all eternity."

The spring and source of grace is God. He clearly defines His enabling grace all throughout the Scriptures. Tucked within each of the following laws of grace are seeds ready to be sown into the lives of our families. Three specific areas will be discussed:

Moments of Grace: This is grace for everyday life.

Seasons of Grace: This is grace for special circumstances.

A Legacy of Grace: Each moment added to each season produces the sum of a life lived in grace.

MOMENTS OF GRACE

"And God is able to make all grace abound toward you (place your name here), that you (place it again), always having all sufficiency in all things, may have an abundance for every good work. Now may He who supplies seed to the sower, and bread for food, supply and multiply the seed you have sown and increase the fruits of your righteousness."
—2 Corinthians 9:8,10

In music, a grace note is a note of embellishment, usually written small.

The grace note, of no consequence on its own, when added to the whole work makes the composition more lovely. Moments of grace, then, add to the composition of our days; making them more beautiful and lovely.

Moments of grace can be antidotes to all the little irritants of daily life. C. S. Lewis affectionately called these irritants "pinpricks," in *The Screwtape Letters*. Screwtape advises Wormwood to be sure "to build up in that house a good settled habit of mutual annoyance...send daily pinpricks." There will be "daily pinpricks" sent to annoy and hinder. Mark this down: The **Devil** does not want you to move in peace. He does not want your homeschool to succeed. He will do whatever he can to keep your family from peace.

Moments of grace operate when we can: *Overlook an offense, speak the truth in love, be slow to speak and quick to listen, laugh at ourselves, and successfully handle unplanned interruptions, such as broken down cars or dead batteries.* They come, one-by-one, with the promise that God is our Source and Supply—His grace will be sufficient.

SEASONS OF GRACE

Sustaining grace. This is grace for the long haul. *Difficulty. Struggle. Special Circumstances.* All for the purpose of growing in maturity. "Sustain" is derived from the Latin root, *sustineo*, sub, and *teneo*: to hold under. God's grace promises to sustain us when we are under a heavy burden. He will uphold us (Psalm 119:116-117); He will keep us from sinking into despondence (Psalm 3:5); He will give power and great ability (2 Corinthians 12:9, Acts 4:33); He will give more grace (James 4:6).

Andrew Murray in *Raising Your Children to Know Christ* adds further understanding to this sustaining grace:

> "Noah's deliverance from the flood was to be the introduction of a new dispensation—the first great act of God's redeeming grace on behalf of a sinful world. In this act God manifested the great principles of the economy of grace: mercy in the midst of judgment; life through death; faith as a means of deliverance, and the one channel through which the blessing comes. And further, it was at this time revealed that the family was to be one means of grace.
>
> The relation of parents and children, which had become the great means for transmitting and establishing the power of sin, was much more to become the vehicle for extending the kingdom of God's grace.... The believing father is to regard himself as the appointed channel and steward of the grace of God. God always gives grace proportionate to the duty He requires."[1]

When the difficulty comes, it comes with the promise that God is the Source and Supply—and His grace is sufficient.

A LEGACY OF GRACE

Each moment added to each season produces the sum of a life lived in grace. Andrew Murry goes on to say:

"God's Word should be woven into the fabric of every parent's heart. His Word is more than a handbook to consult in times of crisis—it should be so internalized and ingrained as to well up from within. *Could a person be an effective physician without an intimate knowledge of physiology? Neither can a parent be effective in spiritual training without an intimate working knowledge of Scripture.*"

—J. Otis Ledbetter, "Miracle Workers: The Role of the Parent in Spiritual Training," E-article, HeritageBuilders.com

"The concept of grace is one that Christians experience each day of their lives, whether they realize it or not. It's the audacious but biblical idea that we can have a personal relationship with a holy eternal God that requires no work on our part, only accepting for ourselves the work of Jesus Christ. Even though our wrongdoing should result in lethal punishment, we are offered forgiveness and life—a second chance to go out there and get it right. The outrageous gift of grace is not to be hoarded, but is to be extended in all our relationships."

Our children will thrive in a home where grace permeates each room. (2 Corinthians 2:14-15, NKJV) proclaims, "Now thanks be to God who always leads us in triumph in Christ, and through us diffuses the fragrance of His knowledge in every place. For we are to God the fragrance of Christ among those who are being saved and among those who are perishing."

Our children need to have the grace of God extended to them so that they may have a safe environment in which to grow to maturity. As we've said, grace is an antidote to sharp tongues, harsh words, belittling looks and comments, useless chatter, and idle negativity. Mothers and fathers, grow in the grace and knowledge of our Lord and Savior Jesus Christ (2 Peter 3:18 NKJV). Then sow these seeds into your families, in order to reap the plentiful harvest of righteousness in the next generation.

End Notes

[1]Andrew Murray. *Raising Your Children For Christ.*

Foundation Stone 12: Creativity
The Power of Play

Janell Rardon

"Laughter heals anger. Laughter creates love. Laughter restores our perspective on all of life."

—Archibald Hart

Allow me to be totally vulnerable with you. Let's pretend you and I are sitting around my kitchen table, engaged in a heart-to-heart conversation about the first years of homeschooling. Having just returned from the Home Educator's of Virginia (HEAV) State Convention, your hands are full of catalogs and your mind full of questions. You ask, "What are the absolute essentials that I should plan to build into my child's early education schedule? My neighbor is sending her little Mary to a traditional school, then swimming lessons, pre-ballet, t-ball (in the spring) and soccer (in the fall)."

Hesitating for just a moment, I ask, "And when is little Mary going to have free time to explore and have creative play?" Just curious.

You might respond, "Creative play? Is that really necessary? Isn't it better to have their time fully structured? To provide them with ample building blocks, such as the aforementioned activities, in order to assure that they develop socially, physically, and emotionally? Won't my little one be socially deprived if she stays at home with me?

Questions about socialization have always been a thorn in the flesh of homeschoolers. Recently, I surveyed the homeschooling community, asking, *"What is the greatest challenge you face in homeschooling?"* Some responses addressed concerns about socialization, but most were struggling with issues of time management and "too many activities"—the antithesis of the old worry about social deprivation. Charles Glenn, in a recent review of Mitchell Stevens's *Kingdom of Children: Culture and Controversy in the Homeschooling Movement*, writes:

> *"Both the 'unschoolers' and the religiously-conservative families seek to shelter their children from many aspects of popular culture that permeate the media and the shopping mall. They are suspicious of the peer culture that is so profoundly influential in public and even private schools. John Locke, himself an advocate of homeschooling, expressed the same concern three centuries ago, writing in* Some Thoughts Concerning Education *(1693) that, "tis not the waggeries or cheats practiced amongst schoolboys....that make an able man, but the principles of justice, generosity, and sobriety, joined with observation and industry, qualities*

"What sort of life did Jesus model for us?

Jesus' life was a model of unhurriedness.

Jesus' life was a model of balanced priorities.

Jesus' life was a model of joy."

"The joy of the Lord is my strength." —Nehemiah 8:10

which I judge schoolboys do not learn much of one another...It is impossible to keep a lad from the spreading contagion if you will venture him abroad in the herd and trust to chance or his own inclination for the choice of his company at school.'"

Many experts might suggest that we homeschoolers are "suspicious in nature" or are "sheltering our children from many aspects of popular culture," but very often our own children provide the answers to these accusations. As a veteran homeschooler, I have worn many hats in my homeschooling community, one of which has been local support group leader and Enrichment Program Director. In addition to my own homeschooling, this position carried the responsibility of leading, guiding, and encouraging all the homeschooling families involved; answering their questions; helping new families get assimilated and involved; fielding media inquiries; training and supporting teachers; and managing the business aspects of the support group meetings. Well, on the last day of our Enrichment Program, I learned an amazing lesson from my youngest daughter, who was nine at the time.

Her class was having an end-of-the-year party and she was very excited. Many times that morning, she had reminded me of the party and stressed how much she wanted me to be there. *"Of course, there is no where else I would want to be,"* I responded. After teaching chapel (which ran over), I was off to administer the final exam in my High School Literature/Writing Class (which ran over). Suddenly, I looked at my watch and realized I needed to get to the party. En route, several parents stopped me to discuss issues, so my progress was hindered! Trying not to be rude, I listened, all the while knowing I was missing the party. Finally, I broke away and arrived to find the party coming to a close. Obviously, my daughter was disappointed, but I thought she was overcoming it quite well. Little did I know.

Later that same day, she was bitten by a tick, suffered an allergic reaction, and endured huge welts and hives as a result of the bite. It was an extremely difficult situation. As I was tucking her into bed, about to say our prayers, I felt uneasy. I knew I needed to discuss "the party" issue and resolve any hurt that might be lodged in her little heart. *"Brooke,"* I asked, *"Why was it so important for Mommy to be at your party? Was it because all of the other Mommys were there?"* Hesitating for a moment, she finally spoke through her tears, *"No, I just wanted you there."* I explained the events of the morning (which were all valid) and apologized. She continued, *"Momma, we just don't have any fun anymore. I want to have fun like we used to have. You're always running to the copy store or sitting at your computer. You're always working on something for our enrichment day. I want to go places and play games together like we used to."*

Ouch! Her words pierced my heart and spoke loud and clear, forcing me to take a good, long look at our life. Here was a little girl asking to come back home. Even though she enjoyed the program, she missed her "undistracted" mother and our times of creative learning.

Uri Bronfenbrenner, Ph.D., states, "For a culture built, as ours is, on the Protestant ethic of work and achievement, play presents a problem. We have a difficult time defining play in positive terms, or according it a prominent place in our theories of human behavior and development, not to mention in public policy or practice. At the very most, play for modern man is an avocation, something that mainly children, and sometimes adults, do in their 'spare time.' We reveal our distinctive capacities and character most clearly—be it as individual or groups—in our play, what there is of it." Plato even said, "You can discover more about a person in an hour of play than in a year of conversation."

If our children need anything, they need time to "be." In a culture that is affectionately called "the land of the rushed" by Dr. Richard Swenson, we have a biblical imperative to train our children to *be still and know God (Psalm 46:10 NIV)*.

In many ways, I find myself fighting culture and having to teach my children how to handle stress. I can't avoid it. I found great help in Dr. Archibald Hart's book, *Stress and Your Child.*[1] Two specific pointers he offers are noteworthy:

> *"Avoiding stressful situations is almost impossible today, if you are involved in any group activities."* He suggests, *"We inoculate our children against stress, we expose them gradually, under controlled conditions, to more and more stress, while at the same time showing them how to cope with the stress. Over time, the process helps to build strength of character, a healthy and positive outlook, a sense of personal competence, and a willingness to take on challenges and not avoid risks. When we inoculate them against stress, in other words, we teach them how to be healthier, more effective adults."* He adds,

> *"Allow adequate periods of recovery from periods of overstress. Life is always full of things to do, and there will always be periods of intensified stress or excitement. Such times of high arousal should always be followed with times for recovery. We are not supermen or superwomen, just ordinary mortals with bodies that have their limits and demand recovery time from overuse."*

Amazingly, a study was done of 91 extremely high achievers, some of which were Nobel Prize winners. The general outcome was that most of them revealed "they got started in their free time, messing around at home with nothing to do. There wasn't schedule or structure." University of Chicago psychology professor, Mihaly Csikszentmihalyi, Ph.D., suggests that every child should "have some down time every day, during which she is free to discover and pursue her own interests and inclinations. As long as you provide children with an environment that is flexible and rich, they will find things that are fun and interesting to do. When there's too much structure and not enough choice in a child's day—'now it's time for gym class, next we have a piano lesson'—the child always has to conform to the external demands of schedule. Pretty soon what she's doing is no fun anymore."

The power of play and unbroken routine is dynamic. I don't think we can overestimate the great need for maintaining this necessary spiritual practice. As we close, may the words of Barbara Edtl Shelton from *It's About Time* speak to us:

> *"Unbroken routine seems to be the element most difficult to convince homeschool moms of the need for. So many 'worthwhile' activities necessitate the frequent leaving of the home, breaking the very routine that would provide the child with the needed atmosphere for exploration. She may fear having to deal with the child's boredom, and rightly so! Or she may simply believe in the need to provide their children with 'outside the home' type of activity."* She continues, *"Moms, you may be undermining your efforts to instill a love of learning in your child by providing choppy routines. A lot of time gets wasted with 'the preparing to leave' mentality and 'settling in once again.'*
>
> *Consistent unbroken routine is vital as it will positively affect the overall attitude of your children when they can count on their ability to focus attention on one thing."*

May God give each of us the wisdom and understanding to manage our homes with excellence. Balance will come as we seek Him. In addition, may we all remind ourselves, once again, that God, the Creator of the Universe, took a complete day to rest and enjoy His labor. I believe He would want us to do the same.

End Notes
[1] Dr. Archibald Hart. *Stress and Your Child.*

Tools for Transformation: Resources

he following resources are given as tools of transformation; enabling you to build a strong, stable family.

INTERNET SITES

Debra Bell, author of *The Ultimate Guide to Home Schooling* (Thomas Nelson Publishers): www.debrabell.com.

Susan Wise Bauer and Jessie Wise, authors of *The Well-Trained Mind*: www.welltrainedmind.com and www.peacehillpress.com.

Clay and Sally Clarkson, authors of *The Wholehearted Child* and numerous other works supporting the homeschooling family: www.wholeheart.org.

Catholic Home Schooling Network of America (CHSNA). Catholic Home Schooling Networking. Homeschooling with other Catholic Home Schoolers: www.chsna.org.

Crosswalk.com Homeschool Channel—A Christian homeschool site providing helpful articles, curriculum reviews and purchasing, chat, humor, forums, resources and daily encouragement: www.homeschool.crosswalk.com.

Home School Foundation—Receive their e-mail newsletter, "The Foundation Report." Contact: P.O. Box 1152, Purcellville, VA. 20134; 540-338-8899: www.homeschoolfoundation.org.

Steve and Teri Maxwell, authors of *Managers of Their Homes*": www.titus2.com.

HSLDA (Home School Legal Defense Association): www.hslda.org.

The Rutherford Institute: www.rutherford.org/welcome.asp.

"By the grace God has given me, I laid a foundation as an expert builder, and someone else is building on it. But each one should be careful how he builds. For no one can lay any foundation other than the one already laid, which is Jesus Christ. If any man builds on this foundation using gold, silver, costly stones, wood, hay or straw, his work will be shown for what it is, because the Day will bring it to light. It will be revealed with fire, and the fire will test the quality of each man's work. If what he has built survives, he will receive his reward. If it is burned up, he will suffer loss; he himself will be saved, but only as one escaping through the flames."
—1 Corinthians 3: 10-15, NIV

Christian Homeschool Association of Pennsylvania (CHAP). Excellent site for resources and encouragement: www.chapboard.org.

Home Educator's Association of Virginia (HEAV). Committed to helping parents fulfill their God-given right and responsibility to educate their own children: www.heav.org.

Leadership Resources at Christianity Today International. An excellent website for leadership materials such as "Leaders & Family," downloadable for $9.95: www.BuildingChurchLeaders.com.

Elisabeth Elliot's teachings and encouragements can be located on: www.backtothebible.org/gateway.

Revive Our Hearts Radio Ministry. Nancy Leigh DeMoss, author/speaker. Wonderful encouragement for a mother's heart: www.reviveourhearts.com.

Focus on the Family. Dr. James Dobson. A lifeline of information, cassettes, books, children's material for the homeschooling family: www.family.org. Also visit the Parent's Place website: www.family.org/pplace.

Insight for Living. Dr. Chuck Swindoll and his teaching series, *The Strong Family*, #SFMCS are available online: www.insight.org.

Family Life Ministries. Dennis and Barbara Rainey. Life changing resources for the family. Excellent resources and encouragement via Internet broadcasts and articles, including: *"Growing a Spiritually Strong Family"* by the Rainey's: www.familylife.com.

BOOKS (ALL AVAILABLE ONLINE AT WWW.CHRISTIANBOOKS.COM)

A Godward Life by John Piper. Discover how to live a fully passionate life for God (Multnomah, 1997; ISBN 1576731839).

Sacred Marriage by Gary Thomas. Mr. Thomas discusses how to use marriage as a tool of discipline to love God more (Zondervan, 2002; ISBN 0310242827).

Sacred Pathways by Gary Thomas. How and where do you feel closest to God? This book investigates nine different pathways of expressing worship. Great understanding into how to develop parents' and children's spirituality. Encourages thinking "outside the box" of traditional expectations (Zondervan, 2000; ISBN 0310230926).

Family Practice by R. C. Sproul. Contributing authors include Elisabeth Elliot, Gary Ezzo, Douglas Wilson and many others. R. C. Sproul writes, "To achieve healthy families we must turn to the Great Physician, a 'family doctor' who still makes house calls" (P & R Publishing, 2001; ISBN 0875524982).

Raising Your Children for Christ by Andrew Murray. A classic, must-read for all parents (Whitaker House, 1984; ISBN 0883680459).

Intimate Issues by Linda Dillow and Lorraine Pintus. A deep understanding of the role of intimacy in marriage (Waterbrook Press, 1999; ISBN 1578561493). Also worth having in your cassette library, "Women and Sexuality I-III" as discussed on Dr. James Dobson's radio broadcast, Product Code: #CT421, available at www.family.org. More resources and encouragement can be found on their website: www.intimateissues.com.

The Five Love Languages: How to Express Heartfelt Commitment to Your Mate by Gary Chapman. Re-educate yourself on how to communicate to your spouse. An excellent tool to strengthen your marriage and family (Moody Press, 1992; ISBN 1881273156).

Season's of a Mother's Heart by Sally Clarkson. Reflections worthy of meditation. Perfect for a support-group Bible study (Faithworks, 1998; ISBN 1888692030).

Peace Within Your Borders by Beth Sharpton. A wonderful devotional written specifically for homeschool teachers (WinePress Publishing, 1999; ISBN 1579212190).

How To Care for the Whole World and Still Take Care of Yourself by Peg Rankin. *Foreward by Patsy Clairmont.* A women's complete guide to setting priorities (Broadman & Holman Publishers, 1994; ISBN 0805453709).

The Harried Homeschooler: A Practical Guide to Balancing Your Child's Education with the Rest of Your Life by Christine Field. Learn the art of navigation—combining homeschooling and life! (Shaw Books, 2002; ISBN 0877887942).

The Organized Home Schooler by Vicki Caruana. This book instructs the reader on how to clear the chaos from a home classroom (Good News Publishing, 2001; ISBN 1581343051).

Manners Made Easy by June Hines Moore. A Scripture-based guide to the principles of etiquette and good manners. Includes a reproducible student workbook (Broadman & Holman, 2001; ISBN 0805437703).

A Sacred Foundation: The Importance of Strength in the Homeschool Marriage by Mike Farris and L. Reed Elam. The title says it all (Loyal Publishing, 2000; ISBN 1929125097).

Planning and Record Keeping

Compiled by Karylene Ollenberger

Additional Articles on the CD
BE SURE TO CHECK OUT THESE OTHER GREAT ARTICLES ON THE CD!

Each article in the book and on the CD has been carefully chosen by the section coordinator to increase your knowledge and understanding of this subject, so don't forget to use and enjoy the parts of the manual on your CD, as well as the part you are holding.

Please note that the page numbering on the CD is different from that of the hard-copy manual.

Introduction: Organizing Home, School, and Time

HOME ORGANIZATION, TIME MANAGEMENT, SCHOOL PLANNING, AND RECORD KEEPING

Before a homeschooling parent can begin to organize, certain decisions must be made. The beginning, according to Marilyn Rockett, in an article titled "Organize to Survive," (Wade, 317) is to **know your priorities**. What is important to you and your family? Make a list of the things that are essential to your home and family. Once priorities have been set, it becomes easier to evaluate whether or not certain tasks and functions enhance or detract from them. Priorities that have been written down can be easily reviewed during the school year to help keep you focused.

The next step is to **set your goals**. What are goals? In *Webster's Ninth New Collegiate Dictionary*, a goal is defined as "the end toward which effort is directed." A simplified example of a **family goal** might be to arrive at church on time every Sunday. An example of an **educational goal** might be to be able to name all the states and their capitals by Christmas of the current school year. A **household goal** might be to get the children more involved in cleaning and maintenance around the house. What do *you* hope to accomplish this year in education? in family time? in household management? Once again, write these down. When my goals are not written down, I am often surprised at how often I commit myself to something that displaces my family's priorities, or does not help me reach my desired goals.

At the end of the specified time period, you will need some method of evaluating whether goals have been achieved. One method of evaluation is through the **use of objectives**. The National Writing Institute defines "objectives" as describing "in detail exactly what cognitive (intellectual) changes you anticipate being the result of the lessons." (*Reading Strands*, p. 6.) According to this text, objectives should be verbs (action words) that describe what you hope to accomplish. In the previous goal example, where we hoped to arrive at church on time, objectives might be: to lay out clothing the night before, to bathe children the night before, to set the alarm clock fifteen minutes ahead of the time you would normally get up, to plan simple foods, like cereal, for breakfast, *et cetera*.

Once objectives are determined, it is easy to look at the list and ask, "Have I laid out the clothing? Are the children bathed? Is the alarm clock set? Are milk and cereal available? Ideally, if all objectives are met, then you will be on time. However, plans don't always work as anticipated. When failures occur, it is not the time to "throw in the towel," but just time to re-evaluate. If a record of priorities, goals, and objectives exists and can be referred to, you can rationally evaluate current achievements versus desired goals and adjust accordingly.

After setting priorities, goals, and objectives, parents can know the direction that home and school will be taking. It then becomes much easier to meet the demands of homeschooling and to keep school in balance with the rigorous demands of a busy life. The parent/teacher should now be able to effectively tackle the task of organizing home, school, and time in a manner that will meet the needs of the family.

It is my hope that within the articles that follow, you will find helpful suggestions and valuable information that will enable you to tackle home organization, school-year planning, record keeping, and time management with confidence. You will find general information on these subjects, reprints of topic-related articles, samples and examples of various forms of paperwork, and a small list of resource materials and website locations to help you begin organizing your homeschool. There are many resources available to assist homeschoolers in becoming organized. Not only are there books, magazines, and software available for purchase, but there is also an extensive selection of materials on the Internet. Many Internet sites offer a wide range of planning and organization materials completely free. All you need to do is select the form and print. For the family with Internet access, this may be the most economical way to go. The forms desired can be printed and then taken to a copy center to be reproduced as needed.

—Karylene Ollenberger

Management Tools For Home and School

Gayle Graham

Homeschool record keeping need not be complex. If we save our energy on record keeping we'll have more time for our real job—teaching our children! I'm suggesting a streamlined record keeping system with just three basic components: a *home*-management notebook, *school*-management notebook, and a *child's* notebook.

HOME-MANAGEMENT NOTEBOOK

As an effective home manager, you'll need a portable Day-Timer™/day-planner to keep up with your logistics (as well as everyone else's, *right?*) Look for one with an appointment calendar, daily or weekly to-do pages, an address and telephone-number directory, and room to add your own personalized sections (Bible study, Christmas section, birthdays, personal yellow pages for frequently-called businesses, Sunday-school notes, *et cetera*).

This is your *home* management tool. Don't try to use this to keep up with school management too, or you'll just overload it. (This is *not* where you'll plan your school day—that notebook is next.)

Choose a format small enough to carry with you wherever you go. Next time you're out for a dental appointment and make a new appointment in six months, you can write it directly into your calendar and *not have to fool around with that little card that will surely get lost.* When you see a friend in the grocery store who asks you about switching a meeting time you can jot it down (or resolve the conflict with another appointment) right on the spot. *Less stress!*

Information written down is information you can put out of your mind until needed. This automatically reduces the stress associated with a busy life.

SCHOOL-MANAGEMENT NOTEBOOK

The school-management notebook is a loose-leaf binder which includes all the various details, plans, and schedules that mom needs as teacher/administrator.

Each Child's Program of Study

Perhaps the best starting point is each child's *Program of Study.* When planning a program of study for your child for the coming school year, look first at your goals in reading, written language, math, and unit studies. Then select the appropriate materials to use in those four major areas, balancing your choices.

Curriculum Scope Pages

Next come your set of curriculum scope pages to record the subjects covered in each school year for a particular child. On this sheet, you list, year-by-year, any textbooks used, and the subjects or unit topics covered in a particular grade.

This will give you a continuum. You can look at the past to see where you have been. You can look at the future to see where you are going. It also helps you when you have younger children coming behind the older ones. You can look back and see, *"Now what did I cover with my oldest child when he was in the sixth grade? ...What materials did I use for beginning reading instruction? ...Have I done a constellation unit? ...How old was my third child when we did that? ...Is it time to go back and do it again?"* This will give a long-range scope of where you have been and where you are going—the yearly big picture for school.

In your loose-leaf notebook, you should also have a weekly overview page. I call mine *Mom's Week at a Glance* with the days of the week across the top and the hours of the day down the side. Fill in unchangeables like tutoring sessions, music lessons, co-op days first.

At major planning times (beginning of the school year, *et cetera*) use this sheet as a place to work our your own master schedule. *When do you plan to tutor that beginning reader? When will you spend time with the toddlers? And what will the older children be doing at that time? How will it all fit?*

Use pencil—you'll want to revise your plan along the way. It's very likely that your schedule will occasionally revise as your family changes and grows. *(If you're like me at all, your schedule will change several times in September!)*

Coordinating a Number of Children

If you have a large family, the third thing you will need in your school management notebook is a master plan of how you will coordinate your children. Some families tell me they start their school day at staggered times. This makes for a longer day for the moms, but it might work for you. Other families might start their school year at staggered times. For example, the year I was having another baby, I started my kindergartner early in August anticipating that she would have time off when the baby arrived in January.

(By the way, you might want to conquer a unit during summer. Summer is a great time to study outdoors. You could do insects, pond life, butterflies—the list is endless. Have a summer of science, say a summer of life science, and conquer a unit ahead of time.)

Large families generally individualize only in language arts and math, reaching all the other ages with the same units in science, history, *et cetera*. Many also plan to accomplish five days of academics in four days, taking the middle day (Wednesday) off for field trips, crafts, experiments, *et cetera*. *(Quite a motivator!)*

Large families find it helpful to use the older ones to teach the younger ones. This is especially good if the skill is one that the older one has just learned and needs reinforcing. This helps the older child as well as the younger one.

Sometimes, large families will work especially hard for six weeks doing seven weeks worth of assignments and taking the seventh week for just family activities.

To use creative approaches like these, you need to set specific goals ahead of time and be thoughtful as you plan. For example, it is helpful to teach science one semester and history another semester rather than doing the two subjects at the same time. That makes less planning for you and less confusion for your child.

The fourth thing you will want for your school-management notebook is a *record of weekly individual assignments for each reading child.* These sheets are best for children eight and up who are fluent readers. You might use 32, 36, maybe even 40 sheets for each of your children depending on the number of school weeks you plan. On this sheet, record daily assignments for the week. Most moms like to do this on the weekend prior to the week beginning.

As you gain experience you will be able to plan several weeks at once. It helps me to plan one month of these at a sitting. Then I can see if there is a balance of choices over a period of time. Use pencil, though; you'll be making adjustments. Your child uses this as a checklist.

Unit Plans

You also want a record of the plans for the unit studies that you will be doing corporately with your children. This includes all of the rest after teaching individualized reading, written language, and math lessons to the child. It's a great idea to teach your children as a group in the same subject area and vary assignments according to the ages and abilities of the children.

For example, if you are studying the explorers, why not study them with all of your children of different ages? What you will do is keep a record of the plans you have made for corporate studies with the children. Usually one page is sufficient for your records for one week. You will record the projects, the experiments you plans to do with your children, the books you will read aloud, and field trips you will take.

CHILD'S NOTEBOOK

The last component in our management assignment is the *Child's Notebook.* Using a three-ring binder with notebook dividers, keep one section for each unit as it is studied, plus a section for math, spelling, foreign language, or other specifics you are studying. Sample papers are kept in each section. (De-clutter weekly.)

For example, say you are doing a unit on the human body. You might investigate a cow's kidney, write a report about Robert Hook (who discovered cells), draw a diagram of the eye, or take a snapshot while on a field trip to the local hospital lab. Include all of that in this section of your notebook entitled *Human Body*. Perhaps your child writes an imaginary story about a voyage through the circulatory system or reads a biography of Louis Pasteur. Include these also in the *Human Body* unit section.

Other things you might want to include in your child's notebook include a copy of the goals set for the school year, a cumulative list of great books as they are read, a writing checklist of skills to remember when proofing papers, or a daily/weekly schedule sheet. The point is to keep it simple and make it his personal record.

What about projects too large for the binder? Photograph them and then give them to charity in the wee hours of the night.

No more clutter! No more loose, flying papers! Your children will have less busy work as homeschoolers and the papers and records they keep will be more meaningful. *Paper production does not equal good schooling.*

BOTTOM LINE

Whew! How much time does all this planning take? It takes approximately one and one-half hours per week of planning time alone to coordinate your school and home management notebooks, and to fill in the children's assignment sheets. (Double this time the first month you try it.)

Think of planning time as an investment. The time you spend planning will be more than repaid to you in accomplishment during your school week. I recommend that first-year homeschool moms spend half a day per week outside of the home for reflection and planning. This can be spent in the library (or, as I do, in the park). We're more productive if we pull away from a situation and reflect.

© Gayle Graham. This article was excerpted from *How to Homeschool* by Gayle Graham, reprinted in *Homeschooling Today* July/Aug 94. Used by permission.

Homeschool and Housework

Tamara Eaton

D oes the combination of homeschool and housework seem like oil and water—they just don't mix? It used to seem to us that we were either successful in homeschooling or housework but never both in the same day. It's easier now—our kids are older, we have a good system and most importantly—**lower standards!** We would never make the cover of *Better Homes and Gardens* but at times we could qualify for *Cluttered Homes and Jungles!*

Here are some tips that have worked for our family:

SIMPLIFY & DECLUTTER!

- **Make a list** of everything that needs to be done then work on it. Don't despair over the things still undone but know you'll get to it eventually. In the meantime, maintain what you've already accomplished so it doesn't get so cluttered again.
- **Be RUTHLESS**—get rid of things you don't use or need! Organize into three boxes: Throw away, Give away, and Put away.
- **Invest in inexpensive storage containers** for things you must keep. We purchased 19-gallon rectangular storage boxes with lids for $5 each from K-Mart and use them to store homeschool supplies, library books, clothes, "treasures," Legos™, toys, *et cetera.*
- **Don't try to do too much at once.** Focus on one area at a time and set reasonable goals. Such as one room or one closet a week. This way the rest of your routine doesn't suffer as much and you're not totally exhausted.
- **Limit "knickknacks"** and go for clear spaces to make cleaning easier. We already have plenty of educational clutter to "decorate" our homes!
- **Take 15-30 minutes** to do some of the dirty jobs that you've been putting off. Clean one window, or one drawer, then stop and get back to the normal routine.

OUR DAILY HOUSEHOLD ROUTINE:

In earlier years when my children were too young to help out much around the house, I neatened up the house before bedtime each evening. That helped us get off to a better start the next morning. After breakfast I would get them started playing while I quickly did the morning chores. Afterwards, my day was free to play with them, teach them, care for them and enjoy them. I loved it! I stayed home a lot, which was my main secret for success.

Now that my children are older, they have regular kitchen chores that don't change more than two or three times a year so everyone knows what is expected. I can also tell at a glance who has done his job—no more confusion about which child is responsible for each chore. Then each child picks a part of the family room to clean quickly. I neaten the bathrooms, living room, and master bedroom and help the youngest two clean their room.

We set 9 AM as our deadline each morning to have all chores completed and the main living area picked up. Then we schedule quick pick-ups: after lunch, before supper, and before bedtime. Friday mornings are for deep cleaning—many hands make light work, then we have "computer school" or do educational projects for the rest of the day.

If the house is a wreck and standards are creeping way too low, we take off from school and other activities and concentrate on getting things in order. Instead of nagging the children, we politely and firmly tell them what needs to be done. (In our home, children who don't follow instructions get added jobs or responsibilities.)

TRAINING CHILDREN TO HELP:

It's been my experience that young children are the most enthusiastic helpers! It's important not to overwhelm them, though, because what looks like a small task to us can seem enormous to them. It's best to have them work along beside us. Even a two-year-old can fold bath cloths; pick up toys and books, and so on, with mom working close at hand.

I rarely tell young children (seven and under) to do something without staying to see that it's done and working right beside them. This helps create good work habits. As they get older, I give them more responsibility and expect them to complete a task whether I am there or not.

It's easier to be consistent if I assign small jobs and make sure they are done. Otherwise, they get into the habit of not obeying right away, or not finishing a job. I use the same principles to train older children who have poor working habits. Many parents don't like the way their kids clean up, but they don't take the time to demonstrate more efficient ways to do it. We want to help our children learn to do a job well.

William and I have also put on training workshops for our children." We pretended to be a couple of the children and demonstrated poor working habits, contrasting them with good working habits. The children thought it was hilarious! Then we purposely messed up the den and allowed each child to come in and clean it as fast as he could, timing him. We demonstrated timesaving methods and encouraged them to use them. They all did a good job, from oldest to youngest. The (at that time) three-year-old won the contest!

Young children are notorious for messing up the house. It helps to keep an eye on their activities during the day as a preventative measure—otherwise they start many different activities and forget to put anything away. Or they scatter their things all over the house. It also helps to create special play areas using a small quilt or child-sized table and chairs in the main home-schooling area. This confines toys to a specific area and they enjoy being in the center of things. They can be taught to play quietly, or to go to another room if they're distracting the rest of the children.

Be consistent in training children to help with chores. I had years when I wondered if my kids would EVER get to the point where they wouldn't need supervision or reminders. Eventually consistency paid off. They aren't perfect yet (kids usually don't see all that moms see!), but they generally do their jobs without reminders and can manage the whole house, if necessary. (At least the teens can—the younger two are still in training!)

Two years ago, I was very sick and for several months my older four children did all the housework and most of the cooking and helped take care of the younger two children. It made all the difference in the world, and was good training for them. They practiced teamwork and since then, have viewed our home as a joint responsibility—they often tell me to go do something else and let them take care of the clean up. Hang in there, it is worth it!

BAD ATTITUDES:

If anyone **whines** or **complains** about working, I give them a little **extra work.** If they keep on, I add more. It nips it in the bud! Bad attitudes are catching, so I try to keep a positive attitude about work. We put on peppy music and get it done as fast as we can. Teamwork is great!

If someone is purposely dragging his chores out and not cooperating, a little extra work solves this problem, too. We always seem to have an area beneath a couch that needs cleaning or a porch to sweep!

CHILDREN'S BEDROOMS:

I have organized the younger children's room so that it is easier to keep neat. We use large Rubbermaid™ tubs with lids to organize their toys. Their favorite toys stay out, but everything else is stored in their closet, which is off limits to them. Occasionally we rotate toys.

They have Legos™ in one container, little cars and trucks in another container, and dolls and accessories in another. They each have a "treasure drawer" where they keep special treasures (bird feathers, pretty rocks, letters, drawings, pogs, *et cetera*). *Each morning I help them straighten their room, then check it several times a day.* It stays neat this way and they enjoy playing there. If I weren't involved, it would constantly be a mess.

Older children sometimes need encouragement, too. They look at their disorderly bedrooms and don't know where to begin! It helps for them to have a routine to follow. This is what we do:

1. Make beds.
2. Pick up all clothes.
3. Pick up all books.
4. Pick up any toys.
5. Pick up any paper or trash.

By this time the room should be presentable and they can vacuum and dust. What was once a insurmountable task becomes possible!

QUICK PICK-UP GAMES:
- **Around the World**—Usually we divide the family room into parts and each child has a part to clean, but sometimes we play "Around the World". Each person works his way around the room clockwise until everything is neat and clean.
- **The Age Game**—Everyone picks up the same number of items as his own age, then if there are items left over, they do it again. Only problem is when they want the parents to pick up the same number of items as their age—whew!
- **Mr. Jones is Coming!**—We clean up the house as fast as we can, pretending that Mr. Jones is coming over at a specific time. If we finish in time, we celebrate with a tea party. If we need more time—well sometimes "Mr. Jones" gives us a call and says he has been delayed for a bit! Sometimes Dad dresses up as "Mr. Jones" and comes around to the front door and rings the bell. Inspection time follows!

KEEP YOUR PERSPECTIVE!

I find that I go in cycles—there are times we're caught up in other projects and we let the housework go, only doing the basics. Other times, I get in the mood (or force myself!) to make our standards higher and in the process, usually move some furniture around and make it cozier by redecorating. I do the same thing with extra baking and elaborate cooking.

William has told me many times that although he appreciates having the house extra neat and clean and cooking extra-special meals, he also appreciates the time and effort that is going into homeschooling and discipling our children. He also encourages me to write, work on the computer, keep up with my reading, and do other things. I appreciate his balanced view because sometimes I feel guilty over simple meals or never-done laundry. But we are enjoying our family so much, and we know we won't have many years left before they will no longer be under our roof!

Elisabeth Elliot shared the following essay (written many years ago by an unknown mother) in one of her newsletters (*Elisabeth Elliot Newsletter, P.O. Box 7711, Ann Arbor, Michigan 48107-7711; $7 year.*) She says that while not too many women iron sheets these days, it is still possible to let many other things take precedence over the primary task.

"I am sadly concerned that thousands of mothers are so over-burdened that the actual demands of life from day to day consume all their time and strength. But of two evils, choose the lesser: which would you call the lesser—an unpolished stove or an untaught boy? Dirty windows, or a child whose confidence you have failed to gain? Cobwebs in the corner, or a son over whose soul a crust has formed, so strong that you despair of melting it with your hot tears and fervent prayers?

I have seen a woman who was absolutely ignorant of her children's habits of thought, who never felt that she could spare a half-hour to read

or talk with them—I have seen this woman spend ten minutes in iron-
ing a sheet, or forty minutes icing a cake for tea, because company was
expected.

When the mother, a good orthodox Christian, shall appear before the
Great White Throne to be judged for the "deeds done in the body," and to
give her report of the master's treasures placed in her care, there will be
questions and answers like these:

"Where are the boys and girls I gave thee?"

"Lord, I was busy keeping my house clean and in order, and my
children wandered away."

"Where wert thou while thy sons and thy daughters were learning
lessons of dishonesty, malice and impurity?"

"Lord, I was polishing furniture and making beautiful rugs."

"What hast thou to show for thy life's work?"

"The tidiest house, Lord, and the best starching and ironing in all
our neighborhood!"

Oh these children, these children! The restless eager boys and girls
whom we love more than our lives! Shall we devote our time and strength
to that which perishes while the rich garden of our child's soul lies ne-
glected, with foul weeds choking out all worthy and beautiful growths?
Fleeting indeed, O mother, are the days of childhood, and speckless win-
dows, snowy linen, the consciousness that everything about the house
is faultlessly bright and clean will be poor comfort in that day wherein
we shall discover that our poor boy's feet have chosen the path that shall
take him out of the way to all eternity."

—Author Unknown

If I'm tempted to be discouraged over the state of my house, I remember
the scripture I prayed many years ago when I was unable to conceive: *"He*
maketh the barren woman to keep house, and to be a joyful mother of children.
Praise ye the Lord!" (Psalm 113:9) I am filled with thankfulness that the Lord
so abundantly answered our prayers with six precious children! They are
MORE than worth ALL the work involved in keeping house for them! Give
your children a hug and offer up a prayer of thanksgiving for them and don't
forget to greet your dear husband with a hug and kiss and a cheerful hello
when he gets home from work—chances are, he won't even notice how the
house looks!

Tips for Managing Time Wisely

Mary Corsi

o teach us to number our days, that we may apply our hearts unto wisdom. (Psalm 90:12)

YOUR HOME

One of the greatest challenges the homeschool mother faces is how to get the schooling done and also keep the house in order. You are now a working mother with a full-time job and as such have less time for housework. Unlike the career woman, however, your children are home all day, making more messes than ever. Add that to the fact that homeschooling seems to lend itself to all sorts of wonderful projects which now beautify your house instead of a classroom across town.

Your house will probably never look like a magazine cover again. At least not for very long. On the other hand, most people work better in a tidy environment. It's easier to do math when you can find the pencils! Here are some suggestions:

- Get rid of clutter. The less you have, the less you have to clean. If you don't use it but can't stand to get rid of it, at least put it in your basement, garage, or attic where you won't have to deal with it as often. But first, really try to get rid of it.
- Get your children involved. Assign chores.
- Each day, try to keep the front areas of the house clean, including the guest bathroom.
- If possible, assign a room as a schoolroom. Even if you don't do school work there, it gives you a place to keep all the supplies and projects.
- Every three months have a "shovel out" day. Go through the house and get rid of all the stuff that has accumulated in the wrong places. Pay special attention to the children's bedrooms. It really helps if Dad takes the children out while you do this!
- If you have a freezer, consider "30-day-cooking." This way your dinners are pre-prepared, and stress is reduced during a time of day when you are most fatigued. Two terrific cookbooks to teach you how to do this are: *The Once a Month Cookbook* by Mimi Wilson and Mary Beth Lagerobord, and *The Good Steward Cookbook* by Lisa Walsh.

YOURSELF

- Get adequate sleep. The best lesson plans in the world will be useless if they are prepared at 3:00 a.m., as the teacher will be cranky and impatient.
- Try to rise before your children. It helps you to mentally prepare for the day. This isn't always easy when your children are young.
- Dress yourself and the children for the day before you start school. Again, this is not always easy when they are very young.

FRIENDS

- Try, try, try to convince your friends, your sister, and your neighbors not to call during your school hours. Since they will anyway, get an answering machine, and USE IT!

SCHEDULING

- A great variety of opinions exist as to just how structured homeschooling should be. Some have detailed schedules and can tell you what subject they will be studying at any given time. Others have no schedule at all. Some organization is appropriate for beginning homeschoolers, even if you lean toward the "unschooling" approach. It helps to make sure that you are getting enough educational time in each day. Scheduling also can teach your child self-discipline. At least set school hours and maintain them for a while. After you homeschool a while, and your children are used to a routine, you can be a bit more flexible.
- Most elementary-age children do best if they study academics in the morning when their minds are fresh. If you have an infant or toddler, however, you may find that their naptime is the best time to work with your older children. Discover what works best for you, and then stick to it for awhile. As circumstances change, be prepared to adapt.
- An ideal (it never is exactly like this) weekday schedule for someone with elementary-aged children might look something like this:

7:00 a.m.	– get dressed, have breakfast
8:00 a.m.	– do morning chores
8:30 to 10:00 a.m.	– book work
10:00 to 10:15 a.m.	– break
10:15 to 11:30 a.m.	– book work
12:00	– lunch, clean up morning's work
1:00 to 3:30 p.m.	– projects, music practice, field trips
3:30 to 5:30 p.m.	– play time, sports, errands, housework
6:00 p.m.	– dinner, tell Dad about the day
7:00 p.m.	– meetings, game time, go for a walk
8:00 p.m.	– clean up, baths, read-aloud time, mom reviews lesson plans for the next day
9:00 p.m.	– kids in bed

Time Management

Tamara Eaton

ime management has always been an interest of mine, but when I had four children in four-and-a-half years, it became more than an interest; it was a matter of sheer survival. I couldn't possibly do everything, so I had to learn to establish priorities, to find creative ways to do the necessary things, and to put everything else on hold.

Homeschooling moms everywhere face the same challenge: How do I juggle homeschooling, housework, cooking, mothering, some personal time, and being a good wife all into one 24-hour period? (Not to mention getting a little sleep, as well.)

We now have six children, tot to teen, and have always homeschooled. This year, we have children in all levels of schooling: nursery school, kindergarten, elementary, junior high, and high school. I have even more reasons now to exercise creative time-management skills. Here are some tips that have helped me over the years.

- As each new year begins, write down priorities and goals. Once you have a working plan, you can modify it as needed, but having one helps you feel more in control of your time. The goals will seem more manageable and you will feel less overwhelmed. You can't do it *all*, so do the important things first.
- Make sure the goals you set are reasonable; otherwise, you are setting yourself up for failure.
- Simplify your life. Develop a system for keeping your house as neat as possible at least in the important areas. Get the kids to help. Start them while they're young. Lower your expectations. Perfection is not a realistic goal with children in the house.
- Simplify your meals. Some of the healthiest meals are the simplest meals. During the homeschool year, we keep breakfast simple, with cereal or oatmeal and toast. Lunch is also simple, consisting of sandwiches or soup and fruit. The children also make their own lunches. Paper plates are used for quick clean-ups. Dinners are kept simple on Mondays, Wednesdays, and Fridays. Many times the children help prepare these meals. I prepare something more elaborate on Tuesdays and Thursdays, but even then it's often something that I can put in the oven or on top of the stove earlier in the day and have ready for dinner without a lot of last minute preparation.

- De-clutter your home. To decrease frustrations, have a place for all homeschooling materials, pencils, papers, books, scissors, *et cetera.*
- Work on children's attitudes and training, don't just let things go. Deal with them so they don't get worse. Summer is a good time to train them to help out with the household chores and cooking. Sometimes it's necessary to take off for a day or two for training in these areas during the homeschool year. It's important that our children learn to be responsible, and to realize that it takes the whole family working together to make our homeschool and household run smoothly.
- Tackle the areas that bother you the most at first; think of ways you can avoid problems in the future, and of ways you can correct any problems now.
- Don't try to do too much all at once. Focus on one area at a time. For example, right now, my closets all need re-organizing and de-cluttering. A realistic goal has been for me to do one closet a week until they are all finished.
- Take 15-30 minutes to do some of the "dirty jobs" that you've been putting off for ages, yet bother you every time you think about them. Clean one window, or one drawer. Then stop and get back to the normal routine.
- Limit outside commitments. Trips take a large chunk out of your day. I try to stay at home during the week as much as possible. It's especially needed with small children in the household. If we go out too much, it upsets their routine and it's difficult to do schooling or housework.
- Begin each school year early to allow time to take breaks when needed.
- Watch your attitudes. They set the tone for the children's attitudes.
- Don't feel guilty if your homeschool doesn't sound as educational, organized, or perfect as your friends' homeschools. Very likely theirs is not as picture-perfect as it sounds. They have their trials and struggles at times. It's very difficult to be objective about your own homeschool, especially if you are just beginning. Talk to other homeschooling families and get their perspective. This should provide encouragement and give you some fresh ideas.
- Don't think that you have to tackle fifty projects and unit studies a year to be productive. There are many ways to learn and busy homeschooling parents can't always find time for all the projects they'd like to do, especially when there are younger children in the household. Elaborate unit studies and hands-on projects are great, but you might have to limit them if you don't feel you can handle them at this stage in your homeschooling adventure.
- Field trips are also something that some families have a difficult time scheduling during the busy homeschooling months. We try to do some in the summertime when things are less hectic.

Review your homeschooling from time to time. Ask yourself these questions.
- *Am I overdoing it?*
- *Am I trying to make something simple complicated?*
- *Do I need to find a new method to teach a needed skill?*

- *Am I committed to too many outside activities?*
- *What can I eliminate in my life right now?*
- *What is essential?*
- *Am I being consistent with the children?*
- *Do I need to take some time to work on their manners? Or teach them to be more responsible?*
- *Would I do better to postpone certain projects or unit studies until later? Next month? Next summer? Next year?*

For most families, homeschooling requires charting their own course, their own road map, instead of following the traditional methods of education set forth by public or private schools. Fortunately, we have many examples in the homeschool community, and we can learn much from them, but ultimately each family has to decide upon the right approach for themselves.

Give yourself time to adjust and to find the best plan for your family. Look toward the long-range goals instead of expecting to see quick results in every area, although there will be good fruit that you can see already. Some of the fruit of your efforts won't be seen for years. Hang in there. It will be worth it.

School Planning

Karylene Ollenberger

here are many different philosophies about preparing for the school year. The goal of this section, however, is to help you to prepare in the way that best meets your needs. If you have set your priorities, assessed your goals, and stated your objectives for your homeschool, you can determine the role homeschooling will play in your life, and decide whether you will be doing all teaching yourself, hiring a tutor, or enrolling your child in a correspondence program. Now, you must **plan what material you need to cover this school year.**

PLANNING EDUCATION

There are several resources that provide a scope-and-sequence of school subjects as they are studied in the public schools. While these do not have to be closely followed, the Math and Language Arts Standards of Learning (SOL) Objectives can be helpful for parents who want to know what is taught in each grade in the public schools—they can provide guidance as you plan what to teach. Internet users may download a copy of the SOLs at www.doe. virginia.gov/testing/sol/standards_docs/index.shtml.

A paper copy of the booklet may be ordered from the Virginia Board of Education at:

> Commonwealth of Virginia
> Board of Education
> PO Box 2120
> Richmond, VA 23218-2120

Many of the major publishers of homeschool textbooks, such as *A Beka* or *Bob Jones University Press*, have a scope-and-sequence available which states exactly what will be covered in each grade. Many of these companies offer their scope-and-sequence free or at a very reasonable rate. Even if you are not using a specific publisher's material, their scope-and-sequence can be useful in deciding what to cover when.

PURCHASING MATERIALS

Once the subject matter is decided, the next step is to **decide where you will obtain the materials.** The library is an excellent source for detailed information on almost any subject, and the Internet has unlimited potential for research. It is important to closely supervise a child's use of this wonderful tool. It takes one wrong click of a mouse for damaging and unforgettable materials to be accessed. If possible, consider a filtering service such as Cybersitter. Even adults can hit the wrong key, and believe me, there are some shocking things out there!

Of course, there also are many curriculum publishers who would like to have you use their complete line of products, and some even supply pencils and paper. When selecting curricula, be sure to consider your student's learning style, consult your subject list, keep your goals and objectives handy, and keep an eye on your pocketbook! Homeschooling is big business. The cost of school "necessities" can add up quickly. Be aware of your budget for the school year and track how far into it you have traveled.

Prepare yourself to make wise purchases. List the materials you already have on hand. Peruse catalogs and flyers to get a general idea of what is available and how much it costs. Price differences between companies can sometimes be substantial. I keep a list of the items I loan to others from my education shelf, and check it before I purchase something new. Before making this a habit, I often found myself the proud owner of two sets of materials—the one I had just purchased and the one that was returned to me after I purchased the new one! Research products you have not heard much about. Ask friends, read reviews, talk to someone who has used what you are considering. This helps a great deal in deciding if something is right for you. Mix and match. Just because a company offers six supplements to their sixth-grade history course does not mean you need them.

ACHIEVING GOALS

Now you know what subjects you are going to cover, and you have the materials with which to cover them. Next, you need a **plan for achieving your goals**. Are you going to have instruction four days a week? five? six? Are you going to cover every subject every day or have an alternating schedule? Do you take extended family holidays during the school year? Do you plan to educate during the traditional school year? all year? an unusual school year? All of these things should be taken into consideration when planning your school year. Use a calendar as you make your yearly plans, and block out vacation days, holidays, or any special events that might affect your schooling. Planners such as DayTimer™, student planners, and teacher plan books can also be helpful in planning the school year.

SCHEDULE EACH SUBJECT

The easiest way to schedule a subject is to divide the number of pages in the textbook by the number of class days in your school year. This is a good way to judge how much material needs to be covered in a day or a week (for those who are alternating subjects during the week day) in order to complete the material to be used. This method also works on a smaller scale. For example, if you have found a particularly interesting chapter on tropical fish in a library book but you only have three weeks to cover the material, you would divide the total pages in the chapter by the number of school days available during the three-week period. This will indicate how many pages you need to read each school day in order to complete the chapter by the time the book must be returned.

The following resources are also helpful when planning the school year:

Daytimer®-type organizers,

Student planners,

Teacher plan books.

As you plan, remember that this is your school. Do what works for you and your family. **Be flexible**. Do not feel that the work must be completed just because you went to all the trouble to figure out the schedule (read the article, "The Learning Moment," in the Teaching Tips section). **Plan re-evaluation time** into your schedule, and **re-evaluate often**. Take the time to **review your priorities, goals, and objectives** to see if the coursework is on the mark. Do not be afraid to change your original plan if it is not working out. If your child is struggling to complete five pages a day, slow down, and change the daily goal. Remember, you are working toward an education, not toward finishing a marathon.

TIPS ON SCHOOL PLANNING

- Make a list of the subjects to study for the school year.
- Plan the materials to be utilized.
- Check off all materials already on hand.
- Mark with a "B" any materials that can be borrowed from friends.
- Mark with an "L" any materials to be utilized from the public library.
- Circle in red remaining materials to be purchased.
- Check costs against your budget; narrow down if necessary.
- Check used-book stores and curriculum sales for remaining items.

A TIP FOR OVER-ACHIEVING HOMESCHOOL MOMS...

According to my friend Suzanne, who is, like myself, overzealous at the start of every school year, the best way to remain realistic is: "Once you have decided your subject list for the year, cut it in half!"

Unit Studies

Jane R. Boswell

Homeschooling parents today are faced with a jungle of choices when searching for the right resources for their children's studies. Curriculum confusion abounds, and a common mistake that we make is thinking that "curriculum" means a certain set of textbooks and workbooks. In actuality, "curriculum" is any person, place, or thing that is used to help facilitate learning. The word "curriculum" comes from a Latin root that means "a course to be run." Curriculum should be an individualized plan of study determined by the "course" each particular student is to "run." Even though most new (and veteran) homeschooling parents are determined to break the mold of the traditional experience, many turn—sometimes in frustration—back to the methods and materials that they were familiar with as kids: textbooks and worksheets. Keep in mind that even though curriculum planning can begin with textbooks, it should develop into learning experiences far beyond the pages of a book. From our personal schooling experiences, we identify with textbooks...and until recently, there were very few other resources readily available to assist parents.

A COMMON SCENE

You've bought all those brand new, shiny, colorful textbooks (with teacher's manuals, of course) and you are feeling really in charge—confident. You're excited about your first homeschool support group meeting, which is well known as a group guaranteed to build you up and shape you into a first-rate home educator. You managed to get a baby-sitter (so you KNOW this is God's will) and you only had to drive around the block twice before you found the correct address. But to be on the safe side, you waited until people started arriving, checked them out to make sure they looked like homeschoolers. (This could be a trap set by the local superintendent's office.) Safe inside, you are greeted by warm, responsive people-that-look-like-parents. You instantly sense an air of camaraderie and feel comfortably accepted—like the time you joined a secret club when you were a kid. The small talk begins and, as always, the first question that comes up in any starter conversation among homeschool parents is "So, what are you using?" (referring to curriculum). You happily explain your professional teaching manuals and beautiful textbooks and make sure to mention the great deal you got on the workbooks—you really need to make a good impression—even if you are a rookie. Looking around for approval, you notice the couple over on the couch whispering and glancing at you with sympathy-filled eyes. The lady next to you shakes her head and pats your hand reassuringly. Suddenly, you feel as though you have just announced that you are dying of a dreaded disease. Then the lady sitting on the other side of you pulls a huge yellow book out of her standard-issue homeschooler's duffle bag. It is bigger than any coffee table Bible you have ever seen, yet smaller than the New York City Yellow Pages. And speaking of coffee tables, suddenly you notice a four-inch thick binder on the one in front of you. From its cover, a child's happy face smiles serenely up at you. For some reason, you're not getting the approval you anticipated, and to make matters worse, everyone begins speaking at you simultaneously. They're using words like "units," "integrated," "hand's-on," and something foreign sounding like "Konos" and what was that other one..."Weaver"? Maybe you've stumbled into a local crafter's club...you begin to feel hot with embarrassment.

Sound bizarre? I have witnessed similar scenes in other support group meetings. New homeschooling parents are still not familiar with the unit method of teaching, even though their children have been learning that way since birth. Although the unit-study approach is gaining popularity with the advent of wonderful unit-study materials, too many homeschoolers are trying to reproduce a system at home that is based on regular "school," which is usually a failure at home just as it is in the schools. Too many parents are settling for crumbs when, with the homeschooling advantage, they have been invited to a smorgasbord.

The homeschooling adventure gives parents the daily opportunity to explore new avenues of learning, and to experiment with methods that work best for each child. It's about families learning together, without the confines of over-structure and constricting molds. The *key* to successful family learning is balance. Finding the mix which will give mom and dad the confidence they need, while providing the children with materials and methods tailored to their need to learn. Because textbooks abound, and because they represent a certain comfort level, most new homeschoolers start out with them. Textbooks provide that needed feeling of security. But the danger of frustration and failure is ever present when homeschooling parents try to copy traditional schooling methods at home. Too many parents and children become discouraged and burn out, trying to use methods and materials that are neither necessary nor productive in the tutorial environment of the family-school. I write these words from experience.

The unit-study method, considered the "Rolls Royce of learning" by master teachers, can easily be integrated into any homeschool program, and before long, your children will be begging you for more "school"!

UNIT STUDIES...

"Unit Studies," "Project Studies," or "Integrated Learning"—whatever it's called, this method takes advantage of the child's natural curiosity and works with the natural learning processes to produce real education that's also fun! This approach integrates several subjects and skill areas while focusing on a central theme. Combining a variety of books, resources, and learning tools, it fosters interest, creativity, thinking and reasoning skills, research skills, in-depth learning, and motivation for learning. The whole family can participate. Each child can work around the same theme, but work on different activities according to their individual skill level. Even mom and dad can get into the act.

I am not going to tell you to throw your textbooks away. No, even textbooks can be useful and can become a starting point. Used as an encyclopedia, they can be valuable for simple research. Since they deal with topics that are normally covered in most school systems—this gives you a track to follow with your children. One textbook can be used for several children, and for different aged children. You can even mix and match—taking topics out of various textbooks—finding related stories in reading texts—using other textbooks just for map work or research like you would use encyclopedias. (Good high-school texts are particularly useful for this.) Look through various levels of textbooks for similar topics and create an index for reference purposes, or better yet, take the texts apart, label them by grade level, and file the related sections in manila folders. (Yes, cut them apart.)

A PERSONAL ILLUSTRATION

Our family got involved in a unit on astronomy which I thought might last for a week or two, and which actually stretched into about 9 weeks. Jill was around 6th grade level and Jonathan was in 2nd grade. We started by using Jill's science text for basic information. She looked up important scientists and inventors related to the study of astronomy in her textbook chapter, and made a list of vocabulary words for us to study and learn. We decided to begin a simple search of the solar system, so we began with the nine planets.

We each chose three (this was before we knew there might be ten)—mom was included in this project. After reading about the planets in a couple of textbooks we had, the children decided that there just wasn't enough information—Jonathan was particularly interested in Pluto. So we set off for the library and ended up bringing home about 40 books—not only on the planets, but about astronomers, inventions, rocket ships, space travel, some videos, and even some star-chart maps—all different levels, and most with lots of pictures and illustrations. I even found some interesting storybooks with good information, which would be enjoyable as well as educational. Jill decided to read about Galileo and Johannes Kepler. Jonathan wanted to know more about the sun and the moon, and all of us decided we wanted to stretch this learning experience to include the stars and space exploration. And we definitely wanted to build a model of the solar system somehow. So, I knew that the rest of the texts and workbooks would have to be laid aside for a while.

Spelling and vocabulary centered around "astronomy" words. Reading lessons were taken right from the books that they had chosen from the library. Instead of doing a lot of written question and answers, we spent really meaningful time on discussion—on questions that the kids raised as we went along (critical thinking). And instead of me trying to answer the questions, we spent a lot of time looking things up. That, by the way is called "developing research skills." Writing skills were developed in similar fashion, as Jill wrote a paper on Johannes Kepler, and Jonathan dictated what he had learned for me to write down. Our solar system model was the icing on the cake. Of course, the whole unit was a science project that eventually launched us into history. As we read biographies of scientists and inventors we studied periods of history, located countries and cities on maps and began developing a timeline.

We researched the planets, their moons, characteristics, sizes, distance from the sun, *et cetera*. After we decided to use our kitchen ceiling as "space," Jill calculated the sizes and distances of the solar system to scale—which, incidentally, was math—and no easy job. Only one-fourth of the sun would fit in one corner and that took Jonathan almost a whole day to make and paint. The scale of measurement had to be adjusted several times so we would have planets that could be seen with the naked eye. Jill finally decided that the Earth should be 1" and we took it from there. As we became involved with the stars, starting with the sun, of course, that study took us further into space exploration, which led us back to early explorers and the development of navigation. This unit became almost limitless but it propelled us into the new frontiers of outside-the-textbook creativity and unit studies.

Now, here comes the "roll your sleeves up and get to work" part. Are you imagining yourself drowning in piles of books and supplies while all dreams of contact with the adult social world fade into a "unit study fog"? Take heart. It's never as hard as we imagine! Usually.

SCHEDULING YOUR DAY

In planning units of study for your family, one of the most difficult things to envision is the actual scheduling of your day—"How is this going to look on paper?" or "How am I going to justify this as bona fide schoolwork in my lesson planner for the end-of-year assessment?" Just thinking about this can send homeschooling moms into a panic! On pure reflex-action, they reach for that stack of workbooks and start mechanically writing page numbers in their plan book. After studying this common phobia, I came to the conclusion that the nagging fear for most parents was that their children might not be getting the basic skills in a "correct" way.

Although I would really like to convince you that reading, language arts and math skills can be fully developed with the unit study approach (and it is possible), I personally feel that these areas are more likely to be enriched through units. For the sake of parental sanity and discernible progress in the children, I recommend that you set aside a daily "skills" period—perhaps thirty minutes to one-hour per day when the children follow a regular routine in math and language arts. During this time they will practice sequentially the skills that might really need work—again, depending on the needs of your child. A reminder: please avoid the temptation of assigning mounds of superfluous pages and problems just for the sake of filling up your lesson planner.

When looking for materials to build the 3 R's skills, the choices are many. I have personal favorites, as do you, and I tend to favor those materials that will creatively motivate learning. Look for integrated language arts programs that combine spelling, vocabulary, grammar, writing, and penmanship with wholesome, practical reading. Games and hands-on arithmetic materials are always effective and especially important for younger children. In developing any curriculum plan, try to find ways to incorporate three important modalities: hands-on activities (kinesthetic learning), observation activities (visual learning), and listening/verbal (auditory learning). Educational research is proving this to be key in developing the widest range of thinking and learning skills; this is why units are so effective.

RECORD KEEPING

So, with this in mind, when the time to "document" comes along, you will be able to show a separate period for Math and, under Language Arts, reading, spelling, penmanship, writing, grammar. The Unit Studies section of the day or week will form a larger heading and take up more space. Here you will list activities and perhaps code them: (B) Bible (R) reading, (SR) silent reading, (OR) oral report, (WR) writing, (SC) science, (SS) social studies, (M) math, (GE) geography *et cetera*. For instance, under Unit Studies for Tuesday you might write, "...made salt dough relief map of our state (GE, SS); read about our state government and gave a report to dad at dinner" (SS, R, OR).

Don't forget to give credit where credit is due in other areas of learning. Cooking can be (CH)emistry, (M)ath, and (PR)actical living. Hobbies, jobs and recreational activities provide some of the most important learning times, and can be categorized under Home Economics, Auto Shop, Gym, Mechanics, Computer, Woodworking, Economics, *et cetera*. Also, reading in any subject area can fall under the official heading of (R) Reading. Be flexible and creative.

DOCUMENTATION...

Now that you're ready to document your unit-study plan, your next task is to actually plan a unit. Start with the books you have on hand. The grade level doesn't really matter because you are looking for topics. Find a unit or chapter that looks especially interesting—this will motivate you, and your excitement, in turn, will motivate your children. Interest is the first motivator for learning. Find a unit with interesting people to study about or a topic that is particularly appealing. You might go ahead and choose six topics from different textbooks—perhaps three in science and three in social studies...this is only a suggestion for organizational purposes. Choose topics that will lend themselves well to other resources you have on hand. Think: "What kinds of activities could I include under this topic? What kinds of field trips could we plan? Who do I know that might know something about this topic—friends, relatives, neighbors, church members, business owners...the librarian?" Librarians love homeschoolers because we are really interested in finding out about all the free things we can get from the library. They like that. Your community can be your greatest resource.

The next step in planning your study is quite simple. Look through the book, chapter, or unit you have chosen and brainstorm. Quickly scan and write down the things that "jump out" at you. Notice pictures, illustrations, boldfaced words, titles, maps, charts, animals, plants, people, and places... anything that impresses your mind on an initial quick-scan of the chapter material. Take your list—and there might be twenty things or more—and begin to group them into manageable topics.

An example: A typical chapter on Central America may yield a veritable gold mine of topics, but try to limit them depending on the ages of your children. Some likely topics might be: The Original Native Population, Christopher Columbus' Early Explorations, Central American Geography, Central American Plants and Animals, Central America Today. An in-depth learning experience involving 3 or 4 topics is far superior to a shallow perusal of dozens of unrelated facts that are quickly forgotten after the test. This chapter provides enough for social studies, history, geography, geology, natural science and political science. Then go back through the section and pick out a few details to include under each topic, such as these two:

Original Native Population:	Central American Geography:
Tribes	Mountainous Regions
Customs	Desert Regions
Economy	Islands
Education	Rivers
Language	Coastal
Religions	Plains
Food	Jungles
Recreation	

Again, make this as general or as detailed as you like. It is best to sit down with the children and decide which topics really catch their interest. You can encourage each child to choose topics of their choice and let them share their learning with the rest of the family, or you can work together on topics, suggesting easier projects to the younger students, and more complicated ones to the older students. As you become more secure, you'll find the children will be naturally excited about certain areas...so please let them go and explore to their heart's content. And don't even try to keep up!

SKILLS TO INCLUDE:

As briefly discussed earlier, include: vocabulary, reading, spelling, oral reports, written work, research, hands-on experience with the topic, art, music, literature, and practical life application. Start with the vocabulary of the unit or topic; a good text usually includes this somewhere in the chapter—or go through the section and pick out key words—words that will be meaningful to the study of the topic. Assign these to older children for vocabulary building and spelling.

If your topic study will include important people, have the children choose several from the chapter and start researching, taking basics from the textbooks and then locating more information from library books, encyclopedias, interviewing people, or visiting a museum. By all means, mom and dad, try not to have all the answers for your students, no matter how brilliant you want your offspring to think you are. Help them formulate the questions that need to be answered, and lead them in the direction where they'll find the answers. Good teachers encourage young minds to explore and search, and in that process, life-supporting skills are developed.

Reading is topic related. Find a variety of reading materials for the children to explore—books can include fiction, non-fiction, magazines, dictionaries, encyclopedias, almanacs, newspapers, picture files, maps, charts, *et cetera.* Have a period set aside daily where you read something together— either taking turns, or with mom or dad reading. At our house we used to call it STORY STOP, and it was one of our favorite times right after lunch. Then, talk about what you read. Everyone has an opinion, and children need to be encouraged to organize and share their thoughts verbally. You can also get more "reports" and research accomplished if you let the children give more oral presentations and fewer written reports. When it comes down to writing, get creative!

SOME MORE IDEAS ...

Here are some ideas for your children: Instead of simply copying mundane facts and figures, try imagining how certain people felt when particular things happened to them, and how they would describe their situation, or write a journal from someone's perspective, or write a play enacting some things you have learned. Sometimes children don't want to write because they haven't mastered spelling or penmanship, so perhaps you can spark their interest by using a typewriter, word processor, or computer. Younger children need to get their ideas on paper before those thoughts 'escape,' so I encourage you to let them dictate their stories to you or older siblings. The very process of thought organization is an important pre-writing skill. Get your children to think in terms of "Cause and Effects." What really caused this war? ...what really motivated Columbus to do what he did? ...what would have happened if he had turned back...? Children need to learn about decision-making and how the consequences can be of historic proportions.

For hands-on experience, glean ideas from your reading and research for projects and field trips. Make models of things, draw pictures, dress the way they would have during a certain time period, create the menus of various countries, learn customs and try practicing them. Draw maps, real and imaginary, play games—there are all kinds of educational ones available—or use your computer to supplement. Plan field trips, or watch videos or films. If you can, try to include time period art and literature in the study of a famous person or event. This can also encompass the philosophies and religions of an age or a culture. Another effective yet simple activity is the creation of a timeline. Building onto it as you go along over the years is a creative and interesting learning experience.

I hope you can see that one thing always seems to lead to another. Once you get the "hang" of it you will probably be hooked...and it can all start with textbooks. One mother recently wrote me after reading one of my articles,

"Thank you for your encouragement. I started a unit study on Greece and we love it. It's fun and the children are really learning. Although I am still apprehensive, we are trying to break our old ways of using standard worksheets and textbooks. You helped dismiss many of those concerns for which I am grateful." (A. V., MA)

Try, and keep trying. You can achieve unit study success!

Home-Organization Resources

Christian Family's Complete Household Organizer by Greg and Sono Harris. Reproducible household management forms, personal record forms, as well as forms for homeschool planning and record keeping.

Choreganizer—motivational chore chart program to help keep children on track with daily household responsibilities. www.unitstudies.com/about

Clutter's Last Stand by Don Aslett. All about getting your house clean and organized! www.cleanreport.com

Creative Home Organizer by Emilie Barnes. Tips on all aspects of home management. www.morehours.bizland.com

Is There Life After Housework? by Don Aslett. Hints on home organization and cleaning shortcuts. www.cleanreport.com

Keepers at Home Organizer is a three-ring binder, divided into 12 monthly sections, that organizes everything imaginable, including convention shopping list, "company coming" planner, garden layout grid, as well as weekly, monthly, quarterly, and yearly home-maintenance schedule. These forms are NOT reproducible but do come with forms for a year's supply of planning. Refill packs are available. http://home.earthlink.net/~cmautry/keepers/index.html

OrganizedHome.com—A website offering comprehensive organizational tips and tools, including attractive and professional-looking planner pages to download.

Managers of Their Homes by Steve and Terri Maxwell, homeschool parents of eight children. In-depth, how-to book for organizing home, school, and life. Included are sample schedules and a "Scheduling Kit" to get you started. www.Titus2.com

Sink Reflections by Marla Cilley. Complete instructions on how to develop routines and schedules, and how to maintain a clean, uncluttered house. Most of the information is available on the extremely helpful website, www.flylady.net, and you can sign up for daily e-mails to support you and keep you on track.

Mega-Cooking by Jill Bond. Focus not only on plan-ahead, prepare-ahead meals but also on home- and time-management techniques. Includes recipes, methods, and reproducible forms to help you become a professional home manager.

Once-A-Month Cooking by Mary Beth Lagerborg and Mimi Wilson. A user-friendly guide to preparing a month's worth of food at a time. Includes detailed shopping, cooking, and freezing instructions.

Feed Your Family For $12 a Day and *15-Minute Cooking* by Rhonda Barfield. The classic *Feed Your Family on $50 a Week* has been updated and republished, and is full of extremely helpful advice, and Mrs. Barfield's extremely practical 15-minute cooking system is a real time-saver.

TIME MANAGEMENT
More Hours in My Day by Emilie Barnes. Wonderful tips on time management and household organization. www.morehours.bizland.com/tes

The Successful Homeschooler by Raymond and Dorothy Moore. Addresses "burnout" and how to avoid it. www.moorefoundation.com

SCHOOL PLANNING AND ORGANIZATION
Garden Patch of Reproducible Homeschooling Planning and Educational Worksheets contains every type of school form imaginable, as well as some home management. Available at the location below in book format or on CD ROM, so you can print your own.

Harris Homeschool Planner—useful reproducible forms for student and teacher, as well as suggestions for their use.

Home Style Teaching by Raymond and Dorothy Moore. Outlines how to organize and begin teaching your children. Promotes teaching children to work, and includes ideas for home-based businesses for children.

How to Homeschool by Gayle Graham. A guide to organization, goal setting, and teaching. A wealth of excellent ideas and principles. Reproducible forms included.

Relaxed Record Keeping by Mary Hood. Ten comprehensive steps to record keeping so that you may establish your own record-management system.

Teaching Your Children at Home by Virginia Birt Baker. Advice on set-up of your homeschool program, with scheduling and curriculum ideas.

RECORD KEEPING
Homeschooler's Journal—spiral-bound lesson plans and other useful forms intended to provide a permanent record for the school year. Available from Rainbow Resource Center, approximately $9.

Homeschooler's High School Journal—on the same pattern as the previous journal, but with extra lines and an area to record time spent on each lesson in quarter hour increments. Also available from Rainbow Resource Center, approximately $9.

Student Weekly Assignment Book—spiral bound, 7" x 11," 48 pages, five days at a glance. Eight lines for each day of the week. Available from Rainbow Resources .

NOTE: All of the previous resources can be found in either of these two locations as well as numerous other homeschool curriculum supply businesses:

Rainbow Resource Center
Route 1, Box 159A
50 North, 500 East Road
Toulon, IL 61483
1-888-841-3456
www.rainbowresource.com

Lifetime Books & Gifts
3900 Chalet Suzanne Drive
Lake, Wales FL 33853
1-800-377-0390

WEBSITES

For those families with Internet access, the following we sites have a large selection of forms and charts to copy free of charge. Many offer specialty papers for graphing, journaling, or early elementary handwriting. While there are many web addresses out there that may offer these same forms, these listed have an extensive list available *at no charge.*

The first site is easy to use. The list of forms comes up on the home page, just point and click on the type of form you want.

www.donnayoung.org Includes scheduling and planning forms, specialty papers, math grids, and lots more!

These next site has a list on the left side of their home page where you must click the appropriate category to get to the site to download forms.

http://home.att.net/~bandcparker Scroll down to "tools and equipment" and click on Internet resources for homeschoolers.

These remaining sites have items to purchase as well as "freebies."

www.teach-nology.com/web_tools This is an educators website, not just for homeschoolers. BUT, they have made software available to create cross-word puzzles, rubrics, word search puzzles, progress reports, *et cetera.*

www.thehomeschoolshop.com

www.homeschooling.about.com

www.homeeducatorsresource.com (click "free stuff")

www.eddirectory.com

Section F

Teaching Tips

Compiled by Janice Campbell

Additional Articles on the CD
BE SURE TO CHECK OUT THESE OTHER GREAT ARTICLES ON THE CD

Each article in the book and on the CD has been carefully chosen by the section coordinator to increase your knowledge and understanding of this subject, so don't forget to use and enjoy the parts of the manual on your CD, as well as the part you are holding.

Please note that the page numbering on the CD is different from that of the hard-copy manual.

Teaching Tips Introduction

One thing I'd like to make perfectly clear—there is no single perfect way to teach a subject. I've chosen a small selection of articles by homeschooling veterans who present simple, practical ways to teach specific subjects and skills. If you've read the *How to Begin* section, you know that each of your children will have a learning style that is uniquely his own, and you will have a natural bent toward a specific style of teaching. While you work with the special combination of styles that is your family, I hope you will glean some interesting and helpful ideas from the experience of others.

I wish you joy in your homeschool journey.

—Janice Campbell

The Learning Moment

Theresa Willingham

Of all the discoveries I've made while homeschooling my three children over the last seven years, that of what I like to call "the learning moment" is one of the most delightful and useful. The "learning moment" is one of those effervescent occurrences like the precise moment a sunset is at it's most beautiful, a piece of music is at its most moving, or shared time with someone is at its most memorable. It's one of those times you have to seize or lose forever. I guess I would define the "learning moment" as that precise instant when an educational opportunity naturally presents itself interestingly and in context, in such a way that it can be built upon and expanded with the maximum of learning obtained.

It's a "moment" that occurs in everyone's life at various times, and quite frequently in children's lives, but is viable only if recognized. To children ensconced in the artificial environment of a public school, such moments may be few and far between and then seldom caught when they occur. In the homeschool, the "learning moment" can be readily captured if we learn to recognize it, and it can make the difference between grasping a concept forever, or having to repeat it endlessly unless another fortuitous moment brings it home.

We recently experienced a good "learning moment" while the children and I were in a pet shop. "School" was the furthest thing from our minds as we admired the animals. Among the creature treasures was a terrarium with two young rats in it. My daughter, a big rodent fan, wanted a closer look and the pet shop proprietor cheerfully accommodated her, placing one of the rats in her cupped hands. We were enchanted as the creature sat comfortably and groomed itself in her palm. It's fur was silky and soft, its eyes bright and curious. As we were admiring the rat, another child walked by and reaching towards it, exclaimed, "Oh, how cute! What kind of animal is it?"

"A rat," my daughter replied.

As if she'd touched a hot iron, the other child's hand recoiled and she drew back in horror. "Oh, gross!" she cried and hurried away.

My daughter laughed and remarked, "That's funny. She thought it was really cute until she learned what it was."

Just like that, a learning moment was upon us and I automatically seized it. "Yes," I agreed with my daughter. "And is it really any less cute than she thought it was before?"

"No," she replied. "Why should it be?"

"It shouldn't be," I replied. "But sometimes, people have "preconceived" notions about things and that colors how they see things—or how things can seem to change before their eyes.

"What's 'preconceived' mean?"

"That means making up your mind about something based on what you *think* you already know about it, even though sometimes what you know about it may be incorrect."

And now the moment was underway, and as we walked out of the store, our conversation segued into discrimination and prejudice. Now we were talking about how people sometimes feel about other people based on preconceived notions they have about culture and ethnicity. We recalled an event where a family member had enjoyed speaking to someone on the phone and then registered surprise when she discovered the person she had been speaking to was black.

"Why should that change the enjoyment she had when she thought the person she was speaking to had a different skin color?" I asked.

"It shouldn't," my daughter replied.

"Is that any different than what happened in the pet shop?" I asked.

No, my daughter replied. Someone had thought an animal was cute until they found out what the animal was and—though that specific animal itself had done nothing offensive—then it was no longer cute. We were even able to extend the concept to nations and their preconceived notions of one another that drive foreign policy and fuel wars.

That single incident with the rat in the pet shop triggered a wealth of learning and conversation that even found it's way into dinner table conversation when Daddy came home, and he was able to add his own unique perspective to it. I could never have driven home as much information and understanding about discrimination, prejudice, culture, tolerance, and open mindedness from a book as that single incident accomplished "hands on," in context, and in real time. And even that would not have been as effective if we had not had other "learning moments" to recall and build upon (such as the telephone incident we drew on for comparison).

In the homeschool, few lessons will be as meaningful and memorable as those we draw from life itself. The secret lies not so much in knowing what to teach, as it does in recognizing when a learning opportunity has presented itself and acting on it. Lots of moments will escape us, though, despite our best efforts.

A few days ago, my husband found ants carrying aphids onto our citrus trees and called the children out to see. We were working around the house then, and only two of the children came and other things distracted us and we weren't able—or ready—to build upon the moment fully, so it was only partially successful. Other times, a moment presents itself and for various reasons, I can't share it with the children at all. And sometimes, I just plain get it wrong. The lesson I see in the moment isn't something that captures their interest or understanding, or is inappropriate for their ages and intellects.

Sometimes, the "learning moment" is a delicate balancing act.

With practice, though, and if we don't get too caught up in "book learning," we can learn to recognize those all-important learning moments and run with them. Grasping a learning moment is a lot like running with a kite. You run and pull the string and dodge about, trying to catch the right breeze, watching the kite bounce higher and higher until the wind catches it. Then the string goes whistling through your hands and the kite is lofted up into the sky, and your heart just soars with the accomplishment and wonder of it all!

Catching a learning moment makes both your children's and your own heart soar with understanding and delight. It's worth the slight extra effort it takes to recognize such a moment and run with it. And best of all, the memory of flying the kite of knowledge and understanding high and free with your children will be with you a lifetime!

Theresa Willingham is a freelance writer living in Tampa, FL with her husband Steve, and their three children, who have been homeschooled from birth. Theresa writes a monthly "Home Learning" column for the St. Petersburg Times, and has written for *Home Education Magazine* (where this article originally appeared), *Life Learning* and other periodicals. Her first book, the *Food Allergy Field Guide: A Lifestyle Manual for Families* (Savory Palate) was awarded first place in its category by the Colorado Independent Book Publishers Association in 2001.

Multilevel Homeschooling

Tamara Eaton

With experience, most moms of several children become experts at multitasking—although don't let anyone convince you that it's as simple to homeschool a bunch as it is one or two. Those same people use the argument that once you have so many children, adding more doesn't make a difference. Each child makes a difference (otherwise, why does it seem so different if even one or two of them are gone for a while?), but we can trust the Lord to enable us to care for them and homeschool them. The multiplied joy more than makes up for the sometimes-multiplied challenges and trials!

We often are asked how we manage to homeschool multiple learning levels, and I find it difficult to explain. It's like preparing a seven-course dinner: How do you tell someone exactly how to prepare everything in such a way that it's all ready at the proper time and stays the proper temperature?

I suppose you could lead them step-by-step through all the directions and it would be easier, but experience is still the best teacher. And there is no way we could have a "normal" homeschooling day if I had to take the time to write down each and every thing that was said and done. (I'd go crazy well before 9 a.m.—*Wait!! Slow down, children, I'm not getting all of this written down fast enough!*) Besides, each family is unique. No one else will have the exact same combination of personalities, learning styles, number of children, curriculum, and other circumstances that we have.

In the very early years, I worked separately with my oldest child while the younger ones played: Later the next oldest would sit in on what we were doing and start to pick up things, and I would spend a few minutes introducing her to new things, too. We talked about things as we did the laundry, cleaned house, cooked, played, *et cetera*—in all those ways parents teach and influence their children every day.

Eventually, we wound up on several different levels of math and reading, but did history and science together by reading aloud the books and discussing the textbooks that were on one of their levels. We filled in any gaps by extra explanations to the younger one and older one. There would be times when one of the children would leap ahead or others would need extra attention in an area, and then I provided help or used different materials. Since we used a lot of "real books" in our homeschooling (not limited to one grade level), this helped. We also worked to give them the basic tools they needed for independent studies and encouraged them from an early age to spend even five or ten minutes working on something while we were nearby, but not watching over their shoulder.

During one period when my youngest two were babies, I had the older three children in one level of BJU (*Bob Jones University Press Textbooks*) English, which made it much easier. This method worked for three years. Later we used another basic high-school grammar course and writing materials geared more toward independent studies. During this same period, my fourth child used a different BJU English textbook, but she participated in the older girls' history and science studies, while my older son worked independently on a higher level. For example, we used one of BJU's *Heritage Studies* as a "springboard" to more studies using real books for the girls, and my older son did a separate BJU course. This was during a time when I had a very active toddler and a nursing baby, and it was helpful to have a combination of texts and books so I didn't have to spend hours supervising and planning things. So, for some years, we were able to cover some of the same subjects with some of the children at the same time, but it was unrealistic to think we could do this all the time for every subject. Some children also prefer to work alone, rather than in groups.

For several years now, my older children have preferred to do mostly independent studies, with the exception of occasional unit studies. Recently they studied Classical composers and their enthusiasm was so contagious that the younger children wanted to get involved, too! We no longer use as many textbooks, but have a traditional high school program on CD-Rom that the teens are using along with reading a large variety of good books and writing a lot. Our "unit studies" tend to focus on using books and materials to research topics in depth and don't always include hands-on projects. Our older children, though, are involved in our family business and ministry, which is the ultimate hands-on project!

I am now doing very much the same thing with my younger two that I did with my oldest two when they were this age: We do things separately for math and reading, but read aloud and discuss books for history and science. Some things go over my youngest child's head, but that's fine. There is no pressure. Her slightly older brother is advanced in some areas, so we help him research his interests and make sure he stays challenged.

In summary, these are the things that have helped us the most in teaching many different levels simultaneously:
- Training our children to be obedient. Otherwise, what a lot of wasted time goes into, "*JOHNNY, FOR THE TENTH TIME, I TOLD YOU NOT TO DO THAT!*") [See "Training Children (And Parents!)" at www.chfweb.com.]
- Training our children to be responsible and help with the house as they get older so all the burden doesn't fall on Mom—thus freeing up Mom's time to help with all the different children. [See Homeschool & Housework in the *Planning and Organization* section.]
- Not structuring our homeschool to be a "school at home."

- Having a basic structure to our day, yet allowing room for flexibility.
- Staying home a lot.
- Encouraging each child to learn to play alone at times without having to be "entertained" by another.
- Teaching each child to respect our need to sometimes have quiet time to work with another child.
- Giving our children the tools they need for independent studies.
- Choosing curriculum that doesn't require too much advance preparation, and that teaches concepts as simply as possible.
- Teaching children the same subjects together whenever possible and adjusting them to fit each level. (Especially when they're younger and not ready for independent studies.)
- Helping them learn to be self-motivated and responsible in their assignments and, eventually, planning their own schooling—with our direction, when needed. [*For more help on this topic, see* "Let's Get Motivated!" and "Motivation Tips!" on www.chfweb.com.]
- Encouraging them to help each other when needed. Often while one child was waiting for me to have time to explain something, another sibling was able to explain it perfectly.
- Allowing the older ones to tutor the younger ones in favorite subjects or to lead a discussion on what they've been learning.
- Concentrating on the "basics" when the children are young instead of too many neat-sounding projects or tangents. There will be time when they're older to make *papier mache'* models of the solar system, *et cetera*. (Unless you just *love* this sort of thing—in which case, it won't cause you stress!)

Sometimes people read what we've written about our homeschooling experiences and feel overwhelmed—not remembering that we've done these things over a period of many years, not all in one school year. There will be time for projects when the two-year-old is no longer two! I no longer have little ones, so we now have freedom to pursue projects and activities that were once difficult when we had toddlers in the house. Plus we have another advantage now: The children are old enough to clean up their own messes!

Whatever your children's ages or levels, you can be confident that God has a homeschooling plan just perfect for your family. Take time to thank Him today for showing you His path and enabling you to walk in it joyfully.

"Now the God of hope fill you with all joy and peace in believing, that ye may abound in hope, through the power of the Holy Ghost." (Romans 15:13)

"Now unto Him that is able to keep you from falling, and to present you faultless before the presence of His glory with exceeding joy, to the only wise God our Saviour, be glory and majesty, dominion and power, both now and for ever. Amen." (Jude 1:24-25)

The ABC's of Learning to Read

Penny Gardner

During my first year of teaching in a first-grade classroom, I had an unforgettable experience. Two vivacious first-grade girls had been struggling for months trying to learn how to read. Then one day in February, the light turned on in their minds. Things started clicking. They had been crawling at a snail's pace but suddenly they were soaring. This was one of the reasons I decided to teach my children at home—I wanted to be the one who was there to experience each leap in understanding as it occurred. What is more exciting than watching your child learn to read? On the other hand, it may be intimidating to feel the responsibility of helping your child with this critical academic skill. From my three years as a first-grade teacher (set your mind at ease—an innovative teacher), from the research I've done over the years, and from the opportunity to learn from our home-school experiences over the past eleven years, I have some thoughts to share.

A—READ ALOUD.

Reading aloud is one of the most essential and pleasurable ways of sharing the joy of reading. Experts agree that reading aloud is the most important activity we can do to prepare our children to read. We sit with our children crowded around us to read some favorite stories. In our family, we usually have a "chapter" book in progress for the older children. During other sessions, we read picture books for the younger children.

Don't make the mistake of thinking that once your children know how to read that you should stop reading aloud. I remember my elementary teachers reading aloud to the class but it didn't profoundly affect me until my sixth grade teacher read *The Hobbit*. I couldn't wait to come in from lunch recess to hear the next chapter. When Mrs. Colburn finished the novel, I reread it on my own. It launched me into reading more challenging material like *The Three Musketeers*. You never know which book will touch someone's life—or when.

B—DON'T RUSH ACADEMICS.

Some parents seem to base their success on how early their child learns to read. After studying David Elkind's *Miseducation: Preschoolers at Risk*, and books by Raymond and Dorothy Moore, I decided that a late start is often a better start. This has been confirmed several times by our own endeavors.

Ruth Beechick calls the moment of readiness "the optimum learning time." She says if we wait until the child shows readiness and interest, the child will learn faster and easier. In her excellent book, *A Home Start in Reading*, Beechick sites a study where one group of kindergarten children focused on reading skills and another group focused on science, learning about the world around them. Three years later, the science group outscored the reading group in their reading test scores. Many prominent people were late readers, so don't worry if your child is around eight or nine years old before he takes off.

Follow the child's lead; instead of pushing, let him come to you with questions or discoveries. At age two, my daughter was delighted with her magnetic letters. She'd spend hours at her little desk, often asking me what a certain letter was. By age four, she knew most of the sounds, because of her own motivation, so I thought she would be an early reader. Surprisingly, things didn't "click" for her until she was almost eight. Even though she had the tools, she didn't have the maturity to master reading. There is more to reading than simply knowing phonetic sounds. I've heard it said that the ability to read is a gift from God; God does things in his own time.

C—HELP YOUR CHILD UNDERSTAND PRINT.

At the end of the very first day of my second year of teaching first grade, a little girl came up to me nearly in tears. She looked at me and said, "But, Teacher, we can't go home yet. I haven't learned to read." She tugged at my heartstrings so strongly that the next day I came prepared with predictable books and activities so that by the end of that second day of school every child would feel like he or she could read. The little girl was happy to go home the second day as a successful reader—ready to show her parents what she had learned. Every child had a sense of accomplishment and success.

Predictable books are stories where the child can easily guess the text of the book because of a pattern, a rhyme, and/or the illustrations. You may want to try one of the activities below once a week in the early stages of learning to read, or simply enjoy reading predictable books together every day.

Print out songs and sing them, pointing to the words as you go. Write a familiar predictable story or nursery rhyme on a chart. Make three copies of it. Let your child become acquainted with the chart by reading it to him, by reading it together, and by allowing him to explore it on his own. Then help your child cut a copy of the chart into sentence strips. He can place the strips on the corresponding sentences on the chart. Or he can arrange them in order (or a silly order) without the chart. Later, help him cut the third chart into word cards. He can match the words onto the sentence strips or the story chart. Or he can make up original sentences from the word cards. These kinds of experiences help children realize that the whole is broken down into sentences, then into words, then into sounds. This is called global learning or learning from the top down; experts claim it is the way most children learn. Charlotte Mason, always ahead of her time, recommended a very similar approach for teaching reading. In the first volume of her series, she wrote of using 'Twinkle, Twinkle' and 'I Love Little Pussy' and word cards for learning to read.

Several times during the school year, I would post a large chart of a song we had learned together somewhere in the classroom. I wouldn't mention it but quietly watched as the students discovered the new addition. One of the better readers would usually figure it out first. Then even the non-readers would go to the chart, point to each word, and "read" it, since they, too, knew the song. These types of activities start with what the child already knows, a nursery rhyme or song, and reinforces the concept of print. Children may need successful experiences like this throughout the sometimes long and frustrating road to becoming an independent reader.

D—TEACH THE CODE.

You don't need to invest a large amount of money in a phonics program. All you need are homemade flashcards, pencil and paper, lower-case magnetic letters, and an excellent book, *Reading Reflex*, by Carmen and Geoffrey McGuinness. This book and Beechick's book get my highest recommendation.

This is not your typical approach to phonics. The book starts by teaching the "basic code" or what I used to think of as simple phonics. Basic code is one symbol representing one sound, the most common sound. The authors state:

> "*The first step in learning to read is understanding the nature of our written code. There are symbols that represent sounds. Each time we see one of the symbols, we are supposed to say the sound that it represents. We make our way through the word and when we get to the end we have meaning...*
>
> "*[This method] has been researched and proven to work on children age four to adult non-readers. It takes what the child knows, the sounds of his language, and teaches him the various* sound pictures *that represent those sounds.*"

By sound pictures or symbols, the authors are referring to the letter or combination of letters that represent a sound.

Have a few linguistic or easy phonetic readers available. There are stories in *Reading Reflex* but I don't particularly enjoy them. So I have adapted the order that sound pictures are presented to follow Set One of the Bob Books. On my website, http://members.aol.com/PennyGar/, you will find word cards and a bingo sound game to accompany the books. I do wish that Bob Books would come out with a set that gives lots of practice with adjacent consonants (sometimes referred to as blends). There is another set of phonetic readers that I recommend you use as well. *Ready for Reading Ant* and *Ready for Reading Caterpillar* provide more practice with the basic code. This series assumes that the child knows the basic code, whereas the Bob Books introduce sounds gradually. "*Silly Sentences*" is a fun way to get more practice at various beginning levels.

E—SIGHT WORDS.

When a child is learning the basic code, there are common words that don't follow what he has learned so far. A few of these irregular words can be taught as sight words when they occur in the Bob Books or other easy phonetic readers. Some sight words are more phonetic than others so have the student look for clues. Start with these words: *and, has, is, a, the, with, was, to, have, said*. "And" is the easiest word in this list and is met in the adjacent consonant section of *Reading Reflex*. The other words are covered in the advanced code but they are so common that your beginning reader may need to learn them earlier.

Charlotte Mason stressed the importance of habits. If a child spells a word wrong, it may become a habit. Hindsight has shown me that invented spelling is not the best approach with these irregular words. Be thorough by teaching your child to spell each of these "weird words" and reviewing them often as they come up in his writing.

F—FLUENCY.

Rereading familiar books, nursery rhymes, and charts with songs or poems will help the child gain fluency and mastery of reading. Mark Thogmartin, author of *Teach a Child to Read with Children's Books*, suggests starting each reading instruction session by having the child reread a book you have already worked on. Having time to read on his own, as mentioned below, will help the child gain fluency.

Echo reading is wonderful for fluency. I like to do this on material that is slightly above the child's comfortable reading level. Use scriptures and great children's literature that is not predictable for echo reading. Sit close together so you can both follow along in the book. The parent points to each word as parent and child read aloud together, pausing very slightly after each phrase. Sometimes the parent will read a split second after the child, echoing him on the easier parts. Sometimes the parent will take the lead so the child is echoing the parent through the difficult parts. Echo reading helps greatly with fluency and expressive reading.

G—GIVE YOUR CHILD TIME TO READ ON HIS OWN.

John Holt wrote that children need time to figure things out for themselves. Many children have taught themselves how to read because they have been allowed this time. You might try to work in a quiet time after lunch when children may look at books, read, or nap. You might also allow a half-hour or hour of individual reading in bed at night. Perhaps your kids will read the familiar predictable books, nursery rhymes, or songs that you've been enjoying together during these quiet reading times. Once reading is mastered and the student is an independent reader, these silent reading sessions can become your "reading program." Parents should model reading during these and other times.

H—HOME: A WRITING-RICH ENVIRONMENT.

Write stories or experiences down for young children as they dictate to you, soon they will start doing the writing with your guidance. Thogmartin suggests that the child write a one or two sentence story each day as part of the reading lesson. He gives several good suggestions on helping the child to discover strategies for writing unknown words. For example, if the child has already learned to spell the word "my," help the child realize that he can easily spell the unknown word "by."

My children have all enjoyed writing before they learn to read. They ask how to spell certain words to make their own notes or they write a list of all the names of people in our family and extended family. Let children see you writing. Try having written conversations with your children. An early attempt might require only yes and no answers from the child. This may evolve into daily letter writing between family members to express feelings and work out problems.

Use patterns from predictable books to inspire original works. For example, after reading *The Bug in the Jug*, my then five-year-old daughter wrote and illustrated a book. It reads:

"This is a sheep. This is a jeep. This is the sheep in the jeep. This is a star. This is a jar. This is the star in the jar. This is a whale. This is a pail. This is the whale in the pail."

I—USE REAL BOOKS FOR YOUR READING PROGRAM.

Library books, inexpensive paperbacks, Bible stories, and magazines are much more interesting than basal readers. Avoid reading workbooks (typically students complete three to six workbook pages for each story they read) unless you want to instill an aversion to reading. I heard Jim Trelease, author of *The New Read-Aloud Handbook*, say that many Americans are alliterate (able to read but choose not to) because of the thousands of senseless workbook pages associated with reading that they were forced to do in school. Strive for a book-centered approach to reading.

J—RELAX AND ENJOY!

Keep things low-key. Avoid putting pressure on your child to read at a certain age. Don't try to dictate what he may read; we all like to choose our own reading material. If your child reads every book in a particular series, at least he's reading. You can expand horizons through your read-aloud program. Does testing for comprehension really have a place in the home when we can hear our children laugh (or cry) as they read? Discuss books with children informally or have them narrate the story line instead of requiring book reports.

Watching our own children learn how to read is a memorable event. Because of our decision to educate our children at home, we are present to experience the light turning on. We see things starting to click. How thrilling to observe a tentative reader turn into an avid one! Let's soar with our children into the fascinating world of reading.

SILLY SENTENCES: A MIX-AND-MATCH READING ACTIVITY

Silly Sentences provide fun practice with the three levels of code presented in *Reading Reflex*. This game is an enjoyable, homemade addition to your beginning reading program. This activity involves your child physically as he manually places two sentence parts together. Think of Silly Sentences as a reading manipulative. It involves chance and humor; we often chuckle together after reading a Silly Sentence. And the outcome is different each time you play. This game also works for an older child who may need a review of phonics but would be offended by a more "remedial" method. Even after my daughter was an excellent independent reader she would occasionally play Silly Sentences just for fun.

In the game, the child forms sentences by placing a beginning and an ending together. Here's an example of a couple of Silly Sentences placed in a logical arrangement:

The red brick   is here.

Glen   will jump.

Now, if your child happened to mix and match the sentence parts differently, he would end up with a sensible sentence and a ridiculous sentence:

Glen   is here.

The red brick   will jump.

I imagine this animated scene in my mind: A smiling brick, wearing red sneakers on the end of his skinny stick legs, jumps about wildly. Pretty hysterical!

To make your Silly Sentences game, highlight and copy the sentence suggestions you can find on my website and paste into your word processor, or make up your own. Make the print larger and take some care with the spacing so you will end up with spaces between phrases and between lines. All the sentence beginnings at each level should be printed on one sheet. All the sentence endings at each level go on another sheet. It's important to use large print, at least 24 points or larger.

Print out the sheet of sentence beginnings on one color of cardstock and print the sheet of sentence endings on a different color of cardstock. Choose pastel shades so the print shows up clearly. After laminating the sheets, cut into phrases using a paper cutter. Or, you may cut up the sheets you print on regular paper and glue them each to a slightly larger strip of construction paper or cardstock (one color for beginnings and another color for endings) and laminate. You may store the sentence beginnings in one envelope or zip lock bag and the endings in another.

Once the game becomes too easy for your child, it's time to make a more complex set of sentences. Set aside a little time to make these inexpensive, colorful manipulatives. Then let your child mix and match his way to fluent reading with Silly Sentences—and enjoy a few chuckles together along the way.

RECOMMENDED READING FOR PARENTS:

Reading Reflex by Carmen and Geoffrey McGuiness

A *Home Start in Reading* by Ruth Beechick

Simply Phonics by Laurie Hicks

Teach a Child to Read with Children's Books by Mark Thogmartin

Stories, Songs, and Poetry to Teach Reading and Writing by M. McCracken

Honey for a Child's Heart by Gladys Hunt

Miseducation: Preschoolers at Risk by David Elkind

Better Late Than Early and *School Can Wait* by Raymond Moore

Right-Brained Children in a Left-Brained World by Jeffrey Freed [I recommend this book if your child does not catch on to reading by age 9. Perhaps he learns differently.]

You Can Teach Your Child to Write

Janice Campbell

W riting—the art of communicating thoughts to the mind, through the eye—is the great invention of the world...Great, very great in enabling us to converse with the dead, the absent, and the unborn, at all distances of time and space; and great not only in its direct benefits, but greatest help to all other inventions. —Abraham Lincoln (1809-1865)

I have often been asked why students, especially young children, seem to dislike writing assignments. After talking with the parent, I usually find that it is a case of "too much, too soon." Parents often feel that if child can read fluently, he should also be able to write fluently. However, *reading and writing require different mental processes and motor skills.* While reading is primarily a mental process of decoding and comprehending words that have been put together by someone else, writing is much more complex. Not only must the student be able to comprehend words, he must draw upon his own limited knowledge or experience of a subject, organize his thoughts, choose appropriate words (and try to spell them correctly), and use his budding penmanship skills to put it all on paper. It's no wonder that children are overwhelmed by the task!

READINESS

How vain it is to sit down to write when you have not stood up to live!
—Henry David Thoreau (1817-1862)

It *is* necessary that children learn to write, but when should they be taught, and how? The timing varies for each child, depending on his mental and physical maturity level and his home life. A child who grows up in a home where books hold a place of honor—and television is rarely or never watched—will usually be light-years ahead of a child who spend his free time being mindlessly entertained by television or video games. Children who see their parents read and write for pleasure are likely to imitate them at a very young age, thereby increasing their readiness skills. Parents who spend time in conversation, enjoy a variety of creative pursuits, interact with nature and read aloud with the family, are providing for their children a content-rich atmosphere and sensory input that will help the children write with vividness, depth, and insight. Laura Ingalls Wilder is a wonderful example of the effectiveness of this "life-style learning." She was able to translate her rich childhood experience into prose that brings that period of history to life. I doubt that she wasted much of her childhood filling out workbooks and answering often-trivial comprehension questions.

Even though life in the twenty-first century is very different from the life recorded in *Little House on the Prairie*, the requirements for developing writing ability are the same for our children as they were for Laura Ingalls Wilder or any other writer: exposure to language and high-quality literature early in life, conversation and interaction with adults, personal experience with nature, time alone for developing thoughts, and much penmanship practice so that lack of fluency does not limit creative expression. Ideally, all these things (except penmanship practice) will be part of a child's life from the day he is born.

READING: THE FIRST STEP IN WRITING INSTRUCTION

The Six Golden Rules of Writing: Read, read, read, and write, write, write.
—Ernest Gaines (1996)

Even if reading and conversation haven't been a regular part of your home life, it's never too late to unplug the television and begin reading aloud and discussing good books with your child. This is the vital first phase of writing instruction—the construction of a sound foundation of literary experience—and ideally it should last from birth through high school, and even beyond, if the family enjoys it. Hearing good literature read aloud does several things:

- It allows the child to hear words put together in a way that is more powerful and expressive than ordinary conversation;
- It exposes the family to vocabulary they may not normally use;
- It often introduces people and places the family would never encounter in real life, opening an opportunity for exploration and understanding of other peoples and cultures;
- It provides an opportunity to internalize correct grammatical structures in an informal context;
- It often helps to create an atmosphere of emotional intimacy in which personal issues can be discussed in the context of the book's characters and situations.

Reading aloud is foundational, but if for some reason it is not possible to do it regularly, at least provide your family with books-on-tape. These can be borrowed from the library, rented, or purchased. Thousands of titles are available, including fiction, biography, poetry, and non-fiction. Books-on-tape usually have the added benefit of being read with perfect diction, which is not only helpful to understanding, but can also improve personal pronunciation.

BUILD SKILLS THROUGH COPYING AND NARRATION

We are what we write. —Michael Wood (1995)

Most children launch naturally into the second phase of writing instruction with very little prompting from the parent. Fingers clenched around a fat pencil, they work hard to copy the letters of their name, or a title for the drawing they have just created. At this stage, you will often hear, "Mommy, can you write [something] for me?" as they realize that letters put together in a certain order mean something. This is also the stage when they will want to re-tell (often at great length) a story you have read or they have heard on tape. Copying and re-telling, often called narration, are critical to the development of writing skills, as they develop many of the mental processes necessary to good writing.

COPYING

True ease in writing comes from art, not chance,
As those move easiest who have learn'd to dance.
—Alexander Pope (1688-1744)

The importance of copying is often underestimated, and it is discarded as soon as a child is able to write a few words on his own. This is unfortunate, for frequent copying of well-written sentences or paragraphs provides several benefits:

- The opportunity to see and reproduce properly written and punctuated writing many times before attempting to do it independently;
- The opportunity to become familiar with new words in a low-stress learning situation;
- Practice in handwriting without the distraction of trying to create content, and to remember how to format, spell, and punctuate it.
- Multi-sensory input tends to be memorable. If a child *sees* a word written, *says* the word to himself as he *writes* it, he has engaged several senses, and is likely to internalize the information after following the process over time.

The easiest way to approach copying is to use a piece of the child's lined paper—I like the size of the lined paper designed for third and fourth graders—and write a sentence, verse, or quotation, using the style of printing you are teaching your child. Skip a line between each line that you write, so that the child can form his letters directly beneath yours. This is much more practical than simply writing line after line of the same letter. It allows the child to see and copy proper letter and word spacing as well as proper letter formation, capitalization, and punctuation. Do this daily until the child is able to copy neatly and easily—a stage that girls seem to reach earlier than boys. If you want your children to learn italic writing, a beautiful and natural style, you can either learn it yourself in order to make the copy masters, or you can use a handwriting program such as *Fluent Handwriting* by Nan Jay Barchowsky. The logical, easy-to-use textbook is accompanied by a CD with installable fonts for the beautiful Barchowsky writing. It's fast and efficient to type in double-spaced text for your copy sheet, using a point size that is manageable for your child, and then to print out as many copies as needed.

NARRATION

Writing and speaking, when carefully performed, may be reciprocally beneficial, as it appears that by writing we speak with great accuracy, and by speaking we write with great ease.—Quintillion (circa A.D. 35-100)

During this stage of learning, you can use narration to begin working on the writing readiness skills of thought organization and sequencing. Read a story to your child and have him re-tell or narrate it back to you in sequence. Charlotte Mason, the nineteenth-century educator whose methods have been adapted for homeschooling by Susan Schaeffer Macaulay, Penny Gardner, and Karen Andreola, used retelling as a major learning tool and a means of evaluation. As the child listens to a story he chooses those parts that seem the most important, mentally organizes them, and chooses the words with which to narrate the story back to you. Just as writing helps an adult or older student detect gaps in his or her knowledge, so narration helps younger students to discover their strengths and weaknesses in listening and comprehension. Narration also allows the teacher to immediately detect and correct comprehension problems. Once a child has mastered the skills required for verbal narration, he will find it much easier to move into written narration than a child who has never had to organize and focus his thoughts in order to convey specific meaning.

DICTATION SHARPENS WRITING MECHANICS

When the child has gained skill in copying and narration, it is time to begin working with dictation. If you prefer to work with carefully planned and sequenced lessons, there are several good writing curricula such as *Imitations in Writing* and *Language Arts Through Literature* that use dictation as a foundation. Otherwise, you can simply choose a brief verse, rhyme, or quotation from a good book and dictate it to the child. Allow him plenty of time to write, then go over the paper with him, helping him to evaluate and correct the piece. You may be shocked to discover that the neat, careful handwriting the child has developed over the past few months of copying has almost completely disappeared! As the child turns his attention to capturing on paper words he cannot see, he will be distracted from his former focus on careful letter formation. Don't be alarmed—this is normal and with encouragement and practice will soon correct itself.

Continue practice with dictation, increasing the length and difficulty of the dictation pieces until you feel that the child has mastered the skills involved. Once the student is comfortable with dictation, he will be able to use writing as a means of communication, not only in birthday lists and captions for his drawings, but also for letters and stories. If you would like to provide supplemental practice in recognizing and correcting errors in punctuation and grammar, the *Great Editing Adventure* and the *Editor-in-Chief* workbooks are good resources.

COMPOSITION: CREATIVE AND EXPOSITORY WRITING

Next to the doing of things that deserve to be written, there is nothing that gets a man more credit, or gives him more pleasure than to write things that deserve to be read. —Pliny the Younger (circa A.D. 62-113)

The essence of writing is to know your subject.
—David McCullough (1933-)

Once your child has achieved fluency in copying (penmanship), narration (mental organization, sequencing, word choice), and dictation (spelling, punctuation, proof-reading), he is ready to add the skill of composition. This is the writing stage in which the student pulls together all the skills he or she has learned, and applies them to either creative or expository writing. Creative writing, which includes the composition of poetry, stories, and personal essays, usually seems to come more easily to girls than to boys, and it is a skill which has limited use in the adult world, except for the talented few who will become published writers. Expository writing, on the other hand, is useful in many situations throughout life. Expository writing includes reports and articles, descriptive, informative, and persuasive essays, and other non-fiction writing. The composition stage begins earlier for some children than for others, but most students are ready to begin sometime in the middle grades.

There are many textbooks available for teaching composition, but it is possible for a motivated student to become an excellent writer using what I call the "Ben Franklin method." In *The Autobiography of Benjamin Franklin*, Franklin relates how, after his father pointed out his lack of "elegance of expression," he taught himself to write more elegantly and expressively:

> *"About this time I met with an odd volume of the* Spectator*...I thought the writing excellent, and wished, if possible, to imitate it. With this view I took some of the papers, and, making short hints of the sentiment in each sentence laid them by a few days, and then, without looking at the book, try'd to compleat the papers again, by expressing each hinted sentiment at length, and as fully as it had been expressed before, in any suitable words that should come to hand. Then I compared my* Spectator *with the original, discovered some of my faults, and corrected them. But I found I wanted a stock of words, or a readiness in recollecting and using them....Therefore I took some of the tales and turned then into verse; and, after a time, when I had pretty well forgotten the prose, turned them back again. I also sometimes jumbled my collections of hints into confusion, and after some weeks endeavored to reduce them into the best order, before I began to form the full sentences and compleat the paper. This was to teach me method in the arrangement of thoughts. By*

comparing my work afterwards with the original, I discovered many faults and amended them; but I sometimes had the pleasure of fancying that, in certain particulars of small import, I had been lucky enough to improve the method or the language..." (35).

Franklin apparently pursued his self-education in writing during his early teens, and this is a reasonable age for students with a strong foundation in reading and dictation to begin working with more challenging assignments. There are several points to remember when teaching the composition stage of writing:

- It is not a speedy process—a completed composition sequence includes establishing a topic, gathering and organizing information, creating a rough draft, evaluating and improving the rough draft, and presenting a final draft;
- Much of the writing process is mental—leave time for brainstorming, and mental organization of ideas;
- Work with the student's natural learning style—some students enjoy visual organizing methods such as mind maps, others like the structure of an outline, and some prefer to do most of the pre-writing process mentally;
- It is not necessary to go through the entire composition sequence with every assignment, particularly if the student is writing frequently for other class work;
- Integrate writing lessons with other subjects by using the composition sequence for history, literature, or science topics;
- Early composition assignments should be brief—don't spring a five-page essay assignment on a student who is accustomed to dictation of no more than a page at a time;
- The writing process can be made less painful for reluctant writers by permitting them to choose topics they find interesting;
- A rich vocabulary is best developed through reading good literature, but extra instruction can be useful. *Vocabulary from Classical Roots* is by far my favorite of the available vocabulary workbooks series.

EVALUATING WRITING ASSIGNMENTS

Vigorous writing is concise. A sentence should contain no unnecessary words, a paragraph no unnecessary sentences, for the same reason that a drawing should have no unnecessary lines and a machine no unnecessary parts. This requires not that that the writer make all his sentences short, or that he avoid all detail and treat his subjects only in outline, but that every word tell. —William Strunk, Jr. (1869-1946), *The Elements of Style.*

The evaluation process is very important in helping the student learn to write. Ben Franklin apparently evaluated his own writing, using published writing as a standard of comparison. I would not expect most students to be motivated enough to do that, but parents can learn to evaluate by reading extensively. If you are not comfortable with your skill in evaluation, you may be able to find another homeschool mom or a friendly English major to evaluate your student's work and provide feedback. You can also seize the opportunity to improve your own skills, and learn to discern good writing by reading books such as *On Writing Well* by William Zinsser, *Elements of Style* by William Strunk and E.B. White, or *Evaluating Writing* by Dave Marks. Writing is the most permanent form of communication, and when you take the time to improve your own skills, you demonstrate to your students that you believe writing is important.

Finally, remember that the process of teaching writing does not begin with composition, but with reading. Without adequate input, a student cannot be expected to produce high-quality output. In order to avoid frustrating students and causing them to feel that they hate writing, you must provide plenty of information in the form of books to read, plenty of practice with the mechanical skills of copying, narration, and dictation, and plenty of time for the development and organization of ideas. It is just as difficult to wring water from a dry sponge as it is to extract meaningful writing from a child who has not been saturated in the written word. As a homeschool parent, you have the opportunity to gently shepherd your child into a world of literary delight, so relax and enjoy the process. You can do it!

Teaching History Using Literature

Carole Joy Seid

In the early years of being a homeschooling parent, when my son J.J. was a little boy, I would go to book fairs and spend tons of money on tons of things that I took home and never used. It became a very expensive habit. As the years wore on and I *kept* spending money for things that sat on my shelf, I began to ask myself, "Why do I keep buying this stuff?" I never felt comfortable using it, and after a week or two of enthusiasm and exhaustion it would wind up in a closet somewhere. It took a while, but I finally realized that I really didn't want someone telling me I had to do thirty minutes of geography on Tuesday morning at 10 o'clock and an hour of science on Friday at noon. On the other hand, I had friends who had their kids playing educational video games all day long, and their attitude was, "Oh, well! It's getting the job done and it's good for their hand-eye coordination." Other friends had their kids plunked down on the couch in front of educational videos all day. I knew that these methods were definitely not my style either, so I kept looking for my niche. What was my style of teaching and what felt right for me? What could I get up every morning and be enthusiastic about? What would work best for my son?

Over the course of several years, it gradually dawned on me that history is the logical core of all the rest of the curriculum. That is, if you want to build your own curriculum, history is the simplest, most common sense framework to build it on. History makes a great framework for all the other subjects because it follows a progression and covers everything else, such as art, music, science, literature, and so forth.

The other reason I decided history would make a good core curriculum, was that as a school teacher, both in public and Christian schools, I saw that our children are "American Historied" to death. The longer I taught and the longer I studied history myself, the more I realized that most children think the world began in 1492. They picture the history of humanity a lot like those gag maps you can buy that show the United States taking up most of the world, with just a little room left over for some of the other nations, like Mexico and Canada to squeeze on the map. If they study history at all in school (which is unlikely, because schools seldom teach history anymore, they teach social studies instead), children would normally cover

200 years of history in eleven years of school, and 4000 years of history in one year of school. I don't know about you, but I think that is a little unbalanced.

Not only is that approach unbalanced, but it also robs our children of a true understanding of why the world is like it is today. I strongly believe that as a Christian parent, one of my responsibilities is to help my children develop a Christian worldview, a warp and woof through which they see the world, so that when they read a book, see a movie, hear a song, go to a play, or whatever, they can discern the worldview being presented. The only way that discernment can be fully developed is to teach children about Western civilization and lay a foundation historically and philosophically from the time they are very young.

Even if our goal is to have our children love America and know American history, they cannot truly understand American history and thought without having some foundational understanding of the history of Israel, Greece, Rome, and Europe. After all, where do we think the founding fathers got their ideas about how a nation should be governed, about the rights of men, about law and justice? Do we think, "Poof! they came out of a cloud somewhere?" No, it didn't happen that way. Our culture and country were birthed out of a long history of government and thought over the past four to five thousand years. So, if you want to study American history, that's great. But study it chronologically where it belongs, which is at the end of 4000 plus years of Western civilization.

Now, how do we go about making history the backbone of our curriculum?

RECOMMENDATIONS FOR THE EARLY YEARS

I prefer not to jump into a time line and start serious historical study until children are about third grade. If a child is too young, a lot of history can be too abstract and confusing, because the young child hasn't accumulated enough life experiences and associative skills to put some of the pieces together, even with a time line.

In the early years I recommend that you just do a general overview of American history with your kids. Nothing exhaustive, but just enough so that when Aunt Susie says something about the Pilgrims at Thanksgiving, your children don't say, "Who?" It just doesn't look good, and it causes your relatives to start questioning whether you should be homeschooling your children.

At this stage, you are simply going to snuggle up with your children and read to them a lot, but the books you choose will cover everything children of that age need to know about American history. No one will expect them to know much about world history at that age, but they will be expected to know about George Washington, and the Pilgrims, and Abraham Lincoln, and other major figures.

Let me share with you some key authors I've found who will help you study American history during the early years until you are ready to jump into a time line.

Perhaps my favorite authors are a husband and wife team, Ingri and Edgar D'Aulaire. Ingri was from Norway and Edgar was from France and Italy. They met in Munich in art school, fell in love, got married, and moved to America. They have written a series of the most unashamedly conservative and patriotic biographies of famous Americans you could ever find. Each book also reflects a strong Judeo-Christian influence. For example, they share about George Washington's mother praying with him each night, and Leif the Lucky becoming a Christian and bringing Christianity back to his people. They also tell the real story of Pocahontas, who was actually the first non-white convert in the New World, who after she was baptized, changed her name to Rebecca. Our children have been robbed of these truths about famous Americans that the D'Aulaire books still contain.

Every child needs to read the D'Aulaire books. There are seven of them currently in print: *Leif the Lucky, Christopher Columbus, Pocahontas, George Washington, Benjamin Franklin, Abraham Lincoln* and *Buffalo Bill.* The illustrations are beautiful, because the D'Aulaires were artists, and there is a full-page illustration on every other page. So raise your children knowing and loving each and every one of these books.

Keep in mind that any time you can use a biography to teach history, do it. Children have no interest in dates and treaties. They want to know about the people who lived long ago, and they really want to know about children. What did they wear? What were they like? Were they naughty? Did they homeschool, too? All of the D'Aulaire books start by sharing events in the childhoods of these famous people.

Biographies are a wonderful "hook" into history, because once children care about the famous person, then they want to know about wars, treaties, dates, kings and queens, and so on. Once a child has an interest in a famous person, then the child will want to know what was going on in the time in which that person lived. Education, in a nutshell, is studying the people of history.

You need to hang out in the biography section of your library, because many of the most wonderful books are out of print. Get a library card and teach your children how to find what they need in the biography section. But when selecting biographies, always remember that older is better. If a book was written in the 1950s or earlier, you will probably like it. If written in the 60s, it will be "iffy." In the 70s you're on your own, and in the 80s and 90s, don't waste your time. This isn't to say that there are no good books written nowadays, but if you're new at this, just stick to the older books until you build your confidence. Once you know the difference between a good book and a bad one, you can find the good ones in any time period.

Here are some other great authors for the early years:
1. Marguerite de Angeli. She wrote *Door in the Wall, Thee Hannah,* and a number of other wonderful books, many of which are now out of print.
2. Alice Dalgliesh is best known for *The Courage of Sarah Nobel,* but has written many other great books.
3. Laura Ingalls Wilder wrote the *Little House on the Prairie* books. Every child needs to read these books at least twice while they are growing up. These books are "Homeschool in a Box," because you can build a whole year's worth of study around them by getting *The Little House*

Cookbook and *The Laura Ingalls Wilder Songbook.*

4. James Daugherty wrote many fine biographies that are great "read-alouds" for this age group.

5. Margaret Pumphrey wrote a little book called *Stories of the Pilgrims.* This is an absolute treasure of a book that will tell your children things about the Pilgrims they will never find anywhere else.

RECOMMENDATIONS FOR THIRD GRADE AND UP

At around third or fourth grade children are usually reading fairly well, so now is the time to start looking into ancient history. Your two tools for working with third graders and up are time-lines and unit studies.

Timelines

A timeline doesn't have to be anything fancy. You can buy ready-made blank ones or you can just get some shelf paper or butcher paper, mark it off into sections according to what you are going to be studying with centuries or groups of centuries, put the dates in for your children and even do the writing in of the names and events. This way they only have to do the illustration part, which is the fun part to them.

If your children are not creative or artistic, there is no reason they can't draw stick figures or cut up magazines or even an old set of encyclopedias from a garage sale. But they need to do their own illustrations and not buy something ready-made. This way they have a sense of "ownership" in the creation of the timeline.

I've been asked, "How do we choose what to put on the timeline?" Well, you divide it into manageable sections of years based on what you are studying at the time. You don't want it to be overwhelming. The key word is "representative." What events represent, or sum up, what we want to remember about a particular time period?

Unit Studies

Now, let's spend some time discussing the theory behind a unit study. I'm sure most of you have heard the term "unit study." There are many different definitions and expectations for what a unit study should be. When I was new to homeschooling, we tried various prepared unit-study programs that we purchased. I felt very locked in and intimidated and not in my niche. As I became more seasoned at homeschooling, I realized how easy it is for anyone to develop a unit study on their own, for free, using only a Bible and a library card.

History gives a logical progression to build a unit study around. After all, you are not going to keep reading about Ancient Egypt forever, you must move on to Greece, and Rome, the Middle Ages, the Renaissance and Reformation, Modern Times, and American History. So using history as your framework keeps you moving.

The concept of a unit study is studying many different subjects, at many different levels, around a common core. What if you have four children and each child has six or seven subjects to cover? Who could teach four grades of seven subjects at the same time? Not even Superwoman could do it. It's not realistic unless you put each child in front of a TV and feed in educational videos all day. I was a trained teacher with a graduate degree and was only expected to teach one subject each day in public school, and I could hardly keep up with that!

When using a unit study approach, the whole family is studying the same thing at the same time, only at different levels. The younger children may be reading picture books about Ancient Egypt while the older children are independently reading something quite demanding, but they are all covering the same information and studying within the same focus, which is Ancient Egypt.

Where prepared unit studies and I parted was when I was a young homeschooling mother. I was supposed to gather all this stuff, stay up nights preparing all the information and materials, then get up the next morning and spit it all back to my child as some sort of "all-knowing one," then stay up the whole next night and start the cycle all over again. For me, that lasted for about three days, then the unit-study program went in the closet.

Reading aloud

That (above) is *not* what I want you to do. All I want you to do is read out loud with your children, learning with them as you go. Most of us, depending on how much education we have had, know very little about the history of Western civilization. I knew practically nothing. When I became a Christian at the age of 21, I attended a church in California and whenever the pastor would use a historical analogy, like comparing someone in the Bible to Peter the Great, I didn't have a clue who Peter the Great was. I was part of the Baby Boom generation. I went to the best East Coast schools, and we never studied history or read a piece of classical literature. Instead we read authors like J. D. Salinger and Kurt Vonnegut and e e cummings. Heaven forbid that we should ever read something like *The Scarlet Letter*!

One of the beauties of homeschooling is that you get to fill in your own educational gaps. If you never studied a particular era of history before, you get to do it now with your children. But it's not a matter of staying up nights and cramming in a lot of information you never knew before so you can teach it to your kids. That is not what I want you to do. I want you to get up with your children in the morning and read your Bible and then sit and read together for an hour or two. Do some math, then go outside and play or garden or dig ditches, or come back inside and bake and cook. Just live real life. My point is that you are learning with your children, as you go, by reading good books together.

Choosing books to read

What books do you need? First there are source books. These are books you are going to use for every unit that you teach. My desire would be that you take three or four years to get through a study of history from ancient times to the present, so these source books will constantly be there as resources for you to refer to.

The first source book I recommend is *How Should We Then Live* by Francis Schaeffer. Everyone needs to own this book. Francis Schaeffer was a leading Christian theologian who wrote this book as a treatise on the rise and fall of Western culture. Chapter by chapter he covers the history, culture, and worldview of different eras from early Rome through the Age of Reason all from a Judeo-Christian perspective. So he tells you about the artists, painters, sculptors, musicians, and philosophers as well as historical figures, focusing on their worldviews and what was the over-riding premise of the culture they lived in. To my mind, this book is the base of teaching a child how to think Christianly. When our son was growing up, I told him, "J.J., if you can master *How Should We Then Live* and the multiplication tables, I will be a happy camper."

The corresponding book to HSWTL was written by Jane Stuart Smith and Betty Carlson, two women who were Schaeffer's associates. Both women were musicians, and they wrote a book called *The Gift of Music*, which is a history of music starting with King David and moving forward in time through several hundred composers in chronological order. So if you have a child who has any gifting or interest in the realm of music, this is the history of music from a Christian perspective. It is amazing to read this book and discover how many of the early composers were believers. For example, Bach wrote at the beginning of every piece, "To the Glory of God," and he signed each piece with "By the Grace of God." These are things we were never taught in school. It's such a joy to learn them now with your children.

Other resources you will be turning to again and again are *Men of Science, Men of God* (biographies of famous scientists), *Streams of Civilization, Volumes 1 and 2* (history of the world from a Christian perspective) and *Kingfisher History Encyclopedia*. Also, *A Child's History of the World* by A. V. Hillyer is a great book if you ignore the first four or five chapters. These are all books you will keep zeroing in on through the years.

Another book that makes my heart sing is by Os Guinness. He and his friend Dr. Louise Cowan, who is a professor in Texas, have compiled *An Invitation to the Classics*, subtitled *"A Guide to the Books You Always Wanted to Read."* What they have done is prepare a history of literature by presenting, in chronological order, important literature in the history of Western civilization. They start with Homer, move through the Greek poets, the Romans, the Middle Ages, and so on to the twentieth century. Each chapter analyzes each author's work from a Christian perspective, explaining his or her worldview, and summarizing the plot of some of his or her writings. Some of the authors were Christians and others were definitely not, and your children need to know which are which. This isn't to say you must never read an author who isn't a Christian, but you want you children to know where the person they are reading is coming from so they can be discerning. You don't have to agree with everyone you read, but you do have to be exposed to these different great minds for the purpose of criticism and analysis.

An *Invitation to the Classics* is junior high and high school literature in one book. Not only does it provide a framework of literature to read as you study different historical periods, but it is also such a help to know what the different authors believed, so you can study worldviews at the same time.

HOW DO WE BEGIN?

Now that we have some understanding of what we plan to do, how do we begin? The obvious answer is that you will begin at Genesis, chapter 1, verse 1. Read the Bible, and maybe Ruth Beechick's *Adam and His Kin* until you get to Joseph being sold into Egypt. Then you are going to study Ancient Egypt, then Ancient Greece, then Rome, and so on, moving forward through history, using the Bible and good historical literature.

Egypt is not a super-important historical period as far as a contribution to Western civilization is concerned, but the contribution of Ancient Greece is gigantic. If you had to spend a whole year studying Ancient Greece, it would be time well spent. Greek thought is foundational to all of Western Civilization and is also foundational to the history of Rome. Once you get to the study of Rome, you will find that the Romans didn't have an original thought in their heads! Everything Roman was really Greek, so you will see the time you spent studying Greece was very well spent. Also, the New Testament was written in Greek because at that time Greek was an international language, much as English is today. The Apostle Paul had a classical Greek education, being raised in Tarsus, and he also had a classical Hebrew education, being trained under Gamaliel. The New Testament, particularly the Book of Acts, is going to come alive for you as you study Ancient Greece and Rome. You are going to see Paul and Christ quoting classical Greek writers. That went over my head for years because I had never studied these things before. For example, when Jesus spoke of wolves in sheep's clothing, he was quoting Aesop, a Greek slave, and when Paul said, "Bad communications corrupt good morals," he was quoting a classical Greek writer. You see, if we don't study the classical writings, we don't realize how much involvement there is of the classics in the New Testament.

I also want to expose you to a very important piece of Western literature, probably the most important work of classical literature, and that is *The Iliad* by Homer. Homer was a blind Greek who brought together many of the oral traditions of the story of the Trojan War and wrote them down in the form of an epic poem. Rosemary Sutcliff, a modern British author, wrote a narrative version of *The Iliad* and also of *The Odyssey* (which is the story of the travels of Ulysses). *Black Ships Before Troy* is exquisitely illustrated and made appropriate for children. When you read it you will understand why it has become a modern classic. It is a great story that parents tell me their children read over and over again. And best of all, it's a boy's book. It's sometimes hard to find good books for boys, but this is one that will grab your boys.

WHY STUDY MYTHOLOGY?

The question always arises, "What about mythology? Why do Christian children need to know about pagan myths?" I will agree that it may not be wise to expose young children to mythology, because they have a hard time distinguishing between fantasy and reality. But once a child reaches the age where he knows the difference and has an understanding of truth, Greek mythology becomes no different from any fictional story.

The reason everyone needs to at least be exposed to Greek and Roman mythology (and even some Norse) is that it is alluded to in every piece of classical literature your children will ever read. Mythology has also become a part of the speech of everyday life. For example, they may hear someone say, "He just opened Pandora's box," or "That was her Achilles heel," or "She has a face that could launch a thousand ships." Understanding the myth behind these analogies is knowledge that all well-educated people share in common, and it is part of a body of knowledge that people will expect your children to own if they want to operate in a literate society. People who have been robbed of familiarity with these things, as I was, go through life as though they are seeing with only one eye. When I was a child and read Louisa May Alcott's *Little Women* and *Little Men* and all her allusions to Greek myths, I had no idea what she was talking about. So please give your children this part of a classical education to equip them to function in the realm of great literature.

THE GENEVIEVE FOSTER BOOKS

Now I am going to discuss another author everyone should read. Most of you don't realize that you are living in the Golden Age of Homeschooling and that many books you can get easily were not available to people who homeschooled five, ten, and fifteen years ago. I would have to go through dozens of out-of-print book searches and spend hundreds of dollars to get the same books you now buy from homeschool suppliers for $15.00 each. One of the authors I used to move heaven and earth to find books by is Genevieve Foster. She lived in Illinois in the 1930s and '40s and was deeply concerned about the lack of good historical literature for her children to read. So she decided to write books herself. I think she is the very finest history author of all time for children.

The first book Genevieve Foster wrote was *George Washington's World*. She then went on to write books about the world at the time of Columbus, John Smith, Abraham Lincoln, Augustus Caesar, and many other famous historical figures. Her books are so magnificent because she takes a famous person and covers his lifetime, using that person as a springboard to tell what is going on all over the world during that slice of history. The books give you an international view of history during a specific time period. The concept is terrific, but what really makes Genevieve Foster great is that she is a great writer. Before her death she said, "When I write, I craft every sentence as if it were a precious jewel." So her books don't read like history textbooks, but like great literature.

What you are looking for in teaching history is books that make your child want to stay up late reading them under the covers with a flashlight. Your kids will be begging to read these books, so don't spoil it by telling them they will be "learning history" by reading them. Genevieve Foster's books are irresistible, because she makes you know and understand the people she writes about. With Genevieve Foster's books you can cover from Ancient Rome forward, and most of American history. Her *Augustus Caesar's World* is the perfect core book for a study of Ancient Rome.

THE MIDDLE AGES AND THE RENAISSANCE AND REFORMATION

After Rome, you will move to the Middle Ages, which seems to be every little boy's favorite period. Boys would be happy to stay in the Middle Ages until they graduated from high school. There are many great books about knights, particularly the *Arthur* series by Rosemary Sutcliff, and *A Boy's King Arthur* by Sidney Lanier.

After the Middle Ages, go to the Renaissance and Reformation. This is when you will introduce your children to Shakespeare. Years ago in England, there was a writer named Charles Lamb who had a sister named Mary. They were both gifted, brilliant people, concerned that the children of England were not becoming acquainted with the works of Shakespeare. So the Lambs decided to retell Shakespeare's plays in a narrative form easily understood by children. Their book, *Tales from Shakespeare*, has become a classic and is the perfect introduction to Shakespeare for children. When you read it with your children, start with the comedies, like "Taming of the Shrew." Read it. Act it out. Go to a play. Stick to the comedies first, then move on to the tragedies and you will discover why Shakespeare is called "the Bard of the Bible" because his work is so biblically based in the Judeo-Christian ethics of right and wrong and sowing and reaping. You will also discover why he is the best-selling playwright of all time. But don't tell your children, "Oh, this is hard!" or "Oh, this is good for you!." Just read the plays and let your children fall in love with Shakespeare as countless people have done before them.

MODERN WORLD HISTORY AND AMERICAN HISTORY

From the Renaissance and Reformation, you can move on to modern world history, and finally reach American history after you've built an understanding of the history of Western Civilization. When you study American history, your core resources will be the series by Peter Marshall and David Manuel: *The Light and the Glory, From Sea to Shining Sea,* and *Sounding Forth the Trumpet.* Read these in the original versions, not the children's versions, for the Christian backdrop to events from Columbus to the last century.

Three other resources will help you find books that are appropriate for each time period and age level. The first is *Honey for a Child's Heart* by Gladys Hunt. The second is *Books Children Love* by Elizabeth Wilson. And the third is *Turning Back the Pages of Time* by Kathy Keller, which deals only with American history. All three provide booklists by historical period and age group, but each takes a slightly different approach and lists books that the others don't, so it is best to have them all.

Teaching Science: First Naturalists, Then Scientists

Ellyn Davis

cience often intimidates parents who want to teach creatively. There are several reasons for this. First, modern science has become so highly specialized—each branch with its own vocabulary, techniques, paraphernalia, and "ivory tower" mentality—that we think it is beyond the understanding of the average person. Cold fusion experiments and quantum theory are the stuff of which government grants are made, not concepts that seem relevant to everyday life.

The second major reason science seems difficult to teach is that modern man is out of touch with the natural world. We no longer interact with plants, animals, or the environment in ways that allow us to learn and apply scientific principles. What former generations knew about animals because they kept livestock, or about the weather because they spent a lot of time outdoors, we now have to learn from books. What once was a natural part of life has become very unnatural and even forced.

The third reason for dreading science is that most science teaching materials are laboratory-oriented and information-intensive. Things are taken out of their natural setting and studied in parts, laboring over details and bits and pieces. All of the information is "second-hand," because the student never interacts with the real plant, animal, or whatever in its natural setting. Even the physical science experiments tend to stress entertainment or acquisition of information.

How can teaching science be made interesting, creative, and less intimidating? We believe that there are seven foundational principles involved in teaching science in the homeschool.

PRINCIPLE #1:

The natural world tells us about God. Suppose someone asked you, "How can I know what God is like?" What would you say? The Bible tells us three ways God has revealed Himself. The first two ways are through His Word: His written word (the Bible) and His Living Word (the life of Jesus reflected in Christians). The third revelation of God is found in the created world: "For since the creation of the world His invisible attributes, His eternal power and divine nature, have been clearly seen, being understood through what has been made..." (Romans 1: 20). The apostle Paul, who wrote this verse, thought nature's revelation of God is so clear that those who ignore it are "without excuse." Furthermore, those who fail to notice God in creation tend to fall into all sorts of sin. This is why Creation Science is so important. Without a Creator, one has no perceived need for a Savior.

The major areas of scientific study are built upon the contributions of men who believed that the world was created by a reasonable, orderly God Who placed certain laws within His creation. Francis Bacon developed the scientific method; Carolus Linneaus began biological classification; Johann Kepler founded physical astronomy; Robert Boyle began the modern study of chemistry; Isaac Newton laid the foundations of physics and developed calculus into a comprehensive branch of mathematics.

> *"Living within the concept that the world was created by a reasonable God, scientists could move with confidence, expecting to be able to find out about the world by observation and experimentation."*
>
> —Francis Schaeffer in *How Shall We Then Live*

We too can be confident that whatever we study in science can teach us what God is like.

PRINCIPLE #2:

Nurture a sense of wonder. The poet Gerard Manley Hopkins wrote: "The world is charged with the grandeur of God!" Small children innately understand this. They are quick to marvel, to "oooh" and "aaah" over an interesting cloud formation, a pile of autumn leaves, a puddle filled with tadpoles, a variegated rock, a wriggly newborn kitten. Sadly, as they grow older, children have such hectic schedules, so many man-made experiences, and so much electronic stimulation that they often have to be trained to appreciate nature. We feel that science *as* science should come after the development of a sense of wonder about nature. Elementary aged children should explore, observe, collect, and marvel at the natural world without parents being teachy about it.

PRINCIPLE #3:

Develop naturalists first, then scientists. Scientists take things out of their natural setting and study their parts, teaching details, dissecting and analyzing. This fragmenting of something alive and fascinating can strip it of its allure. In contrast, the naturalist studies plants, animals, rocks, in their natural settings. He appreciates the uniqueness of each created thing, learning its habits, its patterns, its interaction with other created things. He develops a sense of wonder about nature. Many of the parables Jesus told were addressed to people who understood the patterns of living things, of the seasons, and of the weather. We've lost those understandings because we no longer interact with the natural world on a daily basis. Helping our children become naturalists will restore understandings of the attributes of God which creation can teach us.

PRINCIPLE #4:

Create a context for learning to occur in the most natural way. Keep good books about animals or about people and animals (not textbooks, but interesting stories). Subscribe to a nature magazine for children. Invest in field guides. Maximize your opportunities to interact with nature through nature walks, field trips to nature centers, camping, and spending a lot of time outdoors. Let children cook, fool around with magnets and compasses, wire a light socket, move loads using simple machines, *et cetera*.

PRINCIPLE #5:

Don't expect your children to be what you're not. Don't make them who they are not. If your great love and talent lies in music, chances are your children will be more musically inclined than scientifically inclined. Conversely, some kids just do not like spiders, snakes, hikes, and so forth. Don't force these things on them.

PRINCIPLE #6:

Focus on wisdom and knowledge, not on information. What do our children really need to know? Science curricula are developed to fill one hour a day, 180 days a year. Even if a concept takes only 5 minutes to communicate, a textbook has to devote a classroom session to it. Not only is there a glut of information, but the information tends to be "predigested," telling the child what it all means and what he or she is to think about it. This is what we call "informational overkill." We have to be realistic about our children's needs. Do they show a real bent towards science or nature study? If so, our teaching can be more in-depth in those areas. If not, we need only cover essential concepts and knowledge. A very helpful book for determining the necessary science skills is *What Your Child Needs to Know When*. It lists science concepts the child should cover at each grade level through eighth grade. You will find that many of these concepts can be communicated simply by reading books, taking nature walks, and letting your children help around the yard and the kitchen.

PRINCIPLE #7:

Be open to God's lessons. We don't have to search for spiritual meaning in what we teach. If we are seeking the Holy Spirit's direction, God will create opportunities to use whatever we are studying to bring us closer to Him. I'll give you a personal example involving tadpoles. One day two years ago, when our family was experiencing severe financial difficulty, I took a walk in a pasture near our home. Our financial pressures were weighing heavily on my mind, but I noticed that the pasture was dotted with small puddles of water and each puddle was teaming with frog eggs or tadpoles in various stages of development. There were millions of potential frogs in that one pasture, but I knew that most of the puddles would dry up before the tadpoles could fully mature. I began to think what a waste it was for God to create all those little lives only to have them die, and I asked, "Why did you do this? You knew these tadpoles wouldn't have a chance of survival!" Even as I was asking I began to understand that what I was seeing was the lavishness of God, the "exceeding abundance" that Scripture speaks of concerning Him. A line from a hymn came into my mind: "His grace has no measure, His love has no limit, His power has no boundaries known unto man: For out of His infinite riches in Jesus, He giveth, and giveth, and giveth again." At that moment I knew God would be sufficient for all of our needs. Now every time I see a tadpole I am reminded of this lesson.

SCIENCE RESOURCES

1. Boy Scouts of America. The Boy Scouts offer merit badges in many areas of science and nature (Botany, Reptiles and Amphibians, Birds, Wilderness Survival, Astronomy, *et cetera*). There is an inexpensive booklet for each merit badge. These booklets are packed with information and wonderful project ideas. Contact the Boy Scout office in your area.

2. 4-H. Contact your local Agricultural Extension Service about the many 4-H activities available in your area. We have found 4-H to be very open to homeschoolers forming their own clubs. Project booklets are available in dozens of science areas such as entomology, forestry (focusing on trees found in your state), wildlife, livestock, *et cetera.* The project books are arranged by grade levels, starting at 4th grade, and contain lots of ideas for science study. Our 4-H allows us to have the project booklets even if we are not enrolled in a particular project. The entomology booklets are the best introductions to insect collecting we have ever seen.

3. Wildlife Resources Agencies. Your state probably has an agency dedicated to preserving wildlife. These agencies can help you with free literature (even nature-film rentals) and give you addresses of other state and federal organizations that have nature resources.

THE ELEMENTARY GRADES: NURTURING A SENSE OF WONDER

1. Read lots of books about animals. An annotated list of good literature about animals is on the pages that follow. Subscribe to a nature magazine. Ranger Rick is for elementaries, and is published by The National Wildlife Federation. It occasionally mentions evolution and is definitely conservationist in tone, but is filled with interesting stories about animals and lots of wonderful full-color photos. *Nature Friend Magazine* is a Christian counterpart to *Ranger Rick* (Pilgrim Publishers, 22777 S.R. 119, Goshen, IN 46526). For older students, *National Geographic* and *National Wildlife* focus on nature study. Most states have wildlife magazines that feature plants, animals, and scenic wildlife areas of that state.

2. Collect the tools of the trade. This includes field guides, binoculars, magnifying glasses, an insect net, pinning board and pins, a plant press, an aquarium with wire mesh lid, magnets, a quality compass, and—if finances allow—a microscope.

3. Invest in field guides. Sure, you can check them out of the library, but children live in the now and you lose the critical nurture point for interest if you postpone studying the critter until you can get the field guide from the library. Start with the field guides in areas of greatest interest and in areas you are most likely to study—usually birds, insects, trees, reptiles and amphibians. We prefer the *Audubon Pocket Guides* for beginners because they have photographs, their compact size is appealing to children, and they cover only those animals, plants, or minerals children are likely to see. For more advanced study, we like the big, comprehensive Audubon Society Field Guides.

4. Expect short attention spans. Since it is hard for children to be quiet and still, start with created things that can't run away—rocks, flowers, trees, stars, clouds and weather. Insects are also easy to study because they are so abundant. Progress to animals that require patience and quiet, like birds, reptiles, amphibians, and mammals.

5. Teach taxonomy. Even young children can learn that there are five types, or Kingdoms, of living things (plants, animals, fungi, bacteria, and protists) and that each of these Kingdoms is made up of different kinds of organisms. This doesn't have to be formally taught, but can be communicated when you are walking ("Look at that! Some trees lose their leaves in winter and some don't. Trees that lose their leaves are called deciduous; trees that don't are called evergreens. Ferns are plants too, but they are different from trees. Have you noticed ways they are alike? Ways they are different?")

6. Make your own field guides. Since our children were very young we have kept an index-card box to catalog their "finds." Whenever one of the boys brought home a critter, we would look it up in a field guide and write out its common name, its classification, and its scientific name. For example, the card on a box turtle reads: "Box Turtle, Terrapene carolina. Kingdom: Animalia, Phylum: Chordata (has a spinal cord), Subphylum: Vertebrata (has a backbone), Class: Reptilia (cold-blooded, with scaly skin), Order: Chelonia (has shell and horny beak), Family: Emydidae (pond and river turtles), Genus: Terrapene (pond turtle with movable hinge on lower shell)." After doing this a short while, the boys clearly understood the major taxonomic groupings. We also have traced, cut out, or photocopied the pictures from field guide coloring books and then colored them to make our own field guides. (It is permissible to photocopy the drawings for personal use if you have purchased the book.)

7. Take frequent nature walks. Agree on rules beforehand, like hand signals instead of talking, what the children are to look for, what they are not allowed to do. Don't expect much the first several walks, but after awhile you will notice your children becoming more observant, patient, and quiet.

8. Involve all of the senses. Invest in audiotapes of bird songs, frog calls, and night sounds. Learn to recognize signs that animals have been about, through their tracks, scat, or markings. Hear things, smell things, touch things, even taste things.

9. Keep a pet in a jar. Some critters make good pets. Consult a field guide as to which ones are better kept in captivity. Habitats can be as simple as a large glass jar and as elaborate as a landscaped terrarium. The book *Pets in a Jar* has instructions for collection and care of many small wild animals.

10. Start a nature journal. This may be as simple or as elaborate as you like. It can focus just on trees, or on birds, or can cover as many life forms as you choose. It can be a combination diary, picture album, field notebook, or whatever you wish. Two excellent examples of nature journals are *The Country Diary of an Edwardian Lady* and *A Naturalist's Notebook*.

11. Keep a garden. A garden allows you to effortlessly teach many aspects of plant study. If there's not room for a vegetable garden try a small patch of flowers. Consider choosing varieties that attract butterflies and hummingbirds, or that have medicinal value.

12. Breed animals. Allowing your child to have a pet will open many doors into understanding the natural world. If you can breed an animal (dogs, cats, fish, gerbils, or cows, horses, goats, and so forth), sex education, genetics, and many other science lessons become effortless.

A NATURE JOURNAL

Rather than teaching science from a textbook, why not let each child keep a nature journal? *The Country Diary of an Edwardian Lady* is a wonderful example of how nature, art, literature, and history can be interwoven. In 1906 Edith Holden began a nature journal in which she recorded and illustrated what she saw month by month during walks in the English countryside. She began each month's entry with historical events associated with that month and listed major holidays with brief historical explanations. The rest of each month's entry consisted of notes of what she saw on her frequent walks interspersed with drawings of selected wildlife and plants. She also included poems and famous quotations about the month or about the things she saw. Her watercolor illustrations are exquisite and her Victorian penmanship is a delight to read.

There's no reason children could not follow a similar format. If drawing is a problem, buy several of the field guide coloring books and let the children trace and then color illustrations for their journals. Flowers, leaves, and grasses can also be pressed and then mounted to the journal pages with clear Contact™ paper. Classification and detailed study of certain topics, such as the parts of a flower, can be included. Such an approach can incorporate history, nature study, art, weather study, literature, penmanship, and whatever else you can imagine—even personal entries and photographs. It can be done for as long or as short a period of time as you like. If a year seems intimidating, try it for a month, particularly in the spring, summer, or autumn, or during a family trip.

ABOUT EVOLUTION...

Unfortunately, many outstanding books on nature reflect an evolutionary view of the origin of life, promote an "old earth" theory, or contain mystical elements of native American religions. We have chosen to include a few books with references to evolution or Indian methods because we cannot find anything their equal in teaching value, quality of illustrations, or ability to promote interest. When we use these books, we turn the non-Christian statements into opportunities to teach our children that we live in a fallen world and fallen man has come up with false ideas about how everything got here. We refer to Romans 1, which states that God has made Himself clearly known through creation and that people who refuse to acknowledge the Creator suppress the truth about reality. Our children can recognize subtle as well as overt references to evolution, and understand that what a person believes about creation affects how they live.

We also tell them that people without a Creator feel no need for a Savior. As Ruth Beechick says, "This is the message our society needs today. After people believe in a Creator God, we can talk to them about the Savior. If people are in that evolutionary life chain, with no purpose but what they create for themselves, what place is in their thinking for something like the cross? None at all; it is only foolishness. People first need the preaching of the Creator God." The best creationism books we've found are *Unlocking the Mysteries of Creation* and *It Couldn't Just Happen.*

WHY IS IT IMPORTANT TO STUDY NATURE?

Many of us have lived so long in urban environments that not only are we out of touch with nature, but we are suspicious of attempts to get back in touch, thinking them mystical or New Age. We've also been so conditioned by our Western worldview to think of nature as a commodity that we no longer see ourselves as part of the natural world. Our Greek academic heritage has made us "observers of," not "participators in" what God has created. We feel more comfortable bringing a plant into a laboratory, dissecting it, and "mastering" its fragments than we do taking a nature walk and getting to know plants as plants. The Sioux Indians believe that animals and plants talked before the white man arrived. Maybe animals and plants still talk and we just have lost the ability to listen. The Bible certainly assumes that the natural world has a lot to say to us. Scripture gives us two reasons why nature study is important:

1. Observing and understanding nature is one of the ways man can know about God. Romans 1 tells us that God's invisible attributes and divine nature can be clearly seen through what He has made. Psalms tells us that the heavens "declare" and created things "speak" about the glory and wonder of God.

2. Contemplating nature instructs and inspires God's people. Many spiritual truths are explained using examples from nature. Some Scriptures are John 15 (vine and branches); John 10 (shepherd and sheep); Romans 11 (being grafted into a tree); John 12 (a grain of wheat); Matthew

17 (faith as small as a mustard seed); and Matthew 6 (God's care and provision for wildflowers and birds). Jesus often used natural examples to explain the Kingdom of God and He assumed that His hearers were familiar enough with the natural world to understand His examples. Many Biblical writers used plants and animals for moral instruction. (Example: A lazy person was directed to watch the ant and imitate her industriousness.)

Once we know the importance of studying nature, we don't want to just use creation as fodder for Bible studies or character development. This approach is just as fragmenting as laboratory dissection and just as manipulative as seeing created things as commodities. We need a holistic view of nature that includes understanding, appreciation, wonder, and wise stewardship, as well as application in Bible studies.

TEACHING TIPS: THE UPPER GRADES: TIME FOR MORE SERIOUS STUDY

1. Be realistic. Use the elementary grades to study plants, animals, minerals, heat, sound, light, electricity, magnetism, and machines firsthand and spend as much time outdoors as possible. Save the laboratory for high school. By eighth grade you should know your child's scientific inclination. If he or she plans a career requiring a great deal of science, high school is the time for more serious study and independent research projects, possibly in conjunction with a local continuing-education program. If science is not in your child's future, find out your state's (or the future college's) "bare minimum" science requirements and focus on covering those skills and concepts. For the non-college bound, the Usborne Introductions Series (Chemistry, Biology, and Physics) and advanced coloring books (Biology Coloring Book, Botany Coloring Book, Microbiology Coloring Book, *et cetera*) may be sufficient to earn the required science credits for your state.

2. Find help for your weak areas. Find people willing to either tutor your child or help you over the rough spots of high school science. Our former church was filled with retired scientists from the atomic energy laboratories at Oak Ridge, TN. Sometimes they helped one-on-one and other times they taught groups of homeschoolers once a week, giving assignments to be done at home.

3. Give the child more responsibility. We attended a conference where David and Micki Colfax were the main speakers. During a question and answer session, a parent shared his frustration with a teenaged son who hated school. David Colfax told the man to consider having his son build a room addition to the house. We were astounded at this answer, but saw the great wisdom in it. If that boy really did build a room addition, he would learn math, electronics, building skills, thinking skills, financial skills, and who knows what else, plus he would have acquired a valuable trade. The high school years can be a time for practical application of many scientific concepts. The child can keep a garden, raise livestock, build and wire a storage building (or even a

room addition to the house), or any number of other things. If you read the Colfaxes' book *Hard Times in Paradise*, you will understand how their children could win scholarships to Harvard and Yale with very little formal schooling.

NATURE WALKS

Throughout this section we have referred to "nature walks" as the best way to become familiar with the natural world. For those of you to whom this is an alien concept, here are some suggestions and explanations.

Taking a nature walk simply means you are going to place yourself and your children in the context of living, breathing plants and animals. You are going to interact with them first-hand rather than through books or in a laboratory. You don't have to have a National Park handy to take a nature walk. This can be done in your backyard, in your city park, or in a neighbor's field. If your city has a nature center, there will often be a pre-designed nature trail you can walk. However, the trails at nature centers are usually so overused that there is little left to see. If at all possible, find an area that has both open spaces and woods and is near water. Animals have three basic needs food, water, and shelter so if you can find an area with all three, you are more likely to see a variety of wildlife.

1. Prepare beforehand. Find books about the different plants and animals in your area and have some idea of what you will look for. It is better for the children if the first few nature walks actually turn up something interesting, so plan the walk in an area and at a time when the wildlife you want to see will be observable. For example, pick a few common birds, a few common plants, and a few common insects that you are almost guaranteed to see and make them the object of your first few walks. You can prepare the children beforehand with sheets to color (from *Field Guide Coloring Books*), with bird songs to listen to, and with field guides to look at.

    An inspiring book to read beforehand (you can even read aloud to your children) is *Naming Nature*. The author set out to make the acquaintance of her natural neighborhood. She realized that if she learned just the most common plants, birds, and animals around her, she would probably recognize most of what she saw. So she learned one name at a time, a few names a week, for a year. *Naming Nature* chronicles her year of naming things and is a wonderful guide for amateur naturalists.

    Other very helpful books are *The Field Guides to Wildlife Habitats*. These are the only books that take you habitat-by-habitat (sandy beach, lake and pond, swamp, *et cetera*) and tell you what to look for and listen for, and how to find both plants and animals in each different habitat. With these guides you can take a nature walk anyplace in the United States.

    If you live in the city, *Peterson's First Guide to Urban Wildlife* is very helpful because it covers all the creatures a city child is likely to see.

2. Make it enjoyable. If you and your children are not used to spending a

lot of time outdoors, you must prepare beforehand so that it will be a pleasant experience. Pick a time of day when the temperature is comfortable and no one is tired or hungry. Wear the proper shoes and clothes; put on insect repellent and sunscreen; perhaps take drinks and a snack. Start with short excursions of 15 to 20 minutes. The times can be lengthened as interest builds.

3. Invest in the tools of the trade. As finances allow, begin acquiring the following: A pair of lightweight binoculars, a hand lens, a few pocket field guides, stout walking sticks for probing in holes and under rocks and logs, a small field notebook, and something to hold treasures your children may find. If you want to encourage your children to keep a nature journal, have the supplies on hand: a blank journal, pens, colored pencils or markers, *et cetera*.

4. Agree beforehand on the behavior you expect. Nothing is more frustrating than having a unique "nature moment" spoiled by a loud "Hey! Look at that!" Agree beforehand on the behavior you expect: no loud noises, no running ahead or hanging behind, no damage to the landscape, *et cetera*. It is also helpful to develop hand signals for "Gather around," "Look at that," "Go this way," "Stop here," and other frequent communication you may have during your walks.

   Make sure the children understand basic safety rules such as never sticking their hands into a hole or brush pile without first probing with a stick, never entering water without your permission, and so forth. Also be sure they can recognize any poisonous plants (particularly poison ivy), snakes, or insects they might encounter.

5. Gradually increase the level of difficulty. As children become used to nature walks, you can demand longer periods of silent attention, you can take more lengthy excursions, you can go out in uncomfortable weather, *et cetera*. A wonderful book that begins with simple observation techniques and gradually introduces advanced observation, tracking, and survival skills is *Tom Brown's Field Guide to Nature Observation and Tracking for Children*.

Enjoy your nature walks!

Readable Science Resources

Compiled by Karen Rackliffe

PHYSCIAL SCIENCE

Theodoric's Rainbow—Stephen Kramer

Galileo and the Universe—Steve Parker

Exploring the Night Sky—Terence Dickenson

Starry Messenger—Peter Sis (about Galileo)

Archimedes and the Door of Science—Jeanne Bendick

How Do You Lift a Lion?—Robert E. Wells

How Science Works—Judith Hann (Reader's Digest; ages 8-14)

Hiroshima—John Hersey (Jr. High and up)

From the Earth to the Moon: The Annotated Jules Verne—Walter James Miller

Volcano...Mount St. Helens—Patricia Lauber (Newbery winner)

Yellow and Pink—Steig (all ages) evolution vs creation in picture book format

A Guide to the Elements—Albert Stwertka (Jr. High through adult)

Chaos: the Making of a New Science—James Glick (HS), also *Genius* about Feynman

Enigma—Robert Harris (HS, about a mathematician in WWII)

Chemical History of a Candle, Experimental Researches in Electricity—M. Farraday (HS)

Kon-Tiki—Thor Heyerdahl (non-fiction science adventure)

Eureka! It's an Automobile—Jeanne Bendick

The Kid's Science Book—Robert Hirschfield (creative experiences, hands-on fun)

The Kid's Nature Book—Susan Milord, 365 activities and experiences

Science Crafts for Kids—Gwen Diehn, 50 things to invent and create

BIOLOGICAL SCIENCE

How We are Born, How We Grow, How Our Bodies Work and How We Learn—Joe Kaufman (K-6)

Fantastic Voyage—Isaac Asimov

Square Foot Gardening—Mel Bartholomew (all ages)
Kids Wildlife Book

How Nature Works—David Burnie (Reader's Digest) full of hands-on ideas (ages 8-14)

How the Earth Works—John Farndon (Reader's Digest) hands-on ideas (ages 8-14)

Double Helix:...structure of DNA—James D. Watson (reads like a mystery, HS-adult)

Handbook of Nature Studies—Anna Comstock (reference with teaching suggestions)

Wild Days: Creating Discovery Journals—Karen Rackliffe (that's me!)

Crinkleroot's Nature Almanac;Crinkleroot's Guides—Jim Arnosky

Amateur Naturalist: Explorations and Investigations—Charles E. Roth (upper elementary)

Sky Tree: Seeing Science through Art—Thomas Locker (all ages)

Carl Linnaeus: Father of Classification—Margaret Anderson (upper elementary and up) part of the Great Minds of Science series. Look for *Charles Darwin, Albert Einstein, William Harvey, Marie Curie, et cetera.*

A Thousand Mile Walk to the Gulf—John Muir (very CM)

Walden—Henry David Thoreau (classic for HS and up) also read his essay, "Walking"

Naming Living Things: The Grouping of Plants and Animals—Sarah Riedman (junior high)

Notebooks of Leonardo da Vinci

The Man Who Mistook His Wife for a Hat—Oliver Sacks (stories of mental illness, neurology, psychology [for thinking teens])

Wild Animals I Have Known—Ernest Seton Thomas (not your modern naturalist)

Hollyhock Days: Garden Adventures for the Young at Heart—by Sharon Lovejoy

Chipmunks on the Doorstep—Edwin Tunis (good read-aloud for the family)

The Edge of the Sea—Rachel Carson (exquisite language, awe and wonder for creation, evolutionary content)

The Childhood of Famous Americans for 3rd-6th graders has biographies of Benjamin Franklin, Albert Einstein, and Thomas Edison.

The Sower Series (5th grade and up) includes biographies of Johannes Kepler, Isaac Newton, Robert Boyle, Samuel Morse, and Louis Pasteur. (Focus on Christian faith)

Peterson Field Guides or Audubon Society Pocket Guides are useful reference tools.

Faber Book of Science—Donald Peattie (100 short, lively writings of scientists, arranged historically, for discriminating readers. Contains a strong anti-religion bias.

Some novels by Jules Verne or Arthur C. Clark (2001) are entertaining.

This science article is used by permission of Karen Skidmore Rackliffe, author of Wild Days: Creating Discovery Journals. To view paintings from the notebooks of Karen and her children, go to www.pennygardner.com and click on the nature page. You may order Karen's book from this website.

Testing and Evaluation

Compiled by Sarah Olbris

Additional Articles on the CD
BE SURE TO CHECK OUT THESE OTHER GREAT ARTICLES ON THE CD!

Each article in the book and on the CD has been carefully chosen by the section coordinator to increase your knowledge and understanding of this subject, so don't forget to use and enjoy the parts of the manual on your CD, as well as the part you are holding.

Please note that the page numbering on the CD is different from that of the hard-copy manual.

Introduction

Assessments are often a challenge for students as well as for parents. We hope this section will answer your questions and allay your fears. Three forms of assessment will be addressed: standardized tests, evaluations, and portfolios. I will begin by summarizing the section of the law pertaining to homeschool testing and assessments, then answer many of the frequently-asked questions on this subject.

My husband Dwayne and I have been homeschooling our four children for ten years. I have been testing homeschoolers since the late 1980s, and have been doing evaluations and portfolio assessments since the mid-to-late '90s. I've had experience in the public school as well as in homeschool, and have worked with gifted, average, and special-needs children. I hope that my years of experience will benefit you as you glean information from this section.

—Sarah Olbris

Testing and Assessment Law Summary

SUMMARY OF VIRGINIA CODE 22.1-254.1(C)

The parent who elects to provide home instruction shall provide the division superintendent by August 1 following the school year in which the child has received home instruction with either (i) evidence that the child has attained a composite score in or above the fourth stanine (23 percentile) on **any** nationally normed standardized achievement test or (ii) an evaluation or assessment which the division superintendent determines to indicate that the child is achieving an adequate level of educational growth and progress.

In the event that evidence of progress as required in this subsection is not provided by the parent, the home instruction program for that child may be placed on probation for one year. Parents must file with the division superintendent evidence that they can provide an adequate education and a remediation plan for the probationary year. Acceptance of this plan is up to the discretion of the division superintendent.

WHO MUST BE ASSESSED?

Homeschoolers must provide evidence of progress if they have complied with §22.1-254.1 of the Virginia Code by filing a "Notice of Intent to Provide Home Instruction" form or filing a letter with the school division. However, there is an exception for parents who have filed the Notice of Intent: children who are not six years old as of September 30 of the school year are not required to be tested regardless of the grade level. Also, those who are under the religious-exemption provision §22.1-254 (B) (1) or have complied with the certified-tutor statute §22.1-254 (A) are not required to test.

WHY DO I NEED TO SHOW EVIDENCE OF PROGRESS?

There are several reasons to provide an evaluation. One of those reasons is that if you are registered, the law requires test results, or an evaluation, to be turned in every year. There are, however, other good reasons, such as accountability and getting a clear picture or confirmation of your child's academic standing.

Most of us are held accountable to someone—God, our spouses, the government, our bosses, our children, our parents, and the list goes on.

Evaluating our homeschooled children is another way to show our accountability, and it enables us to present clear results to someone to whom we may feel accountable—including ourselves.

Many of us think we have a clear grasp of what our children know and don't know. We are often right, but unfortunately we are sometimes surprised. When we evaluate our children, we receive objective information on what our child knows in a very specific subject area. If there are any weaknesses, they can also be pointed out. We are then able to use those results to make corrections and changes in the appropriate academic areas.

WHAT TESTING ALTERNATIVES DO I HAVE?

Homeschoolers must be tested or evaluated if they have registered under §22.1-254.1 of the Virginia Code by filing a "Notice of Intent to Provide Home Instruction" or a letter with the school division superintendent. The results of a standardized achievement test or an evaluation or assessment must be sent to the division superintendent by August 1 each year. The Virginia homeschool law provides several options for testing and evaluations.

Parents may use one of the following:

1. Any nationally normed standardized achievement test or
2. An evaluation or assessment, including, but not limited to,
   a. an evaluation letter from a person licensed to teach in any state, or a letter from a person with a master's degree or higher in an academic discipline, or
   b. a report card or transcript from a community college or college, college distance learning program, or home education correspondence school.
   c. A portfolio is not specifically mentioned, but may be accepted by a superintendent because evaluations or assessments are not limited to the above mentioned letter, report card, or transcript.

WHO IS NOT REQUIRED TO BE TESTED OR EVALUATED?

Testing is not required for the following:

1. children who are under the age of six as of September 30 of the school year;
2. students who are under the religious-exemption provision §22.1-254(B)(1);
3. students being taught under the certified tutor statute §22.1-254 (A); or
4. students who have graduated, regardless of age.

PRIVATELY ADMINISTERED STANDARDIZED ACHIEVEMENT TESTS

Private standardized testing is the most commonly used option. You may use any nationally normed standardized achievement test. Students must score in or above the fourth stanine or 23rd percentile. Parents may choose from a variety of tests such as—the *Stanford Achievement Test*, the *Comprehensive Test of Basic Skills* (CTBS), the *California Achievement Tests* (CAT), the *Iowa Test of Basic Skills* (ITBS-TAP), *Science Research Associates*

(SRA), *Peabody, Metropolitan, Wide Range Achievement Test,* and the *Woodcock-Johnson Educational Battery.*

These tests may be administered in a group setting or on an individual basis. Some private schools offer testing for a minimal cost to homeschoolers when they test their own students. There are many private testers and co-ops that will test groups of homeschoolers. Costs will vary.

Individual testing companies may impose restrictions on test usage, i.e., who can administer it, to what size group, which grades can be grouped together, if it can be given individually, and so forth.

EVALUATION

If an independent evaluation or assessment is chosen, the evaluation letter must be completed by a person licensed to teach in any state, or a person with a master's degree or higher in an academic discipline who has knowledge of the child's academic progress. It must state that the child is achieving an adequate level of educational growth and progress.

The evaluator may choose to administer a criterion-referenced test (teacher-made test based on subjects that have been taught or based on the Virginia Standards of Learning). He may interview the child, review samples of his work, and type a one-, two- or three-page report indicating whether there is enough progress to go on to the next grade.

An evaluation or assessment may also include a report card or transcript from a community college or college, college distance learning program, or home education correspondence school.

The division superintendent or his designee will determine if the child is achieving an adequate level of educational growth and progress.

PORTFOLIO EVALUATION

Because a portfolio is not specifically mentioned as a form of evaluation, some superintendents may be reluctant to accept it. However, the law does not limit the methods of evaluation to only those listed. If a portfolio is used, it should be evaluated by a person licensed to teach in any state, or a person with a master's degree or higher in an academic discipline who has knowledge of the child's academic progress. It must state that the child is achieving an adequate level of educational growth and progress.

The portfolio is a compilation of samples of the student's progress in work from the beginning to the end of the school year. If this method is used, a system for choosing and organizing samples of each student's work should be started at the beginning of the year. An evaluator may review the portfolio and write a letter of review for the parent to send to the division superintendent. In some cases, the parent has been known to submit the portfolio itself to the superintendent.

Note: Occasionally, local school administrators devise policies that ignore these provisions in the law. HEAV suggests parents submit all evaluations in a timely fashion, know the law, and contact support-group leaders who are familiar with local policies. Seek legal counsel if necessary.

Tests and Testing Q & A

HO CAN TEST MY CHILD?
The state law does not address who must administer the tests for homeschooled students; neither does it require preapproval of the tester.

Although the law contains no specific requirements for test administrators or evaluators, if testing is done privately, parents are responsible for adhering to the test publisher's standards and instructions. This may include a requirement that the test be administered by a person other than the parent or by a person with a college degree or other credentials. Others may require a certain number of children in the testing group or may require the test to be administered individually.

The law also does not require that test administrators or evaluators be approved *in advance* by the local division superintendent. The only authority the superintendent has is to determine 1) if the student has attained a composite score (math and language arts) in or above the fourth stanine or 23rd percentile on ANY nationally normed standardized achievement test, or 2) if the evaluation "indicates the child is achieving an adequate level of growth and progress." There is no "cut off" score under the evaluation option.

If you test your child, you must be careful to use good testing ethics and be careful to abide by the test publisher's guidelines. If you compromise the rules and ethics of testing your own child, you could be making this kind of testing very difficult for other homeschoolers in the future.

Many parents opt to have their students tested by someone else so they are unquestionably above reproach. Even though the tester's name usually does not appear on the test scores, and the school system has no way of knowing who administered the test, it is sometimes preferable to have someone other than a parent give the test. Reasons for considering having someone else test your child are 1) your child may request extra help from you during the test; 2) he may try harder for someone else; and 3) it may be less frustrating for you.

WHAT KIND OF CREDENTIALS SHOULD THE TESTER HAVE?
If someone other than you will be testing your child, it may be beneficial to have a certified teacher or tester (the certification can be from any state)

who has a bachelor's degree and understands testing principles and ethics.

WHERE CAN I LOCATE PRIVATE TESTERS OR EVALUATORS?

Testers can be found through friends, family, support groups, local homeschool newsletters, church, or other homeschoolers. Local support groups are the best source for information about evaluators and testers in your area. To connect with a local group, visit www.heav.org/support/index. html or contact the HEAV office at office@heav.org or 804-278-9200.

WHAT TEST SHOULD I USE?

There are many tests that will meet the needs of homeschoolers. To name a few: *Iowa Test of Basic Skills, Stanford Achievement Test, California Achievement Test, Peabody, Metropolitan, Woodcock-Johnson, Wide Range Achievement Test*, and many more. Any of these tests will meet the requirements of testing for language arts and mathematics.

Take a look at your child's learning and testing styles. Can he read well? Can she sit still for 30-50 minutes at a time? Can he fill in a bubble sheet without losing his place or coloring outside the lines? Does she do her work within a "normal" amount of time or does she usually take a long time to complete assignments?

You may need to ask other questions like: Can I administer this test myself? Does the test have current norms? (Some school systems are getting picky about this.) Are there any rules the publisher may have that would prevent me from administering the test to my own child?

HOW DO THE TESTS DIFFER?

The *Stanford, Iowa,* and *California* are the most popular of the tests, and are fairly easy to obtain. A complete battery will take anywhere from 2-5 days to administer. The *Stanford* has a reputation for being more rigorous, probably because there are a lot of inductive-reasoning questions in the Reading Comprehension section, and some of the sub-tests have time limits as long as 45 minutes, beginning as early as the third grade. (For some children, this is a very long time to have to sit still and concentrate for one sub-test.)

The *Iowa* has the reputation for being a good "middle-of-the-road" test. The sub-tests range from 9-30 minutes in length, and there is a good mix of inductive and deductive reasoning questions in the Reading Comprehension section.

Testers must be qualified but the restrictions are not quite as severe for the *Iowa* as for the *Stanford*. The *California* has had the reputation for being the easiest of these three tests. However, the newest of the *California* tests, the CAT-5, seems to be more comparable to the *Iowa*. There are no restrictions on the tester's qualifications for this test. Older versions may be obtained through other sources.

Most other standardized tests are designed to be given individually or in a group setting. They may be obtained through various sources. Check with the vendors about necessary tester qualifications. A qualified person who owns the test must administer tests such as the *Wide Range Achievement*

Test and the *Woodcock-Johnson.*

It is a good idea to check on norm dates so that you will be using the most up-to-date tests. It has been said that the older tests are more difficult. Consider, however, that word meanings have changed since the '70s and '80s. Also, students are now required to do higher levels of math at earlier ages. If you choose to administer the complete battery, which includes science and social studies, remember that a lot of changes have occurred in technology and history since you were in school.

DO KINDERGARTNERS HAVE TO BE TESTED?

Children who are NOT six by September 30 of the school year do not have to be tested: grade level is not the prerequisite—age is. "The [testing] requirements of subsection (C) shall not apply to children who are under the age of six as of September 30 of the school year" § 22.1-254.1 (C). Therefore, a five-year-old kindergarten student will not have to be tested; however, a six-year-old kindergarten student will have to be tested if his birthday is before September 30.

ARE STUDENTS REQUIRED TO TAKE THE ENTIRE TEST?

Testing is only required for language arts and mathematics. Certain subdivisions in language arts and mathematics are necessary for determining the composite score (i.e., vocabulary, reading comprehension, language skills, and work-study skills, reading comprehension, written expression, math reasoning, math computation, *et cetera*.) However, testing is not required for science, history, or any other subject area.

HOW CAN I HELP MY CHILD PREPARE FOR THE TEST?

There are a multitude of test prep materials on the market. Some are sample tests like *Scoring High* and the Bob Jones University Prep Test. These will give your child examples from most sections so that they will know what to expect from a bubble test. This will also give you a chance to teach skills like filling in bubbles, and—for grades 3-4 and up—how to keep your place while going back and forth from a bubble sheet to a test. When choosing these prep tests, be sure to use one that is made for the test that you have chosen for your child, i.e., *California, Stanford,* or *Iowa.*

Other test prep materials may be purchased through www.heav.org/testing/resources.html, local teacher supply stores, or accessed online from testing sites such as www.collegeboard.com. They offer practical testing hints such as:

- Go through all of the test questions as quickly as you can, answering only the ones that you know. Then go back and do the others.
- Do not sharpen pencils to a fine point. Having a dull point will fill in the blanks faster.

WHEN IS THE BEST TIME TO DO THE TESTING?

Testing may be done anytime from February through July. However, make sure if you do a test like the *Stanford, Iowa,* or *California* that you allow enough time for the results to be returned to you. Remember that all results must be turned in to the division superintendent by August 1. It can take about 6-8 weeks from the time you order the test to have the test shipped to you, administer the test, send the test back to be graded, and have the results sent to you.

HOW MUCH SHOULD I EXPECT TO PAY FOR TESTING?

Be prepared to pay $20 to $40 for the test if you are ordering it yourself. Costs for proctoring range anywhere from $0 to $200, depending on who is administering the testing, and whether the student is in a group or an individual setting.

NOW THAT I HAVE THE TEST SCORES BACK, HOW DO I READ THEM?

Most test result have three scores: National Percentile Rank, Stanine Score, and Grade Equivalent.

The National Percentile Rank tells how your child ranked nationally against other students in that grade. If your child scored in the 75th percentile, they did better than 75 out of 100 students.

The Stanine Score tells where your child's score was located on a bell curve. The 1st, 2nd, and 3rd stanines are considered below average, 4th, 5th, and 6th are considered average, and 7th, 8th, and 9th are considered above average.

The Grade Equivalent tells that a child in *that* grade at *that* time of year would have scored as well as your child did. If your child scored 7.2, any child in the 7th grade 2nd month could score as well as your child did. It does not mean that your child is working on the 7th grade level – unless they really are in the 7th grade. This score should be used more like a gauge, i.e., my child is doing really well because they scored 7.2 and they're only in the 4th grade; my child is right on track because they just finished the 6th grade; or my child needs some extra help in that area because they're in the 10th grade.

HOW DO I KNOW IF MY CHILD "PASSED"?

The law states that the child must have "a composite score in or above the 4th stanine (23rd percentile)," for option (i) testing. If one sub-test score is a little below the 23rd percentile and others are above, then, with their formula, it may average out. Look at the area on the test results labeled "Core Battery" or "Composite Score" to find out if your child meets the state's requirements.

What are my options if my child does not make the minimum test score?

If your child does not meet the minimum test score of 23rd percentile you have two options:
- You may send in the low scores and possibly be put on probation for the next school year. At the discretion of the division superintendent, the parent may file a remediation plan for one additional year of home-schooling. The parent must also show that he is able to provide an adequate education for his child. Both the remedial plan and evidence of providing an adequate education must be approved by the division

superintendent. In order to continue homeschooling, the child *must* meet the minimum score of 23 percentile the following year. If he does not meet this minimum score, you may be required to register your child in a formal school setting (not necessarily a public school).

- Another alternative is to have the student re-tested with a different standardized test, or have an evaluation done. If the student is tested by the end of May, there is usually sufficient time to make this kind of decision should it be necessary. If you wait past late May to test, results may not be returned to you until late July. This gives you little time for other options and puts you in a time crunch to get results to the division superintendent by the due date. The results of this second form of assessment may be sent to the division superintendent.

WHAT DO I DO IF MY CHILD HAS A LEARNING DISABILITY?

If you suspect your child has a learning disability, it is very important to have him evaluated by a professional and document the results. If you choose to use a standardized test, it may be helpful to attach a copy of his evaluation results and/or a Student Education Program (SEP). In this case, "adequate progress" may be acceptable. You may also choose other forms of assessment mentioned earlier.

WHAT IF I DISAGREE WITH THE SUPERINTENDENT'S DECISION?

If a parent disagrees with a division superintendent's decision regarding testing, probation, or any other aspect of homeschooling, he may appeal within thirty days to an independent hearing officer. The cost of the appeal will be apportioned by the hearing officer in a manner consistent with his findings.

WHAT DO I DO WITH THE RESULTS OF MY CHILD'S ASSESSMENT?

You are responsible to send the results to the school system. Do not assume that your tester or test vendor will send the results in for you. Send the results to the superintendent or the person in your school system to whom you report, and remember to **keep a copy for your own files.**

WHEN DO THE RESULTS NEED TO BE TURNED IN TO THE SCHOOL SYSTEM?

All test results must be turned in to the division superintendent or his designee by **August 1** after each year of homeschooling.

MUST MY CHILD TAKE THE SOL TESTS?

Because SOL tests lead to a public-school diploma, homeschoolers are *not allowed* to take the tests. If a homeschooled student enrolled in a public school, only then would they be required to take SOL tests just as other transfer students would be required to take them.

Testing Tips

Benita Howell

FOR CHILD—

1. Drink plenty of water.
2. Read all test directions carefully. The testing administrator will go over the directions, usually reading two samples aloud.
3. Look for clue words. Several answers may be good, but which one is best? Watch for the words "always" or "never."
4. Think of an answer before you read the choices. Then read the choices carefully, weeding out the obviously wrong answers.
5. Test the answer by adding it to the question and reading it as a statement.
6. Don't spend too much time on one item. Move on!
7. Go back to questions you weren't sure about and narrow down the answers to make a logical guess. Don't leave an answer blank on the answer sheet. This avoids the possibility of mismarking the next answers by putting the right answer in the wrong box.
8. Only mark one answer bubble per question or it will be counted as wrong. Fully erase errors and stray marks.
9. Try each answer in the blank to help you decide which one sounds right.
10. During the "Reading Comprehension" test, read the questions first, then read the reading passage.

FOR MOM—

1. Make sure your child is well-fed and well-rested on the testing day.
2. Your child shouldn't have a full stomach because the brain needs the fresh and abundant supply of blood which might be helping to digest the stomach's overload of food.
3. Build feelings of confidence in your child rather than anxiety. You need to stay calm about the test so your child will be calm.
4. Practice the test format beforehand by writing out spelling words in groups of four and asking your child to find the one word that is spelled incorrectly.
5. Write a letter to your child, then tell him or her to insert correct punctuation and capitalization; then review it together.
6. When talking with your child use interesting vocabulary words. For example, say aquarium rather than fish tank, or gigantic rather than big.
7. Review how to use a table of contents, an index, an encyclopedia, an

almanac, an atlas, a library card catalog, and a dictionary. Review reading and using maps, charts, and graphs.

8. Throughout every academic year, time your child's math so that he learns to work accurately and efficiently *within time limits*. Do the same with reading selections and comprehension questions.

* You may want to purchase the book, *How to Get Better Test Scores on Elementary School Standardized Tests*, published by Random House. It contains many helpful suggestions and practical ideas. It also includes practice tests.

Note: Contact your local support group for further information. Most groups will be able to direct you to testing resources in your area. Many support groups make special arrangements for members of their own group to be tested together.

Evaluations

Sarah Olbris

Evaluations are an alternative form of assessment. Evaluations tend to be less stressful than standardized tests because they are much more informal (usually an interview style) and nothing is timed. They are extremely beneficial for young children, poor readers, and children with learning disabilities.

There is no set form or format for evaluations and every evaluator will have their own style. Before choosing an evaluator, be sure to ask a lot of questions to be confident that they understand your child and his or her needs.

WHO CAN EVALUATE MY CHILD?

If an independent evaluation or assessment is chosen, the evaluation letter must be completed by a person licensed to teach in any state, or a person with a master's degree or higher in an academic discipline who has knowledge of the child's academic progress. Evaluators may be found through family, friends, other homeschoolers, church, local homeschool newsletters, support groups, *et cetera*.

IS THERE A STANDARD FORM OR FORMAT FOR EVALUATIONS?

No. There are no forms to be filled out. Each evaluator has his or her own way of conducting an evaluation. It is usually done in an interview style with lots of questions to find out how much the student has retained from that school year. A report is written up stating the findings. It must include a statement that the child is or is not achieving an adequate level of educational growth and progress. Ask that the report be sent directly to you. After you have received it, you can forward it to the division superintendent or his designee.

HOW IS AN EVALUATION CONDUCTED?

As stated earlier, each evaluator has his or her own method of conducting an evaluation. They may wish to talk to the parent with or without the student being present, and then speak with the child, or they may not need to speak with the parent at all. They may want a formal portfolio to be presented, or they may just want to see a selection of the student's work, or they may not request to see any of the child's work from that year. The evaluator may use a lot of manipulatives or games. Each evaluator has a specific format to go by, so question potential evaluators on what they will be doing with your child.

WHEN IS THE BEST TIME OF YEAR TO HAVE THE EVALUATION DONE?

Schedule the evaluation when you feel confident that your child will do his or her best. Don't schedule close to vacations or any other time you or the child may feel "pushed." Remember that the evaluation must be sent to the school system by August 1. Be sure to allow enough time for the evaluator to write the report and send it to you so that you can turn it in on time.

HOW MUCH SHOULD I EXPECT TO PAY FOR AN EVALUATION?

Costs will range from $0 to $300 depending on who is doing the evaluation, and what credentials they have. Expect to pay an experienced evaluator more than someone who is just starting to do evaluations. You may be able to barter for the evaluation, or there may be a friend who is willing to do it at no cost. Do not let cost be the only determining factor for which evaluator you choose. Most of the time, it is worth spending a bit more money to insure that your child will have a positive experience, than to save a few dollars and be disappointed with the experience.

HOW DO SCIENCE, GEOGRAPHY, ART, AND OTHER SUBJECTS FACTOR IN?

Since language arts and mathematics are the only two subjects that are required by law, most evaluators will not spend much, if any, time on other subjects. However, it can round out the evaluator's picture of your school year if you mention what has been done above and beyond what the law requires.

QUESTIONS YOU SHOULD ASK WHEN SELECTING AN EVALUATOR:
- What are your credentials?
- What experience have you had in evaluations?
- Are you a homeschooler, and if not, what experience do you have with homeschoolers?
- For my particular situation, do you suggest that my child be tested individually, tested in a group, evaluated, or assessed using a portfolio?
- How will the evaluation be conducted?
- Where will the evaluation be conducted?
- May I be present during the evaluation?
- What do I need to have ready for you?
- What do I need to do to prepare my child for the evaluation?
- Do you need to see a portfolio or will their workbooks/notebooks be sufficient?
- How much do you charge?
- Do you have experience with learning disabilities?
- How do you conduct an evaluation for a non-reader or a poor reader?

This is not by any means an exhaustive list, but it gives you a good start.

Portfolios

Sarah Olbris

A portfolio is not specifically mentioned in the Virginia Code, but it may be accepted by a superintendent because evaluations or assessments are not limited to an evaluation letter, report card, or transcript. A portfolio is probably the form of assessment least stressful to the child because it requires the least amount of interaction with the evaluator. Therefore, this form of assessment is extremely beneficial for children who are: not confident with people they don't know well, poor readers, learning disabled, students for whom English is a second language, and others who may have difficulty with more direct forms of assessment.

Just as there are different ways to conduct an evaluation, there are different schools of thought on portfolio evaluations. Some evaluators want only the portfolio. Others want to see the portfolio and have a short interview with the child. Some want a sample paper from each subject dated at the beginning, middle, and end of the year. Others prefer "scrapbook portfolios containing not only representative work samples but also drawings, a list of books read, photographs of projects and field trips, and anything else that provides a complete picture of the child's education. Be sure to ask the evaluator a lot of questions so that you know what is expected of you and your child, and what should be included in the portfolio.

WHAT IS A PORTFOLIO?

A portfolio is really a scrapbook of your child's progress for that school year. It will not contain everything the child has done for the year, but like most scrapbooks, it will contain the highlights of the year.

WHO CAN EVALUATE MY CHILD'S PORTFOLIO?

If you choose to have a private evaluator look at the portfolio, he or she should be licensed to teach in any state, or a person with a master's degree or higher in an academic discipline who has knowledge of the child's academic progress. It must state that the child is or is not achieving an adequate level of educational growth and progress. Some school divisions will accept a portfolio directly from the parent with no evaluation. However, some have been known to lose or misplace them, so be *extremely* careful if you decide to go this route, and if possible, *keep copies of what you submit.*

IS THERE A STANDARD FORM OR FORMAT FOR PORTFOLIOS?

No. There are no forms to be filled out. You may simply submit your portfolio to an evaluator or to the division superintendent or his designee, however, if you choose to use an evaluator, early in the year, they can give you a list of what they expect to be included in the portfolio. Later, the evaluator will write a report stating their findings. It must state that the child is or is not achieving an adequate level of educational growth and progress. Ask that the report be sent directly to you. You can copy it and forward it to the division superintendent or his designee.

WHAT SHOULD BE IN THE PORTFOLIO?

There are many schools of thought about what should be included in a portfolio. Check with your own evaluator to be sure of what they expect to see in your child's portfolio. Some things that are usually included are:

- A list of all curriculum used
- A list or a sample list of reading materials
- Several samples of the child's work in each subject showing growth and progress. Each evaluator may have different requirements.
- Information on unit studies conducted that year. Include reports, small projects, or pictures of them, and/or a brief description.
- Information about field trips. Information in the portfolio may include anything that the child did in preparation for the trip, a report or coloring project after the field trip, brochures, or pictures taken while there.
- Introduction or summary statement by the student explaining how and why individual pieces were included in the portfolio
- Programs from music recital or dramatic production in which the student has participated
- Copies of community-service awards, contest entries, and anything else that the student is proud of.

Also, allow your child some input as to what goes into the portfolio. They may have enjoyed working on a particular item or be very proud of a particular piece of art that you have forgotten about. Even if you don't like that piece or know they did something else that was much better, allow them to choose at least *some* of what goes in.

WHEN IS THE BEST TIME OF YEAR TO HAVE THE PORTFOLIO EVALUATION DONE?

Schedule the portfolio evaluation toward end of the school year. You may be able to drop the portfolio off to be evaluated, but the evaluator must have ample time to review the portfolio and write the report. Since the report must be sent to the division superintendent by August 1, be sure to allow enough time for the evaluator to write the report and send it to you so that you can turn it in on time.

Note: Even though the portfolio does not need to be finished until the end of the school year, putting things in the portfolio is an ongoing project throughout the school year. If you know at the beginning of the school year that a portfolio will be beneficial to you and your child, begin early to set things aside to put into the portfolio. This will make the task of finishing the portfolio at the end of the school year much less tedious.

HOW MUCH SHOULD I EXPECT TO PAY FOR A PORTFOLIO EVALUATION?

Like an evaluation, costs will range from $0 to $300 depending on who is doing the evaluation and what credentials they have. Expect to pay an experienced evaluator more than someone who is just starting out. You may be able to barter for the evaluation or there may be a friend who is willing to do it at no cost. Most of the time it is worth spending more money if it will gain you the services of the evaluator you want, rather than to save a few dollars and be disappointed with the experience.

SHOULD WE INCLUDE SCIENCE, GEOGRAPHY, ART, AND OTHER SUBJECTS IN THE PORTFOLIO?

Since language arts and mathematics are the only two subjects that are required by law, most evaluators will not spend much, if any time on other subjects. However, if you include anything that has been done above and beyond what the law requires, you will provide the evaluator with a more complete picture of your school year. These areas of study are much easier to include and give appropriate recognition when they are in a portfolio. The evaluator does not need to spend a lot of time asking questions about those sections since there is no great need for interview.

QUESTIONS YOU SHOULD ASK WHEN SEEKING A PORTFOLIO EVALUATOR.

- What are your credentials?
- What experience have you had in portfolio evaluations?
- Are you a homeschooler and if not, what experience do you have with homeschoolers?
- For my particular situation, do you suggest that my child be tested individually, tested in a group, evaluated, or assessed using a portfolio?
- What do you want to see included in the portfolio?
- Do you need to interview me or my child as part of the portfolio evaluation?
- What must I to do to prepare my child for the interview if one is required?
- Do I need to drop the portfolio off to you? If so, when do you want it?
- How much will you charge?
- Do you have experience with learning disabilities?

RESOURCES:

Using Portfolios to Assess Student Performance: Far West Laboratory, 730 Harrison Street, San Francisco. CA 94107.

Student Portfolios and Teacher Logs: Blueprint for a Revolution in Assessment, a twelve-page report; National Center for the Study of Writing, 55134 Tolman Hall, Graduate School of Education, University of California, Berkeley, CA 94720. Request Report #TR-65.

Testing Resources

EST PREPARATION MATERIALS

For a more complete listing of test preparation materials, be sure to visit the HEAV website at www.heav.org/testing.

Scoring High, from SRA, 250 Old Wilson Bridge Road, Suite 310, Worthington, Ohio 43085; or from Home School Resource Center at www.hsrc.com.

Bob Jones University Press Practice Tests, from BJUP, Greenville, South Carolina 29614. www.bju.edu

How to Get Better Test Scores on Elementary School Standardized Tests (published by Random House). It is out of print but contains many helpful suggestions and practical ideas and includes practice tests. You might try eBay, Half.com, AAABookSearch.com, or other used-book resources.

SOURCES FOR TESTS:
BASIC ACHIEVEMENT SKILLS INVENTORY (BASI)
Family Learning Organization
www.familylearning.org
homeschool@familylearning.org
P.O. Box 1750
Mead, WA 99021
800-405-TEST
509-467-2552
Cost: $30/student. Shipping is $5 an order, regardless of the number of tests ordered.
Norm Date: 2003

BRIGANCE DIAGNOSTIC INVENTORIES
HSLDA
www.hslda.org/strugglinglearner/BriganceRental.asp
540-338-5600 (ask for Betty Statnick or Faith Berens)
P.O. Box 3000
Purcellville, VA 20134-9000
Cost: HSLDA rents the Brigance to their members for $36, plus a $75

NORMING DATES
Some school districts require tests normed within the past eleven years. Check norming dates when ordering if required in your area.

Be sure to visit the testing section of the HEAV website for complete information on testing and test preparation resources. Visit www.heav. org/testing.

deposit to be refunded if the manual is returned on time and in good condition.

To Order: See instructions on the website. You must be a member of HSLDA to rent the Brigance from them; find out more about becoming a member (HEAV members save $20 on HSLDA membership).

CALIFORNIA ACHIEVEMENT TEST (CAT)

Bayside School Services
www.BaysideSchoolServices.com
orders@BaysideSchoolServices.com
137 Clipper Court, P.O. Box 250
Kill Devil Hills, NC 27948
800-723-3057

Grade Levels: Complete battery for K-12th grade; survey (short form) for 2nd - 12th grades.

Qualifications: No special qualifications needed to order the tests.

Cost: Ranges from $45 to $60, depending on the time of year. Discounts available for groups.

Time: Tests vary from 2 to 5.5 hours

Subjects Covered that make up the composite score: reading vocabulary, reading comprehension, language mechanics, language expression, math computation, and math concepts and applications. Spelling, study skills (word analysis), science, and social studies are optional subtests. The available Test of Cognitive Skills is a separate test which measures academic aptitude.

To Order: Call 1-800-723-3057 or e-mail orders@baysideschoolservices.com.

Norm Date: 1991

Christian Liberty Press
www.christianlibertypress.com/services.htm
502 W. Euclid Avenue
Arlington Heights, IL 60004
800-832-2741, option 6

Grade Levels: Available for 2nd-12th grade

Qualifications: No special qualifications needed to order the test.

Cost: $25-$30 per student depending on whether you use the online or the paper test.

Time: 2.5-3 hours to complete test

Difficulty: Easier than some other tests. Percentage scores may show higher when compared with other tests.

Subjects Covered: READING: vocabulary and comprehension; MATHEMATICS: computations, concepts and problems; LANGUAGE: mechanics, usage, structure, and spelling.

To Order: Call Christian Liberty and request their testing-service form to order the test. Tests can also be ordered through the above website.

Norm Date: 1970s

NORMING DATES
Some school districts require tests normed within the past eleven years. Check norming dates when ordering if required in your area.

Be sure to visit the testing section of the HEAV website for complete information on testing and test preparation resources. Visit www.heav.org/testing.

Family Learning Organization

www.familylearning.org

homeschool@familylearning.org

P.O. Box 7247

Spokane, WA 99207-0247

1-800-405-TEST or 509-467-2552

Cost: $35 per student. Shipping is $5 an order, regardless of the number of tests ordered.

Norm Date: 1992

Piedmont Education Services

www.pesdirect.com

www.pesdirect.com/cat5.html

service@pesdirect.com

1629 Turfwood Drive

Pfafftown, NC 27040

336-924-2494

Cost: Ranges from $48 to $58, depending on the time of year. Discounts available for groups.

Norm Date: 1993

Seton Testing Services

www.setontesting.com

1350 Progress Drive

Front Royal, VA 22630

540-636-1250 or 800-542-1066

Grade Levels: Available for K-12th grade

Qualifications: No special qualifications needed to order the tests.

Cost: $25 per student

Time: 2.0-2.5 hours

Also available: Spectrum Preparation booklets, 1st - 8th grades ($10 plus s/h); not required, but recommended.

To Order: Order online, call and order by phone, or download order form and complete and mail in with payment.

Norm Date: 1988

COMPREHENSIVE TEST OF BASIC SKILLS (CTBS)

The Sycamore Tree

info@sycamoretree.com

www.sycamoretree.com

2179 Meyer Place

Costa Mesa, CA 92627

800-779-6750

Cost: $50/student plus shipping.

Availability: Tests are available to purchase between April 1 and May 5 and again between July 1 and August 5. Tests must be administered

NORMING DATES

Some school districts require tests normed within the past eleven years. Check norming dates when ordering if required in your area.

Be sure to visit the testing section of the HEAV website for complete information on testing and test preparation resources. Visit www. heav.org/testing.

and returned to the company within three weeks to avoid a $25 late fee. The Sycamore Tree sends all tests out for machine scoring at the end of the testing period; if you need the test sooner, they can hand score it for an additional $30.

IOWA TEST OF BASIC SKILLS

Bob Jones University Press
www.bjup.com
Greenville, SC 29614
1-800-845-5731

Grade Levels: Available for K-12th grade

Qualifications: Anyone can place an order for the tests, but materials will only be shipped to a qualified tester who must administer the test and return for scoring. The test scores will be returned to the person who initially ordered the test. Test administrator must have four-year degree, or be a certified teacher, or be a working teacher in a conventional school.

Time: Depends on age of student and testing conditions

Subjects Covered: May vary according to grade level. READING: vocabulary, word analysis skills, and comprehension; MATHEMATICS: concepts and computation; LANGUAGE: spelling, capitalization, and punctuation; WORD STUDY SKILLS: map reading, graphs, tables, knowledge, and use of reference materials.

Cost: Depends on tests ordered. Call Bob Jones to order their testing booklet, which includes information on the tests and order forms, along with qualifications needed to order.

Also available from BJU Press: The Test of Achievement and Proficiency (TAP), the Stanford Achievement Test, and practice tests/previews

Norm Date: 1995

NOTE: Must provide proof of homeschooling in the form of a signature on the order form. Form available on their website.

Summit Christian Academy
www.SCAHomeschool.com
info@SCAHomeschool.com
P.O. Box 2769
Cedar Hill, TX 75106
1-800-362-9180

Grade Levels: Complete battery for grades 3-12

Cost: $50 (non-members); $45 (Summit members)

Qualifications: No special qualifications required to order test, but someone with a college degree must administer. Tests in March on Iowa Basic, so orders must be in by the end of February.

Norm Date: 2000 (Form A)

NORMING DATES
Some school districts require tests normed within the past eleven years. Check norming dates when ordering if required in your area.

TIP: *When looking for someone for counseling, testing, or tutoring of your child (including children with special needs), be sure to check the list for Tutoring, Counseling and Testing Resources in Section G, page G-32 on the CD. This list is by no means exhaustive, and these contacts are not HEAV representatives. Each contact will supply you with their fee structure and requirements.*

Triangle Education Assessments
www.HomeSchoolerTests.com
5512 Merion Station Drive
Apex, NC 27539
919-387-7004 (M-F, 8 a.m.-5 p.m. EST)
877-843-8837
Iowa Tests Offered: ITBS, ITED, CogAT, and Interest Explorer. Practice tests also available.
Grade Levels: Available for grades K-12. (Woodcock-Johnson administered on-site for any age; prices vary, but the basic test runs about $90.)
Cost: $40 per student.
Group discounts: 25 to 40 - $2 off; 41 to 65 - $4 off; 66+ - $6 off
Qualifications: Any homeschool family can order but a bachelor's degree is needed to administer.

PERSONALIZED ASSESSMENT SUMMARY SYSTEM (PASS)

Hewitt Research Foundation
www.hewitthomeschooling.com
Washougal, WA 98671
800-890-4097 or 360-835-8708 (M-Th, 8 a.m.–4 p.m., PST)
About This Test: Hewitt Research Foundation offers a special test that is accepted in some areas. (Superintendents must accept ANY nationally normed test, but since this test is not nationally normed, it is subject to approval. Check with your county superintendent to see if is an acceptable method of evaluation before ordering.) According to the publishers, the test was "developed specifically for home schoolers." It is not timed, can be administered by parents at home, and includes a placement test, allowing children to be tested at their actual level instead of forcing them to take a test with problems both above and below their level.
Grade Levels: Available only for 3rd-8th grade. Order the grade level with which you want your child compared.
Qualifications: No special qualifications are required to order or administer this exam.
Cost: $26 per student. The test fee pays for a placement test to determine which test level is needed, the actual PASS exam, scoring, and a detailed analysis and suggestions for dealing with areas of difficulty.

PSYCHOLOGICAL ASSESSMENT RESOURCES

PAR
www.parinc.com
800-331-8378
Cost: Introductory kit (includes everything needed to test 50 children) is around $250 plus shipping. This source does not sell in smaller quantities.
Qualifications: To place an order, you will need to submit an application and be approved. To be approved, you must have, "A degree from an accredited 4-year college or university in psychology, counseling,

speech-language pathology, or a closely related field, PLUS satisfactory completion of coursework in test interpretation, psychometrics and measurement theory, educational statistics, or a closely related area; OR a license or certification from an agency that requires appropriate training and experience in the ethical and competent use of psychological tests."

STANFORD ACHIEVEMENT TEST (SAT)

Bob Jones University Press
www.bjupress.com/services/testing
Greenville, SC 29614
1-800-845-5731
Cost: $44/without OLSAT; $63.50/with OLSAT.
Qualifications: Only pre-approved Stanford administers can order; see website for details.
Norm Date: 2002 (Stanford 10)

WIDE RANGE ACHIEVEMENT TEST (WRAT)

Summit Christian Academy
www.SCAHomeschool.com
info@SCA.com
P.O. Box 2769
Cedar Hill, TX 75106
800-362-9180
Cost: $30/student.
Qualifications: No special qualifications required to order test. College degree required to give the test. Summit will evaluate the test and return the results to parent unless it is being used as a pretest for placement test.

WOODCOCK-JOHNSON TEST TESTS OF ACHIEVEMENT – (WJ3)

Qualifications: This test can only be administered by someone certified on the test. Look at the HEAV online list of Counselors, Testers, and Tutors for testers that mention the Woodcock-Johnson (www.heav. org/testing/counselingtestingtutoringresources.html).

(List compiled by the Home Educators Association of Virginia and the Bayith Educator. Updated by HEAV with the help of Sarah Olbris in February 2009.)

QUALIFIED EVALUATORS AND PRIVATE TESTERS

Local support groups are the best source for information about evaluators and testers in your area. For a listing of local support groups, visit www. heav.org/support, or call HEAV at 804-278-9200. You may also wish to view HEAV's listings of Counselors, Testers, and Tutors at www.heav.org/testing/counselingtestingtutoringresources.html.

SUPPORT GROUPS

For more information on who can give tests and evaluations in your area, contact your local support group. [See "Support" at www.heav.org/support for lists of support groups throughout the state.]

Section D

High School
at Home

Compiled by Anne Miller

Additional Articles on the CD
BE SURE TO CHECK OUT THESE OTHER GREAT ARTICLES ON THE CD!

Each article in the book and on the CD has been carefully chosen by the section coordinator to increase your knowledge and understanding of this subject, so don't forget to use and enjoy the parts of the manual on your CD, as well as the part you are holding.

Please note that the page numbering on the CD is different from that of the hard-copy manual.

Teaching Teens at Home

D eciding to teach your teen at home may be one of the scariest—and most rewarding—decisions you'll ever make. This section brings you the wisdom of experienced parents and educators, and is designed to help you think through the many issues involved in teaching your teen at home.

Doubts about the value and fitness of home education can be assuaged by reading John Taylor Gatto's *The Underground History of American Education* [available from HEAV]. Gatto traces the development of our current education system and reveals the systematic dumbing down of our children—he will give you the boost you need to make the break from traditional schooling.

The teen years are an exciting time of growth and maturity—a time when our young people are trying to make sense of the world around them and their relationship to it. Home education provides a solid, nurturing framework in an age-integrated environment that largely does away with the debilitating effects of peer pressure. Our children are free to develop their talents and interests through independent study and meaningful work and service.

This is not to say, however, that the teen years are without their challenges simply because we homeschool. Trials will come, but as parents, we must persevere. We must stand firm in our beliefs, while at the same time having tender hearts of compassion and understanding for our teens. We must fight for our children, knowing that the time we invest in them will never be wasted!

—Anne Miller

Understanding the Purpose of High School

By Sandy Lundberg

In the early years of our country, most people's education ended at eighth grade or before. Soon afterward, they entered adulthood, either through marriage, employment, or apprenticeship. Many young women started teaching school when they were fifteen. Many young men entered college at sixteen. It was not until the beginning last century that what we now call "high school" came into existence. From its roots as a method of training workers and assimilating immigrant children, it has now evolved into a basic educational entry level into society—either directly into the world of work, or to further studies at the college level.

In order to get the most benefit from these years, take your focus off the specific subjects young people study in high school, and step back far enough to look at the bigger picture. What kind of adult would you like your child to become? What are his interests, passions, and gifts? What areas of special ability does he demonstrate? Involve your teen in the discovery process. During the elementary years, you took the primary responsibility in setting the direction for your child's education. In high school, this responsibility should begin to shift to the child. It is almost impossible to motivate a young person to work and strive toward a challenging goal if it is one for which he feels no personal ownership.

Hopefully, you will have provided a wide range of studies and experiences in the younger years so that your young person has an idea of what interests him. Together through prayer, reading, evaluating, and asking many questions, you and your teenager can begin to sketch out a future destination.

The most important thing you can do to help your teen as you prepare him for life, is to encourage good character. The young person who is honest, prompt, alert, and interested, takes initiative, knows how to learn, can follow instructions, gets along with other people, and acts responsibly will have no problem getting a job, being promoted, succeeding in college, or eventually running his own company. Use the high school years to cement these character traits into your teenager.

The second way you can help your teenager during these years is by a gradual increase in his level of personal responsibility. A teen needs to take more and more responsibility for his own learning, finances, time, relationship with God, and personal growth. Help him to develop these skills under your guidance and direction, providing the structure and opportunity for trial and error without irreversible repercussions.

Be sure your teen is prepared to function independently with his life skills. Consider all the skills you take for granted: your teen should be able to maintain a checking account, drive a car, cook dinner, sew on a button, care for the yard, pay bills, book airline tickets, and so many other acts of self-sufficiency. Don't let your teen leave home without these basic skills.

Your young person must also be prepared to compete in the larger arena of differing worldviews. Now is the time to introduce the conflicting ideas and arguments that he will encounter in college and in the work place. Study David Nobel's book *Understanding the Times*, or *Let Us Highly Resolve* by David Quine. Subscribe to *World* magazine. Familiarize your teen with national and world events, and with current modes of thinking, such as postmodernism. Have deep discussions about poverty, feminism, euthanasia, the role of government, the environment, welfare, abortion, violence and crime, and what constitutes a family. Alert him to the dangers of pornography, alcohol, and drugs. Together, look for answers to tough questions in the Scriptures.

Finally, don't just worry about what your young person needs to know, teach him how to learn. This might include how to conduct research, read for information, study efficiently, take notes, outline a book or lecture, then skillfully communicate what he has learned verbally and in writing. Help him develop his vocabulary. Study logic and thinking skills. Teach time management. A young person who is skilled in these areas will be a lifelong learner. Since most adults change careers several times during their working life, these skills are necessary for survival.

Once you have considered the bigger picture, you are ready to start thinking about academics; but even in this area, don't limit your thinking to your own high school experience. There are so many creative ways to reach your goals. The more clearly you define the destination, the more efficiently you can map out the route. Your teen has only a limited amount of the precious commodity "time." Focus his efforts on reaching the final goal.

Homeschool Is Best for Teens

Mary Schofield

Something odd happens to many homeschool families when their children become teenagers. They begin to revisit the same questions that newcomers to homeschooling usually ask. We've all heard them, found the answers, and then moved on—when our children were little. But when they become teens, it seems we take up the old issues as if they were suddenly relevant again.

By homeschooling teens, are we shielding them from the "real" world? Are we depriving them of socialization among their peers? Are we trying to cover academic areas best left to "experts"? What if they don't learn all they should? The insecurities we left behind when our children were in the primary grades creep in again.

THE REAL WORLD

The "real world" question is as much a non-issue for teens as it was for kindergartners. The *real* world still isn't found in high schools. High schools promote pooling the unrealistic ideas and values of teenagers.

High schools promote comparing oneself with others and trying to outdo one's peers rather than serving them. Many high schools promote the idea that education is simply acquiring knowledge, and that any idea is a good one as long as you like it.

By contrast, the real world is learning to put others first, to manage a home, and to love one's family. It is learning the value of work, responsibility, honesty, and commitment. These are best learned at home.

TEEN MISSIONARIES

What about the idea that our teens make such great missionaries to the public schools? If a teen truly had a call to be a missionary to his peers, would enrolling him in the local high school really be a good way to fulfill that call?

I know that relationships are developed with peers when one sits in classes and works on group projects with them over a period of time, and certainly some students are saved through the witness of their Christian friends.

But wouldn't a more direct approach work for just as many? Teens working with their families and their churches have found wonderful ways of ministering to their peers without wasting hours upon hours listening to evolutionist theories in science classes, humanistic ideals in history, and psychological garbage in literature courses.

SOCIALIZATION

How about the "socialization" question? Is it any more relevant now than when we began homeschooling years ago? Yes, I believe it is. It is a far *more* relevant issue for teens than for elementary-aged children. Yet, the reason it is more relevant now is not because our children need to be around peers *more* when they reach their teens; it's because just the *opposite* is true.

Studies of school children show that among elementary-aged children, parents still have by far the greatest influence even though their children are around their peers all day. But as they reach junior high, the balance changes; teens in schools are influenced more by their peers as each year goes by.

Now look for a moment at those peers. You may be blessed to have a nice group of friends for your teens, but how mature are they really? Are their decisions the ones you want your teen to follow? Are they the consistent examples of godly wisdom and maturity that you would choose to disciple your teen?

If these peers begin to turn from the Lord's way, and your teen is spending hours daily with them, will he see the slight veering from Truth that begins a downward spiral?

At what age were *you* most tempted to sin? Most of us went through a time of major decision making in our teens. Maturity is reached *after* going through this process, not before and not during.

By expecting our teens to be fully responsible adults, we are short-changing them. They still have much need of guidance during their teens.

Look closer at what teens are missing in the high school social scene. Which activity makes you feel you may be depriving your teens? The *a cappella* choir? The orchestra? The yearbook? The school paper?

What was it about these events or activities that makes them such great memories for us? The camaraderie, the teamwork, the commitment to finish a task? The feeling of accomplishment when the game is won, the performance receives a standing ovation, and the yearbook is finished?

Wouldn't our teens be better off learning the blessing of a task well done, shared commitment, teamwork, and self-sacrifice through their family, church, and community projects, under the guidance of Christian leaders and with the aim of pleasing God—not man or self?

ACADEMICS

What about academics? Isn't it intimidating to look at chemistry books if you didn't do well in chemistry or if, like me, you never took chemistry at all? Relax. Student who take an interest in this field will likely surpass their parents' knowledge of chemistry early on in the course (unless Dad is a chemist, in which case you have no cause for concern). Students at this level are rarely limited by their parents' lack of knowledge.

There are many helpful resources available from which the teen can learn any subject. If you teach your teen how to find and use resources well, you will not need to be overly concerned about trying to master every subject yourself.

What exactly is it that teens should be learning anyway? Is it mostly academics? Look in the Scriptures to see what older women are to teach the younger. Timothy says it is to love their husbands and children, to keep a home, to practice hospitality. Will your daughter learn this in a traditional high school?

What are older men to teach the younger men? Look at the example in Proverbs. Solomon taught his son about being a faithful husband to one wife, about seeking wisdom, about knowing when to hold his tongue, and about what to do when he had offended someone.

Yes, there is a place for academic knowledge and a place for experts in various fields of study. One doesn't need to attend a campus school in order to make use of the knowledge of masters. Check the library, the yellow pages, your church members, and your support group. If you have a need or an interest in a technical academic area, you'll find that those who have acquired the knowledge you need are glad to share it.

What about "gaps" in your teen's education? I have discovered that in every single person there are educational gaps. Did you learn everything you ever needed to know in high school? Have you learned everything now? There is no such thing as an education with no gaps.

The perfect education, the perfect course of study, the perfect text-book—these are all unattainable for sinful man who sees only in part. We will not learn it all or know it all while we are on the earth.

There *will* be gaps; but they are not deadly. When you come across a lack of knowledge in your own life, what do you do? You get out the cookbook, the car manual, the VCR instructions, or you go to the library. Teach your teens to do the same. Teach your teens to be researchers, and when they find a gap in their education, they'll know how to fill it.

Sending teens off to an institutional school program after homeschooling is like abandoning a project just before completion.

Many homeschoolers are turning their children loose too early out of fear of depriving them or out of pressure from their teenagers. But your young people are more likely to be more deprived if they miss out on your training in these important years.

Paul and Mary Schofield homeschool in Placerville, California.

Beginning Homeschooling in the Teen Years

Teri Spray

When a teenager leaves a private- or public-school setting he or she may experience some fear and misgivings. Many teens are afraid of losing social contacts when they begin homeschooling. If their friends have not been a negative influence, be sure to welcome them to join your family for special outings, or to sleep overnight occasionally. There are many "after-school" activities in which your child may still be able to participate.

START STRUCTURED

Begin each day at the same time for the first quarter of school, no matter what! After years of bells and hall-scurrying, a casual, relaxed format can be a confusing jolt. This leads to incomplete assignments and inconsistent performance. Like any experienced teacher, start tough and then you can loosen up as the year progresses.

If you have rescued your child from a bad situation, remember that there will probably be stages of grief to overcome. A sudden change can bring an initial sense of shock, some vague anger, perhaps depression or isolation, then acceptance, and finally resolution. Counseling with your support group or youth pastor may be helpful to your family during this transition. Be merciful and gracious with one another. You were not an experienced parent when you gave birth, and chances are you won't be a perfect home educator your first year either. But do remember that you are the parent, and try not to let your teen see any anxiety you may feel. If you are kind and loving, yet firm, he or she will accept your decision to homeschool more quickly. It takes time to undo years of bad experiences. Be patient with your children. Love them through their hurts, but don't compromise your principles in the process. Remember: If you approach homeschooling with a "let's try it" attitude, you will likely fail.

Understanding Your Teenager

Inge Cannon

The teen years generally encompass the growth and development which are necessary to the process of moving from childhood to adulthood. Wise parents seek to understand the physical, mental, emotional, social, and spiritual needs during this time to ensure curriculum and life choices that will best bring their children to maturity.

ADOLESCENCE

While adolescence occurs physically during puberty (around 11 to 13 years of age), the effects of media communication and educational strategies can pull some of its characteristics to even younger years.

Physical

Puberty brings rapid and often uneven physical growth. The ensuing tendency to be clumsy demands patience along with activities that develop coordination.

Yet this is an age when children often don't like athletics. They can feel intimidated by team sports. An excellent solution is to encourage adolescents to learn individual sports, or to develop some other means of regular exercise that can be continued throughout life. Such a focus will reinforce the importance of keeping the body fit so it can be equipped with strength and stamina to serve the Lord effectively.

The adolescent usually has a very good appetite. In fact, boys particularly can demonstrate the "hollow leg" syndrome. Nutritious meals and healthy eating habits are especially important during adolescence to help prevent or deal with problems such as acne and obesity, and to support growing bone and muscle tissue.

Parents need to exercise caution and avoid letting their teen engage in overstrenuous activities, selecting activities that are appropriate to each young person's individual physical development. Willpower often exceeds ability, so it is easy to violate sensible limits.

Because adolescents alternate periods of energy and fatigue, parents have the difficult task of discerning between fatigue and laziness. Young teens do need a regular routine, which includes a minimum of 8 to 10 hours of sleep each night.

Mental

The adolescent wants to know the reason behind every task or request. "Why do I have to learn to do this or that?" can annoy a parent, but it is a good reminder that teens are motivated to do their best when they understand how the present task relates to ultimate goals. Parents should orient projects for teens to practical needs.

Sometimes the reason behind a requirement can neither be shared by the parent nor understood by the young person. Such occasions demand a quiet, firm statement that the explanation will be given as soon as possible along with a frank appeal that the young person trust the parent.

Adolescents often love adventure and discovery. The adolescent can do some serious thinking and come to excellent conclusions. Curriculum that emphasizes problem solving and good research skills is important during this time. Parents should direct young people to Scripture for answers to their questions and emphasize scriptural principles as a foundation to every area of academic study.

Adolescents are often known for their tendency to make snap judgements—many times very shrewd ones. But it is crucial that they learn early in life to recognize that the correctness of their observations is not synonymous with a special call from God to straighten out the world around them! Young teens can be very critical. Parents must teach them the difference between a discerning spirit and a judgmental attitude, along with a good understanding of when they should share what, with whom.

An adolescent increasingly wants to make his own decisions. It is important to allow him to choose for himself only in those areas where he is ready and able to take responsibility for the *results* of his choices. When parents do extend decision-making privileges, they must scrupulously avoid neutralizing most painful consequences which may occur. Young people need to understand the cause/effect relationship between decisions and consequences. Experience is a powerful teacher!

Parents can, however, offer guidance and encouragement to work through any situation. And when all is said and done—with the lesson effectively communicated—the matter should be dropped. No constant reminders of past failures.

Social

The adolescent's sense of identity is best developed within the family. Knowing each one's gifts, personality, habits, and points of vulnerability will enable parents to reinforce the special place that each child holds in the family. This strong sense of identity protects young people from going elsewhere to achieve their identity.

Adolescents can be fiercely loyal. So strong is their commitment that if a parent criticizes a young teenager's friend, he may take sides with that friend against his parents. This can break down communication within the family, causing discipline to become ineffective. The solution to this potential struggle is to lead the young person to evaluate potential friendships for himself in light of character qualities or deficiencies explained in God's Word.

The adolescent years lend themselves to hero worship. Parents should provide worthy heroes through excellent biographies and the practice of hospitality. Young teens love to meet missionaries who share "real life" adventures in other cultures [or godly people who are successful in other fields—e.g., business, science, law, music, and writing]. Identifying with such people will create a spirit that seeks God's direction.

Adolescence is a crucial period for building communication. As daughters mature, they can benefit from time spent talking and praying with Dad. This will prepare them for receiving his direction throughout the teen years, and for communication with their future mates. Fathers should also give individual attention to their sons. This is a good time for relating biblical concepts to goals, and for prayer together as young men develop a strong sense of life purpose.

Emotional

A young teenager's emotions can fluctuate from the highest of the high to the lowest of the low in a split second. As a result, self-control can be extremely challenging for the adolescent. Those swings are often precipitated by chemical and hormonal changes in the body.

Does this mean parents should excuse moodiness? No; responsibility for one's behavior must be taught. However, there is a place for understanding and much positive reinforcement. Recognition given for proper responses is a powerful motivator!

Occasionally, surging emotions result in explosive reactions: "If that's how it's going to be, I'm not doing it!" When that happens, parents are wise not to allow young people to storm away and shut themselves up. These experiences open tremendous opportunities for teaching teens that while they may not be responsible for the action done to them, they *are* responsible to God for their reactions.

It is especially crucial to point out the importance of avoiding bitterness and the powerful ministry that a grateful attitude can have in every situation.

An adolescent may want very much to be grown up. While at times he will behave like a child, the wise parent will avoid treating him like one. But neither should he be treated as an adult—he is not yet mature enough for that pressure.

The adolescent tends to focus on the here and now. That's why the pimple on his nose today is the end of the world. Parents need to show him that the present attitude can have an effect upon the future, but at the same time, the present circumstance may not matter in terms of the future.

Since the young person often doubts that anyone cares, an understanding ear goes a long way. Listening without always delivering a lecture to fix the situation is an effective way to communicate love.

Spiritual

Parents are in a unique position to teach their young people to recognize God's design for their lives. A big part of understanding God's design is acknowledging that His work is not finished yet. With love and prayer, adolescents can accept the challenge to trust God with the outcome.

Young teenagers want a practical faith and may even question their faith or experience doubts about spiritual decisions. A wise parent will avoid scolding at such times and answer questions patiently, using the Word of God for direction.

The young teen is able, if properly challenged to do some hard things to demonstrate serious convictions. Adolescence is a time of great idealism, so parents should direct the teen's attention to the Lord Jesus Christ as his model.

Since an adolescent is very sensitive to hypocrisy and will be especially intolerant of it in those who lead him, parents and other authority figures need to practice complete transparency in directly acknowledging failure. Asking forgiveness *with very specific wording* will do much to restore trust in relationships. This will also teach the adolescent how to walk with God since he, too, needs to be honest with his Heavenly Father and in his relationships.

YOUTH

When a teenager appears to be grown up physically, he can present a great challenge to the adults who function in an authority relationship with him. His physical appearance often leads a parent to expect adult behavior from him in spite of the fact that he is not yet mature in other ways.

Physical

The teen years are an important time to form physical disciplines. Parents should stress a proper balance between sleep and exercise along with good nutritional and hygiene habits. Spiritual disciplines must be solidified as well: Bible study, prayer, quiet time, memorization, and perhaps fasting. These will build a young person's faith, and help him order his life.

Because a teenager's stamina will be stronger than it was during adolescence, his incredible energy must be brought under control so that it can serve him well.

Mental

In today's society, most adults don't require enough of teens. It is amazing what young people at this stage in life can do! Because these years offer a crucial period for honing academic and practical living skills, parents must provide appropriate training. This is an excellent time for apprenticeships or career explorations.

Teenagers like argument. In fact, parent may tire of the constant debate. But much of it represents a developmental phase in which the young person sharpens his reasoning and judgement. A wise parent will allow times of intense discussion when the situation is not a contest of wills.

Teenagers often act older than they are. Because a teen's viewpoint often lacks maturity, he is prone to reach wrong conclusions. Patient discussion can lead him to correct premises for his reasoning.

Young people need to learn not to argue when witnessing, however; winning souls requires a different approach.

Parents also need to teach teens how to make wise appeals when they disagree with decisions made by authorities. Young people tend to approach such problems by developing better arguments. This attitude damages the relationship, and produces a negative reputation.

Because teenagers want reasons for everything, these are excellent years for studying Bible doctrine, asking "Why do we make the choices we do?" Parents should lead young people to the Scriptures to research answers and evaluate consequences for various courses of action.

Social

Teenagers tend to be creative and idealistic; thus, they need project assignments that will require them to "stretch and grow." Parents should give them worthy things to do and allow them to experience the responsibility of planning activities and fulfilling goals. If they "drop the ball," effective leadership requires avoiding the bail-out maneuver. Support and instruction will be welcome when it is sought.

Parents should encourage young people to finish what they start or, if necessary, take the appropriate steps to request release from the commitment that was made.

Punctuality problems can result from a teenager's tendency to misjudge how long things take. Parents need to provide a good example of dependability in this area and design projects to develop this habit.

Parents should encourage teenagers to form friendships with the elderly. Such relationships will help young people overcome the tendency to be self-centered by giving them many opportunities to serve others. And older people, especially the kind who listen, can be a real help to the teen. The teen grows in his understanding of how God works in people's lives.

Wise parents provide projects that shift a young person's focus away from his friends, and toward building God's kingdom as he *works with* his friends.

Teenagers are naturally gregarious and at some point will experience attraction to the opposite sex. A strong commitment to moral purity should be taught early and reinforced regularly.

Some teenagers may face serious temptation regarding alcohol, drug use, immoral practices, or improper ethics. Because parents may not know when such an experience might occur, they must teach their young people how to answer suggestions or invitations to participate in evil practices.

A teenager needs to know how to reject the suggestion of wrongdoing without rejecting the person who "offered" it. "I've given my life to Jesus Christ and I'm not able to do that," [spoken in a kind tone of voice] will communicate that there is no other option than refusal.

It is crucial that commitments regarding evil and doubtful practices be made long before the hour of trial comes. In the crucible, it is often too late to evaluate issues and potential answers.

Emotional

The teenager's emotions are often intense and still fluctuating. His security needs to be founded upon the Lord alone. No one can take the responsibility of making another person happy.

This is a good time to reinforce your young person's dependence upon the Lord and motivate him to develop a true hunger and thirst for righteousness.

Since Scripture does not provide any model for the practice of dating as exercised in Western culture, parents do well to develop a healthier procedure for finding a mate.

Most of the things learned in the practice of dating become harmful to future relationships: girls learn to be manipulative, and fellows learn to take advantage in ways they should not. Both parties are tempted to be dishonest or immoral, and saddest of all, young people learn to evade parental counsel. Everyone is undermined.

Help your teenager find a sense of life purpose based on God's will through demonstrating a servant's heart toward others. He will "stumble onto happiness" as he moves forward on the road of duty.

Sometimes when young people are chafing to become more independent than parents believe they are ready to be, it helps to say something like, "You and I have the same goals for your life. I don't expect you to live with your mother and me until you are 70 years old. I want you to be able to produce, to have a family if that is God's plan for your life, to glorify God. You want independence, and I want the right kind of independence for you. So let's get on the same side and work together to achieve it, but you'll have to trust me with the timetable."

Such a conversation should occur sometime between ages 14 and 17, preferably between father and offspring.

Spiritual

The teenager's walk with the Lord is personal. He's beginning to understand that living the victorious Christian life is a challenge that nobody else can fulfill for him. It requires his own personal commitment. Taking that personal responsibility is an important step in growth to maturity.

But he is liable to get discouraged. He'll stumble and fall, and can come to the conclusion that it's no use to try to do right consistently.

Parents need to encourage their teenagers to get up again and again, teaching them to experience God's forgiveness, and to ground their faith in God's promises.

Dr. Ronald and Inge Cannon operate Education PLUS, a speaking and publishing ministry for homeschool families. (www.edplus.com).

The Cannon's primary focus is training parents to implement the many benefits of a discipleship lifestyle in home education. They offer many training tools to inspire and empower parents—particularly in the area of crafting apprenticeship programs, choosing high school curricula, and presenting academic credentials for homeschool graduates (transcripts, resumes, portfolios, *et cetera*). Visit their websites for more information: www.homeschooltranscripts.com and www.edplus.com.

How To Issue a Diploma and Prepare a High School Transcript

Inge P. Cannon

No matter where you attend school, your diploma is granted by the people who supervised your educational program. Therefore, unless a student is enrolled in a correspondence school, the homeschool parent will have the responsibility for issuing a diploma and ultimately certifying the student's status as a graduate.

STEPS TO GRANTING A DIPLOMA

The following simple steps will position homeschool parents to grant diplomas to their graduating high school students.

1. **Check Regulations.** Fewer than half a dozen states specify any restrictions in their education regulations about who may grant a diploma. Check with your state homeschool organization or www.hslda.org to learn if your state is one of these.
2. **Check with Admissions Offices.** If you know that your graduate is college-bound, check with the admissions office(s) of your choice to identify their requirements or guidelines.
3. **Prepare a Transcript.** Summarize your record keeping with a carefully prepared transcript (see below).
4. **Issue a Diploma.** Prepare a written diploma. (See "Resources")
5. **Plan an Event.** Plan a special event to honor this milestone in your child's life.

PREPARING A TRANSCRIPT

Thorough documentation of a student's academic record on a transcript makes the diploma meaningful.

When you prepare your annual tax return for the federal government, you summarize all pertinent financial information on the appropriate form(s). You are not asked to send canceled checks, interest statements, and detailed backup documentation. But this information has to be available should you experience and audit.

A high school transcript is somewhat like that tax return. It summarizes and reports in a concise way the total educational profile of the student's experience.

Behind that transcript should stand a portfolio of work samples, a bibliography of resources used, detailed test information, anecdotal records, recommendations from employers and directors of extracurricular activities, *et cetera*. This further documentation will then be available for any interview where it might become necessary.

WHAT INFORMATION SHOULD BE INCLUDED ON THE HIGH SCHOOL TRANSCRIPT?

The following suggestions are adapted from the transcript form designed by the National Association of Secondary School Principals:

1. **Student's Full Legal Name and Identification Information.** Be sure to designate any alternate surnames used (e.g., stepchildren, adoption situations, legal name changes), and indicate your child's birth date. You will need to report a social security number if your child is applying for any financial aid in connections with college enrollment or is entitled to social security benefits to pay college fees. Indicate the names of parents/legal guardian with a permanent address.

2. **Name of School (optional).** Some people believe that naming their homeschool provides an increased sense of "officialness." Another option is to provide the name of the correspondence or satellite program in which you are enrolled.

3. **History of All Subjects Studied.** Use clearly understood titles for all courses. If courses differ from standard offerings, provide a brief explanation. Subjects studied for more than one year should have "level" designations applied to the course title (e.g., English I, English II, Basic Biology, Advanced Biology). Assign a quality evaluation (grade) to each subject. Most educational systems use a grading scale of *A, B, C, D,* and *F.*

   Pass/fail systems should *not* be used because they have a negative impact on your child's grade point average, a very important computation for college applications.

   Designate the unit accumulation (credits earned) for each subject studied. Conventional schools often assign credits on the basis of the Carnegie unit, a time measurement based on the formula: 36 weeks x 5 sessions of 45-50 minutes per week.

   Administrators tend to assume that the 135-150 hours of classroom instruction will generate another 65-150 hours in outside preparation (homework, required reading, research, study, *et cetera*). Thus, a Carnegie unit or its equivalent normally entails 200 hours of work.

   The Carnegie-unit formula needs wise implementation and adjustment by the homeschool parent, since tutorial education is very different from the conventional classroom in its time requirements.

   For example, it may well be that your child is able to complete the assignments in a geometry textbook in a four-month period even though the book was designed for a year's course. In this case, you would not total your child's time. You would instead declare the contents of the course to be the equivalent of the year and assign the Carnegie unit regardless of the time your child spent.

One other caveat should be applied here. Schools usually assign "academic" subjects such as English, math, science, and history one unit of credit per year while they designate "nonacademic" subjects such as home economics, physical education, music, and art that do not involve extensive homework assignments a half unit for the same period of time.

The reason for the difference is that in the "nonacademic" areas a significant portion of classroom time is devoted to practicing skills rather than receiving additional instruction.

4. **Summary of Academic Standing**. Class rank and class size may be omitted on your transcript, but it is in your best interest to compute your child's grade point average (GPA) and tally the total number of credits earned.

The most common numerical scale is the four-point scale, which assigns points per credit: A=4, B=3, C=2, D=1, F=0.

How to compute a GPA:
- Prepare and fill in a grid for the courses, grades, and credits.
- Compute the grade points per course.
- Add up the total number of credits.
- Add up the total grade points.
- Divide grade point total by credit total.

Do *not* compute GPA's for each school year and then average the years. Make sure that your computation counts each individual course separately.

EXTRACURRICULAR ACTIVITIES AND SPECIAL FEATURES OF THE STUDENT'S EDUCATIONAL PROGRAM

Include all community service activities, cottage industries, well-developed hobbies, church activities, honors, and awards.

College admissions officers, scholarship agencies, and employers look for evidence that a student's training in high school includes more than just "school" work. In fact, military academies refuse to consider any applicant without letters of recommendation from sponsors of extracurricular activities or volunteer service.

REPORT OF TEST SCORES FROM STANDARDIZED ASSESSMENTS

Submit reports for only language, math, and reading composite scores. Include national percentile ranking and stanine numbers and omit all else. Grade equivalents should never be included, since this data is fraught with potential for misinterpretation.

Note: If you have experienced any assessments for special needs, consider these evaluations to be personal and confidential (the same as your child's medical records). Do not include such reports on a transcript.

If your child attended school for at least a semester in a conventional setting, list schools attended with dates and location specified (grade 9 and above only).

In such cases, you will want to include a copy of his transcript or report card from that period of study. List on your official transcript form all courses for which you are "transferring" credits to your school.

SIGNATURES OF SCHOOL OFFICIALS

Someone has to certify that the information is correct and take responsibility for any questions that may arise.

As principal, you can include a father's signature or an officer from your umbrella program that supports homeschoolers. In the space for "Individual Certifying Transcript," include the signature of the student's primary teacher.

This is one situation where you *do* want to include degrees or titles for all signatures if these are available.

GRADUATION DATE

Only a small additional step is left to certify this final piece of educational data—a date of graduation.

One final word of advice: Never send your original transcript away. Always send copies of your original.

If possible, obtain an appropriate "crunch" seal in the style used by notary publics at your local office supply store. Then, crunch the copies to give them "official credence."

Adapted from *Mentoring Your Teen: Charting the Course to Successful Adulthood* by Dr. Ronald Jay and Inge Cannon. Copyright 1998 by *Education PLUS+*, 9321 Brookville Road, Indianapolis, IN 46239; 317-222-1695. Used by permission.

RECOMMENDED RESOURCE:

Creating Transcripts and Issuing Diplomas, a 90-minute audiocassette with 40 pages of notes and diagrams, available from Education PLUS+ for $18.50 postpaid. Contact them at 9321 Brookville Road, Indianapolis, IN 46239; 317-222-1695 (website: www.edplus.com).

© Copyright 2000 by *The Teaching Home*, Box 20219, Portland, OR 97294; 503-253-9633; www.TeachingHome.com. Reprinted by permission.

Dr. Ronald and Inge Cannon operate Education PLUS, a speaking and publishing ministry for homeschool families. (www.edplus.com).

The Cannon's primary focus is training parents to implement the many benefits of a discipleship lifestyle in home education. They offer many training tools to inspire and empower parents—particularly in the area of crafting apprenticeship programs, choosing high school curricula, and presenting academic credentials for homeschool graduates (transcripts, resumes, portfolios, *et cetera*). Visit their websites for more information: www.homeschooltranscripts.com and www.edplus.com.

Transcript Tips: More Counts Than You May Think

Inge Cannon, Education PLUS+

Most of the home-educating parents I meet around the country readily acknowledge that a detailed transcript of a student's high school work is necessary for college admissions, and they strive to include the usual line-up of college-preparatory requirements: e.g., four years of English, three sciences (biology, physics, chemistry), three heritage studies (world and U.S. history, government, economics, and perhaps even geography), at least three math units (algebra, geometry, trigonometry, calculus, *et cetera*), two or more years of foreign language, and perhaps some fine arts (music, art, drama, or public speaking). Of course, Christian parents typically add some credits in Bible courses, too.

While this is an excellent academic program, there are many other dimensions that deserve attention during the high school years and, therefore, should also receive recognition on each student's official transcript. And there are several other options for customizing high school programs to young people's needs. In fact, the current statistic that only one in four high school graduates in the United States goes on to earn a college degree is surprising to most people.

By way of reminder, a Carnegie Unit of credit is the instructional time equivalent of 36 weeks of work, typically organized into 5 sessions of 45-50 minutes each. This represents a total classroom time of 135-150 hours, and most educators generally assume that serious academic courses will require an additional 65-150 hours of outside preparation. Since the tutorial format of home education is usually much more time efficient than the group teaching format of the traditional classroom, you will often find it necessary to ignore time equivalents and concentrate on equivalent achievement when compiling your high school records.

EXTRACURRICULAR ACTIVITIES

College admissions counselors, scholarship agencies, and prospective employers place a high premium on a student's track record in extracurricular activities. This listing of experiences reveals a student's interests, priorities, personality, and basic character. Interacting with others, participation in team endeavors, and many fundamental job skills are learned in this forum.

Be sure to include in your son's/daughter's portfolio evaluations written by coaches, music teachers, mentors, supervisors, *et cetera*, and summarize the highlights of your student's experiences on his/her transcript.

There are times when "extracurricular" activities should be listed for academic credit. Consider the following example. If your sixteen-year old son were to volunteer to work every Sunday morning during his junior year in the preschool class at your church, you would have the option of listing his experience as an extracurricular (community service) project with appropriate letters of recommendation from the department superintendent. You could also turn it into an academic course in child development by giving your son appropriate reading assignments pertaining to training preschoolers and then counting his actual Sunday morning time as "lab" experiences for implementing his research.

Any well-developed hobby, cottage industry, or volunteer project can be handled in a similar manner. As long as a research component is present, log your time for it as instruction and use the implementation time as your "lab." When you cease to have an instructional component for the activity, simply record your student's participation as "extracurricular."

CAREER TRAINING

For the past fifty or more years in the United States, public high schools have offered credit to teenagers under headings such as cooperative education, vocational education, tech prep, two plus two (three or four), and distributive education. During the present decade, government schools are opening options for students to begin formal apprenticeship programs in the trades, arts, and crafts, during their high school years. Since these official apprenticeship programs are often six to ten years long, the prospective tradesman or craftsman receives a considerable head start in his/her training by not being forced to earn a high school diploma prior to its beginning. In such programs, students normally attend classes in the morning and "study" in the work place each afternoon. They then receive credit on the transcript for the work training at the rate of one unit per year (earmarked "distributive education," shop, vo-tech, *et cetera*), are graded by the work supervisor, and enjoy the extra benefit of a modest salary as well.

The flexibility of the home-education schedule offers parents the unique opportunity to mentor their children in such work/training arrangements. If you take advantage of these opportunities, do not hesitate to include them on your son's/daughter's transcript. And, of course, teach him/her how to write a resume that appropriately documents these activities.

BASIC LIFE SKILLS

Home economics, "shop" courses (e.g., woodworking, auto mechanics, small machine repair, electronics), and consumer education (e.g., banking, investments, loans, interest, real estate, taxes) are components of practical life that every teen should master prior to high school graduation. Sometimes these courses are assigned a half unit of credit per year because a significant portion of classroom time is spent practicing the skills (similar to physical education and choir/band credits). Thus, you would log approximately 200 hours of instruction and practice into a journal to earn that half credit and 400 hours to earn a full unit. (Note: There is no hard-and-fast rule about this since schools around the country do vary in their systems of documentation.)

ACADEMIC "DOUBLE-HEADERS" ("TRIPLES" AND "QUADS," TOO!)

Another area where home educators can capitalize on the unique design of their educational programs is to allow major projects to receive time credit across several subjects. Conventional schools are limited in this potential because they are constrained to operate in class periods marked by bells, but you can use infinite creativity as long as you document what you are doing.

Consider this example. Suppose you assign your teen a major research project that involves writing a paper on the significance of a particular period in the history of the arts. You want him/her to study the lives of a musical composer and an artist (e.g., painter, sculptor, architect) from the period, and comment about how each person's work reflects the characteristics of the times and the prevalent worldview perspective. When you being this assignment, you give your student several index cards with one subject indicated on each: history, music appreciation, art appreciation, English (composition and research), and word processing. On the front of the card, brainstorm with the student the various aspects of the task that fall into each category. On the back of the card, have the student keep a time log of his/her efforts in that segment of the project. When the paper is completed, the student gives you the final copy, and the completed time logs on the cards. You evaluate and grade each segment of the project on the appropriate card (give a grade) and file the cards in a small box with tabs for all the main high school subjects that comprise your high school plan. As you accumulate enough hours in a given area (English, art, music, *et cetera*), you pull those cards, create a course title, and list the course on the transcript with the appropriate amount of credit (half or whole Carnegie unit). It's that simple!

One other thought—if you accumulated several advanced-science projects in your card file, but you did not have enough to make a complete unit of physics, chemistry, geology, or microbiology, you could combine them all to make a half or whole unit of advanced science. As long as your labels are accurate and you have documentation of your hours, or the scope of the project (bibliography and portfolio), you can be as creative as you wish to be. The same thing would be true if you have a teen who completes several projects in cooking, sewing, gardening, and family living. You could combine those in a course called "Home Management." One family added projects in balancing a checkbook and maintaining the family car and called their course "Basic Living Skills."

The bottom line is that 20-24 Carnegie units is the total normally needed to earn a high school diploma. If your student is college-bound, check with the institutions they are considering attending for their list of required or recommended courses. If you know your children are not college-bound, feel free to adapt your state requirements (or suggestions) to the needs of your children. Remember, there is nothing wrong with having 25-30 credits on your transcript either!

Adapted from *Mentoring Your Teen: Charting the Course to Successful Adulthood* by Dr. Ronald Jay and Inge Cannon. Copyright 1998 by *Education PLUS+*, 9321 Brookville Road, Indianapolis, IN 46239; 317-222-1695. Used by permission.

Dr. Ronald and Inge Cannon operate Education PLUS, a speaking and publishing ministry for homeschool families. (www.edplus.com).

The Cannon's primary focus is training parents to implement the many benefits of a discipleship lifestyle in home education. They offer many training tools to inspire and empower parents—particularly in the area of crafting apprenticeship programs, choosing high school curricula, and presenting academic credentials for homeschool graduates (transcripts, resumes, portfolios, *et cetera*). Visit their websites for more information: www.homeschooltranscripts.com and www.edplus.com.

ADDITIONAL RESOURCES:

Creating Transcripts and Issuing Diplomas, a 90-minute audiocassette with 40 pages of notes and diagrams, available from Education PLUS+ for $18.50 postpaid. Contact them at 9321 Brookville Road, Indianapolis, IN 46239; 317-222-1695 (website: www.edplus.com).

A **high school diploma**, printed on parchment in a gold-embossed case, is available from Home Educators Association of Virginia, 2248-G Dabney Road, Richmond, VA 23230; 804-278-9200; www.heav.org. You inscribe the graduate's name, date of graduation, and signature of presenters.

The ABCs of Testing

While a home-educated student is not required to take the tests described below (except the GED in some cases), it is to his advantage to add one or several to his portfolio if he is well-prepared. Good scores on the appropriate tests can facilitate a student's entry into programs of higher education, scholarships, apprenticeship, employment, or ministry.

Test-preparation resources for specific tests are available in bookstores. Most tests require pre-registration and prepaid fees. Confirm dates, times, and locations well in advance.

ACT (American College Testing). Three-hour test of English, math, reading, and science reasoning. Used by colleges for determining admission and scholarship eligibility. Offered several times a year at local high schools. *ACT Registration Department, Box 414, Iowa City, IA 52243, 319-337-1270;* www.act.org

AP (Advanced Placement). AP exams measure mastery of 32 college-level courses for high school students. Challenging three-hour exams can be taken without attending courses given at high schools, but prepare thoroughly! Colleges give credit or advanced placement if you reach their "qualifying" score. Exams in May at high schools. *Advanced Placement Program, Box 6670, Princeton, NJ 08541;* www.collegeboard.org

CLEP (College Level Examination Program). Five general exams—English, composition, humanities, math, natural sciences, social sciences, and history—and 30 specialized subject tests. Students can earn college credit for material they have learned on their own. Credit procedures vary from college to college. Free *CLEP Colleges* booklet lists participating colleges and test centers. *CLEP, Box 6601, Princeton, NJ;* www.collegeboard.org

GED (General Education Development). Alternative for certifying high school completion. Test includes writing skills, social studies, science, interpreting literature and the arts, and math. Contact public libraries for information.

GRE (Graduate Record Examinations). Assists graduate schools in admissions and students in their transition to graduate education. Admissions tests include the 2 hour, 15 minute General Test (verbal, quantitative, and analytical reasoning), the Writing Assessment, and 14 Subject Tests. www.gre.org

PLAN (Formerly PACT: Preliminary American College Testing Assessment). Career and educational planning assessment for 10th graders. Preparation for the ACT. English, math, reading, and science reasoning skills. Includes an interest inventory, needs assessment profile, and educational/occupational plans. Offered at high schools. www.act.org

PSAT/NMSQT (Preliminary Scholastic Assessment Test/National Merit Scholarship Qualifying Test). Critical reading, math problem-solving, and writing. Important: Only scores from a student's junior year are used to qualify for scholarships, and the test is offered on only one day per year! Make arrangements at a local high school in early spring. SAT required to advance in competition. *PSAT Student Bulletin* with sample questions free at local high schools. www.collegeboard.org

Regents College Examinations (Formerly ACT PEP). Tests demonstrate knowledge to earn college credit in 41 subjects (including nursing); recognized by American Council on Education and accepted by hundreds of colleges and universities. 888-647-2388; www.regents.edu.

SAT (Scholastic Assessment Test). Six times a year. Three-hour test that measures math and verbal reasoning. Indicates potential for academic success. *Registration Bulletin* free from high schools or call 609-771-7600. The College Board, Box 6200, Princeton, NJ 08541; www.collegeboard.org

SAT II (Scholastic Assessment Subject Tests). Twenty-two one-hour tests for subjects in English, writing, math, world history, foreign languages, and listening. Up to three tests at once. Free guidebook at high schools. www. collegeboard.org

WHEN TO TAKE WHAT

The testing schedule below follows accepted college-preparatory practice. Remember to register well in advance of the times given below.

Freshman. Test-preparation books or software for the PSAT, SAT, and ACT.

Sophomore. PSAT/NMSQT in October as practice. PLAN. Take the CLEP test, AP exam, or SAT II for subjects you excel in. Take the SAT as practice.

Junior. PSAT/NMSQT in October to qualify for scholarships. SAT and SAT IIs. CLEP in June/August.

Senior. SAT to improve score. ACT if desired. GED if required. January/February—ACT, CLEP, or SAT II to place out of college introductory courses, apply for college credit, or satisfy requirements in your state. GED if required.

Graduation

he big moment has finally come, and your child has completed his or her high school education. Now what? Participation in a graduation ceremony can be an important recognition of this milestone event—both for parents and students. It also serves as an appropriate time for family and friends to congratulate and honor the accomplishments of the graduate.

Three possible options for celebrating your student's graduation include: the HEAV Graduation in Richmond, a ceremony organized by a local or regional support group, or a private family ceremony.

THE HEAV GRADUATION

For the last 23 years, the Home Educators Association of Virginia has sponsored a graduation ceremony each year at the state convention. A highlight of convention, this beautiful, formal ceremony includes music, a special commencement speaker, caps, gowns, diplomas, and photographs. The 2010 commencement included 200 graduates and more than 2500 guests! To receive a graduation packet of information as soon as they are available, contact our office by phone (804-278-9200) or by e-mail (office@heav.org).

LOCAL OR REGIONAL CEREMONIES

Many local and regional homeschool support groups also hold lovely annual graduation ceremonies, so check with a group in your area.

PRIVATE FAMILY CEREMONY

A private family ceremony has the special advantage of being a personalized and intimate event. Often held at the family's church with relatives, friends, and church family in attendance, this commemoration might include a poetry-reading, an instrumental or voice solo, or a testimony—the options are almost unlimited.

GRADUATION RESOURCES

See the High School Resources listed on page H-78 (on the CD), for information on suppliers of caps, gowns, and diplomas.

Transferring from Homeschool to Public School

Yvonne Bunn

he transition from homeschool to public school may have some unexpected challenges. The transition may not be easy for you or your child. After all, you're leaving parent-controlled education for government-controlled education. This may be a bigger adjustment than you anticipate. What can parents and students expect? How can parents and students prepare?

ELEMENTARY/MIDDLE SCHOOL ENROLLMENT

An elementary level homeschooler and even a middle school student should encounter few academic roadblocks when enrolling in public school. Standardized test scores will provide evidence of achievement that can be easily recognized by school officials. It may benefit both parent and teacher to have a face-to-face discussion about the academic and social aspects of your home-school experience. It may also be helpful to ask the teacher to explain the daily routine so the child will know what to anticipate.

Parents should expect a period of adjustment. Be patient as your child acclimates himself to group study, classroom noise and distractions, and a very different learning environment.

HIGH SCHOOL ENROLLMENT

Transferring into public school at the high school level often requires course descriptions and documentation. A parent-prepared transcript is very helpful. It may be necessary to take Standards of Learning (SOL) tests and sometimes placement tests to either demonstrate proficiency for grade placement or to verify subject mastery for credit transfer. Substitute tests for earning verified credits are also offered such as AP tests, SAT II tests, ACT, CLEP, etc.
NOTE: Requirements differ from district to district. Each independent school district sets its own criteria.

REQUIREMENTS FOR TRANSFER STUDENTS

According to the Virginia Department of Education (DOE), in order to receive a Standard Diploma, a student must earn twenty-two standard credits with six verified credits. For an Advanced Studies Diploma, a student must earn twenty-four standard credits with nine verified credits. To earn a standard unit of credit, a student must complete 140-hours of instruction and pass the course. *A verified unit of credit is earned by passing a course and its related Standards of Learning (SOL) test or approved substitute test."*

The Standards of Accreditation (SOA) provide flexibility to address the special circumstances of transfer students. According to the DOE,

> *"Students entering a Virginia public high school for the first time during the ninth grade or at the beginning of the 10th grade are required to meet the same graduation requirements as non-transfer students. Students transferring during the 10th grade or at the beginning of the 11th grade are expected to earn a minimum of four verified units of credit as prescribed by the SOA for a standard diploma and six verified units of credit for an advanced studies diploma. Students transferring during the 11th grade or at the beginning of the 12th grade are expected to earn a minimum of two verified units of credit as prescribed by the SOA for a standard diploma and four verified credits for an advanced studies diploma."*

> *"There are currently three SOL test administrations each year (two test administrations during the regular school year and one during the summer). Students transferring into Virginia's schools will have an opportunity at any of the regular administrations to take the tests needed for graduation. Typically, an 11th grader is enrolled in English and U.S. History in that grade level. Both of these content areas have SOL tests that would apply toward graduation. The student may also be enrolled in other SOL tested courses as part of the normal 11th- and 12th-grade program, thus having the opportunity to accrue verified credits required for graduation." **

There is no guarantee that homeschool credits will be accepted towards a public high school diploma. According to the Standards of Accreditation, public schools are under no obligation to accept credits from non-accredited schools such as private schools or homeschools. This can be a major roadblock. Although they are not obligated to accept homeschool credits, nothing prevents them from legally doing so.

Prepare a well-documented transcript. You may also try to prove mastery with independent evaluations or portfolios. Be ready to negotiate.

*For more specific information on graduation requirements and transfers, visit the Virginia Department of Education website at www.pen.k12.va.us/VDOE/Parents/index.html

Preparing Your Teenager to Drive

Bonnie Garrison

Driving is a basic survival skill that our children will have to learn sooner or later. As homeschool parents, we have already taken on the job of training our children in every other subject. Why, then, could we not provide driver's education?

My husband and I wrote our own unit study using the state driver's manual. My husband decided that this was the perfect course for him to teach. He divided the material into five main topics.

1. **Rules of the Road.** The first area that was covered was the rules of the road. Dad took the information from the driver's manual and expanded upon it, explaining the importance of following the rules and the consequences of disobeying. A review and test was given before moving on to the second topic.

2. **Road Signs.** In this second part of the course, each student had to recognize the different types of road signs and be able to tell what his reaction would be to each one.

3. **Emergencies.** The third area covered what to do in case of an emergency.

4. **The Car.** The fourth activity involved a field trip to the driveway, where Dad made sure each student knew the function of every switch and knob in all the family cars. Dad also taught everyone how to change a tire and check the oil level.

5. **The Test.** Finally came the big review and a hundred-question test written by Dad. A 90 percent on the test allowed a qualified student to take the state test for a learner's permit.

After getting a permit, we ask that our teenagers spend 500 miles behind the wheel with Dad in the passenger seat before obtaining a regular driver's license. We also required our teenagers to be 17 and willing and able to pay their share of the insurance costs and gasoline.

Accidents can still happen, but we as parents can ensure they don't happen because of foolishness or inexperience. You can judge for yourself when to let your teens learn to drive, and you can teach them the skills they need to be safe drivers.

High School Resources

Compiled by Teri Spray and Anne Miller

ACT Universal Testing, PO Box 4028, Iowa City, IA 52243-4028; www.act.org

Advanced Training Institute International (ATI), Box One, Oak Brook, IL 60522-3001; 630-323-9800. An alternative educational program for the whole family that includes apprenticeship opportunities. www.iblp.org

Bear's Guide to Earning College Degrees Non-traditionally, 11th edition, $29.95 postage paid. Degree.net, c/o Ten Speed Press, P.O. Box 7123, Berkeley, CA 94707; www.degree.net

Beta Club promotes character, develops leadership skills, encourages service involvement, recognizes achievement, and provides technological advantages to students in grades 5 through 12. www.betaclub.org

The Big Book of Home Learning - Volume 3: Teen and Adult, by Mary Pride. Available for $14.60 from the Homeschool Discount Warehouse, 1-800-775-5422.

Bluestocking Press, Good resource for economics and history materials. P.O. Box 1014, Placerville, CA 95667-1014; 916-621-1123.

Bold Parenting, Jonathan Lindvall; 40793 Blue Oak Drive, PO Box 820, Springville, CA 93265; 559-539-0500. www.boldchristianliving.com

Changing the Heart of a Rebel, by Dr. S. M. Davis. Gives 12 key principles to follow to " turn around a rebel." Available as a booklet, or on audio or video cassette. Park Meadows Baptist Church, Memorial Park Road, Lincoln, IL 62656; 1-800-500-8853; www.drsmdavis.com

Charting a Course for High School by Ellyn Davis. Elijah Company, 888-2-ELIJAH; www.elijahco.com

The Christian College Handbook, Berry Publishing Services, Inc.; 701 Main Street, Evanston, IL 60202; 1-800-388-9915; www.berrypub.com

Christian Home Educators' Curriculum Manual, Junior/Senior High, by Cathy Duffy. Available through the HEAV office, 2248-G Dabney Road, Richmond, VA 23230; 804-278-9200; www.heav.org

CLEP, P.O. Box 6601, Princeton, NJ 08541-6601. College credit through testing. Send for free booklet. www.collegeboard.com/clep

Christian Financial Concepts (Larry Burkett) www.cfcministry.org

Civil Air Patrol, www.capnhq.gov

College Admissions: A Guide for Homeschoolers by Judy Gelner. Poppyseed Press, P.O. Box 85 Sedalia, CO 80135. $7.95 + $3.95 postage and handling.

The College Board, Extra books and helpful ideas for taking college-board tests. Forms for taking the tests can be picked up at your local high school counseling office at no charge. www.collegeboard.com

College Degrees by Mail, by John Bear. One hundred good schools that offer bachelor's, master's, doctorate, and law degrees by home study. $12.95 + $2.50 shipping. Ten Speed Press, Box 7123, Berkeley, CA 94707; 1-800-841-2665; www.tenspeedpress.com/catalog/all/item.php3?id=2014

Constitutional Law for Christian Students, by Mike Farris. Registration is through Escondido Tutorial Services at www.gbt.org; or you may call 619-746-0980. This is an on-line, 24-week course.

Continuing Education Departments are a great resource at many universities. Often the cost is less for these programs, and there are fewer residency or attendance requirements. (There may be age limitations.)

Creating Transcripts by Inge Cannon. Education PLUS+, 9321 Brookville Road, Indianapolis, IN 46239; 317-222-1695; www.edplus.com

Critical Thinking Press & Software, P.O. Box 448, Pacific Grove, CA 93950-0448; 1-800-458-4849. Critical thinking activities in Language Arts, Mathematics, Science, Social Studies, and Methods (K-Adult). www.critical-thinking.com

Education PLUS+ sells a complete tape seminar on apprenticeship. Its covers such areas as: How to determine if college or apprenticeship is best; how to select curriculum to maximize preparation; how to keep records that will open doors of opportunity; how to assess interests, talents, and options; how to write a resume that will earn a hearing; and how to be the best mentor a young person could ever have. The entire course costs only $69.99, and includes six dynamic training sessions, a 137-page syllabus, evaluation and journal worksheets, and an extensive bibliography. 9321 Brookville Road, Indianapolis, IN 46239; 317-222-1695; www.edplus.com

Finding the Career That Fits You by Lee Ellis and Larry Burkett. www.cfcministry.org

The Five Love Languages of Teenagers by Gary Chapman. Elijah Company. 888-2-ELIJAH; www.elijahco.com

The Guidance Manual for the Christian Home School by David and Laurie Callihan. 315-592-7830; www.davidandlaurie.com

High School Handbook by Mary Schofield. Available from Home Educators Association of Virginia (HEAV), 2248-G Dabney Road, Richmond, VA 23230; 804-278-9200; www.heav.org

Home School Plus, 925 Ingleside Road, Norfolk, Virginia; 757-466-3477. Classes, activities, and resources for homeschooling families.

Homeschooling for Excellence, David and Micki Colfax. www.amazon.com

Homeschooling the Teen Years, Cafi Cohen. www.homeschoolteenscollege.net

Home Study International, P.O. Box 4437, Silver Spring, MD 20914-4437; 301-680-6570. High school correspondence school. 12501 Old Columbia Pike, Silver Spring, MD 20904; 1-800-782-4769; www.hsi.edu

Institute for Creation Research (I.C.R.), 10946 Woodside Ave., N., Santee, CA 92071. Has a list of colleges that teach from the creationist point of view. www.icr.org

The Joyful Homeschooler by Mary Hood.

Johnson O'Connor Research Foundation. Provides aptitude testing based on tests of person's abilities to perform certain tasks, rather than on preferences (natural abilities or talents). Website contains helpful articles. Washington, D.C., 1120 Connecticut Ave. NW, Suite 1060, Washington, D.C. 20036; 301-424-9445 or 301-424-9446; www.jocrf.org

Keyboard Enterprises, 5200 Heil, #32, Huntington Beach, CA 92649; 714-840-8004. Algebra course on video tape.

Math-U-See. Basic algebra and geometry; Steve Demme. 1-888-854-MATH; www.mathusee.com

Mentoring Your Teen by Inge Cannon. Education PLUS+, 9321 Brookville Road, Indianapolis, IN 46239; 317-222-1695; www.edplus.com

National Center for Home Education. Excellent packet of college information for $22.50. P.O. Box 3000, Purcellville, Virginia 20134; 540-338-7600.

PEERS Test (Politics, Economics, Education, Religion, and Social Issues) 1-800-948-3101. Tests the Biblical worldview of your teen. www.nehemiahinstitute.com

PSAT/NMST are only offered once a year at high schools—usually in October. Registration is in September. This test allows students and parents to see if other entrance exams are necessary or advisable. www.collegeboard.com

SAT Program, P.O. Box 6212, Princeton, NJ 08541-6212.

Saxon Math. Saxon Publishers, 1320 W. Lindsey, Norman, OK 73069; 1-800-284-7019.

Senior High: A Home-Designed Form+U+La, by Barb Shelton. From Farm Country General Store for $39.50; 1-800-551-FARM.

Summit Ministries, P.O. Box 207, Manitou Springs, CO 80829; 719-685-9103. Offers two-week leadership training course, teaching students to recognize the different world views they will encounter in college, literature, and the world in general. They are also taught to understand and defend a biblical world view. A special training session for homeschooled teens is offered in early and late summer. www.summit.org

Teaching the Trivium by Harvey and Laurie Bluedorn. Trivium Pursuit, PMB 168, 429 Lake Park Blvd., Muscatine, IA 52761; 309-537-3641; www.triviumpursuit.com

The Teenage Liberation Handbook, Grace Lewellyn, P.O. Box 1014, Eugene, OR 97440; 541-686-2315; www.LowryHousePublishers.com

The 21 Irrefutable Laws of Leadership Book and Workbook Bundle by John Maxwell, www.injoy.com

The Ultimate Guide to Homeschooling by Debra Bell. Available from HEAV, 804-278-9200; www.heav.org

Westminister Academy offers homeschool tutoring. Has a full range of classes for both middle- and high school students. Seeks to provide, "Academic excellence under the Lordship of Christ." 600 Forest Avenue, Richmond, VA 23229; 804-285-4523.

Worldwide Guide to Homeschooling by Dr. Brian Ray. Available from HEAV, 804-278-9200; www.heav.org

DRIVING RESOURCES

Your State's Driver's Manual. Includes rules of the road and driving laws for your state. Most states are moving toward progressive licensing, requiring a certified driving course and/or more behind-the-wheel training and practice time with a parent or licensed driver.

"Help for the Teenager Who Wants to Drive" is a driver training course designed for parents to teach their own teens to drive. The program includes teacher and student workbooks, free use of videos, toll-free help line, and insurance discount certification. The course consists of seven phases of training with both classroom and behind-the-wheel sections, objective evaluation standards, and a parent's section dealing with how to instruct. Complete program, $149 ppd., subsequent siblings, $134. National Driver Training Institute, Box 948, Monument, CO 80132; 1-800-327-3444; www.national-drivertraining.com

AAA Teaching Your Teens to Drive is a 50-minute video or CD-ROM containing 13 lessons that should be viewed *before* behind-the-wheel training begins. The 88-page handbook follows the sequence of the video lessons. AAA members, $24.95; nonmembers, $37.95. 1-800-327-3444.

Teaching Teen Driving. Free mini-course on the Internet is designed for parents to teach their teenager to drive. Includes lessons, practice, evaluation, and a movie. www.webtrafficschool.com/wts/free/teaching/free_teach.asp

LOGIC AND DEBATE RESOURCES

An Introduction to Argumentation and Debate by Christy Shipe. Covers the fundamentals of formal debate including logic, research, stock issues, affirmative case construction, negative strategies, evidence, delivery, and more. Available from Home School Legal Defense Association, P.O. Box 3000, Purcellville, VA 20134-9000; 540-338-5600; FAX: 540-338-2733; info@hslda.org

Christian Logic Loop, Hans and Nathaniel Bluedorn,www.christianlogic.com

Learning Logic at Home by Nathaniel Bluedorn. A 34-page, information-packed, downloadable PDF file available at www.triviumpursuit.com/catalog/learning_logic_at_home.htm

National Christian Forensics and Communications Association (NCFCA) addresses forensics issues and opportunities. www.ncfca.org;

Traditional Logic: An Introduction to Formal Logic, by Martin Cothran. Book 1 and *Advanced Formal Logic*, Book 2. www.memoriapress.com

Trivium Pursuit, Harvey and Laurie Bluedorn, PMB 168, 429 Lake Park Blvd., Muscatine, Iowa 52761; 309-537-3641, 9am–5pm CST, Monday–Saturday; bluedorn@triviumpursuit.com; www.triviumpusuit.com

RHETORIC RESOURCES

Beginning Public Speaking Student Workpack and Teachers Edition by Teresa Moon. A super-simple, user-friendly, no-experience-needed, easy-to-follow program of introducing and building public-speaking skills for the Christian student and teacher. This is great to use for starting public speaking groups and clubs. www.commforchrist.com

National Christian Forensics and Communications Association (NCFCA) addresses forensics issues and opportunities. www.ncfca.org

Toastmasters Excellent opportunity to learn how to give impromptu speeches, present and organize prepared speeches, and conduct meetings. For information, call 1-800-993-7732, or to speak to a live operator, call 949-858-8255, weekdays between 8:00 am and 5:00 pm, PT; www.toastmasters.org

CAREER/APTITUDE RESOURCES

Discover What You're Best At, Simon and Schuster. www.amazon.com

Test Your Own Job Aptitude, Barrett, Williams. Penguin USA. www.amazon.com

Jist Works, Inc., 720 North Park Avenue, Indianapolis, IN 46202; 1-800-648-5478; www.jist.com

CFKR Career Materials, 11860 Kemper Road, #7, Auburn, CA 95603; 1-800-525-5626; www.cfkr.com

National Board for Certified Counselors, 3 Terrace Way, Suite D, Greensboro, NC 27403; 336-547-0607; www.nbcc.org

The Internet also provides some interesting and useful sites including, www.ncsu.edu/careerkey/index.html and www.explore.cornell.edu

Johnson O'Connor Research Foundation. Provides aptitude testing based on one's skill at performing certain tasks rather than on mere preferences (natural abilities or talents). Website contains helpful articles. Washington, D.C. 1120 Connecticut Ave. NW, Suite 1060, Washington, D.C. 20036; 301-424-9445 or 301-424-9446; www.jocrf.org

Christian Financial Concepts, Larry Burkett. www.cfcministry.org

GRADUATION SUPPLIES: CAPS, GOWNS, TASSELS, DIPLOMAS, RINGS, ANNOUNCEMENTS

Jostens
1-800-839-7125
www.jostens.com

Milligans
109 St. Joseph Avenue
Brewton, AL
1-800-544-4696 for orders
251-867-5895
www.milligans.comDiplomas

Home School Legal Defense Association
P.O. Box 3000
Purcellville, VA 20134
504-338-5600
www.hslda.org
They offer professional-looking diplomas and covers.

Lord's Fine Jewelry
P.O. Box 486
Piedmont, OK 73078
1-800-775-5673

College and College Alternatives

Compiled by Janice Campbell

Additional Articles on the CD
BE SURE TO CHECK OUT THESE OTHER GREAT ARTICLES ON THE CD!

Each article in the book and on the CD has been carefully chosen by the section coordinator to increase your knowledge and understanding of this subject, so don't forget to use and enjoy the parts of the manual on your CD, as well as the part you are holding.

Please note that the page numbering on the CD is different from that of the hard-copy manual..

Introduction

It's a wonderful time to be a homeschooler! Colleges, vocational schools, and businesses have become acquainted with the independence and self-motivation of home-educated students, and they increasingly welcome homeschool graduates. Thanks to home-educating pioneers who paved the way, doors continue to open for non-traditional students.

When I began to homeschool in the late 1980s, the second question people asked me was, "But what if your kids want to go to college?" (The first question was inevitably about socialization.) I was able to point to the example of the Colfax family, whose home-educated sons were admitted to Ivy League schools, as one example of a successful homeschool-to-college transition. Today, I know many teens, including my two oldest sons, who have successfully made the transition from home to independence. Although their educational backgrounds read like a survey of homeschool methodologies—from unschooling, to unit studies, textbooks, co-op classes, video- or satellite-schools—the homeschool graduates I've met have been successful in their move from homeschool to college, tech school, apprenticeships, the military, or the business world. Despite their diverse backgrounds, these students seem to share some common traits that ease the transition: self-confidence, self-motivation, and the ability to work well, both independently and with others. These traits, coupled with the real-world experience many homeschoolers accumulate during their school years, make them increasingly welcome in the public arena.

It's never too early to start researching post-high-school options, and planning for the future. In this section, you will find articles on the college admissions process, resources for researching potential colleges and majors, plus articles on meeting eligibility requirements for college athletics, using college-level exams to bypass a year or two of college, and more. This is only the tip of the iceberg—there is a wealth of information available from libraries, bookstores, homeschool support groups, and on the Internet. Websites, such as www.collegeboard.com and my own www.everyday-education.com, provide useful information and links to other sites. The door to the future is wide open for homeschoolers—step right through!

—Janice Campbell

Choosing Colleges

Wes Beach

SOME GENERAL THOUGHTS
There are some things I'd like to suggest for you to think about when you are in the process of choosing a four-year college. Many people never think beyond [their other state schools]. While these two systems are local, relatively inexpensive, and highly regarded, they do not represent anywhere near the range of choice that you have when choosing a college. You may very well go to a [state school], but I believe that even if you do, you'll have made the wisest pick if it's from the full range of options.

Did you know that there is a highly rated college in California that has an enrollment of exactly 26? That some universities have enrollments of tens of thousands? That there are colleges where you can design your own major, or even your own courses? That there is a fully accredited college in Vermont that accepts only people who have different learning styles (so-called learning disabilities)? That colleges exist in the centers of cities and in very rural locations, and on the plains, in the mountains, and at the edge of the sea? That financial aid can put expensive private colleges within your reach? That at some schools you can study some very unusual subjects, like pulp and paper science; horsemanship; puppetry; and hotel, restaurant, and institutional management? That you can earn a degree from a fully accredited college without ever setting foot on the campus? That some colleges you never heard of can provide you with an education that is better in many ways than what you can get at Stanford, UC Berkeley, or Harvard?

HIGH PRESTIGE / A GOOD FIT
There are 2600 separate studies reported in *How College Affects Students,* by Ernest T. Pascarella and Patrick T. Terenzini, both college professors, that provide evidence that going to a selective and prestigious college does not necessarily provide you with any kind of significant advantage in your life. Your intellectual, emotional, and social growth depend much more on your individual interests and talents. These authors say this, also: "In the area of earnings, even our most liberal estimate is that less than two percent of the differences in earnings are attributable to college quality." You can safely choose a solid college that fits you without worrying about whether or not its reputation puts it at the very top of the heap.

TAKING TIME OUT

One thing you may have heard is that it's dangerous to take time off from school, that it's really hard to get going again when you've been out of school for a while. Interestingly, many college admissions officers are offering exactly the opposite advice. Here is a passage from a book titled *Getting In*, by Bill Paul. "Hargadon" is Fred Hargadon, Dean of Admission at Princeton.

> The majority of applicants...haven't had...compelling [life] experiences. For them, Hargadon has a suggestion: Take a year off between high school and college—a gap year, he calls it. A gap year builds character and exposes a young person to a different way of life, he said in a speech to parents of students at Princeton High School.
>
> "There are all kinds of programs that one can participate in" during the gap year, Hargadon told the parents. "One can go to the American Field Service and spend a year in another country. One can go off and help build a cabin in the mountains. One can work on a sheep ranch in Australia. All sorts of things. One can go to a foreign country and concentrate on the language of that country, working in a menial way to earn the money to live there." It's been his own experience, the dean said, that young people who take a year off between high school and college enter college with more perspective and maturity, and "slightly more" wisdom. "If I had my way," he added, "I think it would be great" to admit a class of students who, almost without exception, had had a gap year.
>
> For some people, the gap can turn out to be more than a year. I graduated from UCLA in 1961 and began work on a master's degree in 1987 at age 48. You can go to college, or back to college, at any point in your life.

GETTING ADVICE

You will probably work, at least briefly, with a high school or community-college counselor, and you may want to initiate an extended dialogue. This can be very beneficial, but there are some things to watch out for. Some people I've worked with have felt that the counseling they've gotten has been very informative and supportive, while others think they've received superficial attention and bad advice. Not long ago I called a community college counselor to get some information about preparation for admission to medical school, and I was told stuff that I knew was wrong.

If you ask for advice, from counselors or anyone else, ask several people, and expect different answers in many cases. If the issue is a purely subjective one, listen to everything, then take the advice that fits you. If the issue revolves around getting correct information, you've got to seek out the necessary facts, get them from as close to the source as possible, ask focused questions, get at what you're seeking in more than one way, and double-check it. Don't, however, get paranoid and paralyzed. Life goes on, and it is never possible to know absolutely everything before acting.

Here, by way of example, is what I mean by getting information from as close to the source as possible. If you're attending Sunshine Community College and you want to transfer to Rainbow University, the counselors at

Sunshine may (or may not) be willing and able to give you useful information, but the source of the information is at Rainbow U, and conversations with a counselor there would most likely yield the most complete and accurate information. Reading literature from Rainbow and talking to more than one person would also be useful things to do.

GUIDEBOOKS

I'm going to suggest that you begin your search with a set of books. The ones I recommend are listed below. Take a look at them, and, if you can afford to, buy the ones that seem most useful. This way you can use the most recent ones (many are updated yearly), take notes in them, highlight important sections, *et cetera*.

- *Cool Colleges for the Hyper-Intelligent, Self-Directed, Late Blooming, and Just Plain Different,* by Donald Asher. This is an energizing, rich, creative, thought-provoking book about choosing colleges.

  Asher has provided a book that almost requires stretching one's thinking about college admission. It isn't—like many other guides—simply an introduction followed by an alphabetical listing of colleges and universities. Schools are grouped and discussed according to type. College profiles and lists are complemented with a lot of other material. Eleven essays by other people are scattered throughout the book; three of them are "What Is Intelligence?," "Why Kids Aren't Happy In Traditional School," and "Secret to Finding Scholarships––There Isn't One." Asher reviews twelve additional books; some of them are also college guides, while others address various issues related to college choice and attendance. Wide-ranging asides in bold type occur throughout; some are a full page, others are two or three sentences. Numerous quotes are in the margins, from many sources and on many topics. Asher even includes a few cartoons––not many, but, like everything else, they add to the mix and provoke thought. A unique design allows all this to fit together in a visually stimulating way.

  Cool Colleges is, in my opinion, the best book to start a college search with, but it's not sufficient. There is, for example, a six-page profile of Prescott College emphasizing, among other things, the environmental studies Prescott offers. The Evergreen State College in Washington is mentioned as another good school for those interested in focusing on the environment, and there are five other mentions of Evergreen throughout the book. But there is no profile of Evergreen, so another book will be necessary if you want to learn more about it.

- *The Fiske Guide to Colleges,* by Edward B. Fiske. This, like *Cool Colleges,* is a "subjective" guide; it is nevertheless based on surveys of college officials and students; 300 of the "best" schools are included. Each campus is described in two or three pages of English prose, giving you a sense of the feel of the place. (In the end, you'll want to base your choices on a more personal set of observations; this book is only a starting point.) Basic facts like strongest programs and cost are also given.

- *The College Handbook,* by The College Board. This book includes all colleges, not just ones selected by the author, as the guides by Asher and Fiske do. It includes objective information such as majors offered, special programs, enrollment at each school, *et cetera.* This book is a very useful reference tool to supplement the more subjective guides mentioned above.

- *Looking Beyond the Ivy League, and Colleges That Change Lives,* by Loren Pope. The first book refutes myths (for example, the myth that you need a high school diploma to get into a good four-year college or university); provides thought-provoking arguments and solid data indicating that you can get a better education at many relatively little-known liberal arts colleges than at high-prestige places such as UC Berkeley, Stanford, and Harvard; and offers valuable guidelines and advice about preparing college applications. The second book presents some of Pope's favorite colleges. He provides detailed descriptions of the 40 schools he includes in the book. What he writes is interesting and useful, but of course you're not Loren Pope, and your preferences may be different from his.

- *Bear's Guide to Earning Degrees by Distance Learning,* by John B. Bear and Mariah P. Bear. The title describes what the book is about. You'll learn in it, for example, that there are fully accredited, state supported colleges from which you can earn a degree without spending any time at the school. They have no campuses, no faculty, and no classrooms; what they do, basically, is award degrees based on portfolios. I give my students a high school diploma based on a minimal portfolio because I believe that they are filled with solid personal attributes and that high school is empty. The colleges I'm referring to here won't award a college degree without a very rich portfolio; I wouldn't either if I were running a college rather than a high school.

- *Index of Majors and Graduate Degrees,* by the College Board. This book lists schools where majors are available. For example, if you want to major in dance, you turn to this section and find all the schools in the country that offer a major in dance. (But see the cautionary note below.)

- *California Colleges and Universities, 2000,* Report 00-01 of the California Postsecondary Education Commission, not only lists and profiles all public and private colleges and universities in California, including community colleges, but also, under "State-Approved and Exempt Institutions," includes schools like the Golden State Culinary Institute and the San Diego Golf Academy. In addition, there are lists of schools by county. You'll also find lists of programs, so you can find all the schools that offer programs in biology or East Asian studies or massage, *et cetera.* It's free! (The first copy is free; additional copies are $6.50 each.) You can order a copy (or copies and be billed) by e-mail at publication-request@cpec.ca.gov. Mail orders should specify the number of copies ordered, include a check for multiple copies, and be sent to Publications Unit, California Postsecondary Education Commission, 1303 J Street, Suite 500, Sacramento, CA 95814-2938. There's an online version at www.CAcollegeGuide.com.

There are all kinds of college guidebooks you might find useful. There is a guide devoted entirely to art programs and schools, and another somewhat broader one on visual and performing arts (this is where I learned that you can earn both a bachelor's and a master's in puppetry at the University of Connecticut). There's a guide to hospitality programs, and there's one on vocational and technical schools.

Arco publishes a guide titled *100 Colleges Where Average Students Can Excel.* Most bookstores have a section devoted to college guides; scanning these sections will give you an idea of what's available.

Of course, I think these books are useful; otherwise I wouldn't recommend them. But I want you to know that I have never found college guidebooks to be entirely comprehensive or accurate. For example, one student I worked with wanted to major in creative writing, so I went through *Fiske* and found all the schools listed as having strong programs in this field. I then discovered that some of these schools were not even listed in *Index of Majors.* Use guidebooks as you begin your search, but when you narrow down your choices, begin to read publications from the colleges themselves––and read their real stuff, like catalogs, not their glossy public relations material. Any school can show you gorgeous photographs of its students and its campus and make grandiose statements about its programs in its advertising, but its course catalog will tell the real story.

USING GUIDEBOOKS

When you've got your guidebooks, start looking at them. I can't prescribe any particular way of attacking them; You go at them in your style. Very few people will sit down and read these books from cover to cover, especially not *The College Handbook,* but if that's your style, do it. I would be much more likely to look at the tables of contents, then start browsing more or less at random.

Fairly soon, as a result of systematic reading or of rummaging around in the guidebooks, you'll discover things that will give direction to your search, and pretty soon you'll be hunting for specific features in schools. Of course, I can't predict what these things will be, but you'll discover them. You may decide that geography is (or is not) very important, or the size of the school, or flexibility of programs, or anything else. One of my former students went to UCLA so he could "study with my hero, the legendary guitarist Kenny Burell, who directs the jazz studies program." You may wind up looking for a small school in a rural setting that offers a flexible program in sociology, or a huge school in a large city that offers a highly structured program in chemical engineering.

AN INFORMATIVE E-LIST

There's a listserv titled "Transition of homeschooled students into post-secondary education." Part of the announcement of this list said, "This list is intended for homeschool students and their parents, admissions officers, financial aid officers, and members of admissions associations. We hope that this list will broaden communication and understanding about the issues facing homeschool students in their transition to college.

"This list is sponsored by the Center for Urban Education of the School of Education of Pace University (NY), and by the Executive Board of the New York State Association for College Admission Counseling, and its Human Relations Committee.

"Please feel free to circulate information about this list. Here's how to join."
Send an email message to:
listserv@list.pace.edu
and in the message area type:
Subscribe HSC-L (Your Name)

GETTING MORE INFORMATION

Don't overlook other sources of information. Family members, friends, teachers, and other people you know may have gone to colleges you'd be interested in, and they can tell you a lot about their schools. Remember, however, that this is *your* education, and what may have been a perfect school for your third cousin may not be appropriate for you at all.

When you get to the point where you are seriously interested in specific schools, call or write or e-mail for information from them; phone numbers and addresses are in the *Handbook* and in *Fiske*. Feel free to call these schools with any questions that you have.

HOW MANY SCHOOLS SHOULD YOU CONSIDER?

I don't know how many colleges you're going to actively and seriously consider––three? eight? One very good piece of standard advice is to apply to several schools and to choose at least one where your chances for admission are almost guaranteed. One of my former students applied to exactly one college––Sarah Lawrence––and figured that if she didn't get in, she'd attend a community college for a year and apply again and to other schools the following year. (She was admitted.) As with all parts of this process, you're making the rules, and you get to decide what's "right."

VISITING COLLEGES

My own belief is that, beyond whatever basic considerations you have, the most important thing is the *feel* of the place where you'll go to school. By far the best way to determine this is to visit each college on your final list.

Pope provides, in *Looking Beyond the Ivy League*, an excellent chapter (Chapter 7, "Sample and Test the Merchandise") on college visits. I'd like to recommend this to you and simply comment on a few aspects of what Pope says.

He suggests that during college visits you should ask the questions that are important to you, and of course I agree. He goes on to list very many questions to ask, and he suggests that you spend a day and a night at "at least a couple of the colleges if possible." I would prefer, instead, to visit every college I was seriously interested in, even if this meant just visiting for part of a day (but surely for several hours). And trying to ask all the questions Pope suggests, while ideally a good idea, would be impossible. Again, you decide what's important.

Pope writes, "Reactions to a visit may be as much visceral as cerebral, as are the major decisions of life, but the viscera will operate more truly if the brain is informed." He then goes on in this chapter and describes exclusively how to fill your brain. I think you also need to give your gut a chance. When you visit a college campus, in addition to conducting the kind of inquiry Pope recommends, just be there for some period of time: sit under a tree and watch the campus world go by, or wander around aimlessly, or sit with a cup of coffee and give your brain a time to drift and sort without your pushing things into any kind of shape.

IF YOU CAN'T VISIT...

If you can't possibly visit college campuses (or all of the ones you've chosen), try to obtain as much information of the kind Pope suggests in other ways. Of course you can't sit under a campus tree without being there, but you can call various people on campus, you can read a lot in various books and in school publications about the campus, and you can talk to a number of people who have some first-hand knowledge of the place. Just as Pope tells you to knock on faculty members' office doors and ask questions, you can also call faculty members and ask the same questions over the phone. You can get their names from the college catalog, and their office numbers through their department offices; for example, call the History department office at the college where you might wind up majoring in history. (Start, if necessary, with the general number of the school.) Look at course titles in the catalog and call professors who teach the things you're most interested in. You can also get phone numbers for students' associations and dormitories and get students on the phone. If you have access to the Internet, use that.

SORTING IT ALL OUT

From time to time during your search, mentally stack your options in front of you, examine them in a somewhat detached way, and let them sort themselves out. Sooner or later you'll know where you want to go to college. Do keep an eye on deadlines, and make sure you're doing specific things that will keep your options open: take required tests like SAT I and II or the ACT, line up people to write recommendations, begin to think about writing essays (and look in a book titled *Essays That Worked*, by Boykin Curry & Brian Kasbar), and gather application materials.

Planning Tips for the Post-High-School Years

Debra Bell

I t is hard to believe that I am already wrapping up home education with two of my four children. I'd be more sentimental about this if it weren't for all the decision-making associated with the senior year. My forerunners had warned me that it is never too early to start working on post-graduation plans, but like most folks we just don't tackle things on our "To Do" List until the pressure mounts.

Choosing a college, choosing a career: these seem to be the only discussions at our house this year. It's a lot of fun exploring all the options until it actually gets down to decision time. It was so much simpler when I was in their shoes.

TIP #1: MAKE CAREER EXPLORATION A PART OF YOUR PROGRAM

At our co-op, the Learning Center, we ran a career exploration elective a few years ago. Most of the kids were just entering high school, so this started them thinking in plenty of time about career paths; and yet they were old enough to already discern some of their interests.

We used YES! (Youth Exploration Survey) from Larry Burkett's ministry (www.cfcminstry.org), *What Color Is Your Parachute?* by Richard Nelson Bolles, and *Do What You Are* by Paul and Barbara Tieger as our main resources, picking and choosing the portions we thought most helpful. One of our moms was trained to administer the DISC personality survey and we had a lot of fun and outrage with the kids taking that. (You can take a free version of this test online at www.cfcministry.org.) We emphasized though that this was just one of many tools they could use to help them evaluate possible career interests. A lot of kids didn't agree with the assessment's conclusions about themselves, though they did agree with the conclusions about others.

A DAY IN THE FIELD

The best activity by far was shadowing someone in a field of interest for a day. Kids got ready for this by first identifying what interesting places they might visit in our community, then generating questions together that each one ought to ask during the day. Everyone reported back at the next co-op. It was a big success, generating a lot of enthusiasm for using the shadowing technique again in the future. More than one student returned with the realization that their glamorized career interest had some real negatives to consider.

Many of the older students then set up an internship or apprenticeship as the next logical step after shadowing for a day. From my observation, that experience either solidified their career direction, or made them realize they needed to go back to the drawing board.

APPRENTICESHIPS AND INTERNSHIPS

Apprenticeships are making quite a comeback. I've found that once an employer tries one with a homeschooler; he is inclined to do it again. By and large, our kids have a work ethic that is missing among many teens today. Internships, on the other hand, are in place at most colleges, and major companies use this tool to evaluate students before tendering a job offer. However, I know of homeschooled high school students who have gotten internships intended for college students.

What's the difference between the two? Apprenticing is a much longer time commitment, with the expectation that the apprentice will enter the work force directly after the apprenticeship. Interning is usually no longer than a semester and is intended to expose the student to the various aspects of a business or career so that he can decide if he likes the environment. In most cases, your best bet will be approaching folks within the homeschool community. But I know kids who have had no trouble setting up experiences in many different fields. And as I mentioned above, these usually result in the employers looking for more homeschooled kids.

When approaching a business or professional about these options, first decide which type of on-the-job training you are looking for. Here are some questions to answer as you design an apprenticeship or internship:

1. **Will this be a paid position?** In some cases, the experience is all the business or professional can offer. But because that experience will clarify a career path or open doors in the future, foregoing the pay is worth it in exchange for the skill learned. In other cases, the pay may be less than the going rate for teen labor. Again, I feel the opportunity to acquire a lifelong skill should be seized before spending a summer working at the local teen haunts. You also should evaluate the example other employees are going to set as well. My sons have been positively influenced by working alongside hard-working homeschool dads who provide for their families through their small businesses.

2. **How will the apprentice or intern be evaluated?** If a business does not routinely use these methods with their young employees, then you can help provide definition and written documentation of the experience. Draw up a simple form ahead of time with the employer. List the skills that should be mastered or introduced; and list the habits of a good employee that your teen should cultivate. For example, initiative, timeliness, customer service, poise, written and oral communication skills, professional appearance, telephone skills, *et cetera,* are qualities colleges and future employers will be interested in seeing documented.

And if your student sees the evaluation form ahead of time, he'll have a clear understanding, too, of where he needs to excel.

3. **Will the student have progressive exposure to all aspects of the business?** If you don't ask this question at the get-go, you may be disappointed to find that the internship is merely organizing a warehouse or stuffing envelopes—jobs no one else wants to do nor has time for. I think, realistically, you'll find these kinds of assignments are a part of most experiences. But if you politely make it clear ahead of time that your intention is to acquire some skills in exchange for hard work and below-market labor, you can exact a commitment to that.

Final advice: Older teens should set up their own apprenticeships or internships. It is important for them to learn to negotiate with a prospective employer and to be poised in important social situations. Our sons are headed into business. Spending time with their father, who works for a Fortune 200 company; working at our family business; and working for several other self-employed homeschool families has clarified their career path. About two years ago, I stopped making phone calls for my sons; they've had to talk to colleges, talk to admissions directors, talk with prospective employers, and negotiate some important opportunities for themselves. At first, they were reluctant to make phone calls or set up appointments. I understood the insecurity. But today, at 17, they are embarrassed if I try to handle a situation for them. "Mom, I can do this myself," always makes me smile. And just the fact that they do take responsibility in these situations has caused many adults to perceive them as more mature than their peers; and thus, ready for more responsibility and opportunities.

LOOKING AHEAD TO POSSIBLE CAREER CHOICES

First, I've spent considerable time reading futurists such as Faith Popcorn and John Nesbitt. I really enjoy prognosticators, especially Nesbitt who predicted in the early '80s that homeschooling would become a major trend. These folks aren't always correct, but they are better than most at looking at cultural and consumer trends and then predicting future employment needs. I've shared with my kids, as I've been reading, about growth industries and job opportunities.

At one point, our son Mike was serious about criminal justice. However, a little research showed a huge glut in this area, with most jobs involving long hours, odd shifts, and other factors not conducive to family life. On the other hand, these futurists predict real opportunity in the service industries. As folks lead busier and busier lives, many are using such time-savers as laundering, house-cleaning, and lawn-care services. These are great opportunities for self-starting entrepreneurs, and I know several homeschooled teens who've started a service-type business in high school that has now turned into full-time employment. In some cases, a college degree helped them better prepare to grow their business; but in others, the degree was essentially not necessary. They were acquiring enough business sense through their own reading and questioning of other entrepreneurs, and they decided to forego the expensive education.

Second thought: Help your kids think about the lifestyle they envision for their future, not just their career. Many of today's prestigious and in-vogue careers are completely incompatible with family life. Does your son want to have time to spend with his family? Does he want to earn enough to support a wife and children? Does he want to have time to invest in his local church or Christian ministry? Does he want to travel, or not? Kids need to think through the impact of career choices on others in their future lives.

WHAT ABOUT OUR DAUGHTERS?

Now what about our daughters? A more difficult question for most of us. But my husband and I have concluded our daughters also need a marketable set of skills. A college degree is certainly one way to acquire that, but there are other venues to achieve this as well. While we certainly are encouraging our girls to prepare for marriage and motherhood, we believe it is presumptuous to assume our daughters will marry. I have also seen firsthand that widowhood is not something Christians are immune from. Research has shown that women, on average, must support themselves independently at least seven years of their adult life. As responsible parents, we want to make sure our daughters are in a position to do so if it becomes necessary.

On the other hand, we have faith that our girls will someday be happily married mothers, free to stay home with their children. They both still talk about pursuing college or additional training after high school. And we don't see this as only necessary to protect them from future disaster; rather, we see this as an opportunity to acquire skills they can use in running their homes well, or in service to their local church. As I talk with them about the full range of possibilities, we are also evaluating careers in terms of their adaptability to home management and ministry; or perhaps part-time work from their homes.

CHOOSING A COLLEGE:

Here are two good questions to answer.

1. How will this college choice possibly affect your teen's spiritual growth? I don't think we can take this for granted. The kids I know who are doing the best spiritually are those who knew where they would be fellowshipping before they left for school. Have you identified a local church that is a good fit for your teen? Active campus ministry? I prefer knowing that grounded adult leadership is available. At least from my experience in college, I find campus ministries that are student-led can easily get into imbalances and even serious error. Visiting the local churches and ministries would seem as important to me as visiting the school prior to deciding.
2. If your teen is planning to live on campus, how confident are you in his or her foundation? I've been sobered by the number of young people just in our circle of friends who have been tripped up by the secularism of the university environment—even on some Christian campuses.

Another area of "land mines" is dating: One freshman I know has been surprised to find how much dating is promoted by the administration at her school—a school, I might add, very popular with homeschoolers. One reason I'm teaching a Church History course to my sons and their graduating friends this year is because I wanted one more chance to cement the foundations of their faith. In the course of our studies, they are seeing that the same heresies and excesses just keep getting recycled. I trust they will be equipped to recognize and reject these wherever they find them in their future.

FINANCING COLLEGE

1. A college education is an investment in the future of your child that statistically should yield a good return. If the choice is between no college education and going into debt to have one—I'd still choose the college education in today's job market. However, going into debt should never be taken lightly. I've heard this from a number of young married couples starting out life together with the burden of college loans hanging over their heads. What they borrowed to get an education didn't seem like much—until combined! In some cases, pregnancy and parenthood came much sooner than expected, and now they are retiring those debts on a single income. Though they think I'm teasing, I tell my sons I'm praying right now that their future wives are not going into debt to get an education. *Consumer Reports* recommends that students not go into debt beyond what they anticipate their starting salary to be the first year out of school. We're using this as a rule of thumb, though I am skeptical of the starting numbers admissions directors are throwing out at my sons, both of whom are planning to major in marketing.

2. Merit scholarships are on the increase at many schools. And this is good news for homeschoolers. There are many avenues, other than just high board scores, to earning these. Essay contests abound. Go to www.fastweb.com to find these. Have your teens fill out the profile form, and Fastweb will notify them regularly of scholarships for which they may possibly qualify. Sign up before the senior year! Lots of deadlines fall early. Cafi Cohen, author of *And What About College?*, has posted examples of excellent college essays on her Website: www. homeschoolteenscollege.net.

3. Colleges are also looking for the student with the distinctive background. Homeschooling in itself used to be enough to make the student exceptional. But schools no longer view this as unusual. Admissions directors say they are looking for kids with unique experiences—they've studied or traveled abroad, are fluent in a second language, have volunteered or initiated community-service projects, started businesses, been involved in local campaigns, **et cetera.** Make a list of the distinctive experiences your teen has had during high school and find a way to draw attention to these somewhere in the college application.

I find a lot of kids overlook the obvious because they are so used to the uniqueness of their family. For instance, if your family provides foster care, has adopted special-needs children, or serves in ministry at your church, highlight this in the essay, letters of recommendations, or separate a addendum to the application if it just doesn't fit anywhere else.

WRITING THE COLLEGE ESSAY

Finally, the essays your child writes for college admittance are critical. First, type these and rubber cement them to the page. Don't hand print. Admission personnel are reading hundreds, and they are scanning them at best. So second, write an opening with real impact and surprise. Start with an anecdote, strong quote, or question. Get some outside advice if necessary (though make sure the essay remains your teen's own words.)

The critical component of the college essay is this: It should be self-revealing and reflective. That means it gives an honest glimpse into the inner workings of your child's mind and personality. Is this a student who thinks deeply, and recognizes the inner impact of life's experiences upon who he is and hopes to become? Is this a student who can analyze and apply what she has read, experienced, or thought about?

I'm not only currently helping (and frustrating) my sons in their never-ending saga of writing essays, but also teaching teens an advanced composition class at our co-op. Almost without exception, kids simply narrate the events that have happened to them. That's the first draft. Good place to start, I tell them, now go back and tell me what you thought about as these events were transpiring. Then think about how your past experiences influenced your response to these events; and then think about how the events you are focusing on have shaped who you are today: what you value; how you think; who you want to become. That should be the focus of your essay, not the actual events that transpired. You're on your way!

© Debra Bell, author of *The Ultimate Guide to Homeschooling*. Reprinted by permission. Visit the Homeschool Resource Center at www.debrabell.com

College-Level Exams Provide Credit and Credibility

Janice Campbell

One of the nicest things about homeschooling is that there is an option for everyone. From unschooling to unit studies to accelerated education, homeschoolers are all over the educational spectrum. What we have in common, however, is a willingness to take advantage of tools that make education—and life—easier or more interesting. One tool we have at our disposal is the College-Level Examination Program (CLEP). (There are other college-level exams available, but I will focus on CLEP exams in this article.) Many colleges grant credit for acceptable scores on college-level exams, making it possible to earn up to a year's worth of college credit while still in high school. Of the many good reasons why homeschoolers might want to take a few college-level exams during the high school years, the most compelling are credibility, time, and money.

SHOW WHAT YOU KNOW

While diversity is one of homeschooling's greatest assets, it can also be perceived as a liability. Pity the poor college admissions officer who has to wade through hundreds of applications and transcripts each week. When dealing with an accredited public or private school, he has some idea of the standards each is using to assign grades. When dealing with a homeschooler's application, though, he has no idea how objectively or by what standards grades are assigned. It makes it difficult to measure a homeschooler against someone who has been more traditionally schooled. When a student is hoping for an acceptance letter, he doesn't want to be seen as a problem by the admissions officer.

So how can a student measurably and credibly demonstrate his learning? A parent-created high school transcript is a start, but it doesn't tell the whole story. When an admission officer sees on a transcript that a home-schooled student has taken English Literature and earned a 'B,' he has no way of knowing the scope and depth of the student's work. However, if the transcript lists a CLEP score along with the grade, the admissions officer immediately understands what the student has studied and how well he understood the material. This gives him an objective point of reference, and as a bonus, may also impress him.

A MINUTE INVESTED IS AN HOUR EARNED

I recently read a study reporting that it's taking longer than ever to earn a four-year college degree. Some students are juggling jobs and school, while others have had difficulty settling on a major. Imagine what an advantage a student would have if he entered college with a year's worth of credit accumulated during the high school years! He could choose to graduate early, or to spend a year exploring classes that look interesting. He could opt for a double major, or spend time as an intern or volunteer. By investing some time during high school, he has given himself extra time to try out different options and decide how he wants to spend his future.

The beauty of the CLEP exams is that they don't have to cause a lot of extra work. Any high-school subject can be broadened and deepened to college-level, especially a subject in which the student has a natural interest. (I wrote about how to do this in an issue of *HELM*.) The exams measure whether a student has acquired knowledge and understanding that is approximately comparable to what he would learn in an introductory-level college course. If a student loves a subject and has read extensively on his own, he may be ready to pass a CLEP without much further study. My two oldest sons took their first CLEPs at sixteen and fourteen. The history buff chose to take the *History of the United States I* exam, and the literature buff took the *Analyzing and Interpreting Literature* exam. Neither studied before the exam, but both passed with remarkably high scores and percentile rankings. This doesn't mean that the exams are easy; it just means that it's possible to learn at a very high level by reading and studying independently.

And when a student feels ready, it's convenient to take CLEP exams. They are offered at hundreds of test centers on college campuses nationwide. Most test centers are open to the public and offer a testing session at least once a month. The test itself lasts ninety minutes. Not a bad time investment for 3-6 college credits!

A CHEAPSKATE'S DELIGHT

CLEP exams are an incredibly inexpensive way to earn college credit. Each exam costs $46 plus a test center fee of $12. That works out to less than twenty dollars per credit hour for three-credit exams, and less than ten dollars per credit for six-credit exams. Compared with other credit-earning options such as distance learning or community college classes, CLEP exams come out way ahead.

SO IS THERE A CATCH?

It's true that the best things in life are free, but some of the cheap things are pretty good too. CLEPs are convenient—you can take them when *you're* ready. They're cheaper than most other ways of earning college credit. They're objective, they're widely accepted (most, though not all colleges accept at least some of the CLEPs—check first if you have your heart set on a particular college), and they don't take a big chunk of your time. And your scores are maintained on a CLEP transcript for twenty years so that you can have them sent to any schools you wish at any time during those years.

The only potential downside I see is the pain of missing out on all the introductory-level college courses that your fellow freshmen have to take, and starting out in more advanced classes. Wait! That's actually another asset. Higher-level classes are usually more specialized and interesting than the survey-level (introductory) courses.

As you can tell, I'm sold on the benefits of college-level exams, and CLEPs in particular. As outsiders in the education establishment, homeschoolers often face a credibility gap. While this needn't affect our educational choices, it's nice to be able to provide objective proof of learning in a way that is non-intrusive. CLEP exams are a cheap, accessible way of earning college credit, and of proving that homeschoolers can teach themselves nearly anything they want to know.

Trades and Vocations: An Alternative to College

Matthew Mariani

How many people would object to a raise in pay? Not many. Everyone agrees that high earnings are better than low earnings. Statistics show that high-earning workers are likely to have a bachelor's degree or more education. But not everyone wants to spend four or more years in college. In fact, most workers do not have a bachelor's degree.

The good news is that many workers without bachelor's degrees have high earnings. High earnings are defined here in two ways. Both depend on medians: the point at which half the workers earned more and half earned less. The first measure of high earnings sets the cutoff at the median for earnings of all workers. The second measure raises the cutoff to the median for earnings of workers with a bachelor's degree.

Many workers who don't have a bachelor's degree earn more than the average college graduate. But earnings are only one measure of what makes a job good.

Some people worry that high-paying jobs are no longer available for those without a bachelor's degree. Many high-paying jobs in manufacturing, telecommunications, and some other industries have been eliminated. For men without a bachelor's degree, earnings adjusted for inflation have fallen over the past 15 years, due in part to these declines in high-paying jobs. Rising requirements for some professional, managerial, and other jobs have made entry without a degree even more difficult. An oversupply of college graduates has also displaced some less educated workers from high-paying jobs, which have not traditionally required a bachelor's degree.

Despite these trends, over 9 million, or 15 percent, of the full-time wage and salary workers age 25 and older who didn't have a bachelor's degree in 1998 earned more than $821 a week. That's more than the median for college graduates.

Earnings are one measure of what makes a job good. But choosing the right career involves many factors. Job characteristics, such as the nature of the work and working conditions, are also important. This article identifies occupations in which many highly-paid workers do not have a bachelor's degree and points out other things that make for a good job.

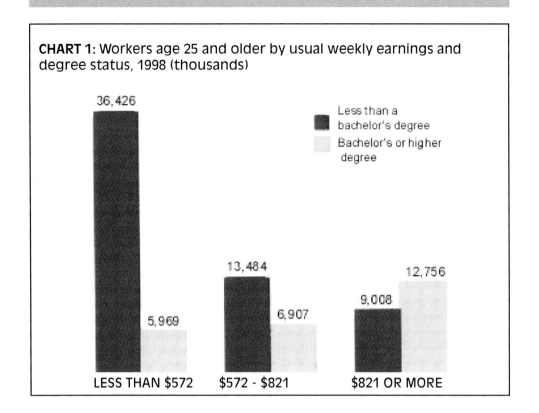

CHART 1: Workers age 25 and older by usual weekly earnings and degree status, 1998 (thousands)

Less than a bachelor's degree

Bachelor's or higher degree

36,426

5,969

13,484

6,907

9,008

12,756

LESS THAN $572 $572 - $821 $821 OR MORE

WHO HAS HIGH EARNINGS?

Median weekly earnings for full-time workers age 25 and older were $572 in 1998. The median for those with at least a bachelor's degree was $821. The low figure is over two and a half times the expected weekly earnings of a full-time employee paid the minimum wage ($ 5.15 an hour), and the high figure is almost four times higher.

In 1998, 22.5 million workers without a bachelor's degree earned $572 or more a week, and 9 million earned $821 or more. (See chart 1.) Thirty-eight percent of workers without a bachelor's degree earned more than the median for all workers ($572 per week). Fifteen percent of those without a bachelor's degree earned more than the median for workers with a bachelor's or higher degree ($821 per week). (See chart 2.) In several occupations, more than 10 percent of the workers without bachelor's degrees earned over $1,000. (See Table 1.)

Fifteen percent of workers without a bachelor's degree earned more than $821 per week.

In part, earnings reflect the skills and innate talents of a worker. Other factors, such as location, urban or rural environment, industry, size of the facility, and unionization, also affect earnings. Three additional factors significantly affect the proportion of workers who have high earnings:

- Occupation
- Age
- Education and training.

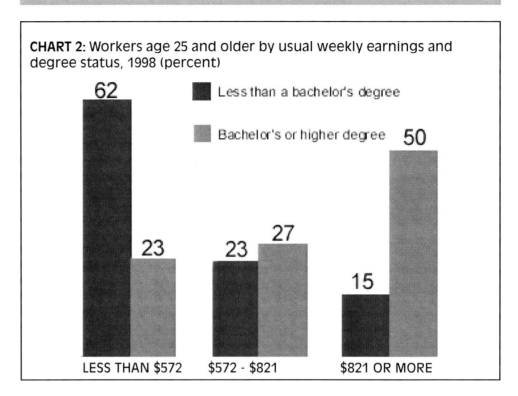

CHART 2: Workers age 25 and older by usual weekly earnings and degree status, 1998 (percent)

Less than a bachelor's degree

Bachelor's or higher degree

62 23 23 27 15 50

LESS THAN $572 $572 - $821 $821 OR MORE

OCCUPATION

Tables 1, 2, and 3 list all occupations that have more than 50,000 full-time wage and salary workers age 25 or older who usually earn $821 or more a week. These tables exclude small occupations—occupations with fewer than 50,000 employed—in which workers have high earnings. Two examples are elevator installer and air traffic controller.

In addition to total employment, Table 2 shows the number of workers who do not have a bachelor's degree and their share of the total. Table 3 lists the same occupations but shows the number of high-earning workers who do not have a bachelor's degree—those earning $821 or more per week. Table 3 also describes the employment of these high-earning workers as a share of all workers and as a share of those who do not have a bachelor's degree.

Earnings vary within occupations. Not every worker in a high-earning occupation makes a lot of money. Consider the example of freight, stock, and material movers. Although some of these workers enjoy high earnings, most do not. This occupational group appears in Table 3 because 54,000 of these workers did not have bachelor's degrees but earned more than $821 a week. However, these workers accounted for only seven percent of all freight, stock, and material movers who did not have bachelor's degrees. As noted in Table 1, freight, stock, and material movers had median weekly earnings of $379, much less than the median for all workers.

Some occupations have higher earnings than others, but earnings vary within occupations.

Remember that first impressions may mislead. Annual earnings for seasonal occupations may be lower than implied by weekly earnings: Spells of unemployment reduce annual earnings in these occupations. Excluding part-timers and workers under 25 results in higher earnings numbers because these workers typically earn less. In addition, putting in extra hours in some occupations more readily translates into higher earnings than in others, in part because some workers receive overtime pay.

AGE

Earnings tend to increase with age as workers gain experience and seniority. (See Chart 3.) This upward trend usually peaks between the ages of 45 and 54. The number of high wage earners is thus concentrated in the

---

TABLE 1

Usual weekly earnings of wage and salary workers age 25 and older with less than a bachelor's degree, 1998

OCCUPATION	MEDIAN EARNINGS	MINIMUM EARNINGS OF THE TOP 10 PERCENT
All occupations	$486	$ 939
Accountants and auditors	547	914
Administrators and officials, public administration	628	1,140
Aircraft engine mechanics	790	1,200
Assemblers	403	773
Automotive mechanics	520	938
Carpenters	518	988
Computer programmers	777	1,306
Computer systems analysts and scientists	860	1,389
Construction laborers	404	820
Electrical and electronic engineers	882	1,343
Electrical and electronic equipment repairers, except phone	630	1,060
Electrical and electronic technicians	665	1,088
Electrical power installers and repairers	847	1,227
Electricians	694	1,094
Financial managers	648	1,241
Firefighting occupations	751	1,194
Freight, stock, and material movers, hand	379	742
Health technologists and technicians	492	805
Industrial machinery repairers	612	1,023
Investigators and adjusters, insurance and other	475	759
Machine operators and tenders, except precision	413	782
Machinists	608	985
Mail carriers and postal clerks	665	870
Managers and administrators not elsewhere classified	721	1,373
Managers, food serving and lodging establishments	511	987
Managers, marketing, advertising, and public relations	762	1,517
Managers, medicine and health	587	955
Material moving equipment operators	515	949
Mechanical engineers	897	1,406
Other financial officers	607	1,112
Plant and system operators	686	1,168
Plumbers, pipefitters, and steamfitters	628	1,056
Police and detectives	635	1,026
Real estate sales occupations	618	1,582
Registered nurses	705	1,002
Sales occupations, other business services	586	1,220
Sales representatives, finance and business services	587	1,257
Sales representatives, mining, manufacturing and wholesale	639	1,174
Sales workers, motor vehicles and boats	595	1,133
Secretaries	394	686
Supervisors and proprietors, sales occupations	520	1,035
Supervisors, administrative support occupations	566	915
Supervisors, construction occupations	710	1,156
Supervisors, mechanics and repairers	738	1,148
Supervisors, production occupations	632	1,089
Supervisors, protective service occupations	729	1,229
Telephone and telephone line installers and repairers	767	1,143
Tool and die makers	802	
Truck drivers	540	963
Welders and cutters	542	930

35 to 44 and 45 to 54 age groups. Some of these highly paid workers without bachelor's degrees entered the job market years ago, when educational requirements for entry were lower and more high-wage manufacturing jobs were available. However, some younger workers without a bachelor's degree also enjoy high earnings. For example, 24 percent of workers age 25 to 29 who did not have a degree earned $572 or more a week. About 7 percent earned $821 or more.

EDUCATION

Many workers who lack bachelor's degrees have other postsecondary education or training. Training other than a bachelor's degree provides the best preparation for some high-paying jobs. Workers with more training usually earn more. Some high-wage occupations are difficult to enter without training, and within occupations, the most highly trained workers tend to collect the largest paychecks and have a better chance of advancing into supervisory jobs.

HIGH WAGE EARNERS DEVELOP SKILLS THEY NEED IN MANY WAYS.

High wage earners develop skills they need in many ways—through associate degree programs, college courses, postsecondary vocational schools and technical institutes, apprenticeships, or other formal employer training, informal on-the-job training, and Armed Forces experience. Earnings data are not available for workers with these types of training, but Chart 4 shows that earnings increase with education. What's good besides earnings? Everyone needs money. Still, hardly anyone chooses an occupation— or a particular job within an occupation— based solely on salary. The perfect career recipe for any individual contains many ingredients besides money. These include the following:
- Benefits
- Projected growth and openings
- Job security
- Advancement potential
- Nature of the work.

Depending on the mix you prefer, a job with lower earnings might please you more than any other.

BENEFITS

Many employers provide some benefits that add to the quality of a job. These may include health insurance, life insurance, child-care subsidies, paid holidays and vacation time, sick leave, and employee discounts. Benefits have become a major part of the compensation workers receive. In March 1998, benefits averaged about 28 percent of total compensation costs. *Benefits make up a significant portion of total compensation for many workers.*

Some benefits, such as health and life insurance or subsidized child care, are as good as cash. Without them, workers would have to pay expenses out of pocket. Some employers, like airlines, provide free or subsidized travel, while retailers may provide discounts on merchandise. Paid holidays and vacation and sick leave improve quality of life.

Depending on the benefits package, a job with lower earnings might provide better total compensation than a job offering just a large paycheck.

TABLE 2

Employment of wage and salary workers age 25 and older by occupation, 1998 (numbers in thousands)

OCCUPATION	TOTAL	NUMBER WITH	PERCENT LESS THAN A BACHELOR'S DEGREE
All occupations	84,549	58,917	70
Accountants and auditors	1,211	427	35
Administrators and officials, public administration	579	246	42
Aircraft engine mechanics	134	117	87
Assemblers	1,005	955	95
Automotive mechanics	536	513	96
Carpenters	743	712	96
Computer programmers	491	194	40
Computer systems analysts and scientists	1,205	366	30
Construction laborers	536	517	96
Electrical and electronic engineers	580	146	25
Electrical and electronic equipment repairers, except phone	437	363	83
Electrical and electronic technicians	378	312	83
Electrical power installers and repairers	119	114	96
Electricians	608	575	95
Financial managers	628	244	39
Firefighting occupations	198	177	89
Freight, stock, and material movers, hand	871	823	94
Health technologists and technicians	1,161	908	78
Industrial machinery repairers	503	480	95
Investigators and adjusters, insurance and other	1,117	820	73
Machine operators and tenders, except precision	3,852	3,721	97
Machinists	458	437	95
Mail carriers and postal clerks	605	514	85
Managers and administrators not elsewhere classified	5,087	2,565	50
Managers, food serving and lodging establishments	797	618	78
Managers, marketing, advertising, and public relations	710	256	36
Managers, medicine and health	617	324	53
Material moving equipment operators	918	899	98
Mechanical engineers	301	88	29
Other financial officers	599	262	44
Plant and system operators	251	224	89
Plumbers, pipefitters, and steamfitters	375	360	96
Police and detectives	982	735	75
Real estate sales occupations	337	194	58
Registered nurses	1,439	694	48
Sales occupations, other business services	442	234	53
Sales representatives, finance and business services	1,609	778	48
Sales representatives, mining, manufacturing and wholesale	1,182	674	57
Sales workers, motor vehicles and boats	254	206	81
Secretaries	2,054	1,837	89
Supervisors and proprietors, sales occupations	2,895	2,081	72
Supervisors, administrative support occupations	654	469	72
Supervisors, construction occupations	460	409	89
Supervisors, mechanics and repairers	241	210	87
Supervisors, production occupations	1,096	958	87
Supervisors, protective service occupations	210	147	70
Telephone and telephone line installers and repairers	242	219	90
Tool and die makers	123	117	95
Truck drivers	2,216	2,132	96
Welders and cutters	479	473	99
All other occupations	40,024	27,073	68

TABLE 3

Employment of wage and salary workers age 25 and older with less than a bachelor's degree and usual weekly earnings of $821 or more by occupation, 1998

OCCUPATION	NUMBER (THOUSANDS)	PERCENT OF ALL WORKERS	% OF WORKERS W/LESS THAN A BACHELOR'S DEGREE
All occupations	9,008	11	15
Accountants and auditors	65	5	15
Administrators and officials, public administration	75	13	30
Aircraft engine mechanics	51	38	44
Assemblers	63	6	7
Automotive mechanics	87	16	17
Carpenters	135	18	19
Computer programmers	91	19	47
Computer systems analysts and scientists	196	16	54
Construction laborers	50	9	10
Electrical and electronic engineers	84	14	58
Electrical and electronic equipment repairers, except phone	95	22	26
Electrical and electronic technicians	79	21	25
Electrical power installers and repairers	62	52	54
Electricians	203	33	35
Financial managers	76	12	31
Firefighting occupations	74	37	42
Freight, stock, and material movers, hand	54	6	7
Health technologists and technicians	83	7	9
Industrial machinery repairers	104	21	22
Investigators and adjusters, insurance and other	60	5	7
Machine operators and tenders, except precision	30	48	8
Machinists	96	21	22
Mail carriers and postal clerks	74	12	14
Managers and administrators not elsewhere classified	1,022	20	40
Managers, food serving and lodging establishments	95	12	15
Managers, marketing, advertising, and public relations	112	16	44
Managers, medicine and health	63	10	19
Material moving equipment operators	138	15	15
Mechanical engineers	51	17	58
Other financial officers	64	11	24
Plant and system operators	78	31	35
Plumbers, pipefitters, and steamfitters	89	24	25
Police and detectives	200	20	27
Real estate sales occupations	56	17	29
Registered nurses	187	13	27
Sales occupations, other business services	61	14	26
Sales representatives, finance and business services	196	12	25
Sales representatives, mining, manufacturing and wholesale	199	17	30
Sales workers, motor vehicles and boats	56	22	27
Secretaries	65	3	4
Supervisors and proprietors, sales occupations	365	13	18
Supervisors, administrative support occupations	80	12	17
Supervisors, construction occupations	135	29	33
Supervisors, mechanics and repairers	79	33	38
Supervisors, production occupations	269	25	28
Supervisors, protective service occupations	57	27	39
Telephone and telephone line installers and repairers	93	38	42
Tool and die makers	53	43	45
Truck drivers	383	17	18
Welders and cutters	75	16	16
All other occupations	2,426	6	9

PROJECTED GROWTH AND OPENINGS

The projected growth rate and number of job openings affect the ease or difficulty of finding a job in an occupation and, perhaps, the opportunities for promotion, as well. The Occupational Outlook Handbook and "The 1996-2006 Job Outlook in Brief" in the spring 1998 provide vital information on projected occupational employment. In some cases, additional information on competition for jobs is given.

Some high wage occupations that do not require a bachelor's degree, such as machinists, are not expected to grow. Others are expected to grow about as fast as the average for all workers, including truck drivers, police and detectives, automotive mechanics, material moving equipment operators, and mechanical engineers. Computer programmer, registered nurse, and most health technologist and technician occupations are projected to grow faster than average.

The projected growth rate and number of job openings affect the ease or difficulty of finding a job in an occupation.

For many occupations, projected growth significantly enhances job prospects. Even so, employment growth usually produces fewer openings than those resulting from the need to replace workers who transfer to different occupations, retire, or stop working for other reasons. For example, the employment of secretaries is projected to increase by 25,000 jobs by 2006, but net replacement needs are expected to provide more than 23 times as many openings.

Lack of growth in an occupation does not always mean a lack of job openings. For example, machinists have favorable prospects despite their lack of employment growth, because of the shortage of skilled machinists in the labor market.

JOB SECURITY

Workers in some occupations and industries are less vulnerable to losing their jobs as a result of economic downturns, seasonal variations in production, or changes in the technologies used to accomplish work. Occupational unemployment rates provide one measure of job security. Workers in occupations with low unemployment rates are less likely to become unemployed. Some occupations having high unemployment rates still qualify as high paying, but workers who desire security may prefer a smaller but more reliable paycheck.

Unemployment rates reflect two kinds of unemployment: cyclical and long term. Recessions and seasonal changes in production create cyclical unemployment in many occupations. During slack periods, workers may face temporary layoffs but can expect to resume work when conditions improve. On the other hand, long-term unemployment or even permanent job loss may result from restructuring or plant closings. Jobs in organizations or industries with good long-term prospects are obviously more desirable. If you lose your job, you will likely find another one in such an industry.

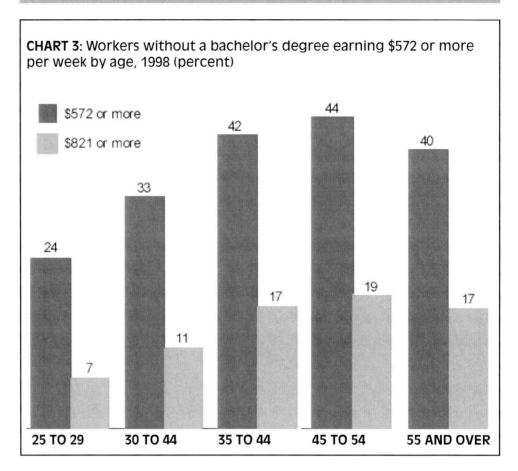

CHART 3: Workers without a bachelor's degree earning $572 or more per week by age, 1998 (percent)

- $572 or more
- $821 or more

25 TO 29	30 TO 44	35 TO 44	45 TO 54	55 AND OVER
24	33	42	44	40
7	11	17	19	17

ADVANCEMENT POTENTIAL

Some occupations offer a natural path for career advancement. For instance, an electrician apprentice becomes a journey level electrician and then, perhaps, an electrician supervisor or contractor. Workers in other occupations may need to blaze their own trail to success. Still other occupations or jobs offer few, if any, chances for advancement.

Promotion potential varies from employer to employer. In general, fast growing occupations and organizations offer better promotion prospects. Large employers often provide better prospects, but small organizations may offer broader responsibilities and opportunities to learn a wider range of skills. The most successful workers look for opportunities and seize them when they arise.

NATURE OF THE WORK

What type of work holds the greatest appeal? It all depends on the person. Different occupations correspond with varying individual, social, and physical characteristics. Everyone weighs these factors in their own way when deciding what makes a job good.

Individuals like doing tasks that interest them, use their skills, and satisfy their needs in other ways. What interests you? Is it cars, music, children, or any one of thousands of other subjects? Do you like taking risks, or do you desire security? Does stress motivate you or make you sick? Different personalities crave different types of activities, such as the following:

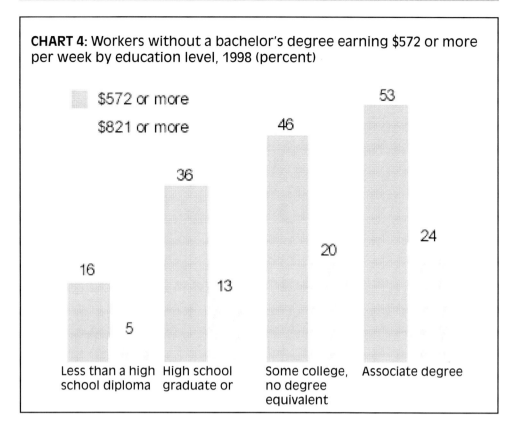

CHART 4: Workers without a bachelor's degree earning $572 or more per week by education level, 1998 (percent)

$572 or more
$821 or more

	Less than a high school diploma	High school graduate or	Some college, no degree equivalent	Associate degree
$572 or more	16	36	46	53
$821 or more	5	13	20	24

- Helping others
- Analyzing data or information
- Coordinating events and activities
- Teaching or mentoring
- Selling or persuading
- Operating or fixing machinery
- Creating new concepts, designs, or works of art
- Running an enterprise
- Managing the efforts of others
- Organizing ideas or programs.

Individuals have their own ideas about the work environment they prefer. Some people like dealing with customers or coworkers all day long, whereas others would rather work alone more often than not. But in either case, having a good supervisor and friendly coworkers may count for a lot.

Important physical characteristics of work include the level of physical exertion necessary, cleanliness and safety of the workplace, and ability to control the pace of work and the methods used. Geographic location also matters. For some people, a good job is one that is near their home.

Different workers value the idea of paid work differently. The hours that high pay demands may clash with what a worker wants. Some only want part-time work so they can devote their energies to family responsibilities, school, or other pursuits.

To learn more about the many distinguishing characteristics of occupations, see "Matching Yourself With the World of Work, 1998," in the fall 1998.

To obtain a reprint of this article, call the Consumer Information Center at 1-888-878-3256.

ARE YOU READY?

The data reveal many good jobs for those who do not have a bachelor's degree—not only jobs with high wages, but also jobs that are good for other reasons. Every job has its positives and negatives. One factor seldom makes a job good or bad.

Find out all you can about occupations that interest you. Research the entry requirements and other characteristics so you will know what to expect. Above all, choose a career that meets your definition of good. The demand for skilled workers will remain strong. Are you ready?

© Occupational Outlook Quarterly, Fall 1999. Reprinted by permission. Matthew Mariani is desktop publisher for the Occupational Outlook Quarterly.

A Lifestyle of Learning Lays the Foundation for Entrepreneurial Success

Rhea Perry

When our oldest son, Drew, was 14, the Lord led my husband to send him to Idaho for a month of entrepreneurial apprenticeship with our friend, Chris Verhaegh. That month changed Drew's life and ours. The seeds Chris planted in our young son's mind soon began to bear fruit. Drew's respectful questioning of my philosophy of education caused me to rethink my methods.

Like some boys, Drew has never been the most academic guy, and that frustrated me for several years. But, when I began to let him explore his interests and pursue his own projects, he became a very productive young man. He's now learning to fearlessly convert his mental vision and knowledge into physical goals and reality.

Now that Drew is 20, he is a member of the local Toastmaster's Club, oversees the manager and the bookkeepers for our 12 rental properties, has his own website, www.fsbo-tnvalley.com, started a local investment real estate club with a friend, and has bought seven houses on his own. He also loves the Lord. But, he doesn't want to spend his life like so many men he sees who are miserable as they trade their time for dollars and their lives for security.

WE DISCOVER REAL ESTATE

Over a year ago, Drew and I took an Internet class in which we were encouraged to read the book, *Rich Dad, Poor Dad*, by Robert Kiyosaki. We also met a new friend who owned investment real estate. Within a month, our family had found and purchased 13 houses in one real estate transaction that was priced well below appraised value. Drew, then 19, was managing our farm and inherited management of these houses.

A week later, the pipes thawed and burst in the only empty house. So, the next day, Drew bought a cell phone, hired all the necessary contractors to repair the house, ran an ad in the daily paper, and rented the house. Some of the contractors asked Drew how old he was. When he returned home from getting the rental house ready, he declared, "Mom, I love this!"

This began his adventure into the field of investment real estate. His father and I started flying and driving with him to various seminars and ordered audiocassette courses that he requested. His education has been somewhat expensive, but less than college and perfectly tailored for what God created him to do.

A FEW INTERESTING IDEAS

One day after we had been out to eat, Drew drove the family to a great neighborhood and parked the van on the side of the street. He took his dad and me to a house that needed some major repairs and ushered us inside. When we asked him why we were in someone else's house, he replied, "I just bought it. What do you think?" Then, he explained that he had purchased the house for $4,300 on a credit card." Three weeks later, Drew sold that house for $6,000 to an investor who rehabs houses.

He then bought a house in the country for $22,000 and began the repairs himself. He hired an interior decorator to advise him about which colors to paint the house. He found, however, that he wasn't able to focus on his other properties while spending his days working on the house. So, he hired a painter and other contractors to finish the job. A lady soon bought the house because she fell in love with the variety of colors. Sale price: $58,000.

Some friends of ours moved south from Pennsylvania and left their house for sale with a real-estate agent. Two years later, they bought a house here but their house in Pennsylvania had not yet sold. Drew taught their 17-year-old son, Dewayne, how he could sell the house. Dewayne spent the month of September in Pennsylvania where he placed an ad in the local daily newspaper. Within a week or two the house had sold. The buyer gave this teenager a $47,000 down payment and agreed to pay off the balance in two years. Everyone was thrilled!

WILL'S STORY

Will, our 14-year-old son, earns his own passive income from gumball machines. He bought and placed four machines in businesses in the neighboring town. Once a month, he hires one of the family's drivers to take him to service the machines. Gumballs cost 2 cents each and sell for 25 cents each; so, the gumball machines paid for themselves in about six months.

Will also sells books and coins on eBay. This is our favorite method for utilizing practical business skills such as marketing, typing, html, creative writing, shipping, and inventory management. Will also built our website, www.educatingforsuccess.com, that we hope will encourage young people to think "outside the box."

DOG DAYS

Our favorite entrepreneurial pastime, where our children learn to create their own money and business opportunities, is to spend holiday weekends at Dog Days. Dog Days is an outdoor flea market on the Tennessee/Alabama border where folks sell more than just yard-sale items. People come from all over to buy and sell farm animals, including hunting dogs. That's how it got the name "Dog Days." We usually drive there the night before and sleep in the van. The little boys pitch a tent just outside. Then, before the sun comes up, the children join the traders with flashlights in hand.

Once Drew bought 50 rabbits that were dehydrating in the summer heat for $1 each. He resuscitated them by separating them into smaller cages he bought from the neighboring vendor and moved the rabbits to the bank of the creek near our campsite. The next day, he sold them for $3.00 each and later in the day, for $2 each plus the price of the cage. Unfortunately, the rabbits we brought home to sell later eventually ate up our profits. Lesson learned: "A fast nickel is better than a slow dime." —Chris Verhaegh

At Dog Days, I give every child $5 and tell them they can buy and sell all they want; but, at the end of the day, they must give back my $5. They may keep anything they have gained. My youngest children are still learning the difference between spending and investing. Experience is the best teacher. But, the best success we ever had with this project was when our friend Ben joined us.

I loaned 10-year-old Ben $5 at 0% interest and we didn't see him for two hours. When he and his brother returned, he ran up to me with a big grin on his freckled face and declared, "Here's your $5 back!" I said, "Show me what you've got, Ben." He had one large animal cage that was worth about $5 AND two chickens worth about $4-$7 each AND a $1 bill. Plus, he gave back my $5. Another lesson learned: Teach them to fish and you feed them for a lifetime.

STUDY TO STAY ENCOURAGED AND INSPIRED

Moms have asked me how we come up with such zany projects. To stay encouraged and keep my focus in my early homeschooling days, I had to surround myself with positive influences. Marilyn Howshall, Sally Clarkson, Chris Davis, and the Colfaxes were my daily vision-givers. Now, Richard Maybury, Robert Kiyosaki, and Terry Dean encourage me. Although I've only met one of these guys, I owe my daily mindset to them and others like them.

It is all too easy to become distracted and begin to think I need to do what I see public school students on my left doing or what I see homeschoolers on my right doing. If I just follow what the Lord has put in my heart for my children and look straight ahead at Him, we'll all be where we are supposed to be. When I didn't listen, I paid the price.

REAL ACTIVITY DEVELOPS THE MIND

Drew is convinced that playing with Legos helped him learn to think. He says, "A boy can't have too many Legos." He even built a wide, shallow box for the little boys to keep under the bed so they can spread out their Legos in one place. Drew started learning about real estate from playing Monopoly.

But, his favorite game and the best resource that reinforces his vision is "Cashflow 101," designed and produced by millionaire Robert Kiyosaki. Not only do players learn to read a financial statement, they see how anyone with a steady job can work his or her way out of The Rat Race with a little diligent study, effort, and faith. Life is one big field trip for me, so we budget money for real books, games, and seminars.

FIND YOUR LOVE

Solomon, the wisest man who ever lived, said:
1. Be happy with the wife of your youth.
2. Be happy with what you hands find to do.

To find a young person's life purpose may take some time and attention, so I have decided to enjoy the journey and not dread, fear, or rush it. Nothing is a failure unless you don't learn something from it. If one of my children dislikes the current project, then I'm thankful we discovered that BEFORE we invested heavily in it. When one of them loves it, we encourage him or her to pursue it further, even if it's only for a season.

My job is to encourage and help each child so that he or she can channel individual interests into a ministry to others, and into streams of income. Their dad's job is to finance the project, and mentor the children by his example. When the venture becomes self-operating, like Will's gumball machines, we can start another project, if the child so desires. I want my children to continue learning and enjoy building their lives forever.

INVEST IN YOUR CHILDREN

Books, tapes, and games have helped me learn to think outside the box. They can literally change your life. In fact, the Elijah Company Catalog is one of the most life-changing resources available to homeschoolers today. If you haven't read it, make sure you request one with your order.

CONTACT US

If you'd like to follow the Perry kids and some of our crazy friends on our journey into entrepreneurial America, join us on our weekly newsletter. We also share the books and resources we discover to be useful. Subscribe by visiting our website, www.educatingforsuccess.com. And we'd love to have you join us on our email discussion group for young entrepreneurs. Just send a blank email to: entrepreneursathome-subscribe@yahoogroups.com

"The mind of man plans his way, But the Lord directs his steps."
[Proverbs 16:9]

© Rhea Perry. Reprinted from the Elijah Company. www.elijahcompany.com.

Homeschoolers in the Military: Enlisting Help

Jeremiah Lorrig, HSLDA

"My son just wants to serve his country, but the recruiter is asking for all these documents and a letter telling them why I homeschooled him. Can he do that?"

This is typical of the calls we receive from Home School Legal Defense Association members whose homeschool graduates are trying to enlist in the United States Armed Forces. There is confusion among parents (and recruiters) about what homeschoolers need to do to enlist. Problems arise not because of discriminatory policies, but because too many recruiters are still not familiar with the homeschool policy instituted on June 1, 2007.

From the outset, we want to clarify that the vast majority of homeschoolers enlisting in any of the armed service branches do not encounter problems but complete the process as easily as any other enlistee. A good number of recruiters know the policy and love homeschoolers.

There are, however, those who do not understand the U.S. Department of Defense's policy. We are writing this article for homeschoolers who are interested in joining the armed services, in order to familiarize you with the requirements and simplify the process for both you and the recruiter.

If you want to enlist as a homeschool high school graduate, there are a few things you need to keep in mind:

- **You must be a homeschool graduate having been homeschooled during the last nine months of your academic year.** Do not try to enlist if you have not completed your high school program as outlined by your parents. You also cannot drop out of high school your senior year and have your parents "graduate" you from homeschool. Be honest. Be wise.
- **You must fulfill the regular requirements**, including the physical tests that all enlistees must pass.
- **You must provide a copy of your high school diploma.** We highly recommend a professional-looking diploma, such as those available through the HSLDA bookstore. Although it carries no extra legal weight, since the enactment of the 2007 policy, we have never had a problem with a recruiter accepting a diploma in HSLDA's format, while we have had

MAKE SURE YOUR TRANSCRIPT INCLUDES:

- *Personal information of the graduate*
- *School information*
- *Dates of each school year and grade levels*
- *List of courses completed for each grade level*
- *Credits earned for each course*
- *Grades given for each course*
- *Grade point average (GPA)*
- *Dates for each class (semester/quarter and year is sufficient in most cases)*
- *Date of graduation*
- *Parent/school administrator's name and phone number*
- *Parent/guardian's signature*

many problems with diplomas printed off a home computer. We strongly discourage presenting a non-professional looking diploma.

- *You must provide a transcript.* You can find templates for a homeschool transcript on HSLDA's high school web pages. Do not be overly creative with a transcript. The most important thing is that it be clear and concise. While notarization is not required for a transcript, we recommend that you notarize it. We have not had the military question a notarized transcript.
- *You must provide transcripts from other institutions attended*, including but not limited to community college, freshman year in a public high school, private school, etc.
- *You will often need to show verification that you were homeschooled legally under the laws of your state.* If you are in a state that requires a notice of intent, a copy of that should suffice. This is only applicable for the high school years. If necessary, HSLDA can write a letter on behalf of members.
- *You must score 50 or above on the Armed Services Vocational Aptitude Battery (ASVAB).* If your score is below 50, you will be able to retake the test at 30-day intervals. There are practice tests and test-taking tips available online. Additionally, some recruiting centers offer classes and/or coaching to help recruits score well on the test.
- *You must take the Assessment of Individual Motivation* (a.k.a. the AIM test). Although homeschoolers are required to take this test, the results do not impact your enlistment. Recruiters are not allowed to use the results to qualify or disqualify homeschool graduates.

In closing, we'll leave you with a few tips. When speaking to a recruiter, tell him or her that you are a homeschool graduate. You will only confuse the recruiter if you say that you are technically private schooled in your state. The military does not care. They call homeschool graduates, "homeschool graduates," regardless of whether your homeschool is technically a private school, umbrella school, satellite school, or any other classification in your state. It is a common misconception that homeschoolers need a GED or college credits. You are a homeschool graduate. If you want to enlist as category tier 1 (a high school diploma recipient), do not take the GED.

Lastly, it might be tempting for you to say that your diploma is from an "accredited" organization. But flee the temptation—it only leads to confusion and makes the process more difficult! To some recruiters, "accredited" means an online school, which is problematic because they do not accept online school graduates. They want someone who has had a real-life teacher. If you did do some online schooling, let them know that you did that along with homeschooling by showing them how you homeschooled under the state law.

Most of the time, you will find that the military loves working with homeschool graduates. However, if you still run into problems, please call HSLDA. We love serving our members.

Reprinted with permission of Homeschool Legal Defense Association (HSLDA). © HSLDA 2010. www.hslda.org/docs/nche/Issues/M/Military_Enlistment.asp

For more information regarding military entrance for homeschoolers, visit the website of the branch of the military that interests you, then search the site for "homeschool."

Section J

Special-Needs Education
Compiled by Judith Munday

Additional Articles on the CD
BE SURE TO CHECK OUT THESE OTHER GREAT ARTICLES ON THE CD!

Each article in the book and on the CD has been carefully chosen by the section coordinator to increase your knowledge and understanding of this subject, so don't forget to use and enjoy the parts of the manual on your CD, as well as the part you are holding.

Please note that the page numbering on the CD is different from that of the hard-copy manual.

Special Needs
Dedication

T his special-needs section is dedicated first to our precious Savior, Jesus Christ, without whom all my worldly effort would amount to nothing. Next, I want to dedicate this to the parents of each child with special disabilities. All children have special needs, but some children's needs are so unique that they will not succeed without the persistence, faithfulness, and energy of tireless parents who have taken on the God-given responsibility of educating them. This section has been assembled with a prayer that it will encourage, enlighten, and equip all the parents of special-needs children for the precious job that they have undertaken.

INTRODUCTION TO SPECIAL-NEEDS SECTION

The completion of this section must stand as a testimony to the faithfulness of an awesome God who works in the midst of hectic and busy lives. When I was approached by HEAV about coordinating this section, I had just had surgery on my right hand and it was going to be in a cast at least a full week beyond the deadline I was asked to meet. Normally, I would have told them, "Impossible!!" God, however, had gone before. He already had put it in my heart to ask HEAV whether I might add some articles to the existing manual's section where I had noted that some topics had not been addressed! So, I saw the request as God's answer to my heart's desire, and I agreed to take on the challenge—and a challenge it turned out to be! Typing the new articles was mostly done with one hand and a bit of voice dictation. My husband, John, pored over my work seeking errors in typing, making ideas clearer, and editing for consistent style and format. His patience and persistence have certainly earned him *at least* one crown to toss into that crystal sea in Heaven. I thank him for his effort, because he added the editing work to a schedule already overloaded with doing the housework that I was unable to do with my cast. He never complained! Without his diligence, this section would never have happened.

I also want to thank Deb Pegram. Without my having to ask, she submitted a whole collection of articles that beautifully rounded out topics where the manual needed more substance. God met unspoken needs through her. Her generous cooperation was a sweet gesture and a great help to getting the task completed. We are already planning an expanded and more comprehensive section for the next revision of the manual. Janice Campbell, the HEAV contact, also was a blessing in her willingness to allow a small extension of a very rapidly approaching deadline, so that I might fulfill the vision God had planted in my heart for this section. Janice forwarded some wonderful material from the Colorado Home Educator's Manual that further completed the vision. Again, God provided. Special thanks, as well, to Betty Statnick, at HSLDA, for her input and encouragement. She provided useful resources and contacts. I appreciate her ministry to the special-needs families as she helped me whenever I asked. Thanks also to all those parents who graciously reviewed articles and gave helpful feedback. Without the help of so many caring people, this section would not have been completed. Our God is truly an awesome God!

—Judith B. Munday, HIS Place for Help in School

How Does a Parent Know When To Get Outside Help?

Judith Munday

There is a range of "normal" performance for development, social skills, and behaviors. Most parents rather intuitively sense when "everything is OK" when they observe their own children or compare their child to someone else's child. Keep in mind, however, that what is "normal" for your child may be exceptional for your neighbor's child.

There are subjective ways to characterize "normal" used by attentive parents as they observe the growth and development of their child. There are also more objective ways to determine what is "normal" in academic development, and when it is time to seek help. In many cases, both are important sources of information for considering whether a child's academic performance requires more than re-teaching, review, or stricter study habits.

There are many kinds of "normal" learning differences, and a wide body of information is available within homeschool and other literature on topics of learner differences, commonly referred to as "learning styles." There are other—sometimes more subtle, other times more obvious—differences from typical development and learning behaviors of a child at a certain age or grade range. We are going to explore the more commonly-encountered difficulties in development, behavior, and academic performance that have made it difficult for the child with average to above-average intelligence to perform up to their God-given capacity.

WHAT ARE THE CHARACTERISTICS OF A "NORMAL" STUDENT?

1. The child is working somewhere within the age-appropriate grade-level materials.
2. The "normal" student probably has some relative strengths and weaknesses that will be seen within the first year or two of school.
3. He or she makes progress in mastery of skills at a rate approximately equal to one grade-level of material per school year attended, given reasonably adequate instruction and curriculum.
4. He or she demonstrates increasing self-control, self-discipline, and organizational skills.
5. He or she is not laboring under handicapping conditions of health-related limitations (such as hearing impairment, vision limitations, or severe emotional issues). The "normal" student is not trying to learn in

a second language or new cultural setting, and does not have severe limitations in intellectual capacity.

6. He or she is making adequate progress in developing appropriate social skills for interactions, play, and communications in a variety of situations.

7. He or she has a healthy, normally-functioning brain as indicated by normal childhood progress through walking, talking, vision, hearing, self-help, and social interactions.

With all those descriptors, most parents are probably wondering if there is such a thing as a "normal" student. When a child is not communicating or talking well in the early years, the mother and/or father is usually inclined to wait and see if the child matures. This can be a reasonable choice for some early academic problems, but in areas of language and communication lags, *time is of critical importance.* The earlier the issue is evaluated, specifically diagnosed, and therapies begun, the better it will be for the long-term intellectual and communication needs of the child.

WHAT ARE THE KEY AREAS OF ACADEMIC DIFFICULTIES?

First, the home-teaching parent typically notices one of two things:

a. Difficulties with reading, writing, or math processing: These are often associated in the parent's mind with "learning disabilities," but it may not be that simple.

b. Difficulties with attention and/or activity levels: These are often seen as an Attention-Deficit Disorder with or without hyperactivity.

There may be multiple factors that can affect the child's attention—behaviors that are *not* going to be diagnosed as ADD, even though they may appear to have many of the "behaviors" found in most "checklists." For example, language processing may cause the child to appear distractible or inattentive, just as in ADD/ADHD.

There are many other conditions that affect children's learning, and some are becoming more frequently diagnosed, such as autism and Asperger's syndrome—a type of high-function autism. There are also some less common conditions, some of which are being found to be strongly linked to exposure to environmental toxins—either before and after birth. Some of these are lifelong disabilities that require both medical and academic remedies. Recent legislation has prompted more active research and protective action, to both prevent and cure these conditions. Just to illustrate: Our nation has approved over 25,000 chemicals to use as food additives, medicines, and pesticides, as well as for industrial and farm uses. Only about 2,000 have ever been tested for their impact on the health of CHILDREN, and research is making a stronger case that some of our children's learning and behavior problems may be linked to this "chemical soup" in which we live. The 2000 Learning Disabilities Association Convention spent over three full days addressing these matters.

WHAT ARE THE DANGER SIGNS FOR EARLY COMMUNICATION OR LANGUAGE PROCESSING DELAYS?

Difficulties may exist in either receptive language (what the child understands) or in expressive language (what the child can say and explain). Some common warning signs include:

a. The child has difficulty expressing him/herself
b. The child does not seem to hear you when you speak softly or from a distance
c. The child has problems with normal speech sounds—at the normal age
d. The child has difficulty maintaining eye contact with you in conversations
e. The child does not seem to understand requests or commands
f. The child makes gestures or sounds instead of trying to speak at age level
g. The child has trouble repeating simple sentences by age four
h. The child has trouble answering simple questions when read a story
i. The child has had frequent ear infections and/or allergies as a young baby or toddler
j. The child seems to be having an unusual number of behavior problems—defiance, acting out, or poor social skills. Research indicates that many children with emotional problems have poor language or listening skills.

Refer to: *Childhood Speech, Language, and Listening Problems: What Every Parent Should Know*, by Patricia McAleer Hamaguchi.

WHAT ARE THE WARNING SIGNS OF A VISION PROBLEM?

There can be several types of vision problems. The most simple is a lack of sharp vision, or visual acuity. The child does not have what is called 20/20 vision. In a school setting, however, there may be other factors that affect a child's ability to use the eyes for reading, copying, or following a line of print without getting lost or skipping words and lines. Visually handicapped children can also have limited fields of vision or reduced accuracy in near or distance vision.

Many homeschool parents have had their children evaluated and treated with vision therapy. Doctors who work with such problems are called "behavioral optometrists," and they specialize in treating some vision problems with exercises that may strengthen specific functions of the eye and its ability to coordinate with the brain during visual activities. While there is a lack of agreement in the research about the benefits of visual therapy, there is no disagreement that children's eyes are an essential part of the learning equation.

For healthy children who have healthy eyes, the following can be signs of a vision problem that can contribute to learning problems. A vision problem is indicated when a child:

a. Holds books too closely
b. Squints when working on "close" work
c. Frequently loses place in copying from chalk board or books
d. Reports frequent headaches after eye-work

e. Frequently rubs or blinks eyes during close work
   f. Seems bothered by working in bright lights or on certain colors of paper

There may be more serious health issues that can also mimic or cause visual disturbances. These may be a result of traumatic injury to the brain, concussions, and cerebral palsy. Some problems associated with these causes can include blurred vision, sensitivity to light, reporting that words are moving, or difficulty with memory.

Parents interested in more specific details need to check the website for the Optometric Extension Program at www.Healthy.net/oep/brain.htm.

***Please note that the intelligence of the child is not related to whether the child may have a vision or language/communication difficulty.*

HOW CAN I TELL IF MY CHILD HAS ADD?

Most parents do not have any difficulty agreeing that both vision and speech can be measured and assessed objectively. Another area less easy to measure is the wiggly or fidgety child. Many parents of young children wonder: Is my child hyperactive or even ADD? There are criteria that may help you evaluate whether to seek a formal evaluation. The American Academy of Pediatrics has put out a general recommendation.

Children with inattention, hyperactivity, impulsivity, academic underachievement, or behavior problems should be considered for more evaluation. Diagnosis should be based on the criteria found in the *Diagnostic and Statistical Manual of Mental Disorders IV*, published by the American Psychiatric Association. Called the DSM by most professionals, the book covers the entire spectrum of mental and emotional difficulties. ADHD was first included in the third edition, and the definitions have been refined since then in the fourth edition. The disorder now has several sub-types described, which explain that some forms of attention deficit are found without hyperactivity or impulsive behaviors. The APA requires that six or more of several categories of inattention and hyperactivity be present for at least six months to a degree that is maladaptive and inconsistent with the child's developmental level. Impulsivity should have been causing impairment in more than one setting since before the child was seven years old.

Many checklists and parent magazines describing ADD/ADHD can be found on the Internet, but proceed with caution and use careful research with rigorous standards when trying to determine if your child is truly ADD/ADHD. Consult a specialist. Even psychiatrists find it challenging to accurately identify ADD or ADHD in children under the age of four or five because of the wide range of "normal" behaviors, so their checklists include very specific criteria that must be present at a certain frequency and intensity to find a diagnosis of ADD/ADHD. (Just a cautionary note: Many pediatricians are not as familiar as psychiatrists with these subtle differences in types. Therefore, a parent should avoid seeking a diagnosis of ADD from a pediatrician, unless the doctor is well trained in the specialty of ADD/ADHD behaviors and in managing both medication and counseling.)

The psychiatrist or psychologist will carefully observe external behaviors. Often learning problems, dietary or environmental allergies, emotional issues, or immaturity can masquerade as an ADD set of behaviors. Thus, one has to look at the "whole child"—in the context of the family setting and educational requirements—to consider whether ADD/ADHD is the major factor that may be affecting educational or social achievement.

One fascinating new area of research is the use of MRI (magnetic resonance imaging) scans on children's brains. Research indicates that there are defined areas of the brain affected by ADHD. The part of the brain typically associated with "inhibition" is affected, and in fact the entire right cerebral hemisphere in boys with ADHD has been found to be smaller than in normal, non-ADHD children. Some connection is seen with history of prenatal, perinatal, and birth complications. Other researchers are looking into genetic markers associated with ADHD, and are finding some evidence there—some researchers indicate there may be more than one gene responsible. Boys are up to nine times more likely to have ADD-ADHD. Parents must understand that ADD difficulties with attention, focus, and impulse control continue into adult life, sometimes affecting job capability and relationships.

WHAT IF MY CHILD HAS A LEARNING DISABILITY?

When a child seems to be experiencing difficulty doing schoolwork, the typical questions most parents ask include: Am I doing something wrong? Is there something I'm not doing well? Is the child just "slower" than my other children? Does my child have a different "learning style" than I'm using?

These questions are a useful place to start. If you have tried honestly and objectively to look at your skills in organization, and are thorough in presenting information in a reasonably well-sequenced program, then you need to step back and look harder for an explanation for your child's problem. You may need to look at the actual program you have chosen—not all curriculum packages are well designed or logically organized. Some don't give enough practice, others don't give the foundational skills **your** child needs to move ahead. (Note: the program may work just splendidly for another child; that does not indicate a deficit in your child.)

After you have examined "external" considerations, as just described, then you should begin looking at your child. I have described several essential factors that must be working in a healthy way in order for the child to benefit from instruction. We have also discussed several very common problems—communication, vision, and attention. It should come as no surprise, since we are both fearfully and wonderfully made, that it may be impossible to come to a clear explanation for many children's learning behaviors.

Typically, professionals evaluating a child for learning difficulties will begin by taking a history of the child, including birth complications, early childhood illnesses or emotional trauma, early learning behaviors, and social skills. They will then begin asking the parent to describe the specific academic behaviors that have caused concern. When you initiate a comprehensive evaluation of your child's learning and physical history, try to be as thorough as possible in your replies to questionnaires. Small details are often of great significance to an evaluator or physician, and they can open up new diagnostic considerations that may be very important.

Once the history-taking has been completed, the child's evaluator will make recommendations for a battery of diagnostic tests and observations to learn more about how the child performs under certain standardized conditions or on standardized tests. These evaluations are then scored and the composite of information is carefully considered and weighed to form a diagnosis and recommendations for your child's educational program. Your input is a valuable part of this entire process, and you should be certain that your ideas are included in the final report. The final report should provide you with specific and understandable ideas for working to help your child make progress in areas of weakness, as well as continuing progress in areas of strength. If you find you need more direction about working to help your child, seek further input from the evaluators. Their expertise and experience should be available to help you create an educational plan for your child.

Once you have current data about your child's strengths and weaknesses, you should seek the advice of an educational consultant to help you create a year-long plan with individualized and appropriate educational goals for your child. In public schools, such a plan is called an IEP (Individualized Educational Plan). To distinguish a year-long plan of educational goals for homeschool students, we use the term Student Education Plan (SEP). An annual plan will describe the child's present levels of performance in academic, social, behavioral, and if necessary, speech and physical development. There will be goals for the child based on these "starting points" that state where the child is expected to be performing by the end of the present school year.

The long-range goals are broken into smaller units, sometimes called benchmarks. Because they are arranged in a logical sequence, these smaller sections clarify what to teach first and what will come next. They will also show what skills the child has mastered. If necessary, the SEP will include any necessary accommodations or modifications that the student requires. (See section of "Writing the SEP" for more details.)

You know, as home educators, that public-school administrators seek to monitor your child's progress. Typically, their expectations are based on a *normal* student who is learning at a typical rate. The child with identified special needs may not be capable of maintaining that level or rate of performance. The IEP provides the individualized statement of expectations for your child and the manner in which both learning and testing will be conducted. The administrator should take into consideration your child's limitations and weaknesses in determining if enough progress has been made. For example, a child with reading skills on the second-grade level and math skills at the sixth-grade level should not be tested on all sixth grade objectives. The IEP should state that math testing be carried out for sixth grade content, but that materials (even on math tests) that require reading might be read aloud to a child, and that reading itself would be assessed at second-grade level. In this way, the child's progress in each area of academic performance can be monitored individually.

If you believe your child needs special help, it is best to seek a comprehensive evaluation of his or her academic skills, overall ability, and areas of weakness. A well-informed parent is always more confident and better equipped to help the child. When selecting a therapy provider, it is useful to point out that not all popular programs provide scientific evidence of their effectiveness. Some therapists' treatment plans can be very costly, and the wise parent should be aware that there is a well-known issue in educational research called a "Hawthorne" effect—it states that ANY treatment applied can produce changes, if only because the participants in a study are looking for changes, and there is no way to measure what would have happened if nothing had been done. The Hawthorne effect makes it difficult to prove that a "treatment" caused the changes in question. Some educational therapies fall into that category. If you personally have used particular treatment programs, and you are satisfied your child's skills improved as a result, there is no argument with what you experienced. Anecdotal stories of success may indicate the utility of certain treatments in effecting improvements, but careful research may be needed to demonstrate that those treatments will be effective for others.

Used with permission: www.hishelpinschool.com

Getting Started and Gathering Materials

In Depth: Getting Started

Judith Munday

When parents choose to educate their children at home, there are many challenges. When parents choose to educate a *special-needs child* at home, those challenges are multiplied many times over. The Homeschool Legal Defense Association (HSLDA) estimates that over 10% of today's homeschooled children have special needs! ("Court Report," an on-line newsletter, vol.16, no.6.)

No matter which path has led to a family's decision to homeschool, the most important thing to remember when teaching a special-needs child is that the family is the best place for them to be. A loving environment with one-on-one attention from a caring parent is bound to bring forth good fruit in the child's life.

It is not enough, however, to simply educate the child at home. The parents must be prepared for the hard work of selecting appropriate curricula and materials, coordinating extra help from caring professionals, learning specialized teaching strategies, and fulfilling rigorous demands for record keeping. Is it worth it? YES! Can it be done successfully—even without special training? YES! No one knows the needs and strengths of a child better than a parent, and there is a wealth of support to teach and encourage the willing parent. Many homeschool parents of special-needs children report that the child opens up and becomes enthusiastic about schoolwork after enduring years of frustration. The child gradually becomes free from the difficulties caused by the stress of ongoing failures. The opportunity to succeed in the homeschool environment is like water poured on the child's thirsty soul. While it will not prove to be an *easy* job, if it is done with prayer, persistence, and patience, parents can successfully educate the special-needs child in the home.

THE CHALLENGES

Parents who decide to educate a special-needs child at home face additional time commitments and expenses for diagnostic testing, individualized assessments, therapy and/or tutoring, and specialized learning materials. There are also additional pressures on relationships within the family, as the special-needs child may appear to receive more attention than other siblings or even the spouse. Parents struggle to find enough time to help each child, get chores done, and find time for personal refreshing. Time management is a daily uphill struggle, especially when it takes so much extra effort to work with most special-needs children.

Parents who decide to teach a child at home have reached that decision in many different ways. The unique needs of some children are apparent from birth, or soon after they begin their education. Other children do not begin to manifest learning problems until several years after beginning school. The child may not appear to respond to a regular curriculum or teaching methods. The child may need more time to master basic skills or seem unable to remember new material for even a short time. Parents may notice other subtle indicators of a learning difficulty, but the child's special needs may never have been formally diagnosed.

Recently, many children have been withdrawn from public school special-education programs to begin homeschooling. The parents are dissatisfied with the child's progress, or they became weary of fighting administrative roadblocks. They finally decide that they need to do the job themselves.

STEPS TO A SUCCESSFUL HOMESCHOOL EXPERIENCE FOR THE SPECIAL-NEEDS CHILD

Several components are essential for a successful homeschooling experience. Knowing them can relieve a significant amount of pressure. When children with special needs start in homeschooling, they typically will need some form of diagnostic testing to determine their present level of achievement in key academic areas. It is *essential* to know a child's weaknesses and grade levels for each academic subject to simplify the choice of an appropriate curriculum. (See *"Choosing Curriculum for the Special-Needs Child", elsewhere in this Special Needs section.*) Parents also should maintain careful and accurate documentation to demonstrate progress. It is important to seek support and helpful resources. It is essential that parents should seek the wisdom and strength of the Lord.

WHY TEST? I DON'T WANT TO "LABEL" MY CHILD!

Parents of children with special needs frequently protest that they do not want to have their child labeled with a label such as "L.D." They may say that they do not wish to have a child suffer embarrassment or become stigmatized. They may even fear that the label will become the "fact" that comes to mind first when others think about the child.

Furthermore, when a child has special needs, the child is usually keenly aware of being different. Such children probably realize they must work harder to learn or do other life tasks. Few students are blissfully unaware of this. Many students start to ask themselves if there is something "defective" about them or if they are simply "stupid." Children can and do make many unfounded conclusions about life as they observe it, and they end up suffering unnecessarily from those misconceptions. These are legitimate issues, and they bring up valid issues for discussion.

Providing diagnostic testing can provide accurate information to the parents about the nature of the child's limitations and probable causes for the child's academic struggles. Diagnostic test results can be lovingly and truthfully shared with the child, while answering their questions and giving them the truth. Parents can put the facts into a loving context for the whole child, emphasizing that God does not make mistakes. The discussion should focus on the ways that the child can excel, so that they don't dwell on the problems they have to deal with. An educational consultant can be enormously helpful in providing a knowledgeable description of the problem to both parents and the child.

Parents will also benefit from accurate information. Without a diagnosis, parents will have trouble locating resources appropriate for the specific disability. Therapists and support personnel are best located when parents know the correct terminology. A "label" can have no negative power over a child or parent unless the label is used as the primary description of the child. Misuse of a label is a choice made in the head—not the heart.

TESTING, ASSESSMENT, AND EVALUATION

Measurement is at the heart of monitoring a child's *progress* in education. Educators should continually gauge whether a child is mastering new content and retaining earlier learning. This is usually done informally by asking a few review questions at the start of a daily lesson. Formal assessments, in contrast, provide information needed to choose an appropriate curriculum, plan lessons, and select teaching material.

Assessments must be part of weekly and monthly lesson planning, and are expected to be more formal and cover more material—such as written work or a project. All through the school year, it is vitally important for parents to have accurate data on the child's current performance. If a child is taught some new material and there is no assessment, the teaching parent does not have any way to tell whether the child is ready to go ahead. It is not enough to make informal guesses such as, "He seems to understand the material," or "She must need more practice because she was so frustrated today."

At the end of each school year, Virginia statutes require that *most** home educated students be assessed to demonstrate progress, and that this information be submitted to the local school division superintendent by August 1. (See Virginia Compulsory Attendance and Home Instruction Related Statutes, excerpted from the code of Virginia 1950, as amended, online at www.heav.org/testing/testingfaq.html. Without such accurate information about the child's *current* level of academic skills, parents will find it difficult to document progress at the end of the year, because there will be no data for comparison. For children with complex learning problems, these year-end tests should be conducted in one-on-one testing situations with trained professionals, and there are several acceptable options for these assessments. Children whose needs are less serious can participate in group testing.

ISSUES FOR SPECIAL-NEEDS STUDENTS WITHDRAWN FROM THE PUBLIC SCHOOLS

Parents who decide to teach their special-needs children at home and withdraw them from the public school system often encounter a great deal of opposition. The child's special needs have already been identified, so additional formal assessment by the school is *not* necessary, yet these parents may face ongoing requests from the child's former public school administrators, who may even tell parents that regular school assessments are "requirements." The parents may be told they "must have the child re-evaluated every year or every three years," "attend regular meetings" to monitor the progress of the child, or that the school "cannot accept parent-supplied IEPs."

These are *not* legitimate requests under Virginia statutes.

Parents are likely to have a copy of the school's most recent eligibility evaluation and/or the child's latest IEP. If the public school's test results have not been given to the parents, it is important for them to request *in writing* a complete copy of the child's educational and testing records from all available sources. Parents may legally be asked to pay for making these copies, but the schools must provide copies when asked.

If parents believe that the public school's test data are incomplete or inaccurate, additional evaluations from qualified professionals should be sought. A complete picture of a child's strengths as well as weaknesses is essential; it enables parents to create an instructional program that meets the child's needs. In many cases, health insurance will approve payment for certain educational evaluations, but it is wise to check in advance.

FORMER PUBLIC SCHOOL STUDENTS AND THE IEP

Parents who withdraw the special-needs child often do so because they have found significant problems in their child's public school Individual Educational Plan (IEP), or problems in the way that it is being implemented. A child's present levels of performance, and appropriate remediation plans, should be contained in the IEP, yet in many public schools in Virginia, IEPs reflect grade-level Standards of Learning (SOLs) *more than remedial individualized plans for the child*.

If the parent simply starts homeschooling while retaining the school IEP, then when it is time for end-of-the-year testing, the goals may be unmet because they were unrealistic, unattainable, and not relevant to the child's needs. If the child is below grade level and standardized testing scores fall below the 23rd percentile, the homeschool might be placed on probation. What do to?

The parent who starts homeschooling a special-needs child may realize that their child is *not* on grade level in all key areas of academic skill. They may believe that by keeping the school's IEP, they should teach curriculum that contains all the grade-level Standards of Learning content [in Virginia]. This is not so. When a parent determines they wish to teach a child at home, special needs or not, the parent selects the curriculum that is **most appropriate for the child**. A state's standards of learning may be a helpful guide to understanding the sequence of skills that are covered in a typical school year; parents should make choices accordingly.

Parents may elect to keep a public school IEP as a general guide and have a homeschool version created, which would be called a Student Education Plan. The public school created IEP contains a description of the student's present levels of performance, and it can serve as a very helpful starting point for teaching. It is also important to use present levels of performance as a point of comparison for end-of-the-year evaluations. An educational consultant can assess the child's skills at the end of the year and refer to the public school's IEP or the SEP to draw conclusions about whether the child has made "adequate level of educational growth and progress." (Virginia Homeschool Statute §22.1-254.1) An educational consultant can assess the child's progress using either the original IEP or an SEP without having to report actual test scores. In Virginia, this can be a very important, allowable alternative to standardized testing. The evaluator would assess the child's skills and use the data to prepare a report that parents can submit to the local superintendent, in accordance with the law. After the first year out of public schools, however, it is not appropriate to use the public school's IEP, unless the child continues to obtain public-school services in specialized areas such as speech and language therapy or occupational therapy.

No matter what time of year parents withdraw a child from the public schools, it is wise to have the child assessed to determine where the child is functioning and to learn the best approaches and curriculum to use in teaching. An educational consultant can help in this. Ask the consultant to help prepare a Student Education Plan that will help guide teaching throughout the school year and provide helpful accountability. It is not necessary, however, to submit the Student Education Plan to the schools.

DIAGNOSTIC EVALUATIONS—WHO NEEDS ONE?

When parents have tried all that they know to improve a child's learning, but without success, it is time to seek in-depth testing by specialists. Establishing early success in reading and language skills is known by educational researchers to be especially critical for a good long-term outcome. Clinics and specialists offer appropriate testing services. Parents should seek their help rather than taking a wait-and-see attitude. Maturity *can* be an important factor for some children's readiness to learn, but when a child fails to progress after making every reasonable effort, there is reasonable cause to seek a fresh perspective from a trained consultant.

Psychologists and other professionals can carry out comprehensive diagnostic evaluations to reveal the specific nature of the special-needs child's strengths, weaknesses, and limitations. That information is helpful in planning therapy and instruction. Comprehensive testing, called a psycho-educational battery, includes assessments of intellectual ability and academic performance in reading, writing, spelling, and math. For children with complex problems, additional testing may be required to probe skills or weaknesses in areas of speech, language, and neurological, physical, and emotional function. Educational consultants are able to administer many of the educational and screening tests for a wide range of problems, but only a psychologist can properly administer formal, comprehensive intelligence tests.

END-OF-THE-YEAR ASSESSMENTS

Children with special needs not only have unique requirements in instruction, but also in end-of-the-year testing. This can be a major concern for parents who do not wish to be placed on probation, because Virginia law, applicable to most homeschooled children, requires a child to score at or above the 23rd percentile. (The law is inconsistent and unfair by not requiring that public school students meet the same standard.) Many special-needs children do not perform well on standardized testing in their weak skill areas.

If a child has been identified as having special needs (even if it is by the parents recording their own observations of him or her) and has an Student Education Plan (SEP), the parents have acceptable documentation of the child's present levels of performance. To satisfy the law's intent, the child only needs to make *demonstrable progress* toward the objectives written on the SEP. Remember, progress cannot be demonstrated if there are no data about the child's performance at the start of the school year compared to the end of the year!! It is the responsibility of the **parent** to document performance on a regular basis!

Fortunately, the law allows end-of-the-year alternatives for special-needs children, and progress may be documented and assessed in several acceptable ways. In academic subjects where the child is performing within normal levels, it may be appropriate to have the child take part in group testing on standardized tests—but only in areas of strong skills.

Group assessments can be arranged through a local test administrator. Parents should ask the test administrator what skills the child must have in order to succeed in group testing. For example, if the child cannot follow multi-step directions, he or she may perform poorly on group testing, even when knowledge of the subject material is strong. If the child requires specialized accommodations, such as having the text material read aloud, parents should also ask a test administrator when and how the child would be tested in keeping with those limitations.

In skill areas where the child is performing well below average, and the child is very unlikely to score above the 23rd percentile, parents should consider having the child assessed in a one-on-one situation. One-on-one testing may be carried out at the end of the year with a standardized achievement test to meet the testing requirements of §22.1-254.2 option (i). Individually administered tests include the Wide Range Achievement Test (not a very complete assessment), the Kaufman Test of Educational Achievement, or the Weschler Individual Achievement Test, among others. These tests will indicate the child's current level of performance in reading, math, written language, and spelling, and will clearly indicate how much progress the child has achieved.

The child also can be assessed *without* standardized testing. Under option (ii) of §22.1-254.1, parents may submit an independent evaluation or present a portfolio to the division superintendent. If an independent evaluation or assessment is chosen, the evaluation letter must be completed by a person licensed to teach in any state, or by a person with a master's degree or higher in an academic discipline who has knowledge of the child's academic progress. It must state that the child is achieving an adequate level of educational growth and progress.

The evaluator may choose to administer a criterion-referenced test (teacher-made test based on subjects that have been taught or on the Virginia Standards of Learning). He may interview the children, review samples of his work, and type a one-, two-, or three-page report indicating whether there is enough progress to go on to the next grade.

An evaluation or assessment may also include a report card or transcript from a community college or college, college distance-learning program, or home-education correspondence school.

The division superintendent or his designee will determine if the child is achieving an adequate level of educational growth and progress.

Work samples, interviews with the child, and asking them sample questions, which might include checking them for skills included in the IEP (ISP), enables the consultant to compare the child's skill level against the end-of-year goals.

A *portfolio* may be the best end-of-year assessment for children who have serious learning problems. Parents collect samples of the child's daily work into separate folders by subject matter during the school year for end-of-year review. As with other forms of assessment, this must include work from early in the year or there will be no way to prove that the child has improved. In September, start collecting work on a *regular* schedule, such as twice each month. *Parents may read more about portfolio assessment elsewhere in this manual.*

STANDARDS OF LEARNING FOR HOMESCHOOLED SPECIAL-NEEDS STUDENTS?

Virginia's Homeschool Statute does not require parents who educate their children under **Options 1, 2, and 3** to follow the Virginia Standards of Learning. The SOLs may provide a helpful overview for each grade-level's curriculum—and parents may choose to use them for reference only.

If a child has been withdrawn from public school, the school-written IEP may reflect grade level SOLs more than remedial individualized plans for the child.

The homeschool Student Educational Plan (SEP), which replaces the public school's IEP, should address the child's known learning weaknesses and also document the reasons that the child requires specialized education.

DOCUMENTING PROGRESS

No matter how serious the child's needs, it is it is important to be able to keep track of learning. Accurate record-keeping is a priority when teaching a special-needs child at home, because it is unlikely the child will progress evenly in every subject. This discrepancy is likely to catch the notice of school administrators monitoring the child's progress. An accurate set of records will permit the parents to defend their homeschool.

There are numerous resources to help parents choose a record-keeping style. (*See Resources at the end of this unit.*) Simple documentation can be kept in a five-section notebook, which is separated into individual academic subjects, and organized by dates. Informal observations can be jotted down into a separate section of that notebook, with data organized chronologically.

In the various sections, parents can record special achievements and other things the child has done that demonstrate knowledge.

Parents can also create an expandable folder to save samples of work *all through the year* to demonstrate skill improvement. File these samples by organizing the oldest papers in the back and adding newer work towards the front in each section. Because this is going to be a fairly hefty folder, organize it correctly from the start. This will save a lot of work during year-end assessments. Enter dates for filing the child's work on a yearly planner—it will help to discipline filing efforts. It is not enough to grab some end-of-the year work samples to document the child's educational progress!

It is very helpful and rewarding to ask the child to help select the best work samples. (Parents may add other items later!) Choosing work samples is a great way to focus the child's attention on those significant factors that affect quality, and this is often very effective in bringing about *further* improvement because the child will then know how to improve.

A well-written SEP is a reference for helping parents document the scope and sequence of newly learned skills during the school year. Students with an SEP should have quarterly assessments based on the SEP to monitor the child's educational progress. The SEP form should have space where these assessments can be recorded.

The quarterly assessments should be done by an educational consultant. Objective reviews of the child's work are similar to the use of familiar landmarks in monitoring progress on a journey. Sighting a familiar landmark provides reassurance that the child's educational journey is going at the appropriate speed and heading in the right direction. Parents can use the results of quarterly evaluations to make sure the child is heading in the right direction. The outcome of these evaluations should be specific and concrete, giving direction for the next educational steps.

Parents should discuss the results with the consultant to learn what is necessary for the child to improve. It may be necessary to change the curriculum or grade levels of material. If progress is not seen, parents will easily discern that a mid-course correction must be made to help the child get on track.

Special-needs students tend to make uneven progress in the different areas of their education, and they are frequently below grade level in at least one area. The SEP is a road map for advancing the child's strengths and remediating their weaknesses. Parents can use the SEP, in combination with other written data, to document the child's progress and make any necessary adjustments to how and what is taught.

The SEP provides ongoing feedback to parents regarding the effectiveness of their teaching. When the child fails to progress, it may be time to seek help from a qualified educational consultant or teacher. Remember, Virginia requires that students must have made "an adequate level of educational growth and progress." It does not require the child to be at his or her age-expected grade level on all skills. If a public school administrator seeks to pressure the parent to prove the child is "on grade level," remind them of the law, and if they continue to apply pressure, consider contacting Home School

Legal Defense Association for assistance. Keep in mind, good documentation is essential both for guiding effective instruction, as well as protecting your rights to homeschool.

CHOOSING AN EDUCATIONAL CONSULTANT AND OTHER PROFESSIONALS

It is important to find professionals and an educational consultant who can provide one-on-one individualized assessments or evaluations for a special-needs child. Parents of a child with special needs will probably already have had many contacts with professionals such as speech-language pathologists and physical therapists.

A consultant can advise about what kind of assessments would be best for the child, and then can carry out diagnostic assessments, end-of-the-year testing, or portfolio assessments. Once the child's present level of performance has been documented, with strengths and weaknesses identified, parents can plan the child's educational program for the coming year. The consultant can help in writing and monitoring an SEP. Further, a consultant can help parents to learn more about the nature of the child's learning problems, provide referrals for additional testing, and suggest helpful teaching strategies. Finally, a consultant can provide a general wealth of information and resources. Appointments with a consultant should be entered on a long-range planner after confirming dates with the consultant.

In selecting a consultant or advisor, parents will want to interview the consultant. (After all, the consultant is going to be working for the parents!) Ask about background, training, and fees, as well as the consultant's attitude toward homeschooling. It is helpful to learn about the consultant's educational theories or favorite therapies to see if there will be a comfortable fit. A consultant who strongly favors specific remediation practices might not be a good fit if the parent has the child enrolled in a program that views that particular remediation from a very different philosophical point of view. So, ask lots of questions. Share a bit about the child and ask for some ideas about a typical problem to see whether the consultant is well informed and can give advice that is useful and appropriate. Make sure that there is a feeling of trust and compatibility—this individual will (or should) be interacting with the parent several times a year at a minimum.

Optimally, parents should locate a consultant who is within reasonable driving distance, to ensure that regular monitoring of the child's progress can be maintained. However—in this technological age—when a nearby consultant cannot be found, the essential information and samples of the student's work can be copied and sent by fax, e-mail, or postal service. Once the consultant has reviewed the material, a phone consultation can be very helpful. The Home Educators Association of Virginia (HEAV), the Homeschool Legal Defense Association (HSLDA), and local support groups have lists of qualified educational consultants who are sympathetic to home-educators' needs.

FINDING SUPPORT FROM OTHERS

The challenge of working with a special-needs child (or more than one!) is stressful at times. Both parents and child need to have regular contact with others outside the immediate family for emotional, spiritual, and educational support. Parents may need to be resourceful in locating this support, and it may require persistent effort. The research may end up feeling like work needed for a term paper, but the rewards are so important!

The best place to start is within the local churches. If the family church does not have a homeschool support group, the parent will have to contact other local churches or homeschooling families. The HSLDA, NAATHAN, and Specially Gifted organizations maintain lists of support groups for different areas of special needs. The Home Educators Association of Virginia (HEAV) also maintains a current list. (As an aside, if a parent becomes aware of a new group or starts a new group, it is an important outreach ministry to notify the statewide organizations about that group, so others may learn about it too.)

The Internet is an important resource for locating organizations helping special-needs children. There are several websites maintained for home educators, including specific disability websites that have homeschool sub-pages, all of which can be very informative. Some websites may not be distinctively Christian nor directed by home educators, but they may still have a wealth of information, links, and reading materials that will be helpful.

Follow up leads, and contact some of these resources, to learn more about what is available nationwide and locally. In many locations, counseling centers can provide information about support groups for special-needs areas. Likewise, physicians and occupational/physical therapists may know of support groups.

Parents of special-needs children should also seek to integrate the child's activities as much as possible with non-special-needs children. This can provide just as much support as talking with parents in a similar situation, and it helps maintain a sense of perspective. The essential thing is to get in touch with some others who can lighten the load and provide help—both in prayer and in support activities.

Used with permission: www.helpinschool.net

Behavior First

Teri Spray

When it comes to behavior, the basic rules should be the same for children *with* special needs as they are for those *without*. However, just as a two-year-old would not be expected to behave the same as a fifteen-year-old, do not expect behavior of a child with special needs to be beyond his developmental level of understanding. Strive for the level of behavior for which the child is developmentally ready. It may take longer to accomplish, but it is not in the child's best interest to allow misbehavior *and blame it on the disability.*

If things are not going well in the behavior department, here are some things to consider:

- Have a list of house rules. They should be simple and few. They should be enforced consistently. Inconsistency leads to confusion and rebellion [because it makes rules seem arbitrary and unfair].
- Be sure the child *knows* the rules—(is not just able to recite them)—and how they apply in his life.
- Be sure the child knows the consequences. These should be consistent and relevant to the rule. Example: If the rule is: "We obey the first time we are told to do something," and the child does not obey when, say, told to pick up toys, it is more relevant to lose the toys for a given period of time than to be grounded from the television for a week. (The child should still be made to pick up the toys, however.) The *purpose* of the consequence should be to train and encourage the child to do the right thing.
- Review the rules with the child periodically—especially if the situation changes. For example, say to the child, "We are going into the library now. Do you remember the special rules in the library? Talking softly; staying together; being gentle with the books."
- When giving instruction, direction, or correction: Gain and maintain eye contact. Have the child repeat the instruction. Allow for questions, but do not allow interruptions. Follow up and make sure the task is completed. Speak softly; this can encourage the child to listen more carefully.
- Deal with infractions promptly. Waiting may disconnect the deed from the consequence for the child and therefore the learning of cause and effect is lost.

- Remain calm; do not lose your temper. A frightened child will not hear your words, only your anger.
- Be ready to follow through with a consequence. If the consequence for a temper tantrum is removal from the situation, are you ready to leave a field trip to enforce the rule? Is there someone else who can bring your other children home? If your children are like mine, they look for opportunities to get you over a barrel.
- Do not carry a grudge. Sometimes when we are feeling overwhelmed with the responsibility of parenting, we emotionally reject a child who is creating stress. We do not do this deliberately, but the child feels it just the same. You may actually be expecting the misbehavior because "that's what he always does." When you find this happening, remind yourself that he is just a child. Scripture says, "Foolishness is bound in the heart of a child." Remember that you are the adult. Once you have corrected the child, and forgiveness has been received, move on. Do not keep digging up past offenses.

PRINCIPLES OF CHANGING BEHAVIOR

"Pick it up! Right now! Did you hear me? Why aren't you doing it? If you don't pick ii up right now, you'll be sorry! Did you hear what I said? All right! That's it! One... Two...." Sound familiar? In homes across our country scenes like this are being played out every day. Children and parents are constantly at odds. Children are challenging their parents' authority. What happened to picnics at the lake, trips to the museum, and looking at constellations on a clear summer evening? Who cares any more? It's hard enough to get all the basics done—like earning a living, keeping the house in order, and seeing that the kids have clean clothes.

There's not enough time in the day to find a minute to gather your thoughts, sigh in relief, and put your feet up, or consider what type of music you'd like to listen to. All the while, there's that constant quibbling, arguing, or even downright yelling and fighting. There are ways to circumvent confrontations and prevent or avoid the seemingly inevitable blow-up. Frequently, it is a matter of taking control, communicating that control, and recognizing some of your children's basic needs when planning and making decisions.

CHILDREN NEED COMMUNICATION

Both parents *must* agree on which behaviors will be acceptable, which behaviors will not be tolerated, what discipline or punishment is appropriate, and where and when it will he administered. First, parents must communicate with each other to set the tone and establish priorities. Later they will need to communicate the ground rules to the children. This takes time and may need to be done in stages.

In many families, schools, work places, and churches, rules are never stated clearly. Sometimes both the rules and the enforcement of them may differ depending on which person is in control at the moment. This approach gives all of us—but children in particular—a feeling of insecurity and lack of control. It feels to them like walking on a surface of Jello. They're never sure how sturdy it is or when they will slip up and get hurt. They need to know that there is a boundary *and* that there is something or someone stronger than them, someone who can set reasonable limits and then keep them within those limits. I believe this is crucial to their understanding of a loving but firm God. If they find no one capable of making and enforcing rules while they are small, then they have difficulty as adults understanding that there is any God who has the power, or the right, to impose limits on their behavior.

Both parents need to agree on what rules they are willing to enforce. Rules should be stated as clearly as possible. The consequence of breaking the rules should be made clear as well. Whenever possible this should he a natural consequence such as: "If you are not dressed properly when we are ready to leave, you may not go with us." For younger children, a poster with pictures or symbols of appropriate behaviors may be helpful (the "If-Then" chart from Doorposts is an excellent example—see the Resources section). Don't have more rules than you are willing to enforce. Don't try to establish a host of rules all at once. Multiple instructions create multiple confusions. Here are some possible, reasonable, family rules stated in positive terms:

1) Our family will show respect for each other and for other people and their belongings.
2) Our family will speak calmly and carefully try to explain our feelings.
3) Children in our family will be in bed by 9 p.m., unless the parents agree on extenuating circumstances.

I have seen families with too few rules and families with too many rules. God initially presented Ten Commandments. Jesus summed them up into two, and added the "Golden Rule." There are two "universal laws" which are also helpful: Do what you say you will do and do not hurt anyone. There is only one Biblical rule specifically directed toward children: "Children obey your parents" (Ephesians 6:1).

Stating rules in positive terms helps children desire to work with them rather than rebel against them. Stating them in terms of "our family will..." gives ammunition against the retort, "but everybody else is," when it surfaces.

[NOTE: Always state a directive in a positive form. Say, "Keep clean." If you say, "Don't get dirty," the child often hears only "get dirty." If you say, "Don't..." anything, often what follows the "don't" is acted upon. So, "Be kind," not, "Don't fight," and "Be neat," not "Don't be messy."]

CHILDREN HAVE A NEED TO MOVE

We need to build action into the way children can respond to what we ask them to do. Instead of paper and pencil, let them manipulate magnetic letters. Instead of saying "yes" or "no," have them clap or jump. Allow a wiggly active moment between two quiet, serious times. For example, if the situation (mental math, spelling words, or reciting facts) demands that the child listen, think, and give an oral response, have her first stand quietly to listen and respond. Then, if the answer is correct on the first try, allow a physical response. Have her do a jumping jack, touch her toes, or run around the table. If the answer is correct on the second try, then allow a slightly less physical response. She may bend from the waist, clap her hands, or kick one foot. The next week let her sit on the floor to listen and jump to her feet for a correct response. Plan for variety! Keep things moving!

CHILDREN HAVE A NEED TO RECEIVE ATTENTION

In many homes, children are clamoring in inappropriate ways for attention. They whine and wiggle and hit and cry. They get on our nerves, and *then* we give them attention! Unfortunately by then it is negative attention, and everyone is upset and unhappy. Children really need attention, and it is our job to give them positive attention *before* they demand attention in negative ways. Spend a few minutes after breakfast in a controlled, planned activity— whether your child is six months old or six years old. By then, they'll probably be only too happy to play quietly on their own. Make sure they have appropriate playthings; that does not necessarily mean the newest, most colorful, and noisiest toy on the market. It may be measuring spoons and cups and a box of dry coffee grounds or colored cornmeal.

CHILDREN NEED TO "DO IT THEMSELVES"

Whenever possible, rather than doing something for your child, let them do it themselves; even if it takes longer and the results are not as neat. If you always do it, when will they hone their own skills? Sometimes they learn valuable lessons by trying the impossible. Sometimes they succeed in doing the impossible! On the other hand, they will never even do the possible if they are not allowed to try. It is not okay to never try. Give them the time and space they need to grow.

Reading and Dyslexia

Judith Munday

What is *dyslexia?* It is a difficulty either with receptive oral language skills, expressive oral language skills, reading, spelling, or written expression. It is the *most common neurobehavioral disorder* in the USA, affecting about one child in five. There is a strong family link, although it has also been associated with prematurity, complications in pregnancy, and accidents. Typically, research shows there is a known difference between the two sides of the brain. Research indicates for dyslexic readers, certain areas of the brain may be "underdeveloped" even though higher order thinking skills for some of these "disabled readers" may be intact. (Dr. Jeff Stern, LDA Convention, 2000, Reno, Nevada.) Some say it is a "left-brain related" problem. It is usually based on congenital deficiencies in phonologic processing or phoneme awareness. This means inability to learn typical rules that govern English (such as adding prefixes, suffixes). It typically includes problems in auditory memory, distinguishing speech, memory of sounds and analyzing sounds – such as "what is the first sound in…." ("Critical Discoveries in Learning Disabilities: A Summary of Findings by NIH Research Programs in L.D.," Research Centers Report at the LDA 1996 conference," Barbara McElgunn, Research Committee.)

Over the years, several reading programs have had greater success in teaching reading to dyslexic students . There is no one "magic bullet" for instructing children with dyslexia, and the best program for your child may be one that uses certain elements of more than one of these listed below. Some dyslexics, for example, have done well learning sight words with very little use of phonics.

MULTISENSORY PROGRAMS

Sometimes called VAKT programs, these programs allow students to work at the same time on as much of each sense modality as possible: Visual, Auditory, Kinesthetic, and Tactile.

1) *Orton Gillingham*—The "classic" and best-known of the multi-sensory teaching programs for dyslexics.
2) *Wilson Program*—12-step remedial program (uses O/G); very systematic.
3) *Linnamood-Bell*—Focuses on auditory (phonemic) awareness; little re-

search with a control group exists to compare results; appears to be effective.

4) *The Spalding Method*—Total language arts aiming at spelling, writing, and reading all integrated together.

5) **S**lingerland Approach—Follows the Orton Gillingham model. It is seen as both preventive and remedial in addressing reading. It is totally multi-sensory. It is not "curriculum specific." Rather it is an *approach* to handling a curriculum in the VAKT manner.

PHONICS-BASED

1) *A Beka*—The primary model of phonics-based instruction at the earliest levels – it is information-intense and may move too quickly at upper levels.

2) *Open Court*—Based on alphabetic and phonological awareness. Research shows positive effects on reading.

3) *SRA*—DISTAR and Reading Mastery. Very effectively sequenced. Lays out phonological processing and builds on it. Research shows positive effects on reading achievement.

4) *Alphabetic Phonics*—Multisensory (360 tapes). Aimed at dyslexic students. Structures patterns in English language. Research has shown consistently positive results.

5) *Sing-Spell-Read-Write*—Popular for its use of VAKT, including effective motivational materials and music. There are some areas of concern, however, for dyslexic readers. First, the *pace* of newly introduced sounds becomes too rapid after the first few booklets, and students may become unable to get enough practice before getting new material. Secondly, the sequence of introduced sounds works with all 26 letters at first, which may prove an overload. Also, the first books are written with the short vowels "e" and "i" in back-to-back order, which frequently confuses children who have difficulty establishing a relationship between sound and print. For non-dyslexic readers, these concerns may be unimportant.

In March 2001, an article appeared citing research into the nature of dyslexia and the brain. It found that English, as a language, has proved very difficult for dyslexics. There are identical neurological signatures for dyslexics around the globe, but there is a difference in the level of difficulty encountered in cultures where one symbol represents one sound, and in English, where we have 1100 ways to spell our forty sounds. The test sample was small, but there are far fewer dyslexics in countries with consistent sound/symbol relationships than in the USA. The researcher concluded that having to learn to read the English language alone accounts for the increased difficulty dyslexic readers face. *(Virginian Pilot, March 16, 2001, p. 1, A-14.)*

When do you suspect dyslexia if a child is having trouble with reading? Typically by the end of first grade, children who fail to learn with traditional instructional methods should be evaluated—especially if there is any history of reading difficulty in any member of your extended family: uncle, aunt, parent, or siblings. There can certainly be additional factors to consider, such as immaturity, lack of ability to focus, or even allergies can contribute to a child's inability to benefit from reading instruction. Recent findings, however, note that unless readers establish good fluent reading habits by age nine, most children will remain noticeably behind—even as late as high school. Drs. Stolhard and Hulne, in 1996, suggest, "decoding predicts the volume of reading." In other words, the ease of decoding that a child demonstrates is closely linked to the ease with which that child can read fluently and easily. Therefore, it is usually best to follow up suspicions of suspected dyslexia at an earlier age. (*Merck Manual, Section 19 Ch.262, Developmental Problems.)*

Used with permission: www.hishelpinschool.com

Strategies for Teaching Children with Learning Disabilities

Teri Spray

 EADING DIFFICULTIES
If reading has been coming slowly for your child, consider the following concepts.

MATURITY

Is my child ready to read? Children do not all walk at the same age, yet many in education think they should all read at the same age—not true! A child is ready to read when letter shapes are easily recognized; letter sounds are easy to discriminate through rhymes and mimicking; and when the child indicates a desire to read through noticing words on packages, signs, and books. If your child is not yet ready to read, relax! Pushing will not help your child to mature any more than yelling at plants will produce fruit faster. However, like the plant, children need a fertile ground for growth and maturity. Nurture your child by:

1) Reading aloud every day.
2) Playing games and making words with magnetic letters on the refrigerator.
3) Teaching nursery rhymes and making up your own rhymes.
4) Teaching Bible memory verses.
5) Playing with pencil and paper (dot-to-dot games, tracing, drawing, copying shapes, coloring).

VISION

This is a very important factor for reading. Please remember that children are farsighted until about 11 years of age. Your child's eyesight may be excellent, but his or her vision may be poor. After the age of six, children begin to focus their eyes more effectively. This is the time when vision difficulties can really surface. If children read with only one eye at a time, they will often scramble or misread letters. If one eye dominates the other eye, letters will reverse easily and letters and words may seem to move around on the page. Reading will be very difficult if the eyes move in short jerks and jumps and cannot track or follow an object smoothly.

When these problems are present, the child must concentrate very hard just to keep the letters on the page still.

Children with vision problems wiggle a great deal while learning to read. They also complain of headaches, that reading is "boring," and are easily distracted. If you suspect a vision problem, take your child to an optometrist who is also a vision therapist. Many vision therapy exercises can be done at home as a part of your school day. Here are a few helpful hints:

1) Use a white card to reveal only one or two lines of reading at a time.
2) Try various colored transparencies over the writing. Some colors make reading easier for children.
3) Limit reading time to short periods in the morning.
4) Be as patient as possible when your child misreads. Remember, it is not laziness or inattentiveness. That "b" really does look like "a."
5) Look for curriculum with large print.
6) Keep plugging away! Though reading may be hard, and your child is resisting, it's worth every bit of the battle. Drill, drill, drill. Make small incremental rewards for your child like the Pizza Hut "Book-It" program—available through support groups or directly from Pizza Hut.
7) Continue to listen to your child read each day, even as he gets older.
8) Intensive phonics should be your first choice in a reading curriculum.
9) Have your child practice eye exercises every day by following a pencil tip or the tip of his thumb left-to-right across the body. Also, have him try following his thumb in circles on the left, right, and center.

AUDITORY PERCEPTION

The third reason for reading difficulty is auditory perception. Your child may be able to hear well, but confuses sounds easily. A child with this problem will confuse the message or often mispronounce words. When sounding out words, they read "C-A-T" and then *say* "tap." You can help this child to read by:

1) Reading a passage slowly together over and over until the sounds begin to register.
2) Cupping the hand behind the ear will also help to amplify the letter sounds to the child for spelling. Suggested curriculum might include the "Lady Bird" books, and other books with limited vocabulary, simple-to-read stories, and colorful pictures.
3) Do not neglect to use phonics. A child with auditory perception problems will not learn to spell without a good phonics base. Even though phonics will not be easy for your child, keep working because the results will be worth all the effort.

VISUAL PERCEPTION

The fourth reason for reading difficulty is a deficit in visual perception. Unlike vision problems mentioned above, the child with visual perception difficulties may see the item clearly, but the message gets scrambled in the brain. As a result, the child misreads and misunderstands what has been read. Strategies for assisting visual perception difficulties can also be learned from vision therapists. Another alternative is *Brain Integration Therapy Exercises* (Child Diagnostics, Dianne Craft, www.diannecraft.org, 303-694-0532).

Curriculum recommendations include the DISTAR approach to reading found in *Teach Your Child to Read in 100 Easy Lessons*, by Engleman, Haddox, and Bruner.

MATH CHALLENGES

Dyscalculia—This is the educational term for a child who cannot remember basic math facts, even after long periods of drill. It seems as though the brain has become a sieve, and the math facts just slip through.

1) Continue daily drills by making many copies of one drill page. Give the same page to the child for a brief, allotted time every day. Note the progress the child makes each day as he or she completes more problems. You may wish to chart his progress in a colorful way with incentives and rewards. (*Calculadder* makes great drill books.)

2) Place a number-line somewhere in the house which is accessible at all times. Staircases are good places for number lines. Use color for emphasis of facts, and plastic toys to "jump" on the number-line. This will give the child both visual and hands-on memory hooks for the math facts.

3) *Learning "Wrap-Ups"* are another hands-on tool for drilling math facts. These are plastic rectangles with an attached string that links a set of math problems physically. Multiplication, division, addition, and subtraction "Wrap-Ups" are sold individually.

4) "Triangle Flashcards" depict math facts in family groups. Three numbers appear in the corners of the cards. As each corner is covered, the question changes from addition to subtraction, or from multiplication to division. For example, the card might have the numbers 3, 5, and 8. Cover the 8, then 3+5 = 8, cover the 5, and 8-3 = 5, or cover the 3, and 8-5 = 3.

STORY-PROBLEM STRUGGLES

In addition to direct reading challenges, there are a lot of reasons children will struggle with story problems. To find the answer for a story problem, a child will need to recognize key words, and then identify the process needed to solve the problem. Some children will solve story-problems by drawing pictures for themselves. Others will solve them in their head and not realize how they arrived at the answer. Help your child identify the key words in the problem by underlining those words when they appear. Key words and phrases would include: sum, difference, more than, less than, each group, total, *et cetera*. The Saxon Math series has an excellent set of story problems in each daily "Problem Set."

WRITING STRUGGLES

Pencil Resistance—Many children seem to struggle with holding a pencil. Pencils often fall from their fingers, penmanship might be inconsistent, and the entire process of handwriting is laborious. When children struggle with pencil resistance, consider the problem to be physical more than attitude. The child will benefit from pencil exercises and fine-motor exercises to develop pencil control—use Legos®, LightBright®, peg boards and colorful dot-to-dot books.

Dysgraphia—This is a problem in which there appears to be a short circuit between the brain and the hand. A child with dysgraphia will have a great idea, but will be unable to put that idea on paper. Children with this problem will not show their work in math, will write one sentence and call it a "paragraph," and will beg to give their book reports orally! Dysgraphia is apparent when letters are formed with great stress, high pencil pressure. and inconsistent shape and/or placement on the line. Strategies to help the dysgraphic child include:

1) Low-stress writing. This means copying easy-to-read material onto lined handwriting paper in small daily assignments.
2) Use a white board or chalkboard to let the child make letters and numbers large and easy to write, and in that way to practice gross motor functions.
3) Allow your child to dictate a story first, then edit and recopy it in short writing sessions. Note: If your child struggles with spelling, this type of exercise can help build success in both spelling and the creative process.

Writer's Block—"I don't know what to write!" Whenever children say these words, the problem usually lies with inadequate experience or limited vocabulary. Prepare your children for writing through stimulating conversation, experiences, books, film/videos, or trips. As you are experiencing adventures, be sure to keep a journal of terms and names. These become the resources for the child's story. If your child still can't think of anything, generate a list of questions to be answered in the assignment. I have seen good success with the *"Writing in Narrative"* curriculum authored by Dr. Les Simonson, of W.I.N., 417 Doe Circle, Franktown, CO 80116, 303-688-0573.

VISUAL-MEMORY DEFICITS

When a child has poor visual-memory skills, spelling, reading, and math facts become very difficult to master. Each time the child looks at a word or math problem, it might as well be a "new" task. Visual memory means holding a "picture" in the mind. Children with strong visual memory skills will often look upward to remember how to spell a word. They're recreating the "picture" of the word they've stored. Here is a strategy for helping your children to remember what they see:

1) Write words to be memorized on heavy cardstock, or other stiff paper, using eye-catching colors and illustrations.
2) Hold the card in front of the child at about eyebrow level.
3) Hide the card, then see if the child can describe it to you in detail.
4) Bring the card back again and again until the child can "see" from memory exactly what the card looks like.

When the child is able to spell a word forward, backward, and inside-out, you know the visual "picture" is firmly in place.
Note: Visual-memory skills are not "visualizing." Visual memory is simply recalling what has been seen. Visualizing and visualization techniques have

often been used as "stress management" therapy and are based on imagination and fantasy.

AUDITORY-MEMORY DEFICITS

Children with auditory-memory deficits often confuse and mispronounce terms. Memory verses can be extremely difficult for these children because they say the words again and again, yet cannot remember the verse. They often confuse directions and instructions. Remembering more than two things at once is usually very difficult. You can help by always repeating your instructions—having eye contact with the child—and then having your child repeat the instructions back to you once or twice. Repeat new terms many times V-E-R-Y S-L-O-W-L-Y. It is also wise to write terms on cards to use in word games and drills.

ATTENTION-DEFICIT DISORDERS (ADD)

This is a "new" diagnosis that has been greatly misunderstood in recent years. Perhaps if we begin by defining ADD by exclusion, it will help clarify the picture:

1) Attention Deficit Disorder is not only a motivation problem, though children can learn to compensate for the disorder when they are highly motivated.
2) Attention Deficit Disorder is not a food allergy, even though some children naturally become extremely restless when they eat sugar, brightly colored food, dairy, wheat, corn, or other foods.
3) Attention Deficit Disorder is not a discipline problem only, though logical consequences and firmly set boundaries will benefit this child greatly.
4) Attention Deficit Disorder does NOT mean your child is lacking in ability or intelligence. Many children with ADD have exceptional intelligence.

Attention Deficit Disorder occurs in children who have a malfunction in the sensory input areas of the brain. Stimuli are apparently not filtered properly and consequently the children cannot focus well mentally. It is thought by many neurologists that the frontal lobe (focus area) is not processing as well as it should. The receptive area in the back of the brain (occipital region) is doing extra work. Sometimes just bending over from the waist and dangling the arms for one-minute intervals can help students to focus.

Children with Attention Deficit Disorder have a great deal of trouble focusing their attention. *Everything* seems to grab at their attention. They battle with over-stimulation. Even as little babies, these children often seem to be hypersensitive to their environment. Children with ADD take an extremely long time to finish a simple task. They may forget something the minute after it happens, such as a fact of learning or instructions that were just given. ADD children will often not seem to be aware of the consequences of their behavior, even though they were clearly defined. Pediatricians can sometimes assess ADD or can refer you to someone who can.

ATTENTION DEFICIT DISORDER WITH HYPERACTIVITY

A child who has these symptoms is known well by all. This child will struggle terribly with structure of any kind. The hyperactivity is present because the "stop it" signal in the brain is not functioning properly. Consequently this is a child who is stimulated by everything and has the impulse to pursue, touch, run, explore, and discuss everything under the sun. Parents of these children may seek medical support to help maintain family relationships. Counseling may be necessary at some point during this child's development due to the many issues that arise daily. A child's self-esteem is seriously harmed when he or she hears nothing but "Stop it," "Settle down," "That's enough," and "Don't!" all day long. A principal once said, "We don't worry about hyperactive students at our school, we let them get out their energy by running around the track about two laps, then they're just fine!"—an interesting thought.

LIVING AND LEARNING WITH A LATE BLOOMER

Sometimes the greatest teaching tool we can use with a child is time. Some children need a very long time to be able to develop academic skills. These children we call our "late-bloomers." Think about that name for a moment, and you can picture a beautiful flower which waits until the little spring pansies are fading to produce its late-season blossoms in the glow of late summer and early fall. The late blooms are nonetheless beautiful. You will know if your child is a late bloomer when these things happen during school:

1) After careful, patient instruction and concentrated effort, the information cannot be used or retained.
2) Whenever you try to build upon a concept, all is lost.
3) Your child cannot focus on material.
4) Your child shows no inclination to read, and does not recognize signs, or symbols.

HELPFUL HINTS FOR WORKING WITH A LATE BLOOMER

1) When working with a late bloomer, focus on that which they *can* do, not what they cannot. Often these children are great at building and experimenting.
2) Help your children to develop their skills and become all that they can be.
3) Work heavily on character. Teach the fruit of the Spirit: love, joy, peace, patience, kindness, goodness, gentleness, faithfulness, and self-control.
4) Be your child's advocate by writing a letter to all relevant parties, explaining the curriculum in which your child is working, and cautioning them to keep disparaging comments to a minimum.

CHALLENGING THE GIFTED LEARNER

It may be difficult to determine if a child qualifies as a "gifted" learner. Here are some clues:

1) Highly intelligent children will be excellent at applying what they know.
2) On tests, they often score much higher in comprehension than in vocabulary.

3) They may score higher in problem solving than in calculation or arithmetic operations.

4) They are often strong in language-usage skills because they seem to know what "sounds right."

5) Their highest scores are often found in the general knowledge areas of science, history, literature, and art. Exceptionally bright students may be high in any or all of these areas depending on their level of interest.

6) They may have begun reading with little or no instruction.

7) They may not complete drills well. Repetition may be as difficult for gifted children as processing challenges are for the learning impaired.

8) Gifted children are more comfortable *without* a challenge. Since most things have come easily to them, they may not understand how to study or really apply themselves.

9) They are easily bored and seek stimulation often. You may run hard to keep this child busy.

STRATEGIES FOR TEACHING THE BRILLIANT CHILD

Remember that your child is still a child. His rates of emotional and physical development have not changed even though his academics are advancing rapidly.

Allow for playtime—including imaginative play—and quiet spaces for reading, and self-directed creative or intellectual pursuits. Don't hurry this child unless he is seeking more stimulation.

Encourage your child to pursue the studies for which he has a "bent."

Don't be intimidated by your child's abilities or potential! You will become the director of learning, not the instructor. Give your child assignments and projects to research, experiments to do, and opportunities from which he or she can learn something new. Help your child organize his time, his data, and his results. You do not need to know more about the information than your student!

For more information, refer to the Gifted Education chapter in this book.

Writing the Student Education Plan (SEP)

Judith Munday

WHAT IS AN IEP? OR IS IT AN SEP?

There are several acronyms for the individualized plan of educational interventions created for a special-needs child. The one that arose from federal legislation aimed at helping educate children with disabilities is the IEP—Individualized Educational Plan (program). Public school students who have identified special needs receive services described in an IEP through the public schools. Homeschooling parents call this a "Student Educational Plan" (SEP), and sometimes an "Individualized Student Plan" (ISP). In all cases, the reference is to the same written program of interventions written specifically to strengthen the weaker areas of a child's educational and life skills. Preschool students have an IFSP—Individualized Family Service Plan. Adolescents also usually obtain an Individualized Transition Plan (ITP) to accompany their SEP and prepare them for success after ending formal education. Throughout this Special-Needs section, we use the term IEP primarily, but interchangeably, with the other acronyms.

WHERE DO YOU START?

When you write an SEP for a child, it can be a very simple process or a complex one. It CAN seem almost impossible the first time you attempt to get your knowledge of your child down onto paper, because it is something so close to the heart that it can be difficult to be objective. It will be very helpful to write answers to the following questions as if you were describing the child to a stranger. Putting the information down in writing truly helps focus, and almost forces a parent into greater clarity when trying to evaluate, "Just what DOES the child need in order to benefit from an education?" The following steps look intimidating, but once the information is organized in front of you, the rest of the process will be much easier than if you had just tried to jot down some ideas in a disorganized approach.

So take some notebook paper and start writing: one page for each response. Draw a line across the paper after you complete each page. (You will be coming back to these sheets.)

1. You start where the child is now! In note form, write answers to the following questions.

a. In what grade is the child? What grade level material is the child working on for each subject? Identify the present levels of performance. Use any documentation, such as previous testing, early report cards, observations made informally, and samples of student work.

b. What are the skill areas that need special help?

c. What is the learning style that meets the need?

d. What kind of curriculum or approach works best with this child?

e. What environment helps this child perform well?

f. What are the child's strengths?

g. What special accommodations or modifications are important for the child to do his/her best?

2. Go back to the answers for items "a-g". Use the answers for each question to write a paragraph that describes the child's strengths and weaknesses. You are explaining why the child needs special individual educational planning (although ALL children really do!). This is called a "narrative summary" of strengths and weaknesses. This Summary of Strengths and Weaknesses is to be attached to the SEP. It provides documentation for why the child needs specially designed educational approaches, pacing, materials, and accommodations to succeed.

SETTING ANNUAL GOALS

1. Spend some time thinking about where you want to see the child by the end of one full school year in each area of weakness. Ask the Lord's guidance and wisdom. For some children, those with severe limitations, there will have to be some difficult reality checks, and it may be necessary to pray for God's peace to see how these long-term goals are going to help the child move forward in meeting God's plans for his/her life. If you feel unclear about what a reasonable expectation or specific goal should be, use a Scope and Sequence approach (for details see *Choosing Textbooks* in this section) to understand what is typically taught, and to adjust it for your child.

2. Now narrow down your list so you can state what behaviors (skills) you want to see in five or six essential areas of weakness or need. These areas should be the long-term "big picture" items. These will be your major focus in your child's SEP. Make sure that you don't get bogged down early with too many ideas or creative ways to reach the one-year goals you identified! Keep in mind that, with appropriate accommodations, the child may be capable of working close to grade level in weaker areas! (To find articles about *Accommodations and Modifications*, see below.) If there is a proper place for creativity in teaching the special-needs child, it is particularly in selecting which accommodations fit into the plan to help your child reach the long-range goals. (Make notes here on which accommodations you think of using.)

3. It is helpful to consider the possible accommodations at this early point in SEP writing, because *with* accommodations and modifications, a greater range of achievement is possible for many areas of learning! This will affect the goals that you set for your child—the highest levels, realistically, that your child can achieve by the end of the year. Accommodations can be and will be important, because they are usually permitted for the child's use on many standardized tests! If they are not part of an SEP, it looks like a parent is just asking for accommodations on the test date to make the testing easier in order to improve scores! Type out the accommodations and modifications and add them to the SEP goals later.

4. Once long-term "big picture" goals are written out, sit down with the Scope and Sequence for the upcoming year. Decide how much of the material in detail the child might realistically complete. Then split that content up into four approximately even sections, similar to a school's marking periods. The end of each section is a cut-off "checkpoint." The four checkpoints function like mileposts to see how much distance you have driven. At the checkpoints, you find out whether the child is moving along fast enough to meet your selected year-end goals. If not, it may be necessary to revisit the long-term goals and revise them. Write these checkpoints down on the SEP form under Checkpoints (see the suggested form).

WRITING SEP GOALS FOR EACH IDENTIFIED WEAKNESS

1. Write a goal for each of the five or six weaknesses. Called a teaching "objective," each goal should give four key facts:
   a. What grade level should the child be working at by the end of the year?
   b. What should the child be doing? This requires an ACTION word. *Examples: write, recite, state, describe.*
   c. What will you expect as a "mastery" level? *Examples: 4 out of 5 times; 86%; every time the child is asked; does it all the time without asking.*
   d. What you will do or use to measure this skill? This takes practice! Examples of measurement can be as simple as counting sit-ups to use of complicated scoring plans, such as a rubric. Standardized test scores or weekly spelling test scores can be used as the means of assessment.

2. Decide how often the child will be evaluated for mastery. For some skills, it might be a daily check of whether the child is holding a fork at meals, or writing in complete sentences. Other goals would be longer range, such as reading a third-grade, sight-word list by January, or, when asked a question, communicating orally in complete sentences that are grammatically correct.

3. Finally, determine what will be used to measure whether the child has reached *mastery* of a skill. It may be a physical action, a written essay, a recitation, or a musical performance, to name just a few examples. Some evaluations are informal, but data should still be recorded at some kind of regular time interval to satisfy the local administrators. A daily notebook is very helpful for recording short notes. Parents know all too well how easily exciting events get "lost" with the ongoing excitement of family living; then years later, it becomes hard to recollect them. It is also helpful for the parent to have a running record of progress. In homeschooling special-needs students, a local superintendent may be asking for documentation of how you KNOW that the child has learned a skill, and the notebook will be valuable.

Acceptable Goals ensure that you **KNOW** whether the child can do what he was asked to do, or knows in fact what you "think" he has learned. You should be able to:
1. **Observe** the behavior or skill being demonstrated.
2. **Measure** the level of performance (to compare with the child's previous performance).
3. **State when** you expect (hope) to see the skill mastered. This sets a temporal target to aim for (so you know how long it is taking to get to the goal). (If there is no demonstrated progress by each checkpoint, it is clear that changes must be made in teaching technique, goals, materials, or accommodations. In other words, it is time to make mid-course corrections.)

A helpful model for writing goals follows. Parents should fill in each blank with a goal for the coming school year that will work on strengthening a significant weakness. A suggested SEP form is on the last page of this article, and contents of the "template" can be placed into the appropriate places.

_____
(child's name)

will be able to_____
(action word)

at the ____ grade level with _____
(percentage or ratio—such as 4 out of 5)

success/accuracy in _____
(number of trials)

EXAMPLES OF APPROPRIATE GOALS
The following goals are observable, measurable, and time-limited:
- Jon will be able to read aloud 25 words correctly from a fifth-grade Dolch reading word list with no more than four errors.

- Jean will be able to underline proper nouns when given a set of 15 sentences with mixed parts of speech with 90% mastery.

Goals that are too vague
- Joseph will "recognize" circles in a fourth-grade math book.
  (What behavior would Joseph demonstrate so you KNOW he "recognized circles? This goal could be made specific by stating that Joseph can point to circles nine out of 10 times when shown a page of different shapes.)
- Julia will understand main ideas in reading.
  (There is no way stated here for a parent to KNOW whether Julia understands, because there is no standard describing what "understanding" would look like. Revise by stating that Julia will answer ten questions based on the main idea & details with 90% accuracy.)
- Julio will identify short vowels in lists of words.
  (Is the parent expecting Julio to point to the short vowels, to read them aloud, or sound out the words using short vowels? The conditions for "identifying" are too unclear—and that means the parent can't state for sure whether he has mastered the task.)

When you have completed writing out your goals for your child, read them through to determine if they are clear, observable, and measurable. Show them to another person who knows the child and ask for feedback. Pray about them and see that you sense God's peace. When the document is finished, it will be a very helpful road map, with checkpoints along the way to help keep your child on a forward path towards success.

REVIEW: WHAT SHOULD THE FINAL DOCUMENT HAVE IN IT?

When you have finished your work, you should have the following components assembled in your child's Student Education Plan (SEP):

1. Biography page. This page should contain the essential data about your child: name, parent names, address, birth date, and grade level.
2. Narrative Summary page. A Narrative Summary page (the same page as above or on a separate sheet) should contain the Narrative Summary of (educational) Strengths and Weaknesses of your child. Be sure to expand on ways in which the "weaknesses" impact learning, but be equally complete in describing the strengths.
3. Goal pages. You should have a collection of "goal pages" (see suggested form at the end of this article, or use one from a different source, including software versions!). On each page, you should state a long-range visionary learning objective you hope to see the child attain within the next school year. Remember: *The SEP does NOT have to contain all the curriculum you are going to be teaching*, nor all the SOLs for that grade level. In fact—**the Student Education Plan (SEP) technically ONLY needs to have goals for strengthening the weaknesses you described in your narrative of strengths and weaknesses!**

4. Benchmarks for each goal. Check that each "long-range" goal has several "benchmark" points or skills that you will use to check achievement at your time-line checkpoints (end of "marking periods"). These can be called the "short-range" goals, and it is helpful to write them underneath each "long range goal." Each short-range goal should be measurable and observable, defined in terms of what your standard is going to be. This helps YOU, and it satisfies the local school authorities.

5. Checkpoints and Measurement Methods. You should place on paper- when and how you plan to measure achievement for each and every benchmark.

6. Accommodations and Modifications. Finally, you should have a sheet on which you explain or list the accommodations and/or modifications you are going to use to teach each area of weakness. Examples—a Braille calculator, taped books, voice-dictation software, or lower/higher than grade level texts. This assures you the right to use the same accommodations on formal, standardized testing, later in the year.

Congratulations! You have just completed your child's SEP!! Well done!

MODEL SEP FORM FOR _____ (STUDENT NAME)

SEP GOAL # FOR CHILD'S LEARNING (Fill in one of the major long-term goals.)	HOW IT WILL BE MEASURED? BY WHAT?	WHEN? 1ST 9 WEEKS PUT A DATE	WHEN? 2ND 9 WEEKS	WHEN? 3RD 9 WEEKS	WHEN? 4TH 9 WEEKS
(1) Will be able to _____ _____ _____ at the ___ grade level (if appropriate) with ___ at ___ mastery level.	Will you give objective tests, ask oral questions, accept a project, watch child do a task, et cetera?	Where do you expect to be at this point? Write in projected chapter #, skill level, _____. Write in PRESENT level of mastery	Where do you expect to be at this point?	Where do you expect to be at this point?	Where do you expect to be at this point?
(2) Will be able to _____ _____ _____ at the ___ grade level (if appropriate) with ___ at ___ mastery level.					
(3) Will be able to _____ _____ _____ at the ___ grade level (if appropriate) with ___ at ___ mastery level.					

SAMPLE OF AN SEP FORM FOR A HAPPY HOMESCHOOLER

We will assume we are looking at this SEP in December. You can see at a glance looking at this SEP that Happy Schooler is weak in his written language (probably in part because he hates to write longhand and in part because of weak spelling and composition skills). We know that because these areas were included as short-term goals to help him strengthen his Written Expression and Spelling. We can also see that he is not yet working at a level of mastery that is given in the goals, so the parent/teacher knows there is more to do in each of these areas. In other words, we know what skills we are looking to see Happy be able to do, and we can see whether he can do it at this point in time! We can SEE what Happy does, we can MEASURE it, and we know how often to check his progress. If Happy did not show much progress in composition, Mom would probably have to adjust the amount of the Language Arts text that she expects Happy to finish by June. Goals **can** be changed!

SEP GOAL # 1 WRITTEN LANGUAGE AND SPELLING Happy needs keyboarding to accommodate special needs.	METHOD OF EVALUATION	1ST 9 WEEKS PUT A DATE NOVEMBER 15	2ND 9 WEEKS JANUARY 20	3RD 9 WEEKS MARCH 20	4TH 9 WEEKS MAY 15
(1) Happy will be able to compose complete sentences with correct punctuation and capitalization on the computer using MS Word at the 5th grade level with 90% accuracy.	Evaluate printouts of work from Language Arts work book (scanned into computer to allow Happy to work on them) and teacher-made tests.	We should be at Chapter 4, Language Arts. November 15 RESULT: 75% grade average for sentence writing	We should be at Chapter 7, Language Arts.	We should be at Chapter 10.	We should be at Chapter 14.
(2) Happy will be able use SpellCheck to correct spelling errors circled on a rough draft typewritten paragraph at the ___x___ grade level (In this case it would be hard to give a grade level to the words that were misspelled) and correct 100% of the mistakes.	Mom will circle words on rough draft and Happy will look them up and grade the final printout paper for accuracy.	We should be at Chapter 4, Language Arts. November 15 RESULT: 75% grade average for sentence writing	We should be at Chapter 7.	We should be at Chapter 10.	We should be at Chapter 14.
(3) Happy will be able to spell a list of 20 words from The Natural Speller using words at the 5th grade level at 90% mastery level.	Weekly 20 word spelling tests using keyboarding.	We should be through 1/4 of the fifth grade word list. RESULT: Average 85% on weekly tests	We should be through 1/2 of the fifth grade word list.	We should be through 3/4 of the fifth grade word list.	We should be through all of the fifth grade word list.

Assistive Technology

Judith Munday

Children with special needs have greater opportunities in these technology-rich times in which we live. There is an abundance of modern technology to assist the disabled learner to have a more level playing field. Parents are often unaware of the extraordinary ways in which such assistance can open the minds and hearts of students who are used to being limited by their disability. For example, a child with severe dyscalculia who cannot seem to master memorization of number facts or attain simple success in written work may find success with the use of calculators, and with programs that will allow the child to *speak* math into the computer and see it appear as a written problem. Students with severe motor limitations are liberated into developing their written expression with voice-dictation software. Dyslexic students with intellectual skills far above their reading and spelling level can benefit by working on grade level with the right combination of technology helps, instead of being forced to work with childish lower-grade-level reading material.

Choices must reflect the genuine need of an individual student, and it is not always in the best interests of a child to simply replace basic learning foundations with technological programs and aides. However, when selected and used appropriately, technology opens up a wider range of opportunities for the child to take in new learning, as well as to demonstrate learning with a greater range of choices.

READING-TECHNOLOGY DEVICES AND PROGRAMS

Reading technology opens doors to some material that was formerly not available to students with certain special needs, such as the visually handicapped, blind, and dyslexic. Assistive technology includes magnification software with/without speech, screen-reading software, Braille software, and keyboard software. Through technology, speech can be sensed by a microphone, typed by a word processor, and read back to the learner. Optical-character-recognition (OCR) technology enables written text to be converted into electronic documents that can be brought up in most word-processing programs. Printed-text material can be scanned, routed to a word processor, and then read and manipulated on the screen. Tape-recorded books are always a wonderful way to teach poor readers at their true ability level of comprehension instead of at their limited reading level.

Parents can use these devices in several ways. Text can be enlarged and reprinted for students with visual limitations. Text can selected and copied into free downloadable programs that will read the text aloud to the student in several choices of voice. These do sound a bit "robot-like," but the programs are able to read the text accurately—even web-page content that is copied. Check www.readplease.com for more information. Another such program is at www.webspeakster.com/browser_ware.htm (note underscore), which carries the "Code-It" software program (American Indian themed—It also has a huge set of links for American Indian information). Available for free download.

Other programs—much more complex and expensive—read text from the screen, highlight text by parts of speech or selected criteria, and incorporate word-processing programs. Links for a few of these programs include:

www.kurzweiledu.com

www.accessiblebookcollection.org—A $49.95/school year access subscription gives students with disabilities access to a wide range of books in digital format.

www.rfbd.org—Recordings for the Blind and Dyslexic. Since almost 50% of client requests were from the dyslexic population, the organization recently changed its name. Learners must be "certified" as needing reading assistance, and a consultant, physician, or teacher can provide certification. A minimum fee is charged yearly for unlimited access to a wide range of materials, and if the necessary text is not available, it will be taped for the child! There is a special tape player necessary, but there are organizations that provide grants for supplying assistive technology!

www.nextup.com—Links to many options for learning with listening—users can even save files in MP3 format.

www.ldresources.com—This is a rich storehouse of links to technology and its applications for students with special needs.

WRITING DEVICES, HELPS, AND SOFTWARE

Technology provides a big assist to writing. There are programs that anticipate content and type it in without the student having to finish the word, programs that read aloud as the student types in material, others where speech is transformed into typewritten content, and many other options. Some parents worry that children with some disabilities should have to learn cursive, but in today's modern world, if they have become proficient in writing with computer assistance, the only reason they might be required to do so would be to sign forms and checks! Parents must ask themselves, "What am I trying to assess—content and ideas, or penmanship skills?" If penmanship skills are seriously limiting a child's ability to demonstrate learning, then good stewardship of that learning capability would indicate that the child should be given a level playing field (with computer help) to show what they know! For "reluctant" writers, the computer may release their ideas when they can type more easily, and use visual organizers to help prepare the topic ahead of composition.

SOME EXAMPLES OF WRITING-ASSISTANCE TECHNOLOGY INCLUDE:

- The ubiquitous word-processing program is a well-known technology. Examples include *Microsoft Word* or *WordPerfect*.
- Voice-to-text dictation software uses a microphone to create a printed text using a word-processing program, such as *Dragon* and *Naturally Speaking*.
- *Franklin Spell-Check*, employing hand-held spell-check technology, can be purchased in most office-supply stores
- *Write Outloud* and *Co-Write* word-prediction software reads text out loud as it is typed, and predicts which word the student may employ to complete an idea. The word-prediction software uses the first letter typed, and shows a drop-down menu of words as options, requiring only a click of the mouse to insert into the document. This is very efficient for students who cannot spell and/or who hate to write by hand. Website discounts on pricing. Free 30-day trials, www.Donjohnston.com/index.html or 800-999-4660.
- *Inspiration* software visually "maps" the student's pre-writing ideas in many different ways. It creates visual printouts to help children organize ideas and plan content, with appealing colors, shapes, and clip-art. It can be obtained from Inspiration Software, Inc.; 800-877-4292; www.inspiration.com
- *e-Mind Maps* by Mindjet.com creates visual concept diagrams, like "wheel" charts, for organizing ideas. It is similar to *Inspiration* software but with fewer options, so that it is easier for students to learn. Downloadable online from www.Mindjet.com

MATH TECHNOLOGY

Students with special needs demonstrate a wide range of difficulties in math—some cannot retain facts, some cannot write the work legibly or it sprawls all over the page with no columns at all, and others cannot see the materials. Dyslexic students cannot read the directions and word problems. The needs for technology are therefore different. Again, the parent must ask, "What skills am I trying to assess: writing, memorization of data, or understanding of operations and math concepts?" The answers to that question will determine which technology devices are most appropriate and helpful. Many students cannot learn math facts by memory, yet with the assistance of a calculator, they are capable of working much closer to grade level content! Students with serious motor-control problems need a range of adaptations, from raised lines, to guide-writing work on the paper, all the way to problems read aloud.

SOME HELPFUL TECHNOLOGY INCLUDES:

- Calculators
- Talking calculators with answer screens and built-in speech synthesizers that state a number or math symbol
- Talking math worksheets that position the cursor and speak the numerals that are seen on the screen.

Check out the following sites for links about math-assistive technology:

www.orbitresearch.com—Talking graphing calculator for algebra and geometry at upper levels of math.

www.tsbvi.edu/math/tools-lv.htm—Lists multiple suppliers of products for the blind and visually handicapped.

GENERAL RESOURCES

Assistive Technology for Children with Learning Difficulties. Marshall Rasking, Ph.D., Schwab Foundation for Learning, 1650 South Amphlett Boulevard. #300, San Mateo, CA 94402. www.schwabfoundation.org. Provides a comprehensive summary of assistive technology options.

Assistive Technology in the Student's Individualized Education Program: A Handbook for Parents and School Personnel. Joey Wallace, Ph.D., compiler, Virginia Assistive Technology System (VATS), P.O. Box 1475, Richmond, VA 23218; 804-786-7765. TDD 804-786-7765. Provides a summary of assistive technology options, legal mandates, and funding options.

www.gucchdgeorgetown.net/UCEDD/documents/ATResources.doc. This organization maintains a large site where parents can learn more about assistive technology for augmentative- and alternative-communication products and technology. There are descriptions of the technology, and a listing of ongoing workshop locations open to parents and educators.

Used with Permission: www.helpinschool.net.

Understanding the Unique Legal Issues of Special-Needs Students

Homeschooling and Special-Needs Children

Christopher J. Klicka

Teaching a child with special needs is a privilege—but it is also hard. It requires much sacrifice, patience, and unconditional love on the part of the parents.

We cannot forget to consider what the child with special needs experiences. Living with a handicap such as blindness, cerebral palsy, a speech impediment, autism, retardation, a disease, or one of many types of learning disabilities is difficult. It is a daily struggle emotionally, mentally, and many times physically. The child's self esteem is constantly challenged. Some handicaps or learning disabilities can be overcome with consistent and focused effort. Other handicaps can only be managed and may never go away.

Living with multiple sclerosis helps me appreciate the struggles of a physically handicapped person. Every day it is hard for me simply to walk, put my socks on, or stay in 80-degree weather for any length of time. The emotional drain is intense. The need to think and plan for logistics to achieve normal movement is a heavy burden. The quality of life from a human perspective is diminished. Hiking in the woods or camping is too hard, going to the beach is incapacitating, and participating in most sports that I love is out of the question.

Personal attention and love from my family is more important to me than ever before. For a *child* with special needs, this extra support and reassurance is essential. Homeschooling your special-needs child makes that intense, loving support possible.

We have seven children including a set of twins who were supposed to have died in the womb. Yet God answered our desperate prayers in a miraculous way. Amy, whose head was caved in, spine twisted, and not receiving adequate nutrients, completely recovered in the womb and was born alive at 2 lbs., 13 ounces. Although Amy was miraculously delivered, she is mentally much slower than her twin sister, Charity. At six years old, Amy is not ready to read like her sister and requires much more time, attention, and love. Sending her to an institutional school would devastate her fragile self-confidence. Teachers juggling the demands of a busy classroom could not possibly give her the one-on-one attention and love she needs.

In light of these experiences, I am convinced that homeschooling children with special needs is the most effective way to teach them and provides the ideal environment in which they will learn and thrive.

PARENTS EXCEL IN TEACHING THEIR SPECIAL-NEEDS CHILDREN

Objective studies have demonstrated that many parents are providing a superior form of education for their special-needs children by teaching them at home.

For example, in one of the most thorough studies performed thus far, a team of researchers led by Dr. Steven Duvall conducted a year-long investigation involving eight elementary and two junior high students with learning disabilities. He compared one group of five students who received instruction at home, with a group of five students who attended public schools. He was careful to match the public school students to the homeschool students according to grade level, sex, I.Q., and area of disability. Using a laptop computer, Duvall sat in on teaching sessions and took an observation every 20 seconds, creating tens of thousands of data points that were then fed into a statistical-analysis package. His research usually included a second observer who double-checked Duvall's readings.

Duvall recorded and analyzed the time students were academically engaged during instructional periods. He also administered standardized achievement tests to measure gains in reading, math, and written language. His results showed that the homeschooled special-needs students were academically engaged about *two and one-half times as often* as public school special-needs students! He found that the children in the public school special-education classrooms spent 74.9% of their time with *no* academic responses, while the homeschool children spent only 40.7% of their time with no academic responses. He also found that homeschools have children and teachers sitting side-by-side or face-to-face 43% of the time, while public education classrooms had such arrangements for special-needs children only 6% of the time. This was a tremendous advantage for the homeschooled students.

His study further found that the homeschooled students averaged six months' gain in reading compared to only a one-half month's gain by the public school students. Furthermore, the homeschooled students gained eight months in written language skills during the year-long study compared to the public school counterparts who gained only two-and-one-half months.

DUVALL SUMMARIZED

These results clearly indicate that parents, even though they are not certified teachers, can create instructional environments at home that assist students with learning disabilities to improve their academic skills. This study clearly shows that homeschooling is beneficial for special-needs students.[1] Contrary to the claims of the education elite, parents do not have to be specially certified or have special qualifications to teach their handicapped children at home.

An interesting historical example is Thomas Edison, who was expelled from public school at age seven because he was considered "addled" by his public school teacher. He lasted only three months in formal schooling. Over the next three years, his mother taught him the basics at home, and as Edison himself stated, "She instilled in me the love and purpose of learning."[2] Without any special qualifications, Mrs. Edison helped her son overcome his disabilities to become a great inventor.

Once again, we see that homeschooling can work for any child.

THE HOME IS THE IDEAL ENVIRONMENT FOR SPECIAL-NEEDS CHILDREN

All children need to know they are loved. For children with special needs, it is even more important. Homeschooling gives these children teachers who truly love them, and intimately know their weaknesses and strengths. This motivation and insight gives parents a tremendous advantage in delivering an effective educational program to their children.

Homeschooling also affords parents the opportunity to instill spiritual values. Having a handicap is a daily struggle. A handicapped child is constantly aware of his weakness and inabilities, and this can often lead to chronic feelings of worthlessness and inadequacy. In homeschooling, parents can spend much time teaching their special-needs children that they were created in the image of God. They have worth and value because God loves them. Their struggles and difficulties have purpose in glorifying God and being conformed more into the image of His Son, which is God's goal for all Christians.

They can learn "not to lose heart. Though our 'outward man' is decaying, our 'inward man' is being renewed day by day. For this momentary, light affliction is producing for us an eternal weight of glory far beyond all comparison, while we look not at the things which are seen but at the things which are not seen; for the things which are seen are temporal, but the things which are not seen are eternal" (II Corinthians 4:16-18). If they accept Jesus as their Savior, believing that He died on the cross for their sins and rose again, they will be healed one day in Heaven, if not before.

Weakness and disability remind us of our mortality, and of our great need for a Savior. The spiritual object lessons to be drawn from our children's handicap are endless and of eternal value to them as well as to the whole family. I can truly say that my multiple sclerosis and Amy's limitations are blessings that are reaping tremendous spiritual growth. God is teaching us to walk by faith, not sight (II Corinthians 5:7).

CAN I LEGALLY HOMESCHOOL MY SPECIAL-NEEDS CHILD? AND WHAT ARE MY RIGHTS?

The Homeschool Legal Defense Association, since 1983, has worked to win and protect all parents' right to teach all their children at home, including special-needs children. When HSLDA began, it was only clearly legal to homeschool in approximately five states. Families now have this freedom in all 50 states. Even though parents are teaching their special-needs children well, and fully within the law, these families are still faced with numerous challenges.

When Israel left Egypt, the Amalekites attacked Israel. However, they would rarely attack armed forces or the main group of the Israelites. Instead they would pick off the stragglers, who were often made up of the sick or weak.

Some public school authorities, unfortunately, seem to have adopted the tactics of the Amalekites when dealing with handicapped children who are being homeschooled. When they find it difficult to pick on homeschoolers who are average or above average students, they turn to harassing the handicapped or special-needs homeschooled children. Going after handicapped children who are homeschooled is somewhat easier, since it is more difficult for the family to prove educational progress. It is easier to intimidate these parents into thinking they are not qualified. The incentive is also greater, since special-needs children are worth *nearly twice as much* in state and federal tax dollars that would be sent to the local school district.

As a result, homeschool families with children with special needs or handicaps are often harassed and restricted more than other homeschool families. Because of this discriminatory treatment, many homeschoolers with special-needs children begin to think they have fewer parental rights than other families. Constitutionally, this could not be further from the truth. Parents with special-needs children live under the same U.S. Constitution as all other citizens. Therefore, they have the protection of the First and Fourteenth Amendments.

For example, one HSLDA homeschool member family in Colorado had their child enrolled in special-needs classes in the public school. After awhile, their child basically stagnated, as the classroom atmosphere became unbearable. The parents, having decided that they could do a better job themselves, notified the school district that they were going to homeschool their child. Although it was legal to homeschool in the state, the local school district refused to disenroll the child, asserting that the child's Individual Education Plan (IEP) recommendation could not be fulfilled by a "mere" mother. It called the family nearly every week, pressuring them to return for more meetings and more conferences with public school specialists. The mother resisted the intimidation, but began to doubt herself. HSLDA was called, and we were able to convince the school district to withdraw unnecessary demands and recognize her right to homeschool privately.

In Illinois, a family disenrolled their child from all special-needs programs except speech therapy. Again and again, the school district tried to pressure the family to come into various meetings in which the child would be evaluated and recommendations given. The school district believed the parents were not qualified. Finally, the district initiated a due-process proceeding, pursuant to the Individuals with Disabilities Education Act (IDEA). District officials believed the family was under the jurisdiction of that Act because the child was still receiving speech therapy. The family followed HSLDA's advice and withdrew their child from speech therapy, breaking all ties with the school district in a written statement. After we further negotiated with the district, the family was left alone.

In Indiana, a couple who educated nine adopted handicapped children was harassed repeatedly by school officials. Scores of other families were homeschooling in the area, but this family was singled out because all the children had special needs; the school district was losing a lot of money.

Many other instances could be cited from HSLDA's experience defending the parents of handicapped children who are harassed simply for homeschooling. In most cases, HSLDA attorneys resolved the situations without going to court. Because of the parents' love, dedication, and unique insight into their children's special needs, these students flourished in the homeschool environment.

RESOURCES FOR TEACHING CHILDREN WITH SPECIAL NEEDS

Homeschoolers can choose between two options to receive help: private special-needs resources, or resources from the public schools through the federal IDEA program. Some homeschool families use a combination of both.

At this time, the U.S. Department of Education's Office of Special Education Programs (OSEP) has interpreted the law to mean that IDEA special education resources only have to be made available to students in public schools or private schools. They specifically explain that homeschooled students cannot qualify. This policy letter from OSEP, however, seems contrary to the purpose of IDEA "to assist States...to provide for the education of ALL children with disabilities." 20 USC section 1400(d)(C).

Therefore, HSLDA has filed suit in federal court to end this discrimination, and we are urging the administration of President George W. Bush to issue a new policy letter from the OSEP, recognizing that *all* homeschoolers may qualify for special-needs services.

Meanwhile, certain states have passed regulations allowing homeschoolers to participate. In a state that recognizes homeschools as private schools, the homeschoolers can generally get special-needs assistance.

However, parents should consider the possible side effect of taking government special-needs services—*loss of freedom.* That common adage, that "government controls nearly always follow government money," often becomes reality for homeschoolers who receive public school services for their special-needs children. Many times the controls are not immediately visible, but they usually surface as soon as parents begin to disagree with public school "recommendations" for new therapy or a different educational approach.

At the very least, homeschoolers who receive public school services for their special-needs children place themselves under the jurisdiction of federal IDEA and local state regulations that implement that Act.

IDEA's intent is to provide statutory guidelines for local public schools to make available a free public education to the handicapped. The Act is *not* a compulsory-attendance statute for handicapped children. It is clearly apparent, therefore, that parents who do not want to take advantage of a free public education for their handicapped child are not required to do so. Such a mandate would also violate the parents' fundamental right to direct the education of their children, as guaranteed under *Pierce v. Society of Sisters.*[3] In *Pierce*, the U.S. Supreme Court declared parents have the right to choose a private education program for their children, and, as a result, the Court struck down an Oregon law that mandated only public school attendance.

Parents of special-needs children are *not* required to use any public educational services. To privately educate their special-needs child is the parents' choice. If they choose to educate their special-needs child privately, they may do so without any state control or interference under IDEA.

HOMESCHOOLING WORKS

Though homeschooling special-needs children takes a tremendous effort on behalf of parents, HSLDA receives regular reports of the consistent success that these parents are achieving—often far beyond the progress the same special-needs child made in the public school. One of the major reasons for success seems to be the fact that parents know their children best and, therefore, can best meet the needs of their handicapped child.

Below is a list of a few resources for more information on teaching special-needs children. HSLDA members may also contact our office and speak with our full-time special-needs coordinator for assistance with questions and finding resources.

In summary, parents who homeschool special-needs students privately will have the least risk of government intervention. Those who choose to work with public schools should exercise great caution. Homeschoolers should also carefully monitor their state legislatures in order to oppose any attempts to create excessive regulations for handicapped children being homeschooled. All homeschooling families need to stand together to protect special-needs homeschoolers from being separately and excessively regulated.

Notes:
1. Steven F. Duvall, *The Impact of Home Education on Learning Disabled Children: A Look at New Research* (report presented to the Homeschool Legal Defense Association, Purcellville, VA, August 30, 1994). Full research published later as "An Exploratory Study of Homeschool Instructional Environments and Their Effects on the Basic Skills of Students with Learning Disabilities," in *Education & Treatment of Children* 20, no.2 (May 1997): 150-172.
2. Christopher J. Klicka, *Homeschooling: The Right Choice* (Twin Sisters, OR: Loyal Publishing, 2000), p. 168.
3. 268 U.S. 510 (1925) [Also see *Meyer v. Nebraska*, 262 U.S. 390 (1923) and *Wisconsin v. Yoder*, 406 U.S. 205 (1972)].

Christopher J. Klicka, Senior Counsel for the Homeschool Legal Defense Association. HSLDA News, December 28, 2001, Adapted from an article in *Practical Homeschooling*, March/April 2001.

Resources for Special Needs

Compiled by Judith Munday

BOOKS

All God's Children: Ministry to the Disabled—Gene Newman and Joni Eareckson Tada. Zondervan Publishing House, Grand Rapids, MI; 1981. A compassionate look at the needs of special children and adults. A gentle, Christ-centered view of the heart and mind of those with extra challenges.

Answers to Questions Parents Ask Most About Homeschooling—Deborah MacIntire and Paul Windham. Creative Teaching Press, Cypress, CA. This book is especially helpful because of the useful forms and suggestions for time management and lesson planning. There are other helpful topics ranging from "balancing family time and education" to "legal concerns."

Assessing Children for the Presence of a Disability—National Center for Children and Youth with Disabilities.

Assistive Technology Guide—Explains the ways different technologies can enable special-needs children to "show what they know" in the best way possible. Free from Schwab Learning, 1650 S. Amphlett Boulevard, Suite 300, San Mateo, CA 94402-2516; 800-230-0988. www. Schwablearning.org

Bridges to Reading Kit: What To Do When You Suspect Your Child Has a Reading Problem—Free kit consisting of five separate booklets for parents to use. Additional reference guides are full of practical suggestions. Order from Schwab Foundation for Learning; 800-230-0988.

Choosing and Using Curriculum: Your Guide to Home Education—Joyce Herzog. A good overview for helping parents understand the perspectives and choices for curriculum styles, selecting materials, and monitoring progress. Recently updated to include more resources. www.JoyceHerzog.com

Christian Home Educators' Curriculum Manual: Elementary Grades (Grades K-6) and companion volume for *Junior/Senior High*—Cathy Duffy. Grove Publishing/Home Run Enterprises, 16172 Huxley Circle, Westminster CA 92683; 1997. Updated annually. A comprehensive presentation of goals, materials and methods organized by study area. Extensive references with lengthy annotations.

Helping Struggling Readers: Successful Reading Techniques—Susan Fondrk and Cheryl Frasca. Good Year Books, Parsippany, NJ; 2001. This resource is packed with solid, research-backed techniques for helping early readers as well as older students who need material presented in different ways. Very well done.

Homeschooling Children with Special Needs—Sharon C. Hensley. Noble Publishing Associates, Gresham, OR; 1995. A practical and realistic manual for the parent of a special-needs child. Decidedly Christ-centered.

How Do You Know They Know What They Know?—Teresa Moon. Grove Publishing, Westminster, CA; 1997. A practical guide to many forms of assessment. Not targeted for special needs, but the tips and principles apply to all students. There are many very useful scoring/grading checklists and forms to use. An important resource for documenting student progress for all students—but particularly for special-needs students.

Learning In Spite of Labels—Joyce Herzog. Greenleaf Press, Lebanon, TN; 1994. A practical set of tips for teaching special children. Offers a Christian view of education and lots of encouragement for new homeschooling families as they consider God's word.

Mathematical Disabilities: What We Know and Don't Know—David C. Geary; 1999. This LDOnLine exclusive article examines the current state of research in the area of math disabilities.

Mathematics and Dyslexia, International Dyslexia Association—An overview of the many ways mathematics learning can be impaired, plus the competencies necessary to instruct students with mathematics learning disabilities.

Math Learning Disabilities—Kate Garnett Ph.D. This article breaks math difficulties down into different types, explains why common teaching practices can perpetuate or exacerbate these problems, and provides ways to structure learning experiences to overcome difficulties in math.

NATHHAN Resource Guide—Provides listings on teaching magazines, organizations and local support groups, testing and assessment information as well as listing of legal organizations and more. P.O. Box 39, Porthill, ID 83853; 253-318-8824.

Parental Rights—Available free as a download from the Virginia Department of Education website under Most Requested Sites: Special Education. Provides the full text of parental rights under the Virginia law's newest revision, in February, 2001. Useful for parents disengaging from the public school or seeking to use public schools for related services. www.doe.virginia.gov.

Phonemic Awareness in Young Children—Marilyn Jager Adams, Barbara R. Foorman, Ingvar Lundberg, and Terri Beeler. Paul Brookes Publishing, Baltimore, MD; 1998. Not *intended* for homeschooling parents, but a rich resource for parents of children suffering from dyslexia and other severe reading problems. The activities presented provide extra reinforcement for those areas of weakness affecting most dyslexic non-readers. Also, this book is a great help for parents who want to help young children beginning to learn about print.

Solving the Puzzle of your Hard to Raise Child—William G. Crook, M.D., and Laura Stevens. Random House, New York, NY; 1987. Dr. Crook exposes the intricate interactions among allergies, foods, and systemic yeast infections that can wreak havoc with a child's ability to focus and learn. Children who have repeatedly suffered respiratory illnesses, ear infections, and allergic reactions may be suffering from the long-term after effects of treatments for their illnesses. Dr. Crook suggests straightforward remedies and steps to bring dramatic improvement.

Special Education: A Biblical Approach—Dr. Joe P. Sutton, ed. Hidden Treasure Ministries, Greenville, NC; 1993. A thorough and Biblical exploration of principles for working with special-needs children. Intended for all educators, the homeschooling parent will find a great deal of wisdom and insight.

Special Parent: Special Child—Tom Sullivan. Jeremy P. Tarcher. Putnam Books, New York, NY; 1995. An up-close exploration of the lives of six families with a special-needs child. Provides some perspective and encouragement.

Strategies for Struggling Learners—Dr. Joe Sutton and Connie J. Sutton. Exceptional Diagnostics, Simpsonville, NC. 1995. This volume lays out many useful strategies for teaching the special-needs child. Directed toward the home educator, Dr. Sutton takes the reader from the basics of diagnosis all the way through modifying learning materials, and much more. A valuable resource.

The Attention-Deficit Child—Dr. Grant Martin. Cook Communications, Colorado Springs, CO; 1998. A Christian perspective on management of the behavior, learning, and relationships of the ADD child. Does not address homeschool, but there is a wealth of up-to-date information and ideas.

The Dyslexic Scholar: Helping Your Child Succeed in the School System—Kathleen Nosek. Taylor Publishing, Dallas, TX; 1995. Despite the title's suggestion that this book is for public school children, this book focuses on the whole child with dyslexia. There are good sections on talking about their difficulties, finding support, and planning beyond high school.

The Learning Disabled Child: Ways That Parents Can Help—Suzanne H. Stevens. John F. Blair, Winston-Salem, NC; 1980. While not the most recent work on LD, this volume is easy reading, and it has practical helps that are very parent centered. Helpful.

The Nontoxic Home and Office—Debra Lynn Dadd. Jeremy P. Tarcher. Putnam Books, New York, NY; 1992. Ms. Dadd's book does not directly focus on children with special needs, but she brings to light an important contributing factor to many children's learning problems—environmental pollution and chemical sensitivity. Today's modern homes are inundated with multitudes of chemicals and fumes that can create neurological damage in the unborn and very young. These changes in the neurological system affect children's learning. This book is an eye-opener.

The Out-of-Sync Child—Carol Stock Kranowitz. Skylight Press, Pedigree, New York. NY; 1998. A very helpful book clearly explaining why the collection of idiosyncrasies about a child may be a problem that can be dealt with and helped. Sensory integrative disorder is not widely recognized, yet it affects many children's learning and daily living. If there seems no explanation for those overly sensitive (or under-sensitive) characteristics about your child, this is the place to seek answers.

The Successful Homeschool Family Handbook—Dr. Raymond and Dorothy

Moore. Thomas Nelson Publishers, Nashville, TN; 1994. A how-to-do-it focusing as much on the practical aspects of being a family in the midst of being teaching parents. The Moore's explain how to find effective solutions for making the homeschool a successful one. While it does not focus on special needs, their flexible approach should give a peace to parents who are struggling.

The Way Children Learn—Cynthia Ulrich Tobias. Tyndale House Publishers, Wheaton, IL; 1994. A helpful introduction to the concept of individual learning styles and the way they can be nurtured to help children learn.

DISABILITY WEB SITES

The following websites provide information about major disability areas of special education. Some are directed to individual areas or disabilities, and others are general resources with a large group of related links. All links were working as of April 2002.

Attention Deficit

www.addwarehouse.com—This company carries many informative materials and resources suited to supporting parents and families. They can also be reached by phone at 800-233-9273 (A.D.D. WARE).

www.chadd.org—National organization for Attention Deficit Disorder.

Asperger's and Autism

www.aspergersdigest.com—This site is loaded with resources and current information, but it is a paid subscription. Interested families may find it worth the cost.

www.familyvillage.wisc.edu—Autism and Asperger's Syndrome.

Asthma

www.aaaai.org—American Academy of Asthma, Allergy and Immunology website with up-to-date links about medical research, practical help, and pages with resources just for kids.

www.healthtalk.com/ae—Healthtalk links to medical information about asthma.

General Special-Needs Resources

www.irsc.org:8080/irsc/irscmain.nsf—The main Internet clearinghouse for links related to special-needs children! Start your search here! Links to Internet community chat groups

www.cec.sped.org—Excellent broad range of authoritative information relating to disabilities and education.

www.hishelpinschool.com—Site focused on strengthening teaching skills for the parents of special-needs students. Practical how-to section on modifying curriculum materials and texts, research-based information on reading, spelling, and more.

www.nathhan.com—Special-needs organization: clearinghouse for a wide range of disabilities resources. Local representative is Deb Pegram in Richmond, VA; 804-323-1726.

www.homeschoolcentral.com—Special education database loaded with many helpful resources.

www.nichcy.org—National Center for Children and Youth with Disabilities produces accurate fact sheets for most exceptionalities. Send for free resources. Especially helpful in learning about different disabilities.

www.specialednews.com—General information and current news and developments on a wide range of disabilities.

www.ldonline.org—Despite its name, this site has a rich source on most areas of special needs. Practical, parent-friendly teaching and background information source.

homeschool.crosswalk.com—General; many sources.

www.specialed.about.com—General coverage of most special-needs topics.

www.mhnet.org—Mental Health (banner ads are an annoying problem, but the site is a very rich source of information).

Learning Disabilities and Dyslexia

www.ldanatl.org—Learning Disabilities Association & Dyslexia.

www.interdys.org—Dyslexia treasure chest. This organization has a wealth of affordable references, and informative booklets. Here is help in testing for dyslexia, tips for working with the children, and more.

www.spalding.org—The name Spalding is intimately associated with the earliest periods of teaching dyslexic students to read. The organization can supply information and teaching materials for interested parents. 1-877-866-7451.

www.dyslexia-teacher.com—A very rich resource with material that is practical and easily used.

www.schwablearning.org—Learning disabilities are the primary focus of this site, which offers good resources at no cost. Look for the booklet on Assistive Technology to get ideas for opening up access to regular curriculum with use of technology.

Congenital/Neurological Difficulties

www.pediatricneurology.com—Birth defects, genetic disorders.

www.ucpa.org—United Cerebral Palsy Association.

www.geocities.com/aneecp—Cerebral palsy; general information.

www.4mychild.com/print-staVA.html—Links to Virginia resources for children with cerebral palsy.

Hearing and Vision Impairments

http://deafness.about.com/library/deafness—Deafness, American Sign Language, hearing assistive technology and more.

www.rfbd.org—Recordings for Blind and Dyslexic. Learn how to get books on tape.

www.ndss.org—Down's Syndrome resource and support.

LEGAL RESOURCES

www.reedmartin.com—Reed Martin is an attorney who specializes in special-education law. His website is full of free articles about special-education law as well as a collections of expensive, but very valuable, booklets for sale on specific topics in the field. If you are a parent of a former public school special-education student, this site is for you.

www.wrightslaw.com—Pete Wright is an adult learning-disabled lawyer who has a heart for helping the families of children—usually in public schools—whose rights under IDEA and other laws may have been violated. Like the Reed Martin site, there is an abundance of reading material available for the downloading, along with items to purchase.

www.ideapractices.org—This site is another rich resource of special-education information, much of which is related to the Federal law: Individuals with Disabilities Education Act (IDEA). It is developed in cooperation with several organizations and the Council for Exceptional Children. You can find resources to learn more about the law, contacts for summer camps for the disabled, and much more.

EDUCATION AND LESSON PLANNING WEB SITES

The following sites overflow with ideas for planning lessons for individualized instruction, units of special interest, and enrichment for the gifted. Most are free, or very reasonable in cost considering the value. Content is not screened specifically for Christian values, but all these linked sites focus on filtering and selecting materials suitable for children. Parental wisdom is always required in selecting lesson material.

www.allkindsofminds.org—This site, referred to recently on a special-education list-serve, has high-quality professional articles coupled with a strong parent-friendly tone. There is a great deal of research-backed information about the nature of learning differences. The articles give solid advice on helping children deal with their disabilities. Parents who are interested in learning styles will find much here to complement that perspective.

www.quia.com—This site is loaded with features that will be very helpful for parents who teach their children, as well for professional educators. There are wonderful "field-trip" links, on-line activities, information on all subjects through high school, foreign languages, and tools for making online quizzes. In addition, there is an option for teachers to make their own free web page, administer quizzes, and more. There is a great deal of excellent material free to a registered user, and there are premium options, such as copying sheets and activities for payment of a fee. The home page provides excellent directions and illustrated help for first-time users.

www.schoolexpress.com—This site is one that appears to offer features similar to the QUIA.com site. There are lesson-planning helps, online activities organized by subject areas, and worksheet printers and printable activities. KONOS users might enjoy some of the Thematic Units. The content is not expressly Christian, but the site appears to have sound educational merit and there does not appear to be anything out of line. As with all sites, parental wisdom and discretion is the key to finding good material. There are some intriguing links to other teacher-friendly materials as well. There are a number of links to online stores.

specialchildren.about.com/parenting/specialchildren—This secular site has current links to almost every area of special needs except home-schooling. There is a great deal of current research and educational helps here.

www.theeducatorsnetwork.com—Rich database on lesson planning, organized by grade and subject matter.

www.schoolhousetech.com—A very reasonably priced site for endless possibilities of teacher-customizable worksheets in math (including high school topics). Vocabulary and Maps are other products. There is a free trial period to experiment with the material before purchase.

www.k12.com—Dr. William Bennett's newest commercial program to promote values-friendly educational programs and curricula. Many materials recommended come from existing publications collected into grade levels.

www.kn.pacbell.com/wired/bluewebn—Another collection of unique and interesting lesson-related websites that are suitable for students. Interested parents can also subscribe (free) for weekly newsletter. Publisher does not share e-mail addresses.

http://westcler.org/wv/geigerj—On this rather cute site, a young child will find many activities that foster learning the alphabet. (Included here because of its special appeal.) There are printable pages, songs associated with each letter and many ways to teach each one. It might be appropriate for older students (maybe age 10) who need more reinforcement to learn their letters with an infinitely patient tutor.

ORGANIZATIONS

Tourette Syndrome Association, Inc.—1301 K Street, Suite 500 East Tower, Washington, D.C. 20005; 202-408-3160. tsdc@tsa-usa.org

Home Educators Association of Virginia (HEAV)—2248-G Dabney Road, Richmond, VA 23230-0745; office@heav.org; www.heav.org

National Challenged Homeschoolers Associated Network (**NATHHAN**)—P.O. Box 39, Porthill, ID 83853; 253-318-8824. NATHHANEWS@aol.com; www.NATHHAN.com

Homeschool Legal Defense Association (HSLDA)—P.O. Box 3000, Purcellville VA. 20134-9000; 540-338-5600. info@hslda.org; www.HSLDA.org

PUBLISHERS

Academic Therapy—20 Commercial Boulevard, Novato CA 94949-6191. Great collection of materials for special students working below reading grade level. Free resources for parents, and visual tracking practice books available. www.academictherapy.com

Educator's Publishing Service—75 Moulton Street, Cambridge, MA 02138-

1104; 800-225-5750. www.epsbooks.com

GlobeFearon / Pacemaker—Normally available through schools, but possibly available through bookstores or "umbrella" schools. Alternatives to regular academic texts that cover basics of upper-grade subjects with lower readability and clean, user-friendly layout.

Lingui-Systems, Inc.—3100 4th Ave., East Moline, IL 61244-9700; 800-776-4332; TDD Phone: 800-933-8331. service@linguisystems. The "*Exclusively LD*" catalog is loaded with good activities, learning games, and informative books suitable for LD, Autism, pervasive developmental disorders, language and auditory processing delays, and much more. Background-information books are sold covering a wide range of syndromes and disabilities.

Remedia Publications—15887 N. 76th St. #120, Scottsdale, AZ; 800-826-4740. Superb collection of teacher-made materials for students at basic skills level. Many resources are suitable for older students.

Steck-Vaughn Publishers—Great publisher for high-interest, lower reading vocabulary materials in the basic skills. Good workbooks and specific skill materials at reasonable costs. www.steck-vaughn.com

SOFTWARE FOR TEACHING

Color Phonics—Eve Engelbrite Education. 1996. Available new through Alpha-Omega Publications and through Amazon.com. Current research led to this program, incorporating sound awareness, multi-sensory input, and high motivation for learners through grade six. Five CD's track student progress, review content answered incorrectly, and print out progress charts. A very effective program with a good teacher center for tracking progress. Priced very reasonably. First CD may require parental assistance to explain some unusual vocabulary choices that illustrate new sounds.

Ultimate Phonics Reading Program: Words and Sentences—Spencer Learning, San Diego, CA; 2000. www.spencerlearning.com. This program is short on cute games or distracting graphics. It is exactly what it calls itself: a systematic introduction to the sounds of the written language taught in phonetically consistent words that are then used in sentences. The child listens to carefully pronounced sounds and then repeats what is heard. Great initial teaching or reinforcement.

Used with permission: www.helpinschool.net.

Gifted Education

Compiled by Beth Wright Bess

Additional Articles on the CD
BE SURE TO CHECK OUT THESE OTHER GREAT ARTICLES ON THE CD!

Each article in the book and on the CD has been carefully chosen by the section coordinator to increase your knowledge and understanding of this subject, so don't forget to use and enjoy the parts of the manual on your CD, as well as the part you are holding.

Please note that the page numbering on the CD is different from that of the hard-copy manual.

Homeschooling Your Gifted Child

INTRODUCTION

For many years, the homeschooling community has been reluctant to "label" kids as gifted. Perhaps the popularity of the sentimentality, "all children are gifted," has conditioned parents to feel embarrassed about wanting to identify their gifted child's special abilities. Perhaps our public school system's egalitarian leanings have stigmatized giftedness as wanting to appear to be better or more deserving than others. Perhaps parents are loath to be called "stage moms," or "pushy."

Whatever the reason, there exists little gifted education literature designed specifically for homeschoolers. With so little guidance, what are parents to do when they suspect their young one may be gifted? How do they meet his academic and emotional needs? What if he is exhibiting behaviors that do not respond to typical parental guidance or discipline?

Thankfully, answers to all of these questions, and more, exist in the gifted education research that has been amassed for over eighty years. Applying these answers to homeschooling is easy. Many gifted education researchers tout homeschooling as the best educational option for gifted children. Some researchers even believe parents are best equipped to determine their child's giftedness. Researchers trust parents' perceptions of their gifted children's abilities and needs, and they recommend homeschooling for the one-on-one attention it affords the little learner.

—Beth Wright Bess
beth@smartkidathome.com
www.smartkidathome.com

Characteristics of Giftedness:
How Can You Tell if Your Child is Gifted?

Beth Wright Bess

Gifted people possess a specific set of variable traits. Using those traits as identification, parents can begin to view their child's behaviors, needs, and abilities in light of possible giftedness. Since, however, many parents of gifted children are themselves gifted, it may be hard for the parents to see their child's accomplishments as unusual. Using objective criteria for determining giftedness behavior and accomplishment, parents will be able to see the child as gifted, and perhaps, for the first time, understand him.

The following *Characteristics of Giftedness Scale* is provided courtesy of the Gifted Development Center, in Denver, Colorado.

Several studies were conducted between 1981 and 1986 to determine the validity of this set of characteristics, and the list has been refined to incorporate the research findings. The following 25 characteristics have resulted:

CHARACTERISTICS OF GIFTEDNESS SCALE
1. Good problem-solving/reasoning abilities
2. Rapid-learning ability
3. Extensive vocabulary
4. Excellent memory
5. Long attention span
6. Personal sensitivity
7. Compassion for others
8. Perfectionism
9. Intensity
10. Moral sensitivity
11. Unusual curiosity
12. Perseverant when interested
13. High degree of energy
14. Preference for older companions
15. Wide range of interests
16. Great sense of humor
17. Early or avid reading ability
18. Concerned with justice, fairness

19. At times, judgment seems mature for age
20. Keen powers of observation
21. Vivid imagination
22. High degree of creativity
23. Tends to question authority
24. Shows ability with numbers
25. Good at jigsaw puzzles

If a child demonstrates more than three-fourths of these traits, it is likely that he or she is gifted.

The key to identifying giftedness lies not in the assumption that giftedness produces accomplishment. For many gifted children, factors such as uneven development or attendant learning disabilities may keep them from accomplishments that are socially accepted as indicative of giftedness. For this reason, researchers, educators, and parents agree that giftedness may be described instead as advanced cognitive ability, intensity, and curiosity, combined with heightened sensitivity to self, others, and the world.

CHARACTERISTICS OF LEARNING BEHAVIORS

How can you tell if your child has advanced cognitive ability if he is an underachiever, learning disabled, or pre-vocal? There are many signs of high learning ability. Knowing what to look for is the key.

Keep in mind that giftedness characteristics become more pronounced with each successive level of giftedness—the characteristics are epitomized by an eagerness, an intensity, a drive, and a concentration bordering on passion. The gifted child may not display a passion for math, but may become obsessed with learning to identify all types of birds or spiders. He may spend many hours in deep concentration while constructing a Lego® creation, building a sand castle, or putting together a puzzle. He may endeavor to read books twice his grade level or quickly master a skill commensurate with years of study.

Intellectual intensity may be demonstrated by the toddler who sits quietly on the sofa looking at book after book for hours. Or, you may see higher cognitive ability in obvious ways, such as a ten-year-old who is eager to learn calculus. Whatever the variation, advanced cognitive ability affords gifted children an ability to reason, extrapolate, make connections between seemingly unrelated concepts, and create systems of logic in order to grasp a unifying order for specific subjects.

Use the following checklist to see if your child exhibits any of the described behaviors. This checklist of giftedness learning characteristics is reprinted courtesy of Western Australia's Department of Education.

LEARNING:
- Is a rapid learner who understands advanced topics easily
- Shows insight and fantasies about cause-effect relationships
- Persists in completing tasks

- Sees the problem quickly and takes the initiative
- Learns basic skills quickly and with little practice
- Is reluctant to practice skills already mastered
- Follows complex directions easily
- Constructs and handles high levels of abstraction
- Can cope with more than one idea at a time
- Has strong critical-thinking skills and is self critical
- Has surprising perception and deep insight
- Is a keen and alert observer, notes detail, and is quick to see similarities and differences
- Displays intellectual and physical restlessness; once encouraged, is seldom a passive learner
- Has a remarkable range of general (or specialized) knowledge in one or more areas
- Possesses extensive general knowledge (often knows more than the teachers) and finds classroom books superficial
- Explores wide-ranging and special interests, frequently at great depth
- Has quick mastery and recall of information, seems to need no revision, and is impatient with repetition
- Learns to read early and retains what is read, can recall in detail
- Has advanced understanding and use of language, but sometimes hesitates as the correct word is searched for and used
- Sees greater significance in a story or film and continues the story
- Demonstrates a richness of imagery in informal language and brainstorming
- Can ask unusual (even awkward) questions or make unusual contributions to class discussions
- Asks many provocative, searching questions which tend to be unlike those asked by other students the same ages
- Has exceptional curiosity and constantly wants to know the reasons why
- Displays intellectual playfulness
- Often sees unusual, rather than conventional, relationships
- Can produce original and imaginative work, even if defective in technical accuracy (e.g. poor spelling or handwriting)
- Wants to debate topics at greater depth
- Mental speed is faster than writing ability, so is often reluctant to write at length
- Prefers to talk rather than write and talks at high speed with fluency and expression

ASYNCHRONY:

Asynchrony is uneven development in the abilities of a gifted person. Asynchrony accounts for many of the misconceptions about giftedness. In average children, cognitive abilities are on par with emotional maturity levels and the result is a good social fit. The average ten-year-old acts and thinks like an average ten-year-old. The gifted ten-year-old, however, may act like a ten-year-old and think like a fifteen-year-old. Depending on the level of giftedness, asynchrony may be mild or pronounced. Exceptionally gifted children with an IQ of 160 to 180, may, at ten, converse with adults, read Plato, and fight with a brother over an action figure.

Asynchrony makes life with the gifted anything but dull.

Identification Methods:
Do You Need IQ Tests?

Beth Wright Bess

So, you suspect that your child is gifted, but you would like concrete proof? Perhaps testing would be an appropriate choice for your child. In order to make that determination, you need information about proper testing instruments, correct testing ages, and how to find a qualified tester.

DO YOU NEED IQ TESTS?

IQ tests have been the darlings of psychologists and educators for decades. Used to route and sort children, they are the tools of special services program directors hoping to appropriately accommodate every child. With so many children in attendance, schools need a method for determining who needs special help and who is normal.

But, do homeschooling parents need to know their child's IQ? Why would a homeschooler need a test score? Many homeschooling parents don't feel the need for "proof" of their child's intellect, see IQ scores as irrelevant to their daily lives, or are wary of a score that may give their child a sense of superiority over others.

Many well-respected gifted education researchers say that when parents suspect their child is gifted, they are rarely wrong! However, some parents feel unsure of their informal assessment of their child, and for various reasons desire an official verdict from a trained professional. For them, receiving proof of IQ is crucial to the education of their child, enabling them to acknowledge the child's need for radical acceleration options and curriculum flexibility.

There are also logistical reasons for obtaining an IQ score. A child who wants to take special classes may require IQ scores for entrance. Some national gifted-education programs require an IQ score in a specific range, i.e., Davidson Young Fellows and Davidson Fellowship offered by the Davidson Institute for Talent Development. Gaining entry into certain organizations such as MENSA requires an IQ score. And, some children use the scores to gain financial aid from organizations like the National Gifted Children's Fund, which requires an IQ score of 150 from applicants who wish to qualify for grants.

WHAT CAN BE LEARNED FROM TESTING?

Many gifted children are also learning disabled and parents turn to testing in order to determine their child's special needs. The subtests on tests such as the WISCIII may provide clues for understanding the child's problems, and when ceilings are reached on those instruments, then an instrument with a higher ceiling will accurately determine the child's level of giftedness. Savvy testers turn to the Stanford Binet Form L-M, and the recently published Stanford Binet 5, for further testing when there is significant subtest scatter on the WAIS or WISCIII. These IQ tests allow for maximum sensitivity to high verbal ability, a trait many exceptionally and profoundly gifted children posses.

Highly, exceptionally, and profoundly gifted children often ceiling even the Stanford Binet L-M after the age of eight, so testing with the SB L-M is generally recommended for children ages three to eight. While an older child may be tested with the L-M, and an IQ score derived, if he is very gifted, his score will be depressed and not reflective of his abilities.

That's why testers have begun using the new Stanford Binet 5. Using the SB5 enables the tester to deliver a close-to-accurate score when the child is assumed to be highly, exceptionally, or profoundly gifted. Children scoring in such ranges benefit most from radical acceleration, and gaining an accurate assessment of their abilities is essential to parents as they seek to meet the child's needs academically.

According to Riverside Publishing (the company that publishes the SB L-M and SB5), "The features of the Stanford Binet Intelligence Scales, Fifth Edition (SB5) make the test useful for the assessment of high abilities in both general and gifted assessment. These features include high ceilings for standard ability scores, continuous testing of abilities in a single instrument from early childhood through old age, extended IQ scores (with a theoretical upper limit of 225 IQ), and gifted composite scores that optimize assessment for gifted program selection."

ONCE THE IQ SCORE IS ATTAINED, WHAT TYPE OF CLASSIFICATION DOES EACH LEVEL RECEIVE?

Gifted education researchers have designed an IQ chart, with attendant monikers, for describing the cognitive abilities of gifted children. Abilities vary between these levels, with the general characteristics of giftedness increasing in intensity as the IQ rises.

GIFTEDNESS CLASSIFICATIONS AND THE IQ SCORE CHART

130+	gifted
130-145	moderately gifted
145-160	highly gifted
160-180	exceptionally gifted
180+	profoundly gifted
200+	sometimes jokingly referred to as terminally gifted

FINDING THE RIGHT TESTER

Finding the right tester is absolutely essential if you are to gain an accurate numerical representation of your child's abilities. While mildly and moderately gifted children may not be terribly shortchanged by an inept assessment, highly, exceptionally, and profoundly gifted children can be found to have scores that grossly under-represent their abilities if the tester is not familiar with proper testing procedures for that population.

Don't take your child to the local college education department tester or public school psychologist and expect accurate results. Even professionals who claim to be gifted education experts may not be capable of assessing your profoundly gifted child. Use the wrong tester and you could go home with a score that isn't even high enough for your child to be classified as gifted using the aforementioned chart. For children in the higher gifted ranges and those with learning disabilities, such a disparity between actual ability and score is almost assured. If the need for an IQ score is important enough to warrant the trouble and expense of testing, make sure your result is accurate!

See Hoagies Gifted Pages website for testers in various states and countries and for articles about testing. www.hoagiesgifted.org/psychologists.htm

RECOMMENDED TESTERS

There are several highly recommended testers on the East Coast who will be capable of helping you, should you choose to have your child tested. These testers have well-established reputations and are either published or lecture in their field:

New York
Julia Osborn
Clinton Street, 1K
Brooklyn, NY 11202
Phone and FAX: 718-522-4824

Virginia
Nadia Webb, Psy.D., Clinical Neuropsychologist
Nadia Webb & Associates, LLC
312 South Main Street
Harrisonburg, VA 22801
Phone: 540-433-6886, FAX: 540-433-0248
e-mail: NadiaWebb@aol.com

Maryland
CTY Diagnostic and Counseling Center
Johns Hopkins University
Phone: 410-516-8301

Curriculum Options:
What Kind of Curriculum Should You Use?

Beth Wright Bess

L ooking back at our first section about giftedness characteristics, we notice that many gifted children learn very differently from non-gifted children. This fact requires parents to meet their children's academic needs through methods that accommodate that difference. Forcing your gifted child to learn through methods that are alien to him will not only frustrate him, but could turn him off to learning entirely.

Lateral thinking, global thinking, abstract thinking, visual-spatial thinking, and other terms have been used to describe the way that gifted people think. From the top down, or the opposite of sequentially, the gifted child's learning process requires an overview before the details, the big picture before the first puzzle piece. What are the implications of such neural "hard-wiring"?

These kids are bored silly by repetition, A-Z fact accumulation, sequential skill mastery, and other popular public school pedagogy. They become frustrated with textbooks that break information down into bite-size pieces because they are starving for the whole story. This need for speed flies in the face of all conventional academic wisdom. Children have to be led to the facts, told what to believe, and then drilled until they memorize them. Right?

Wrong, if your child is gifted.

Gifted children are capable of understanding complex subjects intuitively. They grasp underlying patterns of logic. They see the theory, the concept, and the gestalt.

How then, is the homeschooling parent to teach such an unusual learner? Respect for the child's learning process is a first step in the right direction. Believe in his ability to make intuitive leaps. Know that he wants to achieve. Then, present him with the tools to do so.

SO MANY HOMESCHOOLING METHODS!

Which method should parents choose for their gifted child? The answer to that question depends upon too many factors to allow for a one-size-fits-all answer. The child's learning style, personality, birth order, and any attendant disabilities combine to form unique academic requirements. However, some generalities may be made about the three methods that represent the homeschooling method spectrum.

TRADITIONAL TEXTBOOKS

Parents love traditional textbook-based curricula because they are all-inclusive and help parents to avoid those dreaded "holes" in subject-skill mastery. However, traditional textbook-based curricula can become black holes for gifted kids in the homeschool when parents are afraid to allow the child to learn outside the tightly controlled circle of chapter readings, chapter tests, workbooks, and such. Many parents feel like failures when their gifted child wants to stop following the prescribed order for subject study and move on to more exciting subjects. When parents force the child to stick with the curriculum's schedule, some gifted children develop behavior problems and parents may think that sending them to regular school is the answer.

UNSCHOOLING

The opposite extreme from textbook-based curricula, unschooling may provide the gifted child with the freedom to pursue any subject he wishes, to the depth he desires. Often, when combined with mentorships, apprenticeships, lots of museum and library study, unschooling is a fine educational method that meets the needs of the ever-changing gifted child. Most appropriate for the family that is less-structured, rigid, or schedule-oriented, unschooling suits parents with little investment in "acting like a school."

However, not all gifted children thrive when unschooling. Some may need more structure in order to find their momentum. Some, due to disabilities, may need parents to establish order and rules for their learning. Some children with especially concrete sequential learning styles may need a more orderly presentation of academic materials.

ECLECTIC HOMESCHOOLING

This method seems to offer the best of both worlds. The eclectic method offers the parents control over core subjects. The 3 R's become the cornerstone for the homeschool and parents insist on the child's mastery of each. Parents tailor the type of materials and approach to the child's learning style and keep the child on track with respect to work accomplished. Eclectic method is flexible enough to allow for the very visual-spatial child who learns math with manipulatives, the sequential child who prefers workbooks, and the highly intuitive global child who learns through radical acceleration with a mentor.

Beyond the 3 R's, eclectic method allows the child to choose the subject focus for science and history, enjoying a collaborative process of choosing materials, venues, and enrichment with the parent. Eclectic method may be the perfect homeschooling method for gifted children as it keeps mom and dad in charge of the direction, focus, and scheduling of learning, while affording the child as much input as he desires.

HOW TO TEACH GIFTED CHILDREN?

Homeschooling affords parents the luxury that public school teachers never have. No gifted program can approximate the same wonderful circumstances you possess in your home. What is your advantage? You can spend time with your child; one-on-one, concentrated, focused time. Research indicates that tutorials are the most effective mode of information communication. Just one more reason why homeschooling is the best way to educate your child!

Because many gifted children, especially high-IQ children, hate to write, spell badly, and love to play with math, there are specific accommodations and strategies parents may use to facilitate their child's academic success from an early age. Very abstract children may need special accommodations in other subjects, as well. The following list suggests some tips and strategies:

- Allow your child to dictate stories to you.
- Do not force him to write. It may be either painful or frustrating for him
- Sloppy handwriting is not necessarily a sign of laziness
- Some young gifted children enjoy practicing lovely handwriting as an art form, but develop bad handwriting once writing is used as a means of communication.
- Speak well! Many gifted children learn proper grammar through conversation.
- Horrible spelling is often the calling card of the highly gifted.
- Remediation exercises for bad spelling and poor handwriting may make your child feel stupid.
- *Alpha Smart* word processors are being used widely in school systems as an accommodation for handwriting difficulties.
- Buy a typing tutorial computer program for your gifted child.
- Typing is an acceptable substitute for handwriting.
- Very abstract children may need help gathering their thoughts aloud to parents or to a tape recorder before beginning an outline for a paper.
- Writing outlines may be VERY difficult for some abstract gifted children to accomplish (even verbally-fluent children).
- Allow your child to dictate math solutions to you.
- Allow your child to skip "showing his work" in math problems as long as he gets the answer right.
- Do not force your child to use the "school" method of functions and equations if he can utilize his own method for the same problem.
- Allow your child to do math work that is not in sequential order.
- Trust that the child who is flirting with algebra, trigonometry, or calculus "before he is ready," is ready.
- "Drill and kill" usually is an inappropriate pedagogy for gifted children.
- Allow your child to read above grade level.
- Do not force your child to write summaries about every story or book he reads; he processes so many thoughts about the story that retrieving those thoughts after the fact may be maddening for him.
- Encourage your child to chat about what he reads, thereby providing you with an informal summary of his reading without frustrating him unduly.
- Provide him with reading material that is commensurate with his interests.
- Allow him to choose books from the adult section of the library, even if

he only looks at the pictures.

- Encourage him to read adult-level magazines about his favorite subject; don't provide only children's magazines on the subject.
- Read to him, even after he can read for himself.
- Textbook reading material may be boring and superficial: read library books on key subjects instead.
- Don't be afraid to let him read a book that is "too hard for him" if he picks it.
- If he drops a book after only a cursory pass at reading it, don't panic, he is flexing his mental muscles and gearing up for the next pass. He may not re-approach that book for a year or more, let him take his time. [In fact, in his "cursory pass," he may now know more about the book than most readers—or even the author! (For instance, that it is poorly written, inaccurate, or a waste of time for him.)]

Curriculum Options:

Curriculum Compacting: A Necessity for Academic Advancement

by Del Siegle,
University of Connecticut, Storrs, Connecticut

U nfortunately, the reward for many students who master course work quickly is more of the same. It is little wonder that academically advanced students often report feeling bored and unchallenged (Plucker & McIntire, 1996). Instead of completing work quickly that they know they have already mastered, they sometimes become disenchanted, mentally drop out, and fail to finish even the simplest of assignments. From 5 to 15% of secondary students could benefit from some form of curricular modification.

Curriculum compacting is one of the most common forms of curriculum modification for academically advanced students. It is also the basic procedure upon which many other types of modification are founded. Compacting is based on the premise that students who demonstrate they have mastered course content, or can master course content more quickly, can buy time to study material that they find more challenging and interesting (Renzulli & Reis, 1985).

Both basic skills and course content can be compacted. Although basic-skills compacting is easier for teachers new to the process, the latter is probably more common in secondary schools. Basic-skills compacting involves determining what basic skills students have mastered, and eliminating the practice or repetition of those skills. For example, beginning chemistry students who have demonstrated mastery of the periodic table would have little need for further drill and practice in its use and would be better served by advancing to more complex course content.

Sometimes, academically advanced students may not have mastered course content, but they are capable of doing so at an accelerated pace. They may have some understanding of the content and may require minimal time or instruction for mastery. In these cases, content compacting is useful. Perhaps a sophomore class is reading *To Kill a Mockingbird* and reflecting on the societal ramifications of racial prejudice. Some students read at a much faster rate and are able to cover the novel more quickly than others or are able to demonstrate mastery of the objectives associated with the novel. A former student of mine relayed the following story about his sophomore experience with the novel.

Josh loved to read and was excited when his sophomore teacher distributed *To Kill a Mockingbird* on Friday afternoon. She assigned the first few chapters for weekend reading. Josh was scheduled to play a basketball game that evening and decided to start reading the book on the bus trip to the game. He became engrossed in the story and finished reading the novel that evening after returning from the trip. Monday morning he reported to his literature teacher that it was a great book.

"You didn't finish it already," she commented. After a short conversation, she was convinced he had.

"What are we reading next?" he asked. She gave him the next novel. He finished it in a couple of days and asked for the next one.

She hesitated, "I don't want you mixing up the stories when we discuss them in class, so I'm not going to give you the next one."

"...I'm not going to mix up *To Kill a Mockingbird* with—" the other widely different book, he said. He enjoyed the class discussion and didn't want to miss it. He simply wanted to continue reading interesting literature. This young man would have been a good candidate for content compacting.

I once explained compacting to several junior-high students who were part of a study being conducted by The National Research Center on the Gifted and Talented. One asked, "What is it again?"

I explained that their teacher was planning to test them on their school material and they would then not be required to do worksheets or workbook pages for the material they already knew. One young woman looked at me rather puzzled and said, "Well, that just makes sense." Curriculum compacting does "just make sense." Each year thousands of students coast academically as they repeat material that they already have mastered or which they could easily master in a fraction of the time.

Imagine that you've just finished vacuuming your home and your spouse arrives. After complimenting you on how nice the house looks, your spouse suggests that you vacuum it again. When you question your spouse, s/he responds that you might forget how to vacuum and you ought to practice. After you refuse, your spouse tells a friend that s/he can't understand why you didn't want to vacuum the house again. Your spouse notes that s/he knows that you know how to vacuum but can't understand why you "just won't do it." While this story may seem absurd, may of us have heard teaching colleagues complain about one of their students who knows how do a particular worksheet or homework assignment, but the student "just won't do it." Perhaps, like the vacuuming incident, if the student has demonstrated that he or she knows the material, it doesn't need to be repeated again.

The compacting procedure is simple: Determine what the students already know and what they still need to learn, and replace it with more challenging material that they would like to learn (Starko, 1986). Generally, two basic principles are recommended when compacting. First, grades should be based on the material compacted (what the student has mastered), rather than the replacement material. Students may be reluctant to tackle more challenging material if they risk receiving lower grades that may reduce their chances for academic scholarships. This is not to say that replacement activities should not be evaluated. Second, replacement material should be based on student interests. Since replacement material will require greater student effort, the task commitment and responsibility necessary to work independently (which is often, but not always, the learning situation) mandate that the student have a vested interest in the content.

There are eight basic steps to curriculum compacting.
1. Determine the learning objectives for the material.
2. Find an appropriate way to assess those objectives.
3. Identify students who may have already mastered the objectives (or could master them more quickly).
4. Assess those students to determine their mastery level.
5. Streamline practice or instruction for students who demonstrate mastery of the objectives.
6. Provide small-group or individual instruction for students who have not yet mastered all of the objectives, but are capable of doing so more quickly than their classmates.
7. Offer more challenging academic alternatives based on student interest.
8. Maintain a record of the compacting process and instructional options provided. (Reis, Burns, & Renzulli, 1992a)

Educators new to the process should consider the following recommendations:
- Start with one or two responsible students.
- Select content with which they feel comfortable.
- Try a variety of methods to determine student mastery of the material (a brief conversation with a student may be just as effective as a written pretest).
- Compact by topic rather than time.
- Define proficiency based on a consensus with administrators and parents.
- Don't be afraid to request help from available sources such as community volunteers. (Reis, Burns, & Renzulli, 1992b)

Curriculum compacting works best when adopted by a school district as a regular part of good teaching practices. When superintendents, principals, and other administrators support and encourage the process it is certainly much easier. All students, including those who are academically advanced, are entitled to an education in which instruction is geared to their needs, interests, and developmental levels.

Being a teacher is an awesome responsibility. It means being given charge of the nation's most valuable resource, the talent of its youth, and helping develop it. It means working with future O'Keeffes or Einsteins or Steinbecks at a time when they are most vulnerable, when they are learning about themselves and their talents. If those talents are not developed and recognized, the loss is not only to the nation, but to the individuals who, when not challenged, often fall into patterns of underachievement and bore-dom. By providing an appropriately modified and differentiated educational experience, such as curriculum compacting, the buds of youth do open into radiant blooms of productive and fulfilled adults.

REFERENCES

Plucker, J. A., & McIntire, J. (1996). Academic survivability in high-potential, middle school students. *Gifted Child Quarterly, 40,* 7-14.

Reis, S. M., Burns, D. E., & Renzulli, J. S. (1992a). *Curriculum Compacting: The Complete Guide to Modifying the Regular Curriculum for High Ability Students.* Mansfield Center, CT: Creative Learning Press.

Reis, S. M., Burns, D. E., & Renzulli, J. S. (1992b). *A Facilitator's Guide to Help Teachers Compact Curriculum.* Storrs, CT: University of Connecticut, The National Research Center on the Gifted and Talented.

Renzulli, J. S., & Reis, S. M. (1985). *The Schoolwide Enrichment Model: A Comprehensive Plan for Educational Excellence.* Mansfield Center, CT: Creative Learning Press.

Starko, A. J. (1986). *It's About Time: Inservice Strategies for Curriculum Compacting.* Mansfield Center, CT: Creative Learning Press.

Early College:
Options, Options, Options...

Beth Wright Bess

H ere are some of the things you need to consider as you plan to use college classes for your child: watch the grade-skipping if you plan to use dual-enrollment status; make a transcript that reflects all of your child's work; utilize non-matriculating courses; don't overlook auditing courses; and learn to take their "no" in stride!

DON'T "SKIP" OUT OF DUAL-ENROLLMENT STATUS:

For all of you parents thinking of radically accelerating your child right out of school, emancipating him or her, so to speak, think again. If you plan to ease them into college one class at a time, dual enrollment is the way to go. Many parents use dual enrollment at first, as it is the easiest and least-formal method of gaining college credits for children.

"Our local community college's handbook only had a restriction as to what 'grade' the student was enrolled." Said Beverly, "At the time, we listed Conner as a senior in high school and enrolled him under their 'dual enrollment' category for gifted high school juniors and seniors. All I had to do is prove he was gifted since we homeschooled him. That I did with a 'homebrewed' complete transcript listing every class he ever took at the high school level (54 semester hours by my count, 34 or 38 by the official transcript we got from Clonlara, a school that also offers distance enrollment to home-schoolers), which included complete course descriptions, his official transcripts from Stanford University's EPGY and Northwestern University's LetterLinks programs, as well as his Stanford Achievement scores and SB-LM score."

How did this family fare when they approached the college? "They were taken aback when we approached them; it did take five months to find approval and they had to go all the way to the president's office for approval, but there was nothing in their student handbook that said a nine-year-old senior in high school (albeit homeschooled) could not enroll in classes," said Beverly.

Other parents have used the dual-enrollment status to their advantage as well. Since dually enrolled students are typically between the ages of 16 and 18, most colleges, it seems, will want proof of the child's giftedness. You may provide this proof by your child's school system's classification of your child as gifted, IQ test scores, an avalanche of homeschooling projects and advanced subjects studied, or even a personal interview with the dean of admissions.

HOW TO PREPARE YOUR CHILD'S TRANSCRIPT:

High school transcripts are documents designed to demonstrate the subjects accomplished by the student. Transcripts assign a specific number of points to each completed high school class or semester for every year the student is in high school. High school transcripts never include courses taken in middle school. So, how do you document your profoundly gifted child's work when he may have been "officially" in the first grade when he accomplished the work?

I turned to several popular books designed for homeschoolers preparing for college. While much of their advice was targeted to the older child, it was very useful for the organization of the subjects and such. One of those titles, *The Homeschooler's Guide to Portfolios and Transcripts*, by Loretta Heur, M.Ed., offers this astute advice: "Before you get down to the brass tacks of writing your curriculum, acquire a copy of a high school course selection handbook. This should be a public document available through your state's department of education, your superintendent's office, or your local high school's guidance department."

As you prepare your child's transcript, keep in mind the type of subjects offered by the local high school. These are the types of courses you should highlight. If you have one of those kids who obsessed over one subject for three years, it may be a little tricky to show the level of work he accomplished. Perhaps you can break down those three years into several subjects and show them as separate entities. My son's study of ancient Rome really incorporates a good bit of generalized world civilizations studies and I would note that as a separate course from the Roman History. His extensive readings in the subject of Roman and Greek mythology also qualify as a separate subject as he spent as much time reading those as he would have if he had been taking a college class on the subject. The year he spent 10 hours a day reading physics books? AP (Advanced Placement) physics! The year he spirited away my husband's college chemistry textbook, reading it all day, every day, memorizing the periodic table of elements and working chemistry problems for fun? AP Chemistry for sure! See how easy it is to make a transcript?

Beverly made Conner's transcript with the help of Cafi Cohen's book, *And What About College: How Homeschooling Leads to the Best Colleges and Universities*. She tells, "I took every course Conner had done at the high school level and wrote a complete course description of it to include in the transcript. In the case of courses done through Stanford's EPGY and Northwestern's *LetterLinks*' program, I just had to copy down the course description they provided when we first enrolled in the classes. The same was done for the college classes he took. I listed all special camps, with a brief description of what the camp was about and how many hours Conner attended. The camps were similar to attending workshops and conferences, so credit was given here, too."

"I included any special awards Conner had earned, as well as any publications of his work. An admissions committee should note them. Theatrical performances, musical recitals, clubs, organizations, and special interests were all noted in his transcript as well. Finally, I also included a reading list in the transcript. This was a list of all high-school-level reading Conner had done (much of it through the Junior Great Books Program we did for his English credits)," Beverly adds.

Like all unschoolers, I love options, and Cafi Cohen offers an endless variety in her wonderful book, *Homeschooler's College Admissions Handbook*. She writes, "Fortunately, there is no One Right Way to write a homeschool transcript—or any transcript, for that matter. Examine transcripts from your relatives, friends, and family to see what I mean. From small private schools to large public schools to charter schools to homeschools, transcripts assume an incredible variety of forms. They use different grading systems—or no grading system. They report academics by semesters or, more simply, by completion date. Some look professional. Others—including some from large, well-known high schools—use a bare-bones format."

I made a transcript for Octavian, and it was fun and easy. Since we have always used portfolios for yearly homeschooling evaluations, all I had to do was go through them to verify his work, book titles, textbooks used, projects, awards and anything else I wanted to include. The college preparation advice I found in *Gifted Children at Home* reminded me to include my son's jewelry business on the transcript, even though he developed it when he was only seven!

I used the advice offered in Cohen's book about rewarding credit for subjects studied unconventionally, and managed to come up with a whopping 67 credits! I was excited about using this transcript in August, when we met the admissions officer at the local community college (the one that turned him away three years ago due to his age) to attempt to secure his admission there as a part time student. I'm learning!

NON-MATRICULATING COURSES:

One of the coolest tricks I have heard for gaining college admission for young profoundly gifted kids comes from Cathy, "Community college in our state seems to be easier to get into than high school. Moira entered via a 'back door'—an open enrollment theatre class/group—at 8 (the director simply looked at her, commented 'The costumers are going to love you,' and went on about directing the play) and has since taken language courses, art, and a world history class..."

Some community colleges are sticklers for adhering to their minimum-age requirements and finding creative solutions to this problem may take some thought. Apparently one such loophole is whether or not the child is degree-seeking. Cathy found that their local community college's policy was, "...no questions asked; as long as she isn't in a degree program or seeking college credit, they only need an address and a social security number."

What kind of classes could a profoundly gifted child find in a not-for-credit program? Cathy's daughter was, "taking classes that are not part of their associate degree program, like Italian I and Theatre (they also have Vegetarian Cooking, Knitting, *et cetera*) and most of the people taking the classes are adults taking them for pleasure or in preparation for travel. The question of auditing, etc., didn't come up: she just signed up and paid a registration fee."

The courses not listed with attendant credit hours fit the bill when it comes to this type of community college entrance. The credit hours are noted in the course catalogue as numbers beside the name of the course. Many community colleges offer adult-enrichment classes that have no such credit-hour designation. My twelve-year-old son, Antony, plans to take a web-design class like this in the fall through a university's program called "Center For Community Learning."

THE DRY RUN: AUDITING COLLEGE COURSES

Auditing may be an ideal solution to the trepidation parents feel about the early-college-class dilemma. When your child audits a course, you register him, pay the course fee, and procure the professor's permission for your child's attendance. However, he does not receive a grade to be recorded on a transcript.

Why would you want to spend good money for your child to take a class for which he will not receive credit? Some kids need a "dry run." A chance to do the work, take the tests, and write the reports without the pressures of a grade and a permanent record; an audited course may give your gifted child a confidence boost. Once he sees that he can accomplish the work, he may feel confident enough to conquer another class.

Our son audited his first college class, Latin Literature. He found the readings easy, his note-taking skills adequate (surprise, surprise!), and the exams challenging but manageable. I'm not fond of tests, so the Latin Literature exam was his first academic test in a classroom setting. We asked the professor to grade all of his work and his final grade was a B+, even though it does not appear on his permanent record. With his newfound confidence, our son tackled a senior-level course the next semester.

Since the audited course serves as a validation of your child's readiness for college classes, choosing the right course is crucial. It is best to allow your child to choose a favorite subject. Do not try to cover potentially boring core material such as writing or math, unless your child loves these subjects. Be aware of your child's relative mental age and choose accordingly. Many freshman-level courses may be too superficial to meet your child's need for an in-depth treatment of the subject.

Chat with the respective professors of your child's chosen classes, asking about such matters as class size (the smaller the better), his teaching style (discussion format being best), course textbooks, and how he feels about a youngster in his class (beware of professors who hold unfavorable biases against children). Once you have weighed all the options, choose the class that meets your child's needs and watch him soar.

Extracurricular Activities

Compiled by Darlene Levy

Additional Articles on the CD
BE SURE TO CHECK OUT THESE OTHER GREAT ARTICLES ON THE CD!

Each article in the book and on the CD has been carefully chosen by the section coordinator to increase your knowledge and understanding of this subject, so don't forget to use and enjoy the parts of the manual on your CD, as well as the part you are holding.

Please note that the page numbering on the CD is different from that of the hard-copy manual.

Introduction

o find unlimited opportunities for fun and inexpensive local activities:
- Read the local paper daily, or access their Arts Section online;
- Belong to a homeschool group that e-mails activity information regularly;
- Online, do local searches of museums, malls, history, cities (see: The Search for Extra-Curricular Activities);
- Pick up every free local publication you see;
- Watch bulletin boards, posters, and signs as you go around town.

Homeschoolers are *not* under-socialized: Parents and children find themselves busy from dawn to dark with home, school, church, and extra-curricular activities. So, before committing your valuable time and energy, there are many topics to be considered wisely:
- Are you looking to be involved in the activity, run the program, or serve the group?
- Do you want to drop the kids off, or make it a family activity?
- How often do you want to be involved…once, occasionally, daily, weekly, monthly, seasonally?
- How will this commitment fit into your school day (and life)?
- Are you looking for a secular or religious environment?
- How much are you willing to spend in time, finances, and transportation?
- Are you willing for your children to be under someone else's leadership and influence?
- Is this a contracted commitment, or are you leaving yourself an "escape" clause if it doesn't work out?
- Are you prepared for possible social and moral conflicts with your family's values?
- How many family members will be going in different directions at one time?
- Does your family or children *really need* this experience?

Most of this section was compiled from memory, as I've "been there, done that" for most of the listings over the past fifteen years. Friends and acquaintances call me the "Information Person," constantly asking "How do you hear about all this stuff?" Well, I read everything around me—newspapers, signs, ads, posters, *et cetera*. If it's free, I do it! If it's an annual event, I mark it in my calendar as such. If there's a catch, I find it. If it's worth the effort, I e-mail everyone I know*....

—Darlene Levy

*T.H.I.S. is a free bi-weekly announcement I e-mail to homeschoolers in the Tidewater area of Virginia and beyond. To receive it, go to http://groups.yahoo.com/group/Tidewater_Homeschool_Info_Support/join. It contains classifieds, websites, homeschool support info, events, missions, prayer requests, *et cetera*. You can also access back issues online, as well as view my links, photos, *et cetera*.

The Search for Extracurricular Activities

Darlene Levy

When I began this article, I fully intended to list every museum, historical site, lighthouse, ferry, fort, and amusement in Virginia. A few pages into it, I realized I was wasting my time and effort, plus pages of the HEAV Manual. Everything we could possibly want to know is already published on the Internet, in a much more extensive form than I could put together! The bonus is that most of the options listed below not only apply to Virginia, but to each state that you might move to or visit.

First, if you don't have a computer at home, go to the local library and use theirs—they're fast and free! Set yourself up a free e-mail account (www.hotmail.com or www.yahoo.com are just two of the many available). You can use any search engine www.google.com, www.yahoo.com, www.mamma.com,) Some web addresses are common sense, like www.colonialwilliamsburg.com; some can be found by trial and error, such as by trying www.charlottesville.com or www.leesburghistory.org to see what you get. Depending on who owns the domain name, you may get a state visitor center, a commercial tourist site, a website still for sale, or a complete dud that says it can't load the page! When you do get a good "hit," it should be full of information to direct you around the Commonwealth of Virginia's attractions and services.

For starters, **look up the state or city** you want to visit or research, using "com" and "org" as possible endings: www.virginia.com, www.richmond.org, www.virginia-beach.com.

Try your state slogan: www.virginiaisforlovers.com or www.virginiaisforlovers.org. If that doesn't work, try again, but abbreviate the state: www.vaisforlovers.com or www.vaisforlovers.org.

Do a **search for places in your city and/or state**: "Virginia and Suffolk" or "Virginia." You can also check out the relevant sites the search engine brings up, and also links from each of *those* sites. Try www.virginiatech.com, www.uva.edu, or www.vacommonwealthuniversity.org.

Even if the site doesn't otherwise interest you, it may lead you to more info on the city or state for which you are looking.

STATE AND CITY GOVERNMENT

- All websites end with .va.us (some may use .gov).
- Just to keep us guessing, the **Commonwealth of Virginia** website can be accessed with www.myvirginia.org. Technically, it is the same web address as www.state.va.us, just easier to remember. Either way, it will link you to everything in the Virginia state and city government, from the Governor to the Gloucester City Council.

- www.lva.lib.va.us will lead you into the **Library of Virginia** system. Links galore will send you to state and federal government agencies, but— most importantly—to all Virginia city and county libraries.

- www.so.cc.va.us is the **Virginia Community College System** (VCCS) website, which will provide you with all you need to know to attend any Virginia Community College.

- www.vpep.state.va.us is the **Virginia College Savings Plan** website. It will give you a taste of everything you need to know about financing a college education, about the prepaid education program, *et cetera*.

- www.oag.va.us takes you to the **Virginia Attorney General's** homepage.

- www.legis.va.us will link you to every government official in Virginia, as well as **legislation** information.

- www.vec.va.us is the **Virginia Employment Commission.**

- www.dmv.va.us is the **Department of Motor Vehicles** web address. This is especially handy if you have a teen getting ready to take the driver's permit test. You can look up ALL the requirements beforehand, rather than make four trips to DMV (as we did!).

- www.vdot.va.us is the **Virginia Department of Transportation**—the best place to find out about road closings when there are storms and flooding, or just traffic and construction delays.

- www.virginia-beach.va.us or www.hampton.gov will both take you to **state-sponsored city websites** for Virginia Beach and Hampton, respectively. Substitute any Virginia city for the "Hampton" part of the address, and you'll often get good results. On this type of page, you'll find resident information, visitor information, business information, a calendar of events, employment listings, city government listings, *et cetera*.

- The **Virginia Department of Education** website is www.pen.k12.va.us. (Each U.S. state should be accessible by substituting their own state abbreviation for "va.") There is SO much on this page—links to other

Virginia sites, SOL info, scholarships, contests, technology, parent links, instruction links, technology links, NASA, educational directory, and so forth.

- www.ext.vt.edu takes you to the **Virginia Cooperative Extension** which has ties to Virginia Tech and Virginia State University, so they use links interchangeably. Widely known for 4-H programs, an extension office is available in most cities, with services that are usually free of charge. Their web page lists local city offices, educational programs, resources, camps, employment opportunities, *et cetera.*

- www.newspapers.com is searchable by city and lists **newspapers from all over the USA and the World.** Most city newspaper sites have local attractions, events, museums, and clubs listed in an entertainment-type section. For example, www.dailypress.com covers Eastern Virginia and part of the North Carolina coast. Choose a city or topic such as "museums," "children," or "history" to search, and you'll end up on an entertainment page with more listings than you can possibly use!

- www.virginiausa.com is a **commercial site**, and lists each U.S. state separately. Unfortunately, if local city businesses don't list (advertise) on the website, there's not much to look at—try another state and see.

- www.vahistorical.org takes you to the **Virginia Historical Society**'s website. Many states, and even some larger cities may have similar web addresses to their historical societies.

- www.gatewayva.com is a site maintained by **Richmond Newspapers, Inc.** It links to several Central-Virginia newspapers, listings of local television stations, movies, autos, TV listings, classifieds, *et cetera.*

- www.virginia.com is a complete listing of most **Virginia cities'** libraries, religions, schools, services, travel, airports, real estate, maps, and "Travel Paks" to order prior to a trip.

- www.areaparks.com contains all **U.S. national parks**, listed by state. Each state lists what you need to know when visiting their parks.

- www.virginia.org is **THE complete Virginia site** to surf! It lists history, mountains, beaches, sports, museums, arts, gardens, zoos/parks, wineries, lodging, weather, monthly calendar, family fun, *et cetera.*

- www.stateinformation.com will take you to www.stateofvirginia.com. **Virginia's government agencies** use this site to link you to topics such as health, commerce, higher education, human rights, agriculture, and many more.

- **All national and regional TV stations** have websites such as www.wavy.com, www.wvec.com, and www.abc.com. The national sites should link you to the local stations. On the local sites, you can access news, weather, sports, events, attractions, *et cetera*—just as on television.

- **Colonial Williamsburg** can be accessed many different ways, but they have one link that is unusual: www.pastportal.com is a digital library of archived books, manuscripts, newspapers, *et cetera*, from the colonial period of history. Most are Williamsburg-related, but the site does claim to cover "Virginia History." FYI: www.history.org is the official Colonial Williamsburg "tourist" site.

- Public-library computers have a **reference resource** available at www.stategeography.abc.clio.com. You can search by state and pull up maps, flags, geography, government, history, events, biographies, and other useful information.

No matter where you live, where you want to visit, or what attractions you are looking for, you'll find it on the Internet! The information may begin in a newspaper, TV, or office building, but it ends up accessible by everyone who does a web search or randomly chooses web addresses. Explore—first on the web, then with your family!

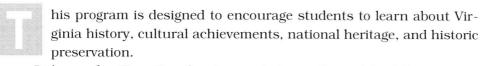

Virginia Time Travelers Passport

Darlene Levy

This program is designed to encourage students to learn about Virginia history, cultural achievements, national heritage, and historic preservation.

- Pick up a free Time Travelers Passport at any city or state visitor center.
- The brochure has an incredible amount of museum information in it, but check the website for up-to-date listings.
- Each year, the program runs from April 1 through November 15.
- The state is divided into five regions with each museum in that area listed as free, discounted, or "Art Explorer."
- City addresses and phone numbers are also provided for each site.
- A stamp is placed on the passport at each museum entrance.
- When students have visited six of the listed sites, they can send in a copy of their passport to receive an *official signed Time Traveler certificate* (DO NOT send the original).
- For an optional $7 shipping fee, the student will also receive a Time Traveler T-Shirt.
- "Art Explorers" is an additional challenge for students.
- If they visit two or more of the art museums as part of their six choices, they receive a special free patch with their certificate.
- For families on a budget, this can be done completely free of charge: The passport is free, then choose free-admission museums, visit two of the free-admission art museums, and mail in for your free certificate and free patch.

Explore Virginia today! www.timetravelers.org

Creative Field Trips

Darlene Levy

TIP: Behind-the-scenes tours are always interesting, even at an everyday place like the post office or the grocery store. Most will have treats for the children at the end of the tour. Places that charge an entry fee often allow groups in free, or at a discount. Some trips may not warrant an "official" tour guide; just explore on your own in approved areas. Always remember your family is representing the homeschooling community, so dress and act accordingly. When we travel overnight, I pack a unit study (Nags Head = Ocean Unit). Field trips don't always have to be taken as a group. It can be as much fun with just your family.

- **Local speakers:** a bird watcher, a chain saw artist, a photographer, a computer whiz, a pastor, a car mechanic, a carpenter, or anyone else with an interesting job or hobby. Go to their home or your church, or reserve a meeting room at a library or community center).

- **Walk a nature trail:** Have parents or teens "planted" along the trail with snacks, drinks, silly string, water balloons, and information. Be sure to pick up any leftover mess.

- **"Heavy-Duty" Hike:** Check out local park five-mile trails, or even a section of the Appalachian Trail!

- **Have an informal soccer or baseball game at a local park:** Each family can bring a snack and drink to share.

- Make an obstacle course or stage "Olympics" **at a park or local school yard after school hours. This is fun, as well as educational, for birthday parties.**

- **"Step Over the Border" Day Trips:** Baltimore, Maryland (Aquarium); Kitty Hawk, North Carolina (Wright Brothers Museum and Memorial); and Nags Head, North Carolina (parks have sand dunes to climb, hang-gliding, and a Junior Ranger Program).

- **"Find An Adventure"**: Search out water towers with city names to photograph as you travel, discover the Eastern Shore lighthouses.

- **Historical Site Day Trips:** Colonial Williamsburg; Jamestown; Yorktown; Fredericksburg; Richmond (Capitol Tour, Delegates Offices, City Statues, Visitor's Center, lunch in a park); DC (Capitol, White House, Smithsonian, FBI, Treasury, Holocaust Museum, Washington Monument, Lincoln Memorial, Arlington National Cemetery, Vietnam Memorial, Monuments and Statues around town); Chincoteague Island.

- **International/Ethnic:** Market, store, restaurant, church, festival.

- **Factories/Manufacturers:** Pepsi, Ball Metal, Tyson, Dollar Tree, Lillian Vernon, *et cetera*.

- **Parks:** Playground, picnic area, boating, fishing, walking trail, junior ranger, hug-a-tree programs, *et cetera*.

- **Chuck E. Cheese/Burger King/McDonald's/Chick-Fil-A:** lunch and playground.

- **Fairs/Festivals:** $ Community fairs and festivals, State Fair of Virginia (Richmond).

Sporting Events
Botanical Gardens
Airports
Aquariums
Zoos
Museums
Plantations
Forts
Farms/Dairies
Malls
Marinas
Beachs
Police Stations
Fire Departments
Art Galleries
Amusement Parks: $
Nursing Homes

Hospitals
Post Offices
Restaurants
Grocery Stores
Caves
Animal Shelters/SPCA/Humane Society
Colleges/Universities
Newspaper Offices
Nurseries/Greenhouses
City Offices
Libraries
Airplane Rides
Plays/Concerts $
Ferry/Boat Rides/Tours $

Clear Communication Enhances Field-Trip Experience

D. Krueger

W hen making arrangements for a field trip, it can be very helpful to offer the contact person at your destination some advance information about your group. The following letter is a sample of one a support group uses to cover all the bases and make certain that the field trip is a pleasant experience for all concerned. A similar letter could be shared with all the field-trip participants, so that everyone is reminded of the group's procedures and standards.

Dear [Field Trip Contact],

As you may know, the practice of homeschooling is increasing at a rapid rate in this country. The U.S. Department of Education estimates that there are over 1 million children in the U.S. being educated at home, by their parents. Our homeschool group was formed so that homeschooling families can offer moral support, share tips and advice, hold-co-op classes, and arrange field trips.

Our needs and requirements are different than those of public (and private) schools in the following ways:

1. Homeschoolers travel in family groups, so the students are often of varying grade levels and abilities. They each come with their own personal teacher, who can translate to their grade level, if necessary. Please do not feel that you have to give a tour that is appropriate for every age group we represent! As long as the material is suitable for the parents, the knowledge can be passed on effectively.

2. Parking—We require more parking than does a school bus. When you see a trail of minivans, you'll know we have arrived. We generally meet in the parking lot of the place we're touring, do a head count, remind the children of the behavior rules, and then enter as a group. If there are parking restrictions or advice you can give us, or special rules we need to be aware of, please let me know in advance so I can make arrangements.

3. Small children—We usually have a few! I have found that our group is generally well-behaved, infants are carried by their

mothers (or in a stroller, if there's access), and promptly removed or fed if they cry. We have a few 2-5 year olds who travel with our pack and one of the mothers generally removes them all to the outdoors, or an appropriate area, if their presence becomes distracting or inappropriate. We have found that keeping a tight rein on children of this age prevents inappropriate behavior and they generally benefit from the field trip as well.

4. We have no time restraints. School field trips generally have an ending time, or a time when they all pack up and leave—we can stay all day. If this is a problem, please let us know. We tend to linger when we have had a good trip, or when there are interesting things to look at.

5. We pre-study whatever topics we feel will maximize our educational experience, therefore we ask a lot of questions, and are generally very interested in understanding the answers. If you have materials to recommend, or resources that we can duplicate for our members, we would sincerely appreciate having that knowledge before we arrive. If you have a website, also, that often proves helpful.

6. Many of our children send thank-you cards to tour guides, so if you can have a few business cards on hand, along with a mailing address, it would be greatly appreciated.

7. Last but not least—flash photography. Please let us know *before* we arrive if it is acceptable to take photographs during our visit.

We look forward to our field trip on [date].

Sincerely,
[Name]
Homeschool Field Trip Coordinator

Athletic Scholarships, High School Sports, and Physical Fitness

Cafi Cohen

"What are the possibilities of homeschoolers earning athletic scholarships? My son plays basketball, and we cannot see any alternative to his attending high school to make him eligible for athletic scholarships." So ran a recent query on one of the on-line services.

A fair question, I thought. My initial reaction was tongue-in-cheek: "Be careful what you wish for: You might get it." Parents and teens should not let the monetary awards blind them to some of the problems that plague athletic-scholarship recipients.

Case in point: My son Jeff's first roommate at the Air Force Academy was a recruited quarterback. Every evening, while Jeff was studying, this cadet attended football practice. Unfortunately, while the cadet met admissions criteria, his qualifications for entering the Academy had been borderline. It was all too much. Like many recruited athletes, the football player left after a year because he could not keep up academically.

I am sure a book could be written about the problems of attending any college or university on an athletic scholarship. For example, counting on an athletic scholarship presumes that the athlete will remain healthy and uninjured. Anyone who saw the excellent documentary *Hoop Dreams* knows the problem here. Trading athletic prowess for educational dollars looks attractive on the surface, but, in many cases, may be detrimental. I question the wisdom of attending high school solely for the purpose of competing for an athletic scholarship, especially if school attendance jeopardizes a teenager's education and attitude towards learning.

While it may be difficult for a budding homeschool football player to win an athletic scholarship, homeschooling actually favors the training schedule faced by elite gymnasts or figure skaters. Not surprisingly, cases of gifted athletes homeschooling in order to accommodate the intense training demands of their sports are becoming more common.

The point here? There are really no simple answers, just the opportunity to look at homeschooling versus school attendance for students who are serious about athletics. Let's assume that you are already well-versed in what local schools can provide, and focus on opportunities in the community and at home for homeschoolers. [See High School at Home section for more articles on this subject.]

The out-of-school, the homeschooling options—many of which have been discovered by homeschoolers simply looking for high-school-level team sports or physical fitness opportunities—are more plentiful than you might think. How do these homeschooled teenagers access team sports and fitness activities? An interesting corollary question I would like to address is: are physical activities an essential part of education, or just add-ons; something you do if you have the time?

In the two states where my kids were homeschooled, New Mexico and Colorado, high school sports programs were open to homeschoolers. We knew a homeschooled teenager on the high school track team in New Mexico and several homeschoolers in Colorado who played high school softball. My kids never took advantage of these opportunities. The larger communities offered so much more.

Both kids played Little League baseball and softball in their middle school years—both sports organized in the community. During his high school years, Jeff participated on a U.S. Diving Team sponsored by the local parks and recreation department (his diving was good enough that the coach at West Point tried recruiting Jeff for diving). Tamara took Tae Kwon Do at a local military base, and played volleyball with a church league.

While I was glad these outlets existed, something else was far more important to me than the kids excelling with a particular sport (or winning an athletic scholarship). I wanted to instill the attitude that lifetime fitness is important, and that time and effort devoted to physical fitness would yield big payoffs.

My line to the kids was: "If you don't have your health (and exercise is key to staying healthy), everything else is that much harder—not impossible, but harder." Additionally, daily intense physical activity was a stress buster for everyone.

What options for team sports and physical fitness do teenagers have? A little networking, trial-and-error, and creativity go a long way. We found, and the experience of our fellow home educators has shown us, that older homeschoolers *can* participate in invigorating, fun, fitness activities. The only problem is locating them. Here are some suggestions:

- Check all sorts of community agencies. We found swimming, diving, yoga, martial arts, and aerobic dancing with parks and recreation departments; hiking and synchronized swimming through community education classes (usually run by local school districts); Red Cross Water Safety Instructor (WSI) and lifeguarding classes at the YMCA; volleyball and bowling with church leagues.

  As homeschoolers (and, in our case, as a family who moved a lot), we learned to look beyond our teenagers' immediate preferences. The dictum, "when in Rome…." applies here. Diving was not our son Jeff's first choice (probably not even his tenth choice). But he felt he needed sports team participation for his academy applications. Through the recommendation of other home educators, we found a U.S. Diving Team run by an excellent coach very near our home. The outstanding coach could and did make everyone (including Jeff) enthusiastic about diving. If the ideal sport is unavailable, look for alternatives which boast good instructors, coaches, and programs.

- Many communities have adult leagues that welcome older teenagers. Examples are baseball teams, basketball teams, and bowling leagues. Ask personnel at large sporting-goods stores for contacts for these opportunities.

- Special-interest groups are another option. Most notable are the distance running, walking, and biking groups that exist even in relatively small communities. These clubs usually welcome participants of all ages and provide expertise and focus for very inexpensive lifetime sports. Gifted high school age runners may even find enough training support in running clubs to qualify for athletic scholarships in track and cross-country.

    In this vein, our family very much enjoyed the outings of a cross-country ski club in Denver. The group seemed made for homeschooling families. All ages were welcome, and everyone participated in mountain treks of various lengths. Club members happily took unlimited amounts of time to share their expertise and enthusiasm.

- Some youth groups offer sports, including team sports, as part of their programs. At Civil Air Patrol, our son Jeff trained (mile run plus push-ups and sit-ups) for periodic physical fitness testing. Some 4-H groups field volleyball and other types of teams. Our daughter Tamara learned basic archery through 4-H. Other youth-oriented outlets include scouts, Camp Fire, and Police Athletic League programs.

- Do not overlook sports at government schools. A few state statutes specifically permit participation of homeschooled teenagers in high school sports extracurriculars. In many other states, no policy has been set; and cases are simply handled on an individual basis, as they occur. Contact a local or state homeschooling group for information *before* talking to your school district about this. They can tell you which laws, if any, apply, and what the experience of local homeschoolers has been.

    Also, even if a negative policy has been set (i.e. no homeschooling participation in sports) or if the school seems confused about your teenager's request to participate in sports, rules are bent all the time. A persistent homeschooler's enthusiasm has won over many a reluctant coach or administrator. Look for loopholes. Perhaps your homeschooler could train with the team as long as he did not compete. With his foot in the door, that teenager may eventually be invited to compete, all rules and regulations to the contrary. Truly talented athletes often prove irresistible.

- Private schools present additional opportunities. Many private institutions allow and encourage participation of homeschoolers on their sports teams. There usually is a fee involved. Suggest it to them. Most coaches will go for anything if you suggest putting it "on a trial basis."

- Community colleges offer classes in various sports and may allow participation on certain teams, especially for older homeschoolers. Kill two birds with one stone: earn college credit and enhance physical fitness at the same time.

- Private clubs and private lessons are the principal outlet for certain sports: fencing, martial arts, gymnastics, dance, and golf fall into this category. While expenses, at first, may seem prohibitive, seek creative solutions. For example, kids can trade golf lessons for caddying, or teach younger gymnastics students in exchange for more advanced lessons. As previously mentioned, some of these activities are so time-consuming at advanced levels (gymnastics, especially) that homeschoolers will find they have a distinct advantage over those who have to spend most of their day in school.

- Homeschool support groups, as they increase in size and in the number of older kids served, are organizing their own sports teams. Often these groups make arrangements to compete with private school teams or other homeschooling groups. If something like this has not been started in your area, consider doing it. Alternatively, your teenagers may prefer a more recreational approach—simply meeting with other older kids twice weekly to play volleyball or to go skating.

- When all else fails, improvise. Some activities need no external support. Older kids can devise and set up their own physical conditioning programs with an aerobic activity (running or walking) plus some strength training. (Check out library books and fitness magazines for ideas on how to achieve this at home.) Others may prefer working with aerobics or weight-training videotapes. Keeping a training log keeps many "on track."

If you are still with me, but yawning because you know nothing will overcome your older kids' inertia when it comes to physical activity, here are a few suggestions.
- Discuss goals for lifetime fitness. Why does it matter?
- Using the above suggestions, brainstorm ideas for sports participation in your community. Urge your teenager to try new activities and find one he or she likes.
- Schedule fun, weekend family activities like hiking and biking. Make time for a daily family walk.
- (Caution: this one is difficult!) Model desired behavior. If you, the homeschooling parent, are doing nothing now, consider a daily 20-30 minute

walk (with malls available, bad weather is no excuse). Why should teenagers put a priority on fitness if you do not?

- Keep records. Some people are very motivated by records showing their progress. Examples are a log of distances run, a journal listing tennis skills mastered, records of competitions, and photos.

- If all else fails, do things the hard way. Suggest that your teenager become an active non-athlete. Take the stairs instead of the escalator, walk or bike rather than drive, grow your own vegetables (gardening is excellent exercise), knead your own bread (a stress-buster and upper-body workout), and shovel snow by hand instead of using the snow-blower.

For us, encouraging lifetime fitness meant making daily aerobic and strengthening activities priorities. To that end, our kids, almost every day, did something physical. Despite my strong unschooling inclinations, daily physical activity was like household chores—no choice. We tried many things, but cycling, hiking, and cross-country skiing were our favorites. Yard work was a constant necessity and invigorated everyone in the family.

Now at college, both Jeff and Tamara continue to make fitness and associated recreational activities a part of their lives, so I feel like an unqualified success in that area—if not in some others! Jeff runs, lifts weights, and hikes "small" peaks near the Academy. Tamara plays rugby on a college varsity team plus recreational racquetball and tennis. Without a car, she also does a lot of walking—a clear case of less is more.

Being a "model" for so many years stuck with us as well. I seldom miss my daily walk and enjoy gardening and the occasional nature hike. My husband works out on our cross-country ski machine in inclement weather, and bikes or walks the neighborhood in good weather. He also does the bulk of the heavy yard work.

As a former couch potato, it all makes me wonder who was homeschooled—the kids or us!

From Home Education Magazine, July/Aug, 1997 Older Kids column, by Cafi Cohen. *Shared freely from the NHEN Article Clearinghouse - www.NHEN.org*

Clubs and Organizations

Darlene Levy

TIP...check out ALL aspects of the group, program, or camp.

Virginia Cooperative Extension is a state agency under the U.S. Department of Agriculture. It is funded with your tax dollars, and the resources available to families are incredible. Each county has its own Extension Service office, so specific offerings may vary.

- www.ext.vt.edu/resources/4h/programs.html
- Free 4-H clubs on 46 topics, from animals to woodworking to gardening to theatre; no uniforms!
- Free science teaching materials, yours upon request
- Free community classes and programs
- Free use of an incubator for hatching chicks
- Hand-in-hand relationship with local museums to set up youth volunteers
- Teen Council to teach leadership skills
- Master gardener certification
- Mum-growing opportunity for youth to learn entrepreneurial skills
- Competition opportunities at the county and state level
- Insect identification
- Soil testing
- Summer camps

Camps may be for a day, a week, or longer. They can have a cute theme or just be a staple of summer. Most are expensive, especially if you have multiple children! Concerns might be: 1) the adults in charge 2) the safety of the transportation 3) the influence of other children.

- Triple-R-Ranch: Christian "frontier" atmosphere, horses! www.tripler-ranch.org
- Church/Faith sponsored camps: Affordable; scholarships often available; usually very trustworthy
- Boy and Girl Scout Camps (See "Girl Scouts" and "Boy Scouts, below)
- Homeschool Sponsored: Family Camp, Creation Camp, Homeschool Retreat, *et cetera.*
- Privately Run "Camps": Usually days only, expensive (Space Museum

Camp, Computer Camp, Local Zoo Camp, Math Camp, Theatre Camp, *et cetera*)
- 4-H Camp (*see Virginia Cooperative Extension Section*)
- Summer Adventure Clubs: City-Sponsored (often with a theme, basically seasonal day care)

Red Cross offers year-round local opportunities at a reasonable cost. Most are invaluable lifetime skills. Community Service opportunities are flexible and often family-oriented. www.redcross.org
- CPR, Lifeguard, Disaster, Babysitting: Classes and Certification
- Community Service: Meals on Wheels, Food Pantry, rides to medical appointments, homeless shelters
- Youth Service: Youth Disaster Corps, Red Cross Pen Pals, Leadership Education, Fund-raising

Girl Scouts emphasize "leadership, social conscience, and values" for girls ages 5-17. Events can be local, regional, national, and worldwide. Adult volunteer leaders play a significant role in the organization. www.girlscouts.org
- Camps: usually on Scout properties, for a week or more
- Clubs offer: weekly meetings, earned badges, field trips, sport clinics, annual cookie sales
- Community Service: environmental stewardship, wildlife conservation
- Mentoring programs: promote literacy, leadership, careers, health, technology
- Global Awareness: cultural exchanges, World Girl Scout Association

Boy Scouts, since 1910 have encouraged "education, character, citizenship, and fitness" for boys 5-20. Events are local, regional, national, and worldwide. Adult volunteer leaders play a significant role in the 300 neighborhood Boy Scout troops. www.bsa.scouting.org
- Events: Jamborees, Conferences
- Programs: Cub Scouts, Boy Scouts, Varsity Scouting, Venturing, National Eagle Scout Association
- Activities: High Adventure Training, Scout Ranch, Venture Patrols
- Service: National Park Service identified volunteer projects

Mission Opportunities can be a family adventure, a Christmas tradition, or a way of life. They can be: 1) local or international 2) occasional or year-round 3) short- or long-term 4) church or national ministry sponsored. Some are more family-friendly than others.
- Teen Mania (www.teenmania.org). Youth and family mission trips, Acquire the Fire volunteers
- Operation Carelift (www.josh.org). Youth and family mission trips in January and July to Soviet Union; Mega-Family-Friendly service in Lancaster, PA each October (1 day or all 2 weeks, you pick!), packing supplies for January Soviet Union mission trip.
- Samaritan's Purse (www.samaritanspurse.org). Help local support staff;

be a collection-site organizer; volunteer in Charlotte, NC for Operation Christmas Child each November and December

- Nursing Home Visits, Pet Therapy
- Child Evangelism Fellowship (www.gospelcom.net/cef/) Backyard Bible Clubs, Evangelism Training
- Campus Crusade for Christ, Military Ministries: Pack Bible deployment kits for soldiers, kids welcomed

Exchange Students bring the mission field to your own home! Host for a week, month, summer, or school year. Plan on a bit of communication or culture adjustment, a bit of carpooling, possibly even an inconvenience or two. But in the long run, it is guaranteed to be a blessing to the student as well as to your family. www.nacel.org

Watch the local newspaper for "Host Families Needed" ads. Also, most universities have an international student advisor who can point you to an exchange program with the school. This will often be a non-housing arrangement. Just an occasional visit or field trip together. Seventy-five percent of international students return to their native country without having been inside an American home! Collegiate baseball teams often house their players within the community, which could be fun for the sports-minded family—free passes to all the games is a perk. www.peninsulapilots.com

4-H, a division of the State and Federal Extension Service, provides many opportunities for homeschooled students. Besides the traditional agricultural and home0economics project areas, there are many other opportunities and competitions in leadership, speech, talent, environmental education, shooting sports, consumer information, general knowledge, travel, community service, and scholarship.

4-H has many free resources of curricula and support materials (such as electricity kits, sewing machines, videos, incubating machines, and more). Each 4-H club is unique, dependent upon the leaders' areas of expertise, and the membership goals.

For more information, call your local Extension Service by calling the County Government office. To locate a local Extension office: http://www.ext.vt.edu/offices. (4-H information contributed by Karie Dawkins.)

How 4-H Enhanced My School Experience

Lauryn Dawkins

Homeschooling is a wonderful way to be educated. However, there are some areas—such as public speaking, community service, and involvement in community organizations—that seem more open to public-school children than to homeschool youth. For our family, 4-H helped bridge the gap between those skills and activities and homeschooling, while keeping activities family centered—which supports one of the most important reasons many choose to home educate.

In 4-H, we were introduced to public speaking and presentations at a young age, in a controlled environment, in front of multiple ages and with our peers. We were encouraged to do our best, and when we made a mistake, it was tactfully corrected for our benefit. 4-H leaders and parents taught us how to narrow our speaking choices, how to present topics confidently in a logical, fluid manner. In college, I found I was prepared to give my opinions and speeches with poise and confidence. To my surprise, my presentations lacked nothing when compared to those of public-school students.

Most of my community service work was through 4-H, though we were involved in other community-serving organizations as well. Through the contacts the program offered, we were able to supply food for the needy, help local parks, provide programs at nursing homes, conduct safety programs, and help in various State Fair activities. True, these things could have been done outside of 4-H, but 4-H inspired the ideas, gave suggestions on the "how to's," and managed to educate us along the way. 4-H is also an organization people are aware of and willing to donate to, enabling us to do more for others.

4-H opened many doors for interesting, informative, and fun field trips. We went to countless museums, historical sites, environmental excursions, and leadership programs with our 4-H group. Sometimes seeing is believing, and we were able to see a lot. In addition to providing the opportunity to qualify for scholarships based on my 4-H leadership and community service experiences, the 4-H program helped me better learn how to socialize with different age groups, present myself in a clear and confident manner, serve my community, and enjoy more exciting and interactive learning experiences.

Lauryn is a homeschool graduate. She is majoring in chemistry and is a pre-med student at VCU.

Support Groups

Compiled by Tammy Bear

Additional Articles on the CD
BE SURE TO CHECK OUT THESE OTHER GREAT ARTICLES ON THE CD!

Each article in the book and on the CD has been carefully chosen by the section coordinator to increase your knowledge and understanding of this subject, so don't forget to use and enjoy the parts of the manual on your CD, as well as the part you are holding.

Please note that the page numbering on the CD is different from that of the hard-copy manual.

Developing a Support System

Where can you go for support? *God Himself* is your most vital support system! Trust in Him and run to Him first with all your cares. "But those who hope in the Lord will renew their strength. They will soar on wings like eagles; they will run and not grow weary, they will walk and not be faint." (Isaiah 40:31)

You can be your next important support system. Taking care of yourself spiritually, physically, mentally, and emotionally can never be replaced by the support you may receive from others. Develop your own daily disciplines to fill up these personal reservoirs so that you can give to your family, train your children, and be a blessing to others.

Your family, and especially *your spouse*, should be part of your support system. Pray together about the choices you make regarding your children and their education so that you can be in agreement. Be specific with your mate about ways he can help. (Of course, remember you are *his* support system, too!) *Grandparents and other relatives* can offer support, and not at all least, *your own children* can be enlisted on the team of your homeschooling effort. "Serve one another in love." Galatians 5:13

These areas of support are at the center of our lives. They will send ripples into the pool of other strengthening relationships, including our homeschool support groups.

—Tammy Bear

Types of Support Groups

ach group of home educators is unique and may have completely different goals and styles. One may exist as a source of general information for local homeschoolers, another may be based in a church, and be a tightly knit group of church members. Some groups offer a highly organized Friday School co-op in which mothers take turns teaching classes once a week to a group of children; or where teachers are hired from the community and members share the cost. Other groups have a few leaders that organize field trips and meet informally once a month for a Mom's Night Out. A support group might even be a small group of families using the same curriculum. Most groups are for people who are community-based, and have leaders who are also busy homeschooling parents. Aside from the location factor, support groups may differ in other areas such as: size; the members of the family that are supported (moms only, parents together, young children, teenagers, and so on); goals; frequency of meetings and activities; level of commitment between the members; organizational style; and cost of membership.

One of the most important differences between groups is whether it limits its membership to those who share a common faith in Christ, or if it is for all homeschoolers. There are advantages to both of these positions. A group for all might be a vehicle for informing larger numbers of voters about legislation that would affect their common interests. A Christian group would provide other advantages like: freedom to share prayer requests, influences for your children that might guide them spiritually, and a bond that will go deeper than your common interest in home education. This type of group will usually adopt a Statement of Faith that prospective members would sign to indicate their agreement.

Many kinds of support groups are needed in Virginia to serve people with different needs and preferences. We should be able to work together without judging another's reason for belonging to a group that may be different than ours. However, we also need to have the freedom to state our convictions honestly, and to seek others who are like-minded. Most people are looking for this, including non-Christians. They can readily see that the most effective support comes with this kind of philosophical agreement. A Statement of Faith need not alienate anyone if presented graciously. It will, however, present a clear and honest picture of the philosophical principles that unify the group. For many home educators, the desire to share their faith with their children and make that a central part of their education is a primary reason for choosing to homeschool in the first place. Why should that factor not be primary in their support groups? The kind of loyalty that develops when the group is united by this bond will cause each member to feel truly nurtured in the Lord, whereas any other central purpose for the Christian support group may eventually grow thin and weak, and wear out.

[NOTE: For an up-to-date list of support groups in Virginia, visit www.heav. org, or call our office (804-278-9200.)

Adapted with permission from *A Comprehensive Guide to Home Education in Colorado.*

Principles for a Healthy Support Group

Although each homeschool support group is a unique group of home educators, certain basic principles seem to be common among those that are thriving and healthy. Here are seven principles that will help any group in their endeavor.

SEEK GOD IN EVERY AREA

A home education group is not a "church" and differs in many ways from a church, but whenever a group of Christians are together, they can benefit from following the guidelines God has given us for cooperating and working with one another. A group will benefit anytime it seeks God's wisdom in His Word for direction! Some of these guidelines are found in the following places:

- Making love a priority - John 15:12, Romans 12:10, Proverbs 17:17, Matthew 19:19
- Working for unity - Philippians 2:2, Psalm 133:1
- Helping those who are weak - Romans 13:1, Hebrews 3:13, Galatians 6:2
- Using your gifts to serve - Romans 12:5-8
- Wisdom for leaders - Proverbs 15:33, James 1:5-8, Proverbs 15:22, James 3:13
- Solving problems - Matthew 18:13-16

If encouragement of fellow home educators is your purpose, then remember to direct people to the source of that encouragement: God Himself. Prayer is the simplest solution to so many needs, yet it seems to be frequently forgotten. It can bind a group together like nothing else! Small groups can plan time for prayer in their meetings, and larger groups can use a prayer chain or prayer partner network, or divide into smaller groups for a portion of the larger meeting. An e-mail system can be an effective means of support, and prevent problems.

"Therefore, as God's chosen people, holy and dearly loved, clothe yourselves with compassion, kindness, humility, gentleness, and patience. Bear with each other and forgive whatever grievances you may have against one another. Forgive as the Lord forgave you. And over all these virtues put on love, which binds them all together in perfect unity." Colossians 3:12-14

HAVE A WELL-DEFINED VISION

This is crucial for any group. The leaders of any support group can get worn-out if the vision is too broad and the expectations of the members too varied or unending. Each year, review your purpose as a group, and make sure it is clearly communicated to the group members. A lot can be accomplished if everyone is working together towards the same goal!

What should you do if you decide that a change of direction is needed? A good way to address this is to call together the leaders of the group and discuss possible changes. Pray for God's direction, and write down the leaders' decisions and your new goals for the group. You may wish to take this to the whole group and ask for a vote to confirm the decisions the leaders have made. Of course, you will need to apply a lot of prayer and graciousness to this transition time!

PLAN GOALS TO FIT THE VISION

Make sure that the goals you set out to accomplish fit with the purpose and needs of your group. It is better to have just a few goals that are carefully planned than to have a shotgun approach. Too many goals without direction can lead to overload. Remember that your support group is to support already busy homeschooling families, not to overburden them with additional activities. Also, realize that every activity you plan may not meet the need of every family. Allow each family the freedom to make decisions about what is best for them.

CULTIVATE OPEN AND HONEST COMMUNICATION

This principle can make a big difference in the smooth functioning of a group and the prevention of potential problems. Honesty means saying what you mean and meaning what you say. Encourage members and leaders to be honest with themselves and with the group about what they are able to commit to do, and their needs or concerns.

Take time to listen to others and make sure that what you hear them say is what they meant to say. Avoid judging the intentions of the person speaking, but try to understand the meaning of her message.

Confidentiality about concerns that are shared in the group meetings is an important courtesy. This should characterize all meetings and give people the security of knowing that what they share will not be heard outside the group.

Solicit frequent feedback from the group. Be sure to give others an opportunity to share their concerns and needs in a positive light. Being a good listener will foster an atmosphere in which everyone is working together toward a common goal. This can help to keep problems from growing out of proportion.

"Do nothing out of selfish ambition or vain conceit, but in humility consider others better than yourselves. Each of you should look not only to your own interest, but also to the interests of others." Philippians 2:3-4

INCLUDE THE FATHERS

While in most families the mother does most of the actual teaching at home, fathers also need support for their important role in the home educating family. However, if they are not *intentionally* included, they may feel unwelcome to participate in support-group activities. Here are some ideas for including fathers:

Enlist the fathers' help when planning the overall purpose of the group and yearly goals. Dads will feel they can participate more wholeheartedly in what they have helped to plan. Maybe the moms would feel comfortable working out the details of *how* the group will function after the fathers have worked with them to set the *direction*.

Ask fathers to lead a meeting or give a devotional talk. Open a meeting by giving dads a chance to share their favorite homeschooling experience. Include outings for fathers and their children in your plan. Dads might serve their families by treating their wives to a night out while they watch the children at home. This may not seem glamorous, but it will be long remembered!

ORGANIZE YOUR RESOURCES

Taking time to organize your plans, time, activities, and finances will really help prevent problems down the road. Think ahead about how to make the most of your meeting times. Each group will vary in the style it adopts, from a formal Robert's Rules of Order style to an informal, homey style. But *every* meeting will benefit from someone planning and praying about it ahead of time. Organization is especially important in the financial area: Be sure the person with this responsibility keeps accurate records.

Your leadership team needs to be organized, too. Each person should have a clear idea of what his or her responsibilities are, and it is a good idea to write down job descriptions. Leaders should know to whom they are directly accountable. Be sure to specify whether leaders will be elected, be appointed, or volunteer. Decide on qualifications for leadership that will ensure that your leaders uphold the values of the group. You might like to set up an apprenticeship plan, where leaders-in-training assist a veteran for a period of time.

ENCOURAGE EVERYONE TO SHARE THE RESPONSIBILITIES

Many hands make light work, and many hearts and minds sharing in the leadership of a homeschool group make the load light. The important thing to remember is that everyone can do something, and small things can make a big difference in the smooth functioning of a group. Do not think that the most experienced homeschoolers should always carry the group. Sometimes it is the new home educators that have the most enthusiasm and creative ideas. Even children can learn a great deal of responsibility by being given tasks that are overseen by an adult.

Yes, support group leaders need support, too! Sometimes those that have a giving, servant's heart are the last ones to realize that they also need to receive. A healthy leader is one who knows his or her own limitations and is willing to delegate and ask for help and encouragement when needed. Be sure to remind the leaders of your group to put their own family's needs at the top of the priority list, and let them know you appreciate them.

GUIDELINES FOR DELEGATION:
- Be willing to let others do the job in a different way than you would do it.
- Invest in the lives of others by training them for the job: this will pay off later.
- Encourage those to whom you delegate: make it your goal to see that they are successful.
- Thank them for a job well done!

Tasks that can be delegated include, but are not limited to: weekly/monthly activities coordinator; newsletter coordinator; special events coordinator of committee; contact person for any event (to answer questions such as "What time does it start?" or "How do I get there?") Counseling new homeschoolers can also be a delegated task. This job may require more training, but it is key to relieving leaders of some of their workload.

Jobs that should *not* be delegated are: speaking for your group to the media or community; correcting communication problems within the group; sharing your vision with the group; and giving encouragement to those to whom you delegate.

One final note on delegation is to remember that for everything you have delegated that was not done effectively, there are probably ten things that were done better and in a fresh new way. You do not need to give up authority to make final decisions; but allow people the freedom to effectively do the job you give them. And do not forget the value of praise.

Some groups set up a buddy system in which an experienced homeschooling family pairs with a younger family, in order to encourage them during the year. This way, the new families do not "slip through the cracks," and the older ones experience the blessing of giving. And a few families won't get worn out by over-giving.

Adapted with permission from *A Comprehensive Guide to Home Education in Colorado.*

Choosing a Local Support Group

In the community where you live, there may be many different support groups. How do you choose which one you will join? First of all, you must think through your goals as a family, and know the needs you have in reaching those goals. Then, as with any decision, spend some time in prayer asking God for wisdom. It may be that two or more groups look like they are right for your family in different ways, but it is usually a good idea to participate wholeheartedly in one group rather than to be spread too thin with several. The relationships that will be most treasured by you and your children are the ones that will be deepened by commitment and time spent together. This is possible only if involvement is limited to a single support group.

The first place to check for local support groups might be with your church. Find out who the other home educators are, and ask them about groups they belong to. Maybe your church has organized a group. HEAV maintains a current list of support groups around the state, and you can find out about some of the groups that are nearest you by checking the list in this manual, or by calling the HEAV office. You can also check the list by accessing the HEAV website. Of course, HEAV does not evaluate the philosophical positions of groups before adding them to the list, so you will want to do that yourself. Once you know about the groups in your area, you will want to call someone in the leadership of each to determine if it is the best fit for your family. Here are a few questions that might give you a start:

1. Is this group open to new members?
2. Is this group open to any home educator, or is it for families of a certain faith?
3. What are the goals of the group?
4. What is the age range of most students?
5. What activities are planned for the coming year?
6. Are dads involved? And if so, how?
7. What level of commitment is required of the members?
8. What is the cost of membership, both in money and volunteer time?

You will want to prayerfully evaluate the input you receive based on your needs as a family and your focus at this stage in your home education journey. You should also consider what your family has to offer others, and where you might be most effective in serving. Don't choose a group only for what it can offer you, but for how it fits with the goals you have mapped out for your family, and how you and your children can develop your gifts in serving others! Ideally, each family member should have relationships where they can support those who are walking alongside them, learn from those who are more experienced, and encourage those who are less experienced.

"But encourage one another daily, as long as it is called today..."
Hebrews 3: 13a

[NOTE: For an up-to-date list of support groups in Virginia, visit www.heav. org, or call our office (804-278-9200.)

Adapted with permission from *A Comprehensive Guide to Home Education in Colorado.*

Forming a New Support Group

In your search for a support group that is just right for your family, you may discover other families that have not yet connected with a group, or that you have a vision for a group that does not exist yet in your area. Do not think that you have to be endowed with some special ability to start a new group! All you really need to have is a desire to meet the need, and a few basic administrative skills. Take the time to make some decisions now that will set your group on the right path. It is much easier to establish the foundation in the early stages of building than to wait until the walls are up! Here is the simple plan to get you started:

1. Why? Identify the need.
2. What? Set one or more goals to meet the need.
3. Who? Determine the people who will be involved.
4. When? Plan a simple schedule.
5. Where? Find a location at which to meet.
6. How? Decide how the group will function.

WHY WILL YOU COME TOGETHER?

What is the primary need that you see for your group to meet? Your need might be informal fellowship with other moms, encouragement for couples, educational activities for students, or sharing resources with others using the same curriculum. Although you may identify several needs, it is a good idea to focus on just one—at least at first. One central purpose, clearly focused, will be easier to reach than a broad undefined one. You may find later that your secondary needs are being met in natural ways for which you had not planned. Write down your central purpose as a statement of your group's vision. (See the following activity sheet. You will also find two sample vision/purpose statements.)

WHAT WILL BE THE WAY YOU CHOOSE TO MEET THIS NEED?

If fellowship for moms is your need, then you may decide to structure your group around a monthly mom's meeting, or night out for pie and prayer. If your need is to build up couples and help the dads stay connected, then your goal might be to have couples take turns hosting a fellowship in their home, while older children in the group teach the younger ones in another room.

Maybe you will choose regular field trips or oral-report days or a class on a particular subject if your need is educational in focus. When curriculum connection is your defined need, you might try a Friday afternoon co-op. Always try to filter ideas through the vision statement of your group *before* making a decision to attempt them. Add these goals to your vision statement.

WHO WILL BE A PART OF YOUR GROUP?

It only takes two families to form a support group, but you should think through how many families will comfortably form the group. Again, make this decision by referring back to your purpose and goals as a group and pray. Small groups offer the deepest friendships and the ability to share in encouraging all the others, while larger groups may provide more teachers for a "Friday School" type of group. You need to think, at this point, about whether you will be meeting in members' homes, or if you have a church or community facility available to you. Remember that it is easier to start small and grow than it is to downsize later! If you desire that everyone in the group share the same religious convictions, then you will need to establish a statement of faith to which each member must agree. Your church may have a statement like this. You may like to create a membership form for prospective members to sign that includes a release of liability for your group.

WHEN WILL YOUR GROUP MEET?

Setting a regular time to meet helps families plan group activities into their schedule and begin to look forward to each time together. Will you meet weekly, monthly, mornings, afternoons, or evenings? Plan enough time together so that your relationships will truly support each other, but not so much as to seem a burden. It will always be necessary to be flexible, and changes may need to be made in your schedule, but it helps to start with a plan. Some groups try to lay out a rough plan for the year before it begins; others plan one month at a time. Write down your schedule and communicate it to all the group members.

WHERE WILL YOU MEET?

This question is related to the number of people in your group. A small group can easily meet in a member's living room, and this sometimes is the most comfortable place for sharing and prayer. The activities of a larger group can be held in a church, or a community library. If you are meeting in one of these buildings, always make sure you let your group know that they will need to help keep it clean.

HOW WILL THE GROUP FUNCTION?

How will the members contribute to the smooth functioning of your support group? Now is the time to set down any rules or policies that are important to you, including: the type of behavior that will be expected of students participating in activities; whether parents will be required to participate with their children; whether members will be asked to do a job within the group; or whether members pay a membership fee. By the time you have carefully considered your vision and goals as a group, you should have some ideas about the best way to carry them out. It is very important to get these ideas on paper and communicate them clearly at the beginning of the formation of your group. This will help safeguard against problems later. There are more tips that will help you in the section entitled "Principles for a Healthy Support Group."

Now that you have thought through these simple steps, record what you have decided, and you are ready to get started! Pray that God will lead you in all your ways that your pathway will be straight! (Proverbs 3:5-6) Remember that the members or needs of your group may change from year to year: Review your vision statement each year and make changes, if necessary. For long-term support for you and your group, be sure to contact HEAV and let them know about your group.

[NOTE: For an up-to-date list of support groups in Virginia, visit www.heav. org, or call our office (804-278-9200.)

Adapted with permission from *A Comprehensive Guide to Home Education in Colorado.*

Support Group Planning Worksheet

"Commit to the Lord whatever you do, and your plans will succeed."
—Proverbs 16:3

Why? State a vision of your group. You can include the theme of your year or an inspiring verse of Scripture:

What? List the goal(s) of this group:

Who? Describe the number of people you are seeking and the qualifications for membership:

When? List your group's proposed schedule of activities:

Where? Determine your location:

How? Describe the rules of behavior for participating students:

What? Determine the duties of the leaders:

What? Determine the duties or requirements for members:

Ideas for Support Group Events

- Plan a Project Fair so that students can share their accomplishments with the group.
- Have the older teens prepare a lesson for younger children to help out during a family night.
- Let the dads organize a camp-out for fathers and their children.
- Have a square dance.
- Give teens a section of the newsletter in which to publish their writing.
- Plan a day for children to share oral reports or art projects.
- Have a mother-daughter tea.
- Organize a couples' dinner or an evening out.
- Let compatible families trade evenings to allow couples a night alone, or trade afternoons for a moms' break from teaching.
- Plan a year's activities around a certain theme such as American history, state history, character qualities, or science.
- Invite a guest speaker to address your group.
- Pool resources to start a lending library, or set up a table to share curriculum.
- Go on a hike—Virginia has a lot of beautiful places for this!
- Have a "Night of Blessing" in which families (or fathers) speak a blessing to their children and encourage them for the year's accomplishments.
- Have children present a talent program for a retirement center as an outreach project.
- Host a drama presentation by the children or a guest performer.
- Organize a Geography Bee through the National Geographic Society.
- Organize a Spelling Bee so that your students can qualify to participate in the National Spelling Bee.
- Plan a field trip to a local educational place. (A good resource for ideas is the *Yellow Pages Guide to Field Trips*, edited by Gregg Harris.)
- Have a curriculum swap or used-book sale.
- Purchase materials (like this Manual) to lend to new home educators joining your group.
- Create a "New Homeschooler Packet" to present to members just beginning their journey. (See HEAV Resources for beginner packets.)
- Honor homeschool graduates with a graduation ceremony.

The Virginia Law

Compiled by Yvonne Bunn

Introduction to the Virginia Homeschool Law

The Virginia homeschool law and related statutes offer a variety of options for parents who choose to homeschool. The law outlines the requirements to teach at home as well as the rights of parents. Although it may seem complicated and confusing at first, understanding the law can help homeschoolers deal with it.

This section includes numerous reference materials—statutes, opinions, memos, and documents—to help you make decisions regarding the education of your children. These reference materials are from various sources; all affect some aspect of homeschooling. We'd like to suggest you read this entire section, get an overview of the law and its interpretations, then refer to specific areas as needed.

The memos from the Department of Education (DOE) are particularly important because they reflect State School Board policies concerning home education. Although these policies are not law, local school districts adhere to them—sometimes overzealously. Since your local school district's policies are based on these memos, it is wise to become familiar with them prior to making initial contact.

Closely related to DOE memos are Attorney Generals' Opinions. They are just that—opinions, but weighty opinions. Again, it is important to be familiar with these documents. They could be helpful...or they could be used against you.

Although homeschooled students are not required to take the Standards of Learning tests, some parents find the SOLs to be a helpful resource. After parents realize the minimum standards are being met in their homeschools, they feel more confident about their curriculum. Parents may download the SOLs from the DOE website at www.doe.virginia.gov.

As you read, you will observe that the Virginia homeschool statute and DOE policies change from year to year. Hence, various older memos contain both current and outdated homeschool information. Because of this unavoidable problem, make sure you are on HEAV's e-mail Update list. We will notify you immediately by e-mail or through our quarterly news magazine concerning law or policy changes. You may sign up for our free weekly e-mail Updates at www.heav.org.

The information and opinions contained here are not necessarily those of Home Educators Association of Virginia. HEAV does not give legal advice; no part of this section or manual should be construed as such. We recommend you seek legal counsel concerning the application of the Virginia Code to your particular situation.

Virginia Homeschool Laws and Related Statutes

ARTICLE I

Compulsory School Attendance §22.1-254. Compulsory attendance required; excuses and waivers; alternative education program attendance; exemptions from article.

A. Except as otherwise provided in this article, every parent, guardian, or other person in the Commonwealth having control or charge of any child who will have reached the fifth birthday on or before September 30 of any school year and who has not passed the eighteenth birthday shall, during the period of each year the public schools are in session and for the same number of days and hours per day as the public schools, send such child to a public school or to a private, denominational or parochial school or have such child taught by a tutor or teacher of qualifications prescribed by the Board of Education and approved by the division superintendent or provide for home instruction of such child as described in §22.1-254.1.

As prescribed in the regulations of the Board of Education, the requirements of this section may also be satisfied by sending a child to an alternative program of study or work/study offered by a public, private, denominational or parochial school or by a public or private degree-granting institution of higher education. Further, in the case of any five-year-old child who is subject to the provisions of this subsection, the requirements of this section may be alternatively satisfied by sending the child to any public educational pre-kindergarten program, including a Head Start program, or in a private, denominational or parochial educational pre-kindergarten program.

Instruction in the home of a child or children by the parent, guardian or other person having control or charge of such child or children shall not be classified or defined as a private, denominational or parochial school.

The requirements of this section shall apply to (i) any child in the custody of the Department of Juvenile Justice or the Department of Corrections who has not passed his eighteenth birthday and (ii) any child whom the division superintendent has required to take a special program of prevention, intervention, or remediation as provided in subsection C of §22.1-253.13:1 and in §22.1-254.01. However, the requirements of this section shall not apply to any child who has obtained a high school diploma, its equivalent, or a certificate of completion or who has otherwise complied with compulsory school attendance requirements as set forth in this article.

B. A school board shall excuse from attendance at school:

1. Any pupil who, together with his parents, by reason of *bona fide* religious training or belief is conscientiously opposed to attendance at school. For purposes of this subdivision, "*bona fide* religious training or belief" does not include essentially political, sociological or philosophical views or a merely personal moral code;

H. The provisions of this article shall not apply to:

1. Children suffering from contagious or infectious diseases while suffering from such diseases;

2. Children whose immunizations against communicable diseases have not been completed as provided in §22.1-271.2;

3. Children under ten years of age who live more than two miles from a public school unless public transportation is provided within one mile of the place where such children live;

4. Children between the ages of ten and seventeen, inclusive, who live more than 2.5 miles from a public school unless public transportation is provided within 1.5 miles of the place where such children live; and
5. Children excused pursuant to subsections B and C of this section. Further, any child who will not have reached his sixth birthday on or before September 30 of each school year whose parent or guardian notifies the appropriate school board that he does not wish the child to attend school until the following year because the child, in the opinion of the parent or guardian, is not mentally, physically or emotionally prepared to attend school, may delay the child's attendance for one year.

The distances specified in subdivisions 3 and 4 of this subsection shall be measured or determined from the child's residence to the entrance to the school grounds or to the school bus stop nearest the entrance to the residence of such children by the nearest practical routes which are usable for walking or riding. Disease shall be established by the certificate of a reputable practicing physician in accordance with regulations adopted by the Board of Education.

(Code 1950, §22-275.1; 1952, c. 279; 1959, Ex. Sess., c. 72; 1968, c. 178; 1974, c. 199; 1976, cc. 681, 713; 1978, c. 518; 1980, c. 559; 1984, c. 436; 1989, c. 515; 1990, c. 797; 1991, c. 295; 1993, c. 903; 1996, cc. 163, 916, 964; 1997, c. 828; 1999, cc. 488, 552; 2000, c. 184; 2001, cc. 688, 820.)

VIOLATIONS OF
COMPULSORY EDUCATION
§22.1-263. Violation constitutes misdemeanor.

Any person violating the provisions of either §22.1-254, except for clause (ii) of subsection A, §§22.1-255, 22.1-258, or §22.1-267 shall be guilty of a Class 3 misdemeanor. Upon a finding that a person knowingly and willfully violated any provision of §22.1-254, except for clause (ii) of subsection A, or any provision of §§22.1-255, 22.1-258, or §22.1-267 and that such person has been convicted previously of a violation of any provision of §22.1-254, except for clause (ii) of subsection A, or any provision of §§22.1-255, 22.1-258 or §22.1-267, such person shall be guilty of a Class 2 misdemeanor.

(Code 1950, §22-275.5; 1959, Ex. Sess., c. 72; 1976, c. 283; 1980, c. 559; 1990, c. 797; 1991, c. 295; 1996, cc. 891, 964; 1999, cc. 488, 526, 552.)

§22.1-254.1. Declaration of policy; requirements for home instruction of children.

A. When the requirements of this section have been satisfied, instruction of children by their parents is an acceptable alternative form of education under the policy of the Commonwealth of Virginia. Any parent of any child who will have reached the fifth birthday on or before September 30 of any school year and who has not passed the eighteenth birthday may elect to provide home instruction in lieu of school attendance if he (i) holds a high school diploma; or (ii) is a teacher of qualifications prescribed by the Board of Education; or (iii) provides a program of study or curriculum which may be delivered through a correspondence course or distance learning program or in any other manner; or (iv) provides evidence that he is able to provide an adequate education for the child. B. Any parent who elects to provide

home instruction in lieu of school attendance shall annually notify the division superintendent in August of his intention to so instruct the child and provide a description of the curriculum to be followed for the coming year and evidence of having met one of the criteria for providing home instruction as required by subsection A of this section. Effective July 1, 2000, parents electing to provide home instruction shall provide such annual notice no later than August 15. Any parent who moves into a school division or begins home instruction after the school year has begun shall notify the division superintendent of his intention to provide home instruction as soon as practicable and shall thereafter comply with the requirements of this section within thirty days of such notice. The division superintendent shall notify the Superintendent of Public Instruction of the number of students in the school division receiving home instruction.

C. The parent who elects to provide home instruction shall provide the division superintendent by August 1 following the school year in which the child has received home instruction with either (i) evidence that the child has attained a composite score in or above the fourth stanine on any nationally normed standardized achievement test or (ii) an evaluation or assessment which the division superintendent determines to indicate that the child is achieving an adequate level of educational growth and progress, including but not limited to: (a) an evaluation letter from a person licensed to teach in any state, or a person with a master's degree or higher in an academic discipline, having knowledge of the child's academic progress, stating that the child is achieving an adequate level of educational growth and progress; or (b) a report card or transcript from a community college or college, college distance learning program, or home-education correspondence school.

In the event that evidence of progress as required in this subsection is not provided by the parent, the home instruction program for that child may be placed on probation for one year. Parents shall file with the division superintendent evidence of their ability to provide an adequate education for their child in compliance with subsection A of this section and a remediation plan for the probationary year which indicates their program is designed to address any educational deficiency. Upon acceptance of such evidence and plan by the division superintendent, the home instruction may continue for one probationary year. If the remediation plan and evidence are not accepted or the required evidence of progress is not provided by August 1 following the probationary year, home instruction shall cease and the parent shall make other arrangements for the education of the child which comply with §22.1-254. The requirements of subsection C shall not apply to children who are under the age of six as of September 30 of the school year.

D. For purposes of this section, "parent" means the biological parent or adoptive parent, guardian or other person having control or charge of a child.
Nothing in this section shall prohibit a pupil and his parents from obtaining an excuse from school attendance by reason of *bona fide* religious training or belief pursuant to §22.1-254 B 1.

E. Any party aggrieved by a decision of the division superintendent may appeal his decision within thirty days to an independent hearing officer. The independent hearing officer shall be chosen from the list maintained by the Executive Secretary of the Supreme Court for hearing appeals of the placements of children with disabilities. The costs of the hearing shall be apportioned among the parties by the hearing officer in a manner consistent with his findings.

F. School boards shall implement a plan to notify students receiving home instruction pursuant to this section and their parents of the availability of Advanced Placement (AP) and Preliminary Scholastic Aptitude Test (PSAT) examinations and the availability of financial assistance to low-income and needy students to take these examinations. School boards shall implement a plan to make these examinations available to students receiving home instruction.

(1984, c. 436; 1986, c. 215; 1991, c. 306; 1992, c. 131; 1993, c. 992; 1994, c. 854; 1998, c. 435; 1999, cc. 488, 552.)

The Legal Who, What, When, and Where of Homeschooling

Yvonne Bunn

You've decided to homeschool. Of course you want to do things right. After all, it's *your* family's future you're planning. By now, you know it's legal. But how exactly do you comply with the law? What does the law say about homeschooling?

The Virginia homeschool law is very precise in most areas. Among other things, it defines who can teach at home, what requirements must be fulfilled, when to notify the state authorities, as well as where a parent can go if he disagrees with a superintendent's decision.

Although the legalese can sound very complicated, don't be intimidated—help is available! There are many experienced homeschoolers who can offer encouragement. Local support-group leaders who are familiar with the legal atmosphere in your area can tell you what to expect. The *Virginia Homeschool Manual* includes copies of the homeschool laws and related statutes, Attorney Generals' Opinions, helpful forms, and other useful resources. HEAV office personnel will be glad to answer your questions. You may also e-mail your questions to us at office@heav.org.

With these things in mind, take one question at a time and refer to the source material in the *Virginia Homeschool Manual* (especially references to the statute). It's important to understand your rights as a parent and know the correct application of the homeschool law. Here we'll address some of the questions that are asked most often:

- Who is required to attend school?
- What schooling options are available for children?
- What requirements must be fulfilled in order to homeschool?
- Whom do I notify that I plan to homeschool?
- When should I send in my notification?
- Where can I go if I disagree with a decision made by the superintendent?
- What if I am homeschooling because of sincere religious beliefs?

WHO IS REQUIRED TO ATTEND SCHOOL?

If your child will be five years old on or before September 30, and has not passed his eighteenth birthday, he must attend school §22.1-254 (A).

However, there is an important exemption to this statute. If, in your opinion as a parent, your child is not mentally, physically, or emotionally prepared to attend school, you may delay your child's attendance for one year §22.1-254 (H) (5). Your child may be **exempted from compulsory school attendance** if he is not six on or before September 30, **and** you notify the school board that you don't want him to attend school until the following year. If you elect to keep your five-year-old at home, you may still teach your child in a manner suitable for his age and maturity. With this exemption, it's not necessary to submit a "Notice of Intent to Homeschool" form until he is six by September 30.

If you plan to homeschool the following year, you may register your six-year-old child as a kindergartner or first-grader depending on his level of achievement and maturity. Regardless, end-of-the-year testing is not required for students who are five years old on September 30 of the school year. The deadline for filing the "Notice of Intent to Homeschool" is August 15 of the year in which you plan to formally teach at home.

WHAT SCHOOLING OPTIONS ARE AVAILABLE FOR CHILDREN?

According to §22.1-254 (A) a parent may (1) send his child to public school; (2) send his child to private, denominational, or parochial school; (3) have his child taught by a tutor or teacher of qualifications approved by the division superintendent; or (4) provide for home education as described in §22.1-254.1. A child may also be excused from compulsory education because of a religious exemption §22.1-254 (B)(1).

The first and second options for education listed above are self-explanatory. The third option referenced in §22.1-254 (A), also known as the "certified or approved tutor statute," allows a child to be taught in or out of his home by a Virginia certified teacher (either his parent or another teacher) whose qualifications are approved by the superintendent. None of the requirements of the homeschool statute apply (i.e. testing). Any parent who meets the qualification of a certified teacher or approved tutor may teach under this option rather than the homeschool statute (see "Certified-Tutor Provision Clarified" in the *Virginia Homeschool Manual*).

To qualify under the certified-tutor option, a parent should submit his credentials to the Division of Teacher Education, Certification, and Professional Development of the Department of Education to secure a certificate or letter of eligibility. If the approved tutor is the parent, the parent simply sends a letter to the division superintendent with a copy of his teacher certification or letter of eligibility and indicates that he is complying with the third option of §22.1-254 (A).

If the parent who is an approved tutor teaches other children, the names of these children should also be listed in the letter. An approved tutor who is not the parent should send a letter with his certification verification and a list of the children being taught.

The fourth option in §22.1-254 (A) is home instruction. This is defined as the instruction of a child by his parent, guardian, or other person having control or charge of the child. It is not considered a private, denominational, or parochial school §22.1-254 (A).

WHAT REQUIREMENTS MUST BE FULFILLED IN ORDER TO HOMESCHOOL UNDER THE HOMESCHOOL STATUTE?

1) First, according to §22.1-254.1 (A), you must meet one of four options.

You may teach at home if any one of the following conditions is met: if a parent (1) has a high school diploma; or (2) is a certified teacher*; or ((3) provides a program of study or curriculum which may be delivered through a correspondence course or distance learning program or in any other manner; or (iv) provides evidence that he is able to provide an adequate education for the child. These four options are listed on the form entitled, "Notice of Intent to Provide Home Instruction."

*Note: If a Virginia certified teacher complies with option (2) of the homeschool statute as listed on the "Notice of Intent to Provide Home Instruction" form instead of §22.1-254 (A), end-of-the-year testing will be required as part of the homeschool statute.

2) Then, you must provide proof that you have met one of the four options.

Option (1) can be satisfied by attaching a copy of a high school diploma from either parent; option (2) can be satisfied by attaching a certificate or letter of eligibility indicating teacher certification; option (3) can be satisfied by including evidence of enrollment, such as a receipt for payment, letter of acceptance, or enrollment contract; or for an individualized curriculum, a copy of the table of contents or scope and sequence; and option (4) is satisfied by a well-written statement indicating why the parent is able to provide an adequate education for his child.

For the option (iv) statement, you might briefly state that because you are the parent, you know your child best and you are able to determine his academic needs. You might also say you plan to exercise diligence in teaching your child, using a well-planned curriculum. Although the superintendent cannot judge your reasons, he will determine if your statement exhibits a mastery of language, basic grammar, and correct spelling.

For all options, a description of the curriculum must be included. A brief listing of the subjects to be taught and the titles of the books or methods you plan to use should be sufficient. It is not necessary to provide lesson plans or send your textbooks to the superintendent.

3) You must submit evidence of academic achievement.

After each year of homeschooling, a parent is required to submit evidence of academic achievement. This evidence may be in the form of a standardized achievement test or an evaluation or assessment §22.1-254.1 (C) (see Testing and Evaluation in the *Virginia Homeschool Manual*). It must be submitted to the division superintendent by August 1 after each year of homeschooling.

4) You must comply with immunization requirements.

The homeschooling parent must comply with the immunization requirements in the same manner and to the same extent as public schools §22.1-271.4. These records are to be maintained by the parents at home. Immunization exemptions are available (see "Virginia Immunization Requirements" in the *Virginia Homeschool Manual*).

WHOM DO I NOTIFY THAT I PLAN TO HOMESCHOOL?

If you decide to homeschool, you must notify your **local division superintendent or his designee** §22.1-254.1 (B). This can be done by a personal letter, which includes evidence of meeting one of the requirements, or by using the "Notice of Intent to Homeschool" form. This form is included in the *Virginia Homeschool Manual*. It may also be downloaded from the HEAV website at www.heav.org or obtained from the HEAV office, your local division superintendent, or the State Department of Education.

Remember to keep copies of all correspondence. You may want to send your "Notice of Intent" form by registered mail. It's not necessary to deliver it in person.

WHEN SHOULD I SEND IN MY NOTIFICATION?

The division superintendent must be notified by August 15 of each school year. Parents who move into the school division after August 15 or who begin home instruction after the school year has begun, must notify the superintendent of their intent to homeschool as soon as practical and comply with the statute within thirty days of notification §22.1-254.1 (B).

If you decide to homeschool after the deadline, please refer to "Beginning Home Education after the Deadline" in the *Virginia Homeschool Manual*. This article addresses special situations and what you might expect.

WHERE DO I GO IF I DISAGREE WITH A DECISION MADE BY THE SUPERINTENDENT?

If you disagree with a division superintendent's decision, you may **make an appeal to an independent hearing officer within thirty days**. Inform your superintendent that you want to request an appeal. (This process is less intimidating for those who have retained experienced legal counsel.) An independent hearing officer will be chosen from a list maintained by the Executive Secretary of the Supreme Court. After the appeal, the cost of the hearing will be apportioned by the hearing officer according to his findings §22.1-254.1(E).

WHAT IF I AM HOMESCHOOLING BECAUSE OF SINCERE RELIGIOUS BELIEFS?

Most homeschoolers who have religious beliefs are fully accommodated by the homeschool statute, §22.1-254.1. However, according to §22.1-254.1 (D), nothing in the homeschool statute shall prohibit a student and his parents from obtaining an exemption from school attendance because of *bona fide* religious training or belief as referenced in §22.1-254 (B) (1). This statute—known as "the religious exemption statute"—states, "A school board shall excuse from attendance at school any pupil who, together with his parents, by reason of *bona fide* religious training or belief, is conscientiously opposed to attendance at school," §22.1-254 (B) (1). (For a more complete explanation of the terms used in this statute, please refer to the articles entitled "Virginia Religious Exemption" and "Religious Exemption—Demystified" in the *Virginia Homeschool Manual.*)

Both parents must have personal religious convictions against school attendance. While you may have philosophical, political, or sociological objections, or a personal moral code in opposition to school attendance, this cannot be the basis for a religious exemption. You must be conscientiously opposed to attendance at school because of *bona fide* religious training or belief in order to homeschool under §22.1-254 (B) (1). This statute cannot be used for any other reason.

Parents homeschooling under religious exemption should be prepared, if called upon, to testify before their local school board concerning their genuine religious beliefs. It is mandatory that parents have strong religious convictions, not just preferences. Because school boards differ in their understanding of the requirements for religious exemption, adequate legal representation is important. Homeschool Legal Defense Association provides legal services for homeschooling families, but you must be a member *before* a problem arises.

How you comply with the homeschool law is foundational to all other decisions concerning home instruction. Review your legal options carefully. Understand your choices. Then decide what is right for your family.

The purpose of this article is to clarify the statutory procedures for homeschoolers. This information should not be construed as legal advice. HEAV encourages all homeschooling parents to seek legal counsel for specific applications of the law.

Virginia Homeschool Laws
VIRGINIA HOMESCHOOL LAWS

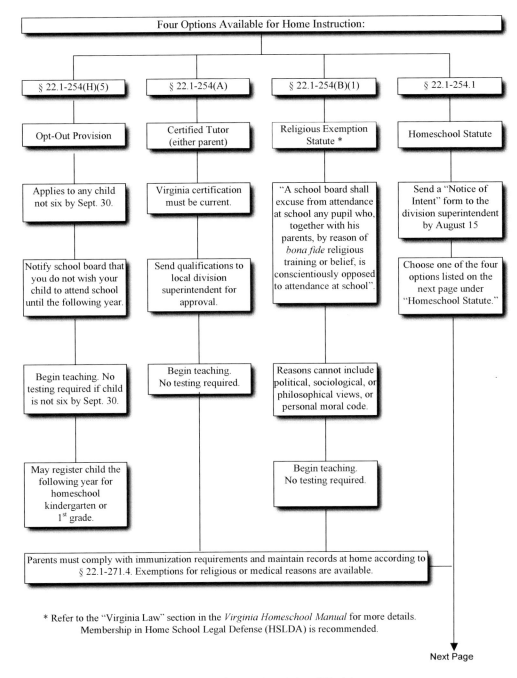

Four Options Available for Home Instruction:

§ 22.1-254(H)(5)	§ 22.1-254(A)	§ 22.1-254(B)(1)	§ 22.1-254.1
Opt-Out Provision	Certified Tutor (either parent)	Religious Exemption Statute *	Homeschool Statute
Applies to any child not six by Sept. 30.	Virginia certification must be current.	"A school board shall excuse from attendance at school any pupil who, together with his parents, by reason of *bona fide* religious training or belief, is conscientiously opposed to attendance at school".	Send a "Notice of Intent" form to the division superintendent by August 15
Notify school board that you do not wish your child to attend school until the following year.	Send qualifications to local division superintendent for approval.		Choose one of the four options listed on the next page under "Homeschool Statute."
Begin teaching. No testing required if child is not six by Sept. 30.	Begin teaching. No testing required.	Reasons cannot include political, sociological, or philosophical views, or personal moral code.	
May register child the following year for homeschool kindergarten or 1st grade.		Begin teaching. No testing required.	

Parents must comply with immunization requirements and maintain records at home according to § 22.1-271.4. Exemptions for religious or medical reasons are available.

* Refer to the "Virginia Law" section in the *Virginia Homeschool Manual* for more details. Membership in Home School Legal Defense (HSLDA) is recommended.

Next Page

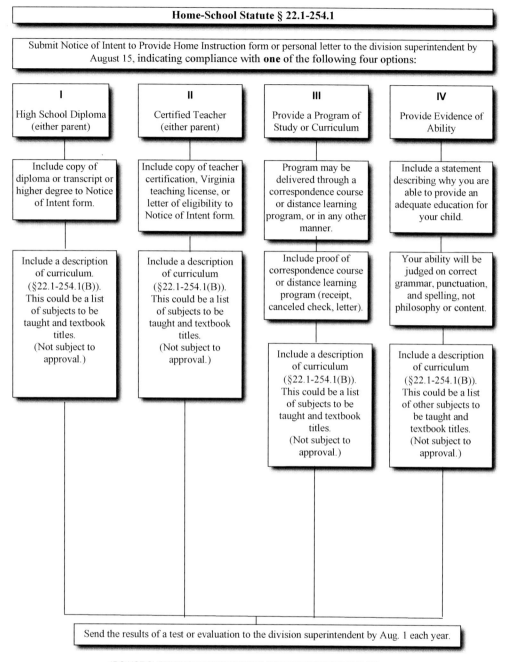

Home-School Statute § 22.1-254.1

Submit Notice of Intent to Provide Home Instruction form or personal letter to the division superintendent by August 15, indicating compliance with **one** of the following four options:

I

High School Diploma (either parent)

Include copy of diploma or transcript or higher degree to Notice of Intent form.

Include a description of curriculum. (§22.1-254.1(B)). This could be a list of subjects to be taught and textbook titles. (Not subject to approval.)

II

Certified Teacher (either parent)

Include copy of teacher certification, Virginia teaching license, or letter of eligibility to Notice of Intent form.

Include a description of curriculum (§22.1-254.1(B)). This could be a list of subjects to be taught and textbook titles. (Not subject to approval.)

III

Provide a Program of Study or Curriculum

Program may be delivered through a correspondence course or distance learning program, or in any other manner.

Include proof of correspondence course or distance learning program (receipt, canceled check, letter).

Include a description of curriculum (§22.1-254.1(B)). This could be a list of subjects to be taught and textbook titles. (Not subject to approval.)

IV

Provide Evidence of Ability

Include a statement describing why you are able to provide an adequate education for your child.

Your ability will be judged on correct grammar, punctuation, and spelling, not philosophy or content.

Include a description of curriculum (§22.1-254.1(B)). This could be a list of other subjects to be taught and textbook titles. (Not subject to approval.)

Send the results of a test or evaluation to the division superintendent by Aug. 1 each year.

*DO NOT SUBMIT MORE INFORMATION THAN IS REQUIRED BY LAW.
When complying with the statute, HEAV encourages parents to use the least intrusive methods of compliance that are acceptable to your superintendent. The flow chart above describes several methods that have satisfied superintendents' requirements.

© 2008 Home Educators Association of Virginia

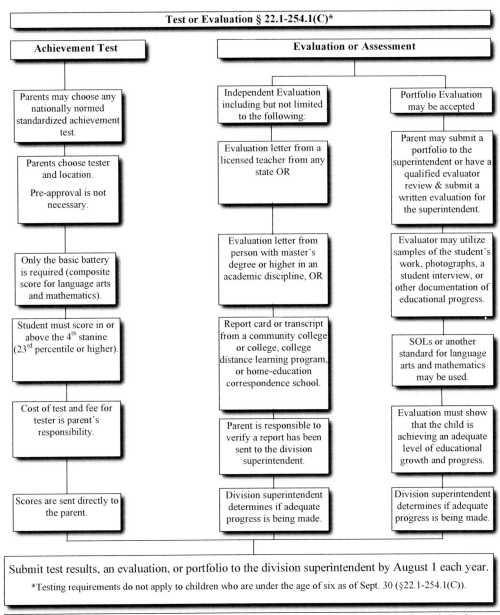

Test or Evaluation § 22.1-254.1(C)*

Achievement Test

Parents may choose any nationally normed standardized achievement test.

Parents choose tester and location.
Pre-approval is not necessary.

Only the basic battery is required (composite score for language arts and mathematics).

Student must score in or above the 4th stanine (23rd percentile or higher).

Cost of test and fee for tester is parent's responsibility.

Scores are sent directly to the parent.

Evaluation or Assessment

Independent Evaluation including but not limited to the following:

Evaluation letter from a licensed teacher from any state OR

Evaluation letter from person with master's degree or higher in an academic discipline, OR

Report card or transcript from a community college or college, college distance learning program, or home-education correspondence school.

Parent is responsible to verify a report has been sent to the division superintendent.

Division superintendent determines if adequate progress is being made.

Portfolio Evaluation may be accepted

Parent may submit a portfolio to the superintendent or have a qualified evaluator review & submit a written evaluation for the superintendent.

Evaluator may utilize samples of the student's work, photographs, a student interview, or other documentation of educational progress.

SOLs or another standard for language arts and mathematics may be used.

Evaluation must show that the child is achieving an adequate level of educational growth and progress.

Division superintendent determines if adequate progress is being made.

Submit test results, an evaluation, or portfolio to the division superintendent by August 1 each year.
*Testing requirements do not apply to children who are under the age of six as of Sept. 30 (§22.1-254.1(C)).

If evidence of progress is not provided by the parent, the home instruction program for that child may be placed on probation for one year. Parents must file with the division superintendent evidence of their ability to provide an adequate education and a remediation plan for the probationary year indicating they will be addressing any educational deficiencies. Upon acceptance of the plan, home instruction may continue for one year. If the plan and evidence are not accepted or the evidence or progress is not provided by August 1 following the probationary year, home instruction shall cease. §22.1-254.1(C)

NOTICE OF INTENT TO PROVIDE HOME INSTRUCTION

I am providing notice of my intention to provide home instruction for the child(ren) listed below in lieu of having them attend school as provided in §22.1-254.1 of the Code of Virginia (1950) as amended.

School Year: 20_____-20_____

NAME(S) OF CHILD(REN)	AGE(S)
_____	_____
_____	_____
_____	_____
_____	_____
_____	_____

I am eligible to provide home instruction under the following option (check one):

_____ I have a high school diploma. (Attach copy of high school diploma or transcript, associate's degree, baccalaureate degree or higher.)

_____ I have the qualifications prescribed by the Board of Education for a teacher. (Attach statement to this effect from the Virginia Department of Education.)

_____ I have provided a program of study or curriculum delivered through a correspondence course, distance learning program, or in another manner. (Attach proof of program or curriculum such as a receipt or letter of acceptance, or a copy of the table of contents or scope and sequence for an individualized curriculum.)

_____ I have attached to this notice evidence that I am able to provide an adequate education for my child(ren). (Attach a statement.)

A description of the curriculum to be followed for the coming school year is attached for each child.

I understand that by August 1 of next year, I must provide evidence of educational achievement for each child listed above who has reached his sixth birthday on or before September 30 of this school year, as prescribed in §22.1-254.1 of the Code of Virginia, which defines the requirements for home instruction.

_____ I would like a copy of §22.1-254.1 on home instruction.

I hereby certify that I am the parent or guardian of the child(ren) listed above.

Signature_____ Date_____

Print or type name and address:

_____

_____

_____

SEND THIS FORM TO THE LOCAL SUPERINTENDENT OF PUBLIC SCHOOLS.

Revised effective July 1, 2008

K-5 Registration

Yvonne Bunn

Kindergarten: to register or not to register? That is the question—at least that's the question most frequently asked of the HEAV office staff during the summer months.

Even if you're a veteran homeschooling parent, you're faced with this question each time a five-year-old's birthday rolls around. Pressure builds as you watch neighborhood children lining up at the bus stop, and it increases even more as "friendly neighbors" (grandparents also) ask questions about beginning school. You still have a choice—even though most parents of public school, private school, and homeschooled students don't know they do!

Most people know, according to Virginia law, if your child will be five years old on or before September 30, and has not passed his eighteenth birthday, he must attend school §22.1-254 (A).

However, there is an important exemption to this statute. If, in your opinion as a parent, your child is not mentally, physically, or emotionally prepared to attend school, you may delay your child's attendance for one year §22.1-254 (H) (5). Your child may be **exempted from compulsory school attendance** if he is not six on or before September 30, **and** you notify your local school board that you do not want him to attend school until the following year.

If you elect to keep your five-year-old at home, you may still teach your child in a manner suitable for his age and maturity. With this exemption, it's not necessary to submit a "Notice of Intent to Provide Home Instruction" form until he is six by September 30.

The following year, you may register your six-year-old child as a kindergartner or first-grader depending on his level of achievement and maturity. Regardless, **end-of-the-year testing is not required for students who are five years old on September 30 of the school year.** The deadline for filing the "Notice of Intent to Provide Home Instruction" is August 15 of the year you plan to formally teach at home.

A call to the local superintendent's office asking what procedure you should follow in notifying the local school board may be helpful. Sometimes this initial phone call is all that is necessary, and at other times a letter is required. Procedures vary from district to district. Don't even be surprised if the secretary tells you that you can't do this—just quote the statute reference above.

What is the advantage of not formally filing a "Notice of Intent to Provide Home Instruction" form for a five-year-old kindergartner? Some children are not ready for school at age five. An extra year will give a child time to mature and continue to develop pre-reading skills and eye-hand coordination. For some children, an additional year may lay the foundation for a successful school experience—a school experience without the frustration of being forced to learn skills he is not ready to learn. Remember, when you homeschool, you do what is best for your child. You don't have to force him to do what everyone else is doing. Home education is individualized instruction—one-on-one tutoring—working with a child at his optimal level of learning.

Beginning Home Education after the Deadline

Yvonne Bunn

A ugust 15—D-Day for filing the "Notice of Intent to Homeschool" form. What can you do if you missed the deadline? Maybe you didn't even know there was a deadline! Do you have to wait another year to begin? Or what if you moved to Virginia after school started and you want to homeschool? Or maybe you want to begin homeschooling in the middle of the year? The fact is, you want to begin homeschooling...*now*. What should you do? What *can* you do?

BE PREPARED

No matter what the circumstances, get complete and accurate information about **all** homeschooling options **before** you contact local officials. Please consider purchasing the *Virginia Homeschool Manual.* There is no better reference on home educating in Virginia—from the requirements of the homeschool law to approved correspondence courses, from socialization to preparing high school transcripts—it's all included! The manual will put the most complete homeschooling information at your fingertips. Well-meaning friends may or may not have the all the facts. The Department of Education will gladly give you information but may add policies beyond the requirements of the law. By being well-informed, you'll know what to expect and be better prepared to make important decisions.

NEW SCHOOL DIVISION RESIDENTS

If you're a new Virginia resident or you've moved within the state from one school district to another, you should comply with Virginia statute §22.1-254.1 (B) as stated below:*

"Any parent who moves into a school division or begins home instruction after the school year has begun shall notify the division superintendent of his intentions to provide home instruction as soon as practicable and shall thereafter comply with the requirements of this section within thirty days of such notice."

Simply stated: When things settle down after the move, inform your local division superintendent that you are in his district. You then have thirty days to comply with the homeschool statute §22.1-254.1.

CURRENT RESIDENTS

Virginia parents who decide to homeschool after the August 15 deadline may also homeschool. According to the language in §22.1-154.1 (B) above, parents are allowed to begin homeschooling after the August deadline. However, this change in the statute does not mean that parents who already teach at home can be lax about the deadline. It clearly refers to parents who **begin** to homeschool for the first time after the school year has begun. The August 15 deadline can be enforced if a family willingly avoids or carelessly neglects to notify the division superintendent

PREPARING FOR THE CHANGE

If you are withdrawing your child from public school in order to begin to homeschool, it is helpful if you understand and are ready to meet the requirements of the homeschool statute **before** withdrawing your child. By being properly prepared, you may avoid the possibility of truancy charges (up to a $100 per day fine and six months in jail). Here's what you need to do:

First, contact a local support group in your area. HEAV networks with more than 220 support groups throughout the state. We will gladly put you in touch with a support-group leader near you. The local support group is familiar with the "homeschool climate" in your area and can usually tell you what to expect. Experienced parents in the group can also offer encouragement as you get started.

Second, obtain a "Notice of Intent to Provide Home Instruction" form from our website at www.heav.org, the HEAV office, the *Virginia Homeschool Manual*, or from your local division superintendent's office. When submitting this form, you must show evidence of: (1) a high school diploma (attach a copy), **or** (2) Virginia teacher certification, (attach documentation) **or** (3) a program of study or curriculum which may be delivered through a correspondence course or distance learning program or in any other manner (attach a payment receipt, letter of welcome, or enrollment contract, or for an individualized curriculum, a copy of the table of contents or scope and sequence, or (iv) evidence that you are able to provide an adequate education for your child (attach a well-written statement). See related articles for more details concerning the four options listed above.

Third, it is best to have materials and a curriculum plan **before** withdrawing your child from school and **before** submitting the "Notice of Intent to Provide Home Instruction" form to the division superintendent. The "Notice of Intent" form requires limited documentation of curriculum. If you are prepared, there will be fewer questions and a smoother transition. Taking your child out of a public school without some type of notification by the parents could result in a truancy investigation. However, the law does not require a parent to wait for "approval" from the division superintendent before withdrawing the student: Virginia is not an "approval" state. The law requires notification of your intent to homeschool.

If for some reason the superintendent responds negatively, you have thirty days to appeal his decision before an independent hearing officer. The cost of the hearing will be apportioned by the hearing officer in a manner consistent with his findings. **Never** ignore official correspondence or telephone calls. For your protection, you should request that all communication be documented in letter form and mailed to you.

It is important for you and your child to begin your homeschooling experience on a positive foundation. Know the law. Know your rights as a parent. Know what to do and how to prepare for success. Yes, you can homeschool...now!

*If your religious convictions cannot be accommodated by this statute, please contact the HEAV office or read related articles in the Virginia Homeschool Manual *for more information.*

[Neither HEAV, support group leaders, nor homeschool proponents should give legal advice. The information in this article should not be construed as such; however, our purpose is to inform interested parents of their options under the Virginia statute.]

Certified-Tutor Provision Clarified

HOMESCHOOLER WINS CASE IN VIRGINIA

After all the years Homeschool Legal Defense Association has spent fighting teacher-certification requirements for homeschoolers, it is ironic to find ourselves in court defending parents' right to homeschool under the certified teacher provision.

Charles and Nancy Berlin, of Manassas, Virginia, have two children and have been homeschooling for three years. Until this year, however, their oldest child had not been of compulsory school age. Since Mrs. Berlin is a state-certified teacher, they chose to operate their homeschool under Virginia's certified teacher statute (§22.1-254(A)).

The Prince William County School Board, however, challenged the right of the Berlins to homeschool under the certified teacher statute, insisting that they operate under the homeschool law. Virginia's homeschool law, of course, imposes several other requirements, including testing, which are not required of the certified tutors under the statute.

On November 24, 1993, Prince William County School Board v. Charles Berlin was argued in Circuit Court before Judge Richard Potter. The school-board attorney argued that the certified-tutor option was really only for non-parents. The school board also asserted that the homeschool law, passed in 1984, was the exclusive option for parents who were choosing to homeschool.

Attorney Klicka, defending the Berlins, pointed out that the school board's argument ignores the fact that parents can legally homeschool under other options, including the religious-exemption option, the five-year-old exemption option, and the health exemption. Furthermore, Klicka argued that the Virginia legislature specifically intended the certified-tutor option to apply to parents who homeschool their children as well as to non-parents. In an earlier Virginia Supreme Court case in 1982, the Court specifically stated that the certified-tutor option was available to parents who homeschool their children. In fact, at that time, that was the only way homeschoolers could legally operate in the state of Virginia. Klicka emphasized that there was no conflict between the homeschool law and the certified-tutor option. Parents who qualified under the certified-tutor option could choose it over the homeschool statute option. HSLDA asked the Circuit Court to deny the school board's motion for a summary judgment.

The Prince William County Circuit Court ruled in favor of the Berlin family and stated,

> *"Now, in plain reading, it seems to me this gives a parent four choices; you send your child to public school, you send your child to a private school, you have you child taught by a tutor or teacher, either in the home or outside the home, by the parent or by a non-parent, or you provide for home instruction as described in 22.1-254.1. The Court notes that the term "tutor" or "teacher" is not defined as parent or non-parent. The term "tutor" or "teacher" is not defined as in the home or out of the home, but I did note that in the Grigg case, the Court found that it was an intent, that was to include in home teaching (emphasis added)."*

The Court is simply stating here that according to the Virginia legislature's intent, the Virginia Supreme Court's decision in Grigg, and the plain reading of the statute, the certified-tutor option applies to parents as well as non-parents. Therefore, any parent who meets the qualifications of a tutor or teacher under §22.1-254 can legally teach their children under this option rather than under the homeschool statute. The Court concludes:

> *"I don't think these two code sections are in conflict. I think these two code sections are very clear. I think it gives you four alternatives. The fourth alternative is described in §22.1-254.1. That fourth alternative, by definition in §22.1-254.1, was not meant to define the other three alternatives, nor do I see any legislative intent to limit the tutor or teacher either to the home as a place of location or to the non-parent. So clearly, the statute provides for teaching within the home by a tutor or teacher of qualifications prescribed by the Board of Education and approved by the Division Superintendent. The facts as stipulated to me for the purpose of this summary judgment motion, I must deny the motion for summary judgment at this time. If, in fact, those facts are proven, it seems to me that this woman meets the third alternative which is to be a teacher within the home who is qualified pursuant to the requirements of the Board of Education and has been approved by the Division Superintendent, and she need not meet the requirements of the fourth alternative, which are defined in 22.1-254.1."*

Finding no conflict between the homeschool statute and the certified-tutor statute, the Prince William County Circuit Court ruled in favor of the Berlins. The court's ruling clearly states that these were just two options from which parents could choose if they were qualified. The Court then signed an order denying Prince William County's motion for summary judgment. As a result, the Prince William County School Board formally dismissed their declaratory-judgment action.

©*From the* Homeschool Court Report*, January/February 1994. Reprinted with permission.*

Certified-Tutor Summary

§22.1-254(A) of the Code of Virginia identifies the ways parents can comply with Virginia's compulsory attendance requirements. This includes a provision that allows a parent to satisfy compulsory attendance requirements by having "...such child taught by a tutor or teacher of qualifications prescribed by the Board of Education and approved by the division superintendent..." as an alternative to attendance at a public or private school.

Parents who are certified teachers may teach their own children under this provision, known as "the certified tutor" option, instead of the home instruction statute found in §22.1-254.1.

Under the certified tutor provision:
- The tutor or teacher must have current teacher certification prescribed by the Virginia Board of Education
- Certification must be approved by the division superintendent
- A parent or non-parent who is certified may teach using §22.1-254(A)
- The tutor may teach his/her own children or other children
- Instruction may take place in the home or outside the home
- End-of-year assessment is not required
- Yearly notification is not required as long as certification is current; new or up-dated certification should be submitted.

Notification should take place in the form of a letter to the division superintendent. Certification documents must be included for the superintendent's approval. In the letter, be sure to clearly state that you are in compliance with §22.1-254(A).

If you choose to use the certified tutor statute, DO NOT FILE a Notice of Intent form. DO NOT check option (ii) on the Notice of Intent form although it shows "certified tutor" as the second option to homeschool. Tutors who use the NOI form indicate they are in compliance with §22.1-245.1, the homeschool statute. The homeschool statute requires end-of-year assessment.

Because a certified tutor option is also included on the Notice of Intent form, understandably, some division personnel are confused. Be prepared to explain the difference if there are questions.

Tutor Provision v. Home Instruction Provision Memo

Supt. Memo 121- Compulsory Attendance Statutes

COMMONWEALTH OF VIRGINIA
DEPARTMENT OF EDUCATION
P.O. BOX 2120
RICHMOND, VIRGINIA 23216-2120

SUPTS. MEMO. NO. <u>121</u>
July 8, 1994

<u>INFORMATIONAL</u>

TO: Division Superintendents

FROM: William C. Bosher, Jr.
           Superintendent of Public Instruction

SUBJECT: Compulsory Attendance Statutes

Section 22.1-254 of the <u>Code of Virginia</u> identifies the mechanisms by which parents can satisfy the compulsory attendance requirements. This Section includes a provision which allows a parent to satisfy compulsory attendance requirements by having "... such child taught by a tutor or teacher of qualifications prescribed by the Board of Education and approved by the division superintendent ..." as an alternative to attendance at a public or private school. A number of parents around the state have sought approval to teach their own children at home under this provision instead of the provisions of the home instruction statute found in Section 22.1-254.1 of the <u>Code of Virginia</u>.

Historically, the Department's interpretation of the entire compulsory attendance statute has been that the tutor provision was not applicable to parents who wish to teach their own children at home. On November 24, 1993, the Circuit Court of Prince William County, in <u>Prince William County School v. Charles Berlin</u>, Case No. CH-34982, ruled that parents have all four options of the compulsory attendance statute available to them. The Department has reexamined its interpretation in light of this case and, by this Memorandum, is revising its interpretation. Parents who wish to teach their children at home have either the home instruction provisions of Section 22.1-254.1 or the tutor provision in Section 22.1-254 to use with the authorization of the division superintendent.

If you have questions regarding this issue, please do not hesitate to contact Robert L. Stokes, Associate Director for Accreditation, at (804) 225-2097, or Charles W. Finley, Specialist for Accreditation, at (804) 225-2747.

WCBJr/cwf

Virginia Religious Exemptions

Christopher J. Klicka, Senior Counsel of the HSLDA

I. The Law

The availability of a religious exemption from public school attendance is guaranteed by law in Virginia Code §22.1-254. The Code states:

B. A school board shall excuse from attendance at school:

1. Any pupil who, together with his parents, by reason of *bona fide* **religious training or belief**, is conscientiously opposed to attendance at school. For purposes of this subdivision, the term *bona fide* religious training or belief does not include essentially political, sociological or philosophical views or a merely personal moral code.

It is the school board itself, not the superintendent or any other administrator, who is charged with the duty of excusing those who are entitled to the benefit of the statute. The statute does not permit a school board to insist that a parent submit a particular form as a condition to receiving the benefit of the statute. The statute does not permit a school board to compel a family to submit annual requests. Once the excuse is granted, it is in effect indefinitely. Furthermore, once the excuse has been granted, it is applicable in any other Virginia county to which the family may relocate. This is because the school board acts as the agent of the state in granting the excuse, and the excuse is in relation to state law, not merely county policy.

Section 22.1-254(H)(5) states that children who are excused under the religious exemption above are excused from all provisions of the compulsory attendance law, including the homeschool requirements of §22.1-254.1. Families who are excused need not file an annual notice of intent or a year-end assessment.

To wrongly prohibit a family from operating their homeschool according to their convictions not only would violate §22.1-254(B)(1) but also would violate their First Amendment right to freely exercise their religious beliefs. [See *Wisconsin v. Yoder*, 406 U.S. 205, (1972); *State v. Whisner*, 47 Ohio St. 2d 181, 351 N.E. 2d 750 at 761, (1976); and *Sherbert v. Verner*, 374 U.S. 398, (1963).] The intent of §22.1-254(B)(1) of the Virginia Code is to protect the right of families to freely exercise their religious beliefs in the context of educating their children.

II. Three Areas of Inquiry

The first issue is whether the parents' opposition to public school attendance is based on personal **religious** beliefs as opposed to merely political, sociological or philosophical views or a merely personal moral code.

The second issue is whether the parents' religious beliefs concerning the education of their children are *bona fide* **or sincere.**

The third issue relates to the children themselves. The statute grants a right to an excuse to any pupil, who together with his parents, by reason of *bona fide* religious training OR belief, is conscientiously opposed to attendance at school. The use of the word "or" was an intentional change from the federal law (see below) on which the Virginia statute was based which required religious training AND belief. With this purposeful change from "and" to "or", it is clear that parents have a statutory option to either (1) allow their child to personally express his or her religious belief; or (2) demonstrate that they are training their children to be conscientiously opposed to attendance at public school. If parents so choose, they can decide to only give evidence as to their child's religious training instead of having the child try to express his or her religious belief. As long as the parents teach their children the same religious beliefs as they themselves hold, the children need not describe their beliefs.

If a school board finds that a particular family satisfies these three criteria, the board shall excuse their children. This is not discretionary; it is a mandatory legal duty.

Several key cases and an attorney-general opinion must be followed by the board each time they determine whether a family's beliefs are religious and *bona fide.*

III. The Case Law Defining What is a Religious Belief

When drafting the religious exemption statute in 1950, the Virginia Legislature used the same (nearly identical) language that was used two years earlier in the federal Universal Military Training and Service Act of 1948. Section 6(j) of that act [50 USC App. 456(j)] provides a religious exemption from military service for conscientious objectors. It states in part that persons **who by reason of their religious training and belief are conscientiously opposed** to participation in war are exempt from combatant training and service in the armed forces of the U.S. Because of the very close relationship between the federal conscientious exemption and Virginia's exemption, court decisions construing the federal exemption are commonly used to shed light on Virginia's exemption.

The federal exemption defines the phrase "religious training and belief" as an individual's belief in relation to a Supreme Being involving duties superior to those arising from any human relation, but not including essentially political, sociological, or philosophical views or a merely personal moral code. In *U.S. v. Seeger*, 380 U.S. 163 (1965), the U.S. Supreme Court defined the phrase "religious training and belief" (the same language used in §22.1-254(B)(1)) to mean a sincere and meaningful belief which occupies in the life of its possessor a place parallel to that filled by God (*Seeger*, 380 U.S. 176). The Court further declared,

> *Within that phrase would come all sincere religious beliefs which are based upon a power or being, or upon a faith, to which all else is subordinate or upon which all else is ultimately dependent.*

Id., at 176. The Court also explained that a belief is not religious if it is essentially political, sociological, or philosophical or based merely on a personal moral code. The Court explained that " a merely personal moral code" means one which is only personal and which is the sole basis for the individual's belief, and which is in no way related to a Supreme Being. Based on this holding, we understand that a family's beliefs are "religious" when their entire belief system is dependent on a supernatural God and His revelation.

IV. The Case Law Defining *Bona fide* and Sincere

The U.S. Supreme Court has offered some guidelines on determining whether an individual's religious beliefs are sincere or *bona fide*. In *Thomas v. Review Board*, 450 U.S. 707, (1980), the Court stated religious beliefs need not be acceptable, logical, consistent, or comprehensible to others in order to merit First Amendment protection (*Id.* at 714). Furthermore, in *U.S. v. Ballard*, 322 U.S. 78 (1944), the Court declared in applying the Free Exercise Clause, courts may not inquire into the truth, validity, or reasonableness of a claimant's religious beliefs. Also according to the U.S. Supreme Court in *Hobbie*, the timing of one's religious beliefs are irrelevant and immaterial.

> *So long as one's faith is religiously based at the time it is asserted, it should not matter, for constitutional purposes, whether that faith is derived from revelation, study, upbringing, gradual evolution, or some source that appears entirely incomprehensible.*

Hobbie v. Unemployment Appeals Commission, 480 U.S. 136, 144 n.9 (1987).

Furthermore, it is important to emphasize (as the Attorney General also emphasized below), that the First Amendment also protects personal religious convictions which are not held by the all members of the particular religious sect. The Court ruled that they must allow for intrafaith differences because:

> *The guarantee of free exercise is not limited to beliefs which are shared by all of the members of a religious sect. Particularly in this sensitive area, it is not within the judicial function and judicial competence to inquire whether the petitioner or his fellow worker more correctly perceived the*

commands of their common faith. Courts are not arbiters of scriptural interpretation.

Thomas v. Review Board, 450 U.S. 707, 715-716 (1981).

A family is entitled to the exemption even if their convictions are not supported by a tenet or doctrine of their church or denomination. In *Frazee v. Illinois Department of Employment Security*, 489 U.S. 829 (1989), the U.S Supreme Court held that in order for a religious belief to be legitimate or *bona fide*, the religious belief may be personal rather than mandated by a church. The Court held that whether or not the individual's church formally supports the religious belief held by the individual is irrelevant in determining the legitimacy of that religious belief (489 U.S. at 833).

This case involved a man (Frazee) who, although not part of any particular church or denomination, claimed he was a Christian and that his religious convictions prohibited him from working on Sunday. He refused a job that would have required him to work on Sunday. When he applied for unemployment, his application was denied because the Illinois unemployment agency had a policy that would not recognize personal religious beliefs, but only religious beliefs that were based on a tenet of a church or denomination. The U.S. Supreme Court ruled that Frazee's personal beliefs were legitimate and protected by the First Amendment. As a result, Frazee was permitted to collect unemployment. The Court held:

> *Undoubtedly, membership in an organized religious denomination, especially one with a specific tenet forbidding members to work on Sunday, would simplify the problem of identifying sincerely held religious beliefs, but we reject the notion that to claim the protection of the Free Exercise clause, one must be responding to the commands of a particular religious organization.*

489 U.S. at 834.

The Court emphasized that a person's religious beliefs can be *bona fide* and legitimate even though they are not supported by any particular church tenet. Personal religious beliefs are *bona fide* and are protected by the U.S. Constitution and Virginia Code §22.1-254(B)(1).

Several earlier cases involved conscientious objectors who were members of religious organizations where the beliefs in question were held in common, but the *Frazee* Court clarified those cases:

> *It is true, as the Illinois court noted, that each of the claimants in those cases was a member of a particular religious sect, but none of those decisions turned on that consideration or on any tenet of the sect involved that forbade the work the claimant refused to perform. Our judgments in those cases rested on the fact that each of the claimants had a sincere belief that religion required him or her to refrain from the work in ques-*

tion. Never did we suggest that unless a claimant belongs to a sect that forbids what his job requires, his belief, however sincere, must be deemed a purely personal preference rather than a religious belief.

103 L Ed 2d at 919.

A Virginia state court case, *Commonwealth of Virginia v. Foreman*, Fifteenth Judicial District, June 5, 1987, relied on several Supreme Court free-exercise rulings in reaching a decision on a religious-exemption case. In that case, the local school board wrongfully denied the family's religious exemption. The District Court overturned the school board and granted the exemption.

In essence, §22.1-254(B)(1) is nothing more than an acknowledgment by the Commonwealth of Virginia that it has no jurisdiction over the educational program of families who have sincerely held, *bona fide* religious convictions opposed to public school attendance. This is very similar to the legal status of private schools in the Commonwealth, which the state has no authority to regulate.

V. Legislative Intent and the Virginia Supreme Court

One comment needs to be made concerning the relation between the homeschool law and the religious exemption statute.

The homeschool law (§22.1-254.1), which was passed in 1984—over 30 years after the religious exemption statute—was not meant to replace the religious exemption or to make the religious exemption more difficult to obtain. The sponsor of the homeschool law, Delegate Dillard, has stated under oath that in sponsoring the law, he had no intention whatsoever of requiring families seeking the exemption to prove anything more than what was required before passage of the new homeschool law.

This is confirmed in the homeschool statute itself, in §22.1-254.1(D), which states that nothing in this section shall prohibit a pupil and his parents from obtaining an excuse from school attendance by reason of *bona fide* religious training or belief pursuant to §22.1-254(B)(1).

This was further confirmed in *Johnson v. Prince William County*, 404 S.E.2d 209 (Va. 1991). Although the Virginia Supreme Court ruled 4 to 3 that the Johnson's beliefs were philosophical rather than religious, the Court unanimously ruled that the sole test is the *bona fides* of their religious beliefs (404 S.E.2d at 211 and 214). The Court condemned portions of two attorney general opinions that improperly required families seeking a religious exemption to prove that homeschooling and private schooling does not accommodate their religious beliefs (*Id.* at 211 and 212). The Court said the sole test is whether public school attendance violates the family's *bona fide* religious beliefs.

Furthermore, the *Johnson* Court explained that the state's interest in seeing that children are educated is not permitted to be a factor in deciding whether an exemption should be confirmed. The inquiry and consideration of a school board can proceed no further than religious beliefs. The Court held that, in the context of a religious objection, the state waived its interest in the education of a child by enacting the religious exemption statute.

Although the Johnsons lost at the appellate level, they subsequently reapplied for a religious exemption. On the second application, the Prince William County School Board properly applied the religious-exemption statute in accordance with the *Johnson* case, and the exemption was granted.

In *Dusan v. Cumberland County School Board* (Chancery No. 2102, Cumberland County Circuit Court, September 15, 1993), the school board denied the Dusans' request in a 2-to-1 decision without any reason. The Dusans appealed to the Circuit Court, and Judge Snoddy reversed the denial, finding that the School Board's decision was arbitrary and an abuse of its discretion. The Cumberland County Circuit Court relied heavily on the fact that the family had submitted affidavits from pastors and letters from friends who vouched for the fact that their beliefs were religious and sincere. Since the record showed the Board had no evidence to the contrary, the Court ruled in favor of the Dusans.

VI. Attorney General Opinion: November 18, 1988

The Attorney General Opinion of November 18, 1988 emphasizes that religious beliefs, in order to be *bona fide*, do not need to be part of the form of worship of a particular sect. (See p. 2 of the Attorney General Opinion of November 18, 1988.) In fact, "there is no legal requirement . . . that a . . . religious belief meet organizational or doctrinal tests in order to qualify for constitutional protection" (*Id.* p.2). Furthermore, the Attorney General states:

> A believer's articulation of his religion should not be dissected and rejected simply because it is not as sophisticated as it might be, nor should interfaith differences determine what is a religious belief and what is merely a personal philosophical belief [Thomas v. Review Brd.,450 U.S. 707 at 715]. The guarantee of free exercise is not limited to beliefs which are shared by all members of a religious sect. Id. at 715-16.

Id. p. 2.

It is irrelevant whether other people in the family's church believe differently concerning the education of their children.

EDUCATIONAL "MONITORING" IS NOT ALLOWED. THE OPINION STATES:

> Under the provisions of Section 22.1-256(A)(4) [now 22.1-254(H)(5)], however, the General Assembly has provided a complete exemption from compulsory school attendance for a child excused on religious grounds. It is my opinion, therefore, that a school system lacks the authority to monitor the educational growth of a child through regular testing . . .

Id. p.5.

In other words, only the religious beliefs can be examined, not the educational progress. This assertion is consistent with §22.1-254(H)(5), which exempts families with religious exemptions from all the other compulsory attendance requirements, including testing. The Attorney General also declares:

> There can be no question that local school boards must respect a bona fide religious objection to school attendance made by parents on behalf

of their children. Parents have the right to direct the religious growth of their children, and there are no facts presented that would outweigh this parental right.

Id. p. 4.

VII. Who is a "parent"?

Logically, only those under a statutory obligation have any need for an excuse or exemption. According to §22.1-254.A, the group of persons who have a duty to comply with the compulsory-attendance statute are: "Every parent, guardian, or other person in the Commonwealth having control or charge of any child... ." It would be logical to define the group of persons entitled to an excuse or exemption in exactly the same way as the group under the obligation is defined. This is precisely what the Virginia legislature has done by including a definition of "parent" in §22.1-254.1.D as follows:

> D. For purposes of this section, "parent" means the biological parent or adoptive parent, guardian or other person having control or charge of a child.

Therefore, the person or persons who are entitled to the religious exemption are the same persons who would otherwise be under obligation to comply with the compulsory-attendance statute. To determine who may request a religious exemption, we need only look at who could be charged with a violation of the compulsory-attendance statute. In a non-traditional or one-parent family, the parent or other person having actual control or charge of the child is entitled to the benefit of the statute.

VIII. Conclusion: How School Boards Should Apply the Religious Exemption Law

All of the above authorities point to a single conclusion. If parents express a sincere religious belief that they would be disobeying God to send their children to public school, the school board must grant them a religious exemption. Courts will reverse school boards that fail to perform their statutory duty in this regard.

The major consideration of the Board is to determine whether the parents' religious objections to public school attendance are genuine or fraudulent. If the beliefs are genuine and *bona fide*, the family shall be granted a religious exemption. Neither the logic of that religious belief nor the timing of that religious belief can be considered. Nor can the church membership of the parents be considered.

The school board cannot consider whether it believes religious exemptions in general are a good idea, whether the board thinks the parents will do a good job teaching their children, or whether they believe homeschooling in general is a good idea. The school board cannot consider whether the family's religious beliefs can be accommodated in any other manner. A school board is not permitted to insist that a particular form be filled out as a precondition.

The vast majority of school boards in Virginia handle religious exemptions as an administrative matter, without a hearing, making a decision simply upon a family's submission of documents establishing their *bona fide* religious beliefs. A letter from a parent can establish his or her religious beliefs. An affidavit from a pastor or religious expert can suffice to establish that the beliefs are "religious." Letters from individuals who know the family can establish the sincerity of the beliefs. Nonetheless, a parent may establish that their beliefs are sincere and religious with only their own statement.

The Virginia legislature has determined that where parents have sincere religious convictions against placing their children in public school, it is more important to respect those religious convictions than to require compliance with the compulsory attendance statute. The legislature has delegated to local school boards the administration of compulsory-attendance exemptions. It is not, however, the prerogative of a school board to second-guess the wisdom of the legislature. A board's duty is to apply the law in an objective, even-handed manner consistent with precedents.

© Christopher J. Klicka, Senior Counsel of the Homeschool Legal Defense Association. This paper was originally presented in 1989 to the Virginia Association of School Board Attorneys.

Understanding Religious Exemption

Yvonne Bunn

s homeschooling continues to grow, so does the number of parents who teach their children at home under religious exemption. However, religious exemption is not for everyone.

Since 1984 the Virginia Code has included language defining the ways parents can teach their children at home. Even before that time, the law included a provision allowing parents to exempt their children from public education because of their religious convictions.

WHO QUALIFIES?

A religious exemption is for parents who have sincere convictions against sending their children to public school. The Virginia law states in §22.1-254 (B) (1):

> "A school board shall excuse from attendance at school: any pupil who, together with his parents, by reason of bona fide religious training or belief is conscientiously opposed to attendance at school. For purposes of this subdivision, 'bona fide religious training or belief' does not include essentially political, sociological or philosophical views or a merely personal moral code;"

There are two issues parents must be prepared to prove: Are your beliefs religious, and are they *bona fide*? The school board, not the division superintendent, must establish that the parents' opposition to school attendance is based on religious beliefs. A religious belief must be one held in relation to a Supreme Being. Your belief system must be dependent on a supernatural God and His revelation.

The parents' religious beliefs must be *bona fide* (meaning sincere). The courts have established that religious beliefs are not to be scrutinized by a school board as to truth, validity, or reasonableness. In order to be sincere, they must be religiously based at the time they are asserted. It is not required that you have always held these beliefs in order to be valid. Your beliefs do not have to be held by all members of a particular group (i.e. a church).

The courts have established that the only true test of *bona fide* religious beliefs is whether or not a family demonstrates through their lifestyle that

God is supreme in every area. Do you have a conviction that it would be a sin to send your child to a public school? If so, religious exemption may be for you.

These beliefs cannot be political, sociological and philosophical views, or a personal moral code, no matter how strongly held. You may disagree with the curricula or the methods of teaching in a public school. You may be concerned with safety issues. You may object to Family Life Education or the lack of character instruction. All of these are good reasons to homeschool—but not good reasons to homeschool under religious exemption.

If the school board concludes that a family's beliefs are *bona fide* and religious, they shall (or must) recognize a religious exemption to compulsory school attendance. Their decision cannot be based on your qualifications to teach, the methods you use, the curricula you choose, how well your children are doing, or any other issues pertaining to education.

WHEN AND HOW TO NOTIFY?

The religious-exemption statute does not address the topic of when or how to inform the local school board of your religious conviction. There is no deadline for notification as in the general homeschool statute.

Some families send a letter describing their religious beliefs. If a letter is sent, it should be directed to the school board, not the division superintendent. Some letters include an affidavit from a pastor or religious expert verifying their beliefs are religious, or letters from individuals vouching for the sincerity of their religious beliefs.

WHAT TO EXPECT

If you determine that your family has a *bona fide* religious conviction against attendance at school, then you must be prepared to articulate your beliefs before your school board. Not all parents will be required to testify before a school board concerning their religious convictions, but some will. This would be a stressful experience for any family—it would be even more stressful if your decision to homeschool under religious exemption was not based on a *bona fide* religious conviction. Make sure you know the law. Make sure you have good counsel.

Virginia is the only state that has a law specifically allowing a religious exemption from compulsory school attendance. If parents use the religious exemption statute inappropriately—for any reason other than *bona fide* religious convictions—the state legislature will be more inclined to impose restrictions on religious exemption or even repeal the law completely.

All of us must know the law and apply it correctly, not only for our own protection but for the protection of all homeschoolers.

*This article is not intended to be construed as legal advice. HEAV recommends that homeschoolers who are interested in pursuing religious exemption obtain proper legal counsel or join Homeschool Legal Defense.

Original Intent of Religious Exemption

Commonwealth of Virginia)
) ss.
County of Fairfax   )

JAMES DILLARD II, being first duly sworn on oath deposes and says:

1. I am a member of the Virginia House of Delegates.

2. I was the prime sponsor of the Virginia homeschool legislation which is now codified as § 22.1-254.1 Code of Virginia.

3. It was not the intent of the new homeschooling law to change in any manner whatsoever the requirements necessary for obtaining a religious exemption under § 22.1-257 Code of Virginia. It was not our intent to make the requirements for a religious exemption either less stringent or more stringent than had been the case prior to the adoption of the new homeschooling law.

4. If a family has religious objections to the concept of the new homeschooling law, to wit: The Commonwealth of Virginia retains the ultimate right and control over the education of the children residing in this State; then they would need to proceed under the provisions of the religious exemption statute.

_____
JAMES DILLARD II

Subscribed and sworn to before me this 28th day of October, 1986.

_____
NOTARY PUBLIC
COMMONWEALTH OF VIRGINIA

My Commission Expires Aug 25, 1988

Court Ruling on Religious Exemption - Judge Fiddler

COMMONWEALTH OF VIRGINIA
FIFTEENTH JUDICIAL DISTRICT

THE WESTMORELAND COUNTY JUVENILE AND DOMESTIC RELATIONS DISTRICT COURT
BOX 451
MONTROSS, VIRGINIA 22520

WALTHER B. FIDLER, Judge
MS. LYNN COATES, Clerk
GEORGE H. BEANE
Juvenile Probation Officer

(804) 493-8911
EXT. 320

June 5, 1987

Mr. William A. Beeton, Jr.
Attorney At Law
3817 Plaza Drive
Fairfax, Virginia 22030

Mr. Lynn C. Brownley
Attorney for the Commonwealth
Montross, Virginia 22520

Re: Commonwealth of Va. Vs. Terry Foreman and Joyce Foreman

This case comes to the Court upon a criminal summons charging that the defendants on or about March, 1987 did unlawfully fail to comply with the compulsory school attendance law Section 22.1-254 of the 1950 Code of Virginia as amended by failing to send four of their children, who are of school age, to a public, private denominational or parochial school.

The defendants plead not guilty to this misdemeanor charge for the reason that they and their children were conscientiously opposed to attendance at any school because of their bona fide religious training or belief.

The applicable code section 22.1-257 A2 states "(a) school board shall excuse from attendance at school any pupil who, together with his parents, by reason of bona fide religious training or belief, is concientiously opposed to attendance at school." Paragraph C. of this code section states "as used in paragraph A2 of this section, the term "bona fide religious training or belief" does not include essentially political, sociological or philisophical views or merely personal moral code."

The evidence is uncontroverted that the defendants have not sent their children to any school, outside of their home, since March 1985. The evidence indicated that the defendants were not basing their claim on membership in any organized religious group, sect or cult, but claimed merely the indentity as Christians who believe in and follow the teachings contained in the Bible and the word of their God as he speaks to them. They insisted that their belief and faith in these two sources directed and controlled their life and in the manner in which they lived and taught their children. They testified that the Bible clearly tells them that they should teach their own children at home and that God has spoken to them in the same way; that they should shiled their children from the unacceptable secular influences of any school and that all teachings should be based on the fact that God is the creator of all things and is the source of all truth; that public schools under the First Amendment to the U. S. Constitution cannot teach from a God oriented standpoint and that private denominational or parochial schools teach their own personal brand of religion which is totally unacceptable to them.

The exemption contained in Section 22.1-257 A2 enacted by the General Assembly of Virginia many years ago, is among the broadest religious exemptions from school attendance contained in the laws of any state. By virtue of that, the issue in this case is considerably narrowed to a question of whether the defendants have such a bona fide religious belief that causes them to conscientiously oppose attendance at school.

The Virginia statute for religious Freedom enacted by the General Assembly on January 16, 1786 (Section 57-1 of the Code of Virginia), well before the adoption of the U. S. Constitution, sets the tone and direction of Religious Liberty in this State. Article I Section 16 of the Constitution of Virginia spells out in rather inescapable language what the Free Exercise of Religion means, "All men are equally entitled to the free exercise of Religion, according to the dictates of conscience"----" but it shall be left to every person to select his religious instructor."

In Wisconsin vs Jonas Yoder etal 406 U.S. 205 (1972) the U. S. Supreme Court stated, "However, in evaluating the quality of the claims of the petitioner, the Court must be careful to determine whether the Religious faith of the petitioners and their mode of life are inseparable and interdependant." The evidence in this case convinces me that the beliefs of the defendants do affect, direct and to a significant extent control their lives and that their beliefs and the effects of these beliefs on their lives are inseparable and interdependant.

In U.S. vs. Seegar 380 U.S. 163 where the words "Religious Train-ing and Belief" in the Selective Service Act were being construed the court stated " The test might be stated in these words: A sincere and meaningful belief which occpuies in the life of its possessor a place parallel to that filled by the God of those admittedly qualifying for the exemption," or as the Court said in Thomas vs. Indiana 450 U.S. 707 (1981) the determination of what is a religious belief---" is not to turn upon a judicial perception of the particular belief or practice in question; religious beliefs need not be acceptable, logical, consistant or comprehensible to others in order to merit First Amendment protection."

The defendants testified that their beliefs have become stronger over the years and have changed in some respects from what they were a few years ago. In Thomas vs Indiana above the Court states, "Courts should not under take to dissect religious beliefs because the believer admits that he is "Struggling with his position"---.

Under the broad classification of Christianity the defendants indicated their approval of the teachings of Paul in the New Testament who emphasized that people change as Christians and continued growth in spiritual matters is a hallmake of the practicing Christian.

A three page handwritten letter, written by the oldest daughter, outlining her religious beliefs was admitted in evidence without objection. The Attorney for the defendants and the Attorney for the Commonwealth stipulated that the religious beliefs of all the children involved coincided with and were the same as their parents.

To some it may appear that the scriptural interpretations of the defendants are faulty or defective; that the their concept of God and his wishes for mankind are impractical or that the defendants are not acting in the long range best interest of their children in fact. Such contentions while appealing to many, are really missing the mark in this case. In Thomas vs. Indiana 450 U.S. 707 the Supreme Court plainly states, "Courts are not arbiters of scriptural interpretation."

Neither County School Boards not Courts have any peculiar qualifications for deciding cases involving matters of deeply held religious beliefs. Our system of civil government however, requires such decisions and by virtue thereof becomes the primary protector of the very religious freedom these defendants seek.

Implicit in the language of Section 22.1-257 A2 and the other sections in Chapter 14 of Title 22.1 is the proposition that if the defendants and their children are entitled to be excused from attendance at school because of their bona fide religious beliefs they are exempt from any other laws, rules or regulations of the local School Board with reference to public education matters.

This Court is satisfied from the evidence that the Religious beliefs of these defendants and their children are genuine, deeply held and sincere. They are not being asserted in any flippant, phony or casual fashion which is also attested to by the extraordinary time, attention and effort they have expended during the past two years in educating their children at home. This is a task that requires a great deal of dedication whatever the motivation.

The Court concludes that the defendants and their children by reason of bona fide religious beliefs are conscientiously opposed to attendance at school and are therefore, excused from such school attendance pursuant to Sec. 22.1-257 A2 of the Code of Virginia.

Having found this exemption applicable to them the Court finds them not guilty of the criminal charge of violating Sec. 22.1-254 of the Code of Virginia.

Date: June 5 , 1987

Walther B. Fidler, Judge

True Copy Teste: _____
CLERK, WESTMORELAND CO. JUVE...
& DOMESTIC RELATIONS COURT

Homeschool Immunization Requirements

STATUTE REFERENCES*: VIRGINIA CODE §22.1-271.1 TO .4 AND §32.1-46
Health requirements for home-instructed, exempted, and excused children

All home-educated children in the Commonwealth of Virginia are required to be immunized, including those taught by a certified tutor and those under religious exemption. However, there are exemptions.

- "In addition to compliance with the requirements of subsection B, C, or H of §22.1-254 or §22.1-254.1 any parent, guardian or other person having control or charge of a child being home instructed, exempted or excused from school attendance shall comply with the immunization requirements provided in §32.1-46 in the same manner and to the same extent as if the child has been enrolled in and is attending school." §22.1-271.4

- "The parent, guardian or person standing *in loco parentis* of each child within this Commonwealth shall cause such child to be immunized by vaccine..."§32.1-46.

DESIGNATED IMMUNIZATIONS

The Commonwealth requires the following immunizations:

§32.1-46. The parent, guardian or person standing *in loco parentis* of each child within this Commonwealth shall cause such child to be immunized by vaccine against:

- Diphtheria, tetanus, whooping cough and poliomyelitis before the age of one year;
- Haemophilus influenzae type b before he attains the age of thirty months;
- Measles (rubeola), German measles (rubella) and mumps before the age of two years;
- Hepatitis B before their first birthday for children born on or after January 1, 1994;
- A second dose of measles (rubeola) vaccine prior to first entering kindergarten or first grade and a child who has not yet received a second dose of measles (rubeola) vaccine must receive a second dose prior to entering the sixth grade;
- Varicella zoster (chicken pox), not earlier than the age of twelve months

for children born on or after January 1, 1997; children who have evidence of immunity as demonstrated by laboratory confirmation of immunity or a reliable medical history of disease are exempt from such requirement.

- After July 1, 2001, all children who have not yet received immunization against hepatitis B shall receive such immunization prior to entering sixth grade.
- After October 1, 2008, three doses of properly spaced human papillomavirus (HPV) vaccine for females. The first dose shall be administered before the child enters the sixth grade. Because the human papillomavirus is not communicable in a school setting, a parent or guardian, at the parent's or guardian's sole discretion, may elect for the parent's or guardian's child not to receive the human papillomavirus vaccine, after having reviewed materials describing the link between the human papillomavirus and cervical cancer approved for such use by the Board.

REPORTING

Parents are NOT required to submit proof of immunization unless the local division superintendent has specifically requested it.

"Upon request by the division superintendent, the parent shall submit to such division superintendent documentary proof of immunization in compliance with §32.1-46" §22.1-271.4.

ADMINISTRATIVE AGENTS

A physician, registered nurse, or health department personnel may give immunizations.

"The parent, guardian or person standing in loco parentis may have such child immunized by a physician or registered nurse or may present the child to the appropriate local health department, which shall administer the required vaccines without charge" §32.1-46.

RECORDS

Persons giving immunizations must provide documentation of the type of immunization given, numbers of doses, date, and any further immunizations required.

"A physician, registered nurse or local health department administering a vaccine required by this section shall provide to the person who presents the child for immunizations a certificate which shall state the diseases for which the child has been immunized, the numbers of doses given, the dates when administered and any further immunizations indicated." §32.1-46

INFORMATION SHARING

Certain designated persons may share confidential immunization information including the child's name, address, phone number, birth date, social security number, and the parent's names.

"For the purpose of protecting the public health by ensuring that each

child receives age-appropriate immunizations, any physician, licensed institutional health care provider, local or district health department, and the Department of Health may share immunization and child locator information, including, but not limited to, the month, day, and year of each administered immunization; the child's name, address, telephone number, birth date, and social security number; and the parents' names. The immunization information; the child's name, address, telephone number, birth date, and social security number; and the parents' names shall be confidential and shall only be shared for the purposes set out in this subsection" §32.1-46. (E).

EXCEPTIONS

Parents may obtain both religious and medical exemptions to immunizations. For a religious objection to immunizations, a Certificate of Religious Exemption (Form CRE 1) may be obtained from a local health department or from HEAV. For a medical exemption, you must have documentary proof from a physician or local health department that one or more immunizations may be detrimental to the student's health.

No proof of immunization shall be required of any child upon submission of

(i) an affidavit to the division superintendent stating that the administration of immunizing agents conflicts with the parent's or guardian's religious tenets or practices or

(ii) a written certification from a licensed physician that one or more of the required immunizations may be detrimental to the child's health, indicating the specific nature of the medical condition or circumstance that contraindicates immunization" §22.1-271.4.

DEFINITIONS:

For the purpose of §22.1-271.2:

- "Admit" or "admission" means the official enrollment or reenrollment for attendance at any grade level, whether full-time or part-time, of any student by any school.
- "Admitting official" means the school principal or his designated representative if a public school; if a nonpublic school or child-care center, the principal, headmaster or director of the school or center.
- "Documentary proof" means written certification that a student has been immunized, such certificate to be on a form provided by the State Department of Health and signed by the licensed immunizing physician or an employee of the immunizing local health department.

*Excerpted from the Code of Virginia, 1950, as amended; revised July 2001.

Certificate of Religious Exemption to Immunization

COMMONWEALTH OF VIRGINIA
CERTIFICATE OF RELIGIOUS EXEMPTION

Name_____ Birth Date_____

Student I.D. Number_____

The administration of immunizing agents conflicts with the above named student's/my religious tenets or practices. I understand, that in the occurrence of an outbreak, potential epidemic or epidemic of a vaccine-preventable disease in my/my child's school, the State Health Commissioner may order my/my child's exclusion from school, for my/my child's own protection, until the danger has passed.

_____ _____
Signature of parent/guardian/student   Date

I hereby affirm that this affidavit was signed in my presence on

this_____ day of _____

Notary Public Seal

Form CRE-1; Rev. 09/92

Legal Memo on the Unconstitutionality of Home Visits

HOME SCHOOL LEGAL DEFENSE ASSOCIATION

MICHAEL P. FARRIS, ESQ.
PRESIDENT
LICENSED IN DISTRICT OF COLUMBIA
AND WASHINGTON STATE

J. MICHAEL SMITH, ESQ.
VICE PRESIDENT
LICENSED IN DISTRICT OF COLUMBIA
AND CALIFORNIA

MAILING ADDRESS: P.O. BOX 159, PAEONIAN SPRINGS, VA 22129
STREET ADDRESS: 17333 PICKWICK DRIVE, PURCELLVILLE, VA 22132
PHONE: (703) 338-5600   D.C. METRO: 478-8530   FAX: (703) 338-1952

CHRISTOPHER J. KLICKA, ESQ.
SENIOR COUNSEL
LICENSED IN VIRGINIA

DEWITT T. BLACK, III, ESQ.
SENIOR COUNSEL
LICENSED IN ARKANSAS
AND SOUTH CAROLINA

JORDAN W. LORENCE, ESQ.
STAFF ATTORNEY
LICENSED IN MINNESOTA, VIRGINIA
AND DISTRICT OF COLUMBIA

LEGAL MEMORANDUM ON THE UNCONSTITUTIONALITY OF HOME VISITS

By Christopher J. Klicka

Certain school districts in various states have taken the liberty of imposing a "home visit" requirement on home schoolers. Home schoolers who refuse to allow home visits are "disapproved" and often charged with criminal truancy. Usually under a home visit requirement, a school official can visit a home school at any time, observe instruction in the home, inspect facilities, and demand certain changes.

These school districts which have home visit requirements are in states where the education statutes **do not mandate** home visits. In other words, the various state legislatures have never delegated this authority to the school districts in the first place.

The purpose of this analysis is to establish that home visits should not be practiced in any state because they are inherently **unconstitutional** for four basic reasons.

I.
HOME VISITS VIOLATE THE HOME SCHOOLERS' PRIVACY AND FOURTH AMENDMENT RIGHTS

Home visits are a violation of the home school family's **right to privacy** and their right to be free from warrantless searches and seizures as guaranteed by the **Fourth Amendment**.

On August 7, 1986, in *Kindstedt v. East Greenwich School Committee*, State of Rhode Island, HSLDA won a case striking down the practice of home visits, setting precedent for the entire state. The Commissioner held in a written opinion,

> It is our view that both the 4th Amendment and also the constitutionally derived right to privacy and autonomy which the U.S. Supreme Court has recognized, protect individuals from unwanted and warrantless visits to the home by agents of the state.

(*Kindstedt*, p. 5, ft.nt. 12). Furthermore, he stated, "In view of the legal and constitutional considerations, we are unable to perceive any rationale whereby a home visitation requirement would be justifiable under circumstances such as these." (*Kindstedt*, p. 7).

It is clear that home visitation cannot be mandated by public school officials over parental objection. The privacy of the parents, family, and home is at stake. Such privacy of the parents was protected by the U.S. Supreme Court in *Griswold* v. *Connecticut*, 381 U.S. 479 (1965).

A school official can only inspect a home schooler's home if the family voluntarily allows them to come in or if the state official has a warrant or court order. Any home school family who does not want to voluntarily participate in home visits cannot be required to do so without violation their Fourth Amendment and privacy rights.

It is a fundamental principle of due process that if a government official comes into one's home for the purpose of making a determination as to whether or not a criminal law is being complied with, then such an intrusion into the home is a search within the meaning of the Fourth Amendment. Since violation of the compulsory attendance law is a crime, a home visit by a public school official to determine compliance with the law is a violation of the home schooler's Fourth Amendment rights.

It is obvious that one's own home is a zone which creates a reasonable expectation of privacy and therefore warrantless searches thereof are ordinarily illegal. "Except under special circumstances, we have consistently held that the entry into a home to conduct a search or make an arrest is unreasonable under the Fourth Amendment unless done pursuant to a warrant." *Steagald* v. *United States*, 451 U.S. 204, 211 (1981). It seems apparent that home visits are unconstitutional.

Most school district officials seem to treat their demand for a search of a person's private home as an inconsequential request to which consent should be readily given. Fortunately, our founding fathers thought otherwise. One of the greatest American jurists, Justice Harlan, (the first), said in *Boyd* v. *United States*, 116 U.S. 616, 635 (1886):

> Though the proceeding in question is divested of many of the aggravating incidents of actual search and seizure, yet, as before said, it contains their substance and essence, and effects their substantial purpose. It may be that it is the obnoxious thing in its mildest and least repulsive form; but illegitimate and unconstitutional practices get their first footing in that way, namely, by silent approaches and slight deviations from legal modes of procedure. This can only be obviated by adhering to the rules that constitutional provisions for the security of person and property should be liberally construed. A closed and literal construction deprives them of half their efficacy, and leads to gradual depreciation of the right, as if it consisted more in sound than in substance.

It is proper to take constitutional offense at warrantless searches such as home visits.

2

There is neither statutory authority or constitutional justification for the demand to yield to a few "inconsequential" searches.

II.
HOME VISITS VIOLATE THE FIFTH AMENDMENT
REQUIREMENT OF DUE PROCESS

During the last several years, four states, New York, Pennsylvania, South Carolina, and South Dakota, were engaging in home visits of home schools even though it was not specifically mandated by law. In all these states, the practice of home visits were abruptly discontinued by case precedent and subsequent legislation.

A. In New York, two county court decisions, *In the Matter of Dixon*, No. N-37-86, Family Court of Oswego County, Nov. 21, 1988, and *In the Matter of Standish*, No. N-125-86, Oswego County, Dec. 23, 1988, both held home visits to be unconstitutional. In *Dixon*, the Court held:

> ...this Court firmly believes that the insistence of the Hannibal Central School District authorities to effect the desired on-site inspection was arbitrary, unreasonable, unwarranted, and violative of the Respondents' [home school parents] due process rights guaranteed under the Fifth Amendment of the Constitution of the U.S. The school district cannot expect to put itself in the position of conducting the inspection and then turning around and impartially or objectively determining whether the program subject to that inspection meets the required criteria for valid home instruction.

Dixon, Slip Op. p. 5. Regarding protection from self-incrimination, the Court explained:

> The Respondents, further, cannot reasonably be put in a situation where they in effect are being forced to give evidence that might be used against them at a future date...

Dixon, p. 5. The Court concluded that the home visit requirement is both "unconstitutional" and "unenforceable." This reasoning of the decision was confirmed in *In the Matter of Standish*, *supra*.

In order to cure the vagueness in the New York compulsory attendance law, the State Education Department issued "Regulations of the Commissioner of Education" for home schooling. The regulations give the local school boards no authority to conduct home visits (unless the home school is on probation), thereby ending the practice of routine home visits.

B. In Pennsylvania, at least one quarter of the 501 school districts were mandating home visits although not required by law. HSLDA, as a result, sued eleven school districts for violating the civil and constitutional rights of the home schoolers. The Federal Court ruled in

3

our favor, *Jeffery* v. *O'Donnell*, 702 F.Supp. 516 (M.D. PA 1988), and declared the law "unconstitutional for vagueness." The legislature subsequently passed § 13-1327.1 which clearly ended the practice of home visits.

C.   South Carolina also sought to impose home visits on home schoolers even though not mandated in the law. On February 27, 1989, the Attorney General said such a practice of mandatory home visits was prohibited by the intent of law:

> Because the amendments do not expressly provide for an on-site visit and because the only reference to the site is the "description" of the place of instruction, a reasonable reading of the whole statute (<u>Sutherland Statutory Construction</u>, Volume 2A, sec. K6.05) indicates that the legislature's intent was not to authorize blanket requirements for on-site visits.

OAG, p. 2. This option effectively ended the practice of home visits on home schoolers in South Carolina.

D.   In South Dakota, HSLDA brought a federal civil rights case *(Davis* v. *Newell School District*, U.S. District Court, Western Division, January 20, 1993) challenging the state's compulsory attendance law which allowed school district to require home visits of home school parents up to three times a year. This case served as a catalyst for the legislature to pass House Bill 1260 during the 1993 legislative session. This bill <u>repealed</u> the unconstitutional requirement of home visits. As a result, home schoolers in South Dakota no longer are subjected to home visits.

In conclusion, where home visits are not clearly mandated by law, local school district policies that have tried to impose such requirements are routinely found to be arbitrary, unreasonable, unwarranted, a violation of the Fifth Amendment, not the intent of the legislature, unconstitutional, and in several instances, based on unconstitutionally vague laws.

III.
THE HOME VISIT REQUIREMENT VIOLATES THE FIRST AMENDMENT PROHIBITION OF ESTABLISHMENT OF RELIGION

The home visitation requirement violates the First Amendment prohibition of establishment of religion. Approximately 85-90% of home schoolers are operating home schools based on their religious convictions. In effect, these families are operating religious schools in their homes.

In *Aguilar* v. *Felton*, 87 L.Ed. 2d. 290 (1985), the U.S. Supreme Court held that the establishment clause bars the use of federal funds to send public school teachers and other professionals into religious schools to carry on instruction or to provide clinical and guidance services. The Court further ruled that use of state and federal aid to assist religious schools violated the establishment clause by creating an **excessive entanglement** of church and state,

4

since the aid was provided in a pervasively sectarian environment.

In addition, the aid, which was in the form of public school teachers and professionals, required ongoing public inspection in order to insure the absence of a religious message. This inspection would require pervasive state presence in the religious schools who utilized the advice of these public school teachers. Justice Powell went so far as to say that such guidance by public school teachers in religious schools constituted direct state subsidy to those schools.

The Court specifically condemned the fact that "agents of the state must visit and inspect the religious school regularly." 473 U.S., at 413. It also found unconstitutional that religious schools "must endure the ongoing presence of state personnel whose primary purpose is to monitor teachers and students..." Id.

Most local home visit provisions give the local public school system the right to come into the religious home school, review their religious instructional materials, discuss the families' religious instructional program, and to observe the actual instruction. This service is provided with the use of state and federal money. Since many home schools are pervasively religious schools engaged in pervasively religious instruction, such home visits and their subsequent cost to the state, constitute **excessive entanglement with the religious home schools.**

In the sensitive area of First Amendment religious freedoms, **the burden is on the school district** to show that implementation of home visits will not ultimately infringe upon and entangle it in the affairs of a religion to an extent which the Constitution will not allow. *Surinach*, 605 F.2d 73, 75-76 (1st Cir. 1979). See also Committee for Public Instruction, 444 U.S. at 646.

Furthermore, the home visits are not an end in themselves, but they are part of a regulatory scheme likely to lead official efforts to alter the operations of that religious school. In some instances, the home visit results are used to close down the home school. Such entanglement by the school district is excessive and severely condemned by the U.S. Court.

IV.
HOME VISITS ARE NOT THE LEAST RESTRICTIVE MEANS OF FULFILLING THE STATE'S INTEREST IN EDUCATION

The requirement of home visits effectively denies a majority of parents their fundamental right to teach their own children which is guaranteed by the U.S. Constitution.

First of all, the Fourteenth Amendment guarantees all citizens the right to liberty. In a long line of cases, the U.S. Supreme Court has interpreted this right of liberty to include the concept of parental liberty. The U.S. Supreme Court and many state and federal courts have held that "parents have the fundamental right to direct the education and upbringing of their children." (See *Wisconsin* v. *Yoder*, 406 U.S. 205, 232 [1972], *Pierce* v. *Society of Sisters*, 268 U.S. 510, 534-35 [1925], *Ohio* v. *Whisner*, 351 N.E. 2d 750 [1976], *Ellis* v. *O'Hara*, [1985,

5

E.D. Mo.], 612 F. Supp. 379, 380-381, *Mazenac* v. *Judson-San Pierre School Corp.*, 614 F. Supp. 1152 [1985]).

This fundamental right to teach their children is guaranteed because they are parents -- **not** because they have been specifically "approved" by a local school official during a home visit.

Secondly, the First Amendment guarantees all citizens and families the right to freely exercise their religious beliefs. For at least 85-90% of all home schoolers, they must home school in order to be faithful to their religious convictions. These families believe they have been called by God to personally teach their own children, applying God's Word to every subject. They believe they cannot delegate this authority to either a public or private school because they would be violating God's command.

All home schoolers who are home schooling for religious reasons, therefore, are prohibited from exercising their First Amendment rights by the requirement of a home visit. Their religious convictions will not allow them to be visited in their home by a public school official.

All the above First Amendment claims demand the application of the well-known compelling interest test established by the U.S. Supreme Court in *Sherbert* v. *Verner*, 374 U.S. 398 (1963). This test has been applied again and again by courts throughout the country. This test has four burdens -- two burdens which must be met by the parents and two which must be met by the State.

First, the family must prove their religious beliefs are sincere.

Secondly, the family must prove that the state's action (home visit requirement) burdens their free exercise of their convictions.

Then the burden shifts. The State, or in this instance, the State Board of Education or local school district, **must prove two burdens:**

1) It must prove that its home visit regulation is "essential" or "necessary" to fulfill its compelling interest in education. *U.S.* v. *Lee*, 455 U.S. 252, 257-259 (1982) and *Widmar* v. *Vincent*, 454 U.S. 263, 270 (1981). The interest of the State has been defined by the U.S. Supreme Court as being: children will be able to read and write in order to participate in our political system and that the children will become self-sufficient. *Yoder*, supra, at 221.

The courts are clear: the State cannot merely **assert** a claim that its regulations achieve a compelling interest that justifies the violation of the family's constitutional rights. Rather, the State (or local district) must **prove with evidence** that its requirements of a home visit achieve its interest that children are literate.

6

More specifically, the State must present proof that the practice of home visitation has an effect one way or another on the home school student's academic achievement. The State must present such proof before it can justify the violation of the fundamental constitutional right of the parents by the requirement of home visitation.

Until the State can present some hard statistics as to the necessity for home visits, this requirement will not be held compelling by the courts.

2) The second burden the State must prove, (if it is able to prove the first burden), is that its home visit requirements are the least restrictive means for fulfilling its interest that children are literate. **Thirty-two** states have recently passed specific home school laws which have no home visit requirements.

As long as a less restrictive means exists in any state to meet state interest in knowing home schooled children will be literate, mandatory home visits cannot stand constitutional scrutiny.

Prepared by Christopher J. Klicka, J.D. (Educational and Constitutional law attorney)
Senior Counsel for the Home School Legal Defense Association

Driver Education Information for Homeschoolers

If you are age 19 or older and you have never held a license issued by any state, you must provide proof of successful completion of a state-approved driver education program OR you must have held a learner's permit at least 30 days before taking the road skills test at a DMV customer service center.

If you are under age 19, you must provide proof of successful completion of a state-approved driver education program and you must hold a learner's permit at least nine months before you can receive a driver's license. Plus, your parent, guardian or foster parent must certify that you received at least 45 hours of driver practice, 15 of which must have been completed after sunset. You will receive a certificate when you complete the driver education program.

If you are between the ages of 15 years and six months and 19 years of age, you must fulfill the following requirements in order to be issued a driver's license:

STEP 1: OBTAIN A LEARNER'S PERMIT
- When applying for a learner's permit, you must complete the Virginia DMV Driver's License Application form (form DL 1M) for a driver's license and pay the fees for both the permit and license. This application includes written consent of one parent or guardian. You may complete this form before or after coming to DMV.
- You will be required to pass a vision screening and the two-part knowledge exam. The two-part knowledge exam is given in English or Spanish on a computer and tests your knowledge of traffic signs, motor vehicle laws, and safe driving techniques. Exam questions are taken from information in the Virginia Driver's Manual. Students who fail the DMV knowledge test may be retested after 15 days.
- Furnish proof of your social security number if you have been issued one.
- Provide an original identification document that contains your complete name and date of birth, such as a birth certificate, as well as a document showing proof of residency. Applicants under age 19 can have a parent or legal guardian certify their Virginia residency. In order to do

this, the parent/guardian must appear in person with the applicant. The parent/guardian must provide a photo identification card and proof of his own Virginia residency with a document from the residency list, such as one of the following: a cancelled check, Virginia vehicle registration, a utility bill, a receipt for personal property taxes or real estate taxes, or a deed or mortgage, etc. Refer to "Acceptable Documents for Obtaining a Driver's License or Photo ID Card" (DMV 141).

- The DMV will take a digitized photo, obtain organ donor information, and request a one-time payment for the learner's permit and driver's license (approximately $15).

STEP 2: ENROLL IN A DRIVER EDUCATION CLASSROOM COURSE AND A BEHIND-THE-WHEEL DRIVING COURSE

If you are a homeschooled student, there are several options for the classroom and behind-the-wheel portions of driver education.

- A classroom driver education course may be taken at one of the following:
    1) a public school,
    2) a private school,
    3) a Commercial Driver Training School,
    4) or, if homeschooled, an approved correspondence course may be taught by the homeschooling parents. The student must currently be enrolled in a homeschool program acknowledged by the division superintendent.
- The following parent-taught, classroom driver education courses for homeschooled students have been approved by the DOE:

DriversEd.com
Attn: Virginia Home Study Course
436 14th Street, Ste. 420
Oakland, CA 94612
1-888-651-2886
www.DriversEd.com

National Driver Training Institute
4432 Austin Bluffs Parkway
Colorado Springs, Colorado 80918-2934
1-800-942-2050
www.NationalDriverTraining.com

VADETS On-Line Driver Education Course
An Alternative for Home School Students
(757) 591-4603
www.vadrivered.com or www.adtsea.iup.edu/vadets

[List continued on the next page.]

I Drive Safely
294 LaMoree Road
San Marcos, CA 92078
1-800-723-1955
www.idrivesafely.com

DISCLAIMER:

Approval of correspondence courses by the Superintendent of Public Instruction is not an endorsement of the educational or operational philosophy of the school. The approval of the courses is also not intended as an endorsement of the quality of the courses nor is it a conclusion that they are appropriate to meet the educational needs of the student. The Superintendent of Public Instruction assumes no liability for damages or financial loss to parents using any of the courses listed above.

- For information regarding the in-car or behind-the-wheel portion of driver education, refer to the Home-Schooled In-Car Driver Education Information Sheet (HS-3). This form contains information on:
  - Parent/guardian qualifications
  - Instructions
  - Student requirements
  - Issuance of the driver's license
- To apply for authorization to teach the behind-the-wheel portion, the parent must complete the following steps:
  - Complete a Home-Schooled In-Car Driver Education Parental Authorization Application (HS-1);
  - Enclose the original proof of completion of the classroom portion of the Driver Education program;
  - Attach a copy of the "Notice of Intent to Provide Home Instruction" form that was submitted to the local division superintendent or his designee, OR attach a letter from the local division superintendent or his designee acknowledging that the child is homeschooled;
  - Mail the above information to:
    Department of Motor Vehicles
    Commercial Licensing Work Center
    P. O. Box 27412
    Richmond, VA 23269-0001
- A separate HS-1 form, letter, and proof of completion must be submitted for each student.
- The only course approved for behind-the-wheel instruction by the parents is Module 11 - Behind-the-Wheel and In-Car Observation, http://www.doe.virginia.gov/instruction/driver_education/curriculum_admin_guide/module11.pdf.

STEP 3: OBTAIN A PERMANENT DRIVER'S LICENSE

Prior to obtaining a permanent driver's license, a Virginia resident under age 19 must complete a state-approved driver education program and hold a Virginia learner's permit for at least nine months. The minimum age to apply for a license is 16 years and three months of age.

- The homeschool parent must sign a Public, Private, and Home School Certificate of Enrollment. http://www.doe.virginia.gov/instruction/ driver_education/forms/certificate_enrollment_form.doc
- The student must complete the Virginia Driver's License Application, form DL 1M which includes written consent of one parent or guardian.
- Students then take the driver education certificate to any DMV customer service center and take the road skills test. You must provide a vehicle for the road skills test. You may take the road skills test no more than three times in any three-month period.
- Generally, males under age 26 must register with the Selective Service. If required by federal law to register with the Selective Service, the student must authorize DMV to forward personal information to the Selective Service unless already registered. If under age 18, the parent or guardian must sign an application authorizing the Selective Service to register the student when he is age 18.
- DMV will mail the permanent driver's license to the judge of the local Juvenile and Domestic Relations Court located in the student's jurisdiction. The court will then notify the student and a parent to appear before the judge to relinquish his learner's permit and receive his provisional license. The student must be accompanied at the licensing ceremony by a parent or guardian.

For DMV information, you may call 866-368-5436, or go to http://www. dmv.state.va.us/webdoc/citizen/drivers/ed_reqs.asp

For further questions, you may contact Vanessa Wigand, the Virginia Department of Education Principal Specialist for Health, Physical Education, and Driver Education, at 804-225-3300.

DMV www.dmvNow.com
Virginia Department of Motor Vehicles
Post Office Box 27412
Richmond, Virginia 23269-0001

HOME-SCHOOLED IN-CAR DRIVER EDUCATION INFORMATION SHEET

HS-3 (07/01/04)

1. The parent/legal guardian who meets the requirements for home school instruction under Va. Code §§ 22.1-254 (B) or 22.1-254.1 and elects to provide in-car driver education instruction to his or her own child must obtain prior authorization from DMV by completing a "Home-Schooled In-Car Driver Education Parental Authorization Application" form (HS-1). A separate form must be submitted for each child who must be under 18 years of age.

   NOTE: If, for any reason, your status as a home-schooling parent/guardian expires or is rescinded or if your child no longer meets the requirements for home-schooling, it is your responsibility to terminate the in-car instruction for certification purposes and notify DMV.

2. Home-schooling parent/guardian qualifications:
   - Hold a valid Virginia driver's license.
   - Have an accumulation of no more than six demerit points in the last 12 months.
   - Not convicted of driving while intoxicated in violation of Va. Code § 18.2-266 or a substantially similar law in another state in the last 11 years.
   - Not convicted of voluntary or involuntary manslaughter in violation of Va. Code § 18.2-35 or § 18.2-36 or a substantially similar law in another state in the last 11 years.
   - Grant consent to DMV to review and monitor parent's/guardian's driving record throughout the authorization period and until the student successfully completes the DMV road skills test.
   - Maintain proper vehicle insurance as required by the Va. Code.

3. Complete, sign and mail the HS-1 form to:

   Department of Motor Vehicles
   Commercial Licensing Work Center
   P. O. Box 27412
   Richmond, VA 23269-0001

   - Provide one of the following documents acknowledging that the requirements for home-schooled instruction under Va. Code §§ 22.1-254 (B) or 22.1-254.1 have been satisfied (A separate letter must be submitted for each child.):
     o A copy of notification to the school division superintendent or designee of your intent to home-school the child
     o A letter from the school division superintendent or designee acknowledging that the child is home-schooled
   - Enclose the original of one of the following as proof of completion of the classroom portion of the Driver Education program:
     o Certificate from an approved correspondence course
     o CDT-B form from a Commercial Driver Training School
     o DEC-1 form from a public/private school
     NOTE: A photocopy will not be accepted.

4. Within 5 working days of receipt of the HS-1, DMV will mail you:
   - A "Letter of Authorization" to provide in-car instruction to the home-schooled minor
   - A copy of Module 11 of the *Curriculum and Administrative Guide for Driver Education in Virginia* as approved by the Virginia Board of Education (also available online at http://www.doe.virginia.gov/instruction/driver_education/curriculum_admin_guide/module11.pdf

5. After receiving the "Letter of Authorization," you must follow Module 11. Your child must complete:
   - 7 periods (50 minutes each) of driving (at least 50 miles)
   - 7 periods (50 minutes each) of observation
     NOTE: If no other student is taking the course, the child may observe the parent/guardian driving, utilizing the lesson plans in the training module.
   - No more than 2 periods of instruction in any 24-hour period (1 period of driving and 1 period of observing)
   NOTE: Training received prior to the date of the "Letter of Authorization" will not be credited toward the in-car requirements.

6. In addition, a parent/guardian/foster parent must provide at least 45 hours of driving time, 15 hours of which must occur after sunset. An online parent/teacher guide is available at http://www.doe.virginia.gov/instruction/driver_education/parent_teen_driving_guide.pdf

7. Upon the completion of the student's in-car training, you **must** present the "Letter of Authorization" at a DMV Customer Service Center.

8. DMV will administer the final road skills test.
   NOTE: The student must have held a learner's permit at least 9 months and be at least 16 years and 3 months old.

9. Upon successful completion of the road skills test, DMV will issue a "Virginia Home-Schooled In-Car Driver Education Certificate" form (HS-2).

10. The parent/guardian must sign the HS-2. When accompanied by a valid Virginia Learner's Permit, the HS-2 will serve as a Driver's License.

11. The Juvenile and Domestic Relations Court in your jurisdiction will notify the parent/guardian and minor to attend the licensing ceremony at which time the permanent license is presented.

Questions?

Please contact the DMV Customer Contact Center toll-free at 1-866-DMVLINE (1-866-368-5463).

DMV Parental Authorization Application

dmvNow.com
www.dmvNow.com
Virginia Department of Motor Vehicles
Post Office Box 27412
Richmond, Virginia 23269-0001

HS-1 (05/19/04)

Home-Schooled In-Car Driver Education
Parental Authorization Application

The purpose of this form is for a parent/guardian to apply for authorization for home-schooled in-car driver education.
Instructions: Complete, sign and mail to the Department of Motor Vehicles at the address below.

The parent/legal guardian of a home-schooled minor may provide in-car instruction to his or her own child. The student must meet the requirements for home-schooled instruction pursuant to Va. Code §§ 22.1-254 (B) or 22.1-254.1.

(Print in ink or type.)

Student

Student's Full Legal Name	(Last)	(First)	(Middle)

Date of Birth	Virginia Learner's Permit Number

Parent Or Legal Guardian

Parent's/Guardian's Full Legal Name	(Last)	(First)	(Middle)

Principal Residence Address		City

State	Zip Code	Virginia Driver's License Number

☐ Mother ☐ Father
☐ Guardian

I hereby request authorization to provide in-car instruction to my home-schooled child and certify that all facts contained in this application are true and valid. I give consent to DMV to review and monitor my driving record throughout the authorization period and until my child successfully completes the DMV-administered road skills test.

_____   _____
Signature   Date

For DMV Headquarters Use Only

Record checked: _____
Demerit Points: _____
Authorization Date: _____
Clerk's Name: _____
Clerk's Signature: _____
Training Completed: _____

Mail this form to:

Department of Motor Vehicles
Commercial Licensing Work Center
P. O. Box 27412
Richmond, VA 23269-0001

1. Attach a copy of notification to the school division superintendent or designee of your intent to home-school the child OR a letter from the school division superintendent or designee acknowledging that the requirements for home-schooled instruction have been satisfied.
2. Provide proof of completion of the classroom portion of the Driver Education program.

Any person who knowingly gives false information on this form shall be guilty of perjury pursuant to Va. Code § 46.2-105.

Homeschoolers and the GED Testing Regulations

Qualified homeschooled students have legal access to the General Educational Development (GED) high-school equivalency test. Through the work of Home Educators Association of Virginia and Home School Legal Defense, home instructed students age 16 or older may pursue this diploma option.

Virginia Code § 22.1-254.2 describes eligibility for the GED and includes the following references to home instructed students:

§ 22.1-254.2. Testing for general educational development; eligibility; guidelines.

A. The Board of Education shall establish a program of testing for general educational development (GED) through which persons may earn a high school equivalency certificate or a diploma as provided in subsection F of § 22.1-253.13:4. The following persons may participate in the testing program:

1. Persons who are at least 18 years of age and not enrolled in public school or not otherwise meeting the school attendance requirements set forth in § 22.1-254;

2. Persons 16 years of age or older who have been instructed by their parents in their home pursuant to § 22.1-254.1 AND who have completed such home school instruction;

3. Persons who have been excused from school attendance* pursuant to subsections B and C of § 22.1-254;

UPDATED GED REQUIREMENTS

The Virginia Department of Education issued Superintendent's Memo #68, March 23, 2007. According to Memo #68, all previous superintendents' memoranda addressing the GED should be disregarded.

Superintendent's Memo #68 gives the following summary of rules for underage eligibility (students between 16 and 18 years of age) including home instructed students:

1) Homeschooled Students

Applicants under eighteen years of age, but at least sixteen years of age, must provide the GED examiner with documentation signed by the superintendent/designee certifying that the applicant has completed a home instruction program.

2) Students Released from Compulsory Attendance*

Applicants under eighteen years of age, but at least sixteen years of age, must provide the GED examiner with documentation signed by the division superintendent/designee certifying that the applicant has been released from compulsory attendance by the local school board.

Emancipated and adjudicated minors are subject to the compulsory attendance law, unless released by the local school board.

*Homeschoolers described as "released or excused from compulsory attendance" are religiously exempt students. Parents must provide documentation from the superintendent or his designee certifying the student is no longer under compulsory attendance according to the local school board.

GED BATTERY

The GED includes five tests that measure the skills considered to be the outcomes of a high school education. The tests focus on skills and concepts and the general abilities to analyze, evaluate, and draw conclusions rather than focus on specific facts.

Subject areas include:

    Test 1: Language Arts – Writing

    Test 2: Language Arts – Reading

    Test 3: Science

    Test 4: Social Studies

    Test 5: Mathematics

Individuals may take the full battery of tests up to three times during a calendar year to qualify for a General Educational Development Certificate. Test scores may be combined in accordance with GED Testing Service policy.

GED TEST PREPARATION

For information on what you should do to prepare for the GED Test and preparation programs in your area, call 877-37MYGED or 877-376-9433. Visit Virginia's Race to the GED to find information about classes in your area, discover how to study by television or computer, take a practice test, or register for the test.

GED APPLICATION

Testing applicants are not required to be Virginia residents. However, they must provide documentation of their current residence, whether in Virginia or another state.

An individual must make application prior to testing and provide a photograph ID at registration and at the time of testing. More information about GED testing can be found at Regulations Governing General Educational Development Certificates.

You may direct questions to Debbie Bergtholdt, GED state administrator, Office of Adult Education and Literacy at Debbie.Bergtholdt@doe.virginia.gov, or 804-371-2333.

Homeschoolers Go to Work!

Compiled by Yvonne Bunn

an you remember your first REAL job? Whether it was flipping burgers or working in retail—that step into the adult world is burned into your memory.

Many homeschoolers are ready and eager to enter the job market during their teen years. They have lots to offer employers: confidence working with adult customers, good work habits, and honesty.

Before you send your homeschooled teen out of your home and into the workplace, it's a good idea to be familiar with state and federal laws regulating their employment. As you might expect, state and federal labor regulations regarding minors have increased since our first years in the job market. The following summary of the major requirements is taken from the *Guide for the Employment of Teenagers*. It addresses many of the employment questions asked by home-educating parents.

ARE WORK PERMITS ALWAYS REQUIRED?

It is not necessary for 12- or 13-year-olds to have work permits. They may work as newspaper carriers, on farms, in gardens, or in orchards without a permit. Children who are 12 or 13 may NOT work as newspaper carriers before 4 a.m., or after 7 p.m., or during school hours. Work permits are not issued to children younger than 14.

WHO MUST HAVE A WORK PERMIT?

Every teenager 14 or 15 years of age must have an employment certificate or work permit to work at a job. He must have a permit even if he is married or has graduated from high school.

ARE THERE EXCEPTIONS?

Yes, there are some exceptions. Work permits are NOT REQUIRED for the following:
- work at home for parents;
- work on farms, in gardens, and in orchards;
- volunteer work;
- non-agricultural jobs when a parent owns the business;
- occasional work around someone else's home, such as yard work;

- work performed for state or local government;
- work as a page or clerk for the General Assembly;
- and child actors who have a theatrical permit.

WHERE CAN YOU OBTAIN A WORK PERMIT?

You may obtain a permit from a local high school or some private schools, even though your child does not attend these schools. Your school board or Department of Social Services may also issue work permits, but call first. An official "Issuing Officer" must give you the permit.

WHAT DOCUMENTATION SHOULD YOU BRING?

In order to obtain the two forms that must be completed prior to obtaining the work permit, the teen must bring evidence of his age. One of the following would be acceptable:
- birth certificate
- Bible or baptismal record
- insurance policy at least one year old
- passport

WHAT WILL YOU RECEIVE?

You will be issued two forms: 1) Intention to Employ, and 2) Permission for Employment. The Intention to Employ form is taken by the teen to the employer. The employer is responsible to fill out the kind of work to be done and the number of days and hours the teen will be expected to work. This must be returned to the official. The Permission for Employment form is filled out by the parent and teen and signed in the presence of an official "Issuing Officer."

WHO KEEPS THE WORK PERMIT?

Three copies of the work permit are issued. The teen takes the first copy to the employer who keeps it at the workplace. (If the teen changes jobs, he must obtain another permit.) The second copy is kept on file in the office of the "Issuing Officer." And the third copy is sent to the Department of Labor and Industry along with the Intention to Employ and Parent's Permission forms.

ARE THERE HOUR LIMITATIONS FOR WORK?*

There are state and federal laws limiting the times and hours a teen can work. Teens who are 14 and 15 MAY NOT WORK the following:
- more than 3 hours a day on a school day;
- more than 18 hours a week in a school week;
- more than 8 hours a day on a non-school day;
- more than 40 hours a week in a non-school week;
- before 7 a.m. or after 7 p.m. except between June 1 and Labor Day, when they can work as late as 9 p.m.;
- during school hours, unless enrolled in a school work-training program;

Moreover, the following also apply:

- The teen must be given a 30-minute rest- or meal-period after five hours of continuous work;
- Although homeschoolers often have schedules that differ from public school schedules, according to the Virginia Department of Labor and Industry, homeschooled employees may only work when public schools are NOT in session. This is a federal law with which the Virginia Department of Labor and Industry must comply. Homeschoolers must confine their working hours to hours outside the local public school schedule.

WHAT TYPES OF WORK ARE ALLOWED FOR 14- AND 15-YEAR-OLDS?

Work in the following businesses is permitted, but teens are prohibited from operating certain machinery that may be considered hazardous:

- Restaurants
- Retail stores
- Office work
- Radio and TV stations
- Gasoline stations
- Bowling alleys
- Skating rinks
- Hotel food-service departments
- Concessions at swimming pools
- Dry-cleaning stores with no processing
- Veterinary establishments
- Kennels
- Cutting grass
- Caddies
- Kitchen work, tray service, and hall cleaning in hospitals and nursing homes
- Greenhouses and nurseries
- Insurance and real estate
- Advertising agencies

ARE THERE SITUATIONS WITH NO RESTRICTIONS ON HOURS OF WORK AND AGE?

Yes, the following jobs have NO HOURLY RESTRICTIONS for ANY AGE teen:

- Working in a non-agricultural business owned by a parent;
- Working around the home for a parent;
- Working for state or local government;
- Working as a General Assembly page or clerk
- Working on farms, in gardens, and in orchards owned or operated by a parent;
- Performing activities for a volunteer rescue squad;
- Working as a child actor with a theatrical permit.

MUST A 16-YEAR-OLD HAVE A WORK PERMIT?

No, students age 16 and older are not required to have work permits. They may be employed in any job allowed by law that does not endanger the teen's health and safety. They may work in many types of jobs—construction, auto repair, dry cleaning, manufacturing, radio and TV repair, printing, hospitals, hotels, theaters, warehouses, fairs and carnivals, etc.

Also, 16- and 17-year-olds have no restrictions on their hours of work. Due to health and safety concerns, however, certain occupations and job tasks are prohibited for teenagers. For an extensive list, see the *Guide for the Employment of Teenagers* published by the VA Department of Labor and Industry.

WHAT TYPE OF ENFORCEMENT IS THERE?

Work permits can be revoked if they are obtained by misrepresentation or by mistake.

The Department of Labor and Industry may inspect a business at any time during business hours. They may examine records such as time cards and works permits, as well as interview any employees. If the employer is found in violation, he may be fined up to $1,000 for each violation.

If you have specific questions, you may call the Virginia Department of Labor and Industry at 804-786-2386. You may also request the free booklet, *Guide for the Employment of Teenagers*, on-line at www.doli.state.va.us.

Public School Access for Homeschoolers

S ome public school districts will allow non-public students to take classes on a part-time basis. Since 1997, school districts can receive a portion of ADM (average daily membership) funding from private school and homeschooled students who choose to attend public schools on a part-time basis. However, local school boards retain the authority to grant or deny part-time access.

> §22.1-253.13:2(N) Students enrolled in a public school on a less than full-time basis shall be counted in average daily membership (ADM) in the relevant school division. Students who are either (i) enrolled in a nonpublic school or (ii) receiving home instruction pursuant to §22.1-254.1, and who are enrolled in public school on a less than full-time basis in any mathematics, science, English, history, social science, vocational education, fine arts, foreign language course, or health and physical education shall be counted in the average daily membership (ADM) in the relevant school division on a pro rata basis as provided in the appropriation act. However, no such nonpublic or homeschool student shall be counted as more than one-half a student for purposes of such pro rata calculation. Such calculation shall not include enrollments of such students in any other public school courses.

IS ACCESS MORE AVAILABLE NOW?

The availability of access is very limited. It varies from district to district. Homeschool parents may appeal to local school boards for public school access for their children. School boards are not required to make public school classes available to private school or homeschooled students. They still retain that discretion. However, school boards and public schools now have an incentive to allow part-time enrollment—partial funding. Part-time students will now be counted in the average daily membership (ADM), and schools will receive up to one-half ADM funding for each part-time student.

WHO MAY ENROLL PART-TIME?

Part-time enrollment is open to both private school and homeschooled students. Only homeschoolers who are registered under §22.1-254.1 may enroll in classes. A religiously-exempt student does not qualify for part-time enrollment because he, together with his parents "by reason of *bona fide* religious training or belief, is conscientiously opposed to attendance at school," §22.1- 254(B)(1). Part-time enrollment is limited to the space available.

WHAT CLASSES CAN BE TAKEN?

Qualifying students may take mathematics, science, English, history, social science, career and technical education, fine arts, foreign language, health education or physical education.

HAVE ACCESS POLICIES BEEN DEVELOPED?

VSBA (Virginia School Boards Association) has adopted the following policies that reflect a framework from which member school boards may create local policy:

- ADMISSION: Part-time students (private-school or homeschool students) who want to enroll in academic courses must designate upon enrollment each extracurricular or club activity in which they wish to participate.
- ENROLLMENT: High-school students must enroll in at least one academic class; elementary- and middle-school students must enroll in one instructional unit for each extracurricular or club activity. If no activity is sought, a minimum of two classes must be attended. Part-time students must complete all prerequisites for course work or the equivalent required of full-time students. Acceptance is on a space-available basis.
- ACTIVITIES: Students who want to participate in extracurricular or club activities must satisfy the same or equivalent criteria (including Virginia High School League regulations) that full-time students must satisfy. Part-time students must participate in and satisfy all try-out or selection processes required. They also must comply with behavioral, disciplinary, attendance, and other classroom rules. The school may withhold credit or terminate the student's participation for noncompliance.
- TRANSPORTATION: Parents of part-time students are responsible for transportation to and from school, including any expenses.
- ACADEMIC CREDIT: Class ranking and grade-point-average shall not be computed for part-time students and such students shall not be eligible to graduate or receive a diploma.

COULD THERE BE OTHER REQUIREMENTS?

In addition to these policies, parents may expect local school divisions to implement regulations of their own. Of course, these policies will vary from district to district. Part-time students may have to meet some of the following requirements:

- prove academic achievement by submitting records,
- take placement tests for individual subjects or to verify grade level,
- attend "home-room" in order to report attendance for state funding,
- maintain a designated grade-point average in order to qualify for extra-curricular activities, or
- take specific courses at home in order to be allowed to participate in interscholastic activities.

WHAT ABOUT INTERSCHOLASTIC SPORTS AND TEAMS?

VSBA suggests that students who want to participate in extracurricular or club activities must satisfy the same or equivalent criteria, including Virginia High School League regulations that full-time students must satisfy. However, according to current Virginia High School League policy, homeschoolers are disqualified from participation in VHSL activities for a variety of reasons. Here are some sample policies:

> The Bona Fide *Student and Enrollment Rule—The student shall be a regular bona fide student in good standing of the school which he/she represents.*

There is an obvious problem for homeschoolers with this rule: According to VHSL policy, a "regular" student is considered a full-time student who is in regular attendance.

> *The Scholarship Rule—The student shall: For the first semester be currently enrolled in not fewer than five subjects, or their equivalent, offered for credit and which may be used for graduation and have passed five subjects, or their equivalent, offered for credit and which may be used for graduation the immediately preceding year or the immediately preceding semester for schools that certify credit on a semester basis.*

There are numerous difficulties with the Scholarship Rule: (1) The take-five-pass-five standard is not met by VSBA's recommendation of enrolling in one class. (2) VHSL further clarifies the Scholarship Rule by stating that credit for the five subjects must be recognized by the State Department of Education. Courses completed at home would not transfer to meet the Scholarship Rule. (3) Because homeschoolers are transferring from another school, scholastic eligibility "may be established only by an official certificate or transcript from that school." Transcripts from homeschoolers are not considered "official" by the Department of Education. Public schools are also not required to accept credits from non-accredited schools such as private schools or homeschools.

Another limiting factor, other than VHSL regulations, is high school eligibility to participate in interscholastic sporting events. Allowing ineligible students to participate on interscholastic teams has serious consequences for public schools. It could result in the entire school losing its eligibility to compete in interscholastic activities—something public schools are not likely to jeopardize

Because of Virginia High School League policies and high school eligibility requirements, participation in interscholastic sports or other interscholastic activities is not open to homeschoolers.

As a last resort, parents who are interested in their children playing on high school sports teams have turned to the courts for relief. Law suits in states with similar restrictions have not resulted in favorable outcomes for nonpublic students.

Section 0

Great Resources

Compiled by Susan Brooks and Janice Campbell

Our thanks to Christian Home Educators of Colorado and Susan Brooks for allowing us to adapt the "Great Resources" section of *The Comprehensive Guide to Home Education in Colorado.*

Introduction

The wonderful thing about the world of homeschool resources is that any listing such as this one is obsolete by the time it is printed. Why is this a wonderful thing? It means that new books and homeschool products are constantly appearing on the market. This section will direct you toward some of the most valuable homeschool classics, and give you a place to begin your homeschool research. When you contact a publisher to request materials, please let them know you read about their product or organization in the *Virginia Homeschool Manual.*

ABOUT THESE RESOURCES

We have selected the materials and sources here to provide you with an idea of what is available. Inclusion in this list does not constitute an endorsement by HEAV of each product in the supplier's catalogs—we've just tried to include a representative sampling of sources. We trust that each family will exercise judgment in choosing products compatible with its educational philosophy and beliefs.

Resources are organized according to categories. Because of space limitations and rapidly changing contact information, we have provided only telephone and website information for most resources. Most of the organizations and companies listed have extensive websites with a great deal of information and often, a complete online catalog. If you wish to request a printed catalog or brochure, there is usually a spot on the company's website where you can quickly and easily request information. Many companies also offer free e-newsletters, so we recommend using the website resource as a first point of contact. If you cannot access the Internet from home or from your local library, please be considerate when contacting small organizations by phone. Most companies provide toll-free numbers for orders only, so please do not use these for product inquiries, as these companies must pay for each call they receive at the toll-free number. Complete address information is listed for a few key organizations and suppliers.

—Janice Campbell

Parent Resources
National and State Organizations

HOME EDUCATORS ASSOCIATION OF VIRGINIA (HEAV)
2248-G Dabney Road
P.O. Box 6745
Richmond, VA 23230
804-278-9200
www.heav.org

HOME SCHOOL LEGAL DEFENSE ASSOCIATION
Provides legal defense and a monthly newsletter to members.
P.O. Box 3000
Purcellville, VA 20134-9000
540-338-5600
www.hslda.org

HSLDA'S FEDERAL RELATIONS DEPARTMENT
An arm of the Home School Defense Association involved in research and public policy.
One Patrick Henry Circle
Pucellville, VA 20132
540-338-5600
nche.hslda.org

NATIONAL CHALLENGED HOME SCHOOLERS ASSOCIATED NETWORK (NATHHAN)
Includes membership, directory, lending library, and bi-annual magazine for those educating special-needs children at home.
208-267-6246
www.nathhan.org

NATIONAL BLACK HOME EDUCATORS (NBHE)
Dedicated to supporting black families as they prepare tomorrow's leaders through home education.
13434 Plank Road, PMB 110
Baker, LA 70714
www.nbhe.net

NATIONAL HOME EDUCATION RESEARCH INSTITUTE
Dr. Brian Ray's clearinghouse for research, reports, and statistics on home education.
P.O. Box 13939
Salem, OR 97309
503-364-1490
www.nheri.org

ORGANIZATION OF VIRGINIA HOMESCHOOLERS
Statewide secular homeschool organization.
www.vahomeschoolers.org

Parent Resources
Periodicals

HOME EDUCATION MAGAZINE
Bimonthly secular publication with an unschooling emphasis; offers free homeschooling guide.
P.O. Box 1083
Tonasket, WA 98855
800-236-3278
www.homeedmag.com

HOME SCHOOL DIGEST
Quarterly print publication with a Christian perspective.
P.O. Box 374
Covert, MI 49043
www.homeschooldigest.com

HOME SCHOOL ENRICHMENT
A bi-monthly magazine.
P.O. Box 163
Pekin, IL 61555
www.homeschoolenrichment.com

HOME SCHOOL TIMES MAGAZINE
A free e-mail magazine.
homeschooltimes.com

HOMESCHOOLING TODAY MAGAZINE
Bimonthly magazine with many practical ideas.
P.O. Box 244
Abingdon, VA 24212
276-628-1686
www.homeschooltoday.com

THE LINK HOMESCHOOL NEWSPAPER
Free bimonthly national newspaper for home educators.
741 Lakefield Road, Ste. J
Westlake Village, CA 91361
www.homeschoolnewslink.com

THE MOORE REPORT
Based upon the work of Raymond and Dorothy Moore.
508 Washington Street, Suite 12B
The Dalles, OR 97021
541-296-4926
www.moorefoundation.com

PRACTICAL HOMESCHOOLING
An interesting, opinionated bimonthly magazine by Bill and Mary Pride and their family.
Home Life, Inc.
P.O. Box 1190
Fenton, MO 63026-1190
800-346-6322
www.home-school.com

THE TEACHING HOME
The print magazine is no longer being published, but the website contains article archives and information. They offer a free e-mail newsletter.
www.teachinghome.com

UNITED STATES GOVERNMENT INFORMATION
Publications, periodicals, and electronic products available.
www.pueblo.gsa.gov

THE VIRGINIA HOME EDUCATOR
HEAV's free quarterly news magazine.
804-278-9200
www.heav.org

Parent Resources
BOOKS

The books suggested here are available from many of the homeschool materials sources listed in the *Curriculum Providers* portion of this Resource Section. In addition, many are available from the HEAV resource center (www.heav.org/store) and/or major booksellers such as Barnes and Noble, Borders, or Amazon.com.

100 Top Picks for Homeschool Curriculum: Choosing the Right Curriculum and Approach for Your Child's Learning Style by Cathy Duffy
Cathy Duffy's most up-to-date manual provides brief, personal reviews of many of the products available to homeschoolers.

The Basic Steps to Successful Homeschooling by Vicki A. Brady
A guide to beginning homeschooling.

Better Late Than Early
Home Grown Kids
Home School Burnout
Home Spun Schools
Home Style Teaching all by Raymond and Dorothy Moore

The Christian Home School by Gregg Harris
Biblical reasons for homeschooling and practical advice.

The Complete Home Learning Source Book by Rebecca Rupp
An 843-page resource guide covering every subject from arithmetic to zoology.

Good Stuff: Learning Tools for All Ages by Rebecca Rupp

Dr. Beechick's Homeschool Answer Book by Dr. Ruth Beechick
Answers to parents' questions about homeschooling.

Educating the Wholehearted Child by Clay and Sally Clarkson

For the Children's Sake by Susan Schaeffer Macaulay
A sensitive look at the foundations of education.

Government Nannies: The Cradle-to-Grave Agenda of Goals 2000 and Out-come-Based Education by Cathy Duffy

The Homeschool Journey by Susan and Michael Card
A look at the joys of homeschooling.

Home Schooling Children With Special Needs by Sharon Hensley, M.A.

The Homeschooling Father by Michael Farris

Homeschooling For Excellence by David and Micki Colfax
The story of one family who homeschooled their four sons into Ivy League colleges.

Hothouse Transplants by Matthew Duffy
This book provides a look at the lives of several homeschool graduates.

The How and Why of Home Schooling by Raymond E. Ballman

Learning In Spite of Labels: Practical Teaching Tips and a Christian Perspective of Education by Joyce Herzog

HomeSchooling: The Right Choice: An Academic, Historical, Practical, and Legal Perspective by Christopher J. Klicka
Answers questions about why and how to homeschool.

The Socialization Trap by Rick Boyer
Protecting your children from age segregation and other pitfalls.

A Survivor's Guide to Home Schooling by Luanne Shackelford and Susan White. A humorous look at how to survive homeschooling.

Teaching Children: A Curriculum Guide to What Children Need to Know at Each Level Through Sixth Grade by Diane Lopez

The Three R's (1st-3rd grade set)
You Can Teach Your Child Successfully (4th-8th) by Dr. Ruth Beechick
Books that teach you how to teach.

The Ultimate Guide to Homeschooling by Debra Bell

Parent Resources
Curriculum Providers

Compiled by: Vicki Bentley, Susan Brooks, Janice Campbell, & Rachel Ramey

Most of the subject-specific resources can be ordered from the major curriculum suppliers listed in the Homeschool Material Sources, but publisher websites are indicated where appropriate. Publisher websites often offer additional product information, articles, links to other sites, and free e-newsletters.

Packaged Curricula/Correspondence Programs

A BEKA BOOK PUBLICATIONS/VIDEO SCHOOL
An accredited Christian textbook approach, with video school option.
877-223-5226
www.abeka.com

ADVANCED TRAINING INSTITUTE INTERNATIONAL/TELOS INSTITUTE INTERNATIONAL
Interdisciplinary, character-training curriculum based on biblical principles.
630-323-ATIA (2842)
ati.iblp.org

ALPHA OMEGA PUBLICATIONS
LIFEPAC curriculum, Switched-On Schoolhouse (computer-based curriculum), *The Weaver* unit study, and more.
800-622-3070
www.aop.com

BOB JONES UNIVERSITY PRESS
An accredited Christian textbook approach, with a satellite school option.
800-845-5731
www.bjupress.com

CALVERT SCHOOL
High-quality traditional education. Complete package includes everything needed.
888-487-4652
www.calvertschool.org

CHRISTIAN LIBERTY ACADEMY
Full-service program or on-line classes.
800-348–0899
www.homeschools.org

CHRISTIAN LIGHT PUBLICATIONS
A Mennonite publisher of homeschool curriculum for grades 1-12.
877-226-8010
540-434-0750
www.clp.org

CLONLARA SCHOOL
Private school that offers homeschool enrollment and support.
734-769-4511
www.clonlara.org

COVENANT HOME CURRICULUM
Classical, eclectic K-12 programs tailored to individual needs.
800-578-2421
262-246-4760
www.covenanthome.com

ESCONDIDO TUTORIAL SERVICE
Internet tutorials in classical Christian education.
760-746-0980
www.gbt.org

GRIGGS UNIVERSITY & INTERNATIONAL ACADEMY
Pre-K to college, focus: Seventh-Day Adventist.
800-782-4769
www.hsi.edu

LANDMARK FREEDOM BAPTIST CURRICULUM
800-700-LFBC
www.landmark/fbc.com

ROBINSON SELF-TEACHING CURRICULUM
K-12 books printable from CD-ROM. Inexpensive and traditional.
517-546-8780
www.robinsoncurriculum.com

ROD AND STAFF PUBLISHERS, INC.
Mennonite curriculum. High-quality coloring books.
606-522-4348
www.anabaptists.org/ras

SCHOOL OF TOMORROW
Textbook and multimedia products published by Accelerated Christian Education (ACE).
972-315-1776
www.schooloftomorrow.com

SETON HOME STUDY SCHOOL
Traditional Catholic education at reasonable cost.
540-636-9990
www.setonhome.org

SONLIGHT CURRICULUM, LTD.
Literature-based unit-study approach, with full curriculum or individual items available. Website

forums are active and helpful.
303-730-6292
www.sonlight.com

SUMMIT CHRISTIAN ACADEMY
K-12, electives, offers a complete curriculum package, testing, & diploma.
800-362-9180
www.scahomeschool.com

SYCAMORE TREE
Accredited, text-based program for homeschoolers.
714-668-1343
www.sycamoretree.com

UNIVERSITY OF NEBRASKA AT LINCOLN
Offers high school courses via distance delivery for enrichment or credit as well as college independent study courses.
866-700-ISHS
www.highschool.unl.edu

Bible/Character Training

The primary resource for learning about God is the Bible itself, but the following resources can be helpful in learning to apply God's Word to everyday life. The items suggested here are only a beginning—request catalogs from companies listed in the *Homeschool Material Sources* for many, many more helpful resources.

Beautiful Girlhood by Mabel Hale, revised by Karen Andreola

Character Building for Families, vols. 1 & 2 by Lee Ann Rubsam

Character Sketches Volumes 1-3 Advanced Training Institute International

Christian Manhood by Gary Maldares
An organized course of study for parents to teach Christian character to their sons.

Dating With Integrity by John Holzmann of Sonlight Curriculum
www.sonlight.com

DEEPER ROOTS PUBLICATIONS
Firm Foundations (elementary), *Discovering...* (junior high), and *Rooted & Grounded* (senior high) Bible curriculum.
www.deeperroots.com

Family Tool Chest series from Heritage Builders
Available from Focus on the Family.

For Instruction in Righteousness
Plants Grown Up
Polished Cornerstones
Bible-based resources by Pam Forster. (Other resources also available.)
www.doorposts.net

I Kissed Dating Good-bye by Josh Harris
A look at alternatives to traditional dating during the teen years.

His Perfect Faithfulness
Romance God's Way
When God Writes Your Love Story by Eric and Leslie Ludy
Books, tapes, and videos available.

Memlok / PC Memlok Bible Memory System
The word picture way to learn verses on cards or the computer: 700 verses and 48 topics. Recommended by Mary Pride, Gregg Harris, and Cathy Duffy. Available in several translations.

Passion and Purity by Elisabeth Elliot
Learning to bring your love life under Christ's control.

PEARABLES
Character-building books and stories for Christian young people.
www.pearables.com

PLAIN PATH PUBLISHERS
Distributes books about Christian character traits. Very conservative, KJV only.
www.plainpath.org

POSITIVE ACTION FOR CHRIST
Bible curriculum for grades K-12.
www.positiveaction.org

SanctiFinder
Bible drills help students learn the order of the books of the Bible.
www.providenceproject.com

Shepherding A Child's Heart by Tedd Tripp

Star Ways
Bible program designed for grades 1-6, but adaptable up to 9th.
www.praisehymninc.com

Stick Figuring Through the Bible
Using simple, colorful stick figures and symbols, this program teaches the Old and New Testament timelines. Several levels are available.
www.grapevinestudies.com

SUMMIT MINISTRIES
Worldview education for all grades.
www.summit.org

Training Hearts, Teaching Minds: Family Devotions Based on the Shorter Catechism by Starr Meade
Devotions based on the Westminster Shorter Catechism. Most conservative Christian families will find the majority of the questions/lessons useful, and can skip the few that may disagree with their doctrinal position.

WALK THROUGH THE BIBLE MINISTRIES
Offers Bible-teaching resources for parents. They offer two seminars that "walk" through both the Old and New Testaments; you will learn by doing! They also have *Kids Walk Thru Seminar* that runs concurrently with the adult sessions.
www.walkthru.org

WYCLIFFE BIBLE TRANSLATORS
www.wycliffe.org

YOUTH WITH A MISSION
Local opportunities for outreach through the King's Kids program.
www.ywam.org

Phonics/Beginning Reading
Alphaphonics
Samuel Blumenfeld's simple, classic method of teaching phonics.
www.alpha-phonics.com

BRITISH BROADCASTING CORPORATION
The BBC site offers free games and phonics-teaching support.
www.bbc.co.uk/schools/wordsandpictures

EAGLE'S WINGS EDUCATIONAL MATERIALS
Alphabet Island Phonics program.
www.eagleswingsed.com

EDUCATORS PUBLISHING SERVICE
Secular materials with strong phonics base and remedial focus.
www.intervention.schoolspecialty.com

The Gift of Reading by Trudy Palmer
Understanding the six stages of reading development with daily lesson plans and spelling rules.

Phonics for Reading and Spelling
Uses Spalding's *Writing Road To Reading* method.

THE PHONICS GAME
Six educational games to teach phonics and reading skills.
www.games2learn.com

PLAY 'N' TALK
A multi-sensory, easy to use, phonics-based reading and spelling program based on word families, such as the "at" family (at, bat, cat, fat, hat, mat, pat, rat, sat).
www.play-n-talk.com

Reading Made Easy by Valerie Bendt
Fully scripted, Christian phonics-based reading curriculum.

RIGG'S INSTITUTE
A non-profit literary agency that carries materials based on the methods of Orton and Spalding.
www.riggsinst.org

SAXON PUBLISHERS
Secular phonics program from the publishers of the well-known math texts.
www.saxonpub.com

Scaredy Cat Reading System by Joyce Herzog
Multi-sensory program with songs, storytelling, and games.
www.joyceherzog.com

Sing, Spell, Read & Write
An award-winning, multi-sensory program for teaching reading, comprehension, spelling, handwriting, grammar, and creative writing to pre-K through elementary-age students.
www.pearsonlearning.com

STARFALL
Online phonics lessons.
www.starfall.com

TALICOR (ARISTOPLAY)
Offers various phonetic/spelling games.
www.talicor.com

Teach America to Read and Spell (TATRAS)
An easy way to teach phonics using the *Saltmine & Hifwip Reading Program,* which uses vertical phonics, teaching all the sounds of a phonogram at one time, rather than learning short sounds or hard sounds first, then long sounds or soft sounds later.
www.verticalphonics.com

Teach Your Child to Read in 100 Easy Lessons by Engelmann, Haddox, and Bruner
Step-by-step, ultimately simple method for teaching phonics and reading at the same time.

Victory Drill Book
Phonics drill curriculum for beginning readers, including remedial work.

The Writing Road to Reading by Romalda Spalding
Teaches phonics, spelling, grammar, and much more. Can be challenging to use.

Writing Road to Reading: Putting the Steps in Sequence
Designed for teaching *Writing Road To Reading.*
www.spalding.org

Grammar
A CACHE OF JEWELS AND OTHER COLLECTIVE NOUNS
Kites Sail High, A Book About Verbs; Many Luscious Lollipops, A Book About Adjectives; Merry-Go-Round, A Book About Nouns
All these books by Ruth Heller teach grammar through poetry and beautiful art.

Challenges
A grammar card game for two levels of play.

Daily Grams
Grades 2-6. Daily review of all grammar rules.

Easy Grammar
Grades 4 and up.

The Grammar Key
CD-ROM course with workbook.
www.grammarkey.com

Great Editing Adventures and *Great Explorations in Editing*
Written by the creators of *Learning Language Arts Through Literature.* Students learn and review grammar as they search for the errors in several fun stories.
www.commonsensepress.com

Harvey's Elementary Grammar and Composition
Grades 4-6.

Jensen's Grammar
An incremental approach using a storyline to teach grammar, with incremental review incorporated as in the Saxon math curriculum.

KISS Grammar
This developmentally-based grammar curriculum is freely available online. home.pct.edu/~evavra/ED498/IM/index.htm
Additional helpful site navigation information:
www.titus2homemaker.com/2005/08/kiss-grammar-making-sense-of-the-site

Language Arts at Home: The Homeschooler's Guide to Teaching English Grammar, Composition, and Literature Appreciation by Rachel Ramey
Provides information to equip parents to integrate language arts into students' other studies.
www.homeworksbest.net

The Latin Road to English Grammar
Available through Schola Publications.
www.thelatinroad.com

Learning English with the Bible by Louise M. Ebner
Otherwise standard grammar textbook uses Scripture as exercises.

Learning Language Arts Through Literature
A complete language arts program including grammar and literature.

Learning Grammar Through Writing
Recommended for use with *Learning*

Language Arts Through Literature.
www.cspress.com

Shurley English
Workbook-based grammar for grades 1-6 and textbook-based grammar for grade 7. Uses jingles.
www.shurley.com

Simply Grammar revised by Karen Andreola
A verbal method of grammar instruction based on Charlotte Mason's books.

Winston Grammar
Multi-sensory approach to grammar.
www.winstongrammar.com

Spelling/Vocabulary
Child's Spelling System
Basic spelling rules.

English from the Roots Up: Greek and Latin Roots
Learning words from their Latin and Greek roots builds vocabulary as well as spelling skills.

How to Teach Any Child to Spell: Teacher's Guide to Tricks of the Trade by Gayle Graham
Strategies, rules, and patterns explained.

Info Please/What Does It Mean?
Search for the meaning of words and add a new word to your vocabulary every day.
dictionary.infoplease.com
www.infoplease.com/wordoftheday

Natural Speller by Kathryn Stout
A simple, non-consumable book with all you need to teach spelling.
www.designastudy.com

Quickword by Aristoplay
A board game of word skills.

Rummy Roots and *More Roots*
Teaches vocabulary through Greek
and Latin Roots.

Spelling Made Simple
Basics of spelling rules.

Spelling Power
Activities, games, and writing for
ages 8-adult. Includes a 338-page
teacher's manual.
www.castlemoyle.com

Spelling Scale For Home Educators
Eight diagnostic spelling tests for
evaluation.

Vocabulary from Classical Roots
An outstanding series of vocabulary
workbooks for middle or high school
students.

Vocabulary Vine
Spiral study of 108 Greek and Latin
roots.

Wordly Wise
www.wordlywise3000.com

GAMES TO PRACTICE SPELLING:
Boggle
Scrabble
Probe
Sum-Words

Literature
The 3Rs Series (K-3rd)
Includes:
A Home Start In Reading
A Strong Start In Language
An Easy Start in Arithmetic by Dr.
Ruth Beechick

BLACKSTONE AUDIOBOOKS
Unabridged recordings of great books.
www.blackstoneaudio.com

Books Children Love by Elizabeth
Wilson
A guide to the best children's litera-
ture for varying age groups.

By Jove / The Play's the Thing
Aristoplay games to teach Greek mythology and Shakespeare.

Children's Literature Web Guide
www.acs.ucalgary.ca/~dkbrown

CHRISTIAN NOVEL STUDIES
Literature study guides.
www.christiannovelstudies.com

The Classics at Home by Ann Ward
Leads you through the works of Beat-
rix Potter, *Charlotte's Web, Winnie-the-
Pooh,* and *The House at Pooh Corner.*

*Classics to Read Aloud to Your
Children* by William Russell

Critical Conditioning by Kathryn
Stout
Teaches literary criticism.
www.designastudy.com

For the Love of Reading by Valerie
Bendt
Share the love of reading with your
children. Now published as part of
Unit Studies Made Easy.
www.valeriebendt.com

Honey for a Child's Heart and *Read
for Your Life* by Gladys Hunt
Utilizing books for building up the
whole child.

Invitation to the Classics by Louise Cowan and Os Guinness
An attractive, readable introduction to the major books and authors of western civilization.

LAUREL HILL VIDEO LIBRARY
Rental videos by mail with an emphasis on literature-based titles.

LOST CLASSICS BOOK COMPANY
Reprinted great old books.
www.lostclassicsbooks.com

MANTLE MINISTRIES
Reprints old books.
www.mantleministries.com

Movies as Literature by Kathryn Stout
A one-year course for high school English or a supplement for grades 7-12.
www.designastudy.com

The New Read-Aloud Handbook by Jim Trelease
How and why to make your child a lover of books.

PROGENY PRESS
Study guides that examine classic and children's literature.
www.progenypress.com

TOTAL LANGUAGE PLUS
Uses literature as the basis for teaching thinking and communication skills.
www.totallanguageplus.com

Writing/Composition
Comprehensive Composition by Kathryn Stout
Composition assignments for grades K-12.
www.designastudy.com

INSTITUTE FOR EXCELLENCE IN WRITING
Variety of language arts programs includes composition, spelling, poetry, and classic literature.
www.excellenceinwriting.com

Stone Soup
A magazine for young writers and artists—a good opportunity for publication.
www.stonesoup.com

Understanding Writing
by Susan Bradrick
An excellent, one-volume writing program for all ages.

Wordsmith Apprentice, Wordsmith, and *Wordsmith Craftsman*
Creative writing for grades 4-12.
www.commonsensepress.com

Write Right!: A Desktop Digest of Punctuation, Grammar, and Style
by Jan Venolia

WRITERS' EXPRESS
Write Source 2000
Writers, Inc.
Reference manuals for middle-grade, junior high, and high school students. Teacher guides available. Website offers writing samples and other helpful information. Company also has materials for younger and older students.
www.thewritesource.com

A Writer's Reference by Diana Hacker

THE WRITING COMPANY
Lesson plans, e-books, and information for writing and literature.
www.writingco.com

THE WRITING CONFERENCE
Provides writing/literature camp for kids grades 6-12 and an annual young writers' contest.
www.writingconference.com

Writing in Narrative (WIN) published by Elijah Company
A simple, step-by-step tutorial on how to write a story.

Writing Strands by Dave Marks
An easy to use, award-winning writing program designed for home-schoolers.
www.writing-strands.com

Handwriting

Barchowsky Fluent Handwriting
Package includes an easy-to-use book and a CD-ROM from which you can print worksheets so that everyone in the family can learn this cursive italic hand. The CD also includes the Barchowsky font, so you can create copy-sheets for your children with the correct handwriting model. Suitable for any age.
www.bfhhandwriting.com

Callirobics
Handwriting exercises set to music to improve eye-hand coordination and fine motor skills.
www.callirobics.com

Draw-Write-Now
Lessons include simple drawing as well as writing.
www.drawyourworld.com

Handwriting Without Tears
Pre-K through cursive.
www.hwtears.com

Italic Handwriting Series by Getty and Dubay
Nine books for grades K-adult. Also includes calligraphy.

StartWrite
Handwriting software for Windows and Mac allows you to create customized handwriting worksheets.
www.startwrite.com

Handwriting is also available from major textbook publishers such as A Beka and Bob Jones.

Math

An Easy Start in Arithmetic by Dr. Ruth Beechick
One of the 3 R's books.

CalcuLadder
Drills to build speed and accuracy.
888-776-8776
www.schoolmadesimple.com

CHALK DUST COMPANY
A DVD program with textbooks.
www.chalkdust.com

Circles: Fun Ideas for Getting A-Round in Math by Catherine S. Ross
Hands-on geometry for older children. Available through Barnes and Noble.

CUISENAIRE RODS
by Dale Seymour Publications
Hands-on math manipulatives to teach any kind of math.

DELTA EDUCATION
Books, games, puzzles, and manipulatives of all kinds.
800-258-1302
www.delta-education.com

Jacobs Math Series

High school algebra and geometry with stories, cartoons, and artwork.

KEY CURRICULUM PRESS

Grades K-12 math program using Miquon Math manipulatives for primary grades, plus the *Key to...series*.
www.keypress.com

Making Math Meaningful by David Quine

Outstanding K-algebra program that explains why, as well as how, math works. Early grades provide scripted narrative instruction method.
972-235-5149
www.cornerstonecurriculum.com

MATH 'N STUFF

Sells math curriculum, manipulatives, games, and puzzles.
85 First Street
Keyport, NJ 07735-1503
www.mathnstuff.com

Math Sense Building Blocks Program by K. S. Koonce and S. S. Simpson

K-6 manipulative program from Common Sense Press.

MATHEMATICS ONLINE
ASK DR. MATH

If you have a K-12 math problem or even a college math problem, you can get an answer from this website. Search the archives or ask your own question.
www.mathforum.org/dr.math

MATHSTORIES

Free math website for children, parents, and teachers, with over 2,000 math word problems classified according to grades and topics.
www.mathstories.com

Math-U-See

Well-designed manipulative-based kindergarten through pre-calculus curriculum with parent videos.
888-854-MATH (6284)
www.mathusee.com

Miquon

Elementary books using math manipulatives to understand math concepts.
www.keypress.com

MOVING WITH MATH

Math curriculum and manipulatives for pre-kindergarten through pre-algebra.
www.movingwithmath.com

MORTENSON MATH

Math curriculum and manipulatives with a Montessori-inspired approach.

Muggins! Math Game by Old Fashioned Products, Inc.

An award-winning math game that is actually fun to play
www.mugginsmath.com

PROFESSOR B ENTERPRISES, INC.

A Christian professor's unique, verbal approach to mathematics uses CDs to teach both the parents and the children.
770-814-8888
800-VIP-MATH
www.profb.com

Ray's Arithmetic

Nineteenth-century textbooks. The first through eighth grade texts are available in hardcover reprints. Upper-level math is available only on CD-ROM.
www.mottmedia.com
www.dollarhomeschool.com

SAXON PUBLISHERS
Well-reviewed, secular K-advanced mathematics texts with emphasis on practice and repetition.
www.saxonpub.com

***Sir Cumference* Books** by Cindy Neushwand & Wayne Greehan
These entertaining stories help teach and reinforce geometry concepts.

Skip Counting video and cassette
Learn the number families while you exercise. Designed for grades K-6 but can be used for all ages.
www.skipcountkid.com

Systematic Mathematics
DVD-based math modules designed to teach math systematically. Available in individual modules or sets of modules.
www.systemath.com

Teaching Textbooks
These math texts are written specifically for homeschoolers so the explanations, directed to the student, are very thorough. Grade 5 through pre-calculus are currently available. The company is working its way down, so lower grades will eventually be available, as well. Textbooks with answer keys and optional CD-ROM solutions.
www.teachingtextbooks.com

True Math by Aristoplay
A game teaching numbers, money, size, scale, geometry, and logic.

U Can Do
Math DVD program.
www.candokids.com

Science

ALPHA OMEGA INSTITUTE
Dave and Mary Jo Nutting provide a biblical framework for teaching science. They publish a bi-monthly newsletter *Think and Believe* and offer a Creation Vacation Bible School, camps, and seminars, as well as a resource center. Young-earth creationists.
(This is not the same as Alpha Omega Publications, which is a curriculum supplier.)
www.discovercreation.org

AMERICAN SCIENCE AND SURPLUS
A catalogue with all kinds of incredible stuff!
www.sciplus.com

AMPERSAND PRESS
Card games teaching biology, astronomy, electricity, and many more subjects.
www.ampersandpress.com

ANSWERS IN GENESIS
Offer books, magazines, videos, and a multitude of young-earth creation resources. Operates the Creation Museum in Kentucky. Focuses on the Word of God as the original source material for the study of science and origins. A ministry of Ken Ham.
www.answersingenesis.org

Answers Magazine
Magazine published by Answers in Genesis. Young-earth creation perspective.
www.answersingenesis.org/articles/am

APOLOGIA SCIENCE
by Dr. Jay Wile
High-quality curriculum written by a Christian scientist.
www.highschoolscience.com

Backyard Scientist **series** by Jane Hoffman
www.backyardscientist.com

BEGINNINGS PUBLISHING COMPANY

The Rainbow: A two-year science curriculum for 12-14-year-olds, with equipment and labs.

The Spectrum: A science curriculum for high school students, based on *The Rainbow* curriculum.
www.beginningspublishing.com

Blood and Guts by Linda Allison
Non-fiction book teaches children about the workings of the human body.

BLUE SPRUCE SCIENTIFIC SUPPLY

Download a catalog for homeschoolers with live specimens, dissection specimens, and equipment.
www.bluesprucescientific.com

CAROLINA BIOLOGICAL SUPPLY COMPANY

Carries just about everything needed for teaching science.
www.carolina.com

CASTLE HEIGHTS PRESS

Offers unit studies and lab books in various sciences.

Considering God's Creation
Natural science adaptable for grades 2-7.

COVENANT HEIGHTS CONFERENCE CENTER

Offers outdoor education classes for grades 4-8.
www.covenantheights.org

Creation and *Journal of Creation (TJ)*
Magazines published by Creation Ministries International. Young-earth creation perspective.
www.creation.com

DELTA SCIENCE MODULES

Life science, earth science, and physical science kits.
www.delta-education.com

EDMUND SCIENTIFIC

Over 4,000 science products.
www.scientificsonline.com

Eyewitness Science **books**
Well-designed books with extensive photographic illustrations.

Facts for Faith
Christian scientific apologetics data update published by Reasons to Believe. Old-earth creation perspective.
www.reasons.org

GREAT SCIENCE ADVENTURES

Subject books (human body, space, etc.) supply activities and reproducibles suitable for use with grades K-8.
www.cspress.com

HOME TRAINING TOOLS

Science equipment and supplies company operated from Christian perspective and run by a homeschooling family.
www.hometrainingtools.com

INSECT LORE PRODUCTS

Lots of BUGS!
www.insectlore.com

INSTITUTE FOR CREATION RESEARCH

ICR publishes a free monthly magazine titled *Acts and Facts,* a daily devotional, has a graduate school for creation science, a museum that portrays natural history from a young-earth viewpoint, and sponsors trips to the Grand Canyon and Mount St. Helens. Offers an apologetics course called Creationist Worldview.
www.icr.org

MAGIC SCHOOL BUS SERIES

Fun instructional books on various fields of science.

MASTER BOOKS

A source of material for children from a young-earth creation science viewpoint.
www.newleafpress.net

THE NASA HOME PAGE

www.nasa.gov

NATIONAL AUDUBON SOCIETY

Contact your local chapter through the website.
www.audubon.org

Nature Friend **magazine**
Monthly Christian nature magazine.
877-434-0765
www.naturefriendmagazine.com

NATURE'S WORKSHOP PLUS

888-393-5663
www.workshopplus.com

LEGO EDUCATION

Lego science kits!
www.pitsco-legodacta.com

SALVATION ARMY OUTDOOR EDUCATION

Will work with families to put together one-, two-, or three-day programs in pond and forest ecology, astronomy, and night hikes. Summer only.

SomeBody™

Games designed to help students learn about the human body.
www.talicor.com

Science Camps
ALPHA OMEGA INSTITUTE FAMILY CREATION SCIENCE VACATIONS

Family camp with teaching on creationism.
www.discovercreation.org

THE SCIENCE COMPANY

A source of scientific supplies especially suited for homeschoolers needing small quantities.
www.sciencecompany.com

SCIENCE MADE SIMPLE

Website with science projects and experiments.
www.sciencemadesimple.com

SCIENCE BOOKS

by Janice VanCleave
A+ Projects in Biology
A+ Projects in Chemistry
A+ Projects in Earth Science
Astronomy For Every Kid
Biology For Every Kid
Chemistry For Every Kid
Earth Science For Every Kid
Physics for Every Kid

SCIENCE-BY-MAIL

You receive three science challenge packets per school year. The pen-pal program pairs scientists with children in grades 4-9.
www.sigchi.org/chi96/proceedings/intpost/Fusco/fm_txt.html

SCIENCE LABS IN-A-BOX

Designed by and for homeschoolers and written from a Biblical perspective. The second sister site offers science supplies.
www.labsinabox.com
www.sciencelabs.com

Science Scope by Kathryn Stout
Scope and sequence for science skills taught in grades K-12.
www.designastudy.com

Solomon Research Guide by Amy Bain
A two-volume science guide for grades K-8.

TOBIN'S LAB

Hands-on science materials for families.
www.tobinslab.com

TOPS (TASK-ORIENTED PHYSICAL SCIENCE)

Science modules for hands-on learning activities for children grades K-12. Website with sample activities.
www.topscience.org

U. S. SPACE CAMP

Camps for kids interested in space exploration.
www.spacecamp.com

USBORNE SCIENCE BOOKS

Concise, colorful overviews of science.

VIRGINIA FOUNDATION FOR AGRICULTURE

Curriculum ideas and activities for elementary and middle school based on agricultural literacy. Topics covered: crops, livestock, water, natural resources, and wildlife.
www.agintheclass.com

History and Geography

AMERICAN CHRISTIAN HISTORY INSTITUTE

Information about the Principle approach to home education.
530-221-1740
www.achipa.com

BELLEROPHON

Historical coloring books, paper dolls, and cut-out buildings from early civilizations to modern monarchs of England.
www.bellerophonbooks.com

CHATHAM HILL GAMES

Historical games, maps, and prints. Game titles include: *The Voyage of the Mayflower, The Battle of Bunker Hill, The Underground Railroad, The Wright Brothers,* and much more.
800-554-3039
www.chathamhillgames.com

Christian History & Biography Magazine
Quarterly magazine devoted to the history and heritage of the Christian faith.
www.christianitytoday.com

Cobblestone and *Calliope*
High-quality history magazines.
www.cobblestonepub.com

DIANA WARING - HISTORY ALIVE!

History tapes and books to make history come alive.
www.dianawaring.com

DOVER PUBLICATIONS, INC.

Carries inexpensive coloring books, craft activities, and paper dolls from various time periods.
store.doverpublications.com

Geography for Every Kid: Easy Activities that Make Learning Geography Fun by Janice Van Cleave
Activity book for teaching geography to grades 3-7.

Geography from A-Z Picture Glossary by Jack Knowlton

GEOSAFARI
An award-winning, interactive electronic game of science and geography.
www.educationalinsights.com

GOD'S WORLD NEWS
Children's newspapers for elementary through high school ages.
www.gwnews.com

Guides to History by Kathryn Stout
K-12 social studies objectives are incorporated into an easy-to-use question guide for the study of any period or culture.
www.designastudy.com

Hands-On Geography by Maggie S. Hogan and Janice Baker

HISTORY CHANNEL
Lots of history news, quizzes, speeches, and study guides.
www.historychannel.com

HISTORY KITS
Each of these kits is a history unit study in a box. The kits include hands-on activities and reproducible notebook pages.
www.handsandhearts.com

HISTORY RESOURCES
From the University of Glasgow's school of history and archaeology.
www.arts.gla.ac.uk/history

History Through Literature by Rea C. Berg
An easy-to-use program for grades 2-6, using the Holling C. Holling books.
www.bfbooks.com

Kids Learn America by Patricia Gordon and Reed C. Snow

Kingfisher Illustrated History of the World
Large reference book in timeline format.

KONOS TIMELINE
A large timeline to hang on the wall.
www.konos.com

The Light and the Glory
From Sea to Shining Sea
Sounding Forth the Trumpet by Peter Marshall and David Manuel

MANTLE MINISTRIES
Richard "Little Bear" Wheeler has living history presentations that are available on audiocassettes. Also carries reprints of classical books that describe America's Christian heritage.
www.mantleministries.com

Mapping the World by Heart and *If the World Were a Village* by David Smith
www.mapping.com

Material World: A Global Family Portrait by Menzel and Mann
An outstanding book that shows a statistically average family from each of thirty nations, interviewed and photographed with all their possessions. Fascinating.

NATIONAL GEOGRAPHIC SOCIETY
High-quality maps, games, and reference books.
www.nationalgeographic.com

ON-LINE BIOGRAPHIES

You can research biographical information on over 20,000 famous people. Geared more toward entertainment figures.
www.biography.com

Our Christian Heritage

History and geography with a biblical approach, grades 1-8.
www.ourchristianheritage.com

THE PILGRIM INSTITUTE

Primary-level text for teaching American Providential history.
574-277-1789
www.pilgriminstitute.org

Runkle Geography by Brenda Runkle

An outstanding, multi-sensory, evolution-free approach for grades 6-12. Available from Geography Matters.

The Story of the World by Susan Wise Bauer

Four volumes cover ancient history through modern times.

Take Off!

An award-winning board game that makes geography fun.

TALICOR (ARISTOPLAY GAMES)

Made for Trade

Travel through a colony shopping for items from that time period.
www.talicor.com

THE TEACHING COMPANY

Outstanding audio and video courses for high school- and college-level learning.
www.teach12.com

The Ultimate Geography and Timeline Guide by Cindy Wiggers

This website has helpful articles, projects, and links.
606-636-4678
www.geomatters.com

UNCLE ERIC SERIES:

"Uncle Eric" Talks About...

Personal, Career and Financial Security

Whatever Happened to Penny Candy?

Whatever Happened to Justice?

Evaluating Books

What Would Thomas Jefferson Think About This?

Are You Liberal? Conservative? Or Confused?

Ancient Rome: How it Affects You Today

www.bluestockingpress.com

Uncle Josh's Outline Map Book by Josh and Hannah Wiggers

More than 100 reproducible maps available in book form or on CD-ROM.

U. S. GEOLOGICAL SURVEY

Excellent source for maps, as well as news about earthquakes, floods, and droughts.
www.usgs.gov

Usborne World History Dates

Book in timeline format.

WALLBUILDERS

David Barton's site for books, videos, audio tapes, and posters on America's Christian heritage.
www.wallbuilders.com

WALL CHART OF WORLD HISTORY

Fold-up chart 15 feet long x 7 inches high when opened out. Can be hung on the wall. Available in book form through Barnes & Noble and Weaver Curriculum.

Where in the World is Carmen Sandiego?
Where In The U.S.A. is Carmen Sandiego?
Fast-paced, geography-based computer games with a detective theme. Published by the Learning Company, which also offers an online game.
www.carmen-sandiego.com

WHITE MOUNTAIN PUZZLES
Learn while working historical and state puzzles!
www.puzzlemaps.com

World Magazine
Adult weekly news publication. Christian worldview.
www.worldmag.com

Art

The Annotated Mona Lisa: A Crash Course in Art History from Prehistoric to Post-Modern by Carol Strickland and John Boswell
Well-done book on art history—not from a Christian perspective.

ART WITH A PURPOSE
Share-a-Care Publications
240 Mohns Hill Rd.
Reinholds, PA 17569

Artdeck
An Aristoplay game available as a game or just as a deck of art reproduction cards.

ARTISTIC PURSUITS, INC.
Incorporates art history with art lessons. Grades 4-12.
303-467-0504
www.artisticpursuits.com

Adventures in Art
This curriculum by David Quine has 51 museum reproductions with compre-

hensive study guides. It helps students visualize significant changes in art throughout history then relate those changes to culture. Ages 6-adult.
www.cornerstonecurriculum.com

Draw Squad by Mark Kistler

Draw Today by Walter Foster
Book and video course.
www.artskills.com

Drawing Textbook by Bruce McIntyre
A simple, inexpensive book that teaches drawing in perspective.

Drawing with Children: A Creative Method for Adult Beginners Too
Drawing For Older Children and Teens: A Creative Method That Works For Adult Beginners, Too by Mona Brookes

GORDON SCHOOL OF ART
Video home-study correspondence course in fine art. Free brochure.
800-210-1220
www.newmasters.com

HOW GREAT THOU ART PUBLICATIONS
Teaches fundamentals of drawing, color theory, and painting. Also available: *God & the History of Art*.
www.howgreatthouart.com

Isms: Understanding Art
A concise guide to the historical art movements. This book provides a good overview of art history.

MILLER PADS AND PAPER
Art supplies and paper.
www.millerpadsandpaper.com

VISUAL MANNA ART
Grades 1-12 art curriculum designed especially for homeschoolers.
www.visualmanna.com

Music
ALFRED PUBLISHING COMPANY
Music instructional books, software, and supplies for instrumentals.
www.alfredpub.com

BAGADUCE MUSIC LENDING LIBRARY
$10/year for lending library that provides music in printed form. Founded in 1983 to collect, preserve, and lend printed music; also provides music education programs.
www.bagaducemusic.org

BELLEROPHON
Carries coloring books of great composers.

Bigwigs of Classical Music: A Complete Guide to the History and Composers of Classical Music by Ben Lansing
Introductory history of classical music for grade 6 to adult that incorporates illustrations and humor to explore the entire span of classical music, from ancient times to today.
www.benlansing.com

DAVIDSON'S MUSIC
Music instructional books and cassettes by Madonna Woods.
www.davidsonsmusic.com

DOVER PUBLICATIONS, INC.
Carries a coloring book of instruments of the orchestra.

Music Maestro II
Aristoplay game of musical instruments.

Music & Moments with the Masters
A five-year music curriculum to help homeschooling families grow in their love and appreciation of great classical music.

Praise Hymns
Grades K-7 music curriculum. (Also sells phonics and Bible programs.)
www.praisehymninc.com
www.cornerstonecurriculum.com

Striving for Excellence by Ron and Inge Cannon
An excellent audiotape and booklet set that examines biblical principles of music.
www.edplus.com

Foreign Language
AUDIO FORUM
Cassette programs for learning more than 90 languages.
www.audioforum.com

BERLITZ
Books teaching French, Spanish, German, Russian, Italian, Japanese, Chinese, and many other languages.
www.berlitz.com

BOLCHAZY-CARDUCCI PUBLISHERS (PUBLISHERS OF ARTES LATINAE)
Teaches Latin and Greek, and publishes reading books in ancient languages.
www.bolchazy.com

GREEK 'N STUFF
Latin and Biblical Greek for children.
www.greeknstuff.com

THE HUMAN LANGUAGES PAGE
Over 1,000 links to foreign language material.
www.ilovelanguages.com

INTERNATIONAL LINGUISTICS CORPORATION/LEARNABLES

Publishes *The Learnables* picture books and cassettes. Offers Spanish, French, German, Russian, Hebrew, Chinese, Japanese, and Czech.
www.learnables.com

Learning How to Read New Testament Greek, with People Just Like You by Randall D. McGirr

Power-Glide **Language Courses**

Language lessons on audiocassettes that take students through second-year college level. Available in Spanish, French, German, Latin, Russian, and Japanese.
www.aop.com

Rosetta Stone

This computer-based language program is used by government agencies and many large corporations. It uses the immersion method of language instruction (only the target language is used), and is available in 27 languages.
www.rosettastone.com

WORLD OF READING

Offers 30 different language books, software, and learning aids.
www.wor.com

Physical Education
CAMP ID-RA-HA-JE

Have special week-long programs for homeschool families.
877-838-5668
www.idrahaje.org

Fitness at Home by David Kidd
A physical education program designed for homeschoolers.

Fun Physical Fitness for the Home by Sono Harris

Logic/Thinking Skills
CRITICAL THINKING PRESS AND SOFTWARE

Offers material to develop thinking skills.
800-458-4849
www.criticalthinking.com

The Fallacy Detective by Nathaniel and Hans Bluedorn
Fun book teaches the recognition of logical fallacies. Recommended for ages 13+.
www.christianlogic.com

Unit Studies
AMANDA BENNETT UNIT STUDIES

Unit studies with daily lesson plans.
www.unitstudy.com

Daily Bread by Rachel Ramey
Bible-based unit-study framework with resource recommendations and reproducibles. Four-year cycle is designed to be used three times, to cover grades 1-12.
www.homeworksbest.net

Five in a Row
A literature-based unit study for elementary school students.
www.fiveinarow.com

Further Up and Further In by Diane Pendergraft
A unit study based on the *Chronicles of Narnia*.

The Heart of Wisdom Teaching Approach: Bible-Based Homeschooling by Robin Sampson
Methodology is a combination of several popular homeschool methods, including Charlotte Mason. Biblically-based.

KONOS

Character-based, hands-on unit study curriculum.
972-924-2712
www.konos.com

The Prairie Primer by Margie Gray
A unit study based on the *Little House on the Prairie series.*

SONLIGHT

A literature-based unit study program.
www.sonlight.com

TAPESTRY OF GRACE

Unit study based on the chronological study of history. Uses classical education stages.
www.tapestryofgrace.com

TRISMS (TIME-RELATED INTEGRATED STUDIES FOR MASTERY OF SKILLS)

Middle school and high school unit studies centered around the chronological study of history. Focused on skills development.
www.trisms.com

Unit Studies 101 by Amanda Bennett
How to create and use unit studies.

Unit Studies Made Easy by Valerie Bendt
Revision and compilation of four earlier unit study books. Tells how to create a unit study and offers samples.

WEAVER

Multi-level unit study based on a chronological study of the Bible.
www.aop.com

Where the Brook and River Meet

A unit study based on *Anne of Green Gables*

Preschool

Before Five in a Row
A resource book to provide you with ideas for use with your 2-4-year-olds. The first section provides activity suggestions based on classic children's books. The second section provides activity suggestions based on daily life.
www.fiveinarow.com

CONSTRUCTIVE PLAYTHINGS

www.constplay.com

DISCOVERY TOYS

www.discoverytoysinc.com

EARLY EDUCATION AT HOME

For ages 3-5. Complete, yet flexible activity-based curriculum guide.

KUMON WORKBOOKS

These workbooks provide practice in skills such as cutting and tracing, helping to develop manual dexterity.

LAURI PUZZLES

Sturdy, textured-foam puzzles are available in a wide range of skill levels. Lauri will replace missing pieces.

Making the Most of the Preschool Years by Valerie Bendt
Lots of activity suggestions to encourage independent play.

Slow and Steady, Get Me Ready by June Oberlander
Week-by-week developmentally-appropriate activities for birth through age five.

Homeschool Material Sources
Places to Purchase These Great Resources

AMERICAN HOMESCHOOL PUBLISHING
Carries material for classical education, K-12.
800-684-2121
www.ahsp.com

AUDIO MEMORY
800-365-SING (7464)
www.audiomemory.com

BEAUTIFUL FEET BOOKS
Publisher of *History Through Literature Approach* study guides and time lines. Carries D'Aulaire children's biographies and Genevieve Foster's *World* titles.
800-889-1978
www.bfbooks.com

BLUESTOCKING PRESS
Historical documents, books, music, toys, and tapes. Publisher of the *Uncle Eric* books.
530-622-8586
www.bluestockingpress.com

BUILDER BOOKS
800-260-5461
www.bbhomeschoolcatalog.com

CADRON CREEK CHRISTIAN CURRICULUM
A catalog of unit studies such as *The Prairie Primer* and *Further Up and Further In,* as well as other quality resources.
575-534-1496
www.cadroncreek.com

CBD
See "Christian Book Distributors."

CHARLOTTE MASON RESEARCH COMPANY
Karen and Dean Andreola have revived this gentle approach to education.
P.O. Box 296
Quarryville, PA 17566
www.charlottemason.com

CHILDREN'S BOOKS
Large selection of good "living" books, most discounted.
800-344-3198
www.childsbooks.com

CHRIST-CENTERED CURRICULUM FOR EARLY CHILDHOOD
Sells early education curriculum and supplies, including phonics, math, and Bible.
800-778-4318
www.christcentercurriculum.com

CHRISTIAN BOOK DISTRIBUTORS (CBD)
Homeschool books and supplies, Christian books, Bibles, music, videos, and software at discounted prices.
800-247-4784
www.christianbook.com

COMMON SENSE PRESS
Carries *Learning Language Art Through Literature, Math Sense,* and unit study material.
352-475-5757
www.cspress.com

CORNERSTONE CURRICULUM PROJECT
David Quine's outstanding music, science, math, and worldview curricula available here.
972-235-5149
www.cornerstonecurriculum.com

CROSS-OVER EDUCATIONAL PRODUCTS

Carries *Snapshot Typing & Quick Piano*.
970-385-1809
www.crossover.ellison.net

DIANA WARING-HISTORY ALIVE!

History tapes and books to make history come alive, as well as *Beyond Survival* and *Reaping the Harvest*.
425-397-0631
www.dianawaring.com

DORLING KINDERSLEY

Colorful, high-quality, educational books.
800-788-6262
www.dk.com

DOVER PUBLICATIONS

31 East 2nd Street
Mineola, NY 11501-3852
store.doverpublications.com

EAGLE'S WINGS EDUCATIONAL MATERIALS

Building a solid foundation in math, phonics, and science.
580-252-1555
www.eagleswingsed.com

EDUCATION PLUS+

Tapes and materials on child development from a Christian perspective, music evaluation, and *Mentoring Your Teen: Charting the Course to Successful Adulthood*. Inge Cannon
317-222-1695
www.edplus.com

ESSENTIAL LEARNING PRODUCTS

800-357-3570
www.elp-web.com

FARM COUNTRY GENERAL STORE

309-367-2844
www.homeschoolfcgs.com

FOUNDATION FOR AMERICAN CHRISTIAN EDUCATION

Information and products for the Principle Approach to home education and the Noah Plan
800-352-3223
www.face.net

GREENLEAF PRESS

Publisher of the Greenleaf Guides carries a large selection of history and historical fiction books. Interesting catalogue.
615-449-1617
www.greenleafpress.com

HARCOURT PUBLISHING COMPANY

Carries full line of K-adult educational material.
800-531-5015
www.saxonhomeschool.com

HEAV RESOURCE CENTER

Wide variety of materials; discounts for members.
804-278-9200
www.heav.org/store

HEWITT HOMESCHOOLING RESOURCES

Catalog for hands-on approach with resources not common to other companies. Based on Raymond and Dorothy Moore's work.
360-835-8708
www.hewitthomeschooling.com

HIS PUBLISHING COMPANY

Specializes in unit study materials.
P.O. Box 1159
Plymouth, NY 13832

HOMESCHOOL RESOURCE CENTER

Debra Bell, author of *The Ultimate Guide to Homeschooling*, offers articles and a catalog.
www.debrabell.com

INSTRUCTIONAL RESOURCES COMPANY

Susan C. Anthony, a former teacher, carries practical resources for almanac usage, encyclopedia, spelling, and math.
907-345-6689
www.susancanthony.com

KEEPERS OF THE FAITH

Conservative books, many old books reprinted, and home of *Keepers at Home* and *Contenders for the Faith* clubs, which are locally-based Christian children's groups similar in concept to secular Scouts organizations.
906-663-6881
www.keepersofthefaith.com

LIFETIME BOOKS AND GIFTS

The *Always Incomplete Catalogue.* You'll find most of the books and tapes listed in this resource section, as well as many more, in this nicely written 391-page catalogue.
305-248-1271
www.lifetimebooksandgifts.com

MOTT MEDIA

Carries wonderful biographies, reprints of 19th-century textbooks, and all books written by Dr. Ruth Beechick.
800-421-6645
www.mottmedia.com

RAINBOW RESOURCE CENTER

Large selection of discounted homeschool books, curriculum, and supplies.
888-841-3456
www.rainbowresource.com

SCHOLASTIC BOOKS

www.scholastic.com

SHEKINAH CURRICULUM CELLAR

903-643-2760
www.shekinahcc.com

SONLIGHT

303-730-6292
www.sonlight.com

THE SYCAMORE TREE

Carries a variety of books and resources.
714-668-1343
www.sycamoretree.com

TIMBERDOODLE

Unusual and creative selection of homeschool books and supplies, including a wide selection of hands-on materials.
360-426-0672
www.timberdoodle.com

TOBIN'S LAB

Science resources and more.
540-829-6906 - Questions
800-522-4776 - Order Line
www.tobinslab.com

TRIVIUM PURSUIT

The Bluedorns' site for classical education includes many helpful articles.
309-537-3641
www.triviumpursuit.com

USBORNE BOOKS

Colorful, educational books from Britain.
800-475-4522
www.usborne.com

VERITAS PRESS

A full-service curriculum provider specializing in classical education.
800-922-5082
www.veritaspress.com

VISION FORUM

Carries classical books and products, including G.A. Henty, as well as government and political studies materials.
210-340-5250
www.visionforum.com

WEEKLY READER

800-446-3355
www.weeklyreader.com

WHOLE HEART MINISTRIES

Clay and Sally Clarkson offer their own books and others, chosen to help families be "whole-hearted."
800-311-2146
www.wholeheart.org

Online Resources

Susan Brooks and Janice Campbell

I f we had devoted this entire book to online resources, we could have listed only a small fraction of those available. The Internet contains a vast array of knowledge, including complete books online, and information and support for virtually every situation you experience in life. So the resources mentioned in this section are only a miniscule drop in the bucket compared to what is available. If you haven't yet explored the Internet, I encourage you to visit your local library or a friend's house, and get acquainted with the wealth of easily accessible and useful knowledge that is available there.

HOME EDUCATORS ASSOCIATION OF VIRGINIA

Web site for the state organization, Home Educators Association of Virginia. Find information on conferences, regional workshops, resources, legislative updates, and local support groups.
www.heav.org

AMBLESIDE ONLINE

This site is home to a free Charlotte Mason-style curriculum. The full text of Charlotte Mason's Original Series is available here.
www.amblesideonline.org

AMERICAN LIBRARY ASSOCIATION RESOURCES FOR PARENTS AND KIDS

Includes links to great websites for kids.
www.ala.org

ASL BROWSER

Video sign language dictionary
www.commtechlab.msu.edu/sites/aslweb/browser.htm

THE BALDWIN PROJECT

Free, online children's literature, including the original illustrations. Includes *Famous Men of Greece, Famous Men of Rome*, and several American history texts.
www.mainlesson.com

BARTLEBY.COM: GREAT BOOKS ONLINE

Free resource offering searchable, downloadable classic books and poetry.
www.bartleby.com

BIBLEGATEWAY

Find any verse in any version of the Bible.
www.biblegateway.com

CHRISTIAN CLASSICS ETHEREAL LIBRARY
Classic Christian books online. Includes writings of the early Church fathers.
www.ccel.org

CROSSWALK.COM
Christian site with multiple topics. Homeschooling section includes curriculum, columns, information, on-line support group, links to organizations, legislative information, *Guideposts* for kids, and resources. Chat site features well-known national participants on various nights, including Michael Farris of the Home School Legal Defense Association.
www.crosswalk.com

CYBERHYMNAL
Online text and music for thousands of hymns.
www.cyberhymnal.org

DONNA YOUNG'S SITE
Free printable forms, articles, and resources—an excellent site.
www.donnayoung.org

ECLECTIC HOMESCHOOL ON-LINE
Articles, resource reviews, state organizations, and support groups, as well as educational material, forms and charts can be downloaded.
www.eho.org

ELIJAH COMPANY
Although the Elijah Company has closed its doors, the 2005 resource catalog is still available for its wealth of articles, and the owners are working on a homeschool resource center online.
www.homeschoolmarketplace.com

EZWORD
Inexpensive, downloadable Bible software. Modules are available for various English translations, Greek and Hebrew versions, and many Bible study tools.
www.ezword.com

EVERYDAY EDUCATION
Janice Campbell's site includes articles, links, and ordering information for *Transcripts Made Easy.*
www.everyday-education.com

FAVORITE RESOURCES FOR CATHOLIC HOMESCHOOLERS
Over 100 searchable pages of free information, plus a link to "Reading Your Way Through History: A Timeline of Worthwhile History Reading in Print," a wonderful resource for unit studies or reading for pleasure.
www.love2learn.net

HOW STUFF WORKS
www.howstuffworks.com

INET LIBRARY
Designed for K-12 educational needs. Includes books, magazines, newspapers, encyclopedias, and specific sections covering chemistry, biology, foreign language, and math. Also includes teachers' lesson plans, college information, and scholarship applications. Subscription required.
www.inetlibrary.com

INTERESTING PLACES FOR KIDS
Good introduction to educational sites for children.
places.to/Browse/forKids

HIGHLAND HERITAGE
The Monroe family offers original unit studies, printables, and timeline ideas.
highland.hitcho.com.au

HOAGIE'S GIFTED EDUCATION PAGE

A comprehensive resource guide for the education of gifted children. Information on giftedness and links to resources on nearly every aspect of gifted education available on the Internet. Also includes lots of annotations and first hand information provided by parents. (Caution: includes links to sites that attack Christian organizations.)
www.hoagiesgifted.org

HOMESCHOOL INTERNET RESOURCE CENTER

All kinds of links to colleges, used curriculum, E-pals, on-line curriculum fairs, and much more.
www.rsts.net

HOMESCHOOL OASIS

Barb Shelton's warm and fuzzy site includes many helpful articles, including her "Season of Re-education and Renewing of the Mind" course for homeschool moms. Also articles by Marilyn Howshall, of *Wisdom's Way of Learning*.
www.homeschooloasis.com

HOMESCHOOL WORLD

Site is maintained by *Practical Homeschooling* and includes homeschool news, articles, books, and reviews. You can also download Daily Devotions, lesson plans, and activities.
www.home-school.com

LIBRIVOX

Volunteers record chapters of books in the public domain and release the audio files back onto the net. Their goal is to make all public domain books available as free audio books.
www.librivox.org

ONELOOK

This site searches over 800 dictionaries, including Webster's 1828 Dictionary and numerous specialized dictionaries, with one click.
www.onelook.com

PROJECT GUTENBERG

Over 17,000 free, downloadable books.
www.gutenberg.org

READING A-Z

Reading resources, including downloadable children's books. Paid membership required.
www.readinga-z.com

REFERENCE MATERIALS

Almanacs, atlases, dictionaries, and other freely searchable reference texts.
www.reference.com

TITUS 2

Steven and Teri Maxwell's Christian message boards, including a board for *Managers of Their Homes*.
www.titus2.com

WORLD ATLAS

Maps, flags, and geography facts and figures.
www.worldatlas.com

The *Great Resources* section was adapted with permission from the resource section of *A Comprehensive Guide to Home Education in Colorado*.

Making the Most of Google®
Rachel Ramey

T o use the Internet effectively, you must be able to search effectively. There are a number of good search engines available, and they are similar, but they all work a little differently. I am most familiar with Google®, so that is the one I will expound on. You can experiment with these tips to see which ones will work with other search engines.

BASIC SEARCHING

The first two things you need to know are that Google® searches are case insensitive, and that the order of your search terms matters. That the search is case insensitive means that it does not matter whether you use uppercase or lowercase letters. Thus, *eddie, Eddie,* and *EDDIE* would all return the same results. (So would edDIe or some other variation, if you're not a good typist!) The order of your search terms matters, as well, so searching for *Virginia trailers* would possibly **not** return the same results as searching for *trailers Virginia.* You will probably want to put your most important search terms first.

Another important note is that Google® automatically assumes you want to search for a page which includes **all** of the search terms you input. A search for *dogs canine bark* will return only pages which contain "dogs" AND "canine" AND "bark," **not** pages which contain only one or two of these terms.

There are several ways to narrow down your search. The first (and the one I use most often) is quotation marks. Anything you put inside quotation marks will be treated as an exact phrase **only**. If you are searching for Thomas Jefferson, for example, your search results will be more relevant if you enclose the name in quotation marks: *"Thomas Jefferson"* rather than just *Thomas Jefferson.*

Another way to limit your search is the use of + and -, which allow you to include or exclude certain terms. You will not usually need the + symbol, as Google® default is to search for every word. The - can be especially helpful, though. If I run a search for the word *bark* (with dogs in mind), the results may include a number of sites about trees. I can exclude (most of) these sites by using the - operator, like this: *bark -tree.* Note that, when using the + or - operators, there should be a space before the symbol and there should **not** be a space after the symbol.

Another operator is *OR*. I have already mentioned that Google® searches for **all** of the search terms by default. If you prefer it to search for **any** of the terms, instead, you can include *OR* between your terms: *dogs OR canine OR bark.*

You may also like to know that Google® has filtering options. By default, the filter is set at moderate. This means that explicit pictures should not show up in the image search, but a text search will return all results. You can change this. Just to the right of the search box, there is a small "preferences" link. If you click on this link, one of the settings you can change is the SafeSearch filter. Because the search database is created electronically, an occasional site may slip through the cracks. You can let Google® know about these so they can investigate them, through the contact link at the bottom of the search page.

ADVANCED OPTIONS

Google® has a number of advanced search modifiers. These precede the search terms and modify the method by which Google® executes the search. The basic rule with these is that anything that is part of modifying the search follows the modifier immediately, with no space. There is then a space between the modifier (and any necessary specifics) and the regular search terms. (This will make more sense as you read the individual explanations.)

site: This is the only advanced option I use regularly for searching, but it can come in **very** handy. With this enabled, Google® searches only the current site. This is helpful for sites, which do not have their own search engines. (I've also used it on Dave's Gardening site, where you are limited to a certain number of searches per day in the plant database, but can browse as much as you want.) To use this option, type *site:* followed by the site's URL, with no space in between. Then add a space and enter your search terms as usual. The following terms would search my website for "cooking": *site:www. homeworksbest.net cooking.*

allinurl: This does what it sounds like it will do; it requires that all the search terms be located in the URL. As you might guess, this narrows down your search quite a bit! Make sure there's a space between the colon and your search terms.

inurl: While this sounds like it will do exactly the same thing as *allinurl:*, this option is a bit different. This requires that the **first** search term be in the URL; the remaining search terms are searched in the normal fashion.

allintitle: and *intitle:* These work in essentially the same manner as *allinurl:* and *inurl:* except that they, obviously, search the page's title rather than its URL.

link: This modifier is particularly helpful if you're managing a website. It searches for pages which link **to** the site you specify. To use this function, type *link:*, followed by the site URL (minus http://) with no space in between (just like for a *site:* search). If I want to find out who is linking to my homepage, I can enter *site:www.homeworksbest.net* into the search box.

filetype: This is a rather specific search option, but I can think of some times it would come in handy. This function limits your search to a particular type of file. To use it, you type *filetype:*, followed by the three-letter extension of the filetype you want to search for, with no space in between. Then space and type your remaining search terms as usual. For example, if I am searching for a map of Israel, but I am only interested in .jpg images, I might type *filetype:jpg Israel map* or *filetype:jpg "map of Israel"*.

define: This is not a standard search at all. When you use this to limit your search, Google® gathers definitions from around the web for your word or phrase.

Excerpted from *Daily Bread: A Comprehensive Unit Study Resource*, by Rachel Ramey.

Daily Bread is a Bible-based unit-study framework that includes resource recommendations and reproducibles. Its four-year cycle is designed to be used three times, to cover grades 1-12. store.homeworksbest.net

Computers and Technology

Susan Brooks

As the computer world has exploded into a source of unlimited information, it is difficult to cover everything offered to homeschool families. This is an attempt to get you started on the right foot as you go "site seeing' on the Internet!

If you do not own a computer, go to your local library and they will be happy to help you start your search. If you do have a computer, you can still start at the library for your first instructions. The journey is filled with buttons to push, so do not be afraid to press one and see what happens!

The library has a wonderful website to get started. Get on your library's home page and go to the Internet site. First go to www.getnetwise.org. It will have tutorial instructions, risks, and age-appropriate tips on safety for your family, how to choose filters for your searches, how to understand the differences between reliable and unreliable sources, safe kids' sites that have been pre-filtered, and more. Provide guidance to your children, as this is a great learning tool for making right choices. Learning to make good decisions is a skill that will last a lifetime in every area of your children's lives.

Go to Kathy Schrock's *Guide for Educators*, which can be reached through the library's home page or school.discovery.com/schrockguide. This site has a categorized list of Internet sites to enhance curriculum. It is updated daily to keep up with the tremendous number of new World Wide Web sites covers a large number of subjects and, best yet, is filtered and geared toward educators.

ACADEMIC SUPERSTORE
Educational software in all subjects for grades K-12.
www.academicsuperstore.com

APPLE COMPUTER, INC.
Homeschoolers can purchase Apple educational software.
www.apple.com/education/k12/homeschool

EDUCATIONAL RESOURCES
Educational software in all subjects for grades K-12.
www.edresources.com

INNOVATIVE LEARNING GROUP, INC.
Multimedia and hands-on products.
919-678-8778
www.thinkingmaps.com

SCHOLASTICS NEW MEDIA
Educational software for grades K-12.
www.scholastic.com

SWITCHED-ON SCHOOLHOUSE
Complete curriculum software.
www.aop.com

UCOMPASS.COM, INC.
Web-based educational programs.
www.ucompass.com

Computer Magazines
MACWORLD
A magazine devoted to the Macintosh computer.
www.macworld.com

PC MAGAZINE: THE INDEPENDENT GUIDE TO TECHNOLOGY
www.pcmag.com

COMPUTER CLASSES
Global SchoolNet Foundation Clearinghouse for distance and Internet-based education for K-12.
www.globalschoolnet.org

TEAMS DISTANCE LEARNING
Satellite distance learning for K-8.
teams.lacoe.edu

LEARNING THE INTERNET
GetNetWise
www.getnetwise.org

KATHY SHROCK'S GUIDE
school.discovery.com/schrockguide

LEARN THE NET
www.learnthenet.com

Internet Tools
BABELFISH TRANSLATOR
Copy-and-paste up to 150 words of text to be translated. Several languages available.
babelfish.yahoo.com

INTERNET ARCHIVE/WAYBACK PROJECT
This project seeks to archive the entire internet. If a webpage you need is no longer available, look for it here.
www.archive.org

SAFESURF
An internet rating system, for filtered surfing.
www.safesurf.org

SEARCH ENGINES
Alta Vista: www.altavista.com
Excite: www.excite.com
GoodSearch: www.goodsearch.com
Google: www.google.com
Webcrawler: www.webcrawler.com
Yahoo: www.yahoo.com

Service Providers
CROSSWALK
Provides filtered Internet service.
www.crosswalk.com

INTEGRITY
Provides filtered Internet service for a fee.
home.integrityonline.com

Materials for Learning English as a Second Language

ALTA BOOK CENTER
Huge offering of ESL and EFL books, magazines, and multimedia resources for teachers, parents, and students.
14 Adrian Court
Burlingame, CA 94010
800-ALTAESL
www.altaesl.com

BILINGUAL BOOKS FOR KIDS, INC.
Commercial publisher of books written with Spanish and English appearing side-by-side. Pre-school through high school level.
P.O. Box 653
Ardsley, NY 10502
800-385-1020
www.bilingualbooks.com

ONE STOP ENGLISH
ESL Teaching resource site. Offering free lessons plans, exams, games, worksheets, and teacher training and support. Also purchase English as a Second Language curriculum from MacMillian publishing for kindergarten to adult learners, beginners to intermediate.
www.Onestopenglish.com

OWL: ONLINE WRITING LAB.
This site, from Purdue University, has many useful worksheets, handouts, instructional powerpoint presentations, and exercises for more advanced adults or high school students. Includes resources for grammar, writing research papers, and more.
owl.english.purdue.edu/handouts/esl/index.html

PASO PARTNERS
Curriculum guide and full lesson plans, in both English and Spanish, designed to help elementary students, K-3, whose primary language is Spanish. Integrates mathematics, sciences, and language. Also may be purchased in book form from SEDL.
800-476-6861
www.sedl.org/scimath/pasopartners/pphome.html

ENGLISH TOWN
Online English course with live chat capabilities for communication practice. Nominal monthly fee gives you unlimited access to teachers and course work. Because of the live chat aspect, only recommended for adults or mature high schoolers.
www.englishtown.com

INGLES SIN BARRERAS
Internet English language course designed specifically for native Spanish speakers. Subscription fees required.
www.inglescursos.com

ESL KID STUFF
For a yearly subscription fee you can access flashcards, worksheets, songs, and other resources specifically for teaching elementary-aged children English.
www.eslkidstuff.com

TESOL (TEACHERS OF ENGLISH TO SPEAKERS OF OTHER LANGUAGES)

This organization offers many resources for teachers of English. Whether the student is pre-school or post-high school, you will find books, lesson plans, reproducible, and other tools for teaching English. The site also list standards for each grade level.

700 South Washington Street,
Suite 200
Alexandria, Virginia, 22314 USA
703-836-0774
888-547-3369
www.tesol.org

Proveedores de Materiales Educativos en Español

A BEKA BOOKS A/C PUBLICACIONES AGUILA EN MEXICO:
Sor Juana Ines de la Cruz # 2
Hgo. del Parral, Chihuahua., Mexico.
Teléfono: 627-522-3150 Fax: 627-522-4949
Correo electronico:
ilap@infosel.net.mx
Fuera de Mexico
Casilla de Correo 15068
Asuncion, Paraguay
Teléfono: 59-52-145-0631
Correo electronico:
abekaspanish@uninet.com.py

ACCELERATED CHRISTIAN EDUCATION
P.O. Box 299000
Lewisville, Texas 75029-9000
www.aceministries.com

CHRISTIAN LIGHT PUBLICATIONS
P.O. Box 1212
Harrisonburg, VA 22803
Teléfono: 800-776-0478
Fax: 540-433-8896
Correo electronico: Office@CLP.org

COLEGIO HEBRON
Apartado Postal 578
Guatemala, C.A.
Teléfono: 502-2333-2615

P.O. Box 4274
Leesburg, VA 20177-8388
Teléfono: 800-527-8329
Correo electronico:
colheb@c.net.gt
www.hebronministries.com

EL HOGAR EDUCADOR EN MEXICO
APDO 17 Arteaga, Coahuila,
Mexico, 25350
Teléfono: 844-483-0377
Fuera de Mexico
1001 South 10th St., Suite G-529
McAllen, Texas 78501 USA
Teléfono: 52-844-483-0377
Correo electronico: vnm@hughes.net
elhogareducador.myshopify.com

HOME EDUCATORS ASSOCIATION OF VIRGINIA (HEAV)
www.heav.org/resources/spanish

LA ASOCIACION AMOS 5:24
Gonzalitos 210-B Norte, Col. Vista Hermosa,
Monterrey, N.L. cp64620 Mexico
Fuera de Mexico
Route 1 Box 1404
Pickton, TX 75471 USA
www.amos524.org

LIBRERIA NUEVA VIDA
APDO 656 Torren, Coahuila,
Mexico, 27000
Teléfono: 871-712-7362
Correo electronico:
robertw@att.net.mx

LIGHTHOUSE CHRISTIAN ACADEMY
P.O. Box 60328
Nashville, TN 37216
Teléfono: 866-746-6534
aceweb.schooloftomorrow.com/
store/dept.asp

LITERATURA MONTE SION
thechurchtoday.org

PUBLICADORA LA MERCED
Apartado 15
Pital de San Carlos
Costa Rica, C.A.
Teléfono: 506-465-0017; Fax: 506-465-0018
Correo electronico:
plmantor@racsa.co.cr.

PUBLICADORES LAMPARA Y LUZ
26 RD 5577
Farmington, NM 87401
Teléfono: 505-632-3521 Fax:505-632-1246
Correo electronico:
lamplight@emypeople.net

RESPUESTAS EN GENESIS
Site de Web:
www.RespuestasEnGenesis.org

VARA Y CAYADO
Hwy 172
Crockett, Kentucky 41413 USA
Teléfono: 606-522-4348
Fax 606-522-4896

MIKE & PAM RICHARDSON
Vida Nueva Ministries
1001 S 10th Street, Suite G-529
McAllen, Texas 78501